The New Zealand
Bed & Breakfast
Book 2002

HOMESTAYS · FARMSTAYS · B&B INNS

Copyright © Moonshine Press

Published by Moonshine Press,
P. O. Box 6843
Wellington, New Zealand
Telephone: 04-385 2615, Fax: 04-385 2694
Website: http://www.bnb.co.nz
Email: bnb@actrix.gen.nz

ISBN 0-9582149-5-6

All information in this guidebook has been supplied by the hosts.
The publishers will not be liable for any inaccuracies.

Introduction

The popularity of B&B in New Zealand has increased each year since we first published *The New Zealand Bed and Breakfast Book* in 1987. The reason for this amazing growth is quite simply that the hosts are such wonderful people. Most hosts who are listed here are homeowners who want to share their love of the country with travellers. Each listing has been written by the host, and you will discover their warmth and personality is obvious in their writing. Ours is not simply an accommodation guide but an introduction to a uniquely New Zealand holiday experience.

Any holiday is remembered primarily by the people one meets. How many of us have loved a country simply because of one or two especially memorable individuals encountered there? Bed and Breakfast offers the traveller who wants to experience the real New Zealand and get to know the people the opportunity to do just that.

Bed and Breakfast in New Zealand means a warm welcome into someone's home. Most of the places listed are homes, with a sprinkling of private hotels and guesthouses. Remember that Bed and Breakfast hosts cannot offer hotel facilities. Therefore please telephone ahead to book your accommodation and give ample notice if you require dinner.

All properties inspected
All B&Bs which are newly listed are inspected to ensure that they meet our required standard. We expect that all B&Bs in *The New Zealand Bed and Breakfast Book* will offer excellent hospitality.

Tariff
The prices listed are in New Zealand dollars and include GST. Prices listed are subject to change, any change to listed prices is to be stated at time of booking. Some offer a reduction for children. Unless otherwise stated this applies to age 12 and under.

Breakfast
Breakfast is included in the tariff. We do not specify the menu, so you will find an interesting variety and you can be sure they will be generous breakfasts.

Self-contained accommodation
Many homes in towns and on farms can offer separate self-contained accommodation. In almost every case linen and food will be provided if required. The tariff will vary depending on your requirements, so check when booking.

Finding your way around - using the New Zealand B&B Book
We travel southwards down the islands listing the towns as we come to them.
We have divided New Zealand into geographical regions and have included a map of each region. We have simply listed the towns as they occur on our southward journey. In areas such as Southland where we travel across more than down, the route we have taken should be obvious.

We wish you an enjoyable holiday and welcome comments from guests.
For more information or to leave comments visit our website www.bnb.co.nz or write to us at P. O. Box 6843, Wellington, New Zealand.

Happy travelling

Moonshine Press

4

About B&B

Ensuite and private bathrooms are for your use exclusively
Guests share bathroom means you will be sharing with other guests
Family share means you will be sharing with the family

Our B&Bs range from homely to luxurious, but you can always be assured of superior hospitality.

The best thing about a homestay is that you share the family's living area.

Just as we have a variety of B&Bs, you will also discover a variety of breakfasts, and they will always be generous.

If you would like dinner most hosts require 24 hours notice.

Most of our B&Bs are non smoking.

The New Zealand Bed & Breakfast Book is online at www.bnb.co.nz

Don't try to travel too far in one day. Take time to enjoy the company of your hosts and other locals.

Make your B&B reservation in advance. It is a nuisance for you if you arrive to find the accommodation has been taken, and besides, the hosts need a little time to prepare.

The most suitable time to arrive is late afternoon and to leave is before 10 in the morning.

Most of our B&Bs will accept credit cards.

To get the feel of a place stay more than one night.

If you have made your first night's reservation from overseas make sure your dates are correct. You might cross the dateline to come to New Zealand.

Please let your hosts know if you have to cancel, they will have spent time preparing for you.

If you are unsure about anything ask your hosts, they are your own personal travel agent and guide.

The difference between a hotel and a B&B is that you don't hug the hotel staff when you leave.

You can order *The Australian Bed & Breakfast Book*. Contact Moonshine Press, PO Box 1, Brooklyn, NSW 2083, Australia. Or visit our website www.bbbook.com.au

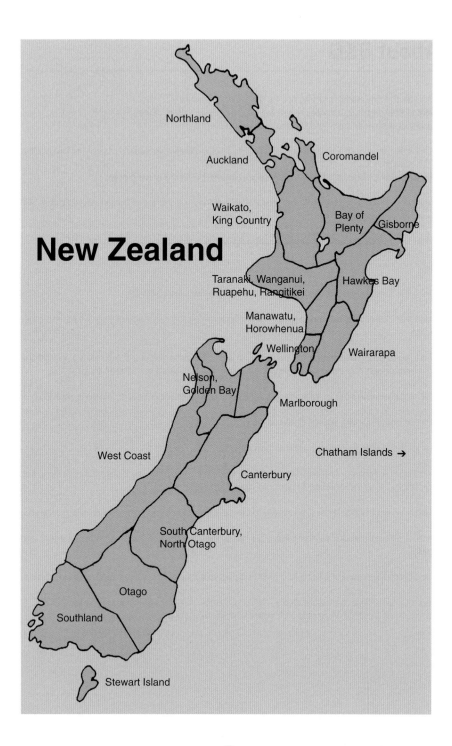

New Zealand

Northland

Auckland

Coromandel

Waikato,
King Country

Bay of
Plenty

Gisborne

Taranaki, Wanganui,
Ruapehu, Rangitikei

Hawkes Bay

Manawatu,
Horowhenua

Wellington

Wairarapa

Nelson,
Golden Bay

Marlborough

West Coast

Chatham Islands →

Canterbury

South Canterbury,
North Otago

Otago

Southland

Stewart Island

Contents

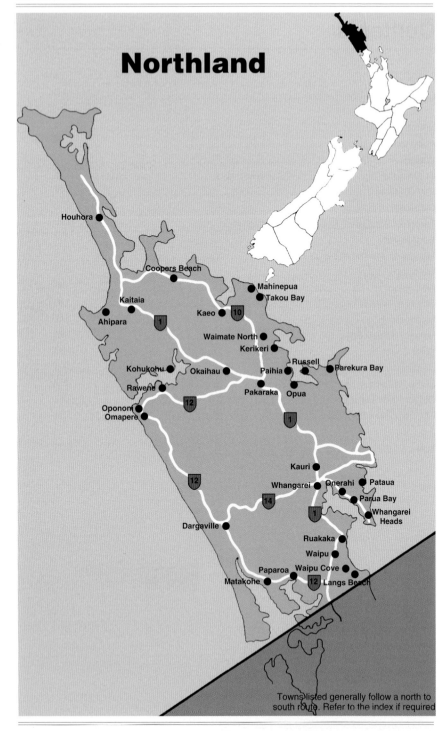

Northland

Houhora

Coopers Beach

Kaitaia

Ahipara

Kaeo ①10

Mahinepua
Takou Bay

Waimate North

Kerikeri

Kohukohu   Okaihau

Paihia

Russell

Parekura Bay

Rawene

Pakaraka   Opua

Opononi
Omapere

①12

①1

Kauri

①12

Whangarei   Onerahi   Pataua

①14

Parua Bay

①1

Whangarei
Heads

Dargaville

Ruakaka

Waipu

Paparoa   Waipu Cove

Matakohe   ①12   Langs Beach

Towns listed generally follow a north to
south route. Refer to the index if required

Houhora

We have fled our largest city with Evie our cat, to live here in paradise on the shores of Houhora Harbour, and are ideally situated to cater for your Far North expeditions. Visit Cape Reinga, enjoy the beautiful beaches and other attractions within easy commuting distance. We can arrange four wheel drive trips, line or deep sea fishing (smokehouse on site) and offer relaxed and quality accommodation. Homemade bread, homegrown fruit, vegetables and eggs. Fresh or smoked fish a speciality. Email, internet and fax facilities available.

Houhora Lodge & Homestay
Homestay
44km N of Kaitaia
Jacqui & Bruce Malcolm
Far North Rd
Houhora, RD 4
Kaitaia

Tel: (09) 409 7884
Fax: (09) 409 7884
Mob: 025 926 992
E: houhora.homestay@xtra.co.nz
W: www.bnb.co.nz/hosts/
houhoralodgehomestay.html

Cost: Double $125 Single $80
Dinner $30 by arrangement
Visa/MC
Beds: 3 King/Twin (3 bdrm)
Bath: 2 Ensuite 1 Private

Ahipara - Ninety Mile Beach

The Siesta is a Mediterranean style house set in private grounds with panoramic views overlooking the sheltered Ahipara Bay, sand-dune wilderness and the magnificent Ninety Mile Beach. Each room has private balcony, queen-size bed and ensuites. Sleep to the sound of the sea with sea-views from your bed, enjoy spectacular sunsets from your balcony. The adjacent villa has 2 luxury self-contained, spacious apartments with spectacular views, and are an ideal base for longer stays. We have a very friendly cat and dog. Phone for directions.

Siesta Lodge
B&B S/C Guesthouse
16km W of Kaitaia
Carol & Alan Harding
PO Box 30
Ahipara Northland

Tel: (09) 409 2011
Fax: (09) 409 2011
Mob: 025 293 9665
E: ninetymile@xtra.co.nz
W: www.ahipara.co.nz/siesta

Cost: Double $140-$160
apartments $200-$250
Visa/MC
Beds: 1 King 3 Queen (4 bdrm)
Bath: 4 Ensuite 4 Private

Ahipara - Ninety Mile Beach

2 Self-contained units with fully equipped kitchens, situated on the water's edge at Ahipara Bay, the southernmost sheltered end of 90 mile beach. BBQ on your covered terrace. Relax and enjoy lovely seaviews from your comfortable unit. Safe swimming, fishing, surfing, walking just across the road. Front door pickup for Cape Reinga and Reef Point tours, fishing trips or quad bikes. Golf course - 5 minutes away. Takeaways and dairies nearby. Enquire tariff for long stays, extra guests. Children very welcome. Sorry no pets.

Foreshore Lodge
B&B Self-contained
17km W of Kaitaia
Maire & Selwyn Parker
269 Foreshore Road
RD 1 Kaitaia

Tel: (09) 409 4860
Fax: (09) 409 4860
W: www.ahipara.co.nz/foreshore

Cost: Double $85-$105
Single $78 Child $10
Visa/MC
Beds: 1 Super King 1 King
2 Double 2 Single (3 bdrm)
Bath: 1 Ensuite 1 Private

Kaitaia

Enjoy a relaxing stay in our 1912 Kauri villa. Wireless Road was once the site of a ship to shore radio station and built to accommodate the staff. Set on 5 acres in a semi-rural setting, we can promise peace and tranquillity. We can also organise a trip along the famous 90 Mile Beach to the lighthouse at Cape Reinga or a horse trek along the 90 Mile Beach. We have 2 children, Elaine and Leigh, 2 cats, 1 dog.

Historic Wireless B&B	**Tel:** (09) 408 1929	**Cost:** Double $70 Single $40
B&B Homestay	**Mob:** 025 268 1353	Child under 13 1/2 price
4km N of Kaitaia	**W:** www.bnb.co.nz/hosts/	**Beds:** 1 Queen 1 Double
Clive & Cherie Johnston	historicwirelessbb.html	1 Single (3 bdrm)
Wireless Rd		**Bath:** 1 Guests share
RD 2 Kaitaia		

Kaitaia - Ahipara

Welcome to our comfortable house. Relax and enjoy views from the deck of Ninety Mile Beach stretching to the Cape. A private walkway 50 metres leads to the beach. Activities Ahipara offers are surfing, swimming, horse riding, golf course 2km drive. For those interested in farming, visit our beef farm at Herikino. Dinner available on request. Directions: Take road to Ahipara from Kaitaia. Turn left at Ahipara School, follow road around corner, 3rd house on beach side.

Beachside	**Tel:** (09) 409 4819	**Cost:** Double $65-$70
B&B Homestay	**Fax:** (09) 409 4819	Single $40-$50 Child $20
15km W of Kaitaia	**W:** www.bnb.co.nz/hosts/	Dinner $20 Visa/MC
Maire & Brian Veza	beachside.html	**Beds:** 1 Twin 2 Single (2 bdrm)
72 Foreshore Road		**Bath:** 1 Ensuite 1 Family share
RD 1 Kaitaia		

Kaitaia - Lake Ngatu

Our lakeside home, set on 10 acres of mature garden, orchard and paddocks, is the ideal centralised Northern retreat. Relax in your upstairs room or private lounge, swim, walk or kayak the Lake, 3 minutes to 90 mile Beach - the choice is yours! 100kms to Cape Reinga, bus tours pass our gate daily, or fishing/diving trips can be arranged. Special continental breakfast with homegrown produce, meals on request, undercover parking and saltwater pool top off the experience - Diane, Graeme and Jif the dog welcome you!

Lake Ngatu Lodge	**Tel:** (09) 406 7300	**Cost:** Double $100 Single $80
B&B Countrystay	**Fax:** (09) 406 7300	Dinner by arrangement
14km N of Kaitaia	**Mob:** 025 624 8412	Visa/MC
Diane & Graeme Jay	**E:** lakengatulodge@hotmail.com	**Beds:** 2 King/Twin (2 bdrm)
Sweetwater Road	**W:** www.bnb.co.nz/hosts/	**Bath:** 1 Private
RD 1, Awanui	lakengatulodge.html	
Northland		

Kaitaia - Pamapuria

Our native timber home is idyllically situated on one and a half acres of English style garden, with a touch of the South Pacific. We offer guests a real get away from it all, stress-free, country stay, within easy reach of all popular attractions. Experience game fishing, dolphins, Cape Reinga, and visit the nocturnal park. Wake up each morning to a delicious, bountiful breakfast, which could include such delights as fresh picked strawberries and raspberries (in season), home made muesli, yoghurt and conserves, followed by a cooked course to boast about. Our 5 cats ensure a mouse-free environment.

Plane Tree Lodge	**Tel:** (09) 408 0995	**Cost:** Double $100-$120
B&B Self-contained	**Fax:** (09) 408 0959	Single $70-$90
10km S of Kaitaia	**Mob:** 025 968 147	Visa/MC
Rosemary & Mike Wright	**E:** reservationsplanetreelodge	**Beds:** 3 Queen
State Highway 1	@xtra.co.nz	3 Single (5 bdrm)
	W: www.plane-tree-lodge.net.nz	**Bath:** 3 Ensuite 1 Private

Coopers Beach

Enjoy a "million dollar" view of Doubtless Bay while you enjoy Mac's smoked fish on your toast. The bus to Cape Reinga stops at our gate, you may visit glow-worms, kiwi house, go on a craft or wine trail, swim with dolphins, go fishing, diving or just relax on our unpolluted uncrowded beaches, there's one across the road. There are several fine restaurants and the "world famous" fish and chip shop nearby. Have a memorable stay with Mac'n'Mo, they will take good care of you.

Mac'n'Mo's	**Tel:** (09) 406 0538	**Cost:** Double $65-$75
Self-contained Homestay	**Fax:** (09) 406 0538	Single $40-$60 Dinner $25
3km N of Mangonui	**Mob:** 025 286 5180	**Beds:** 1 Queen 2 Double
Maureen & Malcolm MacMillan	**E:** MacNMo@xtra.co.nz	2 Single (4 bdrm)
PO Box 177	**W:** www.bnb.co.nz/hosts/	**Bath:** 2 Ensuite 2 Guests share
Mangonui	macnmos.html	

Coopers Beach

Our B/B is 800 mtrs north of the Coopers Beach shops. We are 1 hour north of Paihia. Each room has ensuite bathroom, Sky-Cable TV, fridge, tea and coffee making facilities. We have a guest laundry and barbecue and two pussy cats. We arrange scenic bus tours to Cape Reinga, fishing trips and dolphin watching. Enjoy the sea and rural views of this lovely place where you can visit the many isolated beaches in the area, knowing you are 150 kms from the nearest traffic lights.

Doubtless Bay Lodge	**Tel:** (09) 406 1661	**Cost:** Double $90 Single $65
B&B	**Fax:** (09) 406 1662	Child $20
3km N of Mangonui	**Mob:** 025 275 2144	Dinner $25 by arrangement
Harry & Berwyn Porten	**E:** hporten@voyager.co.nz	Visa/MC
33 Cable Bayblock Road	**W:** www.bnb.co.nz/hosts/	**Beds:** 3 Queen 2 Single
Coopers Beach	doubtlessbaylodge.html	(4 bdrm)
Mangonui 0557		**Bath:** 4 Ensuite

Mahinepua - Kaeo

Would you like a chance to see some of Northland's spectacular scenery. Have we the place for you! Situated on the East coast with views of the Pacific Ocean, Cavailli Islands and home of one of the famous Marlin deep sea fishing grounds. Golf at Kauri Cliffs, sightsee to Cape Reinga, visit the Bay of Islands, Kerikeri, Whangaroa or just relax. We have a dog called Benson and Moppet the cat and we love to entertain and would enjoy meeting you. For more information please phone us.

Waiwurrie	**Tel:** (09) 405 0840	**Cost:** Double $150-$175
Homestay	**Fax:** (09) 405 0854	Single $125 Dinner $35pp
22km E of Kaeo	**Mob:** 025 652 5102	Visa/MC
Vickie & Rodger Corbin	**E:** wai.wurrie@xtra.co.nz	**Beds:** 1 King 1 Queen (2 bdrm)
Mahinepua, RD 1	**W:** www.bnb.co.nz/hosts/	**Bath:** 1 Ensuite 1 Private
Kaeo/ Whangaroa	waiwurrie.html	
Northland		

Kerikeri - Waimate North

"Aspley House" with its old-world charm and family antiques offers a relaxing and comfortable stay. Situated in picturesque rural surrounds of the Atkinson family farms and citrus property. Two large, well-appointed guestrooms open on to a wide verandah with views of landscaped gardens and beyond to rolling farmland. Being descendants of pioneer families we have a good knowledge of local history as well as being widely travelled. We offer quality accommodation and look forward to your stay. Pets: Jake, Jack Russell, Mr Cat. We regret that our home is not suitable for young children.

Aspley House	**Tel:** (09) 405 9509	**Cost:** Double $120 Dinner $30
B&B Farmstay Homestay	**Fax:** (09) 407 7403	**Beds:** 1 Double
8km S of Kerikeri	**W:** www.bnb.co.nz/hosts/	2 Single (2 bdrm)
Joy Atkinson	aspleyhouse.html	**Bath:** 1 Ensuite 1 Private
Waimate North		
Kerikeri, RD 3 Bay of Islands		

Our B&Bs range from homely to luxurious, but you can always be assured of superior hospitality.

Kerikeri

We welcome guests to our home, large garden, swimming pool and citrus orchard. Its a pleasant walk to the historic area and 4 mins by car to township, clubs and craft outlets. David has a vintage car which is used for personalised historic scenic and craft tours. We are 5th generation New Zealanders love to help with "where to go and what to do", can make tour bookings. We enjoy providing a 3 course dinner with wine. Can meet coach or plane, no cost. Directions please phone.

Matariki Orchard	**Tel:** (09) 407 7577	**Cost:** Double $100 Single $50
B&B Homestay	**Fax:** (09) 407 7593	Child $20 Dinner $30pp
3km E of Kerikeri	**Mob:** 025 278 2423	Visa/MC
Alison & David Bridgman	**W:** www.bnb.co.nz/hosts/	**Beds:** 1 Queen 2 Single
Pa Road	matarikiorchard.html	(2 bdrm)
Kerikeri		**Bath:** 1 Guests share
Bay of Islands		

Kerikeri - Okaihau

We farm cattle, sheep, horses and worms on our 310 acres. There are panoramic views of the Bay of Islands area from our home 1,000 ft above sea level. Of 1840's pioneering descent, our interests are travel, farming, genealogy and equestrian activities. We have an extensive library on Northland history and families. Directions: SH10 take Wiroa/Airport Road at the Kerikeri intersection. 9kms on the right OR SH1, take Kerikeri Road just south of Okaihau. We are 4th house on the left, past the golf course (8kms).

Clotworthy Farmstay	**Tel:** (09) 401 9371	**Cost:** Double $80 Single $40
B&B Farmstay	**Fax:** (09) 401 9371	Dinner $25 by arrangement
12km W of Kerikeri	**W:** www.bnb.co.nz/hosts/	Visa/MC
Neville & Shennett Clotworthy	clotworthyfarmstay.html	**Beds:** 1 Queen 4 Single
Wiroa Road		(3 bdrm)
RD1, Okaihau		**Bath:** 1 Guests share
Bay of Islands		

Kerikeri

"Simply superior" wrote one of our guests and at "Kilernan" we strive to maintain that standard. Close to the Kerikeri Village but with magnificent rural views our home offers quality accommodation, your own ensuite; full breakfast; and dinner with all the trimmings. We can also assist with a full range of local tours and sightseeing activities. Together with 'Monty' our pedigree boxer we look forward to extending a welcome and superior hospitality to our guests.

Kilernan Homestay	**Tel:** (09) 407 8582	**Cost:** Double $110 Single $70
Homestay	**Fax:** (09) 407 8317	Child n/a Dinner $35
5km N of Kerikeri	**Mob:** 025 790 216	Visa/MC
Heather & Bruce Manson	**E:** brucemanson@xtra.co.nz	**Beds:** 1 Queen 2 Single
Silkwood Lane	**W:** www.bnb.co.nz/hosts/	(2 bdrm)
RD 2 Kerikeri	kilernanhomestay.html	**Bath:** 2 Ensuite

Kerikeri

Would you like some good old Kiwi hospitality? Our seven bedroom home has superb views, not only of the Inlet, but of Cape Brett and Russell. Our 1100 acre sheep and beef farm borders the Waitangi Forest. It has two lakes and many species of timber trees and natives which we have planted. Enjoy a full breakfast consisting of free-range chook eggs and our own sausages before exploring the many attractions Kerikeri has to offer. Backpackers has 6 bedrooms and a large lounge with kitchen, laundry facilities. Note: Please phone first for bookings, detailed directions or if you need to be picked up. We have two cats.

Kerikeri Inlet View	**Tel:** (09) 407 7477	**Cost:** Double $70 Single $45
Farmstay	**Fax:** (09) 407 7478	Child $15 Dinner $18
8km Kerikeri Central	**Mob:** 025 612 0021	B/packers $25 - no breakfast
Trish & Nolan Daniells	**W:** www.bnb.co.nz/hosts/	**Beds:** 1 Queen 2 Double
Inlet Road	kerikeriinletview.html	2 Single (3 bdrm)
RD 3 Kerikeri		**Bath:** 2 Ensuite 1 Guests share

Kerikeri

Puriri Park has long been known for its hospitality in the Far North. Guests are welcome to wander around our large garden, explore the orange and kiwifruit orchards, sit by the lilypond or feed our flock of fantail pigeons. We have five acres of bird-filled native bush, mostly totara and puriri. We are in an excellent situation for trips to Cape Reinga and sailing or cruising on the beautiful Bay of Islands. We can arrange tours for you or pick you up from the airport.

Puriri Park	**Tel:** (09) 407 9818	**Cost:** Double $85 Single $65
B&B S/C Orchardstay	**Fax:** (09) 407 9498	Child $10 Dinner $30
8km S of Kerikeri	**E:** puriri@xtra.co.nz	Visa/MC
Paul & Charmian Treadwell	**W:** www.bnb.co.nz/hosts/	**Beds:** 3 Double 2 Twin
Puriri Park Orchard	puriripark.html	1 Single (4 bdrm)
State Highway 10, Box 572		**Bath:** 1 Private 2 Guests share
Kerikeri		

Kerikeri

A warm welcome awaits you at our restful homestay ovelooking Kerikeri inlet, magnificent water views and often spectacular sunrises and sunsets. Plenty to see and do in Bay of Islands. We are only too happy to help arrange your trips. Tea and coffee available at all times. Laundry facilities available. Courtesy pick up from bus or airport. Phone, fax or leave phone number on answer phone, we will call you back. One of the best locations in Kerikeri. Do come and share it with us. Evening meals by prior arrangement. None smokers and we have no pets.

Sunrise Homestay B&B	**Tel:** (09) 407 5447	**Cost:** Double $80-$85
B&B Homestay	**Fax:** (09) 407 5447	Single $55 Dinner $30pp
7km N of Kerikeri	**Mob:** 021 774 941	Visa/MC
Judy & Les Remnant	**W:** www.bnb.co.nz/hosts/	**Beds:** 1 Double 4 Single
Skudders Road	sunrisehomestaybb.html	(3 bdrm)
Skudders Beach, RD 1		**Bath:** 1 Ensuite 1 Guests share
Kerkeri		

Kerikeri

Your holiday, a special time to have as many adventures as you can, or simply a wonderful opportunity to relax and spoil yourself. Ironbark Lodge, set in a 20 acre farmlet with tennis court, close to a Kauri forest, and surrounded by imposing eucalypt trees is the perfect base from which to explore. Each bedroom has a private ensuite. You'll love the comfy beds, and a substantial breakfast will ensure a perfect start to every day. Join us for an evening meal by arrangement ($30pp). Kerikeri restaurants are 15 minutes away, Paihia 30 minutes. Pets: 1 cat Directions: Please phone.

Ironbark Lodge
Homestay
10km N of Kerikeri
Rangi & Dail Bidois
Kerikeri

Tel: (09) 407 9302
Fax: (09) 407 9302
Mob: 025 503 231
E: prueb@xtra.co.nz
W: www.bnb.co.nz/hosts/
ironbarklodge.html

Cost: Double $100 Single $55
Visa/MC
Beds: 2 Queen 1 Single
(3 bdrm)
Bath: 3 Ensuite

Kerikeri

Venture down Glenfalloch's tree lined driveway to a peaceful garden paradise. Evalyn and Rick welcome guests with refreshments to be enjoyed in the lounges or outdoors on the decks. You are welcome to wander about the garden, use the swimming pool and tennis court, or just relax in our private retreat. Breakfast can be enjoyed at your leisure outdoors, weather permitting. Laundry facilities available. Directions: travel 0.6km from the Stone Store to second driveway on left after Department Of Conservation Sign.

Glenfalloch
Homestay
2.6km N of Kerikeri
Rick & Evalyn Pitelen
Landing Road
Kerikeri

Tel: (09) 407 5471
Fax: (09) 407 5471
Mob: 025 280 0661
E: glenfall@ihug.co.nz
W: www.bnb.co.nz/hosts/
glenfalloch.html

Cost: Double $80-$90 Single $55
Child $15 Dinner $25pp
Visa/MC
Beds: 1 King 1 Queen 1 Double
1 Single (3 bdrm)
Bath: 2 Ensuite 1 Private

Kerikeri

After extensive travel we have designed and built a new home with guest accommodation and comfort in mind. All bedrooms have ensuites and TV with direct access to our lovely sheltered veranda. Breakfast in our large guest lounge. Historic Kerikeri is surrounded by orchards, farms, and is centrally situated to Bay of Islands and Northland's many tourist attractions. "Graleen" is 200 metres form SH10, only 20 minutes from historic Waitangi and Paihia beaches, 3 minutes from the township, restaurants, golf course and many craft galleries.

Graleen
B&B
3km S of Kerikeri
Graeme & Colleen Wattam
Kerikeri Road
RD 3, Kerikeri Bay of Islands

Tel: (09) 407 9047
Fax: (09) 407 9047
Mob: 025 940 845
E: graleen@xtra.co.nz
W: www.kerikeri.co.nz/graleen

Cost: Double $70 Single $40
Visa/MC
Beds: 1 Queen 1 Double
2 Single (3 bdrm)
Bath: 3 Ensuite

Kerikeri

"Thanks for taking such good care of us" wrote guests from Canada. Stroll 400m into Kerikeri to shops, cafes, restaurants and cinema. We can help you plan your holiday, pointing out areas of interest such as craft trails, wineries and golf courses. Ensuite bedrooms open onto their own private patios for breakfast in the sun. An evening meal can be provided by prior arrangement. We offer a tranquil smoke-free environment. Pixie, our cat is now comfortable with guests and becoming more sociable. Complimentary airport transfers.

Pukanui	**Tel:** (09) 407 7003	**Cost:** Double $90-$100
Homestay	**Fax:** (09) 407 7068	Single $50-$60 Dinner $30
Elaine & Bill Conaghan	**Mob:** 025 942 647	Visa/MC
Kerikeri Road	**E:** pukanui@igrin.co.nz	**Beds:** 2 Queen 1 Twin
Kerikeri	**W:** www.bnb.co.nz/hosts/	(3 bdrm)
	pukanui.html	**Bath:** 3 Ensuite

Kerikeri

If you want tranquillity, relaxing on the deck watching boats come up the Inlet, a warm welcome awaits you, in our large, comfortable bungalow. The adventurous can paddle canoes up to the Stone Store. Our yacht is close by. Bush walks, night kiwi walks, fishing, horse trekking can be arranged. Bird life is abundant, sheep munch next door and we have two pet calves. At Kerikeri roundabout turn right into Hobson, left into Inlet - at 2.3km turn left into Blacks. We're half way down the hill. See you.

Holmes Homestay	**Tel:** (09) 407 7500	**Cost:** Double $75 Single $50
B&B Homestay	**Fax:** (09) 407 7500	Dinner $25 Visa/MC
3km E of Kerikeri	**Mob:** 025 241 9448	**Beds:** 1 Queen 2 Single
Jane & Tony Holmes	**E:** tony_holmes@xtra.co.nz	(2 bdrm)
Blacks Road	**W:** www.bnb.co.nz/hosts/	**Bath:** 1 Private 1 Family share
Kerikeri	holmeshomestay.html	

Kerikeri

An idyllic setting with exquisite accommodation and convivial company at The Summer House, a French Provincial inspired Bed and Breakfast. The perfect retreat for relaxation, to experience Kerikeri's vineyards, cafes and craft shops and to explore the Bay of Islands and the beaches, Kauri forests and historic sites of the Far North. This architecturally designed home is set in a tranquil hectare of citrus orchard and beautifully landscaped sub-tropical garden. Enjoy gourmet breakfasts, warm hospitality and inspiring surroundings. Unsuitable for children. One aristocratic cat.

The Summer House	**Tel:** (09) 407 4294	**Cost:** Double $165-$185
B&B Self-contained	**Fax:** (09) 407 4297	Single $135-$145
1.5 km W of Kerikeri	**Mob:** 025 409 288	Visa/MC
Rod & Christine Brown	**E:** summerhouse@xtra.co.nz	**Beds:** 1 King/Twin 1 Queen
The Summer House	**W:** www.thesummerhouse.co.nz	1 Double (3 bdrm)
Kerikeri Road Kcrikcri		**Bath:** 2 Ensuite 1 Private

Kerikeri

Welcome to 'Oversley' and enjoy magnificent panoramic water views, sweeping lawns and private native bush walks to the water. Our spacious, comfortable home, set in 18 acres, offers a friendly relaxed atmosphere with quality accommodation and laundry facilities. We are an easy going, well travelled, retired couple, enjoy all sports, sailing and fishing on our 13 meter yacht, golfing on Kerikeri's first class course 15 minutes away (Kauri Cliff's course only 35 minutes away) and are animal lovers. Your company at dinner, to share good food and wine with us, is most welcome.

Oversley
Coastal Homestay
12km E of Kerikeri
Maire & Tone Coyte
Doves Bay Road
RD 1 Kerikeri

Tel: (09) 407 8744
Fax: (09) 407 4487
Mob: 025 959 207
E: oversley@xtra.co.nz
W: www.bnb.co.nz/hosts/
oversley.html

Cost: Double $110-$140
Single $90-$120 Dinner $25
Visa/MC
Beds: 1 King 1 Queen
2 Single (3 bdrm)
Bath: 2 Ensuite 1 Private

Kerikeri

Jill and Roger welcome you to Gannaway House. Our comfortable home, set in 2 acres of garden and orchard is situated down a tree-lined driveway, close to town but in the quiet of the country. We offer one large ground floor room with ensuite and private entrance. Upstairs, two rooms (1 Queen and 1 Twin) with shared facilities. Enjoy our beautiful tranquil garden - also the sheep and lambs in the orchard. We are also breeders of pedigree cats. Directions: From S.H. 10 - first driveway on left past Makana Chocolate Factory.

Gannaway House
B&B Homestay
2km S of Kerikeri
Jill & Roger Gardner
Kerikeri Road
RD 3
Kerikeri

Tel: (09) 407 1432
Fax: (09) 407 1431
Mob: 025 798 115
E: gannaway@xtra.co.nz
W: www.bnb.co.nz/hosts/
gannawayhouse.html

Cost: Double $85-$105
Single $55-$75 Child $30
Dinner $30 by arrangement
Visa/MC
Beds: 2 Queen 1 Twin (3 bdrm)
Bath: 1 Ensuite 1 Guests share

Pakaraka

Beautiful 51 acres, stone walls, barberry hedges. Sheep, cattle. Ken trains dogs daily! Enjoy watching help shift animals. Meet and photograph with "Mr Angus" our lovable steer. "Monkey" and "Governor Grey" our cats will enjoy your visit. Swimming pool or cosy warm home in winter. Good Central Base! Tour five golf courses, bowls, beaches, hot pools, shopping! Situated 15 minutes Paihia, Kerikeri, Kaikohe. Welcome to Bay of Islands. Book early or take pot luck! (10 minutes North Kawakawa or 2 south Pakaraka Junction). "Highland Farm" on entrance.

Bay of Islands Farmstay - B&B
Highland Farm
10km N of Kawakawa
Glenis & Ken Mackintosh
Pakaraka State Highway 1,
RD 2 Kaikohe 0400

Tel: (09) 404 0430
Fax: (09) 404 1040
Mob: 025 249 8296
E: Ken@soft.net.nz
W: www.bnb.co.nz/hosts/
bayofislandfarmstaybb.html

Cost: Double $80 Single $50
Child $10 Dinner $18 - $28
Visa/MC
Beds: 1 Double 1 Twin
3 Single (2 bdrm)
Bath: 2 Ensuite

Kerikeri

Our adobe-style masonry villa has stunning rural views, semi-tropical gardens, and is a short stroll along the main street to village cafes and restaurants, or down to the historic Stone Store and beautiful river basin where the nation of New Zealand was born.

Three lovely ensuite guest rooms pamper you in quiet comfort with excellent beds, antiques, stylish linens, fresh flowers, toiletries and evening chocolates. The guest lounge has TV, stereo, video and internet available plus a cheery wood fire crackling away in winter.

Breakfast includes freshly squeezed orange juice and fruit, homemade muesli and muffins accompanied by a selection of eggs Benedict, salmon'n'eggs, omelets, pancakes with bacon and pure maple syrup and traditional bacon'n'eggs.

Kerikeri's sunny climate, central Bay of Islands location and abundant activities make this your perfect holiday destination. We offer friendly personal hospitality and are here to make sure you enjoy our beautiful area to the fullest.

We are a member of New Zealand Heritage and Character Inns.

KERIKERI IS WHERE NEW ZEALAND BEGAN.

Kerikeri Village Inn
B&B
Peter & Jackie
165 Kerikieri Road
Kerikeri
Bay of Islands

Tel: (09) 407 4666
Fax: (09) 407 4408
Mob: 025 744 302
E: kerikeri.village.inn@xtra.co.nz
W: www.bnb.co.nz/hosts/
kerikerivillageinn.html

Cost: Double $145-$165
Extra person $45 Visa/MC
Beds: 3 Queen 1 Single
(3 bdrm)
Bath: 3 Ensuite

Paihia

Our home, on 10 acres, is large and modern, built by Maurice of native timbers. Of English/NZ origins, we have American connections too. Our bedrooms are spacious and private and open onto our large garden. We are close to Haruru Falls, Waitangi, beaches, walks, golf and historic places. Our breakfasts feature homemade breads, preserves, fresh fruit, and more. We can book tours and cruises. Complimentary refreshments on arrival. Heather teaches ceramics and enjoys showing guests over the studio. We have two dogs and one cat.

Puketona Lodge
Countrystay
8km N of Paihia
Heather and Maurice Pickup
Puketona Road
RD 1
Paihia 0252

Tel: (09) 402 8152
Fax: (09) 402 8152
Mob: 025 260 7058
E: puketonalodge@xtra.co.nz
W: www.bnb.co.nz/hosts/
puketonalodge.html

Cost: Double $115
King/Twin $120
Single $90
Dinner $35 Visa/MC
Beds: 1 King/Twin 1 Double
(2 bdrm)
Bath: 1 Ensuite 1 Private

Paihia

...For the sophisticated traveller...luxury with charm. Two scenic ensuite apartments uniquely located on a hilltop reveal breathtaking panoramic views over historic Waitangi, the harbour, Russell the islands and the endless horizon. Start your day with delicious Austrian pancakes, stroll along the beach to Waitangi, ride the ferry to Russell, cruise the islands.... Christine has a degree in Hotel Management, Frank is an international photographer. His latest book depicts the beauty of the Bay. Pleasant ambience, minimum stay 2 nights, please no smoking inside.

The Totaras - Hilltop B&B
B&B
Paihia Central
C & F Habicht
6 School Rd
Paihia

Tel: (09) 402 8238
Fax: (09) 402 8238
E: fhabicht@hotmail.com
W: www.bnb.co.nz/hosts/
thetotarashilltopbb.html

Cost: Double $130-$175
Dinner $40pp Visa/MC
Beds: 1 King/Twin 1 Queen
1 Single (2 bdrm)
Bath: 2 Ensuite

Paihia

Drive in through an avenue of mature Liquid Amber trees to our comfortable timber home on our 10 acre Country Estate growing citrus and pip fruit. The guest wing has views of the fountain, bird aviary, small lake and black swan with the double and twin rooms having private verandah access. Fresh orange juice, fruit and homemade jams are served at breakfast. We are born NZ'ers, sailed thousands of miles living aboard our 50ft yacht in the Pacific and will gladly share our Bay of Island knowledge to make your visit most memorable.

Lily Pond Orchard B&B
(Est 1989)
Countrystay
7km N of Paihia
Allwyn & Graeme Sutherland
Puketona Road, RD 1, Paihia
Lily Pond Orchard sign at gate

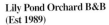

Tel: (09) 402 7041
W: www.bnb.co.nz/hosts/
lilypondorchardbb.html

Cost: Double $85 Single $45
Beds: 1 Double 1 Twin
1 Single (3 bdrm)
Bath: 1 Guests share
Separate toilet

Central Paihia

The Cedar Suite offers first class accommodation in our modern cedar home amidst beautiful native trees. Suites are separate and completed with their own superior ensuite bathroom or shower. Both of us enjoy music, Peter managing the New Zealand Symphony Orchestra for over twenty years, and Jo enjoys photography and interior design. Breakfast we call Kiwi: - continental plus - and local fruit plays a big part in that. There is private parking, comfortable beds, fine linen, a French style room, filtered water and TV.

The Cedar Suite	**Tel:** (09) 402 8516	**Cost:** Double $98-$135
B&B Self-contained	**Fax:** (09) 402 8555	Single $88-$125
Jo & Peter Nisbet	**Mob:** 025 969 281	Visa/MC
5 Sullivans Road	**E:** Cdr.Swt@xtra.co.nz	**Beds:** 3 Queen 1 Single
Paihia	**W:** www.bnb.co.nz/hosts/	(3 bdrm)
	thecedarsuite.html	**Bath:** 3 Ensuite

Paihia

Millennium Sunrise. Welcome to our modern waterfront home, set amongst subtropical gardens with expansive harbour views, just minutes from tourist activities and town centre. Guests enjoy privacy through a clever split-level design. Buffet breakfast with a choice of dining room, garden deck or courtyard. Laundry facilities, ample off-street parking and courtesy pickup from bus available. Descendants of early settlers, we have a good knowledge of local history. Ernie is a Masonic Lodge member.

Te Haumi House	**Tel:** (09) 402 8046	**Cost:** Double $80 Single $45
B&B	**Fax:** (09) 402 8046	Visa/MC
1.5km S of Paihia	**W:** www.bnb.co.nz/hosts/	**Beds:** 2 Queen 1 Single
Enid & Ernie Walker	tehaumihouse.html	(2 bdrm)
12 Seaview Road		**Bath:** 1 Guests share
Paihia		1 Family share

Paihia

The perfect spot for those seeking a quiet, sunny and central location. Discover the Garden Suite and Tree House. Self contained modern units nestled in a garden setting with trees that almost hug you, native birds and sea views. Each unit has ensuite bathroom, fully equipped kitchen for self catering, super king bed, T.V, insect screens and is tastefully decorated to reflect the natural colours of the surroundings. Safe off street parking, all within a five minute stroll to the waterfront, restaurants and town centre.

Craicor Accommodation	**Tel:** (09) 402 7882	**Cost:** Double $120 Single $90
Self-contained	**Fax:** (09) 402 7883	Optional continental
Central Paihia	**E:** craicor@actrix.gen.nz	breakfast $7.50 pp
Garth Craig & Anne Corbett	**W:** www.bnb.co.nz/hosts/	Visa/MC Amex
P. O. Box 15	craicoraccommodation.html	**Beds:** 2 King (2 bdrm)
49 Kings Road		**Bath:** 2 Ensuite
Paihia Bay of Islands		

Paihia

Share with us the best views in the Bay, from the comfort of your quiet sunny units, situated in Bayview Road, overlooking Central Paihia. Conveniently situated to shops, wharf and restaurants. One unit has a double and single bed. Upstairs are the bathroom, lounge, and kitchen. The studio has a double bed, kitchen and ensuite. Both are fully equipped with TV, BBQ and decks for you to relax on and enjoy the panoramic views. We supply generous breakfast provisions each day for you to enjoy at your leisure.

Iona Lodge
Self-contained
Paihia Central
Mary & Malcolm Sinclair
29 Bayview Road
Paihia Bay of Islands

Tel: (09) 402 8072
Fax: (09) 402 8072
E: ionas@xtra.co.nz
W: www.bnb.co.nz/hosts/ ionalodge.html

Cost: Double $85-$115
Single $70 Visa/MC
Beds: 2 Double 1 Single
(2 bdrm)
Bath: 2 Ensuite

Paihia

We invite you to stay and relax in our home, only minutes away from the beach, with bush walks and golf course nearby. On arrival a warm welcome awaits you, with tea or coffee and a chance to unwind. Assistance with your itinerary is offered should you need help. We look forward to the pleasure of your company and ensuring your stay is as comfortable and memorable as possible. Our courtesy car will meet you if travelling by bus.

Bay of Islands Bed & Breakfast
B&B Homestay
1km N of Paihia
Laraine & Sid Dyer
48 Tahuna Road
Paihia
Bay of Islands

Tel: (09) 402 8551
Fax: (09) 402 8551
Mob: 025 657 6815
E: larained@ihug.co.nz
W: www.bnb.co.nz/hosts/ bayofislandsbedbreakfast.html

Cost: Double $70 Single $40
Beds: 1 Queen 2 Single
(3 bdrm)
Bath: 1 Family share

Paihia

Situated in a quiet unique location above the beach in the centre of Paihia, Chalet Romantica offers luxurious, fully self-contained apartments and rooms with tea and coffee making facilities. Each apartment/room features its own private balcony or patio with fantastic views over the Bay of islands. An indoor heated pool, spa and gym adds to the relaxation and comfort of the stay at this remarkable place. For more information please click on to the pictorial website. Honeymooners heaven. Pre bookings are advisable. Wir sprechen deutsch, et on parle francais.

Indoor POOL, SPA, GYM

Chalet Romantica
B&B Self-contained
Paihia Central
Inge & Edi Amsler
6 Bedggood Close
Paihia
Bay of Islands

Tel: (09) 402 8270
Fax: (09) 402 8278
Mob: 025 285 5600
E: chalet-romantica@xtra.co.nz
W: www.bnb.co.nz/hosts/ chaletromantica.html

Cost: Double $99-$143
Single $79-$123
Apartments $116 - $198
Visa/MC
Beds: 2 King/Twin 1 Queen
2 Single (3 bdrm)
Bath: 2 Ensuite 1 Private

Paihia

Anna, Michael and family welcome you to our
RIVERSIDE RETREAT set on the banks of the
Waitangi River.
A peaceful and tranquil haven surrounded by beautiful
native bush. A "BIRD WATCHER'S PARADISE!"
Magnificent river, bush and garden views with all day
sun. Enjoy spacious grounds. Ducks, herons and
shags settle in for the night.
Onto swimming with DOLPHINS, deep sea FISHING,
ISLAND HOPPING or the famous 'Cream Trip",
Historical Waitangi Treaty houses, Waimate Mission
house, Russell, Ninety Mile Beach, MAORI
CULTURE, diving ....restaurants/entertainment.
We are 3 1/2 hours drive north from Auckland.

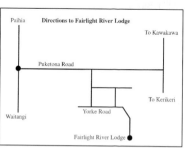

Fairlight River Lodge
Homestay
3km NW of Paihia
Anna & Michael Innes-Jones
107B Yorke Road
Haruru Falls
Paihia

Tel: (09) 402 8004
Fax: (09) 402 8048
Mob: 025 654 0217
E: fairlight@bay-of-islands.co.nz
W: www.bay-of-islands.co.nz/
    accomm/fairlite.html

Cost: Double $100-$165
    Single $100
    Visa/MC
Beds: 3 King 2 Single
    (3 bdrm)
Bath: 2 Ensuite 1 Guests share

Paihia

Paradise Glory: A Romantic hideaway, nestled in virgin native bush with million dollar views over the beautiful Bay of Islands. Great for those wishing to unwind and get away from it all. Balcony at tree top level, gives best views imaginable, while you soak up that warm sun. Paradise View: 1 minute walk to Paihia Village. Outdoor Gazebo. Both Units have microwaves, refrigerators, automatic w/ machines, linen, electric blankets, duvets. Idyllic locality with birds singing, golf course, swimming, fishing, bush walks, boating. Spectacular ocean views.

Paradise View	**Tel:** (09) 402 8458	**Cost:** Double $99 Single $59
B&B S/C Accommodation	**Fax:** (09) 402 8457	Continental b'fast $10pp
71km N of Whangarei	**Mob:** 021 684 580	High season surcharge
Iris Bartlett	**E:** paradiseview@xtra.co.nz	**Beds:** 2 Double 9 Single
34 Selwyn Road	**W:** www.bnb.co.nz/hosts/	(4 bdrm)
Paihia Bay of Islands	paradiseview.html	**Bath:** 2 Private

Paihia

Quiet central location overlooking the Bay, seaviews, stroll to beach, town centre, restaurant adjacent. Free bikes & tennis and off street parking, 3 studio suites & 1, 2 bedroom all well appointed with ensuites. Plus 3 bedroom holiday home, 2 bathrooms, full kitchen, all have TV's, microwaves and fridges. Our interests are golf, fishing square dancing and gardening We have 2 very friendly cats Cleo & Levi. Please no smoking inside. Cooked breakfast is available on our sunny deck with spectacular views to Russell & beyond. Love to have you stay.

Admiral's View Lodge	**Tel:** (09) 402 6236	**Cost:** Double $75-$95
B&B S/C Holiday Home	**Fax:** (09) 402 6237	3 Bdr House $85 - $175
Paihia Central	**E:** admiralsview@actrix.gen.nz	Visa/MC Amex Diners
Robyn & Peter Rhodes	**W:** www.bnb.co.nz/hosts/	**Beds:** 2 Queen 2 Double 2 Twin
2 McMurray Road	admiralsviewlodge.html	6 Single (5 bdrm)
Paihia Bay of Islands		**Bath:** 4 Ensuite

Paihia

Marlin House is a beautiful neo-colonial building with spacious accommodation for eight persons in four self-contained suites with sitting room, fridge, Sky-TV off-road parking. Situated in a quiet tree-clad spot above Paihia with million dollar views of the Bay. It is only a three minutes walk from the beach shops and restaurants. We serve special continental breakfasts either in your suite or on the deck or you may order a full cooked breakfast. Ask us about our special discounts for tours.

Marlin House	**Tel:** (09) 402 8550	**Cost:** Double $90-$130
B&B Self-contained	**Fax:** (09) 402 6770	Single $80-$100
Paihia central	**Mob:** 025 487 937	Dinner B/A Visa/MC
Christopher & Angela Houry	**E:** chris.houry@xtra.co.nz	**Beds:** 3 Queen 1 Twin
15 Bayview Road	**W:** www.bnb.co.nz/hosts/	(4 bdrm)
Paihia	marlinhouse.html	**Bath:** 4 Ensuite
Bay of Islands		

Paihia

A romantic Spanish villa surrounded by a sub-tropical garden of palms and fern trees, enjoying the most spectacular views over the Bay of Islands Our villa makes an ideal accommodation base for your stay in Northland. It is within easy driving or coach distance from all the main sites, and only three minutes from Paihia swimming beaches and shops. We offer a choice of traditional bed and breakfast in our in-house guest wing or the privacy of self-contained accommodation in our holiday apartments.

Villa Casablanca
B&B Self-contained
3km N of Paihia
Barbara & Derek Robertson
18 Goffe Drive
Haruru Falls
Paihia

Tel: (09) 402 6980
Fax: (09) 402 6980
Mob: 021 666 567
E: derek@bestprice.co.nz
W: www.bestprice.co.nz

Cost: Double $160-$180
Single $130 Child n/a
Dinner $35
Seasonal Discounts
Visa/MC Amex
Beds: 1 King/Twin 4 Queen
4 Single (6 bdrm)
Bath: 4 Ensuite 2 Private

Paihia

Secluded yet we are right on the main beach in Paihia. Windermere is an extensive modern home with private self contained units for your personal use. Panoramic views from your own deck plus BBQ is available. We are 10 minutes walk to the centre of Paihia, numerous restaurants and a short ferry ride to historic Russell. We overlook the Waitangi River/Reserve and world famous golf course. A short drive away is Keri Keri, well known for its arts and crafts and citrus orchards. Directions: Please phone Jill or Richard. You will enjoy your stay with us and our friendly cat Ceefa.

Windermere
B&B Self-contained Homestay
0.5km NW of Paihia
Richard & Jill Burrows
168 Marsden Road
Paihia Bay of Islands

Tel: (09) 402 8696
Fax: (09) 402 5095
E: windermere@igrin.co.nz
W: www.windermere.co.nz

Cost: Double $100 - $150
Single $100 Child $25
Visa/MC
Beds: 2 Queen 4 Single
(2 bdrm)
Bath: 2 Ensuite

Paihia

Beaches Bed & Breakfast on the Waterfront offers holidaymakers spacious and comfortable bedrooms with Italian tiled ensuites. Two of our rooms open onto private balconies overlooking the Bay of Islands with panoramic views to Russell and beyond... You may even see dolphins frolic past your window! Centrally located on the corner of Kings and Marsden Roads, Paihia, the numerous restaurants and cafes of Paihia are within easy walking distance - and the Paihia wharf is only 500 metres along the waterfront. Tour Booking Facilities. Not suitable for children.

Beaches
B&B
Paihia Central
Ford & Annie Watson
14 Marsden Rd
Paihia 0252 Bay of Islands

Tel: (09) 402 8650
E: Beaches.BandB@xtra.co.nz
W: www.beachesbandb.co.nz

Cost: Double $100-$175
Beds: 3 Queen (3 bdrm)
Bath: 3 Ensuite

Paihia - Bay of Islands

Welcome and relax in our home. The "Waitangi Reserve" and world famous golf course is five minutes drive away. Enjoy our four poster with private bathroom or King waterbed with ensuite and river frontage. Continental or cooked breakfast is served on our kauri table or the veranda beside our serenely, tranquil, gently tumbling Puketona River frontage with extending, uninterrupted, farmland beyond. We enjoy meeting people and are, ourselves, well travelled. Along with our golden retriever we look forward to making your stay memorable. Tour booking facilities.

Appledore Lodge	**Tel:** 09 402 8007	**Cost:** Double $70-$125
B&B	**Fax:** 09 402 8007	Single $60-$75
6KM W of Paihia	**E:** appledorelodge@xtra.co.nz	**Beds:** 1 King 1 Double
Janet & Jim Pugh	**W:** www.bnb.co.nz/hosts/	(2 bdrm)
Puketona Road	appledore.html	**Bath:** 1 Ensuite 1 Private
Paihia Bay of Islands		

Paihia

Our studio apartment has all the comforts of home, a beautiful sunny lounge with fridge, microwave, TV, tea/coffee facilities, laundry, barbecue and undercover parking. All surrounded by a semi tropical garden. With breakfast upstairs you will enjoy the beautiful panoramic view of the surrounding countryside. Extra twin beds are available upstairs if in a group. We share our home with a small gregarious poodle and 3 reclusive cats. Situated only 3km from main tourist attractions. We offer you a warm welcome.

Fallsview	**Tel:** (09) 402 7871	**Cost:** Double $75-$90
B&B	**Fax:** (09) 402 7861	Single $40-$50 Child $40
3km Paihia	**Mob:** 025 627 1652	Visa/MC
Shirley & Clive Welch	**W:** www.bnb.co.nz/hosts/	**Beds:** 1 Queen 1 Twin
4 Fallsview Road	fallsview.html	1 Single (3 bdrm)
RD 1, Haruru Paihia		**Bath:** 1 Guests share

Just as we have a variety of B&Bs
you will also discover a variety of breakfasts,
and they will always be generous.

Paihia - Opua

We invite you to share our home set in a native bush garden and enjoying extensive upper harbour views. Our guest wing has private entrance and deck area, tea/coffee facilities, microwave, fridge and television. We host only one group at a time to ensure guests' privacy. Don is a retired carpenter and Pat a retired nurse. Our interests include walking, gardening, local history, fishing, sailing and woodwork. We have been hosting guests for many years and look forward to welcoming you to our home.

Rose Cottage
Homestay
5km S of Paihia
Pat & Don Jansen
Oromahoe Road
Opua Bay of Islands

Tel: (09) 402 8099
Fax: (09) 402 8099
Mob: 025 605 9560
W: www.bnb.co.nz/hosts/ rosecottageopua.html

Cost: Double $80 - $100
Single Negotiable
We host only one group
(2-4 persons at a time)
Beds: 1 King/Twin
1 Double (2 bdrm)
Bath: 1 Private

Paihia - Opua

Welcome to my lovely home above Opua harbour. Enjoy panoramic views of water and boat activities - always something happening. Tourist activities are nearby. Relax in the spa after your day's outing. You may like to wander in my garden - my big interest. Downstairs is a 2 roomed unit, separate shower, toilet and private deck with stunning views. Take the Whangarei - Paihia road. Turn right for Opua - Russel ferry. This is Franklin St. My house is clearly visible on the seaward side.

B&B Self-contained Homestay
300m E of Opua
Margaret Sinclair
7 Franklin St
Opua

Tel: (09) 402 8285
Fax: (09) 402 8285
W: bbopua@xtra.co.nz

Cost: Double $65 Single $40
S/C Flat 1 double 2 single
$65 - $85 Double
$10 Single
Beds: 1 Double 2 Single
(2 bdrm)
Bath: 1 Family share

Paihia - Opua

"Seascape" is on a tranquil bush-clad ridge. Enjoy spectacular views, stroll through bush to the coastal walk-way, enjoy our beautifully landscaped garden, experience the many activities in the Bay, or relax on your deck. We are keen NZ and international travellers. Other interests include music, gardening, fishing, boating, and Rotary. Our fully self-contained flat has double bed, TV, laundry, kitchen, own entrance and deck. Join us for breakfast, or look after yourselves. Guest Room with shared facilities also available.

Seascape
B&B Self-contained
5km S of Paihia
Vanessa & Frank Leadley
17 English Bay Road
Opua

Tel: (09) 402 7650
Fax: (09) 402 7650
E: frankleadley@xtra.co.nz
W: www.bnb.co.nz/hosts/ leadley.html

Cost: Double $80 Single $50
S/C $80 - $90 Visa/MC
Beds: 1 Double 2 Single
(2 bdrm)
Bath: 1 Ensuite 1 Family share

Russell

My home overlooks Russell Bay with breathtaking
water and bush views. Born and bred in Northland I
take great pride in showing my guests NZ finest
capital. I love every kind of fishing and frequently
escort my guests out game fishing. Meals are usually
served on the terrace and I find my guests like to
explore and sample the different fish restaurants that
abound in Russell. Lots of lovely walks handy. All I
ask of my guests is to completely relax and use my
home as theirs.

Kays Place
B&B Homestay
4mins N of Russell
Kay Bosanquet
67 Wellington Street
Russell

Tel: (09) 403 7843
Fax: (09) 403 7843
Mob: 025 2723 672
E: kay@bay-of-islands.co.nz
W: www.bnb.co.nz/hosts/
kaysplace.html

Cost: Double $120-$150
Single $65
Beds: 1 Queen 1 Double 1 Twin
1 Single (4 bdrm)
Bath: 1 Ensuite 2 Private

Russell

Our wooden house is by the beach in a sheltered bay.
We recommend walking shoes to our guests because
parking is on the hill, and a footpath leads down to the
house through a tunnel of native fern. A rowing dinghy
is free for fishing or crossing to Russell. Beach walks
start at the door and guests may swim off the beach or
sail to the islands. Breakfast includes fresh fruit,
muesli, yoghurt, hot bread, home-made jams,
marmalade and eggs. Dinner by arrangement. Please
phone or e-mail for directions.

Brown House
Homestay
7km S of Russell
Eva Brown
Major Bridge Drive
RD 1
Russell

Tel: (09) 403 7431
Fax: (09) 403 7431
E: evabrown@voyager.co.nz
W: www.bnb.co.nz/hosts/
brownhouse.html

Cost: Double $80 Single $50
Dinner by arrangement
Visa/MC
Beds: 1 Double 1 Single
(2 bdrm)
Bath: 1 Private

Russell

"The Manaaki" overlooks the picturesque harbour and
village of historic Russell with its delightful seaside
restaurants, shops and wharf a gentle stroll away.
Magnificent harbour, bush and village views are a
feature of guests private accommodation. The Villa is
an attractively appointed sunny spacious de-luxe unit
set in its own grounds (with garden spa) adjacent to the
main house. The Studio is a self contained suite-styled
apartment on the ground floor of our new modern
home. Both units have mini -kitchen facilities and off-
street parking.

Te Manaaki
Self-contained Homestay
Russell Central
Sharyn & Dudley Smith
2 Robertson Road
Russell

Tel: (09) 403 7200
Fax: (09) 403 7537
Mob: 025 972 177
E: triple.b@xtra.co.nz
W: www.bnb.co.nz/hosts/
temanaaki.html

Cost: Double $150-$250
Single $150-$250 Child $20
Visa/MC
Beds: 2 Super King (2 bdrm)
Bath: 2 Ensuite

Russell - Matauwhi Bay

Welcome to historic Russell; take a step-back into a bygone era and spend some time with us in our delightful, nostalgic, immaculately restored Victorian Villa (Circa 1894).

Enjoy your own large guest lounge; tea/coffee and biscuits always available, with open fire in the cooler months, and wrap-around verandahs for you to relax and take-in the warm sea breezes. Each of our four queen rooms have traditional wallpapers and paintwork, with handmade patchwork quilts and fresh flowers to create a lovingly detailed, traditional romantic interior.

Breakfast is served in our farmhouse kitchen around the large kauri dining table or al-fresco on the verandah if you wish. It is an all homemade affair; from the freshly baked fruit and nut bread, to the yummy daily special and the jam conserves.

Our self-contained cottage is set in park-like grounds for your privacy and enjoyment: with two double bedrooms, it is ideal for a family or two couples travelling together. It has a large lounge overlooking the reserve and out into the bay, a sun-room and fully self-contained kitchen.

Wonderful for people looking for that special place for peace and time-out. Max 4 persons. Breakfast is available if required. Complimentary afternoon tea on arrival. Laundry service available.

We look forward to meeting you soon. Our homes are SMOKE-FREE. We are closed June and July. We are a member of NZ Heritage Inns Group.

EXPERIENCE OUR HISTORIC B&B. ENJOY A WORLD OF DIFFERENCE.

Ounuwhao B&B
B&B Self-contained Historic Guesthouse
1km E of Russell
Marilyn & Allan Nicklin
Matauwhi Bay
Russell

Tel: (09) 403 7310
Fax: (09) 403 8310
E: thenicklins@xtra.co.nz
W: www.bnb.co.nz/hosts/ounuwhaobb.html

Cost: Double $150-$200
Single $100-$150
Child $35 under 12 yrs
Detached garden-suite $185
Visa/MC
Beds: 1 King/Twin 4 Queen
2 Twin 2 Single (5 bdrm)
Bath: 4 Ensuite 1 Private

Russell

Quite central position with fine sea views over Russell and the Bay. One of the interesting new homes architecturally designed in keeping with the historic nature of Russell. An all timber construction featuring New Zealand Kauri, Rimu, Douglas Fir and Pine. A special place to stay and share an intimate glimpse of a Russell life style. A look at craftsmanship of today with old world atmosphere combined with modern private facilities and true home comforts.

Friendly and personal attention is assured. Breakfast at our antique Kauri table amongst Rimu wood panelling, old bricks and over 100 years old re-sited arched windows. Furnished with antiques, Persian carpets throughout and examples of Roly's Kauri furniture and cabinetry. Air conditioning and heating for all year round comfort.

Two private spacious suites, each with their own entrance from the main foyer, both have sea views, queen size beds, ensuites, TV, fridge and tea/coffee making facilities. Studio unit with private entrance and own verandah to enjoy the view over Russel and the Bay. Air conditioning, queen bed and one large single, fridge, TV, large ensuite.

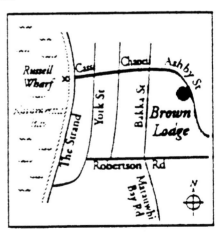

Russell township is easy 3 minute walk to restaurants, shops, wharf. Relax on the front veranda with peaceful sea views to Waitangi and Paihia. We can advise and book restaurants, boat cruises around the Bay and bus trips to Cape Reinga etc.

Smoke free home, safe off street parking, no wheel chair access. Please phone or fax ahead to avoid disappointment.

Brown Lodge
Homestay Studio Unit
0.25km E of Russell
Joan & Roly Brown
6 Ashby Street
Russell

Tel: (09) 403 7693
Fax: (09) 403 7683
E: brown.lodge@xtra.co.nz
W: http://webnz.co.nz/bbnz/
brown1.htm

Cost: Double $160-$180
Single $160 Visa/MC
Beds: 3 Queen 1 Single
(3 bdrm)
Bath: 3 Ensuite

Russell

Our home is situated at the end of Te Wahapu Peninsula. We are surrounded by native bush and tuis & fantails are our constant companions. Kiwis are sometimes heard during the night. Both upstairs bedrooms have beautiful sea views from your bed. Guests are welcome to sit in the spa pool and watch the sun set over Paihia across the Bay. A track through the bush leads down to the beach and the self-contained historic cottage, where you are welcome to use the dingy and barbecue.

Treetops
B&B Self-contained Homestay
5km S of Russell
Vivienne & Andy Nathan
6 Pinetree Lane
Te Wahapu
Russell

Tel: (09) 403 7475
Fax: (09) 403 7459
Mob: 025 272 8881
E: vnathan@xtra.co.nz
W: www.bnb.co.nz/hosts/
treetopsrussell.html

Cost: Double $95 Single $85
Dinner $35
S/C Cottage $95
Visa/MC Amex Diners
Beds: 1 King 1 Double
(2 bdrm)
Bath: 1 Guests share

Russell

Our home is 10 minutes walk to historic Russell and the design inspired by having lived in Greece. In warm weather breakfast on the verandah looking out to Matauwhi Bay and Russell Boat Club otherwise relax in the glassed-in breeze way with fresh waffles and maple syrup. Or you may like a traditional English breakfast using fresh eggs from our chickens. We have only one guestroom with its own entrance, large bathroom and antique bath. Our combined interests include travelling, art, sport and our cat and dog. Welcome!

Lesleys
Homestay
1km E of Russell
Lesley Coleman
1 Pomare Road
Russell Northland

Tel: (09) 403 7099
E: three.gs@xtra.co.nz
Mob: 021 120 9260
W: bay-of-islands.co.nz/
accomm/lesley.html

Cost: Double $95 Single $70
Child $30 Dinner $20
Visa/MC
Beds: 1 Double 1 Single
(1 bdrm)
Bath: 1 Private

Russell - Okiato

"A quiet place to relax." We have sailed half way around the world to find this beautiful quiet place in the heart of the Bay of Islands and would be happy to share this with you for a while. Aimeo Cottage is built on the hill of Okiato Point, a secluded peninsula overlooking the Bay. In 10 minutes you are in New Zealand's first capital, Russell, the site of many historic buildings, an interesting museum and art galleries. Children are welcome. For golfers a complete set of clubs (men) complementary available.

Aimeo Cottage
B&B Self-contained Homestay
3 bedroom holiday home
9km S of Russell
Annie & Helmuth Hormann
Okiato Point Road
RD 1 Russell

Tel: (09) 403 7494
Fax: (09) 403 7494
Mob: 025 272 2393
E: aimeo-cottage.nz@xtra.co.nz
W: www.bnb.co.nz/hosts/
aimeocottage.html

Cost: Double $110 Single $100
Child $25
Dinner by arrangement
Visa/MC
Beds: 2 King/Twin 1 Twin
1 Single (2 bdrm)
Bath: 1 Ensuite 1 Private

Russell - Te Wahapu

Our Home and Garden are hidden among the trees just metres from the water's edge. In the morning awake to bird song and the sunrise over Orongo Bay. A dinghy is at hand for a leisurely paddle and a mooring is available for your boat. We offer warm hospitality and quality smoke free accommodation with fine linen, china, silver and antiques. Meals feature fresh home grown fruit and vegetables and eggs from our free range chickens. Historic Russell's Museum, Cafes and Galleries are just seven minutes away. Come and enjoy this private and tranquil place.

Brisa	**Tel:** (09) 403 7757	**Cost:** Double $100-$140
B&B Self-contained	**Fax:** (09) 403 7758	Single $90-$120
7km S of Russell	**Mob:** 025 58 22 31	Dinner by arr. $30pp
Jenny & Peter Sharpe	**E:** brisa@xtra.co.nz	Visa/MC
Te Wahapu Road	**W:** www.bay-of-islands.co.nz/	**Beds:** 1 King/twin 2 Queen
RD 1 Russell	accomm/brisa.html	1 Double (3 bedroom)
		Bath: 3 Ensuite

Russell - Parekura Bay

Our home is an upstairs-downstairs. Your accommodation is a fully self-contained unit (breakfast upstairs with us), alternatively, there is a double bedroom, share bathroom upstairs. We are situated 25 km from Russell township, 25 km from vehicular ferry which leaves from Opua (Paihia side) to Okiaio, Russell side. The view is great, 5 minutes walk to a safe swimming beach. We can arrange activities for you. Quiet surroundings. Children welcome, under 8 years no charge. We have a dog, yours will be welcome.

Carpe Diem	**Tel:** (09) 403 8015	**Cost:** Double $100 Single $44
B&B Self-contained Rental	**Fax:** (09) 403 8015	Child $10
24km E of Russell	**Mob:** 025 218 0151	**Beds:** 1 King/Twin 1 Double
Jewel & Martin Collett	**W:** www.bnb.co.nz/hosts/	2 Single (3 bdrm)
Parekura Bay	carpediem.html	**Bath:** 1 Private 1 Family share
Russell Northland		

Russell

Secluded waterfront location just 7 mins from Russell village. Choose from the luxury of our lodge - sleeps up to 8 persons - (Qualmark ★★★★ rated 2001/2) Homestay suite (double) and Studio - sleeps 1 double, 2 singles, all fully self-contained with own ensuites. Services include telephone, TV & video library and BBQ's. Pets by arrangement. Complimentary dinghy and kayak for use on our sheltered estuary. Resident Golden Labrador (Tessa). Optional light tackle, saltfly, gamefishing or sightseeing trips on our modern fully equipped charter vessel "MAKO 1"

Mako Lodge &	**Tel:** (09) 403 7770	**Cost:** Double $110 Single $110
Fishing Charters	**Fax:** (09) 403 7713	Dinner by arrangement
B&B Homestay Lodge S/cont.	**Mob:** 025 739 787	Lodge From $170
7km S of Russell	**Tollfree:** 0800 625 669	Visa/MC
Jean & Graeme McIntosh	**E:** makolodge.charters@xtra.co.nz	**Beds:** 1 King/Twin 2 Queen
Box 114	**W:** www.bnb.co.nz/hosts/	1 Double 6 Single (4 bdrm)
Russell	makolodgefishingcharters.html	**Bath:** 4 Ensuite

Russell

LA VEDUTA. Enjoy our mix of traditional European culture in the midst of the beautiful Bay of Islands, historic heartland of New Zealand. La Veduta is the perfect pied-a-terre for your Northland holiday. Relax, or we can arrange a wide range of activities. Restaurants and ferries handy, transport available. We offer our guests a warm welcome and personalised service. French Italian spoken. A large garden for our black poodle. A balcony for sunset lovers with panoramic views. TV room, billiard room, laundry.

La Veduta
Homestay
0.5km N of Russell
Danielle & Dino Fossi
11 Gould Street
Russell
Bay of Islands

Tel: (09) 403 8299
Fax: (09) 403 8299
E: laveduta@xtra.co.nz
W: www.laveduta.co.nz

Cost: Double $130-$150
Single $95-$110 Child $45
Dinner by arrangement
Visa/MC
Beds: 4 Double 1 Twin
1 Single (5 bdrm)
Bath: 2 Ensuite 2 Private
1 Guests share

Russell

Our apartment is adjacent to our home with magnificent seaviews and a lovely garden and is located in a quiet street, 5 mins drive from the village and a 5 min. stroll to beautiful Long Beach. The unit has one double bedroom, plus a sofa/settee in lounge for extra guests, a fully-equipped kitchen adjoining lounge and outdoor decks. We have lived in Russell for 16 years. We share our home with our cat 'Ollie' and a small friendly dog. Friendly hospitality awaits you. We also have a variety of holiday homes available - all fully self contained and self catering and all have spectacular views over the bay.

Paws for Thought
S/C Holiday Homes also available
Russell Township
Eldon & Gill Jackson
4 Russell Heights Road
Russell Bay of Islands

Tel: (09) 403 7109
Fax: (09) 403 7159
Mob: 025 276 2870
E: paws.for.thought@xtra.co.nz
W: www.guesthouse.co.nz

Cost: Double $100
Beds: 1 Queen (1 bdrm)
Bath: 1 Private

Russell

On Te Wahapu Peninsula stay in secluded modern hilltop villa - fully equipped kitchen, liv/din room and bath, to plan day trips by car or bus tour - Cape Reinga; Air or boat tours - Bay of Islands or local ferry boat trips - Russell to Paihia w/shopping, museums return to your 'treehouse' plan picnic track to Tore Tore Island at the end of Peninsula just beyond boat ramp at low tide or stay on your private patio and decks enjoy NZ's natural habitat with ever-changing bay views.

Whare Tainui
Self-contained
7km S of Russell
Eleanor & William Stegall
PO Box 54
Te Wahapu Russell

Tel: (09) 403 8339
Fax: (09) 403 8339
Mob: 025 244 3178
W: www.bnb.co.nz/hosts/
wharetainui.html

Cost: Double $125-$145
Visa/MC
Beds: 1 Queen (1 bdrm)
Bath: 1 Ensuite 1 Private

Russell - Parekura Bay

Overlooking the sea, where sunlight plays with the shade of palms and native trees, the Casa de la Luna is a retreat in traditional Mediterranean style. Ceramic tiled stairs lead to guestrooms, each with sea-facing balconies. Enjoy stunning views, listen to a silence broken only by bird song. Fishing and bushwalks available. Welcome to our smoke free villa in the sun, being also home to two friendly West Highland terriers. Having travelled widely, we understand your needs and look forward to your stay. Children by arrangement.

Casa de la Luna	**Tel:** (09) 828 3524	**Cost:** Double $160-$185
B&B Self-contained	or (09) 403 7333	Single $130 Child B/A
21km E of historical Russell	**Fax:** (09) 828 5964	Dinner B/A Visa/MC
Robyn & Chris Moon	**W:** www.bnb.co.nz/hosts/	**Beds:** 2 Queen (2 bdrm)
Manawaora Rawhiti Road	casadelaluna.html	**Bath:** 1 Ensuite 1 Guests share
Parekura Bay B.O.I.		

Kohukohu

Historic Kohukohu, now a friendly and charming village,is situated on the north side of the Hokianga Harbour. Our beautifully restored Kauri home is set in two acres of gardens and trees and commands a spectacular view of the harbour. The guest rooms, opening on to a sunny verandah, are in a private wing of the house. Meals are prepared using home-grown produce in season. We are interested in and knowledgeable about the history and geography of the area. We have two cats.

Harbour Views Guest House	**Tel:** (09) 405 5815	**Cost:** Double $80 Single $40
B&B Homestay Guesthouse	**Fax:** (09) 405 5865	Dinner $20
80km S of Kaitaia	**W:** www.bnb.co.nz/hosts/	**Beds:** 1 Queen 2 Single
Jacky Kelly & Bill Thomson	harbourviewsguesthouse.html	(2 bdrm)
Rakautapu Road		**Bath:** 1 Private
Kohukohu Northland		

Rawene

The view of harbour and hills beautiful - sunsets breathtaking. Our one acre garden includes tropical flowers and fruit trees. Fresh fruit picked almost everyday. We are retired, Wally an ex naval man. Interests meeting people, gardening, wine making, photography, exploring New Zealand. 1km to shops, hotel, ferry, petrol, hospital. Turn off main road, motor camp sign over hill veer left. At Nimmo Street West turn left to top of hill, flat parking area, easy access. Warm welcome.

Searell's	**Tel:** (09) 405 7835	**Cost:** Double $70 Single $40
B&B Homestay	**Fax:** (09) 405 7835	Child $15 - $20
43km W of Kaikohe	**W:** www.bnb.co.nz/hosts/	Dinner $20 Full breakfast $5
Nellie & Wally Searell	searells.html	**Beds:** 1 Double 2 Single
PO Box 100, Rawene 0452		(2 bdrm)
Nimmo Street West		**Bath:** 1 Private
Rawene		

Opononi

Situated on Koutu Point overlooking the beautiful
Hokianga Harbour, our home has views both rural and
sea. Two rooms have private decks, ensuites, and all
rooms are tastefully decorated and very
comfortable.We are a friendly Kiwi couple, and our
aim is to provide a memorable stay, peaceful, or as
active as you wish. Our friendly dog lives outside.
Koutu Loop Rd is 4.3 kms north of Opononi then left
2.3 kms on tar seal to Lodge on right.

Koutu Lodge
B&B Homestay
50km W of Kaikohe
Tony and Sylvia Stockman
Koutu Loop Road
Opononi
(Postal - RD3, Kaikohe)

Tel: (09) 405 8882
Fax: (09) 405 8893
E: koutulodgebnb@xtra.co.nz
W: www.bnb.co.nz/hosts/
koutulodge.html

Cost: Double $90 Single $55
Dinner $30 by arrangement
Visa/MC
Beds: 1 King 1 Queen 1 Double
1 Single (3 bdrm)
Bath: 2 Ensuite 1 Private

Opononi

Situated on the corner of SH12 and Fairlie Cres,
opposite a beach reserve on the edge of the pristine
Hokianga Harbour, only 20 minutes from "Tane-
Mahuta" the largest Kauri tree in the world. From our
decks there are picture postcard views up and down
and across the harbour to the huge golden sand dunes.
Machine embroidery, patchwork, quilting, fishing,
boating, service clubs activities, indoor bowls, our
quiet dog Toby are our main interests. Come to the
Hokianga- the West Coast diamond.

Opononi Dolphin Lodge
B&B Homestay
57km W of Kaikohe
Rob & Pam Jensen
Cnr SH12 & Fairlie Cres
Box 28
Opononi

Tel: (09) 405 8451
Fax: (09) 405 8451
E: <shirley@xtra.co.nz
W: www.bnb.co.nz/hosts/
dolphinlodge.html

Cost: Double $85 Single $50
Visa/MC
Beds: 1 Queen 1 Double
1 Twin 1 Single (3 bdrm)
Bath: 2 Ensuite 1 Private

Omapere

Our beachfront home on Highway 12 overlooking the
Hokianga Harbour is within walking distance of restaurants
and bars. The beach is 50 metres away. Both rooms have
ensuites, tea making facilities, refrigerators and TV with
separate entrances onto private decks to relax and enjoy
superb views. We're close to the Waipoua Forest, West
Coast beaches and sand hills. With an involvement in
farming, forestry and education. Stay and share our home
and cat. Extra to above a self-contained flat $70 per night,
discounted for longer stay.

Harbourside Bed & Breakfast
B&B
60km W of Kaikohe
Joy & Garth Coulter
PO Box 10
Omapere

Tel: (09) 405 8246
W: www.bnb.co.nz/hosts/
harboursidebedbreakfast.html

Cost: Double $80 Single $50
Visa/MC
Beds: 1 Queen 2 Single
(2 bdrm)
Bath: 2 Ensuite

Omapere

Snuggled into this peaceful private, beachfront location, our new home embraces the continuously inspiring sea scape of the ever changing, dramatic harbour entrance and magnificent dune. Simply relaxing in this harbourside haven is reviltalizing. Bush and forest walks, horse riding, harbour cruising, fishing, river and coastal swimming are some of the natural delights to be enjoyed in this historic area. Our dog will be a willing walking companion. Star gazing in the warmth of the hot tub is a wonderful way to finish the day. Phone for directions.

Hokianga Haven Omapere
Beachfront
B&B
60km W of Kaikohe
Heather Randerson
226 State Highway 12
Omapere Hokianga

Tel: (09) 405 8285
Fax: (09) 405 8215
E: tikanga2000@xtra.co.nz
W: www.bnb.co.nz/hosts/
omaperebeachfront.html

Cost: Double $100-$130
Beds: 1 Queen   (1 bdrm)
Bath: 1 Private

Dargaville - Bayly's Beach

Less than 2 1/2 hours north of Auckland, the sometimes wild, always wonderful West Coast is an ideal place to relax. With a glimpse of the sea, your cottage is two minutes walk from the beach and clifftop walkway. Play 18 hole golf locally, we are en-route to Kai Iwi Lakes and Waipoua Forest. We enjoy a relaxed lifestyle with our two children and cat. Your cottage is sunny, comfortable and has a great shower! Breakfast at your leisure - this is provided in cottage for you. Directions: Drive through the village, you will see our sign at the foot of the big hill.

Ocean View
Self-contained
12km W of Dargaville
Paula & John Powell
7 Ocean View Terrace
Baylys Beach, RD7
Dargaville

Tel: (09) 439 6256
Mob: 025 623 3821
E: baylys@win.co.nz
W: www.bnb.co.nz/hosts/
oceanview.html

Cost: Double $75 Single $45
         Child $10 under 12yrs
         Visa/MC
Beds: 1 Double 1 Single
         (1 bdrm)
Bath: 1 Ensuite

Dargaville

We are in central Dargaville just minutes to various restaurants. Awakino Rd is the road to local hospital and we are just 4 doors from main entrance. Ideally suited to enjoy Kauri Parks, Kai Iwi Lakes, beaches, Pouto Point trips, museums etc. Wallace's main interest is Masonic Lodge. Agnes enjoys meeting people. We enjoy sharing our local knowledge in a smoke free home. Our aim is a "friendly, relaxing, make yourself at home' house. A spoilt cat named "China" lives with us.

Grand View
B&B
Dargaville Central
Agnes & Wallace Bennett
66 Awakino Road
Dargaville

Tel: (09) 439 5163
Mob: 021 1500 910
W: www.bnb.co.nz/hosts/
user2.html

Cost: Double $60 Single $30
         Child $30 Dinner $20
         Visa/MC
Beds: 1 Double 1 Twin
         (2 bdrm)
Bath: 2 Family share

Awakino Point Lodge
Dargaville

Dargaville

This unique property set on its own acreage surrounded by attractive gardens is just a two minute drive from Dargaville. The best features of a boutique motel scheme and a New Zealand bed and breakfast have been amalgamated to produce this "Something a little different".

You will enjoy your own private self contained suite with private bathroom, friendly personal service and a good breakfast most of which is home produced.

The lodge has three well appointed one and two bedroom self contained ground floor units. One of them has a kitchen, bath and log fire which is very cosy in winter.

There are plenty of good eating houses in Dargaville reasonably priced, but if you require a meal at the lodge please be sure to book in advance.

Credit cards can be accepted but travellers cheques or cash would be very much appreciated. Smoking to be kept to the outdoors please. 3 suites all with ensuite bathrooms.

```
         ◄── To Waipoua Forrest
              and the North        ███
──────────────────────────────────────
 1.5 kms to Dargaville  1.5 kms to Lodge
         ◄──                    ──►
   SH 12 to
   Dargaville                 SH 14 to
   and the        SH 12 to    Whangarei
   North          Auckland
```

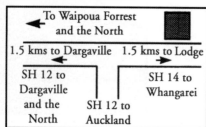

Awakino Point Lodge
Self-contained S.C Units
3km Dargaville
June & Mick
P O Box 168
Dargaville

Tel: (09) 439 7870
Fax: (09) 439 7870
Mob: 025 519 474
E: awakinopointlodge@xtra.co.nz
W: www.skybusiness.com/
awakinopointlodge

Cost: Double $75-$85 (1 bdrm)
4 persons $125-$135
(2 bdrm)
Visa/MC Amex Diners
Beds: 3 Queen 4 Twin (5 bdrm)
Bath: 3 Ensuite

Dargaville

Kauri House Lodge sits high above Dargaville amongst mature trees. The 1880's villa retains all it's charm, style and grace with original Kauri panelling and period antiques in all rooms.

Start your day woken by native birds, walk through extensive landscaped grounds or read in our library. In summer enjoy a dip in the large swimming pool. In winter our billiard room log fire is a cozy spot to relax for the evening.

Join us to explore beautiful mature native bush on our rearby farm overlooking the Wairoa River and Kaipara Harbour.

The area offers many activities including deserted beaches, lakes, river tours, horse treks, walks and restaurants.

Kauri House Lodge
Farmstay B&B luxury
accomodation
1.5km S of Dargaville
Doug Blaxall
PO Box 382
Bowen Street
Dargaville

Tel: (09) 439 8082
Fax: (09) 439 8082
Mob: 025 547 769
E: kaurihouse@infomace.co.nz
W: www.bnb.co.nz/hosts/
kaurihouselodge.html

Cost: Double $175-$225
    Single $150-$160 Visa/MC
Beds: 1 King/Twin 2 King
   (3 bdrm)
Bath: 3 Ensuite

Dargaville

We enjoy sharing our home and local knowledge with guests in our modern, one level home 2ks from Dargaville on SH 12, minutes from quality restaurants. Excellent parking for vehicles, and an expansive garden. We thank our guests for not smoking and offer the use of our enclosed Spa Pool. Our family of three grown children, all live away from home, and interests include Family, Farming, Rotary International, Gardening and Big Game Fishing. Our pets include two cats and a friendly corgi.

Turiwiri B&B
B&B
2km S of Dargaville
Bruce & Jennifer Crawford
Turiwiri
RD 4, State Highway 12
Dargaville

Tel: (09) 439 6003
Fax: (09) 439 6003
W: www.bnb.co.nz/hosts/turiwiribb.html

Cost: Double $70 Single $35
Beds: 2 Queen (2 bdrm)
Bath: 1 Guests share

Dargaville

If you enjoy a good nights sleep, love a nice hot shower and insist on cleanliness then look no further. My Kauri bungalow was built in 1912 has 4 queen and twin bedrooms well decorated for your comfort. A large family lounge with log fire and a lovely modern kitchen, dining room with coal range. I'm close to the town centre which has excellent eating out houses. If it's a friendly homely stay you require call in, your inspection is welcome.

Birch's B&B
B&B
Dargaville central
Walter Rex Birch
18 Kauri Street
Dargaville

Tel: (09) 439 7565
Fax: (09) 439 7520
Mob: 025 586 554
E: birch@kauricoast.co.nz
W: www.bnb.co.nz/hosts/birchsbb.html

Cost: Double $70 Single $45
Child negotiable
Visa/MC
Beds: 2 Queen 2 Twin
(4 bdrm)
Bath: 1 Guests Share

Matakohe

"Maramarie" is a secluded Kauri homestead set in a mature garden. Located 4km from Matakohe and the unique Kauri museum where Kauri history is beautifully displayed and is a must see on your visit to Northland. We are beef farmers and our farm overlooks the Kaipara Harbour. I am Swedish and Tom is a Kiwi with three school age children. We have working dogs and a lazy cat. Come and visit our family and relax on our farm. Please phone for reservations and directions.

Maramarie
Farmstay
4km S of Matakohe
Elinor & Tom Beazley
Tinopai Road
RD 1
Matakohe

Tel: (09) 431 6911
E: maramarie@xtra.co.nz
W: www.bnb.co.nz/hosts/maramarie.html

Cost: Double $80 Single $50
Child 1/2 price
Dinner $20 B/A Visa/MC
Beds: 1 Double (1 bdrm)
Bath: 1 Private

Pahi - Paparoa

We invite you to come and relax in or old Kauri renovated villa built 1880, tastefully decorated for your comfort. We offer water views, all tide boat ramp, wharf, beach reserve home of the biggest Morton bay fig tree, all within 100 metres. We are within minutes of Matakohe Kauri Museum on the twin coast scenic route. Our home is spacious and warm for in-house guests, or a cosy self-contained cottage amongst delightful gardens is available. Our two cats love meeting people, as we do.

Palm House	**Tel:** (09) 431 6689	**Cost:** Double $85 Single $70
B&B Self-contained	**Fax:** (09) 431 6689	Dinner $25 by arrangement
7km W of Paparoa	**E:** palmhouse@paradise.net.nz	S/C Garden Cottage $75
Len & Pam Byles	**W:** www.bnb.co.nz/hosts/	Visa/MC
Pahi Road	palmhouse.html	**Beds:** 2 Queen 1 Twin (3 bdrm)
RD 1, Paparoa Northland		**Bath:** 1 Ensuite 1 Guests share

Whangarei - Parua Bay

Enjoy our Million Dollar Views. The Farm Park is a unique 300 acre farm/housing complex, running deer, cattle and sheep. We have a safe beach, walks, orchard, security gates, adjacent to "The Pines" golf course, with public boat ramp, fishing, tennis and beaches nearby. A spa is available. We enjoy travel, sport, gardening, patchwork. We have resided in UK and Solomon Islands and travel extensively. Dinner is by arrangement and we request no smoking. Phone for directions/gate code. We have a small dog.

Pen-Y-Bryn	**Tel:** (09) 436 1941	**Cost:** Double $115
S/C Farmstay Homestay	**Fax:** (09) 436 1946	Single $80 Dinner $35pp
15km E of Whangarei	**Mob:** 021 932 578	Visa/MC
Tina & Wayne Butler	**E:** wbutler@ihug.co.nz	**Beds:** 1 Queen (1 bdrm)
Headland Farm Park	**W:** www.pen-y-bryn.co.nz	**Bath:** 1 Ensuite
RD 4 Whangarei		

Whangarei

Happily retired, we enjoy outdoors, travel, sport and guests. We have a twin, self-contained studio with en-suite and double room with conservatory and family share bathroom. Spectacular sea and landscape views - tea/coffee facilities, refrigerator, table and chairs, TV, radio, adjoining covered decks. Enjoy gardens, beaches, forest and mountain walks, golf, fishing, boating, swimming. Smoking outdoors or on decks please. DIRECTIONS: From Whangarei city centre, head east to Onerahi (5km) - at BP station, turn left on Whangarei Heads Road, 5km to B&B on left.

Waikaraka Harbourview	**Tel:** (09) 436 2549	**Cost:** Double $50-$70
B&B Self-contained Homestay	**Fax:** (09) 436 2549	Single $35-$45 Visa/MC
10km E of Whangarei	**E:** becksbb@xtra.co.nz	**Beds:** 1 Double 2 Single
Marrion & John Beck	**W:** www.bnb.co.nz/hosts/	(2 bdrm)
477 Whangarei Heads Road	waikarakaharbourview.html	**Bath:** 1 Ensuite 1 Family share
Waikaraka, RD 4, Whangarei		

Whangarei - Parua Bay

Parua House is a classical colonial house, built in 1883, comfortably restored and occupying an elevated site with panoramic views of Parua Bay and the Whangarei Harbour. The property covers 29 hectares of farmland including two protected reserves which are rich in native trees (including kauri) and birds.

Guests are welcome to explore the farm and bush, milk the Jersey cow, explore the olive grove and subtropical orchard or just relax in the spa-pool or on the verandah. A safe swimming beach adjoins the farm, with a short walk to the fishing jetty, two marinas and a golf course are nearby.

Our wide interests include photography, patchwork quilting and horticulture. The house is attractively appointed with antique furniture and a rare collection of spinning wheels.

Awake to home-baked bread and freshly squeezed orange juice. Dine in elegant surroundings with generous helpings of home produce with our own meat, milk, eggs, home-grown vegetables, olive and subtropical fruit (home-made icecream a speciality). Pre meal drinks and wine are provided to add to the bonhomie of an evening around a large French oak refectory table. As featured on TV's "Ansett NZ Time of Your Life" and "Corban's Taste NZ".

Parua House
Farmstay Homestay
17km E of Whangarei
Pat & Peter Heaslip
Parua Bay
RD 4
Whangarei

Tel: (09) 436 5855
Fax: (09) 436 5105
E: paruahomestay@clear.net.nz
W:
www.paruahomestay.homestead.com

Cost: Double $100-$110
Single $70 Child 1/2 price
Dinner $30
Visa/MC
Beds: 2 Queen 3 Single
(4 bdrm)
Bath: 2 Ensuite 1 Private

Whangarei - Onerahi

"Channel Vista" is situated on the shores of Whangarei Harbour. We have 2 luxury self contained units each with their own private decks where you can relax and watch the boats go by. We offer a smoke free environment and have laundry, fax and email facilities available. Salty (dog) and Pepe (cat) are our friendly pets. Local shopping centre is only 3 minutes away. All sports facilities (eg golf, diving, walks, game fishing, bowls etc) nearby. We are only 1 hour from Bay of island, so it is a good place to base yourself for your Northland holiday.

Channel Vista
B&B Self-contained Luxury
9km Whangarei
Jenny & Murray Tancred
254 Beach Road
Onerahi, Whangarei

Tel: (09) 436 5529
Fax: (09) 436 5529
Mob: 025 973 083
E: tancred@igrin.co.nz
W: www.bnb.co.nz/hosts/
channelvista.html

Cost: Double $90-$150
Visa/MC
Beds: 2 Queen (2 bdrm)
Bath: 2 Ensuite

Whangarei

Chelsea House is a 1910 villa walking distance from the central city, Town Basin and restaurant. Opposite is Mair Park featuring walkways through beautiful native bush to the summit of Parahaki. Our double room ($90) has television, ensuite and kitchen (self catering $350 weekly). The twin room ($70) has tea/coffee making facilities and ensuite. Your choice of breakfast menu is served in our family kitchen or in the cottage garden setting. We have two children (11/15 yrs) and Peanut a Jack Russell. Laundry available.

Chelsea House
B&B
1km N of Whangarei
Cathy & Mel Clarke
83 Hatea Drive
Whangarei

Tel: (09) 437 0728
Mob: 021 379 976
Tollfree: 0508 243 573
E: mel.clarke@clear.net.nz
W: www.bnb.co.nz/hosts/
chelseahouse.html

Cost: Double $70-$90
Single $40 Child $20
Visa/MC
Beds: 1 Queen 2 Single
(2 bdrm)
Bath: 2 Ensuite

Whangarei

We welcome you to our turn-of-the century villa lovingly restored to offer comfort and luxury. Mother and daughter team Grace and Linda offer you friendly personal service. Our rooms offer superbly comfortable beds, TV, tea/coffee, heaters and electric blankets. Five minutes to city centre with a wide variety of top class restaurants, 20 minute drive to Tutukaka Coast, handy to spectacular Whangarei Falls. We have a dog and cat. Your pets welcome. Laundry facilities available.

Graelyn Villla
B&B
4.5km NE of Whangarei
Linda McGrogan & Grace Green
166 Kiripaka Road
Whangarei

Tel: (09) 437 7532
Fax: (09) 437 7533
E: graelyn@xtra.co.nz
W: www.bnb.co.nz/hosts/
graelynvillla.html

Cost: Double $80 Single $65
Child by arrangement
Visa/MC Amex Diners
Beds: 2 Queen 2 Single
(3 bdrm)
Bath: 3 Ensuite

Whangarei

We welcome you to our charming country residence at
Maungatapere, within easy driving distances to East and
West Coast beaches. We are a semi-retired couple with two
family pets, and welcome the opportunity to return
hospitality experienced overseas. Our home overlooks a
stream and we are gradually developing the 3 1/2 acres into
lawns, gardens and ponds. The guest wing is private - TV
room - tea coffee making facilities - smoke free area.
Whangarei has excellent restaurants or you can choose to
dine with us and enjoy hospitality.

Taraire Grove
B&B Homestay
16km W of Whangarei
Jan & Brian Newman
Tatton Rd
RD 9
Whangarei

Tel: (09) 434 7279
Fax: (09) 434 7279
E: cooper@igrin.co.nz
W: www.bnb.co.nz/hosts/
tarairegrove.html

Cost: Double $80 Single $50
   Child 1/2 price
   Dinner $12 - $20
   Visa/MC
Beds: 1 Queen 2 Single
   (2 bdrm)
Bath: 1 Guests share

Whangarei

Welcome to our quiet, centrally situated home,
overlooking Whangarei City and Hatea River. Stroll to
the town basin and city centre. Let us recommend a
restaurant or cafe. We are handy to the Airport, Golf
Links and beaches. Our home has swimming pool and
lovely gardens for your enjoyment. Choose between a
cosy detached Bedroom with ensuite or guests
bedrooms upstairs. A TV lounge is provided. We share
our home with "Storm" our cat. Quiet Location.
Privacy Assured.

The Wright Place
Self-contained Homestay
2.3km NE of Whangarei
Selwyn & Margaret Wright
2 Memorial Drive
Whangarei

Tel: (09) 438 7441
Fax: (09) 438 7441
Mob: 025 245 4177
E: wright.place@clear.net.nz.
W: www.bnb.co.nz/hosts/
thewrightplace.html

Cost: Double $75-$80
   Single $50 Visa/MC
Beds: 1 Double 2 Single
   (3 bdrm)
Bath: 1 Ensuite 1 Family share

Whangarei

Our comfortable elevated home is 1.2 km from the
Mall and Post Office. We overlook the Hatea River,
Western Hills with views over city. The Town Basin is
at the bottom of the street with restaurants, cafes and
the Aquatic Centre. Forum North, Whangarei area
hospital is close by. Unfortunately our place is not
suitable for children. Meet Cara our lovable Boxer.
Smokers outside. Pick up from Airport. We look
forward to meeting you. Please phone ahead.

City Lights
B&B Homestay
Kevin McMahon
& Doug Simpson
40A Vale Road Riverside
Whangarei

Tel: (09) 438 2390
Fax: (09) 438 2480
Mob: 025 958 243
E: dougkevin@xtra.co.nz
W: www.bnb.co.nz/hosts/
citylights.html

Cost: Double $80 Single $50
   Visa/MC
Beds: 1 Queen 2 Single
   (2 bdrm)
Bath: 1 Guests share

Whangarei

Enjoy a warm friendly welcome. We have over three acres of beautiful trees, shrubs, bulbs, perennials, succulents and a large variety of bird life. Feel at home in a spacious self-contained unit with fridge, microwave and tea making facilities. Enjoy cooked or continental breakfast in our dining room overlooking the garden. We are 10km from central Whangarei on Ngunguru- Tutukaka highway. 5km from Whangarei Falls. Beautiful beaches, restaurants, diving, fishing and golfing within 10km.

Country Garden Tearooms
Self-contained
10km NE of Whangarei CBD
John & Margaret Pool
526 Ngunguru Road
RD 3
Whangarei

Tel: (09) 437 5127
Mob: 025 519 476
W: www.bnb.co.nz/hosts/
countrygarden.html

Cost: Double $65 Single $45
Dinner $20 by arrangement
Beds: 2 Queen (2 bdrm)
Bath: 2 Ensuite

Whangarei

Come and enjoy the absolute tranquillity of "Owaitokamotu" which is a place of water, magnificent rocks of all shapes and sizes, and pristine native bush awaiting your rambling walks, all set on 10 1/2 acres of easy contour and newly created gardens. Our home is newly built and is wheelchair friendly. Bedrooms have private access form exterior. TV, tea, coffee and cookies. A wide verandah offers pleasant relaxation. Smoking outside only please. Laundry facilities available.

Owaitokamotu
Homestay
12km SW of Whangarei
M & G Whitehead
PO Box 6067
Otaika Whangarei

Tel: (09) 434 7554
Fax: (09) 4347554
W: www.bnb.co.nz/hosts/
owaitokamotu.html

Cost: Double $75 Single $45
Dinner $20
Campervans $10-$14
Beds: 2 King/Twin 2 Queen
(3 bdrm)
Bath: 2 Guests share

Pataua South

Ron & Evelyn Burns invite you to join them as welcome guests and experience their hospitality at their seaside paradise. Our home is situated on the Pataua Estuary with sea views toward the Poor Knight Islands, and offers peace & tranquillity. The estuary has been proved one of the cleanest in the north and is ideal for swimming, with ocean swimming beaches with surf and golden sands are a short walk away. We invite you to breakfast on the deck to enjoy the ever-changing view. BBQ available. We are experience travellers, have hosted guests from around the world and shared travelling experiences with fine food.

Pataua South Homestay & B&B
B&B Homestay
30km E of Whangarei
Evelyn & Ron Burns
PO Box 3008 Onerahi

Tel: (09) 436 1926
Mob: 021 265 4966
W: www.bnb.co.nz/hosts/
patauasouthhomestaybb.html

Cost: Double $85 Single $50
Child $25
Dinner $30 by arrangement
Beds: 4 Double 3 Single
(2 bdrm)
Bath: 2 Family share

Whangarei

"Stranded Mariner", 6km from central Whangarei. In a very peaceful country, native bush surrounding. Walkways lead from boundaries to Museum, 18th century Clarke homestead, Bird Recovery Centre, Kiwi house. Sherwood Golf Course, 3km. Errol handcrafted our home from native timbers (floors, ceilings), featuring leadlight windows, bricked fireplaces. Cottage garden waterwheel, organic vegetables. Breakfast, and evening meals prepared in our kitchen emphasizing freshness-top quality. Whangarei's a great base to explore Northland, Bay of Islands, Kauri forest, Poor Knights Islands are all easy day trips.

The Stranded Mariner	**Tel:** (09) 438 9967	**Cost:** Double $90-$120
B&B Self-contained In House	**Fax:** (09) 438 7967	Dinner by arrangement
6km W of Whangarei	**Mob:** 025 620 9178	Visa/MC BC
Errol & Sharon Grace	**E:** info@strandedmariner.co.nz	**Beds:** 1 Queen 1 Double
State Highway 14	**W:** www.strandedmariner.co.nz	1 Twin 1 Single
RD 9 Whangarei		**Bath:** 1 Ensuite 2 Private

Whangarei - Kauri

Welcome to Karamea House, a magificent colonial homestead, surrounded by parklike lawns, fragrant gardens & native trees. 10mins north of Whangarei, 1.8kms off SH 1,and just 40mins from the famous Bay of Islands. Your hosts delight in having your stay be a special one providing an all weather astroturf tennis court, outdoor swimming and spa pools, a generous breakfast and a relaxing ambience. Children welcome, pets by arrangement. Single party bookings only ensures guests privacy and exclusive use of the first floor.

Karamea House	**Tel:** 09 435 3401	**Cost:** Double $160-$180
B&B Homestay	**Fax:** 09 435 3495	Single $120-$140
4km N of Whangarei	**Mob:** 025 451 961	Child $50.00 per child
Eliza and Denis Snelgar	**E:** snelgar@kcbbs.gen.nz	Visa/MC
184 Apotu Road	**W:** www.bnb.co.nz/hosts/	**Bath:** 1 Private
Kauri Whangarei	karameahouse.html	**Beds:** 3 Queen 1 Single (3 bdrms)

Whangarei Heads

We have a small farm and a large garden, with two quaint old self-contained cabins in the garden. They have comfortable beds and basic cooking facilities. We have a rowboat you are welcome to borrow, a cat, nearby shops and galleries. Laundry available. This is a beautiful area with rocky bush clad hills, harbour and ocean beaches, lots of Conservation land. Or just relax in private. We are the only buildings in the bay. Red mailbox 2487 on the Whangarei Heads Road.

Manaia Gardens	**Tel:** (09) 434 0797	**Cost:** Double $65 Single $50
Self-contained Homestay	**E:** arnoldac@igrin.co.nz	Self Catering $50 - $60
31km SE of Whangarei	**W:** www.bnb.co.nz/hosts/	Extra Person $15
Audrey & Colin Arnold	manaiagardens.html	Visa/MC
RD 4		**Beds:** 2 Queen 1 Single
Whangarei		(3 bdrm)
		Bath: 2 Private

Whangarei Heads

We are a semi-retired couple with dog. We speak
Dutch, French, German, and Japanese and we like to
laugh. Our unusual home with some natural rock
interior walls is on the edge of a safe swimming beach,
and bush reserve with walking tracks and several good
fishing spots. A photographically fascinating area with
wonderful views of coastal "mountains" bay and sea.
Guests have own entrance and sitting room, all sea
views. Enjoyable food and NZ wine. Directions:
Phone, fax, email for reservations and directions.

Bantry	**Tel:** (09) 434 0751	**Cost:** Double $100 Single $55
Homestay	**Fax:** (09) 434 0754	Child 1/2 price under 12yrs
28km SE of Whangarei	**E:** lieffrng@igrin.co.nz	Dinner $30
Karel & Robin Lieffering	**W:** www.bnb.co.nz/hosts/	**Beds:** 1 Queen 2 Single
Little Munro Bay	bantry.html	(2 bdrm)
RD 4 Whangarei		**Bath:** 1 Guests share

Ruakaka

We offer awesome sea views from your own private
terrace plus a free tour by arrangement, over our 160
acre dry stock farm & bush. Cooking facilities
available. Our wetland area is home to the rare brown
bitten. Beautiful beaches, golf course, racetrack where
Vince trains our racehorses and good restaurants are a
short drive from our home. As ex dairy farmers with a
grown up family of four children, other interests
include B&B for the past 11 years, travel, golf
gardening.

Bream Bay Farmstay	**Tel:** (09) 432 7842	**Cost:** Double $70 Single $40
B&B Self-contained Farmstay	**Fax:** (09) 432 7842	Dinner $20 Visa/MC
30km S of Whangarei	**Mob:** 025 419 585	**Beds:** 2 Queen 2 Single
Joyce & Vince Roberts	**E:** robertsb.b@xtra.co.nz	(3 bdrm)
Doctor's Hill Road	**W:** www.bnb.co.nz/hosts/	**Bath:** 1 Private 1 Family share
RD 2 Waipu	breambayfarmstay.html	

The difference between
a hotel and a B&B
is that you don't hug
the hotel staff when you leave.

Waipu

Sleep to the sound of the ocean in a separate efficiency apartment or in guest bedrooms on our 36 acre seaside farm. Explore our limestone rock formations or just sit and relax under the mature trees that grace our shoreline. The beach at Waipu Cove is a ten minute walk along the sea. We are a licensed fish farm, graze cattle and have flea free cats. Glow worm caves, deep-sea fishing, scuba diving and golf available locally. No smoking please. American spoken. Bookings recommended.

Self-contained Farmstay
10km S of Waipu
Andre & Robin La Bonte
PO Box 60
Waipu
Northland

Tel: (09) 432 0645
Fax: (09) 432 0645
E: labonte@xtra.co.nz
W: www.bnb.co.nz/hosts/
labonte.html

Cost: Double $80 Single $50
Dinner $20 Visa/MC
Beds: 1 King 2 Double
2 Single (3 bdrm)
Bath: 2 Private

Waipu

Relax in a charming seaside cottage or with your hosts Gillian and John in their unique solid Stonehouse. Either way you will enjoy the green pastures of our farm, fringed with mature pohutakawa trees and the sound of surf on a magnificent ocean beach. Picturesque rock gardens, croquet lawn and sheltered patios complete the setting. Canoes and dinghys are available for exploring the adjacent lagoon and bird sanctuary. Lots to do, lots to discover and to end each day, warm company around a log fire. German spoken.

The Stone House
B&B Self-contained Farmstay
6km SE of Waipu
Gillian &John Devine
Cove Road
Waipu

Tel: (09) 432 0432
Fax: (09) 432 0432
W: www.bnb.co.nz/hosts/
thestonehouse.html

Cost: Double $80-$100
Single $60 Child $20
Dinner $20 Visa/MC
Beds: 2 Queen 2 Double
3 Single (4 bdrm)
Bath: 1 Ensuite 3 Private

Waipu Cove

Flower Haven is elevated with panoramic coastal views, being developed as a garden retreat. The accommodation is a self-contained downstairs flat with separate access; kitchen includes stove, microwave, fridge/freezer. Washing machine, radio, TV, linen, duvets, blankets and bath towels provided. Reduced tariff if continental breakfast not required. Our interests are gardening, genealogy and meeting people. Near to restaurants, bird sanctuary, museums, golf, horse treks, fishing, caving, walking tracks, oil refinery. 5 minutes to shop, sandy surf beach, rocks. Whangarei 35 minutes, Auckland 1 1/2 hours.

Flower Haven
B&B Self-contained Downstairs
Flat
8km SE of Waipu
53 St Anne Road
Waipu Cove, RD 2 Waipu 0254

Tel: (09) 432 0421
Mob: 025 287 2418
E: flowerhaven@xtra.co.nz
W: www.bnb.co.nz/hosts/
flowerhaven.html

Cost: Double $70-$90
Visa/MC
Beds: 2 Double (2 bdrm)
Bath: 1 Private

Langs Beach

Our great grandfather settled this area in 1853. Our home is the original Lang home, right beside this most beautiful of white surf beaches, lined by Pohutukawa trees. Our sunny guest lounge/kitchen/dining area runs right along the front of the house, looking over the beach, bay and Hen and Chicken Islands. Comfortable rooms with ensuites make this a delightful place for rest and relaxation. Billie & Graham look forward to your company. See more of us at http://mysite.xtra.co.nz/~Lochalsh

Lochalsh Bed & Breakfast
B&B
12km SE of Waipu
Graham & Billie Long
Cove Road
Langs Beach Waipu

Tel: (09) 432 0053
Fax: (09) 432 0053
Mob: 025 203 1660
E: langs@xtra.co.nz
W: www.bnb.co.nz/hosts/
lochalshbedbreakfast.html

Cost: Double $80-$100
Single $60 Child POA
Dinner $20 by arrangement
Visa/MC
Beds: 1 King 1 Twin (2 bdrm)
Bath: 2 Ensuite

Make your B&B reservation in advance.
It is a nuisance for you if you arrive
to find the accommodation has been taken,
and besides, the hosts need
a little time to prepare.

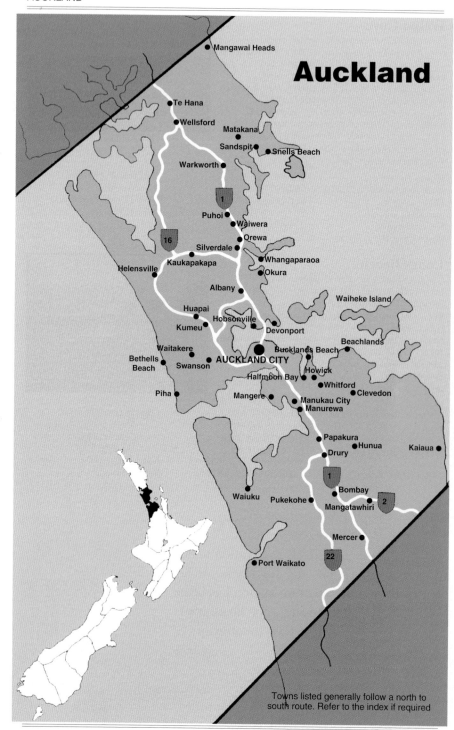

Auckland

Mangawai Heads

Te Hana

Wellsford

Matakana

Sandspit

Snells Beach

Warkworth

1

Puhoi

Waiwera

Orewa

Silverdale

16

Whangaparaoa

Kaukapakapa

Okura

Helensville

Albany

Waiheke Island

Huapai

Hobsonville

Kumeu

Devonport

Waitakere

Bucklands Beach

Beachlands

Bethells
Beach

Swanson

AUCKLAND CITY

Howick

Halfmoon Bay

Whitford

Piha

Mangere

Manukau City

Clevedon

Manurewa

Papakura

Hunua

Kaiaua

Drury

1

Waiuku

Bombay

Pukekohe

Mangatawhiri

2

Mercer

22

Port Waikato

Towns listed generally follow a north to
south route. Refer to the index if required

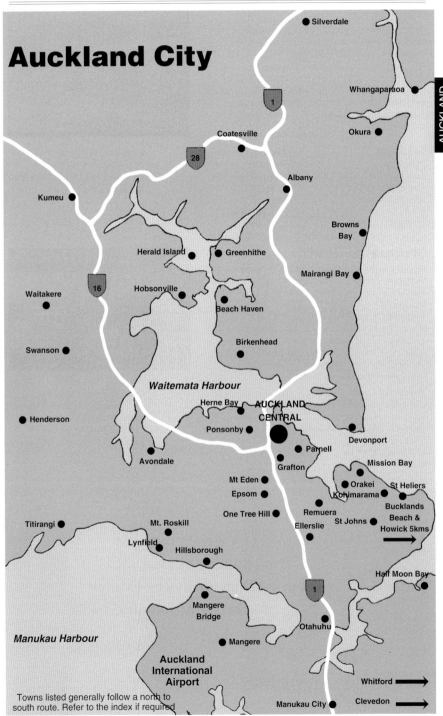

Auckland City

Silverdale

Whangaparaoa

1

Okura

Coatesville

28

Albany

Kumeu

Browns Bay

Herald Island   Greenhithe

Mairangi Bay

Waitakere

16

Hobsonville

Beach Haven

Swanson

Birkenhead

Waitemata Harbour

Herne Bay   AUCKLAND CENTRAL

Henderson

Ponsonby

Devonport

Avondale

Parnell

Grafton

Mission Bay

Mt Eden

Orakei   St Heliers

Epsom

Kohimarama

Bucklands Beach & Howick 5kms

One Tree Hill   Remuera

St Johns

Titirangi

Mt. Roskill

Ellerslie

Lynfield

Hillsborough

Half Moon Bay

Mangere Bridge

1

Otahuhu

Manukau Harbour

Mangere

Auckland International Airport

Whitford ➡

Towns listed generally follow a north to south route. Refer to the index if required

Manukau City   Clevedon ➡

Mangawhai

'A little out of the way, quite out of the ordinary'.
Breathtaking views over rolling pasture to a Pacific ocean
dotted with islands can be seen from our eyrie tucked into
the hills above the seaside haven of Mangawhai. After a
game of croquet or a beach visit for swimming or fishing,
we can share the evening meal. Within our home built with
architectural flair the guestroom is private, has tea and
coffee facilities, a bed with a firm mattress, good heating
and good lighting.

Fallowfield
Homestay
7km S of Mangawhai
Jean & Don Goldschmidt
Staniforth Road
RD 5
Wellsford

Tel: (09) 431 5096
Fax: (09) 431 5063
Mob: 025 829 736
E: goldschmidt@xtra.co.nz
W: www.bnb.co.nz/hosts/
fallowfield.html

Cost: Double $95-$105
Dinner $30 Visa/MC
Beds: 1 Queen 1 Twin (2 bdrm)
Bath: 1 Private 1 Guests share

Mangawhai Heads

Indulge yourself - escape to the tranquillity and magic that's
Mangawhai Lodge. Five stylish guest rooms open onto
wrap-around verandas of this colonial lodge. Spectacular
sea and island views of the Hauraki Gulf, Bream Bay and
white sandy beaches ensure Mangawhai Lodge is the
ultimate "room with a view". Spend your days on the
championship golf course, exploring the beaches and
walkways or curled up reading or watching the boats sail
by. Ideal for groups. Adjacent to award winning cafe,
bowls/golf. Water access 3 minutes.

Mangawhai Lodge - a room
with a view Boutique B&B
boutique bed and breakfast
1km SE of Mangawhai Heads
Jeannette Forde
4 Heather Street
Mangawhai Heads

Tel: (09) 431 5311
Fax: (09) 431 5312
E: mlodge@xtra.co.nz
W: www.seaviewlodge.co.nz

Cost: Double $110-$150
Single $80-$130 Visa/MC
Beds: 3 King/Twin 2 Queen
8 Single (5 bdrm)
Bath: 3 Ensuite 2 Private

Our B&Bs range
from homely to luxurious,
but you can always be assured
of superior hospitality.

Wellsford - Te Hana

Tony and Colleen welcome you to The Retreat, a spacious 1860's farmhouse built for a family with 12 children. Set well back from the road, the house is surrounded by an extensive landscaped garden, including a productive vegetable garden and orchard.

Fresh produce from the garden is a feature in our home cooking. Colleen is a spinner and weaver and our flock of sheep provides the raw material for the woollen goods that are hand made and for sale from the studio. If you haven't got close up to a sheep this is your chance, as we always have friendly sheep to hand feed.

We have hosted guests at The Retreat since 1988 and appreciate what you require. We know New Zealand well, our families have lived in NZ for several generations and we have visited most places in our beautiful country, so if you have any questions on what to see or do, we are well equipped to provide the answers. We host only one group at a time, so you won't have to share a bathroom with someone you don't know.

The Retreat is very easy to find. Travelling North on SH 1 check your speedo as you leave Wellsford, it is just under 5 km to The Retreat, look for the Weaving Studio sign on your left. You will pass through Te Hana before arriving at The Retreat. Kaiwaka is 13km north of The Retreat.

Website; http://mysite.xtra.co.nz/~TonyMoore

The Retreat
Historic Farmhouse
5km N of Wellsford
Colleen & Tony Moore
Te Hana
RD 5, Wellsford

Tel: (09) 423 8547
E: theretreat@xtra.co.nz
W: www.bnb.co.nz/hosts/
theretreat.html

Cost: Double $90 Dinner $25pp
Visa/MC
Beds: 1 Queen 1 Double
1 Single (2 bdrm)
Bath: 1 Private

Warkworth

We live on a 314 acre farm overlooking Kawau Bay and
Mahurangi Heads 80km north of Auckland, farming sheep,
deer, cattle. Private setting, open space, farm walks, bush
reserves and restored old school. Close to safe beaches.
Participation in farming activities welcome. Family home
is 50 years old, comfortable and relaxed with open fireplace.
Rod, commercial pilot, flying instructor, scenic flights
available. Near Goat Island Marine reserve and historic
Kawau Island. We welcome you to share our hospitality
and three course dinner. One cat.

Blue Hayes Farmstay	**Tel:** (09) 425 5612	**Cost:** Double $65-$75
Farmstay	**Fax:** (09) 425 5612	Single $40 Child $20
13km E of Warkworth	**Mob:** 025 776 873	under 12yrs Dinner $20
Rosalie & Rod Miller	**W:** www.bnb.co.nz/hosts/	Visa/MC
44 Martins Bay Road	bluehayesfarmstay.html	**Beds:** 4 Single (2 bdrm)
RD 2 Warkworth		**Bath:** 1 Ensuite 1 Family share

Warkworth

Our home is in a peaceful, quiet garden with views of
Warkworth and the hills. The bed-sitter style rooms
are a good size. Each has own entrance, tea making,
TV and patio with car parking. No cooking. The
rooms are private but feel free to come in and chat.
Breakfast is substantial continental with choice. We
enjoy walking and golf. Ina is an artist. Close to town
and a selection of restaurants. Our home is smoke
free. Please phone. View Road is off Hill Street.

Homewood Cottage	**Tel:** (09) 425 8667	**Cost:** Double $80 Visa/MC
Self-contained	**Fax:** (09) 425 9610	**Beds:** 1 Double 2 Single
0.5km N of Warkworth	**Mob:** 025 235 7469	(2 bdrm)
Ina & Trevor Shaw	**W:** www.bnb.co.nz/hosts/	**Bath:** 2 Ensuite
17 View Rd	homewoodcottage.html	
Warkworth		

Warkworth - Snells Beach

Mahurangi Lodge, a 30 acre farmlet 1 hour Nth of
Auckland (1 1/2 hour International Airport) is set on a
hilltop. Enjoy magnificent views of Kawau, Little Great
Barrier Islands, & Coromandel from large smokefree
rooms. A welcome "cuppa"on arrival, meet our manx cat
relax, dine in or at good restaurants nearby. 20 min from
Goat Island Marine Reserve (some snorkel gear available)
only minutes to Kawau Island Ferry with our special guest
discounts. Many good walks, wineries, craft shops around.
Turn East Warkworth lights, 9km to Snells Beach.

Mahurangi Lodge	**Tel:** (09) 425 5465	**Cost:** Double $50-$80
B&B Farmstay Homestay	**Fax:** (09) 425 5465	Single $25-$40
9km E of Warkworth	**E:** alandrod@ihug.co.nz	Child $10 - $15
Alison & Rodney Woodcock	**W:** www.bnb.co.nz/hosts/	Dinner B/A Visa/MC
416 Mahurangi East Road	mahurangilodge.html	**Beds:** 3 Double 2 Twin
Snells Beach		3 Single (4 bdrm)
Warkworth		**Bath:** 2 Ensuite 1 Guests share

Warkworth - Sandspit

"Sandspit" the perfect stop to and from The Bay of Islands. "Belvedere" has 360 degree views, sea to countryside and is 'awesome' plus relaxing decks, barbecue, garden, orchards, native birds and bush, peace and tranquillity with good parking. Airconditioned, spa, games room, comfortable beds are all here for your comfort. Many attractions are within 7 kms and Margaret's flair with cooking is a great way to relax after an adventurous day with pre-drinks, 3 course meal and wine. Come and stay with Margaret, Ron and our friendly dog "Nicky".

Belvedere Homestay	Tel: (09) 425 7201	Cost: Double $100
Homestay	Fax: (09) 425 7201	Single $65 Dinner $40
7km E of Warkworth	Mob: 025 284 4771	Beds: 2 Queen 1 Twin (3 bdrm)
M & R Everett	E: belvederehomestay@xtra.co.nz	Bath: 1 Ensuite 1 Private
38 Kanuka Road	W: www.bnb.co.nz/hosts/	
RD 2 Warkworth	belvederehomestay.html	

Warkworth

Your hosts, John & Paddy have more than 30 years experience in the hospitality field and have lived in Warkworth for the past 27 years. Our wealth of local knowledge will ensure your stay is both memorable and enjoyable. Willow Lodge boasts tranquil rural views over rolling farmland and is set in two acres of landscaped gardens. We offer superior self-contained accommodation complete with own ensuite , kitchen facilities, TV, BBQ all of which opens onto your own private courtyard. We are well know for our fabulous breakfasts.

Willow Lodge	Tel: (09) 425 7676	Cost: Double $100-$120
Self-contained Homestay	Fax: (09) 425 7676	Single $60-$80 Child $20
4.5km W of Warkworth	Mob: 025 940 885	Dinner $30
Paddy & John Evans	W: www.bnb.co.nz/hosts/	Beds: 1 Queen 2 Double
541 Woodcocks Road	willowlodgewarkworth.html	4 Single (4 bdrm)
Warkworth		Bath: 2 Ensuite 1 Private

Warkworth

Our home and self-contained unit (built 1999) is set on 11 acres nestled beside the Whangateau Harbour. Relax in the extensive gardens and swim in the beautifully appointed pool. Nearby is Omaha Beach, golf course, tennis courts, restaurants, art and craft studios, pottery works, museum, Sheep World, Honey Centre and Kawau Island. This is some of the prettiest coastline in New Zealand. John and Barbara look forward to sharing their little slice of paradise with you.

Self-contained Homestay	Tel: (09) 422 7415	Cost: Double $50-$75 (Seasonal)
13km E of Warkworth	Fax: (09) 4227 419	Single $40-$65
Barbara & John Maltby	W: www.bnb.co.nz/hosts/	Extra persons $12
Omaha Orchards	maltby.html	Dinner $15 - $20
282 Point Wells Road, RD 6		In-house accom. available if
Warkworth		preferred
		Beds: 1 Queen 1 Double bed settee
		Bath: 1 Ensuite

Warkworth

Nestled in a valley beside the Mahurangi Stream with a bush backdrop, Bellgrove is a tasteful country home and farmlet only 3km on a sealed road from Highway 1. Enjoy our large inground swimming pool, hot spa pool, friendly farm animals, manicured gardens and extensive decks. Guest's private upstairs accommodation is separate from the family with rural views. John has been involved in tourism for 10 years and has travelled extensively. Julie's interests include cooking and entertaining. Bellgrove is recommended by Lonely Planet travel guide.

Bellgrove
B&B Country Homestay
3km W of Warkworth
Julie,John & Jessica (aged
11yrs) Bell
346 Woodcocks Road
RD 1 Warkworth

Tel: (09) 425 9770
Fax: (09) 425 9770
E: bellgrove@xtra.co.nz
W: www.bnb.co.nz/hosts/
bellgrove.html

Cost: Double $100 Single $60
Dinner $25 Visa/MC
Beds: 1 Queen 1 Twin
1 Single (3 bdrm)
Bath: 1 Ensuite 1 Private

Warkworth

Secluded intimate retreat on the beautiful Mahurangi Peninsula. Set amongst 2 acres of lovely gardens right on Mahurangi Harbour's foreshore. Idyllic magical place to relax in total privacy, captivating panoramic sea & rural views from our unique spacious apartment. Facilities for weekend or longer stays (self-catering). Sundecks, reclining chairs, bbq, kitchen, TV, ensuite (own entrance). Stroll along the bays to historic Scott's Landing, bush trails, swimming, boating, fishing (rods provided). Friendly village atmosphere, licensed restaurants, shopping and attractions. (Auckland 1 hour)

Island Bay Retreat
Homestay Studio Loft Apt.
9km E of Warkworth
Joyce & Bill Malofy
105 Ridge Rd Scotts landing,
RD 2 Warkworth

Tel: (09) 425 4269
Fax: (09) 425 4265
Mob: 025 262 8358
W: www.bnb.co.nz/hosts/
islandbayretreat.html

Cost: Double $115
Beds: 1 Queen 1 Single
(1 bdrm)
Bath: 1 Ensuite

Warkworth

Our sheep and cattle farm is 50 minutes from Auckland just 1km off SH1, and our spacious home is set in a quiet, secluded valley overlooking native bush and surrounded by gardens. Join in farm activities or just relax. The upstairs guest bedrooms, with extensive farm views, open into a large guest sitting room with TV and tea/coffee making facilities. Local sightseeing attractions include historic Kawau Island and many lovely beaches. We are widely travelled and warmly welcome visitors to our home.

Ryme Intrinseca
Farmstay
6km S of Warkworth
Elizabeth & Cam Mitchell
121 Perry Road
RD 3
Warkworth

Tel: (09) 425 9448
Fax: (09) 425 9458
E: rymeintrinseca@xtra.co.nz
W: www.bnb.co.nz/hosts/
rymeintrinseca.html

Cost: Double $100 Single $60
Child 1/2 price
Dinner $25 by arrangement
Visa/MC
Beds: 2 Queen 2 Single (3 bdrm)
Bath: 1 Private
We only take one party at a time

Warkworth - Matakana

Hurstmere House if full of gracious Old English charm, with timber panelling and magnificent views over surrounding countryside. Suites have antiques, fresh flowers, crisp white linen with TV, fridge, tea/coffee making facilities within minutes drive are restaurants, wineries, famous pottery, beaches, golf, Goat Island, craft market and ferry to Kawau Island. Pets on site. Visit Tawharanui Regional Park and hidden treasurre with beaches and walks. Anne & Bob invite you to enjoy genuine hospitality with complimentary drinks in our beautiful friendly home.

Hurstmere House
B&B Self-contained
10km E of Warkworth
Anne & Bob Moir
PO Box 37 - 186 Tongue Farm Rd
Matakana Northland

Tel: (09) 422 9220
Fax: (09) 422 9220
Mob: 025 820 336
E: hurstmere@ihug.co.nz
W: www.hurstmerehouse.co.nz

Cost: Double $180 Single $140
S/C $200 Visa/MC Amex
Beds: 1 King/Twin 3 Queen
1 Twin 2 Single (4 bdrm)
Bath: 4 Ensuite

Warkworth - Sandspit

Welcome to Jacaranda Cottage, our new house. The views of the Sandspit harbour are magnificent and so close you will feel part of the panorama. We are one hour from Auckland. Warkworth is a picturesque area which provides many opportunities for sightseeing and relaxation, including restaurants, vineyards, art galleries etc. We are a few minutes walk form Sandspit wharf, from where ferries leave for Kawau Island. We have a 9m launch and will take you fishing, by arrangement. Our dog is a border collie.

Jacaranda Cottage
Self-contained Homestay
6km E of Warkworth
Rhondda & Les Sweetman
1186 Sandspit Rd
RD 2 Warkworth

Tel: (09) 425 9441
Fax: (09) 425 9451
Mob: 025 912 281
Tollfree: 0800 80 0 537
E: rhondda@xtra.co.nz
W: www.bnb.co.nz/hosts/
jacarandacottagesandspit.html

Cost: Double $100 Single $70
Child $40 Dinner $25
Self-contained $50 - $80
Visa/MC Amex Diners
Beds: 1 Queen 1 Double
1 Twin (3 bdrm)
Bath: 1 Ensuite 1 Guests share

Warkworth - Sandspit

Imagine sitting on a deck, surrounded by native bush and birds, overlooking 360 degree sea views. "Sea Breeze" is fully self-contained and breakfast is provided in your kitchenette to be enjoyed at your leisure. A bedsette doubles for extra guests. Take a cruise to Kawau Island, bush walks to the beaches, or visit vineyards, local galleries and cafes. Your hosts have travelled extensively and now enjoy living both child and smokefree with their cat, gardening and boating in their spare time. Phone/fax for directions.

Sea Breeze
B&B Self-contained
10km E of Warkworth
Di & Robin Grant
14 Puriri Place
RD 2, Sandspit Heights

Tel: (09) 425 7220
Fax: (09) 425 7220
Mob: 021 657 220
E: robindi.grant@xtra.co.nz
W: www.bnb.co.nz/hosts/
seabreeze.html

Cost: Double $95 Single $60
Visa/MC
Beds: 1 Queen (1 bdrm)
Bath: 1 Ensuite

Warkworth - Sandspit

An enchanting hideaway up a tree lined driveway. This tranquil home on 6 acres has magical views of Sandspit Estuary. The Mediterranean ambience, white linen, tiles, candles and flowers give a sense of romance. All rooms have French doors opening onto private courtyards. Refreshments served on arrival or available in separate guest lounge. Maureen's special three-course breakfast is surpassed only by the view. Boutique vineyards, restaurants, cafes, potteries and beaches nearby. A short walk to Kawau ferry. Golden retriever on site. Smoke free home.

The Saltings
B&B
7km E of Warkworth
Maureen & Terry Baines
1210 Sandspit Road
RD 2 Warkworth

Tel: (09) 425 9670
Fax: (09) 425 9674
Mob: 021 625 948
E: saltings@wk.planet.gen.nz
W: www.bnb.co.nz/hosts/
thesaltings.html

Cost: Double $120-$150
Single $100-$120
Child Unsuitable Visa/MC
Beds: 2 King/Twin 1 Queen
4 Single (3 bdrm)
Bath: 3 Ensuite

Warkworth - Matakana

As a happy family, Claudia, Alex and Julia(10), we welcome you in our brand new home, "CASA ALEGRIA". We have a peaceful setting close to Warkworth, Sandspit and Matakana with an awesome view of Kawau Bay, deerfarm, vineyards. The suite has a seperate entrance, luxurious bathroom, two king single beds, private patio. Claudia serves special breakfasts and as wine and food connaisseurs we offer on request 3-course dinners. Visit top wineries, Kawau, Goat Island, go horseriding, fishing, golfing, or just enjoy being pampered in Claudia's beauty studio...German, French, Japanese spoken.

Casa Alegria
Self-contained Beauty Farm
11km E of Warkworth
Claudia & Alex Schenz
180 Monarch Downs Way
RD 2, Warkworth

Tel: (09) 422 7211
Fax: (09) 422 7833
E: casaalegria@xtra.co.nz
W: www.bnb.co.nz/hosts/
casaalegria.html

Cost: Double $120 Single $85
Dinner $30 Visa/MC
Beds: 2 King/Twin
1 King (2 bdrm)
Bath: 1 Ensuite 1 Private

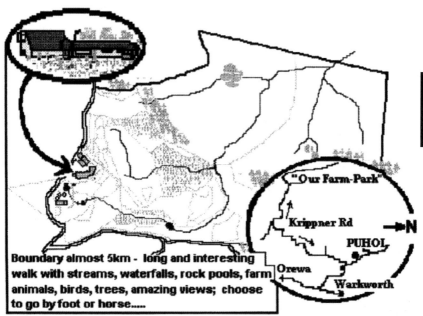

Boundary almost 5km - long and interesting walk with streams, waterfalls, rock pools, farm animals, birds, trees, amazing views; choose to go by foot or horse.....

Puhoi

"Farmstay - the gentle way"
organic farming 40 minutes north of Auckland city, International Airport 1 hour. Peace and quiet high in the hills, panoramic views, fresh air, clean water, comfortable beds, delicious meals. NO-ONE SMOKES HERE.

We farm with kindness, beautiful Belted Galloway cows calves, sheep, horses to ride; ducks, poultry running free... Talk and share knowledge over dinner, walks through trees with views, streams and secluded private places.... Visit our interest filled district. Stay longer for learning experiences - organic farming/ horticulture, "Conversational English"...
info-pictures see www.farmstaynz.com

Our Farm-Park
Farmstay
20km N of Orewa
Nichola(s) & Peter Rodgers
RD3
Kaukapakapa
Auckland 1250

Tel: (09) 422 0626
Fax: (09) 422 0626
Mob: 021 215 5165
E: ofp@friends.co.nz
W: www.bnb.co.nz/hosts/
ourfarmpark.html

Cost: Double $105 Single $90
Child 5-12yrs $10,
$13-17yrs $20
Dinner $25pp
Guest Wing $120 Visa/MC
Beds: 1 Queen 2 Twin (2 bdrm)
Bath: 1 Private

Puhoi

We welcome you to our sunny colonial style home in the lovely Puhoi Valley. We are only 2 minutes by car west of Main North Highway up a small road behind the old pub in this historic Puhoi Village. The homestead has wide verandahs around 3 sides where you can relax as you view the gardens, winding paths and beautiful trees. Nearby are the fantastic Waiwera Thermal Pools, or you could hire a canoe and paddle down the Puhoi River to Wenderholm Beach and Park. Sky T.V. available.

Westwell Ho
Homestay
9km N of Orewa
Fae & David England
34 Saleyards Road
Puhoi
Warkworth

Tel: (09) 422 0064
Fax: (09) 422 0064
Mob: 025 280 5795
E: dhengland@xtra.co.nz
W: www.bnb.co.nz/hosts/
westwellho.html

Cost: Double $90 Single $70
  Child $30 Visa/MC Amex
Beds: 1 Queen 1 Double
  1 Single (2 bdrm)
Bath: 1 Ensuite 1 Private

Waiwera

Puriri Cottage is situated in Waiwera on the Hibiscus Coast 30 minutes drive north of Auckland on State Highway 1. We invite you to come and share our character home on 15 acres of land overlooking the Waiwera valley with views to Saddle & Kawau Island. We have lovely gardens, bush walks, abundant native birds, ducks, fish, chickens, 1 dog & 2 cats. Waiwera Hot Pools, Beaches, Restaurants and other recreational facilities are close by. Unsuitable for children under 10 & we are smoke free indoors.

Puriri Cottage
B&B
8km N of Orewa
Roger & Jacque Fletcher
143 Weranui Road
Waiwera
Auckland

Tel: (09) 426 1503
Fax: (09) 426 1502
Mob: 021 844 822
W: www.puriricottage.co.nz

Cost: Double $110 Single $75
  Dinner by arrangement
  Visa/MC
Beds: 1 Queen 1 Twin
  (2 bdrm)
Bath: 1 Guests share

Orewa

Overlooking the native bush and the sheltered bay of beautiful Hatfields Beach Moontide Lodge offers a high standard of "boutique" accommodation. We are situated on a cliff with beach access. Each of our four luxuriously appointed bedrooms features ensuite or private bathroom and breathtaking seaviews. Enjoy your complimentary tea/coffee and sherry/port in our elegant guest lounge with open fireplace. Breakfast and dinner (by appointment) is served in our formal dining room or on the verandah. German and French spoken. Timmy, our dog, is a friendly extra.

Moontide Lodge
Lodge
2km N of Orewa
Jurgen & Monika Resch
19 Ocean View Road
Orewa - Hatfields Beach

Tel: (09) 426 2374
Fax: (09) 426 2398
Mob: 025 263 0102
E: moontde@nznet.gen.nz
W: www.bnb.co.nz/hosts/
moontidelodge.html

Cost: Double $150-$180
  Single $130-$160
  Visa/MC Amex Diners
Beds: 4 Queen (4 bdrm)
Bath: 3 Ensuite 1 Private

Orewa

For true kiwi hospitality 'Eagles Nest' awaits you. We are located between Orewa and the beautiful Whangaparoa peninsula with spectacular beaches and the gateway to 'Twin Coast Discovery'. Enjoy the vistas over Red Beach and beyond to the Coromandel whilst enjoying a delicious home-cooked breakfast. John, Joy, and Freda our family cat, welcome all nationalities; several European languages spoken. We have extensive knowledge of the local and surrounding areas. Our wish is to make your stay at 'Eagles Nest' a memorable experience.

Eagles Nest
B&B Homestay
1.5km SE of Orewa
Joy & John Bray
18 Eagle Place
Red Beach Orewa

Tel: (09) 426 8862
W: www.bnb.co.nz/hosts/
eaglesnest.html

Cost: Double $65 Single $50
Beds: 1 Queen 1 Single
(2 bdrm)
Bath: 1 Private 1 Family share

Silverdale

Looking for a romantic weekend away or just wanting to relax in elegant surroundings during your travels around New Zealand, then come and stay at The Ambers. Share our tranquil country atmosphere and warm hospitality - unwind with complimentary pre-dinner drinks. We have travelled extensively and enjoy meeting people. Three friendly German Shepherd dogs are part of our family. We are 30 minutes north of Auckland and are minutes from beaches, restaurants and shops. Please phone for reservations and directions. Warm regards, Di and Gerard.

The Ambers
B&B
1km S of Silverdale
Gerard & Diane Zwier
146 Pine Valley Road
Silverdale Auckland

Tel: (09) 426 0015
Fax: (09) 426 5354
E: gzwier@xtra.co.nz
W: www.the-ambers.co.nz

Cost: Double $150 Single $110
Child $75
Visa/MC Amex Diners
Beds: 1 King/Twin 2 Double
1 Twin (4 bdrm)
Bath: 3 Ensuite 1 Family share

Whangaparaoa Peninsula

For an exceptional B&B experience- 'Quality, Hospitality and Value'. Facing the sun, our modern, comfortable, clean hme is elevated with panoramic seaviews, dramatic sunsets. Dedlicious freshly cooked breakfasts. Guest lounge/tea, coffee, balconies. Fresh flowers, sweeties and toiletries. Laundry, parking. The house is for guests to enjoy, hosts have an attached apartment. One min walk to 6 restaurants. Warm sandy beaches, swimming, fishing, walks, golf, Tiritiri bird Island and many other activities. Tourist information. Bird books. Relax to the sound of the waves. Ideal weekends, arrival/departure, airport 1 hour.

Bayview Manly Quality B&B Inn
B&B Inn
35 km N of Auckland
Eddie & Wendy Hewlett
1 Beach Rd Manly Village
Whangaparaoa

Tel: (09) 428 0990
Fax: (09) 428 0990
Mob: 025 280 8346
Tollfree: 0800 101 590
E: bayviewmanly@xtra.co.nz
W: www.bayview-manly.co.nz

Cost: Double $110-$135
Single $95-$120
Child N/A Visa/MC
Beds: 1 Queen 1 Double
1 Twin (3 bdrm)
Bath: 2 Ensuite 1 Private

Whangaparaoa

We offer a comfortable twin studio unit with private bathroom and mini-kitchen with fridge, microwave and top-cook stove. Separate guest entrance and private patio surrounded by trees and garden. TV, linen and towels are provided. Beds have electric blankets and duvets. We are within walking distance to beaches, shops, bowling club and restaurants. Within 5km is Shakespeare Park, Gulf Harbour Marina and golf course. Our home is smoke-free and we have two Balinese cats 'Chino' and 'Phoebe'. Directions - please phone.

Jan & Ernest's Place
Self-contained
40km N of Auckland
Jan Collins & Ernest Davenport
18A Brixton Road
Manly Whangaparaoa

Tel: (09) 424 7281
Mob: 025 264 2962
E: codav@xtra.co.nz
W: www.bnb.co.nz/hosts/
janandernests.html

Cost: Double $65-$85
Single $40-$60
Optional continental
breakfast $5 pp
Beds: 2 Single (1 bdrm)
Bath: 1 Private

Kaukapakapa

Relax in the comfort and warm hospitality of a large Kiwi country home. Set in a large much loved garden, in a quiet rural valley our home has lots of indoor/outdoor living areas. Enjoy, playing pool, petanque or croquet, or a drink in the Summerhouse. There are local bush walks and golf and tennis facilities. Special interest: travel, shell collecting, geology, fossils, botany and art. Whether staying one night or days, let us share the delights of country life. We are non smokers.

Kereru Lodge
Self-contained Homestay
14km N of Kaukapakapa
Mrs B Headford
Arone Farm
RD 3
Kaukapakapa

Tel: (09) 420 5223
Fax: (09) 420 5223
Mob: 025 297 5523
E: Bheadford@xtra.co.nz
W: www.bnb.co.nz/hosts/
kererulodgekaukapakapa.html

Cost: Double $70 Single $45
Dinner $20 Visa/MC
Beds: 1 Queen 1 Double
2 Single (3 bdrm)
Bath: 1 Ensuite 1 Guests share

Helensville

"Rose Cottage" offers comfort and privacy set within the gardens of the beautifully restored Whenuanui Homestead (Kauri villa circa 1908). Whenuanui is a 320 ha Helensville sheep and beef farm providing magnificent farm walks. The family homestead and gardens have panoramic views over Helensville and the Kaipara Valley. Tasteful accommodation includes ensuite, TV and kitchenette. Just 35 minutes from downtown Auckland on State Highway 16. A base to explore the Kaipara region or a great start or end to your Northland tour. Smoking outdoors appreciated.

Rose Cottage
B&B Self-contained
4km SW of Helensville
Dianne & Richard Kidd
2191 State Highway 16
RD 2 Helensville

Tel: (09) 420 8007
Fax: (09) 420 7966
Tollfree: 0800 755 433
E: kidd.home@xtra.co.nz
W: www.bnb.co.nz/hosts/
rosecottagehelensville.html

Cost: Double $95 Single $70
Visa/MC
Beds: 1 Queen (1 bdrm)
Bath: 1 Ensuite

Huapai - Kumeu

Foremost Fruits is surrounded by several top NZ wineries and is on a small orchard with a greenhouse growing export table grapes. We provide comfort and relaxation plus use of a swimming pool. Guests have an upstairs to themselves - 2 bedrooms have TV. Breakfast is of choice and we offer selection of home-made breads and jams. There are several top restaurants in the area plus casual dining and take-away. Local attractions: Beaches, gannet colony, horse riding, golf. Directions from Auckland: Take Northwestern Motorway to end. Turn left to Kumeu (8K) past garden centre — over railway line to Trigg Road (Left before 100 K sign) No. 45

Foremost Fruits
B&B Farmstay Homestay
15km W of Auckland
Andrea & Jim Hawkless
45 Trigg Road
Huapai Auckland

Tel: (09) 412 8862
Fax: (09) 412 8869
E: jrhawkless@xtra.co.nz
W: www.bnb.co.nz/hosts/
foremostfruits.html

Cost: Double $75 Single $50
Child $25 Dinner $20
Visa/MC
Beds: 2 Queen 3 Single
(3 bdrm)
Bath: 1 Guests share

Kumeu

Nor-West Greenlands is 15 acres nestled in a tranquil valley of native bush setting with a large garden, and a flock of tame coloured sheep. A swimming pool and guest lounge compliment the two storied house which is home to Kerry and Kay, three cats, a dog (outside) and various crafts (lessons available). Kumeu has numerous wineries and restaurants, and Muriwai is home to the Gannet Colony. If you want peace and quiet 30 mins from Auckland city we have it.

Nor-West Greenlands
Countrystay
26km NW of Auckland
Kay & Kerry Hamilton
303 Riverhead Rd
RD 2
Kumeu

Tel: (09) 412 8167
Fax: (09) 412 8167
Mob: 025 286 6064
Tollfree: 0800 501 850
E: bed@farm-stay.co.nz
W: www.farm-stay.co.nz

Cost: Double $110 Single $65
Dinner $30 by arrangement
Visa/MC
Beds: 2 Double 2 Single
(3 bdrm)
Bath: 1 Private 1 Guests share

Hobsonville

Eastview is restful, built for sun, and panoramic views towards city over Westpark marina, and upper reaches of Waitemata Harbour. 15 minutes from Auckland, 3 minutes from motorway and Westgate shopping complex. Facilities, guest's private entrance, lounge, 2 large bedrooms with the morning sun overlooking view, tea/coffee, T.V. Sky, video and laundry. Easy travelling to many of Auckland's tourist attractions, golf courses, restaurants. Gateway to routes north. We share our home with a friendly oriental cat and Bischon dog. Phone/fax for directions.

Eastview
B&B Homestay
20 km NW of Auckland
Don & Joane Clarke
2 Parkside Road
Hobsonville
Auckland

Tel: (09) 416 9254
Fax: (09) 416 9254
E: djclarke@xtra.co.nz
W: www.bnb.co.nz/hosts/
eastview.html

Cost: Double $85 Single $60
Child $30 Dinner $33
Beds: 1 Queen 1 Double
2 Single (3 bdrm)
Bath: 1 Private 1 Guests share

Bethells Beach

Drive 30 minutes from Auckland city to one of the most unique parts of the West coast. The Bethell's settled this area 6 generations ago and Trude and John continue the long family tradition of hospitality. They have created two magic cottages and venue in this spectacular place where the best sunsets and seaviews are to be experienced - as seen in - Grace mag. & Elle Aus Feb 2000, Elle Singapore March 2000. Both cottages have a sunny north facing aspect and are surrounded by 200 year old pohutukawa's (NZ Christmas tree). Each one is totally separate, private and has a large brick barbecue. The vast front lawn is ideal for games and the gardens are thoughtfully designed for relaxation. The cottages are made up with your holiday in mind - not only are beds made and towels/linen put out, but Trude and John have attended to too many details to mention and laundry facilities are available. Even the cats will welcome you. As seen in Vogue Australia 1998. Life/The Observer (Great Britain 1998) - 'one of twenty great world wide destinations'. British TV Travel Show 1998. She magazine (February 1999) - 'one of the 10 most romantic places to stay in NZ'. North and South magazine (January 1999) - 'one of the 14 best Bed and Breakfasts in NZ'.

'TUREHU' COTTAGE has a studio atmosphere with double bi-folding doors from the conservatory. For outdoor dining sit under a pohutukawa tree at your own bench and table on the hillside with views over the beach and Bethell's valley. Cork floor in the kitchen, TV and bedroom area, gentle cream walls and white trim. Warm slate floors in the conservatory with lounge, dining table and bathroom (shower and toilet). Kitchen has microwave, large fridge/freezer, stove and coffee plunger, with all kitchen and dining amenities. Suitable for a couple and 1 child or 2 friends.

'TE KOINGA' COTTAGE, this superb home away from home is 80sq m and has 2 bi-folding doors onto a 35sq m wooden deck for outdoor dining and relaxation in this sun trap. Set under the shade of a magnificent spralling pohutukawa tree and surrounded by garden. A fireplace for winter warmth and sixteen seater dining table. The two bedrooms have carpet and terracotta tiles expand to the dining, kitchen, bathroom and toilet. Wood panelled and cream/tan rag rolled walls for a relaxing atmosphere. The bathroom offers a bath and shower. Open planned kitchen has microwave, large fridge/freezer, stove, dishwasher and coffee maker. Suitable for a family, 2 couples or a small function. Trude is a marriage celebrant and Trude and John specialise in weddings, private functions and company workshops. A local professional chef is available for these occasions.

THE WHITE HOUSE. Facing directly west into the sunsets and sea views this cottage is totally private and set among wild grasses and a rocky outcrop. 3 minutes and you are on the beach with a local summer cafe to distract you with home cooking and the best coffees in town. The cottage is completely surrounded with decks which lead you into a two bedroom cottage with superb conservatory off the main lounge. Fully self contained with your holiday in mind, even a cocktail shaker is provided. LOCAL ADVENTURES - Bethell's beach is a short drive or walk. Pack a picnic lunch and discover Lake Wainamu for fresh water swimming and expansive sand dunes or go on a bush walk with excellent examples of New Zealand native flora. If you head in the direction of the beach you may enjoy exploring the caves (at night the magic of glow worms and phosphorescence in the shallows), or go surfing or fishing. You are close to many world class Vineyards and restaurants/ cafes. You may fancy a game of golf - two courses within 10-20 minutes drive from your cottage. Many more activities in a short driving distance. No pets please. Children under 12 half price

Bethell's Beach Cottage
Self-contained Cottages &
100 Seater Summer Pavilion
15km W of Swanson
Trude & John Bethell-Paice
PO Box 95057
Swanson
Auckland

Tel: (09) 810 9581
Fax: (09) 810 8677
E: info@bethellsbeach.com
W: www.bethellsbeach.com

Cost: Double $175 - $275 + GST
Breakfast $20pp
Dinner $35pp B/A
Visa/MC Diners
Beds: 3 Queen 3 Double
5 Single (5 bdrm)
Bath: 3 Private

Waitakere

Guests have sole use of comfortable holiday home - two bedrooms, bathroom, lounge (TV) and large kitchen/dining room with excellent cooking facilities. Additional guests $20 each. Breakfast extra. Foldout double bed available. The main house and guest cottage are surrounded by a large country garden - swings for children. Cattle, two Border collie working dogs, bees and chooks. Located in rural valley in the Waitakere Ranges. Good walking tracks in the area - forest, beach and lake. 30 minutes drive west of central Auckland. Beach 5 minutes.

Greenmead Farm
Self-contained Farmstay
15km W of Henderson
Averil & Jon Bateman
115 Bethells Road
RD 1 Henderson

Tel: (09) 810 9363
Fax: (09) 810 9122
E: jabat@greenmead.co.nz
W: www.greenmead.co.nz

Cost: Double $90
Beds: 4 Single (2 bdrm)
Bath: 1 Private

Swanson - Waitakere City

Private and peaceful with breathtaking panoramic views located high in the Waitakere Ranges on the "Twin Coast Discovery Route". Watch the sun rise across native kauri trees, bush and Auckland City beyond. We are within easy access to over 200 km of walking tracks through 17,000 hectares of native rainforest. 10-15 minutes from West Coast beaches(Piha,Bethells,Karekare Muriwai) wineries and two scenic golf courses, art trails, shopping centers. Indoors non - smoking. A warm welcome awaits you. Please phone for directions. Airport pick up available.

Panorama Heights
B&B Self-contained Guesthouse
4km W of Swanson
Paul & Allison Ingram
42 Kitewaho Road
Swanson, Waitakere City Auckland

Tel: (09) 832 4777
Fax: (09) 833 7773
Mob: 025 272 8811
Tollfree: 0800 692 624
E: nzbnb4u@zfree.co.nz
W: www.bnb.co.nz/hosts/
panoramaheights.html

Cost: Double $110 Single $75
Dinner by request
Visa/MC
Beds: 2 Queen 1 Twin
1 Single (4 bdrm)
Bath: 3 Ensuite 1 Private

Swanson

Our romantic home is set amongst 17 acres of native bush and pasture. We offer a selection of beautifully appointed rooms with fine linen, fresh flowers and chocolates. Our most popular suite boasts a large private bathroom complete with claw footed bath which adds to the romantic charm. We are renowned for our scrumptious cooked breakfasts and wonderful home baking. Tea and coffee facilities available in all rooms. We are a New Zealand family, along with our dog and two cats we offer you a warm welcome and a memorable time.

Abode de Fleur
B&B Homestay
10km W of Henderson
Janice Reece & daughter, Fleur Pridmore
1194 Scenic Drive North
Swanson, Waitakere Auckland

Tel: (09) 833 4288
Fax: (09) 833 4288
Mob: 025 786 788
E: fleursb&b@xtra.co.nz
W: www.fleurs.co,nz

Cost: Double $95-$120
Single $65-$75
Dinner by arrangement
Visa/MC
Beds: 2 Queen 1 Twin (3 bdrm)
Bath: 1 Ensuite 2 Family share

Henderson

Just 15 minutes form Auckland City and five minutes from historical Henderson, The Garrett offers villa style accommodation complete with ensuite and private terrace. Twin beds or king size if you prefer. We are able to accommodate extra guests with folding beds available on request. High ceilings and period furniture and decor create an atmosphere of old in this delightful Homestay. Local attractions include wine trails, Art Out West Trail - including Lopdell House Gallery. Waitake Ranges, bush walks, Aratiki Heritage and Environment Centre, world renowned golf courses. No pets and no campervans.

The Garrett
B&B Homestay Detached B&B
15mins W of Auckland
Alma & Rod Mackay
295 Swanson Road
Henderson Auckland 8

Tel: (09) 833 6018
Fax: (09) 833 6018
W: www.bnb.co.nz/hosts/
mackay.html

Cost: Double $75 Single $45
Child $22
Beds: 2 King/Twin 1 King
2 Single (2 bdrm)
Bath: 1 Ensuite

Piha

Piha Cottage is secluded in quiet bush surrounds near beach and tracks. Its studio style includes a kitchen, dining and living area. We have a young child, Asha, and Floyd the cat. Piha is on the rugged West Coast nestled into native rainforest. The beach is renown for surfing and is patrolled for swimmers in summer. There is a network of outstanding tracks to choose from - spectacular cliffs and wild beaches, streams and waterfalls. We can provide maps and advice on the tracks which we know intimately.

Piha Cottage
Self-contained
20km W of Henderson
Tracey & Steve Skidmore
PO Box 48
Piha, Waitakere City
Auckland

Tel: (09) 812 8514
Fax: (09) 812 8514
E: piha_cottage@yahoo.co.nz
W: www.bnb.co.nz/hosts/
pihacottage.html

Cost: Double $95 Single $95
Child $20
Beds: 1 Double 1 Single
(1 bdrm)
Bath: 1 Private

Piha

Winner of the 2001 Bank of New Zealand Waitakere Eco City "BEST ACCOMMODATION" Award. Situated in the sub-tropical raiforest of the Waitakere Ranges and on the Wild West Coast, Piha has one of New Zealand's top surfing beaches and magnificent sunsets that are legendary. Enjoy the many bush walks, climb Lion Rock, visit the fairytalk Kitekite Falls or relax in the swimming pool, hot spa or games room. Our quality self contained units give you all the comforts of home plus privacy, homemade bread each morning and stunning panoramic sea and bush views. Our two very friendly little Bichon dogs are kept separately.

Piha Lodge
Self-contained
40mins W of Auckland
Shirley Bond
117 Piha Road
Piha

Tel: (09) 812 8595
Fax: (09) 812 8583
Mob: 021 639 539
E: pihalodge@xtra.co.nz
W: www.pihalodge.co.nz

Cost: Double $130 Child $20
Additional adults $30
Visa/MC
Beds: 3 Queen 1 Double
1 Single (4 bdrm)
Bath: 2 Private

Okura

Situated at the "top" of Auckland's North Shore City, Okura is a small settlement bounded by farmland and the Okura River, a tidal estuary edged with native bush. We offer your own spacious living-room with TV, dining area, tea making facilities and fridge. Nearby are a wide variety of cafes, restaurants, shops, Browns Bay and Long Bay beaches, bush and cliff walks, North Shore Stadium, Massey University, Browns Bay RSA and golf courses. Okura is one of Auckland's best kept secrets! Directions on request.

Okura B&B
B&B Homestay
20km N of Auckland Central
Judie & Ian Greig
20 Valerie Crescent
Okura, RD 2
Albany, Auckland

Tel: (09) 473 0792
Fax: (09) 473 1072
E: ibgreig@clear.net.nz
W: www.bnb.co.nz/hosts/
okurabb.html

Cost: Double $75 Single $60
Visa/MC
Beds: 1 Queen 3 Single
(3 bdrm)
Bath: 2 Private

Coatesville - Albany

We are only 25 minutes from Auckland City. Relax in secluded tranquillity, our home opens into beautiful gardens, native bush and stream offering the best of hospitality in a friendly relaxed atmosphere. On the farm we have sheep, cattle and pet lambs Our spacious guest areas consist of the entire upstairs. Guests may use our games room, play tennis on our new court, row a boat on the lake, or just stroll by the stream. Camperdown is easy travelling to the main tourist route north. Directions. Travel North on old highway 1 through Albany, turn left into Coatesvile/Riverhead Highway (28). Transfers are available.

Camperdown
Farmstay
7km N of Albany
Chris & David Hempleman
455 Coatesville/Riverhead Highway
RD 3, Albany Auckland

Tel: (09) 415 9009
Fax: (09) 415 9023
Tollfree: 0800 921 479
E: chris@camperdown.co.nz
W: www.camperdown.co.nz

Cost: Double $105 Single $75
Child $40 Dinner $35
Beds: 1 King/Twin 2 Queen
1 Double 2 Single (4 bdrm)
Bath: 2 Private 1 Guests share

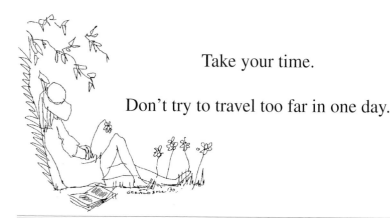

Take your time.

Don't try to travel too far in one day.

Albany

We absolutely guarantee you will enjoy your stay! If you are not absolutely delighted you can renegotiate! When you arrive to awesome river views you will be greeted to a warm welcome, be offered tea, coffee or juice with freshly baked muffins or slice.

You will sleep in luxurious linen, have plenty of soft fluffy towels and all the little extras that will make your stay special!

You will awake to birdsong, the smell of freshly baked bread, you could amble down to the jetty before breakfasting on fresh tropical fruit, your choice of oaty pancakes, French toast and bacon, poached egg with smoked salmon, English or continental breakfast. Restaurants and award winning cafe can be found in Albany Village

"We never think of staying anywhere else " say Barry and Dorothy of Cambridge England (after their third stay). We are 7 minutes from Albany, North Harbour stadium and university, 19 minutes from Auckland and ideal stopover before heading North or South.

Bruce and I look forward to sharing our home with you! Chester our friendly springer Spaniel is housed separately from the guest area.

Directions: From State Highway 1 take Albany exit and go through village on State Highway 17. Turn opposite the "Albany Inn" into the Avenue. Travel 7km then turn left into Attwood Road. 1 km left into Ngarahana Avenue. 1km to cul-de-sac, 2nd house on right, down private road. White colonial styled house.

Albany Country Home	**Tel:** (09) 413 9580	**Cost:** Double $100-$130
Country Home	**Fax:** (09) 413 9583	Single $90-$110
20min N of Auckland	**Mob:** 025 745 898	Child neg Dinner B/A
Patricia & Bruce Fordham	**E:** patricia.fordham@xtra.co.nz	Visa/MC Amex
Birethanti	**W:** www.bnb.co.nz/hosts/	**Beds:** 1 Queen 1 Double
57 Ngarahana Avenue, Albany	albanycountryhome.html	(2 bdrm)
Auckland 1331		**Bath:** 1 Ensuite 1 Private

Albany

No road noise, fresh air, peace and tranquillity.
"Hedingham" a large stately house just off the main North/
South tourist route, one of the closest rural areas (20
minutes) to Auckland Central. Guests have their own
bathroom and lounge. Wake up to chirping birds, freshly
brewed coffee and enjoy a delicious country breakfast. You
may take a stroll in the delightful bush by our river, or you
might like to kayak. John and Angelika can assist you with
your New Zealand travel plans. We invite you to visit our
comprehensive web page. http://www.hedingham.co.nz

Hedingham	**Tel:** (09) 415 9292	**Cost:** Double $105 Single $65
Country Homestay	**Fax:** (09) 415 7757	Dinner $30
7km N of Albany	**Mob:** 021 459 292	**Beds:** 1 Double 2 Single
Angelika & John de Vere	**E:** devere@hedingham.co.nz	(2 bdrm)
446 Coatesville Riverhead	**W:** www.hedingham.co.nz	**Bath:** 1 Guests share
Highway		
RD 3, Albany Auckland		

Albany - Coatesville

Let us make you comfortable in our country home only
15 minutes from the city. Swim, play pool or just
enjoy the quiet after a busy day. Stroll in the bush and
paddocks, meet our horse, goat, pet coloured sheep,
two dogs and cat all very friendly. We can arrange
outings to local attractions including horseriding,
beaches, and nearby stadium. Generous breakfasts, and
coffee and teas are always available, smoking on the
decking please. Sue speaks French and is learning
Mandarin. We have wheelchair access.

Te Harinui Country Homestay	**Tel:** (09) 415 9295	**Cost:** Double $80 Single $60
B&B Country Homestay	**E:** sueblanchard@xtra.co.nz	Child by arrangement
3km N of Albany	**W:** www.teharinui@2fs.com	Dinner $25 by arrangement
Mike & Sue Blanchard		**Beds:** 1 Queen 2 Single
102 Coatesville Highway		(2 bdrm)
RD 3, Albany Auckland		**Bath:** 1 Guests share

Greenhithe

You will be warmly welcomed to Waiata-Tui Lodge. Our
haven of 9 acres is only 15 mins to Auckland City and 6
mins to Albany University. A handy starting off palce for
North. You can relax here. Waken to bird song. Look out
over Kauri to the water below and the more distant
Waitakere range. Walk in our gentle rainforest, enjoy
massive trees a few centuries old. Swim in the pool. Meet
Henry our friendly goat. Therese is a keen spinner adn
wine-maker. We have both travelled extensively in New
Zealand and overseas.

Waiata Tui Lodge	**Tel:** (09) 413 9270	**Cost:** Double $75-$90
(The Song of the Tui)	**Fax:** (09) 413 9217	Single $60 Dinner $25
Homestay	**W:** www.bnb.co.nz/hosts/	Visa/MC
15km N of Auckland	waiatatuilodge.html	**Beds:** 2 Queen 1 Twin
Therese & Ned Jujnovich		2 Single (3 bdrm)
177 Upper Harbour Drive		**Bath:** 1 Private 1 Guests share
Greenhithe Auckland		

Coastal Beach Haven

Welcome to "Port 'O' Call", a secret hideaway
overlooking the tranquil sparkling waters of the
glorious Upper Waitemata Harbour. Enjoy watching
the many water activities or partake in them yourselves. We can take you sailing on our 28' Catamaran
"Akarana Express" or enjoy a leisurely paddle in a
kayak around these calm waters viewing the bird life
that abounds.....

Come and enjoy our warm and relaxed hospitality in
one of two spacious private tastefully decorated
bedrooms with ensuite featuring hair drier, toiletries,
bathrobes, heated towel rail; all leading out to a large
salt water pool and spa pool for your enjoyment, whilst
still enjoying the relaxing views over the water and
soak up the sunshine from the wide verandahs. Tea
and coffee making facilities, fridge, laundry and
ironing facilities, fresh flowers.

To get away for a peaceful read or just to ponder,
discover the "Secret Garden" amongst the tropical
palms and watch the beautiful white doves nesting, or
cuddle up in front of the log fire during winter with a
complimentary glass of fine New Zealand wine.
20 mins from America's Cup Village, Wine/Craft and
Sightseeing Tours, Charter Fishing Trips arranged,
Lunch/Dinner/BBQ's by arrangement.

THE ULTIMATE PLACE TO UNWIND.
P.S. There are three resident cats. Jill and Bernie look
forward to making your stay totally enjoyable.

Port O Call
B&B Homestay
Jill & Bernie Cleal
12 Amelia Place
Coastal Beach Haven
Auckland

Tel: (09) 483 4439
Fax: (09) 483 4439
Mob: 025 227 2639
E: portocall.b&b@xtra.co.nz
W: www.bnb.co.nz/hosts/
portocall.html

Cost: Double $140-$150
Single $80-$100 Visa/MC
Beds: (2 bdrm)
Bath: 2 Ensuite

Herald Island

Your host has home right on waters edge. Upstairs has 2 bedrooms, each with its own sundeck, with views of harbour. Own lounge, bathroom, and tea & coffee making facilities. Downstairs has 1 Twin (large) with own ensuite. Very homely. Easy access. Within 20 mins radius, wine tasting, horse riding, golf course, bush walks, vintage car museum & model world. Close to various restaurants. A small boat is available for fishing or a short cruise. Rooms serviced daily, laundry available. We have 1 dog Emma, 1 cat Tiger. Directions: Please phone.

Harbour View Homestay
B&B Homestay
20km N of Henderson
Les Pratt
84 The Terrace
Herald Island

Tel: (09) 416 7553
Fax: (09) 416 7553
E:harbourviewhomestay@nznet.gen.nz
W: www.bnb.co.nz/hosts/
harbourview.html

Cost: Double $80-$95
Single $45-$65
Child under 12 half price
Dinner $20 Visa/MC
Beds: 1 Queen 4 Single
(3 bdrm)
Bath: 1 Ensuite 1 Private

Browns Bay - Auckland

Spend some peaceful nights in our quiet guest bedrooms with Sky TV, garden and rural outlooks. Separate guest entrance leads into kitchenette with fridge, microwave, washing machine, dryer etc. Adjoining dining room. Internet, e-mail, fax, etc available. We overlook North Harbour Stadium and are minutes from a variety of restaurants, cafes, beaches, shopping and Auckland City Centre with all its attractions. Off street parking, 2 minutes to Motorway. Non smoking. Dinners $10, $20, $30 pp with prior notice.

Amoritz House
B&B
1.5km W of Browns Bay
Carol & Gary Moffatt
730 East Coast Road
Browns Bay
Auckland

Tel: (09) 479 6338
Fax: (09) 479 6338
Mob: 025 806958
Tollfree: 0800 936 338
E: amoritz@ihug.co.nz
W: www.bnb.co.nz/hosts/
amoritzhouse.html

Cost: Double $90-$120 Single
$70-$90 Dinner $10 - $30pp
Beds: 1 King/Twin 1 Queen 1
Double (3 bdrm)
Bath: 2 Ensuite 1 Private

Mairangi Bay - Auckland

Our modernised homestay is a short stroll from village shops, restaurants, cafes, sandy beaches and clifftop walkways. Golf, bowling and other attractions are adjacent. We offer warm friendly hospitality in our non-smoking home with idiot cat onsite. Amenities include ensuite bedrooms, TV lounge, tea coffee, laundry, Internet, phone/fax, barbeque area and offroad parking. Relax in our secluded tranquil garden with solar heated pool and native birdlife. Breakfast is a scrumptious indulgence while, requested, evening meals are legendary for "That cannot be the time" remarks.

Bays Cottage Homestay
B&B Homestay
13km N of Auckland
Jean & Brian Henstock
7 Matipo Road
Mairangi Bay, Auckland

Tel: (09) 479 3822
Fax: (09) 479 3822
Mob: 025 239 3772
E: bayscottage@xtra.co.nz
W: www.mysite.xtra.co.nz/-
bayscottage/

Cost: Double $80-$110
Single $50-$70
Dinner $25 by arrangement
Visa/MC Amex Diners
Beds: 1 King 1 Queen
1 Twin (3 bdrm)
Bath: 3 Ensuite

Mairangi Bay

Our modern indoor/outdoor home is situated in the middle of Auckland's North Shore beaches - walking distance to Mairangi Bay beach, cafes, restaurants and cliff top walks. Our upstairs bedroom has a balcony with gulf views - our downstairs a private garden view. An extra single room is available downstairs in conjunction with the double room. A delicious breakfast is served in our courtyard or dining room. Our interests - wine, golfing, boating and our miniature poodle. No smoking indoors. Off street parking.

Allenby Bed & Breakfast
B&B
1km W of Mairangi Bay
Brian & Pam Bolton
91 Hastings Road
Mairangi Bay
North Shore City

Tel: (09) 478 3477
Fax: (09) 445 3885
E: bbolton@clear.net.nz
W: www.allenby.co.nz

Cost: Double $100 Single $85
Child $50 Visa/MC Amex
Beds: 1 Double 1 Twin
1 Single (3 bdrm)
Bath: 2 Ensuite

Devonport

Welcome to Cheltenham By The Sea Bed & Breakfast. We are located in historical Devonport, Auckland, New Zealand. Adjacent to beautiful Cheltenham Beach. A large contemporary home. A short walk to shops, restaurants, golf course, bowling green, croquet club, tennis and squash courts. We are located 45 minutes from the International Airport and 12 minutes via ferry to downtown Auckland City. We offer our guests experienced advice for their NZ pursuits and a warm welcome.

Cheltenham-By-The-Sea
Homestay
10km NE of Auckland
Gayle and Mark Mossman
2 Grove Road
Devonport
Auckland

Tel: (09) 445 9437
Fax: (09) 445 9432
Mob: 021 251 6920
E: mgmossman@clear.net.nz
W: www.cheltenhambythesea.co.nz

Cost: Double $100-$120
Single $70 Child $30
Beds: 1 Queen 1 Double
1 Twin 2 Single (5 bdrm)
Bath: 1 Ensuite 1 Private
1 Guests share

Devonport

Private sunny garden room with ensuite, own entrance, parking. A few steps from Cheltenham Beach, short stroll to Devonport village. McHughs, Duders receptions nearby. French doors open onto tranquil villa garden. Guests are served delicious breakfast in sunny courtyard of tropical plants or in privacy of room - fresh juices, tropical or local fruits, muesli, yoghurt, warm homemade breads, croissants, muffins, choice of cooked. Crisp cotton sheets, bathrobes, flowers, fruit,selection of teas, coffee bodum, refrigerator, TV, in room - fax/email, laundry in villa, where one king bedroom offered. French/Spanish spoken.We welcome you

The Garden Room
B&B Homestay S/C
1.4km E of Devonport
Perrine & Bryan Hall
23 Cheltenham Rd Devonport

Tel: (09) 445 2472
Fax: (09) 445 2472
Mob: 025 989 643
E: b.hall@clear.net.nz
W: members.tripod.com/
GardenRoom/

Cost: Double $140-$160
Single $110-$120
Child $50 Visa/MC
Beds: 1 King 1 Queen
1 Single (2 bdrm)
Bath: 1 Ensuite 1 Private

Devonport

Tucked away at the end of a quiet cul-de-sac, Karin's Garden Villa - a DEVONPORT DREAM - offers real home comfort with its light cosy rooms, easy relaxed atmosphere and the warmest of welcome from Karin and her family. A beautifully restored spacious Victorian villa surrounded by large lawns and old fruit trees.

Karin's Garden Villa has also been featured on NZ and Australian television advertising for its relaxed, peaceful setting. Just 5 minutes stroll from tree-lined Cheltenham Beach, sailing, golf, tennis, shops and restaurants and only a short drive or pleasant 10 minute walk past extinct volcanoes to the picturesque Devonport centre with its many attractions.

Your comfortable room offers separate private access through French doors, opening onto a wide verandah and cottage garden. And for those visitors wanting ultimate comfort and privacy, there is even a self-contained studio cottage with balcony and full kitchen facilities to rent (min. 3 days). Sit down to a nutritious breakfast in the sunny dining room with its large bay windows overlooking everflowering purple lavender and native gardens. Guests are welcome to join the family barbecue and relax on our large lawn. We welcome longer stays and can arrange favourable discounts accordingly.

Help yourself to tea and German-style coffee and biscuits anytime, check your e-mail and feel free to use the kitchen and laundry. Karin comes from Germany and she and her family have lived in Indonesia for a number of years. We have seen a lot of the world and enjoy meeting other travellers. Always happy to help you arrange island cruises, rental cars and tours.

"See you soon - bis bald - à bientôt". Airport Shuttle Bus to our doorstep or to Downtown Ferry Terminal. Courtesy pick-up from Devonport Wharf. By Car: After crossing Harbour Bridge, take Takapuna-Devonport turnoff. Right at T-junction, follow Lake Road to end, left into Albert, Vauxhall Road and then first left into Sinclair Street.

Come as Guests - Leave as Friends.

Karin's Garden Villa
B&B Self-contained Self-contained Cottage
4 km N of Auckland Central
Karin Loesch
14 Sinclair Street
Devonport, Auckland 9

Tel: (09) 445 8689
Fax: (09) 445 8689
E: stay@karinsvilla.com
W: www.karinsvilla.com

Cost: Double $135-$165
Single $80-$125 Child $20
S/C Cottage $175
Visa/MC Amex
Beds: 1 King/Twin 2 Double
3 Single (4 bdrm)
Bath: 1 Ensuite 1 Private
1 Guests share

Devonport

Devonport Villa Inn, winner of the NZ Tourism Awards for hosted accommodation, is in the heart of Devonport, 2 minutes walk from Auckland's best kept secret, sandy and safe Cheltenham Beach.

There is something special about every aspect of this exquisite historic home built in 1903 by a wealthy retired English doctor. Edwardian elegance, spacious individual rooms with king and queen beds, extensive guest library, rich woollen carpets, restored colonial furniture, outstanding stained glass windows and the guest lounge with its amazing vaulted ceiling and polished native timber floor.

Choose from the unique upstairs Turret Room, the romantic and sunny Rangitoto Suite with its private balcony, the colonial style Beaconsfield Suite with antique clawfoot bath and four-poster king bed or the Oxford and Gold rooms.

Each cosy room is individually decorated with delightful handmade patchwork quilts, firm beds, soft woollen blankets, fresh bouquets of flowers from the garden, plump pillows and crisp white linen. And in the morning you will be cooked a delicious full breakfast, including freshly squeezed juice, natural yoghurt, nutritious muesli, muffins baked daily, Belgian waffles, double smoked bacon with eggs and preserves.....join other guests in the dining room overlooking the garden, or if you like we can serve breakfast in some rooms at a time to suit.

Please ask when booking. Sit in the sunny shell courtyard overlooking the Edwardian style garden with lavender hedges, old roses and spacious lawns. Enjoy a moonlit stroll along the beach to North Head and dinner at a nearby restaurant.

Devonport Villa is within easy walking distance of the major wedding reception venues and the historic sights of Devonport. Let us help you to make your stay in Devonport relaxing, pleasant and unique. Fax and E-mail available. Smoking is not permitted in the house.

Devonport Villa B&B Inn
B&B
8km N of Auckland
Keith & Lesley Wilkinson
46 Tainui Road
Devonport
Auckland

Tel: (09) 445 8397
Fax: (09) 445 9766
E: dvilla@ihug.co.nz
W: www.bnb.co.nz/hosts/
devonportvillabbinn.html

Cost: Double $175-$245 Visa/
MC Amex
Beds: 2 King 2 Queen 2 Single
(7 bdrm)
Bath: 1 Ensuite 6 Private

Devonport

Situated along the water front in the seaside village of Devonport, close to the shops, restaurants, wedding reception venues and ferry to down town Auckland. Quiet and private with off street parking. We offer three lovely fresh spacious bedsitting rooms with ensuite or private bathroom. All have comfortable beds, armchairs, television, tea/coffee and harbour views. Also, guest lounge and delightful garden. Leisurely breakfast with lots of fresh fruit, selection of cereals, breads and teas, juice, fresh coffee and cooked course. laundry, non-smoking inside.

Top of the Drive   **Tel:** (09) 445 3362   **Cost:** Double $120-$140
B&B   **Fax:** (09) 445 9636   Single $70-$120
Devonport Central   **W:** www.bnb.co.nz/hosts/   **Beds:** 1 King 1 Queen
Viv & Ray Huckle   topofthedrive.html   1 Single (3 bdrm)
15C King Edward Parade   **Bath:** 2 Ensuite 1 Private
Devonport   1 Family share
Auckland

Devonport

Our home is a charming colonial villa within easy walking distance of Devonport's numerous cafes, shops, safe swimming beaches, golf course and ferry terminal. Spectacular panoramic views from nearby summit of Mt Victoria. Spacious bedrooms with exceedingly comfortable beds! Double spa bath in one bathroom. Bathrobes provided. Large guest lounge with sky TV, tea/coffee making facilities, fridge and homebaking. Laundry facilities. Outside smoking only. We have travelled extensively both here and overseas and look forward to making your stay in our country an enjoyable experience.

Amberley B & B   **Tel:** (09) 446 0506   **Cost:** Double $100-$130
Homestay   **Fax:** (09) 446 0506   Single $70-$100 Child neg
Mary & Michael Burnett   **Mob:** 025 288 0161   Visa/MC Amex Diners
3 Ewen Alison Avenue   **E:** amberley@xtra.co.nz   **Beds:** 3 Queen 2 Single
Devonport   **W:** www.bnb.co.nz/hosts/   (4 bdrm)
Auckland 1309   amberleybb.html   **Bath:** 2 Guests share

Devonport

Welcome to our charming modern home, built in 1994, surrounded by trees and gardens. Peaceful, spacious and sunny bedrooms with attractive country decor. All rooms have TV and clock radios. Tea and coffee facilities available with delicious home cooking. we are adjacent Waitemata Golf course and 5 minutes from Narrow Neck Beach. Swim, sail and explore. Devonport village is 2 minutes by car and has a variety of restaurants, cafes and antique shops. Hosts are well travelled, informative and enjoy hospitality. Directions: Please phone

Ducks Crossing Cottage   **Tel:** (09) 445 8102   **Cost:** Double $90-$120
B&B Homestay   **Fax:** (09) 445 8102   Single $65-$85 Child $30
1.5km N of Devonport   **E:** duckxing@splurge.net.nz **Beds:** 1 Queen 1 Double
Gwenda & Peter Mark-Woods   **W:** www.bnb.co.nz/hosts/   2 Single (3 bdrm)
58 Seabreeze Road   duckscrossingcottage.html   **Bath:** 1 Ensuite 2 Private
Devonport
Auckland   **1213**

Devonport

Villa Cambria is among one of the finest Bed & Breakfast Inns in Devonport. The elegant, historic Villa is a typical Devonport Victorian home. Built in 1904 of native kauri timber, it has been lovingly restored to its former glory and tastefully furnished with an eclectic mix of antique, asian, interesting and homely items. The Villa is situated in an unbeatable location, just a few minutes walk to beautiful Cheltenham Beach and the picturesque Waitemata Golf Course (18 holes).

Each of the guest rooms is decorated individually. Choose from the romantic Garden Loft with its own balcony, or one of our four beautifully appointed guest bedrooms. From the hand-selected sprigs of lavender in the bathrooms to the complimentary tea, coffee, port and toiletries, you'll be pampered during your stay. All our rooms have phone connections, irons and hairdryers. Breakfast is wholesome, enjoy hand selected fresh fruit, yoghurt, a choice of cooked breakfasts and a selection of continental favourites.

Breakfast is made with fresh produce from the market and is accompanied by home made bread, followed by freshly brewed coffee and a choice of teas. The finishing touch though, is without a doubt the warm, friendly spontaneity of owners Clive and Kate, who live in a completely separate part of the house.

After breakfast you can enjoy the many nearby attractions, take a 12 minute ferry ride into the centre of the city (ferries cross every 30 minutes), or explore the many islands in the Hauraki Gulf. Devonport boasts more than 30 restaurants and offers excellent shopping, a cinema, many lovely walks and one of 49 extinct volcanic cones dotted around Auckland. Indeed Devonport has the enviable reputation of being the 'Jewel in Auckland's Crown' and one of the safest places to live within the city.

Visit our web site at www.villacambria.co.nz for full details and room descriptions.

DIRECTIONS: From the airport take a shuttle bus door to door service. By car: Travelling north, cross Auckland Harbour bridge. Travel 1.5kms and take the Esmonde Road exit Highway 26 to Takapuna-Devonport. Follow signs to Devonport along Lake Road. At the roundabout turn left into Albert Road, then at the T junction turn left into Vauxhall Road, Inn on left.

Villa Cambria	**Tel:** (09) 445 7899	**Cost:** Double $150-$230
B&B	**Fax:** (09) 446 0508	Single $130-$150
2km N of Auckland Central	**Mob:** 025 843 826	Visa/MC Amex
Kate & Clive Sinclair	**E:** info@villacambria.co.nz	**Beds:** 3 Queen 1 Double
71 Vauxhall Road	**W:** www.bnb.co.nz/hosts/	1 Twin (5 bdrm)
Devonport, Auckland	villacambria.html	**Bath:** 5 Ensuite

Devonport

Welcome to our pretty Victorian Villa (1885) nestled in a quiet cul-de-sac on the lower slopes of Mt Victoria. There are three elegant spacious rooms woth ensuites and Sky TV. A hot Spa Pool is available in the garden. We serve a delicious full breakfast and coffe and tea are available at all times. Situated just 100 metres from the Historic Devonport Village, 5 minute walk to the ferry which is a 10 minute ride to downtown Auckland. Directions: Rattray street is the first on the left past the Picture theatre. Not suitable for children or pets. www.rainbowvilla.co.nz, e-mail rainbowvilla@xtra.co.nz.

Rainbow Villa	**Tel:** (09) 445 3597	**Cost:** Double $130-$150
B&B	**Fax:** (09) 445 4597	Single $100-$120
Judy McGrath	**E:** rainbowvilla@xtra.co.nz	Visa/MC Amex
17 Rattray Street	**W:** www.rainbowvilla.co.nz	**Beds:** 1 King 1 Queen
Devonport		2 Single (3 bdrm)
Auckland		**Bath:** 3 Ensuite

Devonport

Welcome to our home. Let us pamper you in our quiet, sunny Victorian Villa furnished with antiques, oriental carpets and memorabilia from our extensive travels. Laze on your Victorian brass bed, soak in your Victorian claw footed bath. Complimentary drinks, chocolates. All bedrooms have ensuite, private bathrooms, bathrobes, toiletries, flowers, teddy bears to cuddle. Self-contained guest wing complete with kitchen facilities. Laundry, airport transfers available. Off-street parking. Stroll to the beach, restaurants, cafes, art galleries, shops, museums. Directions:Please phone.

Badgers of Devonport	**Tel:** (09) 445 2099	**Cost:** Double $119-$149
B&B Self-contained Quality	**Fax:** (09) 445 0231	Single $89-$119 Dinner $35
Accommodation	**Mob:** 025 720 336	Visa/MC Amex
Heather & Badger Miller	**E:** badgers@clear.net.nz	**Beds:** 4 Double 4 Twin
30 Summer Street	**W:** www.badger.co.nz	2 Single (4 bdrm)
Devonport Auckland		**Bath:** 3 Ensuite 1 Private

Devonport

Ivanhoe is a fully furnished B & B apartment. It is on the ground floor of our lovely home which looks out over the waters of the Waitemata harbour off Narrow Neck beach. This is a home away from home with a cozy lounge, kitchenette with cooking facilities, spacious bedroom and bathroom. Super continental breakfast is offered, with tea, coffee, biscuits, fruit for your convenience during the day. The beach, park, tennis, golf all only opposite. Historic Devonport only minutes away enables you to enjoy the restaurants, shopping and walks. A ferry sails to downtown Auckland in minutes. We have an 8yr old Boxer and a cat.

Ivanhoe	**Tel:** (09) 445 1900	**Cost:** Double $120-$140
B&B Self-contained Apartment	**Fax:** (09) 446 0039	Single $85-$100 Child $10
3km NE of Devonport	**E:** ivho@xtra.co.nz	Apartment weekly rates $700
Coralie & Philip Luffman	**W:** www.bnb.co.nz/hosts/	Visa/MC
82B Wairoa Road	ivanhoe.html	**Beds:** 1 Queen 1 Single (1 bdrm)
Devonport Auckland 9		**Bath:** 1 Ensuite

Devonport

A charming and private, beautifully appointed cottage only meters from the sea and park. The ideal location in Devonport. A short stroll along the waterfront in different directions takes you to lovely Cheltenham beach, Duder/McHughs reception lounges and Devonport village. Our cottage is light, serene and airy with full facilities including lounge/bedroom, bathroom, kitchen and private verandah. Full breakfast available on request. We welcome either short term or longer stays. John, Michele and family, including a little dog and cat, warmly invite you to stay.

Devonport Sea Cottage
B&B Self-contained Cottage
1km NE of Devonport
John Lethaby & Michele van Zon
3A Cambridge Terrace
Devonport Auckland

Tel: (09) 445 7117
Fax: (09) 445 7117
E: lethabys@ihug.co.nz
W: www.bnb.co.nz/hosts/
devonportseacottage.html

Cost: Double $120 Single $100
     Child $10
Beds: 1 Queen 1 Single
     (1 bdrm)
Bath: 1 Ensuite

Devonport

Welcome to our cosy smoke-free quiet and private guest cottage. We are right in the heart of historic Devonport Village with all its attractions, cafes, beaches, golf course, scenic walks. The ferry to Auckland City and the Hauraki Gulf is 3 minutes walk away. A breakfast basket is delivered to your door and provides fruit juice, cereals, home made muesli and yoghurt, a platter of seasonal fruits, breads, English muffins, jams, spreads, cheeses, free range eggs, breakfast teas and freshly brewed coffee. TV, fax.

The Jasmine Room
B&B Self-contained Cottage
4km N of Auckland Central
Joan & John Lewis
20 Buchanan Street
Devonport
Auckland

Tel: (09) 445 8825
Fax: (09) 445 8605
Mob: 021 120 9532
E: jasmine@photoalbum.co.nz
W: www.bnb.co.nz/hosts/
thejasmineroom.html

Cost: Double $100
Beds: 1 Queen (1 bdrm)
Bath: 1 Ensuite

Devonport

Recommended by the New York Times, leading tourist guide books and International Interior Design magazines, The Peace & Plenty Inn offers a world of graciousness, romance, comfort, fine food and hospitality.

Situated in an unbeatable location from which to explore all of the Auckland area, The Peace & Plenty Inn is on the waterfront in the seaside village of Devonport, and steps away from many fine restaurants, shopping, museums, galleries, the beach, and the ferry to central Auckland.

Built in 1888, The Peace & Plenty Inn has been impeccably restored with five individual Queen guest rooms in French Country Style with feather duvets, fine linens, plump pillows, oriental carpets, antiques, fine art, fireplaces, all bedrooms with private ensuite bathrooms. Enter a world of comfort with French Marcellas, Belgian chocolates, Italian toiletries, and bouquets of fresh flowers everywhere.

A MEMBER OF

Relax in a private lounge with complimentary Port, Teas, Coffee and cookies. Select from our gourmet breakfast menu - your choice of Eggs Benedict; French Baked Eggs with Brie and Avocado; Waffles; Eggs Devonport with smoked salmon; double-smoked bacon and eggs any way you like them - freshly squeezed orange juice, scrumptious muffins baked daily, homemade yoghurt and fresh tropical fruits.

Australia & New Zealand's Finest B&B's

& Rural Retreats

Proud to be a member of the Heritage Inns of New Zealand and The Small Hotel Company.

The Peace & Plenty Inn	**Tel:** (09) 445 2925	**Cost:** Double $230 Single $200
Luxury Inn	**Fax:** (09) 445 2901	Visa/MC Amex Diners
10 mins Auckland	**Mob:** 025 665 661	**Beds:** 3King 3 Queen 2 Single
Judith & Peter Machin	**E:** peaceandplenty@xtra.co.nz	(5 bdrm)
6 Flagstaff Terrace	**W:** www.bnb.co.nz/hosts/	**Bath:** 5 Ensuite
Devonport	peaceplentyinn.html	

Devonport

Welcome to the luxury and "olde-worlde" elegance of Buchanan's of Devonport, our gracious 2 storey home in the heart of Devonport - a historical, picturesque, seaside village on Auckland's North Shore. Built in 1933 in the Edwardian style architecture and immaculately restored in 1998 to its original era, our home is tastefully furnished throughout with genuine NZ and colonial antiques and artworks.

A private lounge with a gas-log fireplace, tea and coffee-making facilities, filtered water & complimentary biscuits is available for guests' use. Upstairs, we offer 4 luxuriously appointed, colour themed bedroom suites, all with balconies and ensuites with complimentary toiletries, hairdryers & demist mirrors.

Each room has its own unique charm (which sometimes give our guests some difficulty as to which room they want to stay!) and are individually furnished with an antique wooden bed & furnishings, imported fine beddings, plush Egyptian cotton towels , a comfortable couch, fresh flowers, TV, CD player, alarm clock, heater & electric blankets, ironing facilities, tea and coffee-making facilities and complimentary biscuits & sherry. The Honeymoon Suite has an added VCR and matching his-and-hers bathrobes!

Allow us to pamper your taste buds in the morning with a choice of delicious, hearty continental or cooked breakfast, which is served between 7.30am-9.30am in the formal dining room, or outside in the sunny courtyard with Kauri & other native trees and a 3-tier fountain.

And after your day's outing, relax in the warm waters of the spa-in-gazebo to soothe your body and mind. Only a 5-min stroll to the Devonport ferry wharf and a stone's throw away from all the village's international restaurants & cafes, special attractions and amenities, including major wedding reception venues, an 18 hole golf course (advanced bookings required) and lovely white-sand beaches! A complimentary tour of Devonport by your hosts is also on offer.

We can be a venue for small conferences too, with or without catering. 24-Hr. Security/Safety deposit box available. Ample off street parking. Unsuitable for children. A warm welcome awaits you at Buchanan's of Devonport from Eric, Cecille & Helena (our lovely 6 year old daughter who is our pride & joy!).

Please check out our website for a "virtual reality tour" of our B&B Inn.

Buchanan's of Devonport
B&B Inn
B&B Boutique
12km N of Auckland Central
Eric & Cecille Charnley
22 Buchanan Street
Devonport Auckland

Tel: (09) 445 3333
Fax: (09) 445 3333
Mob: 025 207 6738
E: info@buchanansofdevonport.co.nz
W: www.buchanansofdevonport.co.nz

Cost: Double $170-$230
Single $140-$180
Visa/MC Amex Diners
Beds: 1 King/Twin 1 Queen
2 Double (4 bdrm)
Bath: 4 Ensuite

Devonport

This historic accommodation allows you to bask in the glory of a bygone era. Built in the style of an English gothic mansion situated in large park like grounds, the house is complete with high ceilings and arches galore open onto sprawling veranders that are perfect for whiling away sunny afternoons.

A new conservatory in keeping with the style of the house, segures into the recently landscaped garden, redolent with the scent of wisteria, roses and lavender. Close to beaches shops, golf and ferry.

Earnscliff	**Tel:** (09) 445 7557	**Cost:** Double $235-$265
B&B	**Fax:** (09) 445 7602	Single $205-$235
2km N of Devonport	**Mob:** 025 293 7030	Visa/MC Amex Diners
Graeme & Jenny Dickey	**E:** earnscliff@xtra.co.nz	**Beds:** 2 Queen (2 bdrm)
44 Williamson Avenue	**W:** www.earnscliff .co.nz	**Bath:** 2 Ensuite
Devonport		
Auckland		

Birkenhead Point

An historic 1903 Colonial Villa; romantic, elegant, tranquil and private. Located in a quiet street of native and tropical trees,nine minutes to Auckland city by car or ferry, walking distance to cafes, restaurants, boutique shopping, galleries,beaches, coastal and bush walks. Two guests rooms both luxuriously furnished with antigue European and Asian furnishings. China Blue with antigue carved four poster bed,large ensuite dressing room and balcony overlooking the garden, the decor in shades of blue Tuscany Summer with ensuite, in soft cream and terracotta tonings reminiscent of the Tuscany countryside.

Stafford Villa	**Tel:** 64 9 418 3022	**Cost:** Double $245 Single $190
B&B	**Fax:** 64 9 419 8197	Visa/MC Amex Diners
3 KM No of Auckland City	**Mob:** 021 61 3022	**Beds:** 1 King/Twin 1 King
Chris and Mark Windram	**E:** rest@staffordvilla.co.nz	(2 bdrm)
2 Awanui Street	**W:** www.staffordvilla.co.nz	**Bath:** 2 Ensuite
Birkenhead Point Auckland		

Waiheke Island

Waiheke Island is beautiful and different, and Gulf Haven provides exceptional accommodation in an award winning 2 acre waterfront garden, with uninterrupted sea views. Our 2 sunny studio apartments are private and peaceful, each offering luxurious self-contained facilities for 2 people. A path takes you via a dramatic deck to secluded rock pools and deep clear water. We enjoy our Island hideaway and its mild climate and welcome you to experience it with us. We meet you from most ferries, please phone first.

Gulf Haven	**Tel:** (09) 372 6629	**Cost:** Child n/a Dinner n/a
Self-contained S/C Studio Apt	**Fax:** (09) 372 8558	Breakfast optional $8pp
4km E of Oneroa	**E:** gulfhavn@ihug.co.nz	$165 Self contained Studio
Alan Ramsbottom & Lois Baucke	**W:** www.webnz.com/	Visa/MC
49 Great Barrier Road	bbnz/haven.htm	**Beds:** 1 King/Twin 1 Queen
Enclosure Bay		(2 bdrm)
Waiheke Island		**Bath:** 2 Ensuite

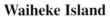

Waiheke Island

Quality bed and breakfast suites in main Lodge or private garden setting all with own bathrooms, private sun decks and TV. Tranquil native bush setting, 150 metres to a beautiful swimming beach, 12 minute walk to cafes and shops. Spa pool. B&B includes continental breakfasts and homemade afternoon teas. Also self contained units with decks and BBQs. Ferry travel, tours etc. organised. Full conference facilities. Free wharf transfers. Minimum two night weekend booking on most accommodation. Off season specials. Two children and two cats - all tame.

Punga Lodge	**Tel:** (09) 372 6675	**Cost:** Double $110-$130
B&B Self-contained Units	**Fax:** (09) 372 6675	Single $95-$110 Child $25
1km E of Oneroa	**E:** pungalodge@hotmail.com	S/C apartments $120 - $210
Dyan Sharland & Rob Johnston	**W:** www.ki-wi.co.nz/punga.htm	Visa/MC
223 Ocean View Rd		**Beds:** 3 Queen 7 Double
Little Oneroa		5 Single (10 bdrm)
Waiheke Island		**Bath:** 5 Ensuite 5 Private

Waiheke Island

We live above Sandy Bay which is 2-3 mins walk away with spectacular sea views. All the rooms of our modest home face due north catching the sun all day, ideal for our spoilt cat. Waiheke caters for adventuring, dining out, sandy beaches, rock pools, which we enjoy after farming and owning a garden centre which our 4 children helped with. We really enjoy our B & B and look forward to sharing our beautiful island with you. Directions: Ferry from Auckland. Car ferry Howick. Complimentary ferry transfers.

Blue Horizon
B&B
David & Marion Aim
41 Coromandel Road
Sandy Bay
Waiheke Island

Tel: (09) 372 5632
W: www.bnb.co.nz/hosts/
bluehorizon.html

Cost: Double $70-$85
Single $55-$70
Dinner on request
Beds: 2 Queen (2 bdrm)
Bath: 1 Ensuite 1 Family share

Waiheke Island - Auckland

Our vineyard guest house, set overlooking one of the oldest and largest stands of pohutukawa trees on the island, has stunning sea views back to Auckland and Rangitoto. The house has complete privacy and is only a short stroll in any direction to any one of many secluded swimming bays and is a 20 minute walk to Surfdale. For wine lovers staying on a vineyard offers an intimate glimpse of the vineyard process and a taste of the wine. The beautifully furnished house includes three bedrooms and two baths and can be rented in smaller units, e.g. one bedroom w/ensuite and kitchen or two bedrooms, lounge with a mini-bar.

Kennedy Point Vineyard
S/C Vineyard Guesthouse
1km NE of Surfdale
Susan McCarthy
44 Donald Bruce Road
Waiheke Island Auckland

Tel: (09) 372 5600
Fax: (09) 372 6205
E: sunsethill@ihug.co.nz
W: www.bnb.co.nz/hosts/
surfdale.html

Cost: Double $175 Single $175
S/C House $300 Visa/MC
Beds: 2 Queen 2 Single
(3 bdrm)
Bath: 1 Ensuite 1 Private

Herne Bay - Auckland Central

Relax and enjoy the hospitality of one of Auckland's grand old homes. Recently refurbished to include all modern amenities but retaining its early colonial charm. Lovely water views, stroll to the Ponsonby cafes and restaurants and beaches. Continental or cooked breakfast supplied. The entire upstairs is available for guests with high water pressure/heated towel rail, drier and toiletries. Gas and electric heating and TV in both bedrooms with free Internet in the adjoining library.

Moana Vista
B&B Homestay
2.5 km W of Auckland central
Tim Kennedy & Matthew Moran
60 Hamilton Road
Herne Bay
Auckland

Tollfree: 0800 08 VISTA
Mob: 021 376 150
E: info@moanavista.co.nz
W: www.moanavista.co.nz

Cost: Double $140-$160
Single $120
Visa/MC Amex Diners
Beds: 1 King 1 Queen (2 bdrm)
Bath: 1 Guests share

Ponsonby - Auckland Central

Chic B&B hotel close to all the razzmatazz of Ponsonby
Road's bars, cafes and shopping. An 1898 villa restored
with bold use of colour and NZ and Pacific art works.
Leisurely breakfasts served from our extensive menu in the
dining room or alfresco on the veranda overlooking the
large garden. Eight double rooms and three suites. Each is
beautiful and comfortable with ensuite, sky tv, DDI phones,
hairdryer, tea making facilities. Some rooms have a
kitchen, cd and video player. This is the place to meet
people and have fun.

The Great Ponsonby B&B	**Tel:** (09) 376 5989	**Cost:** Double $145-$175
B&B - small hotel	**Fax:** (09) 376 5527	Single from $140
Auckland Central	**E:** great.ponsonby@xtra.co.nz	Double Suites $190 - $245
Sally James & Gerry Hill	**W:** www.ponsonbybnb.co.nz	Visa/MC Amex Diners
30 Ponsonby Terrace		**Beds:** 6 King/Twin
Ponsonby Auckland		5 Queen (11 bdrm)
		Bath: 11 Ensuite

Ponsonby - Auckland Central

Prepare to be pampered at the "Ponsonby Potager".
Enjoy a self-help breakfast in the garden room or on
one of the two private decks. You have your own
entrances, bathroom, lounge (with video and book
library), fully equipped kitchen, fresh fruit and
flowers, off-street parking and Sky TV. It is peaceful
here but only a 3 minutes stroll to the shops, cafes and
restaurants of Ponsonby. Marsha, Ray and Danny
(their 4 legged son) respect your privacy but are here if
you need advice.

Ponsonby Potager	**Tel:** (09) 378 7237	**Cost:** Double $120 Single $90
Self-contained	**Fax:** (09) 378 7267	**Beds:** 2 Double (2 bdrm)
Auckland Central	**E:** raywarby@compuserve.com	**Bath:** 1 Private
Marsha & Ray Lawford	**W:** www.bnb.co.nz/hosts/	
43 Douglas Street	ponsonbypotager.html	
Auckland 2		

Ponsonby - Auckland Central

Delightful olde-world charm with modern amenities to
assure your comfort - accent on quality. Hospitable
and relaxing. Quiet with green outlook. Close to
Herne Bay & Ponsonby Road cafes & quality
restaurants. Airport shuttle service door-to-door.
Handy to public transport, city attractions and
motorways. Smoke free indoors. Alternative health
therapies & massage available. Special dietary
requirements catered for. Organic emphasis. Single
party bookings available.

Colonial Cottage	**Tel:** (09) 360 2820	**Cost:** Double from $100
B&B Homestay	**Fax:** (09) 360 3436	Single from $80
Auckland Central	**W:** www.bnb.co.nz/hosts/	Dinner $25 By arrangement
Grae Glieu	colonialcottage.html	**Beds:** 1 King 1 Queen
35 Clarence Street		1 Single (3 bdrm)
Ponsonby Auckland 1034		**Bath:** 1 Guests share

Ponsonby - Auckland Central

Summer Street is very quiet but less than one minute walk from Auckland's busy Ponsonby Road with all its fantastic shops and restaurants. Public transport is close (Auckland centre 15 minutes). Airport shuttles come door to door. Importantly we provide off-street parking, quality queen size beds, linen and towels. A continental buffet breakfast is laid out either in our dining area or in the garden. Alternatively you've got a really great choice of reasonably priced quality cafes and bistros a minute away on the Ponsonby Road.

Summer Street
B&B
Auckland central
Selwyn Houry
6 Summer Street
Ponsonby Auckland

Tel: (09) 361 3715
Fax: (09) 361 3715
Mob: 021 535 635
E: selwyn_houry@hotmail.com
W: www.bnb.co.nz/hosts/
summerstreet.html

Cost: Double $90-$130
Single $80-$100
Child by arrangement
Beds: 2 Queen (2 bdrm)
Bath: 1 Guests share
1 Family share

Parnell - Auckland

10 Parnell Road is a townhouse close to many cafes and interesting shops of the area, the central city and museum is within walking distance. Facilities for guests include private bathroom and sitting room with TV. Smoking outside please. A small park opposite with a view of the city and Sky Tower add to the position of number 10. No pets please.
Children over 12.

Parnell Homestay
B&B Homestay
1km from Auckland
George & Janette Welanyk
10 Parnell Road
Parnell Auckland

Tel: (09) 358 2233
Fax: (09) 358 2233
Mob: 021 377 431
W: www.bnb.co.nz/hosts/
welanykhomestay.html

Cost: Double $90 Single $80
Visa/MC Amex Diners
Beds: 1 Double (1 bdrm)
Bath: 1 Private

The most suitable time
to arrive is late afternoon,
and to leave is before 10 in the morning.

Parnell - Auckland

Ascot Parnell is a convenient, central and quiet location to visit all Auckland city attractions. Also ideal for the business traveller who requires everything nearby. Built in 1910, this large mansion has been carefully restored to its former elegance, maintaining its old-fashioned charm. As a small B&B hotel it offers spacious guest-rooms with European character and style.

The Downtown ferry terminal is 1 mile (2.5km) away, and there is a Link-bus every 8 minutes on the corner of the street. It is an easy walk to the Rose Gardens, Auckland Museum, Parnell Village and Newmarket with its many boutiques, craft-shops, art galleries, cafes and restaurants. The airport shuttle bus will bring you to the door.

There is a choice from spacious superior queen-rooms to modestly priced but comfortable single rooms. All are non-smoking, immaculate and tastefully decorated, they have their own bathroom, hair-drier, telephone and Internet access.

A sumptuous breakfast is served in the morning room overlooking the subtropical garden. Refreshments are offered throughout the day.

Although it is not necessary to rent a car, there is parking in the courtyard.

The friendly hosts Bart and Therese also speak Flemish/ Dutch, French and German and look forward to welcoming you.

Visit http://www.ascotparnell.com/ and use the reservations form.

Ascot Parnell
B&B Small Hotel
1.5km E of Auckland Central
Bart & Therese Blommaert
36 St Stephens Avenue
Parnell Auckland 1

Tel: (09) 309 9012
Fax: (09) 309 3729
E: AscotParnell@compuserve.com
W: www.ascotparnell.com

Cost: Double $165-$185
Single $95-$165
extra person $50
Visa/MC Amex Diners
Beds: 7 Queen/Twin 2 Queen
2 Single (11 bdrm)
Bath: 10 Ensuite 1 Private

Parnell - Auckland

THE REDWOOD offers you a very warm welcome. Stroll through our peaceful inner-city native garden and you will find a stand of tree ferns, Nikau palms and cabbage trees. Native birds frequent the garden and as we do, you shall enjoy their evensong. We are adjacent to the famous Parnell Rose Gardens and Dove-Myer Robinson Park. You are invited to use the lounge and deck from where you will experience our ever-changing view of pleasure craft and shipping over the Waitemata harbour to Devonport and Mt Victoria.

You will have the same views while enjoying our gourmet breakfast having choices of fresh fruit, yoghurt, cereals, daily baked muffins, breads and pastries, and choice of cooked breakfast.

We are located close to many popular attractions, including Parnell Village and its restaurants, the Auckland Domain and museum, Kelly Tarlton's Underwater World, the salt water Parnell pools and the waterfront as well as many golf courses. If you are enjoying a day of sightseeing picnic hampers can be supplied on request. We are just a one-stop bus ride or a twenty-minute walk from the city centre and waterfront, including the yacht basin.

You will enjoy the shopping, galleries, cinemas, theatre and many more restaurants in the down town area. Door to door shuttle buses are available to and from the Airport. We are happy to advise and assist you with onward travel.

Our two bedroom self contained cottage at Tairua on the Coromandel Peninsula with its wonderful views of the harbour and ocean, enables us to help you with accommodation if you are planning to tour in the area. Our rooms are comfortable and have queen, double or single beds with all the conveniences you would expect, including colour TV and tea and coffee making facilities. You will find us well travelled and conversant on many topics of interest, including wine. We aim to provide you with a home away from home and every effort has been made to ensure that your stay - be it business or pleasure - is a pleasant and enjoyable one.

In house pre or post jet-lag therapeutic massage and other beauty therapy treatments are available. Email, fax and office facilities available. German spoken.

Redwood Bed & Breakfast	**Tel:** (09) 373 4903	**Cost:** Double $120-$165
B&B	**Fax:** (09) 373 4903	Single $85-$120
2km S of Auckland Central	**Mob:** 025 758 996	Child $25 Visa/MC
Dawn Feickert	**Tollfree:** 0800 349 742	Tairua 2 bedroom S.C beach
11 Judges Bay Road	**E:** kotuku@wave.co.nz	cottage also available for rent.
Parnell	**W:** www.bnb.co.nz/hosts/	**Beds:** 2 Queen 1 Double
Auckland	redwoodbedbreakfast.html	2 Single (3 bdrm)
		Bath: 2 Ensuite 1 Family share

Parnell - Auckland
VERY CENTRAL SPECIAL BREAKFAST*
UNIQUELY AUCKLAND THEMED ROOMS

Birdwood House is located adjacent to Auckland's
exclusive PARNELL boutiques, 5 minutes by car
from Auckland's central CBD, 4 minutes by car or
a 10 minute flat stroll from Auckland's trendy
fashion centre NEW MARKET, the AUCK-
LAND HOSPITAL, the DOMAIN, and the
MUSEUM, ... we are VERY, VERY CENTRAL.

A regular bus service links Parnell, the CBD,
Auckland Hospital and New Market. The airport
shuttle operates a 24 hour service to our front door
(20 minute ride). Motorway access to Auckland's
Southern, Western and Northern suburbs is only
minutes away. Enjoy with us our 1914 NEWLY RESTORED, 'Arts and Crafts' Charles Rennie Mackintosh
bungalow.

We stand majestically in the prestigious suburb of PARNELL, overlooking Auckland city and the sky tower.
Our elevated back view takes in the Auckland MUSEUM and the luxurious BOTANICAL GARDENS of the
DOMAIN. Parnell village with its range of AWARD winning RESTAURANTS, ART galleries and
BOUTIQUE shops is virtually on our doorstep.

Birdwood House is located on the Parnell Historic Walk in amongst historic houses/buildings. The NEW
MARKET business district is to the south and has a large selection of designer and speciality shops, cinemas
and swimming pool and gymnasium. WAITEMATA HARBOUR with its sandy beaches, water sports and
Kelly Tarltons Aquarium is close by.

We can enhance your stay by arranging tours or by suggesting 'unique' Auckland things to do. At Birdwood
House we embody Edwardian quality and hospitality. A HOME AWAY FROM HOME Birdwood House's
original features include a beautiful KAURI staircase, delightful stained LEADLIGHT windows and a
mesmerising inglenook FIREPLACE.

Every bedroom in the house is decorated on a sumptuous theme such as the museum room which overlooks
the Auckland's museum and the Cathedral room which reflects Parnell's newly renovated Holy Trinity
Cathedral. After a comfortable nights sleep enjoy our healthy SPECIAL BREAKFAST with an emphasis on
FRESH and in season produce.

You can enjoy breakfast in bed if you are feeling decadent.
Business facilities are available should you require to hold
a meeting we have a separate lounge to accommodate your
guests. You may encounter our cat "Chutney" and our
small dog "Mandy", but they are confined to a separate
living area.

OUR Aim is to make your stay in Auckland memorable
and cater for your individual needs. When we first saw this
house it beckoned us to enjoy it, we invite you to join us
and help us do the same.

Birdwood House	**Tel:** (09) 306 5900	**Cost:** Double $150-$185
B&B	**Fax:** (09) 306 5909	Single $130-$160 Visa/MC
1.5 S of Auckland	**Mob:** 025 777 722	**Beds:** 4 King/Twin 1 Double
Barbara Bell & Rosemary Moloney	**E:** info@birdwood.co.nz	(5 bdrm)
41 Birdwood Cresent	**W:** www.birdwood.co.nz	**Bath:** 4 Ensuite 1 Private
Parnell Auckland		

Parnell - Auckland

With its stunning harbour views and perfect, convenient location in prestigeous Parnell, our charming little hotel affords our guests a desirable amount of independence. Our unique and comfortable bedrooms offer the privacy of ensuite bathrooms. Families are welcome, we are non-smoking and guests would be lucky to encounter our elusive cat! Let us help you arrange tours or rental cars. We are happy to negotiate our winter discounts etc and we welcome the opportunity to make your visit to Auckland enjoyable .

Chalet Chevron
B&B B&B Hotel
1.5 km E of Downtown Auckland
Brett & Jennie Boyce
14 Brighton Road
Parnell Auckland

Tel: (09) 309 0290
Fax: (09) 373 5754
E: chaletchevron@xtra.co.nz
W: www.chaletchevron.co.nz

Cost: Double $100-$125
Single $80-$90 Child $20
Family rm - sleeps 4 $130 -
$160 Visa/MC Amex Diners
Beds: 2 King/Twin 1 Queen
5 Double 2 Twin
13 Single (14 bdrm)
Bath: 12 Ensuite 1 Guests share

Parnell - Auckland

St Georges Bay Lodge is an elegant Victorian Villa which has the charm of a by-gone era, with the comfort of modern amenities. There is no better location for your stay in Auckland City. We are minutes from: picturesque PARNELL VILLAGE, designer boutiques and speciality stores, great cafes, restaurants, and night club life, health centres, swimming pools, gardens, parks, and the Museum in Auckland Domain and Holy Trinity Cathedral. Also within comfortable walking distance: Newmarket and the Central City business district and the Casino.

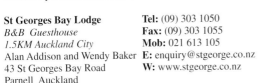

St Georges Bay Lodge
B&B Guesthouse
1.5KM Auckland City
Alan Addison and Wendy Baker
43 St Georges Bay Road
Parnell Auckland

Tel: (09) 303 1050
Fax: (09) 303 1055
Mob: 021 613 105
E: enquiry@stgeorge.co.nz
W: www.stgeorge.co.nz

Cost: Double $195-$245
Single $165-$205
Visa/MC Amex
Beds: 2 King 1 Queen
1 Twin (4 bdrm)
Bath: 3 Ensuite 1 Private

Mt Eden - Auckland

All are welcome at 811 Bed and Breakfast. Your hosts Bryan and David, Pfeni and their Irish Water Spaniels welcome you to their turn of the century home. Our home reflects years of collecting and living overseas. Centrally located on Dominion Road (which is an extension of Queen Street city centre). The bus stop at the door, only 10 minutes to city and 20 minutes to airport, shuttle bus from airport. Easy walking to Balmoral shopping area (banks, excellent restaurants). We have operated a bed and breakfast on a farm in Digby County, Nova Scotia, Canada.

811 Bed & Breakfast
B&B
Auckland Central
Bryan Condon & David Fitchew
811 Dominion Road
Mt Eden Auckland 1003

Tel: (09) 620 4284
Fax: (09) 620 4286
Mob: 025 289 8863
W: www.bnb.co.nz/hosts/
bedbreakfast.html

Cost: Double $75 Single $50
Beds: 2 Double 1 Twin
(3 bdrm)
Bath: 2 Guests share
2 Separate Showers
2 Separate Toilets

Mt Eden - Auckland

We invite you to stay at our charming small hotel offering quality B&B with all modern facilities yet combined with a homely and welcoming atmosphere. Our picturesque, colonial villa with its 11 guestrooms is tastefully decorated with native timber furniture. All rooms have ensuites, quality commercial beds, telephones, desks, suitcase racks. Internet access available. The sunny spacious lounge opens to a private deck and small exotic garden. Situated 2 km from the city centre, yet in serene, historic surroundings.

Bavaria B&B Hotel
Small Hotel
2km S of Auckland Central
Ulrike Stephan & Rudolf Schmidt
83 Valley Road
Mt Eden Auckland 3

Tel: (09) 638 9641
Fax: (09) 638 9665
E: bavaria@xtra.co.nz
W: www.bavariabandbhotel.co.nz

Cost: Double $99-$130
　　　Single $70-$90 Child $12
　　　Visa/MC Amex
Beds: 1 King/Twin 4 Queen
　　　2 Double 2 Twin
　　　4 Single (11 bdrm)
Bath: 11 Ensuite

Mt Eden - Auckland

Peace and quiet in the heart of Auckland. Ideal for travellers, families and groups. Top-rated villa style in sunny garden setting with tennis court. Guest lounge with open fire, Sky TV, internet facilities. Off street parking, laundry and cooking facilities. Close to Eden Park and to shops, restaurants etc. Rated "best by guests" and great value for money.

Pentlands B&B Hotel
B&B Hotel
3km S of Auckland Waterfront
Brian Hopkins
22 Pentland Avenue
Mt Eden
Auckland

Tel: (09) 638 7031
Fax: (09) 638 7031
Mob: 025 339 928
E: hoppy.pentland@xtra.co.nz
W: www.pentlands.co.nz

Cost: Double $79-$89
　　　Single $49-$59
　　　Extra People $20 - $25
　　　Visa/MC Amex
Beds: 7 Double 3 Twin
　　　5 Single (15 bdrm)
Bath: 4 Guests share

Mt Eden - Auckland

We are situated approx 4 km from Auckland City Centre. On a regular bus route. Close to Mt Eden Village and Newmarket, cafes, restaurants and shops. Our Town House has parking and is a level section. Made of concrete and Cedar Wood, TV, coffee/tea making facilities. Non-smoking. 1 Cat.

B&B
4 Central Auckland
Mrs Joan Monkton
2/45 Peary Road
Mt Eden Auckland

Tel: (09) 630 6705
Mob: 021 121 5732

Cost: Double $80 Single $40
　　　Visa/MC
Beds: 1 Twin (1 bdrm)
Bath: 1 Private

Epsom - Auckland

Our home, a spacious 1919 wooden bungalow, is surprisingly quiet and restful, set in a garden suburb in a tree-lined street, 200 metres from Greenwoods Corner Village with its bank, post office, reasonably priced non-tourist restaurants, and bus stop on direct route (15 minutes each way) between the airport and CBD.

There is a short walk to One Tree Hill, one of Auckland's loveliest parks with a playground, farm animals, groves of trees, the Observatory, and a magnificent panorama of Auckland from the summit. A 15 minute walk through the park leads to the Expo centre and Greenlane Hospital.

There are two accommodation areas - either the 'Garden Suite' with its Queen-sized double bedroom, large lounge with 3 single beds, patio, desk and TV, own bathroom, and which is the area we find really suitable for families; or the 'Upstairs' bedroom (king-size, can be converted to twin beds) with own ensuite, desk and TV.

We have travelled widely both in NZ and overseas (our son lives in Finland) and very much like conversing with guests and assisting in making their stay as pleasant as possible in our country and especially in this attractive suburb of Auckland.

We are a smoke-free family. Jim and I were both born in NZ.

Millars Epsom Homestay
Homestay
5km Auckland City Centre
Janet & Jim Millar
10 Ngaroma Road
Epsom Auckland 1003

Tel: (09) 625 7336
Fax: (09) 625 7336
Mob: 025 659 2817
E: jmillar@xtra.co.nz
W: www.bnb.co.nz/hosts/
millarsepsomhomestay.html

Cost: Double $80-$90
Single $60-$70 Child $10
Dinner $30 Visa/MC
Beds: 1 King 1 Queen
2 Single (3 bdrm)
Bath: 1 Ensuite 2 Private

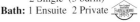

Epsom - Auckland

Our 70 year-old villa is in the residential part of Epsom amidst gracious homes. We offer quiet accommodation in our comfortable home complete with delicious breakfasts. Guest may have sole use of the lounge, TV and library. Tea and coffee are provided. Our self-contained unit with ranch slider opening onto a forecourt has a bedroom wi th queen-sized bed, en-suite, kitchen, lounge with TV. Our Guesthouse is between Gillies Avenue and Manukau Road close to the Motorways, Airport and within walking distance of Newmarket.

B&B Guesthouse	**Tel:** (09) 630 7710	**Cost:** Double $79-$89
Auckland Central	**Fax:** (09) 630 7710	Single $65-$75 Visa/MC
Cloudy Chen	**E:** TYCHEN@ihug.co.nz	**Beds:** 3 Queen 1 Double
18 Epsom Avenue	**W:** www.bnb.co.nz/hosts/	1 Single (5 bdrm)
Epsom Auckland	chen.html	**Bath:** 1 Ensuite 2 Guests share

Epsom - Auckland

We offer home comforts, and bedrooms with views. 2 minutes from the motorway, in a central quiet garden suburb, with many facilities. Airport 20 minutes , on a door to door shuttle bus service. Excellent city bus service nearby. Juice, tea, coffee provided. Laundry facilities. Off street parking. Family group welcome. We are experienced travellers and enjoy our guests. Directions: Leave Motorway at Market Road, travel West, cross over Great South Road, first left into Dunkerron Ave, Tahuri Road 2nd left.

Hey's Homestay	**Tel:** (09) 520 0154	**Cost:** Double $85 Single $55
B&B Homestay	**Fax:** (09) 520 0184	Child neg Dinner $25
6km S of Auckland Central	**Mob:** 021 642 652	**Beds:** 1 King 1 Twin (2 bdrm)
Kathy & Roger Hey	**E:** R.K.Hey@xtra.Co.NZ	**Bath:** 1 Guests share
2/7 Tahuri Road	**W:** www.bnb.co.nz/hosts/	
Epsom 3 Auckland	hey.html	

Epsom - Auckland

Experience warm, friendly hospitality in our large modern home in a quiet tree lined street. Just 5 minutes from motorway and 15 minutes from Airport and City CBD. Our central location is ideally positioned to explore the many attractions, whether by car or one of the nearby bus routes. Perhaps you would enjoy a game of golf with us. Use of full laundry facilities. Telephone, email by request. Evening meals by prior arrangement. We look forward to sharing our non-smoking home with you.

Auckland Homestay	**Tel:** (09) 624 3714	**Cost:** Double $120
B&B Homestay	**E:** aucklandhomestay@xtra.co.nz	Single $60-$90
Isobel & Ian Thompson	**W:** www.aucklandhomestay.co.nz	Dinner B/A Visa/MC
37 Torrance Street		**Beds:** 1 Queen 2 Single
Epsom		(3 bdrm)
Auckland		**Bath:** 1 Ensuite
		1 Guests share

Epsom - Auckland

Nestled on the slopes of One Tree Hill in a tree-lined street, Epsom House is within 4 minutes flat walk of the local Greenlane and National Women's Hospitals, Expo and Conference Centre, Showgrounds and Collectors Markets. Luxurious suites, superior bed and bedding and quality furnishings, ensuite bathrooms with spa bath. Relax in the private sunny courtyard garden or private comfortable guest lounge. All suites have fast internet and e-mail facilities. Tariff includes complimentary continental or gourmet breakfasts, coffee, special teas and juices. Our dog Linny welcomes you.

Epsom House
B&B Homestay
4km S of Auckland
Kathy & Rick
18 Crescent Road
Epsom Auckland

Freephone: 0800 118 448
Tel: (09) 630 0900
Fax: (09) 630 0900
Mob: 025 834 779
E: kathyvb@xtra.co.nz
W: www.epsombb.com

Cost: Double $200 Single $160
Dinner $40 Visa/MC
Beds: 2 King 1 Twin (2 bdrm)
Bath: 2 Ensuite

One Tree Hill - Auckland

A warm friendly welcome awaits you at 39B. Situated 15 minutes from the airport and city centre our large contemporary home in a secluded garden setting on private right of way offers pleasant views and peaceful surroundings. We are close to Ellerslie Racecourse, One Tree Hill Domain, Alexandra Park, Epsom Showgrounds and Ericsson Stadium, Restaurants, Antique shops, Supermarket, and bus service are a short distance away. Our spacious self-contained unit has a large bedroom with king sized bed. Private bathroom lounge with TV, kitchenette, microwave, washing machine and extras. Arrive as a guest - depart as a friend. Directions: Please phone

Self-contained Homestay
5km S of Newmarket
Ron & Doreen Curreen
39B Konini Road
One Tree Hill Auckland 5

Tel: (09) 579 9531
Fax: (09) 579 9531
E: curreenhomestay@hotmail.com
W: www.bnb.co.nz/hosts/
curreen.html

Cost: Double $65-$75 Single $45
Child $12 Dinner $25
Beds: 1 King 1 Queen
1 Double (3 bdrm)
Bath: 1 Private 1 Guests share

One Tree Hill - Auckland

Our comfortable non-smoking home has modern facilities with a huge 400 acre treed park at the end of our street. We have six restaurants in the next street including European ,Chinese, Thai, McDonalds and Wendys. The NZ Expo centre and Ellerslie Conference Centre are nearby. Off street parking. Frequent buses to city. Directions: Exit route 1 at Green Lane East, head west, then left at lights, then second right.

Greenlane Homestead
Homestay
6km S of Downtown Auckland
Clare Ross & Winston Dickey
21 Atarangi Road
Greenlane East
Auckland, 5.

Mob: 025 281 3222
Freephone: 0800 254 419
E: Stay@Paradise.net.nz
W: www.bnb.co.nz/hosts/
dickey.html

Cost: Double $65-$75
Single $40-$50
(Ensuite $10 extra)
Dinner $15
Visa/MC accepted
Beds: 2 Queen 5 Single
(4 bdrm)
Bath: 1 Ensuite 2 Guests share

Remuera - Auckland

Guest book comments "Absolutely purr-fect". "A superb stay". "Very comfortable with stunning food". "A lovely oasis of calm with wonderful breakfasts". "Peaceful retreat with excellent breakfasts". Our breakfasts ARE special using seasonal fruit and produce. Join us for a Cordon Bleu candlelit evening dinner - booking essential. "Woodlands" is very quiet, surrounded by native trees and palms and central to many places of interest. The two guest bedrooms have tea/coffee facilities, heated towel rails, and coloured TV's. Safe off street carparking. Arrive a guest - leave a friend.

Woodlands
B&B Homestay
7km N of Auckland Central
Judi & Roger Harwood
18 Waiatarua Road
Remuera Auckland 1005

Tel: (09) 524 6990
Fax: (09) 524 6993
Mob: 025 602 5592
E: Woodlands@ake.quik.co.nz
W: www.bnb.co.nz/hosts/
woodlands.html

Cost: Double $120-$130
Single $90 Child
Dinner $45 Visa/MC
Beds: 1 King 1 Double
1 Single (2 bdrm)
Bath: 1 Ensuite 1 Private

St Johns Park - Remuera - Auckland

Relax in our lounge, conservatory, or garden . Our warm comfortable smoke free home has off street parking in quiet residential area surrounding the Remuera Golf Course. All bedrooms have smoke alarms, electric blankets, cosy duvets, fans, and for cooler nights, heaters. Laundry and ironing facilities are available. There is a range of restaurants nearby. Bus stop to and from Downtown Auckland at gate. We are handy to Tamaki University Campus and Ascot Hospital. Members of New Zealand Association of Farm and Home Hosts.

Amity Homestay
Homestay
8km SE of Auckland Central
Jean & Neville Taylor
47 Norman Lesser Drive
St Johns Park, Remuera
Auckland

Tel: (09) 521 1827
Fax: (09) 521 1863
E: jean@amity.co.nz
W: www.amity.co.nz

Cost: Double $90 Single $45
Beds: 3 Single (2 bdrm)
Bath: 1 Guests share

Remuera - Auckland

We invite you to stay in our beautiful old home. Longwood is a fully restored farmhouse, built in the 1880's, with all the comforts of the 90's. We have two guest rooms, each with ensuite and our spacious home features sunny verandahs overlooking the gardens and pool. Breakfast to suit - healthy or indulgent or a little of both. We are superbly located close to the shops, galleries, theatres and parks of Auckland City, Parnell, Newmarket and Remuera. We ask no smoking please indoors. We have a friendly cat. The airport shuttle will bring you to our door, or phone for easy directions.

The Brooks, Longwood
B&B Homestay
1km N of Newmarket
54 Seaview Road
Remuera Auckland 1105

Tel: (09) 523 3746
Fax: (09) 523 3756
Mob: 025 744 035
E: longwood@ihug.co.nz
W: www.brooksnz.co.nz

Cost: Single $95-$140 Visa/MC
Beds: 1 Queen 2 Single
(2 bdrm)
Bath: 2 Ensuite

Remuera - Auckland

Omahu House - character 1924 bungalow. Cool summer rooms with fans, centrally heated in winter. 1200m2 garden, off street parking. Omahu House, friendly personal care, comfort plus, complete privacy - luxurious little extras. Leisurely breakfasts taken indoors, by the pool or highly recommended "breakfast in bed" etc etc. Omahu House bakes croissants, bread, fresh daily - real flavours jams, jellies, crispy bacon, eggs your choice. Take Market Rd exit - travel to Remuera Rd, turn right into Omahu Rd. Shirley, Keith welcome you to Omahu House, No. 35.

Auckland Omahu House
B&B Homestay
1km W of Remuera
Shirley & Keith Mossman
35 Omahu Rd
Remuera
Auckland

Tel: (09) 524 9697
Fax: (09) 524 9997
Mob: 025 208 469
E: omahu@voyager.co.nz
www.aucklandOmahuHouse.com

Cost: Double $150-$165
Single $140-$150 Child $20
Dinner B/A Visa/MC
Beds: 3 King/Twin
1 Single (4 bdrm)
Bath: 3 Ensuite
1 Private

Remuera - Auckland

A large warm sunny one-bedroom fully-furnished unit with character in a well-restored classical New Zealand turn of the century villa in Remuera, within walking distance of the shops. A lock-up garage is available. There is a rear service courtyard and a small private front courtyard . The unit is fully equipped. The tariff includes self-serve continental breakfast. A double bed-setee in the living room extends the sleeping capacity to four guests. We live next door and are happy to provide information etc. Dinner by arrangement.

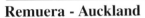

Lillington Villa
B&B Self-contained
Carol and Peter Dossor
2/24 Lillington Road
Remuera
Auckland

Tel: (09) 523 2035
Fax: (09) 523 2036
Mob: 025 927 063
E: Caropet@xtra.com.nz
W: www.bnb.co.nz/hosts/
lillingtonvilla.html

Cost: Double $120 Single $100
Child $20 Dinner $40
full week $520 Visa/MC
Beds: 2 Single (1 bdrm)
Bath: 1 Ensuite

Remuera - Auckland

Experience our comfortable modern home offering the entire lower floor area as guest accommodation. One double bedroom, one twin bedroom. Private bathroom. Sitting room with tea/coffee making facilities, fridge, TV, opening on to sheltered patio and garden with own entrance. Conveniently situated to Parnell, Remuera, Newmarket and CBD. Many of Auckland's prime attractions are nearby and easily accessible by private or public transport. We have Emily, our Birman cat, and request no smoking indoors. It is our pleasure to assist in making your stay memorable. Directions: Phone for easy directions.

Brabingtons
Homestay
3km E of Auckland
Gayle & Jack Brabant
163 Arney Road
Remuera Auckland

Tel: (09) 524 8754
Fax: (09) 524 8614
Mob: 021 432 573
E: gayle.brabant@xtra.co.nz
W: www.bnb.co.nz/hosts/
brabingtons.html

Cost: Double $95 Single $75
Child by arrangement
Beds: 1 Double 1 Twin
(2 bdrm)
Bath: 1 Private 1 Guests share

Remuera - Auckland

An 1847 Historic Regency Mansion, Cotter House is an oasis of peace and quiet close to Newmarket shops and Remuera restaurants. Guests enjoy gourmet breakfasts in the privacy and charm of rose covered verandahs and marble terraces, or simply relax in refined settings amidst a rare collection of French antiques and modern art. Large suites with internet, digital TV, fireplace and marble bathrooms offer refined comfort. The dining and ballrooms are available exclusively for guests' catered entertaining needs, corporate functions and business seminars. French and Spanish spoken fluently.

Cotter House Luxury City Stay	**Tel:** +64 9 529 5156	**Cost:** Double $300-$350
B&B City Stay	**Fax:** +64 9 529 5186	Single $180-$250
8KM E of Auckland City	**Mob:** +64 21 672 989	Visa/MC Amex Diners
Gloria Poupard-Walbridge	**E:** info@cotterhouse.com	**Beds:** 1 King/Twin 1 Queen
4, St. Vincent Avenue	**W:**www.bnb.co.nz/hosts/cotterhouse.html	1 Double 1 Single (4 bdrm)
Remuera, Auckland	www.cotterhouse.com	**Bath:** 2 Ensuite 1 Private

Ellerslie - Auckland

Taimihinga - softly calling o'er the ocean. Answer the call - enjoy the welcome at this comfortable home in quiet garden with pleasant northerly outlook. Ellerslie offers convenient access to Auckland's Business and Entertainment Centres, Scenic and Recreational Attractions. It is close to motorway (1km), transport, racing, parks, hospitals, shops, restaurants. Interests: people, family (now in faraway places), arts, music, travel, church (Anglican), Probus, gardening. Refreshment trolley, hairdrier and bathrobes in rooms. Laundry and fax facilities (small charge). Smoking outside only, please. Directions: Please phone, fax or write.

Taimihinga	**Tel:** (09) 579 7796	**Cost:** Double $80 Single $50
Homestay	**Fax:** (09) 579 7796	Dinner by arrangement
8km SE of Auckland Central	**E:** mlovebnb@ihug.co.nz	Visa/MC
Marjorie Love	**W:** www.bnb.co.nz/hosts/	**Beds:** 1 Double 1 Twin
16 Malabar Drive	taimihinga.html	1 Single (3 bdrm)
Ellerslie Auckland 5		**Bath:** 1 Guests share

Orakei - Auckland

Welcome to our modern spacious home with views, secure parking, laundry facilities and exclusive guest lounge. Post office and bus stops closeby. In a quiet residential area, we're a few minutes to many tourist attractions, restaurants, theatres, casino, beaches, harbour cruises and race courses. Enjoy local scenic walks. A full breakfast is served in the dining room or "al fresco". We've travelled extensively overseas and in New Zealand. Warm friendly hospitality assured. No smoking indoors please. Directions: Airport shuttle to door. Phone/fax.

Sealladh	**Tel:** (09) 522 2836	**Cost:** Double $140-$160
Homestay	**Fax:** (09) 522 9666	Single $100
4.5km E of Auckland Central	**Mob:** 025 211 7186	Dinner by arrangement
Heather and Bill Nicholson	**E:** sealladh@xtra.co.nz	Visa/MC
2/9 Rewiti Street	**W:** www.bnb.co.nz/hosts/	**Beds:** 1 King 1 Twin (2 bdrm)
Orakei Auckland 1005	sealladh.html	**Bath:** 2 Ensuite

Mission Bay - Auckland

We warmly welcome you to our modern split level home. The upper level is for your exclusive use including a private lounge. 5 minutes walk to Mission Bay beach, cafes and restaurants and 10 minutes scenic car or bus ride to down town Auckland and ferry terminal for harbour and islands in the Gulf. We are retired and look forward to sharing our special part of Auckland with you. Please phone for directions or airport shuttle bus to our door. Please no smoking.

Homestay
6km E of Auckland Central
Bryan & Jean Cockell
41 Nihill Cresent
Mission Bay
Auckland

Tel: (09) 528 3809
W: www.bnb.co.nz/hosts/
cockell.html

Cost: Double $85 Single $60
Dinner $25 Visa/MC
Beds: 1 Double (1 bdrm)
Bath: 1 Private

Mission Bay - Auckland

Relax in the quiet comfort of our quality Art Deco house - all new furnishings. All guest rooms have level access, tea and coffee and cookies, fridge, hair dryer, bath robe, comfortable seating, Sky TV, electric blankets and feather duvets. . A cosy fireplace in the Guest Lounge, off road parking. 200 metres to Beach, movie theatre, restaurants, bars and cafes, Kelly Tarltons Underwater Worls and a shopping centre. We offer breakfast in the dining room or trays to your room. Family rates available also for two couples travelling together. No smoking indoors but we have a large covered courtyard.

Patteson Ave. House
B&B
10km S of Auckland City
Ann Curtis
71A Patteson Ave
Mission Bay Auckland

Tel: (09) 528 7278
Fax: (09) 528 7976
Mob: 021 155 6443
E: patteson.avenue.bnb@paradise.net.nz
W: www.bnb.co.nz/hosts/
pattesonavehouse.html

Cost: Double $100-$120
Single $85-$105
Child neg Visa/MC
Beds: 1 King/Twin 2 Queen
(3 bdrm)
Bath: 1 Ensuite 1 Guests share

Kohimarama Beach - Auckland

Kohimarama Beach is a marine suburb central to all Auckland activities. Our chalet overlooks a park and is a short flat walk to 3 beaches for swimming, shopping and restaurants. All year we offer complimentary sailing on the world's finest harbour. We have travelled all over NZ and extensively overseas and delight in showing guests our city. Guests occupy entire floor (private guest lounge, sunny deck). Tea/coffee anytime. Traditional 3 course dinner available (roast lamb). Only one special group at a time - You!

Chalet on the Park
Homestay
8km E of Auckland Central
Trish & Keith Janes & Irish Setter
19 Baddeley Avenue
Kohimarama Beach Auckland

Tel: (09) 521 2544
Fax: (64-9) 521 2542
Mob: 025 397 116
Tollfree: 0800 360 544
E: chalet@bigfoot.com
W: www.bnb.co.nz/hosts/
chaletonthepark.html

Cost: Double $90 Single $70
Child $25 Dinner $25 B/A
Visa/MC Amex Diners
Beds: 2 Queen (2 bdrm)
Bath: 1 Private 1 Family share

St Heliers - Auckland

On holiday or business, relax in our home overlooking
Glover Park. The B&B with Comfort, Convenience
and Conviviality. Enjoy our great breakfasts. 5/10
minute walk from the beach, cafes, shopping and
banks yet only 12 minute drive to the central city.
Visit Kelly Tarltons, Sky City or cruise the Waitemata
Harbour. Tea & coffee available in separate guest
lounge. Handy transport. We are happy to assist with
travel plans, dinner reservations etc. Peter and Jeanne
with Sophie the cat welcome you.

The Totara
B&B Homestay
1km N of St Heliers Bay
Peter & Jeanne Maxwell
1/17 Glover Road
St Heliers Bay Auckland

Tel: (09) 575 3514
Fax: (09) 575 3582
Mob: 025 284 0172
E: maxwell.totara@clear.net.nz
W: www.bnb.co.nz/hosts/
thetotara.html

Cost: Double $120 Single $90
Visa/MC Amex Diners
Beds: 1 Queen 1 Twin (2 bdrm)
Bath: 1 Private

St Heliers - Auckland

Welcome to our modern home with off street parking
in a smoke free environment. One group of guests is
accommodated at a time. Having travelled extensively
ourselves we are fully aware of tourists' needs. 8
minutes walk to St Heliers Bay beach, shops,
restaurants, cafes, banks and post office. Picturesque
12 minutes drive along the Auckland waterfront past
Kelly Tarlton's Antarctic and Underwater Encounter to
Downtown Auckland. Interests including all sports,
gardening and Jill is a keen cross-stich embroiderer.
Not suitable for children/pets.

B&B
10km E of Auckland
Jill & Ron McPherson
102 Maskell Street
St Heliers
Auckland

Tel: (09) 575 9738
Fax: (09) 575 0051
Mob: 025 752 034
E: ron&jill_mcpherson@xtra.co.nz
W: www.bnb.co.nz/hosts/
mcpherson.html

Cost: Double $110 Single $75
Beds: 1 Queen 1 Twin (2 bdrm)
Bath: 1 Private

St Heliers - Auckland

Our character home with pretty cottage garden offers
guests a sunny retreat only a short walk to lovely
beach, village and restaurants. Spacious bedroom with
easy access has ensuite bathroom, Sky TV etc.
Delicious breakfast of fruit, home-made bread/muesli,
and/or full breakfast, espresso coffee/tea. Telephone,
fax, email, hairdryer, laundry, off street parking
available. With Bess our gentle golden retriever and
Bertie our cute toy poodle, we look forward to offering
you a warm welcome to our smoke-free home.

Pippi's Bed and Breakfast
B&B Homestay
10km E of Auckland Central
Pippi & Philip Wells
15 Tuhimata Street
St Heliers Auckland

Tel: (09) 575 6057
Fax: (09) 575 6055
Mob: 021 989 643
E: pswells@xtra.co.nz
W: go.to/pippis

Cost: Double $130-$150
Single $110-$120 Visa/MC
Beds: 1 Queen
1 Double (2 bdrm)
Bath: 1 Ensuite 1 Private

Titirangi - Auckland

Welcome to our home! Situated at Titirangi, the gateway of the Waitakere Ranges and Auckland's historic West Coast with its magnificent beaches and vast native bush areas! Nearby are other attractions such as the Titirangi Golf course, cafes, restaurants and walking tracks. Gaby and Peter, your hosts of German descent, are keen trampers themselves and are happy to introduce you to the highlights of Auckland and its surrounding areas. PS: We have a shy cat called Coco. Non smoking inside residence.

Kaurigrove	**Tel:** (09) 817 5608	**Cost:** Double $85-$90
Homestay	**Fax:** (09) 817 5608	Single $45-$50
20min W of Auckland City	**Mob:** 025 275 0574	Visa/MC Amex Diners
Gaby & Peter Wunderlich	**W:** www.bnb.co.nz/hosts/	**Beds:** 1 Queen 1 Single
120 Konini Road	kaurigrove.html	(2 bdrm)
Titirangi Auckland 7		**Bath:** 1 Guests share

Avondale - Auckland

Kodesh is an ecumenical, cross cultural Christian community of around 25 residents, about 8 minutes by car from downtwon Auckland. Guest rooms in a large modern home have full cooking facilities available, a self contained flat sleeps four. An evening meal is available in the community dining room Monday - Friday. Bookings essential. The atmosphere is relaxed and guests can amalgamate into the life of the community as much or little as desired. No smoking, no pets, children under 12 welcome in self contained unit.

Kodesh Community	**Tel:** (09) 828 5672	**Cost:** Double $45 Single $30
B&B Self-contained	**Fax:** (09) 828 5684	Child $15 Dinner $8
10km W of Auckland Central	**E:** Kodesh_Trust@free.net.nz	Flat $60 - $80
Kodesh Trust	**W:** www.bnb.co.nz/hosts/	**Beds:** 2 Queen 4 Single
31B Cradock Street	kodeshcommunity.html	(2 bdrm & 1 flat)
Avondale Auckland		**Bath:** 1 Private 2 Family share

Mt Roskill - Auckland

Let us entertain you, or if preferable leave you in peace in our spacious home, alternatively commune with our cats in the garden. On public bus routes to central Auckland, cafes, restaurants and shopping centres. We are experienced travellers and wish to provide you with amenities we find comforting when away from home. Ensuite bedrooms have all home luxuries, including tea/coffee making facilities. Dinner by arrangement. Our interests are music, gardening, books and entertaining guests. 20 mins from airport.

BedQuest	**Tel:** (09) 620 1441	**Cost:** Double $120 Single $90
B&B Homestay	**Fax:** (09) 620 1441	Visa/MC
6km S of Auckland Central	**Mob:** 025 329 303	**Beds:** 1 Queen 1 Double
Barbara Letcher and Shirley	**E:** bedquest@ihug.co.nz	(2 bdrm)
Conway	**W:** www.bnb.co.nz/hosts/	**Bath:** 2 Ensuite
11 Quest Terrace	bedquest.html	
Mt Roskill Auckland		

Lynfield - Auckland

Welcome to our impressive lodge, featuring extensive harbour views. We are situated 15 minutes from airport and 20 minutes away from city centre on main bus route. The Lodge also includes a self contained unit, extensive viewing decks, spa pool, BBQ, guest lounge with Sky TV and Internet access. There is a golf course nearby and the spectacular Waitakere rainforest with over 200kms of tracks is 15 minutes away. Stuart has an intimate knowledge of the forest and offers various guided walks to suit.

Manuka Lodge
B&B Self-contained
10km S of Auckland Central
Stuart & Barbara Baker
11 Gothic Place
Lynfield
Auckland

Tel: (09) 627 2659
Fax: (09) 627 2284
Mob: 025 783 744
E: stuartbaker@xtra.co.nz
W: www.bnb.co.nz/hosts/
manukalodge.html

Cost: Double $95 Single $55
Child $25 Dinner by arr.
Visa/MC
Beds: 1 King 1 Double 1 Twin
1 Single (5 bdrm)
Bath: 1 Private 1 Guests share
1 Family share

Hillsborough - Auckland

A warm welcome to our beautifully appointed mediterranean-style home and garden overlooking the Manukau Harbour, just 15 minutes form Auckland Airport. Stay in our delightful spacious upstairs room with ensuite, TV; or in our self-contained apartment (bedroom, bathroom, kitchen, lounge with extra sofa-bed, TV). Relax on your own, or socialise with us as you wish. Breakfast alfresco in the garden, sunny kitchen conservatory, or ask for room service. Ian is an architect, and our interests include travel, people, sport, garden, music, antiques.

Hillsborough Heights Homestay
Self-contained Homestay
10km S of Auckland Central
Sandra & Ian Burrow
434A Hillsborough Road
Hillsborough Auckland

Tel: (09) 626 7609
Fax: (09) 626 7609
Mob: 021 626 760
E: aucklandhomestay@hotmail.com
W: www.bnb.co.nz/hosts/
hillsboroughheightshomestay.html

Cost: Double $110 Single $80
Dinner by arrangement
Visa/MC Amex
Beds: 2 Queen 1 Double
(2 bdrm)
Bath: 2 Ensuite

Mangere Bridge - Auckland Airport

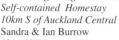

We invite you to share our home which is within 10 minutes of Auckland Airport, an ideal location for your arrival or departure of New Zealand. We enjoy meeting people and look forward to making your stay an enjoyable one. We welcome you to join us for dinner by prior arrangement. Courtesy car to or from airport, bus and rail. Off street parking available. Handy to public transport. Please no smoking indoors. Although we have a cat we request no pets. Inspection welcomed.

Mangere Bridge Homestay
Homestay
14km S of Auckland Central
Carol & Brian
146 Coronation Road
Mangere Bridge
Auckland

Tel: (09) 636 6346
Fax: (09) 636 6345
W: www.bnb.co.nz/hosts/
mangerebridgehomestay.html

Cost: Double $70 Single $45-$50
Child $20 12 & under
Dinner $20 B/A
Beds: 2 Double
2 Single (3 bdrm)
Bath: 1 Guests share
1 Family share

Mangere - Auckland Airport

Clean comfortable home five minutes from airport but not on flight path. Easy walk to shops and restaurants. Ten minutes from shopping centres and Rainbows End amusement park. Aviation golf course near airport, winery and Lakeside Convention Centre nearby. My interests are golf, travel, Ladies' Probus and voluntary work. Beds have woollen underlays and electric blankets. There is a sunny terrace and fenced swimming pool. Courtesy car to/from airport at reasonable hour. Vehicles minded while you're away from $1 day. One timid outdoors cat.

Airport Homestay/B&B
B&B Homestay
2km Mangere
May Pepperell
288 Kirkbride Rd
Mangere Auckland

Tel: (09) 275 6777
Fax: (09) 275 6728
Mob: 025 289 8200
W: www.bnb.co.nz/hosts/
airporthomestay.html

Cost: Double $60 Single $40
Child $15
Beds: 3 Single (2 bdrm)
Bath: 1 Guests share

Mangere Bridge - Auckland Airport

Enjoy breakfast overlooking the harbour/bird reserve from our comfy, peaceful, waterfront home, which is 10 mins from the airport but not on the flight path. Short driving distance to shops, restaurants, takeaways, golf course, swimming pool and lakeside convention centre. City bus stop across the road. Sample wines at Villa Maria Winery, take a stroll up Mangere Mountain, through Ambury park/farm or along Kiwi Esplanade. One student daughter, a cat and small dog are in residence. Airport courtesy car at a reasonable hour.

Tudor House Homestay
B&B Homestay
16km S of Auckland Central
Gill Whitehead
1 Banbury Place
Mangere Bridge
Auckland

Tel: (09) 634 3413
Fax: (09) 622 3238
Mob: 025 605 7257
E: gill.w@xtra.co.nz
W: www.bnb.co.nz/hosts/
tudorhousehomestay.html

Cost: Double $70 Single $45
Child $20 Dinner $20 B/A
King/Twin with ensuite $80
Visa/MC
Beds: 1 King/Twin 1 Queen
1 Single (3 bdrm)
Bath: 1 Ensuite 1 Guests share

Mangere Bridge - Auckland Airport

8 minutes Auckland Airport, 20 minutes Downtown Auckland. Restored Kauri Villa in quiet locality on Mangere Mountain. Enjoy quality decor and expansive harbour views whilst eating a hearty cooked or continental breakfast. Off street parking available, public transport at gate. Our guests say "Thanks for your friendly hospitality and insight into Country affairs. Best bed in NZ". D & MB, Sth Aust. "10/10 for comfort and food. 11/10 for entertainment!!" P & A MacG, Scotland. From Airport travel north along George Bolt Drive, turn left onto Kirkbride Road. Follow Kirkbride straight through to Wallace Road.

Mountain View B&B
B&B Homestay
7.5km N of Auckland Airport
Ian & Jenny, and cat Oscar Davis
85A Wallace Road
Mangere Bridge Auckland

Tel: (09) 636 6535
Fax: (09) 636 6126
E: mtviewbb@voyager.co.nz
W: www.bnb.co.nz/hosts/
mountainviewbb.html

Cost: Double $75-$120
Single $55-$90 Child $15
Dinner B/A Visa/MC
Beds: 4 Queen 1 Twin
2 Single (5 bdrm)
Bath: 3 Ensuite 1 Guests share

Otahuhu - Auckland

We welcome you to the oasis in Otahuhu. We can help you plan your holiday route and rent a car. The motorways, train, bus and airport are minutes away. 70 is a rest stop before your long flights "home". We are collectors of amazing things, cactus, coins of the world, depression glassware, brass birds, Canadian art and a cat called Alice. Washing facilities available. Dinner by arrangement. Phone, fax or write to reserve. Our courtesy van will pick you up at the airport, train or bus.

B&B	**Tel:** (09) 276 9335	**Cost:** Double $60 Single $40
17km S of Auckland	**Fax:** (09) 276 9235	Child neg Dinner $20
Jerrine & Gerard Fecteau	**E:** oasisbb@xtra.co.nz	Visa/MC
70 Mangere Road	**W:** www.bnb.co.nz/hosts/	**Beds:** 1 Queen 1 Double
Otahuhu	fecteau.html	2 Single (3 bdrm)
Auckland		**Bath:** 2 Guests share

Half Moon Bay - Auckland

Endymion Lodge is situated on a sunny slope with sea views above Half Moon Bay marina. We have buses at the door or a 5 minute walk to catch the fast ferry to downtown Auckland. Our area offers nice beaches, golf courses, theatres and a variety of excellent cafes. Self contained area with tea & coffee facilities plus laundry available. We also provide sailing charters on our 42ft charter yacht - day sails or extended cruises in the Hauraki gulf or Bay of Islands. Transfers arranged.

Endymion Lodge	**Tel:** (09) 535 8930	**Cost:** Double $75-$100
Self-contained Homestay	**Fax:** (09) 535 8042	Single $65-$85
3km E of Howick	**Mob:** 025 951 038	Dinner by arrangement
Dave & Helen Jeffery	**E:** helen@sailingholiday.co.nz	Visa/MC Amex Diners
21 Endymion Place	**W:** www.sailingholiday.co.nz	**Beds:** 1 Queen 1 Double
Half Moon Bay		1 Single (2 bdrm)
Auckland		**Bath:** 2 Private

Manukau - Auckland

Our homely country cottage, set in two acres is close to the international airport. The garden loft is separate from the house with ensuite, TV, fridge, overlooking large peaceful gardens and ponds. Accommodation inside the house has its own bathroom. We are 35 minutes from downtown Auckland, close to bush walks, Regional Botanic gardens and restaurants. Delicious home cooked breakfast includes eggs from our free range hens. We have a swimming pool and a friendly dog 'Daisy'. We are non-smoking. Booking is essential.

Tanglewood	**Tel:** (09) 274 8280	**Cost:** Double $80 Single $60
Homestay	**Fax:** (09) 634 6896	Child $10 Dinner $20 B/A
6.5km NE of Manukau City	**Mob:** 025 649 3973	Visa/MC
Roseanne & Ian Devereux	**E:** tanglewood@clear.net.nz	**Beds:** 1 Queen 1 Double
5 Inchinnam Road	**W:** www.bnb.co.nz/hosts/	2 Single (3 bdrm)
Flat Bush Auckland	tanglewoodmanukau.html	**Bath:** 1 Ensuite 1 Guests share

Manurewa - Auckland

Welcome to our sunny, spacious home and meet our friendly Tonkinese cat. We are 15 minutes form Auckland Airport, 20 minutes form Auckland City Centre, by motorway, gateway to the route south and Pacific Coast Highway. Nearby are Manukau City Shopping Centre, Rainbow's End Adventure Park, restaurants, cinemas, souvenir shops, Community Arts Centre, Regional Botanic Gardens (Ellerslie Flowershow), and bush walks. Our interests include Red Cross, teaching, classical music, painting, gardening, photography, Christian interests, reading and travel. We're a smoke-free home. Directions: Please phone.

Hillpark Homestay
Homestay
2km S of Manukau City
Katrine & Graham Paton
16 Collie Street
Manurewa Auckland 1702

Tel: (09) 267 6847
Fax: (09) 267 8718
Mob: 021 215 7974
E: hillpark.homestay@xtra.co.nz
W: www.bnb.co.nz/hosts/
hillparkhomestay.html

Cost: Double $70 Single $50
 Child $20 Dinner $15 B/A
 Visa/MC
Beds: 1 Double 3 Single
 (3 bdrm)
Bath: 1 Ensuite 1 Guests share

Howick - Auckland

Relax with us 50 metres "Above The Beach", Kauri trees and views across the gulf. Auckland: 16km by road, or 35 minute stressfree ferry ride. Airport: 25 minutes. Howick is a delightful village with 16 cafes and restaurants and historic church. Six beaches, two golf courses and ferry within 2 km radius. Feather duvets, electric blankets, heaters, easy chairs, fridge and TV for your convenience. Home away from Home and super breakfasts. Directions: Shuttle from airport. Please phone for directions. Non smokers.

Above the Beach
B&B Homestay
1km NE of Howick
Max & Marjorie Fisher
141 Mellons Bay Road
Howick
Auckland

Tel: (09) 534 2245
Fax: (09) 534 2245
E: kea.nz@attglobal.net
W: www.bnb.co.nz/hosts/
abovethebeach.html

Cost: Double $85-$100
 Single $55 Visa/MC
Beds: 1 Queen 1 Double
 2 Single (4 bdrm)
Bath: 1 Ensuite 1 Private
 1 Guests share

Howick - Auckland

Welcome to "Cockle Bay Homestay", situated in a quiet location at gateway "Pacific Coast Highway", 20 minutes from Auckland Airport/City. Howick is one of the oldest settlements in New Zealand. Breathtaking sea views of the Hauraki gulf. Five minute walk to beach/historic restaurant. Use ferry from Howick to City - delightful way to see the harbour, or bus end of driveway. Guest rooms spacious and comfortable with sea views. Our small dog wins the hearts of all our guests. Off street parking. Laundry facilities available.

Cockle Bay Homestay
B&B Homestay
3km S of Howick
Jill & Richard Paxman
81 Pah Road
Cockle Bay
Howick, Auckland

Tel: (09) 535 0120
Fax: (09) 535 0120
Mob: 021 685 638
Tollfree: 0800 159 837
E: cocklebay@bnbnz.co.nz
W: www.bnbnz.co.nz

Cost: Double $115-$135
 Single $90-$105
 Visa/MC BC
Beds: 1 Queen
 1 King/Twin(2 bdrms)
Bath: 1 Ensuite 1 Private

Howick - Auckland

We offer warm relaxed hospitality in a charming setting with excellent facilities - your own sunny lounge, private bathroom, bathrobes, hairdryer, great breakfasts with homemade foods - muesli, breads, yoghurt, preserves, plus cooked options. Offstreet parking, laundry and office facilities available. Only 30 min from CBD by local ferry or motorway (offpeak) and 20 min from airport. Short stroll to Howick village with many restaurants, cafes, pubs, interesting shops. 10 min drive to 5 safe beaches, historic village, golf courses.

Mellons Bay Lodge
B&B
1/2 k E of Howick
June & Owen Williams
64 Mellons Bay Road
Howick Auckland

Tel: 09 535 0535
Fax: 09 535 2713
Mob: 025 504 352
E: ojw@takeiteasy.co.nz
W: www.bnb.co.nz/hosts/
mellonsbay.html

Cost: Double $105-$115
Single $50-$90 Visa/MC
Beds: 1 Queen 1 Double
1 Single (3 bdrm)
Bath: 1 Private 1 Guests share

Beachlands

Enid and Terry offer you a warm welcome to the Marine Garden suburb of Beachlands which is situated on the East Coast, 40 km South East of Auckland City. Our converted cottage is only 3 minutes walk from the beach at Sunkist Bay, local shops and licensed restaurant. The Formosa Auckland Golf Course and Pine Harbour marina are 5 minutes drive away. We are both in our early 60's, have travelled widely and share our home with a shy cat. Guest accommodation is a large upstairs bedroom with sitting area, TV and a shaded balcony facing the sea. Phone for directions.

B&B Homestay
25km E of Howick
Enid & Terry Cripps
51 Wakelin Road
Beachlands 1705

Tel: (09) 536 5546
Fax: (09) 536 5546
W: www.bnb.co.nz/hosts/
cripps.html

Cost: Double $80 Single $50
Dinner $20 by arrangement
Visa/MC
Beds: 1 Queen (1 bdrm)
Bath: 1 Private

Whitford

Springhill is an 8 hectare farm in Whitford, an attractive rural area approximately 25km SE of Auckland. We are close to a beautiful golf course, beaches and Auckland Airport. We breed Angora goats and pets include a cat and a dog. We have a large comfortable home and spacious garden. Guest accommodation is one detached double room with ensuite, and 1 room with twin single beds. TV, tea & coffee making facilities,and a private spa pool are available. Directions: Left off Whitford Park Road. 1km past Golf Course.

Springhill Country Homestay
Farmstay
25km SE of Auckland
Judy & Derek Stubbs
Polo Lane
Whitford, RD, Manurewa,
Auckland

Tel: (09) 530 8674
Fax: (09) 530 8274
Mob: 021 251 2518
E: djstubbs@ihug.co.nz
W: www.bnb.co.nz/hosts/
springhillfarmstay.html

Cost: Double $95 Single $70
Child $35 Dinner $30pp
by arrangement
Beds: 1 Queen 2 Single
(2 bdrm)
Bath: 1 Ensuite 1 Family share

Whitford

Enjoy a game of tennis on our peaceful rural five acre block. Wake up in your separate self-contained loft to the sound of the birds. We are 30 minutes from Auckland City and within 15 minutes. of cinemas, shopping, restaurants, cafes and craft shops. Nearby is a Marina where sailing/boating and fishing are available by arrangement. We are close to beaches, golf courses and polo ground, or you may prefer a quiet country walk. Unsuitable for children or animals.

Albertine
Homestay
12km Howick
Averill & Bart Allsopp - Smith
298 Clifton Road
Whitford, RD 1, Howick
Auckland

Tel: (09) 530 9441
Fax: (09) 530 9441
Mob: 021 974 119
E: albertinestay@xtra.co.nz
W: www.mysite.xtra.co.nz/
~albertinestay

Cost: Double $90 Single $65
Visa/MC
Beds: 1 Double (1 bdrm)
Bath: 1 Ensuite 1 Private

Clevedon

Willowgrove is located near the rural village of Clevedon on the Pacific Coast Highway - just 40 mins from Central Auckland and the Airport (we are happy to pick-up at a small charge. The house is set in 2 acres of mature gardens, and a further 9 acres is being established as an Olive Grove. We are close to beaches, golf and polo and enroute to the Coromandel. A warm hospitable welcome awaits you. Directions please phone.

Willowgrove
B&B Homestay
40km SE of Auckland
Sallie McDonald and David Hooper
764 Clevedon - Kawakawa Bay Rd
RD5 Clevedon Papakura

Tel: (09) 292 8456
Fax: (09) 534 8465
Mob: 021 991 499
E: mcdonaldsm@paradise.net.nz
W: www.bnb.co.nz/hosts/
willowgrove.html

Cost: Room Rate $90-$120
Dinner $25 Visa/MC
Beds: 2 Queen (2 bdrm)
Bath: 2 Private

Clevedon

Our home is set in 14 acres with extensive rural views. Mangere Airport and Auckland City are 40 mins away. We offer a self contained bed/sitting room ensuite with TV, tea and coffee making facilities and private courtyard. There are beaches nearby along the Scenic Route to Coromandel. Locally polo, winery, horse riding, golf available. Paddy is involved in the fashion industry, Christopher is a retired naval officer. Kennel facilities available on site.

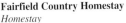

Fairfield Country Homestay
Homestay
7km E of Clevedon
Christopher & Paddy Carl
Clevedon
RD 5 Papakura

Tel: (09) 292 8852
Fax: (09) 292 8631
E: carl.fairfield@xtra.co.nz
W: www.bnb.co.nz/hosts/
fairfieldcountryhomestay.html

Cost: Double $135 Single $100
Dinner $40pp Visa/MC
Beds: 1 Queen (1 bdrm)
Bath: 1 Ensuite

Clevedon

In 1988 Phil and Cathy Foulkes set out to create a dream country home and garden for themselves and their family. Tucked away in their garden are two self contained spacious cottage units where they invite guests to share their hospitality. Set on 10 acres, handy to Clevedon Village each cottage unit offers a queensize bedroom with ensuite, lounge/dining room with double bed settee, laundry and cooking facilities. Clevedon features green pastures, friendly people and old fashioned hospitality within 30 minutes drive from Auckland CBD and International Airport.

The Gables
B&B Self-contained
3km S of Clevedon Village
Phil & Cathy Foulkes
122 Tourist Road
Clevedon RD 2 Papakura

Tel: (09) 292 8373
Fax: (09) 292 8629
Mob: 025 941 249
E: foulkes@xtra.co.nz
W: www.the-gables.co.nz

Cost: Double $100
Single $80 Visa/MC
Beds: 2 Queen (2 bdrm)
Bath: 2 Ensuite

Kaiaua

Our home, "Corovista", is so named because of its commanding views of the Coromandel Mountain Range rising above the sparkling waters of the Firth Of Thames. This locality on the Pacific Coast Highway has its advantages being close to Auckland, Clevedon, Hunua Parklands, the world renowned Bird Sanctuary and nearby Miranda thermal pools. We, your hosts, are widely travelled and offer warm hospitality to overseas and local guests in our smoke-free home. We have one small terrier that lives outdoors. Directions: Please phone.

Corovista
Homestay
72km S of Manukau City
Julia & Bob Bissett
1841B East Coast Road
Kaiaua, RD 3 Pokeno

Tel: (09) 232 2842
Fax: (09) 232 2862
Mob: 025 245 5269
W: www.bnb.co.nz/hosts/
corovista.html

Cost: Double $65-$90
Single $40-$50 Child 1/2
Dinner $30pp Visa/MC
Beds: 1 King/Twin
1 Double (2 bdrm)
Bath: 1 Guests share
1 Family share

Kaiaua

Situated on the water's edge, 4km north of Kaiaua township, the Lodge has panoramic views of the Coromandel across the Firth of Thames. It is ideally positioned for leisurely seashore strolls or more active tramps in the Hunua Ranges. Boating and fishing facilities are available and breakfast includes flounder or snapper, in season. En suite rooms are spacious and the separate guest lounge has a refrigerator and television. The Seabird Coast is renowned for its birdlife, thermal hot pools, nearby Regional Parks and "fish 'n chips".

Kaiaua Seaside Lodge
B&B Lodge
85km SE of Auckland
Fran Joseph & Denis
Martinovich
1336 Pacific Coast Highway
Kaiaua

Tel: (09) 232 2696
Fax: (09) 232 2699
Mob: 025 274 0534
E: kaiaua_lodge@xtra.co.nz
W: www.bnb.co.nz/hosts/
kaiauaseasidelodge.html

Cost: Double $95-$110
Single $65
Beds: 2 Queen 1 Double
2 Single (5 bdrm)
Bath: 2 Ensuite 1 Guests share

Papakura

Welcome to our wilderness on the doorstep of Auckland City. A great place to start or end your NZ holiday. Peace, tranquility, great food, magic sunsets, wild scenery, leafy greenery views, from all rooms. Large comfortable newly decorated home, verandas, lawns, garden, bush and rural setting on 50 acres with sheep, ponies, cattle, birdlife Stay a few days and discover the wonders of Auckland. Fresh food, fresh air, comfortable beds guaranteed. Please phone. Dinner from $25 or $35, 3 courses by prior arrangement. Pets and children welcome.

Hunua Gorge Country House	**Tel:** (09) 299 9922	**Cost:** Double $90-$120
B&B Homestay Country stay	**Fax:** (09) 299 6932	Single $60
5km E of Papakura	**Mob:** 021 669 922	Dinner From $25 Visa/MC
Joy, Ben & Amy Calway	**E:** hunua-lodge@xtra.co.nz	**Beds:** 1 King 1 Queen 1 Double
482 Hunua Road	**W:** www.bnb.co.nz/hosts/	1 Twin 3 Single (5 bdrm)
Papakura Auckland	hunuagorgecountryhouse.html	**Bath:** 1 Ensuite 1 Private
		1 Family share

Papakura

If you are looking for a peaceful location close enough to Auckland to visit city attractions (20 minutes) yet also handy to the airport (15 minutes) or motorway system (2 minutes) our family home will meet your requirements. Our upstairs guest bedrooms and lounge (with TV, library, fridge, tea/coffee facilities) open onto a private balcony overlooking Pahurehure Estuary Reserve. We are happy to assist with any holiday arrangements and offer fax, internet and laundry facilities. We offer a discounted rate for 3+ night bookings.

Campbell Clan House	**Tel:** (09) 298 8231	**Cost:** Double $110 Single $65
Homestay	**Fax:** (09) 298 7792	Child Neg Dinner $25/$35
1.5km W of Papakura	**Mob:** 025 967 754	Visa/MC
Colin & Anna Mieke Campbell	**E:** colam@pl.net	**Beds:** 1 Queen 2 Single
57 Rushgreen Ave	**W:** www.bnb.co.nz/hosts/	(2 bdrm)
Papakura	campbellclanhouse.html	**Bath:** 1 Private
		1 Family share

Hunua - Paparimu

On clear nights, stars shine incredibly brightly - no city lights here - yet still within easy reach of Auckland Airport and City, beaches, hotpools, golf courses and beautiful Hunua Ranges. Handy to State Highway 2 for travel south and Coromandel Peninsula. The self-contained cottage nestles peaceful among mature trees. Guinea-fowl, bantams and Balinese cats potter around the garden. Sheep and cattle graze the paddocks. You are guaranteed a warm, friendly welcome whether you eat a home-cooked meal with us or decide to self cater.

Cost: Double $98
Each additional person $30pp
Dinner $35 by arrangement
Visa/MC

Erathcrih Country Cottage	**Tel:** (09) 292 5062	
Self-contained Farmstay	**Fax:** (09) 292 5062	
20mins S of Papakura	**Mob:** 021 128 1547	
Rob & Gillian Wakelin	**E:** gillrob@voyager.co.nz	**Beds:** 1 Queen
10 Wilson Road, Paparimu	**W:** www.voyager.co.nz/~gillrob/	1 comfortable double bed-
RD 3, Papakura	index.html	settee in lounge
Auckland		**Bath:** 1 Private

Drury

Our spacious, comfortable, and relaxing home is an ideal place to start or finish a NZ holiday. Only 20 minutes from Auckland Airport and 30 minutes from the city centre. Set in expansive lawns and giant oak trees, with wide verandahs, overlooking rolling green farmland, indoor garden and BBQ in a large conservatory, tennis court, swimming pool, spa pool, and games room. 2 or 3 course dinners, including pre dinner drinks and nibbles, wine, and liqueurs with coffee. Laundry facilities. Pets - a family cat.

Tuhimata Park
B&B Homestay
5km S of Drury
Susan & Pat Baker
697B Runciman Road
Runciman, RD 2
Drury

Tel: (09) 294 8748
Fax: (09) 294 8749
E: tuhimata@iprolink.co.nz
W: www.bnb.co.nz/hosts/
tuhimatapark.html

Cost: Double $100-$110
Single $55-$70 Child neg
Dinner $30 - $35 Visa/MC
Beds: 2 Double
2 Single (3 bdrm)
Bath: 1 Ensuite 1 Guests share

Drury

Warm country hospitality in a delightful country setting - the perfect start or end to your holiday. Stroll through the large garden or mingle with the hobby farm menagerie; soak in the Jacuzzi or enjoy a candlelit supper and good company. A restful and private visit is guaranteed. Archie and Sue have travelled extensively and have worked in the food and media industries for more than 30 years. No smoking in the house please. Directions: Please phone. Visit us at www.farmstay.net.nz

Briardale
B&B Farmstay
6km S of Drury
Archie & Sue McPherson
23 Maxted Road
Ramarama, RD 3 Drury
Auckland

Tel: (09) 294 7417
Fax: (09) 238 7592
Mob: 025 736 313
E: sue.mcpherson@icn.co.nz
W: www.bnb.co.nz/hosts/
briardale.html

Cost: Double $100 Single $50
Child neg
Dinner by arrangement
Beds: 1 Queen 2 Twin
1 Single (3 bdrm)
Bath: 2 Guests share

Drury

The Homestead is an early colonial home (1879) with an interesting history. Lovingly restored by Ron and Carolyn this character filled family home nestles on 15 acres with mature native bush and a tumbling stream creating a wonderful peaceful haven, only 30 mins from the centre of Auckland. Close to excellent restaurants or let us cook for you using the best of fresh local produce. Guest lounge and TV, laundry facilities. Family cat and dog. Please phone for directions.

The Homestead
B&B Homestay
3km E of Drury
Carolyn & Ron Booker
349 Drury Hill Road
RD 1
Drury 1750

Tel: (09) 294 9030
Fax: (09) 294 9035
W: www.bnb.co.nz/hosts/
user90.html

Cost: Double $90 Single $60
Child negotiable
Dinner $25 Visa/MC
Beds: 1 King 1 Queen (2 bdrm)
Bath: 2 Ensuite

Drury

Southawk is a secluded country home set in 10 acres with beautiful gardens, swimming pool and petanque. Only 25 mins from Auckland City; 20 mins from Auckland International Airport; 3 kilometres from the Southern Motorway. Close to all Auckland's most famous attractions. Join us for an evening meal or NZ style BBQ. Large modern guest bedrooms, own bathrooms and lounge with TV/music and tea/coffee facilities. Relax around the open fire in the winter and the pool in the summer. A warm welcome awaits you.

Southawk
Homestay
3km N of Papakura
Lynn Lockhart & Rod Campbell
249 Sutton Road, Drury,
Auckland South
PO Box 203, Drury

Tel: (09) 298 0670
Fax: (09) 298 0673
Mob: 021 354 024
E: southawk@xtra.co.nz
W: www.bnb.co.nz/hosts/
southawk.html

Cost: Double $110 Single $70
Child neg Dinner $30
Visa/MC
Beds: 2 Queen 1 Single
(3 bdrm)
Bath: 2 Private 1 Family share

Waiuku

Just 50 minutes drive from Auckland's International Airport and city, "Totara Downs" is found on a quiet country road. Set in large country house gardens with breath taking rural views. We offer feather and downs pillows and duvets, sitting room with open fire, swimming pool, lawn croquet. Historic Waiuku boasts wonderful peninsula beaches and country garden tours. With Flora our westie and two cats we look forward to meeting you. Not suitable for children under 12. Smoke free home.

Totara Downs
Homestay
5km E of Waiuku
Janet & Christopher de Tracy-Gould
Baldhill Road
RD 1, Waiuku
South Auckland

Tel: (09) 235 8505
Fax: (09) 235 8504
E: totaradw@ihug.co.nz
W: www.totaradowns.co.nz

Cost: Double $100-$120
Single $80 Visa/MC
Beds: 1 King/Twin
1 Queen (2 bdrm)
Bath: 1 Ensuite 1 Private

Pukekohe

Our beef fattening 10 acre farm is just 12 kms from the Drury - Pukekohe off ramp, Auckland Airport a 35 minutes drive. We have a dog, Buddy, cat Zoe, hens and ducks. We love meeting people, having travelled throughout NZ, Australia, UK and Continent, where we enjoyed farm-stays. We welcome guests to our home. Directions: Southern Motorway to Drury off ramp. Follow signs Pukekohe-Waiuku. Right turn at Caltex Service Station. First left Ostrich Road, then left Ostrich Farm Road, "Woodside" 2 kms on right.

Woodside Farmstay
Farmstay
6km N of Pukekohe
Evelyn & Les Atkinson
195 Ostrich Farm Road
RD 1 Pukekohe

Tel: (09) 238 7864
W: www.bnb.co.nz/hosts/
woodsidefarmstay.html

Cost: Double $75 Single $40
Child 1/2 price
Dinner $17.50
Beds: 5 Single (3 bdrm)
Bath: 1 Guests share

Pukekohe

We extend to you a warm invitation to relax with us at Deveron, our comfortable country home, set in 11 acres of beautiful native bush and extensive gardens. Guests' wing ensures peace and privacy. In addition we can offer our spacious, comfortable 2 bedroom guest apartment with large lounge and wood burning stove, fully equipped kitchen and laundry and deck with gas BBQ. Breakfast provisions are included. Weekly rates apply. Nearby are several golf courses, excellent restaurants, surf beaches, vintage railway and water gardens.

Deveron
Countrystay S/C Guesthouse
10km W of Pukekohe
Sally & Tony McWilliams
77 Sommerville Road
Patumahoe

Tel: (09) 236 3673
Fax: (09) 236 3631
E: devmark@eudoramail.com
W: www.bnb.co.nz/hosts/
deveron.html

Cost: Double $95-$105
Single $65 Child $15
Dinner $30 Guest Hse $130
$20 extra adult Visa/MC
Beds: 2 King/Twin 2 Queen
2 Single (4 bdrm)
Bath: 1 Private 2 Guests share

Bombay - Auckland

Easily accessed on the Southern Motorway 'Brookfield Lodge' is the perfect place to begin and end your holiday or for a weekend retreat. Relax and savour country cuisine and warm hospitality. The large gracious home is set in an extensive beautiful garden on a 20 acre thoroughbred farm. Attractive bedrooms are adjacent to a Jacuzzi (spa) room. Enjoy wonderful breakfasts. Three course meals by arrangement. Restaurants nearby. Resident Labrador. From North: Pukekohe-Bombay exit. 50 metres into BP Centre. Brookfield access Rd beside McDonalds. 1 minute. From South: 1km past Beaver Rd.

Brookfield Lodge
B&B Country Homestay
25min S of Airport
Noreen & Ray Lee
State Highway 1
RD, Bombay

Tel: (09) 236 0775
Mob: 025 292 1422
Tollfree: 0800 37 75 80
E: mcvicarr@xtra.co.nz
W: www.bnb.co.nz/hosts/
brookfieldlodge.html

Cost: Double $110 Single $80
Dinner $30 by arr.
Beds: 1 Queen 2 Single
(2 bdrm)
Bath: 1 Private

Mangatawhiri

Formerly hosts at Crofthill, Otorohanga, we now farm 50 acres 10 minutes off the southern motorway, on S.H. 2, making us ideally sited for travellers driving to or from Rotorua, Tauranga or the Coromandel Peninsula. Walk across fields, down a country lane or just relax here, approximately 40 minutes from central Auckland or 45 minutes from the airport. Maramarua golf course is 5 minutes away and a pleasant drive will take you to Miranda hot springs and the seabird coast.

Ashcroft
Farmstay
30km SE of Pukekohe
Jim & Jennifer Beveridge
SH 2 RD 1 Pokeno

Tel: (09) 233 6020
Fax: (09) 233 6020
Mob: 025 501 732
E: crofthill@xtra.co.nz
W: www.bnb.co.nz/hosts/
user68.html

Cost: Double $80 Single $45
Child negotiable
Dinner $25pp Visa/MC
Beds: 1 Queen 1 Twin
(2 bdrm)
Bath: 1 Private

Mercer

We live on a cattle farm with a modern brick home.
We have a large swimming pool surrounded by one
acre of interesting garden. We are 3km off the main
Auckland-Hamilton highway. Our views are
panoramic. Very happy to provide dinner - alternative
restaurants available. 30-40 minutes from Auckland
Airport. Directions: Travel SH1 to Mercer. At Mercer
do not enter Mobil Service Centre. Travelling from
north turn left across railway line. Travelling from
south turn right across railway line 3km up Koheroa
Rd - meet Kellyville Rd - House visible on left.

B&B Self-contained Farmstay
24km SE of Pukekohe
Dorothy & Alan McIntyre
233 Koheroa Road
Mercer

Tel: (09) 232 6837
Fax: (09) 232 6837
W: www.bnb.co.nz/hosts/
mcintyre.html

Cost: Double $85 Single $50
Child Neg Dinner $20
Beds: 1 Queen 1 Double
(2 bdrm)
Bath: 1 Private

Port Waikato - Sunset Beach

Sunset Beach - Auckland's undiscovered gem. Magnificent
sunsets, incredible black sand dunes, awesome surf, the
historic Waikato River. Uncrowded beaches. One hour
from Auckland. Nature at its best. We invite you to share
the hacienda on the Beach. Kick back and relax by the large
salt water swimming pool or for the more energetic,
wonderful beach or bush walks, tennis, fishing (river or surf)
whitebait and duck shooting in season, limestone caves.
Onewhero Golf Course nearby. Dine by candlelight in the
courtyard or by the cosy fire during winter. (Dinner extra by
arrangement). We have a small social dog.

Cabana Costena
Homestay
30km SW of Pukekohe
Christine Haber
31 Oceanview Road
Sunset Beach, RD 5 Tuakau

Tel: (09) 232 9665
Fax: (09) 232 9665
Mob: 025 988 487
E: Costena@voyager.co.nz
W: www.bnb.co.nz/hosts/
cabanacostena.html

Cost: Double $75-$95
Single $50 Dinner $25
Visa/MC
Beds: 1 Queen 1 Double
1 Single (3 bdrm)
Bath: 1 Ensuite 1 Private

Most of our B&Bs are non smoking.

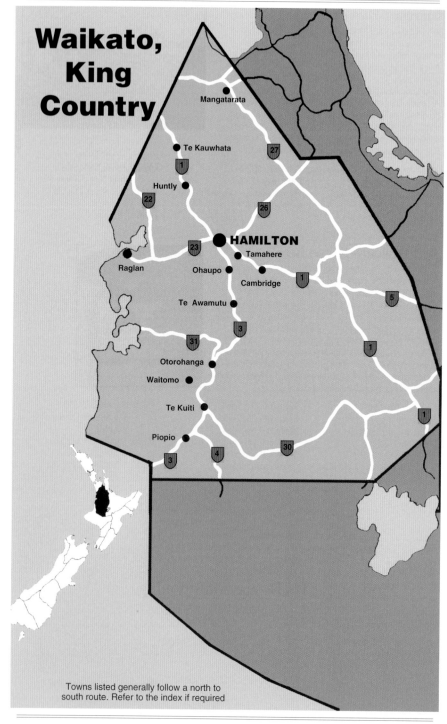

Waikato, King Country

Mangatarata

Te Kauwhata

27

1

Huntly

22

26

23

HAMILTON

Tamahere

Raglan

Ohaupo

Cambridge

1

Te Awamutu

5

3

31

Otorohanga

1

Waitomo

Te Kuiti

Piopio

3

4

30

1

Towns listed generally follow a north to
south route. Refer to the index if required

Mangatarata

Welcome to our beef farm with views of rolling pasture, bush and Coromandel ranges. Our sunny guestroom with TV, tea, coffee, cookies is opposite the bathroom. We are handy to the Hauraki Golf Course, Bowling Club, Seabird Coast, Miranda Hot Pools, Ngatea Gemstone Factory and Thames Coromandel coast. Our friendly dog Becky lives outside and our cat Watson shares our home. We are aged 50ish and enjoy handcrafts, gardening, four wheel driving and vintage machinery. Warm country hospitality awaits you. Non-smoking indoors.

Clark's Country Touch
Farmstay
13km W of Ngatea
Betty & Murray Clark
209 Highway 27
Mangatarata, RD 6 Thames

Tel: (07) 867 3070
Fax: (07) 867 3070
Mob: 021 808 992
W: www.bnb.co.nz/hosts/
clarkscountrytouch.html

Cost: Double $65 Single $40
Child Discount
Dinner $15 Visa/MC
Beds: 1 King/Twin (1 bdrm)
Bath: 1 Family share

Te Kauwhata

Welcome to your home in the Waikato. Our farm and Horse Stud is the perfect setting for your first nights stay. Horses. Livestock, Pets, Ponds and Pinewoods enhance our rural location on Lake Waikare Scenic Drive. Our quality air conditioned Garden Studio gives the opportunity for self catering. Breakfast and Dinner are served in our dining room. For peace and quiet, country walks, honeymoon suite, golfing, horse riding, natural hot springs near by or our pool; the choice is yours. Herons Ridge is a KiwiHost business.

Herons Ridge
Self-contained Farmstay
7km E of Te Kauwhata
David Sharland
1131 Waikare Road
RD 1 Te Kauwhata

Tel: (07) 826 4646
Fax: (07) 826 4646
E: herons_ridge@xtra.co.nz
W: www.webnz.com/bbnz/
heron.htm

Cost: Double $80 Single $50
Child discount
Dinner $30
S/C studio $120
Beds: 2 Queen 1 Double
1 Single (3 bdrm)
Bath: 1 Ensuite 1 Private

Huntly

Parnassus offers you all the calm and beauty of the New Zealand countryside yet is only minutes off SH1. We are a working farm combining dairying, forestry, sheep and beef and have an extensive (1.6ha) garden incorporating formal rose beds, woodland area, orchard, berry fruit courtyard and kitchen gardens. Children enjoy our delightful range of birds and small animals. We're easy to find, from SH1 cross Waikato River just south of Huntly township, right into Harris St 2km, right into Te Ohaki Road, 1.9 kms on LHS.

Parnassus Farm & Garden
Self-contained Farmstay
4km NW of Huntly
David & Sharon Payne
Te Ohaki Road
RD 1 Huntly

Tel: (07) 828 8781
Fax: (07) 828 8781
Mob: 021 458 525
E: parnassus@xtra.co.nz
W: www.bnb.co.nz/hosts/
parnassus.html

Cost: Double $90 Single $45
Child According to age
Dinner B/A Visa/MC
Beds: 2 Double 4 Single
(3 bdrm)
Bath: 1 Private 1 Guests share
1 Family share

Raglan

For romance, relaxation and recreation...Magic Mountain Lodge is on top of a hill country sheep and horse trekking farm. Situated at 328m above sea level (same height as Auckland Sky Tower). The views are 360° - see 3 harbours and 4 mountains. You'll feel on top of the world! The lodge is self contained catering for 2 - 8 people (only one group at a time). Includes log fire, candlelight, CD player, TV, waterbed. Very cosy with <u>all</u> home comforts. Cooked breakfast is served at the picnic table with panoramic views or in the privacy of your lodge. See stunning sunsets and sunrises. Ride our beautiful horses over farmland for 1 or 2 hours or to the Bridal Veil Falls (55m high). Horses to suit novice to experienced riders. Riding instruction given to novices and freedom to run for the experienced. Within a short drive visit famous surf beaches, taste Raglan's cuisine, purchase local art and crafts. Take a scenic harbour cruise or chartered fishing trip. Climb Mount Karioi, view the Bridal Veil Falls or simply relax, soaking up the magical views from your balcony.

Magic Mountain Farm Lodge & Horse Treks
B&B Self-contained Farmstay
20km S of Raglan
Jan-Maree & Marcus Vernon
334 Houchen Road
Te Mata, RD 1, Raglan

Tel: (07) 825 6892
Fax: (07) 825 6896
Mob: 025 756 276
E: bookings@magicmountain.co.nz
W: www.magicmountain.co.nz

Cost: Double $120
Single $90 Child $30
Enquire about group discounts
Beds: 1 Queen 2 Double
2 Single (2 bdrm)
Bath: 1 Private

Raglan

We are fortunate to have our own private beach and farm right on the Westcoast - panoramic views - providing surfing, fishing, hanggliding, bush and mountain walks and scenic drives. We take pride in farming this land for over 100 years. A large garden provides vegetables and flowers. Two cats are our resident pets. Seperate studio and spa. Directions: 1/2 hour Raglan/1 hour Hamilton/2 1/2 hours Auckland. Take Hamilton/Raglan Rd route 23. Turn off at Kauroa/Bridal Veil Falls - turn R) at Te Mata into Ruapuke Rd, Turn L) into Tutu Rimu Rd follow to junction and our entrance 61 on cattlestop and name on letterbox.

Matawha
Self-contained Farmstay
20km S of Raglan
Jenny & Peter Thomson
61 Matawha Road
RD 2 Raglan

Tel: (07) 825 6709
Fax: (07) 825 6715
Mob: 025 162 6405
E: jennyt@wave.co.nz
W: www.bnb.co.nz/hosts/matawha.html

Cost: Double $60-$80
   Single $30-$40 Dinner $20
Beds: 1 Double 4 Single
   (2 bdrm)
Bath: 1 Private 1 Family share
hb

Hamilton

I have travelled extensively throughout New Zealand and overseas and welcome tourists to my comfortable home. I live close to the Waikato River with its tranquil river walks and St Andrews Golf Course. My interests are travel, golf, tramping and gardening. A member of NZ Association Farm & Home Hosts and Probus. I look forward to offering you friendly hospitality. Directions: From Auckland - leave main Highway north of Hamilton at 2nd round intersection into Bryant Road. Turn left into Sandwich Road and 2nd street on right.

Kantara
Homestay
3km N of Hamilton
Mrs Esther Kelly
7 Delamare Road
Bryant Park Hamilton

Tel: (07) 849 2070
Mob: 025 263 9442
E: esther@enlighten.co.nz
W: www.bnb.co.nz/hosts/kelly.html

Cost: Double $80 Single $55
   Dinner $20 Visa/MC
Beds: 2 Single (1 bdrm)
Bath: 1 Private

Hamilton

Welcome to our home two seconds off the city bypass on Routes 7 and 9 at five crossroads. We are adjacent to the showgrounds, Ruakura Research Station and handy to the university and only three minutes from central city. Our home is a 'lived-in' comfortable home, warm in winter and cool in summer, with a pool available. We enjoy, along with our cat, spending time with visitors from NZ and overseas . We have travelled extensively and enjoy helping to plan your holiday.

B&B Homestay
1.5km E of Hamilton Central
Maureen & Graeme Matthews
24 Pearson Avenue
Claudelands
Hamilton

Tel: (07) 855 4269
Fax: (07) 855 4269
Mob: 025 747 758
E: mgm@xtra.co.nz
W: www.bnb.co.nz/hosts/matthews.html

Cost: Double $65 Single $45
   Child 1/2 price
   Dinner $20 Visa/MC
Beds: 3 Single (2 bdrm)
Bath: 1 Guests share
   1 Family share

Hamilton

Only minutes from town centre, our ten year old home has a spectacular view of the Waikato River - New Zealand's longest. We travel extensively and love sharing travel anecdotes, but also respect our guests privacy. Your room has its own tea/coffee facility and private bathroom. Eighty-five minutes from Auckland International Airport appeals to tourists arriving or departing New Zealand. Our interests include gardening, music, sport, travel and people. We don't have young children or pets, and are smoke free.

Homestay	**Tel:** (07) 849 2005	**Cost:** Double $80
Glenys & John Ebbett	**Fax:** (07) 849 8405	Single $55 Dinner $20
162 Beerescourt Rd	**E:** johnebbett@xtra.co.nz	**Beds:** 2 Single (1 bdrm)
Hamilton	**W:** www.bnb.co.nz/hosts/	**Bath:** 1 Private
	ebbett.html	

Hamilton

We are five minutes drive along Clyde Street to Waikato University and in the other direction five minutes from the centre of Hamilton City. Also five minutes away are the Hamilton Gardens. All our guest rooms have magazines to read, tea making facilities and television sets and all beds have electric blankets. In daylight hours we will meet trains or buses and take you back to the station for your return journey. Our home is a no smoking zone and we have off street parking.

B&B	**Tel:** (07) 856 0337	**Cost:** Double $65
2km E of Hamilton	**Fax:** (07) 856 0337	Single $40 Child $15
Mrs V Wood	**E:** VAL.AND.COLIN.WOOD	**Beds:** 1 Double 2 Single
164 Clyde Street	@xtra.co.nz	(3 bdrm)
Hamilton	**W:** www.bnb.co.nz/hosts/	**Bath:** 1 Guests share
	wood.html	1 Family share

Hamilton

Anlaby Manor has been built as a replica Yorkshire stately home after a Sir Edwin Lutyens design. Features a huge central staircase replicated from that of "Gone with The Wind". A formal English garden of 2.5 acres with neo-Roman statuary, fountains, box hedging and roses. A luxury 2 story cottage fully self contained is also available for honeymooners and families. There is a swimming pool, tennis court, sauna and billiard room. Children under 12 years are free. We have no pets.

Anlaby Manor	**Tel:** (07) 856 7264	**Cost:** Double $180 Single $130
B&B Cottage	**Fax:** (07) 856 5323	Dinner $60 Cottage $180
Halina & Pryme Footner	**E:** anlaby.manor@xtra.co.nz	Visa/MC Amex Diners
91 Newell Road	**W:** www.anlabymanor.co.nz	**Beds:** 4 Queen
RD 3		2 Single (4 bdrm)
Hamilton		**Bath:** 2 Ensuite 1 Private
		1 Guests share

Hamilton

Haere mai - Welcome to our comfortable smoke free, homely Lockwood nestled within a quiet garden. Guests have sole access to their bathroom and bedroom. Our aim is to provide a warm environment where guests relax and enjoy themselves. Within walking distance are popular "Cafe en Q", "The Platter Place". Chartwell Square and Waikato River walks. We also have a beach home with magnificent sea views near Opotiki if requested. We share our home with a friendly cat named Zapper. Directions: Please Phone.

Homestay
Hamilton Central
Judy & Brian Dixon
50A Queenwood Avenue
Chartwell
Hamilton

Tel: (07) 855 7324
E: jdixon@voyager.co.nz
W: opotiki2.co.nz/waiotahi

Cost: Double $65 Single $45
Beds: 2 Single (1 bdrm)
Bath: 1 Private

Hamilton - Ohaupo

Warm, comfortable smokefree family home in a quiet rural setting, close to Hamilton, Airport and Fielddays (Mystery Creek). Free pick-up/delivery airport, bus, train terminal all part of the friendly service. 5km to Vilagrad Winery; 2 minutes walk to Gostiona Restaurant. Two storeyd house with guest rooms, lounge downstairs; dining, hosts upstairs. Fresh home baked bread and selection of coffees to suit. Judi lectures statistics, University of Waikato. Earl is a "retired" school teacher. One daughter still lives at home. Non-smokers preferred.

Green Gables of Rukuhia
B&B Homestay
4km SW of Hamilton
Earl & Judi McWhirter
35 Rukuhia Road
RD 2 Ohaupo

Tel: (07) 843 8511
Fax: (07) 843 8514
Mob: 025 848 030
E: judi@stats.waikato.ac.nz
W: www.bnb.co.nz/hosts/
greengablesofrukuhia.html

Cost: Double $75-$85
Single $40-$50
Dinner B/A Visa/MC
Beds: 2 Double 3 Single
(3 bdrm)
Bath: 1 Guests share

Hamilton

Just minutes from Hamilton, Mystery Creek and Cambridge, The Poplars offers a haven of peace and quiet. Set in a majestic three acre garden with internationally acclaimed daffodils, 800 roses and many water features. Each guest room has tea and coffee making facilities, electric blankets and TV. Solar heated swimming pool and spa are adjacent to guest rooms. Hosts Peter and Lesley, themselves seasoned travellers, offer you the charms of country living. A warm welcome shared with family pets awaits you. A unique and special place to stay. Directions: Please phone.

The Poplars
Homestay Home & Garden
4km S of Hamilton
Lesley & Peter Ramsay
402 Matangi Road
RD 4
Hamilton

Tel: (07) 829 5551
Mob: 025 668 0985
E: ramsay@waikato.ac.nz
W: www.bnb.co.nz/hosts/
thepoplars.html

Cost: Double $90 Single $65
Dinner $25pp B/A
Visa/MC
Beds: 1 King 2 Single (2 bdrm)
Bath: 1 Private

Hamilton

Come and join us in our Mediterranean-style Villa, placed for maximum sunshine in a landscaped garden with goats and sheep grazing the gully below. We are a friendly couple and now our family have left home, we wish to share our new surroundings. Having travelled extensively, we understand the importance of hospitality. See our many art and craft interests on display. Our 5 acre farmlet is conveniently 3kms from Hamilton Airport, Mystery Creek and just off SH1. Enjoy tranquillity and glorious sunsets. Please ring for directions.

PORT Williams	**Tel:** (07) 856 2499	**Cost:** Double & Single (Ensuite
Farmstay Homestay B&B	**Fax:** (07) 856 2499	with Double Spa Bath) $110
Farmlet	**Mob:** 025 261 1959	Queen (Ensuite) $105
6km S of Hamilton	**E:** port.williams@clear.net.nz	Dinner by arr.
Roger & Pat Williams	**W:** www.bnb.co.nz/hosts/	**Beds:** 1 Queen 1 Double 1 Twin
Pencarrow Road	portwilliams.html	1 Single (2 bdrm)
Tamahere, RD 3 Hamilton		**Bath:** 2 Ensuites - 1 with
		Double Spa Bath

Lake Rotokauri - Hamilton

Our home is nestled in 3 acres of garden, offering privacy and relaxation. Enjoy magnificent views of Lake Rotokauri and Mt. Pirongia from our upstairs guest rooms where there is a kitchen, lounge and dining area. Our special self-serve breakfast is full of home-made treats. Soak in the hydrotherapy spa or relax having a professional therapeutic massage (available by appointment). We, with our children are keen outdoors people and can direct you to local attractions...the Hamilton zoo with its famous 'free flight' sanctuary is just 2 minutes away. Please phone for reservations and directions.

Self-contained Country	**Tel:** (07) 8499 020	**Cost:** Double $120 Single $90
Gardenstay	**Mob:** 025 202 1978	Visa/MC
4km NW of Hamilton	**E:** dcdewes@hotmail.com	**Beds:** 1 Queen (1 bdrm)
Cathy & David Dewes	**W:** www.bnb.co.nz/hosts/	**Bath:** 1 Ensuite
Exelby Rd Hamilton	dewes.html	

Hamilton

We extend a warm welcome to all visitors. Our home is spacious, clean and comfortable with views over Hamilton City. Quality accommodation in a friendly, relaxed environment. Off street parking, complimentary tea and coffee, laundry facilities, exercise room and swimming pool. Great breakfast guaranteed. Dinner provided by arrangement. On city bus route. Free transport to and from local airport, bus and train stations. Waikato University, Hamilton gardens, river walks, cafes, restaurants and bars minutes away. Our children have flown the nest but Turbo the cat remains.

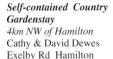

Hillcrest Heights H/stay B&B	**Tel:** (07) 856 4818	**Cost:** Double $75-$85
B&B Homestay	**Fax:** (07) 856 4831	Single $55-$65
Hamilton Central	**Mob:** 025 226 7386	Child $15 Dinner $20 B/A
Barbara & Tony	**E:** hillcrest.bb@clear.net.nz	**Beds:** 4 bedrooms each with a
54 Hillcrest Road	**W:** www.bnb.co.nz/hosts/	Queen & single
Hillcrest Hamilton	hillcrestheightshomestaybb.html	**Bath:** 1 Ensuite 2 Guests share

Hamilton - Tamahere

Lenora and Trevor warmly invite you to relax and to share the comfort of our smoke free home "Lenvor", which is set in a rural area, down a country lane. Sam, our cat, lives outside. Our two storeyed home has guest rooms, small lounge upstairs; dining, lounge, hosts, downstairs. 10 minutes to Hamilton or Cambridge; 5 minutes to Mystery Creek or airport. Lenora's interests are floral art and cake icing. Trevor enjoys vintage cars. Breakfast includes cereals, home made jams, preserved fruits, bacon and eggs.

Lenvor B&B	**Tel:** (07) 856 2027	**Cost:** Double $100 Single $50
B&B	**Fax:** (07) 856 4173	Child $25 Dinner $25 B/A
10km S of Hamilton	**W:** www.bnb.co.nz/hosts/	**Beds:** 2 Queen 2 Single
Lenora & Trevor Shelley	lenvorbb.html	(3 bdrm)
540E Oaklea Lane		**Bath:** 1 Ensuite 1 Guests share
RD 3, Tamahere		1 Family share
Hamilton		

Hamilton

We welcome you to the peace and tranquillity of country life. Our place is central from Te Awamutu and Hamilton and are located in the little farming community of Te Pahu, right under Mount Pirongia. We are in the middle of a block of Chestnut trees and are quite secluded. We have our small dog and two fat cats. Our home is very large and roomy and we have special facilities for the elderly person. Comfort and nice meals is what we offer you.

Country Quarters Homestay	**Tel:** (07) 825 9727	**Cost:** Double $80 Single $40
B&B Homestay	**Fax:** (07) 827 5872	Child $10 Dinner $20
28km S of Hamilton	**E:** graeme.waite@xtra.co.nz	Caravan $15
Ngaere & Jack Waite	**W:** www.bnb.co.nz/hosts/	**Beds:** 1 Queen 1 Twin
No 11 Corcoran Road	countryquartershomestay.html	3 Single (5 bdrm)
Te Pahu		**Bath:** 1 Guests share
Hamilton		Shower room

Hamilton

Welcome to Sefton, a sunny and warm home centrally located on the eastern side of the Waikato River. A mere five minute walk over the river takes you direct to central Hamilton and a large variety of restaurants, shopping and entertainment. Quiet river walks and sporting venues are close by. Sefton is located in an older residential area surrounded by well established gardens and mature trees. Ben, a boxer dog and two cats share our home which is a no smoking zone.

Sefton	**Tel:** (07) 855 9046	**Cost:** Double $100 Single $50
B&B	**Fax:** (07) 855 9041	**Beds:** 1 Queen 1 Single
0.5 E of Hamilton Central	**Mob:** 025 221 4681	(2 bdrm)
Jan Short	**E:** jshort@xtra.co.nz	**Bath:** 1 Guests share
213B River Road	**W:** www.bnb.co.nz/hosts/	
Hamilton	sefton.html	

Hamilton

Away from the "hustle and bustle" yet close to all
amenities. "The Cottage" its self-contained with all
cooking facilities, laundry and phone. Set in 2 acres of
gardens looking out over our 47 acres, with herefords
and suffolk sheep who love the odd slice of bread. We
have two adult children, two cats and two Jack
Russells who will give you a friendly welcome. Our
interests are gardening, sport and travel. Come and
enjoy your stay in our relaxed and informal surroundings. Please phone for directions.

A&A Country Stay
Self-contained Country Cottage
10km E of Hamilton
Ann & Alan Marsh
275 Vaile Rd, RD 4
Hamilton

Tel: (07) 824 1908
Fax: (07) 824 1908
Mob: 025 763 014
E: aacountrystay@xtra.co.nz
W: www.bnb.co.nz/hosts/
aacountrystay.html

Cost: Double $80 Single $50
Extra person $15 Child neg.
Dinner $20pp Visa/MC
Beds: 1 Queen 1 Double
2 Single (2 bdrm)
Bath: 1 Private

Cambridge

Park House, circa 1920, is for guests of discernment who
appreciate quality and comfort. For 15 years we have
offered this superb setting for guests. Throughout this large
home are antiques, traditional furniture, patchworks and
stained glass windows creating an elegant and restful
ambience. The guest lounge features an elaborately carved
fireplace, fine art, library, TV and complimentary sherry.
Bedrooms in separate wing upstairs ensues privacy.
Unbeatable quiet location overlooking village green, 2
minute walk to restaurants, antique and craft shops.
Member of heritage Inns.

Park House
B&B
Cambridge Central
Pat & Bill Hargreaves
70 Queen Street Cambridge

Tel: (07) 827 6368
Fax: (07) 827 4094
E: Park.House@xtra.co.nz
W: www.bnb.co.nz/hosts/
parkhouse.html

Cost: Double $130-$160
Single $120
Visa/MC Amex
Beds: 1 King/Twin 1 Queen
1 Double (3 bdrm)
Bath: 2 Ensuite 1 Private

Cambridge

Our 1930's character farmhouse offers open fires in
guests' sitting room, tennis and swimming pool set in
country garden amongst picturesque horse studs.
Proximity to Cambridge and Lake Karapiro makes
Birches an ideal base for lake users. Hugh, a
veterinarian, and I are widely travelled. Olivia, 9, is
happy to show her farm pets and cat. Little Cherry
Tree cottage (queen/ensuite) is ideal for couples
wanting privacy. The twin room has private bathroom
with spabath. We serve delicious farmhouse breakfasts
alfresco or in dining room.

Birches
B&B Self-contained Farmstay
5km SW of Cambridge
Sheri Mitchell & Hugh Jellie
263 Maungatautari Road
PO Box 194 Cambridge

Tel: (07) 827 6556
Fax: (07) 827 3552
Mob: 021 882 216
E: birches@ihug.co.nz
W: www.bnb.co.nz/hosts/
birches.html

Cost: Double $90 Single $60
Child B/A Dinner B/A
Visa/MC Amex
Beds: 1 Queen 1 Double
1 Single (2 bdrm)
Bath: 1 Ensuite 1 Private

Cambridge

We look forward to welcoming you to our centrally located spacious comfortable home near the Waikato River. Guestrooms have TVs, tea/coffee making facilities and en suite bathrooms. A guest lounge/library/music room is available for guests wanting privacy or join us in our lounge for coffee, a glass of wine or a chat. Easy to find, peaceful and tranquil location. Directions: Cross bridge at south end of Victoria Street (main street) turn right off bridge, Marlowe Drive is first on right.

White's Homestay
B&B Homestay
Cambridge Central
Diane & Paul White
7 Marlowe Drive
Cambridge

Tel: (07) 823 2142
Fax: (07) 823 2143
Mob: 025 963 224
W: www.bnb.co.nz/hosts/whiteshomestay.html

Cost: Double $80 Single $50
Child n/a Dinner B/A
Visa/MC
Beds: 2 Queen (2 bdrm)
Bath: 2 Ensuite

Cambridge

Wanting home comfort and privacy or want to chat you will find it here. Located 5 minutes from the town centre, restaurants, antique and gift shops, harness racing and golf club.This is the centre of the Thoroughbred horse Industry.(Horse studs 5 min drive) Daily leisurely drives to Waitomo Caves 40 mins, Rotorua 55 mins, Hamilton Field Days 10 mins, Lake Karapiro 10 mins and a host of other interesting drives and walks. Children and pets welcome. We're happy to pick you up from the bus stop or Hamilton Airport. Bookings recommended.

Hansel & Gretels B&B
B&B
5min walk Cambridge
Debbie Worth
58 Hamilton Road
Cnr Hamilton Road and Bryce St
Cambridge

Tel: (07) 827 8476
Fax: (07) 827 8476
Mob: 025 537 928
E: HanselGretal@hotmail.com
W: www.bnb.co.nz/hosts/hanselgretelsbb.html

Cost: Double $80 Single $70
Visa/MC
Beds: 1 King 1 Double 2 Single
(3 bdrm)
Bath: 2 Private

Cambridge

Glenleg welcomes you to Cambridge to a new home with quality spacious accommodation - warm quiet and private overlooking Waikato Farmland, with plenty of off street parking. Beds have electric blankets and woolrests. 200 Rose bushes in the garden. 5 Mins to Lake Karapiro. Mystery Creek where NZ National Field Days and many other functions are held is only 15 mins away. Sky TV, laundry facilities available. No smoking indoors please. "Home away from Home". For a brochure and directions please phone.

Glenelg
B&B Homestay
2km N of Cambridge
Ken & Shirley Geary
6 Curnow Place
Leamington Cambridge

Tel: (07) 823 0084
Fax: (07) 823 4279
E: glenelgbedbreakfastnz@hotmail.com
W: www.bnb.co.nz/hosts/glenelg.html

Cost: Double $100 Single $65
Child $20 Dinner $20 B/A
Visa/MC
Beds: 3 Queen 1 Twin
(4 bdrm)
Bath: 3 Ensuite

Cambridge

Welcome to our country home, situated just off State
Highway One. Positioned on a commanding knoll, 20
acres sheltered by mature trees offering the weary traveller
peace and tranquillity. The outlook from the spacious home
provide panoramic views of the surrounding Waikato
countryside. We have an inground swimming pool and
floodlit tennis court. Five minutes to Lake Karapiro, twenty
minutes to Mystery Creek. Within one hours drive to
Tauranga, Rotorua , Waitomo Caves. Please feel at home
with us, farm animals and Possum the cat.

Dunfarmin	**Tel:** (07) 827 7727	**Cost:** Double $90 Single $50
B&B Countrystay	**Fax:** (07) 823 3357	Child $25 Dinner $25 B/A
10km S of Cambridge	**Mob:** 025 611 5247	Visa/MC
Jackie & Bob Clarke	**E:** dunfarmin@zfree.co.nz	**Beds:** 1 Queen 1 Double
55 Gorton Road	**W:** www.bnb.co.nz/hosts/	3 Single (3 bdrm)
RD 2 Cambridge	dunfarmin.html	**Bath:** 1 Ensuite 1 Guests share

Cambridge

Welcome to our beautiful turn-of-the-century Kauri villa,
lovingly restored and recently extended to provide you with
luxury accommodation in peaceful surroundings. Features
include private entrance to each room opening onto mature
gardens, fresh fruit and flowers, own tea/coffee making
facilities and special breakfast. Our home provides an ideal
base for you to stroll into town or explore the surrounding
countryside. We will be happy to provide you with
information about local attractions. Above all, a relaxing
and memorable stay is assured.

The Hedges	**Tel:** (07) 823 4072	**Cost:** Double $100-$120
B&B Self-contained	**Fax:** (07) 823 4072	Single $70-$90 Visa/MC
Cambridge Central	**E:** almitchem@xtra.co.nz	**Beds:** 2 Queen (2 bdrm)
Andrew & Lindsey Mitchem	**W:** www.bnb.co.nz/hosts/	**Bath:** 2 Ensuite
30 Alpha Street	thehedges.html	
Cambridge		

Cambridge

At Thornton House we offer you a luxury accommodation
in surroundings that uniquely reflect Cambridge's character
and charm. Our two recently renovated guestrooms are
fitted with comfortable queen beds and private ensuites
(including a clawfoot bath). Other features include historic
architecture, central heating, luxury robes, fresh flowers,
complimentary confectionery, own tea/coffee making
facilities and CD player/radio and scrumptious breakfasts.
You are also welcome to relax in the well-appointed lounge
and share our local knowledge and passion for fine food and
wine (and burmese cats).

Thornton House	**Tel:** (07) 827 7567	**Cost:** Double $160-$185
B&B	**Fax:** (07) 827 7568	Single $140-$165
Cambridge Central	**Mob:** 025 981 017	Dinner B/A
David Cowley & Christine	**E:** b&b@thorntonhouse.co.nz	Visa/MC Amex Diners
Manson	**W:** www.bnb.co.nz/hosts/	**Beds:** 2 Queen 1 Single (2 bdrm)
2 Thornton Road, Cambridge	thorntonhouse.html	**Bath:** 2 Ensuite

Cambridge

Pamade is a character home, very comfortable with beautiful gardens, swimming pool and spa pool. We are situated 2 minutes from central Cambridge with its wonderful selection of fascinating Art, Craft, Boutique and Antique Shops, Restaurants, Stud Farms and Golf Course. Just around the corner from Lake Karapiro (5 minutes drive), with its water-skiing, rowing and other aquatic sports. Mystery Creek (Fieldays) is only 10 minutes drive away. Self contained unit plus large double room with private exit. Great continental breakfast guaranteed.

Pamade B&B
B&B Self-contained
2km S of Cambridge
Paul & Marion Derikx
229 Shakespeare Street
Leamington

Tel: (07) 827 4916
Fax: (07) 827 4988
Mob: 021 261 7122
E: pamades@hotmail.com
W: www.bnb.co.nz/hosts/
pamade.html

Cost: Double $70-$90
Single $50-$60 Dinner B/A
Beds: 1 King/Twin 1 King
1 Queen 1 Double
2 Single (3 bdrm)
Bath: 2 Ensuite 1 Private

Cambridge

Clanfield House, circa 1900, is a beautifully restored Victorian Villa in the heart of Cambridge. We offer delightfully decorated, separate accommodation with ensuite facilities, and a courtyard with private Spa Pool, in peaceful surroundings. Enjoy an optional evening meal in our elegant dining room, cooked by well known Waikato Chef Wayne Good. All your breakfast provisions are left in your room, to enjoy at your leisure. Our home makes an ideal base for visiting the surrounding countryside. We look forward to making you welcome.

Clanfield House
B&B Self-contained
1km Cambridge central
Wayne Good & Raymond Parker
155 Victoria Street
Cambridge

Tel: (07) 823 2018
Fax: (07) 823 1412
Mob: 025 856 016
E: wayne.good@xtra.co.nz
W: www.findus.co.nz/
clanfieldhouse

Cost: Double $125-$150
Single $90 Dinner B/A
Visa/MC
Beds: 1 Double (1 bdrm)
Bath: 1 Ensuite

Cambridge

Country House Living with Style: elegant, superior accommodation in a peaceful rural setting near Cambridge, in stunning gardens and furnished with quality artwork and antiques (many available for sale in our adjacent interior design studio). Stroll through neighbouring farmland, visit a nearby scenic reserve, or relax with a book in our library. With cat Pusskin we can offer a haven for jet-lagged travellers, being only 90 min from Auckland Airport, and we are within easy reach of many of NZ's major tourist attractions.

Gainsborough House
B&B Homestay
5 NE of Cambridge
Julie and Michael Thorpe
1-103 Maungakawa Road
RD 4 Cambridge

Tel: +64 7 823 2473
Fax: +64 7 823 1678
E: GainsboroughHouse
@xtra.co.nz
W: www.bnb.co.nz/hosts/
gainsboroughhouse.html

Cost: Double $120-$200
Single $90 Dinner B/A
Visa/MC
Beds: 1 King 1 Double
1 Single (3 bdrm)
Bath: 3 Ensuite

Te Awamutu

The 85 acre farm, situated in beautiful country side with cattle, horses, pigs, poultry, sheep, goats and pets. A spacious home welcomes you with swimming pool and tennis court. Large guest rooms with doors to garden. Specials: Horseback riding and gig rides for children and adults. Raspberry picking in season and access to the milking of 500 dairy cows.

Farmstay Guesthouse
4.5km N of Te Awamutu
Mrs R Bleskie & C. Bleskie
Storey Road
Te Awamutu

Tel: (07) 871 3301
W: www.bnb.co.nz/hosts/
bleskie.html

Cost: Double $90 Single $50
   Child $25 Dinner $25
Beds: 1 Double 8 Single
   (5 bdrm)
Bath: 1 Ensuite 1 Guests share
   1 Family share

Te Awamutu

'Leger Farm' is a private residence with country living at its finest. The discerning leisure traveller seeking quality accommodation, in peaceful, relaxing surroundings, will find warm hospitality and every comfort here. Spacious bedrooms share stunning panoramic views of surrounding countryside. Each bedroom has its own balcony with beautiful garden vistas. We farm red deer and sheep, and are centrally based for visiting Waitomo Caves and black water rafting, Rotorua with its thermal activity and NZ's dramatic West Coast and ironstone sands. Golf course nearby for relaxation. Smoke free home.

Leger Farm
B&B Farmstay
2km S of Te Awamutu
Beverley & Peter Bryant
114 St Leger Rd Te Awamutu

Tel: (07) 871 6676
Fax: (07) 871 6679
W: www.bnb.co.nz/hosts/
legerfarm.html

Cost: Double $115
   Single $65 Dinner $25
Beds: 1 Double 1 Twin
   3 Single (3 bdrm)
Bath: 1 Ensuite 1 Private
   1 Guests share

Te Awamutu

We welcome visitors to enjoy our hospitality and the peacefulness of our home 5 minutes from the centre of New Zealand's "Rosetown". Waitomo, Rotorua and Lake Taupo are within easy driving distance from us. Hamilton airport and Mystery creek are 20 minutes away. Te Awamutu is an excellent base for bushwalking, golfing, fishing and garden visits. Gardening, philately and woodturning are among our interests. Prior notice for dinner, would be appreciated. Direction. Please phone or fax for reservations and directions.

Morton Homestay
B&B Homestay
4km S of Te Awamutu
Marg and Dick Morton
10 Brill Road
RD 5 Te Awamutu

Tel: (07) 871 8814
Fax: (07) 871 8865
W: www.bnb.co.nz/hosts/
mortonhomestay.html

Cost: Double $70 Single $40
   Dinner $20 Visa/MC
Beds: 1 Double 2 Single
   (2 bdrm)
Bath: 1 Private

Te Awamutu

Poplar Ridge Farm is a 24 hectare block in the middle of the lush Waikato. It is a maize and dry stock small farm. There are panoramic views and spectacular sunsets. We have traditional gardens with colour all year and in winter lots of native birdlife. Our home has recently been totally refurbished and reflects our passion for NZ art, Persian rugs and English china. See our own toy museum or trout fish twelve minutes away. Rotorua and Waitomo Caves are just sixty minutes. We have two cats and one dog.

Poplar Ridge Farm	**Tel:** (07) 872 7958	**Cost:** Double $90 Single $60
Farmstay	**Mob:** 025 677 4032	Child 1/2 price Dinner $25
19km SE of Te Awamutu	**E:** the.suttons@voyager.co.nz	Visa/MC
Ross & Valda Sutton	**W:** www.bnb.co.nz/hosts/	**Beds:** 1 Twin 1 Single (2 bdrm)
1614 Arapuni Road	poplarridgefarm.html	**Bath:** 1 Guests share
Parawera, RD 2		
Te Awamutu		

Te Awamutu

A warm welcome awaits you at Tregamere, where you'll share our large, well-appointed home, dine as friends and slumber in comfort. Enjoy fabulous sunsets over Mt Pirongia, savour our lush garden, explore the impressive Kahikatea stand, participate in life on our 64 acre dry stock farm or amuse yourself in the games room. Set in tranquil surroundings on Te Awamutu's northern boundary, our central location is great for exploring - west coast beaches, the renowned Waitomo Caves, Hamilton and Rotorua are all within an easy drive.

Tregamere	**Tel:** (07) 870 1950	**Cost:** Double $100 Single $80
Farmstay	**Fax:** (07) 870 1952	Child $30 Dinner $35
1.5km N of Te Awamutu P.O	**Mob:** 025 291 3162	Campervans $30
Bev & Chris Johnson	**E:** c.b.john@xtra.co.nz	**Beds:** 1 Queen 3 King Single
2025 Ohaupo Road	**W:** www.bnb.co.nz/hosts/	(2 bdrm)
Te Awamutu 2400	tregamere.html	**Bath:** 1 Ensuite 1 Guests share

Otorohanga - Waitomo District

Welcome to Meadowland, on State Highway 31, on the right hand side at the top of the second hill. Our accommodation is: a self-contained unit which can sleep up to six. One twin and two double bedrooms in homestead with guest shared bathroom and separate toilet. All beds have woolrests and electric blankets. We have a tennis court, swimming pool and spa pool on site. We are five minutes from the Otorohanga Kiwi House and Aviary, twenty minutes from Waitomo Caves area. We have three outside cats. Non-smokers preferred.

Meadowland	**Tel:** (07) 873 7729	**Cost:** Double $75 Single $50
B&B Self-contained Farmstay	**Fax:** (07) 873 7719	Child $20 Visa/MC
8km NW of Otorohanga	**Tollfree:** 0800 687 262	**Beds:** 2 Queen 1 Double
Jill & Tony Webber	**E:** meadowland@xtra.co.nz	1 Twin 2 Single (5 bdrm)
746 State Highway 31	**W:** http://mysite.xtra.co.nz/	**Bath:** 1 Private 1 Guests share
RD 3 Otorohanga	~Meadowland	

Otorohanga - Waitomo District

Relax and visit First Farm on Waitomo Caves Road (SH37).
5 min to Waitomo, Otorohanga, Te Kuiti, 2 min to two
restaurants. Free Ostrich Farm tour - products for sale.
Don't miss our free nightly glow-worm tour. Early New
Zealand homestead, spacious rooms, veranda/garden area.
Three country cottage s/c units. Ross is a Conservation
Ranger. Ann has "Baraka Crafts" souvenir shop in
Otorohanga with "World's Largest Spinning Wheel" (10%
off for you!). Common comments: "Friendly hospitality -
Home away from Home". Freephone now!

Waitomo Big Bird B&B
B&B S/C Farmstay Homestay
8km S of Otorohanga
Ross & Ann Barnes
17 Waitomo Caves Road
RD 7 Otorohanga

Tel: (07) 873 7459
Tollfree: 0800 733 244
Mob: 025 772 707
E: bigbird.bb@xtra.co.nz
W: www.bnb.co.nz/hosts/
waitomobigbirdbedbreakfast.html

Cost: Double $65-$80
Single $40 Child $15
Family/Group $25-$30pp
Dinner $20 Visa/MC
Beds: 5 Queen 2 Double
2 Twin 3 Single (9 bdrm)
Bath: 2 Private 1 Guests share
1 Family share

Waitomo Village - Waitomo District

Our home is only 100 metres from the Museum of
Caves information office in the centre of the village
and a few hundred metres from the Glow Worm Caves.
Our detached rooms with their individual ensuite
facilities are of the highest standard. With a variety of
cave adventure trips, excellent bush walks and a top
golf course we recommend at least two days to spend
with us. We will arrange your meals. You will find a
place with warm and friendly hospitality.

Dalziel Waitomo Caves
Guest Lodge
B&B Self-contained
Andree & Peter Dalziel
PO Box 16
Waitomo Caves

Tel: (07) 878 7641
Fax: (07) 878 7466
W: www.bnb.co.nz/hosts/
dalzielwaitomocaves.html

Cost: Double $70 Single $50
Visa/MC
Beds: 3 Queen 1 Double
2 Single (5 bdrm)
Bath: 5 Ensuite

Waitomo

Our 550 hectare sheep and cattle property is near the
Waitomo Caves with a view of Mt Ruapehu. A massage
spa/conservatory overlooks the gardens and farm. Our
adult children have largely left home but one cat keeps an
eye on us. Our baby grand and karaoke love attention and
various farm walks and a glow worm/cave night walk can
be undertaken. Peter is a well informed and progressive
farmer while Jocelyn is a Midwife and artist. We enjoy
welcoming visitors to our home.

Forest Hills
Farmstay
8km S of Waitomo
Jocelyn & Peter Boddie
584 Boddies Rd
Te Kuiti

Tel: (07) 878 8764
Fax: (07) 878 8764
Mob: 025 846 464
E: jocpetbod@xtra.co.nz
W: www.bnb.co.nz/hosts/
foresthills.html

Cost: Double $110 Single $80
Dinner $35
Double bed/detached $110
Visa/MC
Beds: 1 King/Twin 1 Queen
1 Double (3 bdrm)
Bath: 1 Ensuite 1 Private
1 Family share

Te Kuiti - Waitomo District

We live only 50 metres off Highway 3. Expect a warm welcome, peace and relaxation in our 1920's bungalow. The bedrooms have tea and coffee-making facilities, quality beds and bedding and heaters. Breakfast can be timed to suit you and includes cereals, fruit, juice and toast followed by cooked English breakfast and brewed coffee or tea. Feel free to use the TV in one of the lounges. We can help you with advice about local attractions including great places to walk or tramp.

Te Kuiti B&B
B&B Homestay
1km S of Te Kuiti
Pauline Blackmore
5 Grey St
Te Kuiti

Tel: (07) 878 6686
W: www.bnb.co.nz/hosts/
tekuitibb.html

Cost: Double $65-$80
Single $50 Visa/MC
Beds: 2 Queen 2 Single
(3 bdrm)
Bath: 2 Ensuite 1 Private

Te Kuiti - Waitomo District

Large, magnificently appointed homestead providing warm hospitality that ensures every comfort. Spacious bedrooms feature vistas of green rolling hills and spectacular outcrops of limestone. 571 hectare sheep and cattle farm. Pet sheep, pig and donkeys. Guests may choose superking/twin beds with bathroom. Separate guest wing consists of superking/twin bed with ensuite and patio. Complete relaxation is the keynote. This is New Zealand at its best. Children not catered for. Dinner served by prior arrangement only. Waitomo 25 min drive. Check in: after 4 pm.

Tapanui Country Home
Farmstay
20km NW of Te Kuiti
Sue & Mark Perry
1714 Oparure Rd
RD 5 Te Kuiti

Tel: (07) 877 8549
Fax: (07) 877 8541
Mob: 025 949 873
E: tapanui@xtra.co.nz
W: www.tapanui.co.nz

Cost: Double $145-$160
Single $135-$150
Dinner $40 Visa/MC
Beds: 3 King/Twin (3 bdrm)
Bath: 1 Ensuite 1 Private
1 Guests share

The best thing about a homestay
is that you share the family's living area.

Te Kuiti - Waitomo District

Raema, Michael and the cat welcome you to our hill top home, overlooking bush clad hills, fertile valleys and distant peaks with golden dawns and spectacular sunsets. We offer comfortable beds and the quiet surroundings of a 30 hectare farm plus 40 years experience of the district and its attractions. Waitomo is 25 mins away, Rotorua, Taupo 2 hours so come and enjoy the company, the scenery and a good night's rest. Arriving or departing from Auckland - we are 2 1/2 hours to the Airport.

Panorama Farm
B&B Farmstay
6km E of Te Kuiti
Michael & Raema Warriner
65 Carter Road
RD 2 Te Kuiti

Tel: (07) 878 5104
Fax: (07) 878 8104
E: panoramab.b@xtra.co.nz
W: www.bnb.co.nz/hosts/
panoramafarm.html

Cost: Double $66 Single $35
  Child $17 Dinner $20
  Visa/MC
Beds: 1 Double
  3 Single (2 bdrm)
Bath: 1 Guests share

Piopio - Waitomo District

Enjoy a peaceful, relaxing time at our large, modern home set in landscaped gardens on a small sheep and cattle farmlet. Our elevated site provides panoramic views of green pastures, trees and limestone rocks. All rooms have a garden or rural outlook. Spacious heated bedrooms have comfortable beds and electric blankets. Our interests encompass gardening, music, sailing and meeting people from all over the world. Piopio 1km and Waitomo Caves just 35 minutes away. Please phone ahead for reservations and directions.

Bracken Ridge
Country Homestay
24km SW of TeKuiti
Susan & Rob Hallam
Aria Road
Piopio 2555

Tel: (07) 877 8384
Mob: 025 610 4001
W: www.bnb.co.nz/hosts/
hallam.html

Cost: Double $80 Single $50
  Dinner $20 by arrangement
Beds: 1 Queen 3 Single
  (2 bdrm)
Bath: 1 Private

Pio Pio - Waitomo District

Barbara and Leo Anselmi own and operate a 1200 acre sheep, beef and dairy farm. You will be welcomed into a 3000 square feet modern home set in picturesque gardens, in a lovely limestone valley.

You will be treated to delicious home cooked meals and the warmth of our friendship. Whether enjoying the excitement of mustering mobs of cattle and sheep, viewing the milking of 550 cows, driving around the rolling hills on the four-wheeled farm-bike, relaxing as you bask in the sun by the pool or wandering through the gardens, you will experience unforgettable memories of breathtaking scenery, a clean green environment.

We have farm pets who love the attention of our guests. The donkeys are waiting to be fed. We look over a beautiful 18 hole golf course which welcomes visitors.

The property is a short distance from Black Water Rafting and canoeing activities, The Lost World Cavern, and the famous Waitomo Caves. Nearby are bush walks and the home of the rare Kokako bird. We can help to arrange activities for people of all ages and interests including garden visits and horse riding. Please let us know your preference.

We are 140 kms from Rotorua/Taupo.

Directions: Travel 19 kms south of Te Kuiti on SH3 towards Piopio. Carmel Farm is on the right. We can arrange to pick up from Otorohanga, Te Kuiti or Waitomo, if required.

Carmel Farm
19km S of Te Kuiti
Barbara & Leo Anselmi
Main Road
PO Box 93
Pio Pio

Tel: (07) 877 8130
Fax: (07) 877 8130
E: Carmelfarms@xtra.co.nz
W: www.bnb.co.nz/hosts/
carmelfarm.html

Cost: Double $100 Single $50
Dinner $25pp
(with complementary wine)
Beds: 2 King/Twin
4 Single (4 bdrm)
Bath: 1 Ensuite 1 Family share

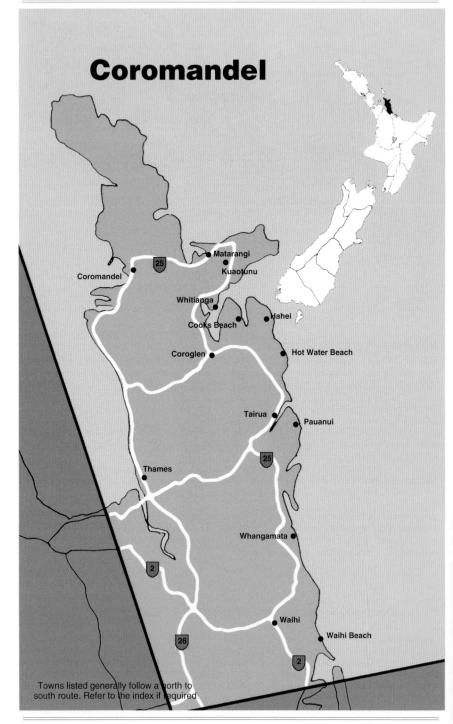

Coromandel

Coromandel

Matarangi

Kuaotunu

Whitianga

Cooks Beach

Hahei

Coroglen

Hot Water Beach

Tairua

Pauanui

Thames

Whangamata

Waihi

Waihi Beach

Towns listed generally follow a north to south route. Refer to the index if required

Thames

For 11 years our guests have enjoyed the beauty of Wharfedale which has featured in Air NZ airwaves and Japans my country magazines. We invite you to share our idyllic lifestyle set in 9 acres of park like paddocks and gardens surrounded by native bush. Delight in private river swimming, abundant bird life, our dairy goats. We enjoy wholefood and organically grown produce. There are cooking facilities in the studio apartment. We have no children or indoor animals. Cool shade in summer and cozy log fires and electric blankets in winter. We look forward to meeting you.

Wharfedale Farmstay	**Tel:** (07) 868 8929	**Cost:** Double $100-$120
Self-contained Farmstay	**Fax:** (07) 868 8926	Single $80 Visa/MC
8km SE of Thames	**W:** www.bnb.co.nz/hosts/	**Beds:** 1 Double 2 Single
Rosemary Burks	wharfedalefarmstay.html	(2 bdrm)
RD 1		**Bath:** 2 Private
Kopu Thames		

Thames

A small elegant lodge nestled in the foothills of the Coromandel Peninsula overlooking the historic gold and timber town of Thames. We are 1 hours drive from Auckland International Airport. The tree lined property offers 4 luxury chalets set apart which have generous decks with magnificent views. Thames is the ideal base to explore the rest of the Peninsula and is away for the hustle and bustle of the city. Included are 2 studios and 2 two bedroom chalets all with tea/coffee, fridge, sinks, and microwave.

Grafton Cottage	**Tel:** (07) 868 9971	**Cost:** Double $110-$150
Self-contained	**Fax:** (07) 868 3075	Single $95 Visa/MC
3km SE of Thames	**Mob:** 021 139 4012	**Beds:** 1 Queen 4 Double
Ferne & David Tee	**E:** graftcot@ihug.co.nz	2 Single (6 bdrm)
304 Grafton Road	**W:** www.bnb.co.nz/hosts/	**Bath:** 6 Ensuite
Thames	graftoncottage.html	

Thames

Share in Thames' early history, stay in our Lovely Victorian House which is comfortable, homely and smokefree. Our large grounds include mature trees, swimming pool (summer) and grass tennis court. The house features large comfortable bedrooms, guest lounge with TV, stereo and extensive library, billiard room, S/S tea and coffee. Our interests include travel, steam trains, embroidery, dancing, reading, gardening and our lovable cat and dog. Directions: Opposite Toyota Plant turn into Banks Street . Right into Parawai Rd and find us 200 m further on left.

Brunton House	**Tel:** (07) 868 5160	**Cost:** Double $95 Single $60
B&B Homestay	**Fax:** (07) 868 5160	Dinner $25 B/A Visa/MC
1.5km SE of Thames	**Mob:** 025 627 4272	**Beds:** 2 Queen 1 Double
Albert & Yvonne Sturgess	**E:** BruntonHouse@xtra.Co.Nz	2 Single (3 bdrm)
210 Parawai Road	**W:** www.bnb.co.nz/hosts/	**Bath:** 1 Guests share
Thames	bruntonhouse.html	1 Family share

Thames

Each guest has an ensuite and tea/coffee facilities.
Relax and enjoy the tranquility of the Valley, hike in
the nearby Forest Park or circle the Peninsula to view
the famous Coromandel scenery. We're in our mid
50's, enjoy meeting travellers, love the rural lifestyle,
grow fruit/vegetables and pamper Bart the cat on our 4
acre property. Turn at BP corner (south end of
township) into Banks Street then follow Parawai Road
into the Valley. We're 8 km s from BP. Just 1 1/2
hours from Auckland.

Huia Lodge
Homestay
8km E of Thames
Val & Steve Barnes
589 Kauaeranga Valley Road
Thames

Tel: (07) 868 6557
Fax: (07) 868 6557
E: HuiaLodge@thames-info.co.nz
W: www.thames-info.co.nz/
HuiaLodge

Cost: Double $75 Single $40
Child $20 Dinner $20 B/A
Visa/MC
Beds: 2 Queen 2 Single
(3 bdrm)
Bath: 2 Ensuite

Thames

Allan and I grow mandarins, olives, native trees & raise
coloured sheep on a small organic farm. Our guest wing
with lounge, fridge, TV and extensive library has bedrooms
with decks overlooking river and mountains. Coromandel
forest park has superb walking tracks or nearby you can
amble over neighbouring farmland or swim in forest pools.
We have a relaxed garden, Jack Russell Roly and cat
Mehitable. We love meeting people often cooking for
guests mostly from farm produce. Come and let us look
after you.

Mountain Top B&B
Homestay
6.4km E of Thames
Allan Berry & Elizabeth
McCracken
452 Kauaeranga Valley Road
RD 2 Thames

Tel: (07) 868 9662
Fax: (07) 868 9662
E: mtopbb@voyager.co.nz
W: www.bnb.co.nz/hosts/
mountaintopbb.html

Cost: Double $90-$95
Single $50 Child 1/2 price
Dinner $20 - $30
Visa/MC Amex Diners
Beds: 1 Queen 1 Double
1 Single (2 bdrm)
Bath: 1 Guests share

Thames

Relax and enjoy the tranquil views from our spacious
home set in 2 acres of park-like grounds. Enjoy a pot
of tea or coffee and home baking on your sunny patio
or relax in our comfortable guest lounge featuring an
atrium and waterfall. At night marvel at the glow
worms - only 2 mins walk. Our interests include
tramping in the nearby "Forest Park", fishing and
gardening. We share our lifestyle with our friendly
German Shepherd, a cat, and some sheep. A warm
welcome awaits you.

Acorn Lodge
B&B
4km E of Thames
Dennis & Pat
161 Kauaeranga Valley
RD 2 Thames

Tel: (07) 868 8723
Fax: (07) 868 8713
E: AcornLodge@xtra.co.nz
W: www.bnb.co.nz/hosts/
acornlodge.html

Cost: Double $95 Single $55
Dinner $25 by arrangement
Visa/MC
Beds: 1 Queen 1 Double
1 Single (3 bdrm)
Bath: 2 Private

Coromandel

Our homestay is near an attractive safe beach. We have a bush setting and beautiful views of Coromandel Harbour. The area is very quiet and peaceful. Vic is a professional furniture/designer maker. Hilary enjoys gardening, spinning, weaving and woodturning. We have a cat and keep a smoke-free home. The house is unsuitable for young children. Take SH25 for 50kms travelling north from Thames. Turn sharp left into Te Kouma Road. After 3kms turn left into Kowhai Drive. We provide dinner by prior arrangement.

Coromandel Homestay
Homestay
11km S of Coromandel
Hilary & Vic Matthews
74 Kowhai Drive
Te Kouma Bay Coromandel

Tel: (07) 866 8046
Fax: (07) 866 8046
E: vc.hm.matthews@xtra.co.nz
W: www.bnb.co.nz/hosts/
coromandelhomestay.html

Cost: Double $80-$90
Single $50
Dinner $30 - $40 Visa/MC
Beds: 1 Queen 1 Double
1 Single (2 bdrm)
Bath: 1 Ensuite 1 Private

Coromandel

Welcome to Jacaranda, a warm relaxing home set on 6 acres of peaceful farmland and beautiful gardens with rural and mountain views. We offer spacious bedrooms, guest lounges and kitchen and ample verandahs. Our meals are delicious featuring home grown organic foods plus local seafood, served overlooking the rose garden whenever possible. Jacaranda is an excellent base close to all the peninisula's attractions. Gayle loves tramping the amazing local trails. Gary loves fishing, golf and tennis and we will happily organise these or any other activities.

Jacaranda Lodge
B&B Homestay
3km S of Coromandel
Gayle & Gary Bowler
3195 Tiki Road
RD 1 Coromandel

Tel: (07) 866 8002
Fax: (07) 866 8002
E: jacarandaCOROMANDEL
@xtra.co.nz
W: http://also.as/bowler
www.bnb.co.nz/hosts/
jacarandalodge.html

Cost: Double $90-$125 Single $50-$100
Dinner $30 - $40
Beach House $80 - $120
Visa/MC
Beds: 3 Queen 1 Double
1 Twin (5 bdrm)
Bath: 2 Ens. 1 Priv. 1 G/Share

Coromandel

We invite you to share our recently renovated home on 1 1/2 acres of rural land. Views of surrounding farmland and bush-clad hills. A long shady verandah provides an opportunity to relax or enjoy breakfast outdoors. Dinner includes home-grown produce, our lamb, local seafood and complimentary NZ wines. Guests have the opportunity to talk to our sheep, make acquaintance with George our cat and explore the Peninsula with its varied attractions. Laundry facilities available.

Huntington Lodge
B&B Homestay
1.5km S of Coromandel
Judy & Bill Lightfoot
1745 Tiki Road
Coromandel

Tel: (07) 866 7499
Fax: (07) 866 7499
E: huntington@wave.co.nz
W: www.huntingtonlodge.co.nz

Cost: Double $90 Single $50
Child neg Dinner $35 B/A
Visa/MC
Beds: 1 King 1 Queen
1 Single (2 bdrm)
Bath: 1 Guests share

Coromandel

Geoff and I are a retired couple who enjoy meeting
people, and invite you to a restful holiday in a country
setting. With newly established trees and gardens,
roses a speciality. You have the independence of 4
units situated apart from our home, all with fold out
sofas, TV, fridge, tea and coffee making facilities. You
have a country touch feeling with only a 10 minute
stroll to Coromandel township, where you can enjoy
our local arts, crafts and restaurants. Come and enjoy.

Country Touch
B&B Self-contained
0.5 N of Coromandel
Colleen & Geoff Innis
39 Whangapoua Road
Coromandel

Tel: (07) 866 8310
Fax: (07) 866 8310
Mob: 025 971 196
E: countrytouch@xtra.co,nz
W: www.bnb.co.nz/hosts/
countrytouch.html

Cost: Double $90 Single $65
Child $10 Visa/MC
Beds: 2 Queen 4 Single
(4 bdrm)
Bath: 4 Ensuite

Coromandel

Be our guests in beautiful Coromandel. We have three
guest bedrooms and guest lounge with TV, tea/coffee
making facilities. Views to the East are bush clad hills
and to the West sea views and spectacular sunsets.
Enjoy breakfast served in the garden. Take a leisurely
5-10 minutes stroll into Coromandel Town with lovely
craft shops and restaurants. Experience a walk in
indigenous forest, ride a unique miniature railway and
visit beautiful gardens. Golf course, bowls and
beaches nearby. Internet/web access. Hosts; Estelle &
Ross.

The Green House
B&B
0.5km S of Coromandel
Ross & Estelle Cashmore
505 Tiki road
Coromandel

Tel: (07) 866 7303
E: rosstelle@paradise.net.nz
W: www.bnb.co.nz/hosts/
thegreenhouse.html

Cost: Double $100 Single $50
Visa/MC
Beds: 2 Queen 2 Single
(3 bdrm)
Bath: 1 Ensuite 1 Guests share

Coromandel

AJ's HOMESTAY with panoramic sea views overlooking
the Coromandel Harbour, spectacular sunsets. Five-minute
walk to a safe swimming beach. Most mornings breakfast
is served on the terrace. Our games room has a billiard and
table tennis table. Dinner can be arranged. Directions,
Thames coast main road (SH25) Approx. 50 mins. At the
bottom of the last hill overlooking the Coromandel
Harbour. Turn sharp left, at the Te Kouma Rd sign. Travel
past the boat ramp, next turn left. Kowhai Dr.

AJ's Homestay
Homestay
10km S of Coromandel
Annette & Ray Hintz
24 Kowhai Drive
Te Kouma, RD
Coromandel

Tel: (07) 866 7057
Fax: (07) 866 7057
Mob: 025 581 624
E: rm.aj.hintz@actrix.gen.nz
W: www.bnb.co.nz/hosts/
ajshomestay.html

Cost: Double $85-$120
Single $70 Dinner $25 - $35
Visa/MC
Beds: 1 Queen 1 Double
1 Single (2 bdrm)
Bath: 1 Ensuite 1 Family share

Matarangi Beach

We invite you to share with us the natural beauty and peaceful tranquillity that is Matarangi Beach. A sun and sea paradise providing an escape from today's busy lifestyles. Activities include swimming, tennis, golf, power cycle rentals, beach and bush walks. Our family of four adults have now been replaced by three cats who own us. The guests' bedrooms are upstairs and are warm and inviting, served by their own bathroom. We look forward to the pleasure of your company and ensuring your stay is a memorable one.

Pinekatz
Homestay
24km N of Whitianga
Glenys & Trevor Lewis
108 Matarangi Drive
Matarangi Beach, RD 2 Whitianga

Tel: (07) 866 2103
Fax: (07) 866 2103
Mob: 021 461 136
E: pinekatz@wave.co.nz
W: www.bnb.co.nz/hosts/
pinekatz.html

Cost: Double $80 Single $50
Dinner $20pp - B/A
Visa/MC
Beds: 1 Queen 2 Single
(2 bdrm)
Bath: 1 Guests share

Kuaotunu

"Country Living with Style and Comfort", with Swiss/Kiwi family on 5 1/2 hectare "Paradise" above the Pacific. Exquisite Meals - Swiss Chef using top quality produce and woodfired oven served in guests dining room or Panoramic Gazebo. Walk to clean, safe, white sandy beaches, enjoy the peace and tranquility of Kuaotunu. Bushwalks, tennis, fishing, kayaking, swimming. Golf and horse trekking nearby. Ideal starting point for exploring glorious Coromandel Peninsula or relaxing. Our daughter and pets will make children welcome.
AND OUR VIEW? JUST THE BEST!

The Kaeppeli's
B&B   Country Stay
17km N of Whitianga
Jill & Robert Kaeppeli
Grays Avenue RD 2
Whitianga

Tel: (07) 866 2445
Mob: 025 656 3442
E: kaeppeli_kuaotunu_nz
@paradise.net.nz.
W: www.whitianga.co.nz/
kaeppeli

Cost: Double $70-$120
Single $45-$70
Children 6-12yrs 1/2 price
Dinner $28 Visa/MC
Beds: 2 King 4 Single (4 bdrm)
Bath: 2 Ensuite
1 Guests share

Kuaotunu

We offer you the upper level of our architecturally designed home with spectacular views over the beach and pohutukawa trees to the Mercury Islands and Great Barrier. The master (or mistress) guestroom has queen bed, window seats and small private balcony. Children love the family guestroom, double bed, two singles, bunks, cot, TV/video, plenty of toys, games, kids' videos. Our lifestlye is enhanced by our Retriever, Poodle and little Foxy. We are two professional women whom also manage 200 Private Beach Houses available for holiday rental.

Blue Penguin
B&B
17km N of Whitianga
Glenda & Barbara
11 Cuvier Crescent
Kuaotunu, RD 2, Whitianga
Coromandel Peninsula

Tel: (07) 866 2222
Fax: (07) 866 0228
E: holidayhomes
@bluepenguin.co.nz
W: www.bluepenguin.co.nz

Cost: Double $95-$110
Single $65 Child $30
Dinner $20 B/A
Visa/MC
Beds: 1 Queen 1 Double 4
Single (2 bdrm)
Bath: 1 Guests share

Kuaotunu

Situated on the coast our new home has been purpose built
for guests with ensuites and underfloor heating. Enjoy
breakfast in the sunny conservatory or on the deck listening
to the waves. The safe beach is just a short walk through
the garden. Ideal for all sea activities, fishing, kayaking or
explore the local art and craft. Whitianga with its
restaurants and tourist activities is a 20 minute drive. Our 10
acre property has a small bush reserve, sheep and a friendly
dog. Welcome.

Kuaotunu Bay Lodge
B&B Self-contained Homestay
18km N of Whitianga
Lorraine and Bill Muir
State Highway 25
Kuaotunu, RD 2
Whitianga

Tel: (07) 866 4396
Fax: (07) 866 4396
Mob: 025 601 3665
E: muir@kuaotunubay.co.nz
W: www.kuaotunubay.co.nz

Cost: Double $130-$150
Single $95 Dinner $35pp
Visa/MC
Beds: 2 Queen 2 Single
(3 bdrm)
Bath: 2 Ensuite 1 Private

Kuaotunu

Welcome is assured at Drift In. This tranquil
comfortable modern cedar home is designed to take
full advantage of the sun and breathtaking views of the
Great Barrier and Mercury Islands, by day and moonlit
night. An unique beach theme pervades our house and
garden. Breakfast is a memorable occasion with sight
and sounds of birds and sea complimenting an
excellent range of home cooking. Only a minute walk
to safe white-sand beaches and rock pools. Drift in,
relax and enjoy this special part of New Zealand.

Drift In B&B
B&B Homestay
17km N of Whitianga
Yvonne & Peppe Thompson
16 Grays Avenue
Kuaotunu, RD 2
Whitianga

Tel: (07) 866 4321
Fax: (07) 866 4321
Mob: 025 245 3632
W: www.bnb.co.nz/hosts/
driftinbb.html

Cost: Double $80-$90
Single $50
Child $30, 5 - 12yrs
Dinner B/A Visa/MC
Beds: 1 Queen 2 Single
(2 bdrm)
Bath: 1 Guests share

Kuaotunu

"PITOONE" is a 30 ha hilly Farm, with 7ha of wonderful
native bush, enjoyable walkways and its own wondrous
waterfall. Five min drive to the beautiful Kuaotunu beach
and Matarangi Golf Course. The very charming chalet,
overlooking the native bush to the Pacific Ocean has full
cooking facilities, open fire place, living area that opens to a
deck where you can imagine sipping a glass of wine as you
listen to the sound of the bush and feel the tranquillity. The
perfect "Get Away".

Pitoone
Farmstay Self-contained Chalet
14km N of Whitianga
Annegrit, Michael
& Jessica (8yrs) Brueck
1120 State Highway 25
Kuaotunu, RD 2
Whitianga

Tel: (07) 866 2690
Fax: (07) 866 2690
E: a.m.brueck@xtra.co.nz
W: www.bnb.co.nz/hosts/
pitoone.html

Cost: Double $130-$155
Dinner by arrangement
Beds: 1 Queen 2 Single
(1 bdrm)
Bath: 1 Private

Whitianga

Welcome to our picturesque two storied cottage filled with feline memorabilia! Relax with complimentary tea or coffee served on the veranda or in the guest lounge. Enjoy a good nights rest in comfortable beds & choose a variety of treats from our breakfast blackboard menu. You will probably like to meet Sylvie the cat or perhaps visit the cat hotel in the garden. A separate cottage is available with Queen beds, bathrooms and kitchen. Friendly helpful service is assured - Hope to see you Soon!

Cosy Cat Cottage
B&B Self-contained
1km S of Whitianga
Gordon Pearce
41 South Highway
Whitianga

Tel: (07) 866 4488
Fax: (07) 866 4488
Mob: 025 798 745
E: cosycat@whitianga.co.nz
W: www.bnb.co.nz/hosts/
cosycatcottage.html

Cost: Double $80-$95
Single $50-$60
Cottage $80 - $95
Visa/MC
Beds: 2 Queen 1 Double
1 Single (3 bdrm)
Bath: 2 Ensuite 1 Private

Whitianga

Welcome to our comfortable modern home and the tranquillity of our garden. Tea or coffee is available at any time. Guests share the lounge/TV room. The shower, toilet and bathroom are each separate rooms for easy access. Bob and Anne are ordinary Kiwis in our 50's, Bob enjoys building and flying radio controlled aircraft, Anne makes pottery, line-dances and gardens. We have two friendly cats. We are a short stroll from the restaurants, shops, beaches and wharf. Free pickup from bus or plane.

Anne's Haven
Homestay
Anne & Bob
119 Albert St
Whitianga

Tel: (07) 866 5550
E: anneshaven@paradise.net.nz
W: www.bnb.co.nz/hosts/
anneshaven.html

Cost: Double $65 Single $40
Child $20 Dinner $20
Beds: 1 Double 2 Single
(2 bdrm)
Bath: 1 Family share

Whitianga

Welcome to our friendly home, which is nestled in a secluded park-like garden, which includes native, and many mature trees. We also offer you a spa and swimming pool and lots of lovely gardens to relax in. You would normally be woken up to the tune of bellbirds, then you settle into a hearty breakfast which will set you up for the whole day. We have a guest lounge and tea and coffee making facilities. We can assure you of a warm friendly welcome and a comfortable stay.

Camellia Lodge
B&B Homestay
3.5km S of Whitianga
Pat & John Lilley
South Highway
RD 1
Whitianga

Tel: (07) 866 2253
Fax: (07) 866 2253
Mob: 021 217 6612
E: camellia@wave.co.nz
W: www.bnb.co.nz/hosts/
camellialodge.html

Cost: Double $90-$105
Single $65 Child 1/2 price
Dinner $25 Visa/MC
Beds: 1 Queen 2 Double 2
Twin (4 bdrm)
Bath: 2 Ensuite 2 Guests share

Whitianga

Looking for comfortable affordable accommodation 3.2km from Whitianga. Hearty cooked breakfast will keep you going all day. 18 hole golf course where hire clubs available is adjacent. Short drive to Whitianga township with many restaurants and your hosts will be only too happy to arrange all holiday wishes. Guest lounge, TV, Tea/Coffee and laundry facilities. Ensuite also available for disabled people. Parking available. Friendly dog and cat. We at A-Hi-way Haven know that you will come as a visitor and depart as a friend.

A Hi-Way Haven	**Tel:** (07) 866 2427	**Cost:** Double $70-$90
B&B Homestay	**Fax:** 64 07 866 2424	Single $40-$50 Visa/MC
3.2km S of Whitianga	**Mob:** 025 627 2044	**Beds:** 1 King/Twin 1 Queen
Joan & Nevin Paton	**E:** hiway@whitianga.co.nz	1 Double 2 Single
1 Golf Rd	**W:** www.bnb.co.nz/hosts/	(4 bdrm)
Whitianga	ahiwayhaven.html	**Bath:** 1 Ensuite 1 Guests share

Whitianga

Welcome to The White House. "When only the Best will do" Relax, sight see and holiday in a friendly comfortable environment. Murray offers a complimentary tour of Whitianga/Mercury Bay. Breakfast is 'special' and pan fried fish and pipi fritters is just one option. Whitianga is a central base to explore the Coromandel and is the nearest town to Hot Water Beach, Cathedral Cove and Shakespeare Cliff. Your hosts Murray & Jessie have backgrounds in Education and Nursing. We are committed to making your stay memorable.

The White House	**Tel:** (07) 866 5116	**Cost:** Double $100-$120
B&B	**Fax:** (07) 866 5116	Single $70
500m Whitianga	**Mob:** 025 341 029	Dinner B/A Visa/MC
Murray & Jessie Thompson	**E:** whitehousebb@paradise.net.nz	**Beds:** 1 King/Twin 1 Queen
129 Albert Street	**W:** homepages.paradise.net.nz/	1 Double 2 Single (3 bdrm)
Whitianga	whitehousebb/	**Bath:** 1 Ensuite 1 Guests share

Whitianga

Enjoy European hospitality in Whitianga's most luxurious Boutique Accommodation. Maria, a ships chef from Poland and New Zealand husband Guy will make your stay a memorable experience. Large luxuriously appointed rooms. Magnificent breakfasts. Superb candlelit dinners or BBQ by arrangement. Laundry, fax and E-mail available. Large guest lounge with Sky TV, books and music. Sunny outdoor area with spa pool.Situated near the beach and next to reserves and farmland ensures absolute peace and quiet. Privacy and discretion assured. You will not regert coming.

At Parkland Place	**Tel:** (07) 866 4987	**Cost:** Double $125-$150
B&B	**Fax:** (07) 866 4946	Single $100 Child Neg
4km N of Whitianga	**Mob:** 025 291 7495	Dinner by arrangement
Maria & Guy Clark	**E:** parklandplace@wave.co.nz	Visa/MC Amex Diners
14 Parkland Place	**W:** www.wave.co.nz/	**Beds:** 2 King 3 Queen
Brophys Beach	atparklandplace	3 Single (5 bdrm)
Whitianga		**Bath:** 3 Ensuite 1 Guests share

Whitianga

Our BEACHFRONT location with a 180 degree view of Mercury Bay from both of our spacious upstairs rooms is unequalled. These rooms offer high quality accommodation with individual tea/coffee making facilities, refrigerators, fans, heaters, table & chairs, TV, radios, electric blankets, reading lights and ensuites with heated towel rails and heaters They open onto a balcony facing the beach where you can photograph the sunrise over the horizon and watch the fishing, sailing and pleasure craft plying our sparkling clean bay.

Our downstairs room faces the garden at the rear of the house. Safe swimming at any stage of the tide, surfcasting or sunbathing is just 30 meters across the grass reserve. Beach lovers can walk the 3km sandy beach, gather shells or just breathe the clean fresh air along the way.

We are just a 5 minute level walk to many waterfront cafes, restaurants, wharf, passenger ferry and the shopping village. Our generous continental breakfasts include something home baked and are served on our covered deck facing the beach (weather permitting).

Our rooms all have secure doors allowing total privacy when required, guests own entrance and off street parking. We are fortunate to have lived in Whitianga for over 40 years and we enjoy sharing our home and our love of the Peninsula with our guests.

Helen is a licensed marriage celebrant, and can arrange a venue and service for couples wishing to marry whilst in the Mercury Bay area.

Our tariff is seasonally priced and we offer a discounted rate for a 3 night stay. Low season rates May to September,we are closed June & July 2002. High season mid December to end February. Courtesy transport to local bus/airfield. Smoke free indoors.

The Beach House
B&B
1km N of Whitianga
Helen & Allan Watson
38 Buffalo Beach Road
P O Box 162
Whitianga

Tel: (07) 866 5647
Fax: (07) 866 5647
Mob: 025 668 2781
E: ahwatson@paradise.net.nz
W: www.bnb.co.nz/hosts/
thebeachhousewhitianga.html

Cost: Double $90-$150
Single $70-$130 Visa/MC
Beds: 1 King/Twin 2 Queen
1 Single (3 bdrm)
Bath: 2 Ensuite 1 Private

Whitianga

You are invited to share our Riverside Retreat beside the waters which run through the beautiful Mahakirau Valley. Your cottage, nestled amongst native trees in 3 acres of landscaped gardens, has fully equipped kitchen, sunny lounge, and queen bedroom on mezzanine floor with views over the garden and river. You can fly-fish for trout, bush walk, or just relax by the river with a book. The perfect place to unwind, soothe the spirit and leave the world behind. Your hosts and moggy "Woz" assure you a relaxing and memorable stay.

Riverside Retreat
B&B Self-contained
6km S of Whitianga
Maree & Richard Prestage
309 Road
RD 1
Whitianga

Tel: (07) 866 5155
Fax: (07) 866 5155
E: retreat@xtra.co.nz
W: www.riversideretreat.co.nz

Cost: Double $120 Single $120
Beds: 1 Queen (1 bdrm)
Bath: 1 Private

Whitianga - Cooks Beach

Mercury Orchard is 5 acres of country garden and organic orchard close to Cooks, Hahei and Hot Water Beaches. Our large guest room opens to private garden and swimming pool, has tea & coffee facilities and ensuite bathroom and adjoining bedroom. Also available - Fig Tree Cottage, self contained country style comfort, opening through French doors into orchard, crisp cotton bed linen, fresh fruit and flowers, breakfast hamper and use of BBQ. We share our smoke-free home with 2 small dogs and a cat. We look forward to making your Coromandel experience a memorable one.

Mercury Orchard
Homestay Rural
17km N of Tairua
Heather and Barry Scott
141 Purangi Road
RD1 Whitianga

Tel: (07) 866 3119
Fax: (07) 866 3115
Mob: 025 283 0176
E: mercorchard@xtra.co.nz
W: www.mercuryorchard.co.nz

Cost: Double $105 Single $75
Dinner $25
S/C Cottage $120 Visa/MC
Beds: 2 Queen (2 bdrm)
Bath: 1 Ensuite 1 Family share

Whitianga - Coroglen

Coroglen Lodge is situated on 17 acres of farmland with cattle, sheep and friendly chickens. Surrounded by hills and nestled in a valley with views of Coromandel Ranges and Whitianga Estuary , this is rural tranquillity. Half way between Whitianga Township and Hot Water Beach there is easy access to both areas and all attractions. We have a garden to roam in, barbecue area with fuel, and full cooking facilities. Two showers, 2 toilets and laundry facilities are available. Guest area is separate and spacious with a large sunny lounge area for your comfort.

Coroglen Lodge
B&B Self-contained Farmstay
14km S of Whitianga
Wendy & Nigel Davidson
2221 State Highway 25
RD 1
Whitianga 2856

Tel: (07) 866 3225
Fax: (07) 866 3235
E: clover@wave.co.nz
W: www.bnb.co.nz/hosts/
coroglenlodge.html

Cost: Double $65-$85 Single
$40-$50 Child $30 Visa/MC
Beds: 1 Queen 1 Double 2
Single (3 bdrm)
Bath: 2 Guests share

Whitianga

Our charming cottage is located opposite the wharf offering peaceful harbour views. A 1 minute stroll takes you to Buffalo Beach. The township, a 2 minute easy walk has excellent restaurants, cafes and shopping. A 4km drive takes you to the 18 hole golf course and busy airfield. Guest share the family lounge with open fire during the cooler months. Breakfast served on sunny deck or room service. Guests own entrance with safe private off street parking. Our lovely home is shared with two quiet cats.

Cottage by the Sea	**Tel:** (07) 866 0605	**Cost:** Double $80-$150
B&B	**Fax:** (07) 866 0675	Single $90 Visa/MC
500m Whitianga	**Mob:** 025 237 6163	**Beds:** 1 King 2 Queen (3 bdrm)
Gayle & Max Murray	**E:** staying@acottagebythesea.com	**Bath:** 1 Ensuite 1 Guests share
11 The Esplanade	**W:** www.bnb.co.nz/hosts/	
Whitianga	cottagebytheseawhitianga.html	

Whitianga

Come and stay view our beautiful million dollar view of the Mercury Bay. Relax on the deck in a hammock, have a spa bath, watch digital Sky TV, or try a Kiwi Experience with a barbeque. Enjoy many beautiful beaches including a hot water beach! Visit our many excellent restaurants and go on many water activities. Ernie is a keen hunter, fisherman and Gaye loves meeting people and is keen on genealogy, history and collecting antiques. We can help people with disabilities as Janet has her National Certificate in Human Services. Children are welcome.

Tranquillity	**Tel:** (07) 866 5005	**Cost:** Double $85-$100
B&B Self-contained	**Fax:** (07) 866 5105	Single $60 Child $30
4km N of Whitianga	**Mob:** 025 279 8174	Dinner $25 B/A Visa/MC
Ernie & Janet Gaye Fraser	**Tollfree:** 0800 005 007	**Beds:** 2 Double 1 Single
2 Cooks Lookout	**E:** tranquillityb&b@xtra.co.nz	(2 bdrm)
Whitianga	**W:** www.dreamland.co.nz/	**Bath:** 1 Guests share
	tranquillity	

Hahei

The Church is Hahei's newest and most unique accommodation and dining experience. The Church building provides a character dining room/licensed restaurant for wholesome breakfasts and delicious evening meals. Ten cosy wooden cottages scattered through delightful bush and gardens offer a range of accommodation and tariffs, with ensuites, fridges and tea and coffee facilities (some fully self-contained). Enjoy our warm hospitality, the wonders of Cathedral Cove, Hot Water Beach, and the Coromandel Peninsula. We live on site with our 11yr old daughter, dog and cat. Seasonal rates. Smoking outside.

The Church	**Tel:** (07) 866 3533	**Cost:** Double $90-$140
B&B Self-contained	**Fax:** (07) 866 3055	Single $80-$100 Child $15
38km S of Whitianga	**Mob:** 025 596 877	Dinner Menu Visa/MC
Richard Agnew & Karen Blair	**E:** hahei4ch@voyager.co.nz	**Beds:** 10 Queen (10 bdrm)
87 Beach Road	**W:** thechurchhahei.co.nz	**Bath:** 10 Ensuite
Hahei, RD 1 Whitianga		

Hahei Beach

Barbara and I live overlooking the sea with panoramic views from the Alderman Islands to the Mercury Islands. We are five minutes from Hahei Beach and are on the road to Cathedral Cove and its beaches, a must when visiting this area. Hot Water Beach is just a short distance away where you can enjoy a warm soak at any time of the year.

The area offers bush walks, surf beaches, fishing and spectacular views for photography. "The Paradise Coast". Most rooms have sea views with ensuites/private bathrooms, all beds have electric blankets and insect screens are fitted to most windows.

We have tea/coffee making facilities and a refrigerator for the use of all guests. We can assure you of excellent meals. My wife is a first class cook, at least, I think so. Weather permitting, our generous continental breakfast is served on our front deck.

We thank you for not smoking in the house. We have no animals.

Please give us a telephone call when you wish to come and we can promise you a most enjoyable stay.

Directions: Turn off at Whenuakite (Highway 25). Grange Road is on left by Hahei Store. We are on left near top of hill. Look for 'Spellbound' signs, follow Service Road. Street numbers not consecutive.

Spellbound Homestay - B&B
Homestay
36km N of Tairua
Barbara & Alan Lucas
Grange Road
Hahei Beach, RD 1
Whitianga

Tel: (07) 866 3543
Fax: (07) 866 3003
Mob: 025 720 407
E: spellbound@whitianga.co.nz
W: www.bnb.co.nz/hosts/
spellboundhomestaybb.html

Cost: Double $100-$125
Single $60-$85 Child by
arrangement Dinner $25
Beds: 2 King/Twin 2 Queen
(4 bdrm)
Bath: 3 Ensuite 1 Private

Hahei Beach

Come and unwind in our comfortable private upstairs studio apartment and enjoy the sea views and relaxing atmosphere. Take a 200m stroll to the beautiful beach and experience the magic of Hahei. Cathedral Cove walkway and Hot Water beach are nearby. Scenic boat/ dive trips are easily arranged with local operators. We have an adult family scattered around the world and two friendly cats. We thank you for not smoking indoors. We enjoy an active retired lifestyle, so please phone ahead for bookings and directions.

Cedar Lodge
Homestay
36km N of Tairua
Jenny & John Graham
36 Beach Road
Hahei, RD 1
Whitianga

Tel: (07) 866 3789
Fax: (07) 866 3978
E: cedarlodge@wave.co.nz
W: www.bnb.co.nz/hosts/
cedarlodge.html

Cost: Double $90 Single $60
Visa/MC Amex Diners
Beds: 1 Queen 1 Single
(1 bdrm)
Bath: 1 Private

Hahei Beach

Relax and enjoy the breathtaking views and the absolute privacy of our Bed and Breakfast. Having Cathedral Cove and Hot Water Beach just 5 minutes away, we are perfectly situated for your stay in Hahei. We offer you a warm, homely stay with excellent breakfast. Our cottage, surrounded by native bush, contains ensuite, tea and coffee making facilities and fridge. Feel free to use our laundry and barbecue terrace. Portacot available. We have two children and a friendly cat. Directions: Please phone for directions.

Bon Appetit Hahei
B&B Homestay Cottage
36km N of Tairua
Andy & Monika Schuerch
Orchard Road
Hahei, RD 1
Whitianga

Tel: (07) 866 3116
Fax: (07) 866 3117
Mob: 025 293 0929
E: schuerch@wave.co.nz
W: www.bonappetit.co.nz

Cost: Double $85-$95
Beds: 1 Queen (1 bdrm)
Bath: 1 Private

Hot Water Beach

Hot Water Beach is a beautiful surf beach. At low tide hot water bubbles up at a particular place in the sand and you dig yourself a "hot pool". Our house is surrounded by huge Pohutukawa trees, 150 metres from the sea. We have a terrier and Joe makes home-brew beer. Apartments are comfortably furnished and we provide tea, coffee, bread, butter, jam, milk and cereals. Guests prepare breakfast at preferred time. Nearest restaurant 10 minutes away at Hahei. Directions: Turn right into Radar Road 200 metres before shop.

Auntie Dawns Place
Self-contained
24km N of Tairua
Dawn & Joe Nelmes
Radar Road
Hot Water Beach, RD 1
Whitianga

Tel: (07) 866 3707
Fax: (07) 866 3701
E: AuntieDawn@MercuryBay.co.nz
W: www.bnb.co.nz/hosts/
auntiedawnsplace.html

Cost: Double $75-$90
Single $40 Child $15
Visa/MC
Beds: 2 Queen 1 Double
1 Single (2 bdrm)
Bath: 2 Private

Hot Water Beach

We have a spacious elevated home with extensive decks, on which you can have fresh coffee or juice, while enjoying sweeping panoramic sea/beach views. Sit under the brilliant southern stars in our spa pool or play on our full sized billiard table. You can swim, surf, dive, fish, kayak, play golf, bushwalk, horse trek or visit spectacular Cathedral Cove or alternatively just dig a hole and soak in the natural hot springs on our beach. We have two cats and a sociable boxer.

Hot Water Beach B&B
B&B Homestay
32km S of Whitianga
Gail & Trevor Knight
48 Pye Place
Hot Water Beach, RD 1
Whitianga

Tel: (07) 866 3991
Fax: (07) 866 3291
Mob: 025 799 620
E: TKnight@xtra.co.nz
W:
www.hotwaterbedandbreakfast.co.nz

Cost: Double $125-$140
Single $100-$120
Dinner $30
Visa/MC Amex Diners
Beds: 2 Queen (2 bdrm)
Bath: 2 Ensuite

Tairua

Situated on the foothills of Tairua. Our boutique accommodation offers Rest and Tranquillity for that perfect "Get Away" break. Our bedrooms have own ensuite with fridge, tea & coffee making facilities. The Guest TV lounge opens onto BBQ area, swimming pool and garden. Breakfast is a house specialty, delicious continental choices served in the dining room with its ever-changing views of Tairua Harbour and Paku Mountain. Enjoy our beaches, bush walks, fishing, diving, and golfing. Good Restaurants. Close to Cathedral Cove & Hot Water Beach. Website www.nz.com/webnzkotuku.

Kotuku Lodge
B&B
45km E of Thames
Pauline and Ian Monk
179 Main Road Tairua

Tel: (07) 864 7040
Fax: (07) 864 7040
Tollfree: 0800 228 997
E: kotuku@wave.co.nz
W: www.bnb.co.nz/hosts/
kotukulodge.html

Cost: Double $90-$125
Single $65-$75 Child $25
Visa/MC
Beds: 1 King 1 Queen
1 Double 1 Single (3 bdrm)
Bath: 3 Ensuite

Tairua

'On The Edge' of Paku Hill, panoramic views of the Pacific Ocean and islands. Ideally situated for walks to Paku Hill with spectacular views of Pauanui and Tairua. 20mins north - Hot Water Beach and Cathedral Cove. Close to 18 hole golf course and good restaurants. Andrea and James have travelled extensively, spending their leisure time diving, fishing and skiing. With their intimate knowledge of the Coromandel Peninsula they can provide a tour of the Coromandel in their green coach. Andrea is a registered nurse and can assist people with 'special needs'. Our adult children are not at home, only our cat.

On the Edge - Tairua
Homestay
30km E of Thames
Andrea Marylin Patten
219 Paku Drive
Tairua Coromandel Peninsula

Tel: (07) 864 8285
Fax: (07) 864 8232
Mob: 025 736 176
E: ontheedge@tairua.co.nz
W: www.bnb.co.nz/hosts/
ontheedgetairua.html

Cost: Double $140 Single $100
Child $50 Dinner $25
Visa/MC
Beds: 1 Queen (2 bdrm)
Bath: 1 Private

Tairua

Beautiful, quiet harbour location with sunbathing beach and safe swimming on the doorstep. Homely hospitality or if desired 'just leave you to it'. Your own private garden area with table and chairs overlooks numerous harbour activities. The apartment is self contained and fully equipped and garage for your car. Ideal for self catering and offers discerning private comfort for up to four persons. Boat launching location and wharf fishing nearby. This is our paradise which we invite you to share for a while. Your stay will be one to remember. Continental breakfast (on request) included in tariff. Not one disappointed guest. Directions: Please phone

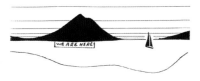

Esplanade Apartment
JH & S Charlton
18 The Esplanade
Tairua 2853 via Thames

Tel: (07) 864 8997
Fax: (07) 864 8997
E: jcharlton@wave.co.nz
W: www.nz-coromandel.com/
tairua/esplanade.html

Cost: Double $65-$95
Visa/MC
Beds: 1 Queen 2 Single
(1 bdrm)
Bath: 1 Ensuite

Pauanui Beach

Pauanui is on the east coast of the Coromandel Peninsula and one of the most magnificently planned resorts in this area with red chip roads to add to the landscape. Activities are catered for by 9 and 10 hole golf courses, 4 tennis complexes each with 4 courts, mini-putt, restaurants. Self help continental breakfast is provided, we have ideal self catering facilites. We have 3 units, each with ensuites, TV, fridge and tea/coffee facilities. Included in tariff are bikes, canoes and windsurfers. We also cater for fishing trips and scenic tours. Nearest town Thames 40 mins, Hot water beach 1 hr, Tairua 20 mins (5 min by ferry). Auckland 2 hrs.

Pauanui Pacific Holidays
Tourist Accomodation
50km E of Thames
Kevin & Kay Flooks
Box 144
7 Brodie Lane Pauanui Beach

Tel: (07) 864 8933
Fax: (07) 864 8253
Mob: 025 971 305
E: pauanui.pacific@xtra.co.nz
W: www.bnb.co.nz/hosts/
pauanuipacificholidays.html

Cost: Double $110-$120
Single $80-$120 Visa/MC
Beds: 1 Queen 1 Double
2 Single (3 bdrm)
Bath: 3 Ensuite

Pauanui Beach

Our relaxing smoke-free home, close to the harbour and walking distance to the ocean beach can be the start of your Coromandel experience. Your room has twin beds, and ensuite bathroom, TV and tea/coffee making facilities. We serve a continental breakfast in the sunroom or garden. There is a choice of local licensed restaurants. Here you can golf, bowl, play tennis or just laze on the beach. We and Misty, our little dog, look forward to making your stay enjoyable.

Ash-Leigh Cottage
B&B
50km E of Thames
Joan & Alan Parker
11 Golden Hills Drive
Pauanui Beach

Tel: (07) 864 8103
Fax: (07) 864 8752
E: ashleighp@wave.co.nz
W: www.bnb.co.nz/hosts/
ashleighcottage.html

Cost: Double $90
Beds: 2 Single (1 bdrm)
Bath: 1 Ensuite

Whangamata

Brenton Lodge provides superior boutique accommodation with style. A superb country retreat for the discerning visitor ..... intimate and personal. Escape & Enjoy, Peace, Privacy & Pampering. Glorious sea views, beautiful gardens & swimming pool, situated just 2 km's from the surf beach and village. Charming Guest Cottages are tastefully decorated, cotton sheets, fresh flowers. Gourmet Breakfasts served in the privacy of your room or alfresco on your balcony.

Brenton Lodge	**Tel:** (07) 865 8400	**Cost:** Double $250 Single $230
Guest Lodge	**Fax:** (07) 865 8400	Extra person $60
2km W of Whangamata	**Mob:** 025 780 134	Visa/MC Amex
Jan & Paul Campbell	**E:** brentonlodge@xtra.co.nz	**Beds:** 3 Queen (3 bdrm)
1 Brenton Place	**W:** www.brentonlodge.co.nz	**Bath:** 3 Ensuite
Whangamata		

Whangamata

Just 5km off SH25 (golf course), across a river ford, you will find the award winning lodge and unique German Black Forest winery style gourmet restaurant set in 2 hectares of native rainforest and park grounds. Two cosy bedrooms with balcony and two spacious suites with private decks. Wentworth Falls walkway and perfect beaches. Ideal for romantic escape! No TV reception! But: water lily pond, Nikau palm glow worm grotto, family cats, outdoor bush sauna, hydrotherapeutic spa pool, massages, beauty treatments. Rest and Relaxation at its best!

Bushland Park Lodge	**Tel:** (07) 865 7468	**Cost:** Double $175-$290
Country Retreat Gourmet Restaurant	**Fax:** (07) 865 7486	Single $175-$290
6km S of Whangamata	**Mob:** 025 200 7972	Dinner $60
Petra & Reinhard Nickel	**E:** bushparklodge@xtra.co.nz	Visa/MC Amex Diners
PO Box 190	**W:** www.wellness.co.nz	**Beds:** 2 King/Twin 2 Queen
Wentworth Valley Road		(4 bdrm)
Whangamata		**Bath:** 4 Ensuite

Whangamata

Experience genuine Kiwi hospitality with Bev & George who welcome you to their comfortable, clean, modern, smoke-free home only minutes from our magnificent surf beach - handy to town, park, golf and surf club. Guests have their own lounge with TV, tea & coffee making facilities, microwave and fridge. Our interests are travel, gardening, sport, fishing, tramping and conservation. Whangamata offers surfing, boating, swimming, fishing, and tramping through beautiful bush. We have Alice - a friendly boxer dog and a cat. Please phone for bookings and directions.

Il Casa Moratti	**Tel:** (07) 865 6164	**Cost:** Double $95 Single $70
Homestay	**Fax:** (06) 865 6164	Dinner $25 B/A Visa/MC
1km N of Whangamata	**Mob:** 021 685 027	**Beds:** 1 Double 2 Single
Bev & George Moratti	**E:** ilcasamoratti@xtra.co.nz	(2 bdrm)
313 Mary Road	**W:** www.bnb.co.nz/hosts/	**Bath:** 1 Guests share
Whangamata	ilcasamoratti.html	

Whangamata

Extra touches, something special. Free Whangamata tour.
Two hours from Rotorua or Auckland. Use our delightful
modern homestay in riverside setting as a base to explore the
superb beaches and bushwalks of Whangamata and the
Coromandel Peninsula. Enjoy quality cuisine with produce
from our garden. Your party will be our only guests.
Children welcome. We will help you share our interests -
golf, fishing, boating, snorkelling, travel, petanque, floral art,
gardening, kite flying. Free guest double kayak. Help with
your itinerary. Individualised tours with licensed operator -
luxury car. Cat.

Waireka Lodge
Homestay
1km N of Whangamata
Gail & Dick Wilson
108 Waireka Place Whangamata

Tel: (07) 865 8859
Fax: (07) 865 8859
Mob: 025 274 1000
E: waireka@whangamata.co.nz
W: www.bnb.co.nz/hosts/
wairekalodge.html

Cost: Double $90-$110
Single $65-$75 Child $25
Dinner $25 Visa/MC
Beds: 1 Queen 2 Single
(2 bdrm)
Bath: 1 Private

Whangamata (Rural)

Character country home situated on 3 acres, at the
Southern end of the stunning Coromandel Peninsula.
Copsefield is purpose built for your comfort, with 3
ensuite rooms. All rooms are non-smoking. Two
beaches close by . Canoes, bikes, walks, spa pool.
Peace and tranquility beside native bush and river.
Guest lounge with TV, tea and coffee. Complimentary
wine. Full breakfast including home grown eggs and
fresh fruit. Your hosts Trish & Richard offer you a
warm and friendly welcome, and personal attention.

Copsefield B&B
B&B
8km N of Whangamata
Richard and Trish Davison
1055 S.H. 25
RD 1
Whangamata

Tel: (07) 865 9555
Fax: (07) 865 9555
Mob: 025 289 0131
E: copsefield@xtra.co.nz
W: www.copsefield.co.nz

Cost: Double $130
Single $90
Child under 5 free
Visa/MC
Beds: 2 Queen 2 Single
(3 bdrm)
Bath: 3 Ensuite

Whangamata

We are ideally located close to the town centre and very
handy to Whangamata's shops, cafes and restaurants,
and an easy stroll to the surf beach, harbour and wharf.
Our home, in its cottage and rose garden setting, has
three tastefully decorated guest bedrooms, all with
comfortable beds, TVs and ensuite bathrooms.
Complimentary tea and coffee available in guest lounge.
Enjoy our extensive breakfast and use our home as a
base to relax and enjoy the natural attractions that
Whangamata and area has to offer. We have a cat.

Sandy Rose Bed & Breakfast
B&B Homestay
200m N of town centre
Shirley & Murray Calman
Corner Hetherington &
Rutherford Roads
Whangamata

Tel: (07) 865 6911
Fax: (07) 865 6911
Mob: 025 711 220
E: sandyrose@whangamata.co.nz
W: sandyrose.whangamata.co.nz

Cost: Double $110 Single $85
Visa/MC
Beds: 1 Queen 4 Single
(3 bdrm)
Bath: 3 Ensuite

Waihi

We offer a friendly restful smoke-free stay in our modern home and garden. Waihi is the gate way to both the Coromandel with its beautiful beaches and the Bay of Plenty. Waihi is a historic town with vintage railway running to Waikino, a working gold mine discovered 1878 closed 1952. Reopened in 1989 as a open-cast mine. Free mine tours available. Beach 10 min away, beautiful bush walks, golf courses, trout fishing. Enjoy a home cooked meal or sample our restaurants. Our interests are gardening, dancing and travel.

West Wind Gardens
B&B Homestay
1km N of Waihi
Josie & Bob French
22 Roycroft Street
Waihi

Tel: (07) 863 7208
W: www.bnb.co.nz/hosts/
westwind.html

Cost: Double $65 Single $35
Child $15 Dinner $20
Visa/MC
Beds: 4 Single (2 bdrm)
Bath: 1 Guests share

Waihi Beach

"Waves" is just a few sandy steps to the Pacific surf. Swimming, fishing, golfing, flying, boating, bowling, tennis, adventure activities are all close by. A great year round holiday place. Waihi is the gateway to the beautiful Coromandel Peninsula and The Bay Of Plenty fruit bowl. "Waves" offers comfortable, friendly Bed & Breakfast or fully equipped self - catering accommodation. Discuss your options with Margaret & George. They are a much travelled, hospitable couple who will help make your stay memorable. "Waves" is smoke free. Children welcome.

"Waves"

Waves
B&B Self catering
13km E of Waihi
Margaret & George Collins
169 Seaforth Road
Waihi Beach

Tel: (07) 863 4771
Fax: (07) 863 4772
Mob: 025 487 603
E: wavesatwaihibeach@yahoo.co.nz
W: www.bnb.co.nz/hosts/
waves.html

Cost: Double $95 $70
Up to 4 people Self catering
$120
Beds: 1 Queen 1 Twin 1 Single
(2 bdrm)
Bath: 2 Private

Waihi Beach

Welcome to my home overlooking Waihi Beach a true living leisure treasure. Breathtaking seaviews from 3 level brick home set in cottage and tropical gardens. Guest lounge with TV, microwave, fridge and tea making facilities. There is a 5 minute walk to beach (about 8km of rippling white sand). Lovely bush walk, two golf courses and a large goldmine in Waihi. Restaurants near by. Waihi Beach is truly the centre of a visitors paradise. My interests are badminton, handcraft, gardening and providing for you.

Seaview
Homestay
10km E of Waihi
Dulcie Cooper
12 Mayor View Terrace
Waihi Beach

Tel: (07) 863 5041
Fax: (07) 863 5041
Mob: 025 217 3584
W: www.bnb.co.nz/hosts/
seaviewwaihibeach.html

Cost: Double $85 Single $60
Child $15 under 13
Dinner $25
Beds: 1 Queen 2 Single
(2 bdrm)
Bath: 1 Private

Waihi Beach

Waterfront Homestay Fully self contained two double bedrooms plus single bed. Very suitable for two couples or small family group. Unit on lower floor of family home. Situated on waterfront of beautiful uncrowded ocean beach. Walk from front door directly onto sandy beach. Safe ocean swimming, surfcasting, surfing and coastal walks. 9 hole golf course with club hire in township, 18 hole golf course 11km away. Restaurant within walking distance of accommodation or use facilities provided with accommodation. Tariff $90 per couple bed & breakfast, $10 per extra persons. Off season rates available.

Waterfront Homestay
Homestay
11km E of Waihi
Kay & John Morgan
17 The Esplanade
(off Hinemoa Street) Waihi Beach

Tel: (07) 863 4342
Fax: (07) 863 4342
Mob: 025 287 1104
E: k.morgan@xtra.co.nz
W: www.bnb.co.nz/hosts/
waterfronthomestay.html

Cost: Double $90 Visa/MC
Beds: 1 King 1 Double
    1 Single (2 bdrm)
Bath: 1 Private

Waihi

Welcome to our new home 300m's off the main highway, quiet, peaceful and situated on an organic blueberry orchard. Look for trout and eels in the bordering stream, sit on your own deck with coffee and blueberry muffins or visit the local organic cafe, restaurants, shops, local historic sites and walk in the beautiful countryside. Enjoy a relaxing breakfast on the deck or in our comfortable dining room. Have a walk in the orchard accompanied our friendly Labrador, or just relax with your favourite book.

Trout & Chicken
B&B Homestay Studio
2km W of Waihi
Michael & Adrienne Muir
9137 State Highway 2
RD 2 Waihi

Tel: (07) 863 6964
Fax: (07) 863 6966
Mob: 025 206 4080
E: trout&chicken@hotmail.com
W: www.bnb.co.nz/hosts/
troutchicken.html

Cost: Double $110 Single $90
    Dinner $30 by arrangement
    Studio $80 Visa/MC
Beds: 1 Queen 2 Twin (2 bdrm)
Bath: 2 Ensuite

Waihi

Modern brick home set on the side of a hill with extensive views and access to trout river. Private guest wing comprising 2 double bedrooms, large private bathroom with shower and bath. Guest lounge with TV, stereo and large selection of New Zealand books. Laundry and separate toilet. The property has eight acres, large attractive garden and pond area. I breed kakarikis, New Zealand's endangered parrots, and doves and pigeons. We also have one house dog. We are situated 2 minutes to centre of Waihi, complete privacy and quiet guaranteed.

Waihi
Homestay
Waihi
Anne & Bill Ashdown
20 Riflerange Road
Waihi

Tel: (07) 863 6448
Fax: (07) 863 6443
W: www.bnb.co.nz/hosts/
Waihi.html

Cost: Double $75 Single $50
    Dinner $20pp
Beds: 1 King 1 Double
    (2 bdrm)
Bath: 1 Private
    1 Guests share

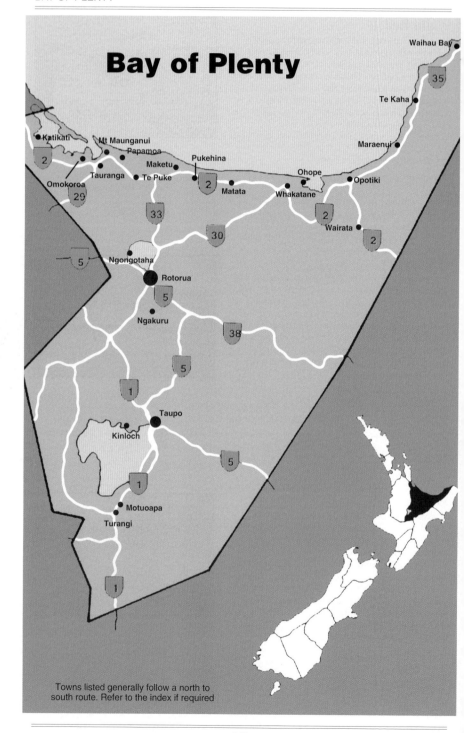

Bay of Plenty

Waihau Bay

35

Te Kaha

Maraenui

Katikati

Mt Maunganui
Papamoa

Pukehina

2

Maketu

Ohope

Omokoroa

Tauranga

Te Puke

Opotiki

29

2

Matata

Whakatane

2

33

Wairata

30

2

5

Ngongotaha

Rotorua

5

Ngakuru

38

5

1

Taupo

Kinloch

5

1

Motuoapa

Turangi

1

Towns listed generally follow a north to
south route. Refer to the index if required

Katikati

Spectacular 360 degree views, from forests and farmlands to mountains and the sea - your introduction to the true spirit of rural New Zealand with its unsurpassed hospitality and warm generosity. Our modest, clean and comfortable family home is on a 5 acre farmlet, 8km south of Katikati Mural Town. Or you may prefer instead our fully equipped, self-catering hillside cottage. We enjoy children 'helping' us with our friendly smallfarm animals. Swimming pool, horses, glowworms at night. Near beaches, tramping, golf, hot pools, birdgardens, winery, restaurants, arts/crafts.

Jacaranda Cottage	**Tel:** (07) 549 0616	**Cost:** House: Dbl. $70 Sgl. $45
B&B Farmstay	**Fax:** (07) 549 0616	S/C Cottage: (2 night min.stay)
Self-contained Cottage	**Mob:** 025 272 8710	Dbl $80 $20 per extra adult
30km N of Tauranga	**E:** jacaranda.cottage@clear.net.nz	Child discount Visa/MC
Lynlie & Rick Watson	**W:** www.beds-n-leisure.com/	**Beds:** House: 1 Queen 2 Single (2 bdrm)
230 Thompson's Track	jacaranda.htm	S/C: 1 Double 1 Single (1 bdrm)
RD 2, Katikati		**Bath:** House 1 Guests share S/C 1 Ensuite

Katikati

This modern self-contained apartment has all amenities including lounge (with convertible divan), fully equipped kitchen and laundry. For a larger family extra bedrooms and a private bathroom are available in the main house. A deluxe continental breakfast is provided for self-service. Other amenities are BBQ, dinghy, games rooms for billiards, table tennis etc. We share our peaceful horticultural lifestyle property on Pahoia peninsula with many birds. There are spectacular views of Tauranga harbour (water's edge 200m away) and sunset over the Kaimai Ranges.

Jones Lifestyle	**Tel:** (07) 548 0661	**Cost:** Double $75
Self-contained	**Fax:** (07) 548 0661	Single $50
20km S of Katikati	**E:** joneslifestyle@clear.net.nz	Child $15 Visa/MC
Thora & Trevor Jones	**W:** www.bnb.co.nz/hosts/	**Beds:** 1 Queen (1 bdrm)
Pahoia Road	joneslifestyle.html	**Bath:** 1 Private
RD 2, Tauranga		

Katikati

Aberfeldy is a large attractive home set in extensive gardens with private sunny guest accommodation. The private lounge opens onto a patio, and has TV and coffee making facilities. One party at a time in guest accommodation. We farm sheep and cattle.Rod's been associated with Kiwifruit for nearly 30 years. Panoramic views of bush-clad hills, farmland and harbour. Activities include bush and farm walks, meeting tame animals especially Sue the Kune Kune pig. Golf course, horse riding, music, cooking. Jax, our Australian terrier will welcome you.

Aberfeldy	**Tel:** (07) 549 0363	**Cost:** Double $90 Single $50
B&B Farmstay	**Fax:** (07) 549 0363	Child $25 Dinner $25 by
3km N of Katikati	**Mob:** 025 909 710	arrangement Visa/MC
Mary Anne and Rod Calver	**Tollfree:** 0800 309 064	**Beds:** 1 Double 3 Single
164 Lindemann Road	**E:** aberfeldy@xtra.co.nz	(2 bdrm)
RD 1	**W:** www.bnb.co.nz/hosts/	**Bath:** 1 Private
Katikati	aberfeldy.html	

Katikati

Waterford House, situated in a quiet semi-rural area, provides spacious accommodation with wheelchair access throughout. A large comfortable lounge with television, stereo-radio, fridge-freezer, microwave and tea/coffee making facilities. Cot and highchair are available. Local attractions include Twickenham Homestead Cafe, Morton Estate Winery, Bird Gardens, Ballantyne Golf Course, Sapphire Springs Hot Pools, Kaimai bush walks, Uretara River Walkway and craft workshops. 32 murals and sculptures depict the history of Katikati "Mural Town", located on Pacific Coast Highway. Our cat is called Matilda.

Waterford House	**Tel:** (07) 549 0757	**Cost:** Double $65 Single $40
(katikati.8k.com)	**W:** www.bnb.co.nz/hosts/	Child discounted
B&B Homestay	waterfordhouse.html	Dinner $20 by arr. Visa/MC
1km N of Katikati		**Beds:** 1 Queen 1 Double 2 Twin
Alan & Helen Cook		1 Single (5 bdrm)
15 Crossley Street, Katikati		**Bath:** 3 Guests share

Katikati

You'll enjoy it here.....Seaviews from every room "complimentary cuppas", 10 acres to explore with: inground pool, gardens, lily ponds, pet cows, hens, birds, kiwifruit & avocado orchard. **Nearby:** Forest & Seaside walks, 3 Golf courses, Horse-riding, scenic flights, hot pools, ocean beach, harbour, gardens, fishing, murals, hikau walkway.
Homemade Breakfast: Breads, fruits, cereals, preserves, eggs, pancakes, baking, fresh juice, filtered coffee, teas. Easy to find, comfortable and accommodating, generous meals, laundry service, pianolas & vintage cars, no smoking or animals indoors. Warm Welcome. Group Discounts

Peaceful Panorama Lodge	**Tel:** (07) 549 1882	**Cost:** Double $85 Single $75
Orchardstay & Private Suite	**Fax:** (07) 549 1882	Child $25 Dinner $25
9km N of Katikati	**E:** wills@bopis.co.nz	Private Suite $110 dble
Heather & Bernie Wills	**W:** www.bnb.co.nz/hosts/	Visa/MC Amex
901 State Highway 2	peacefulpanoramalodge.html	**Beds:** 2 Double 3 Single (3 bdrm)
RD 1, Katikati		**Bath:** 1 Ensuite 1 Private

Katikati

Welcome to our large comfortable home Cotswold Lodge. Built in old colonial style, set in peaceful gardens with beautiful views to the Kaimai ranges and only a short stroll to the harbour. Nearby are hot pools, beaches, wineries, bird gardens, murals and bushwalks. Des is interested in vintage cars and fishing. Alison paints porcelain and makes dolls and bears. We both enjoy golf, walking, gardening and travel and have a friendly Labrador "Boots". Come and stay a while, relax and soak up the tranquillity.

Cotswold Lodge	**Tel:** (07) 549 2110	**Cost:** Double $115 Single $80
Homestay Rural Homestay	**Fax:** (07) 549 2109	Dinner $35 Visa/MC
7km N of Katikati	**Mob:** 025 496 570	**Beds:** 2 Double 2 Single
Alison & Des Belsham	**E:** cotswold@ihug.co.nz	(3 bdrm)
183 Ongare Point Road	**W:** www.bnb.co.nz/hosts/	**Bath:** 3 Ensuite
RD 1	cotswoldlodge.html	
Katikati		

Omokoroa

Walnut Cottage is situated on scenic Plummers Point Peninsula overlooking Tauranga Harbour. We invite our guests to enjoy the tranquillity our "little-corner-of-the-world" has to offer. Relaxing hot mineral pools, a picturesque walk and an estuary with attractive reserve and jetty are a short stroll away. The Kowhai Suite (own entrance and conservatory)has TV and tea/coffee facilities. Breakfast includes freshly squeezed orange juice (in season), homemade bread, muesli and jams. Directions: Plummers Point Rd is opposite Caltex Service Station on SH2.

Walnut Cottage	**Tel:** (07) 548 0692	**Cost:** Cottage $75-$95
Self-contained Homestay Cottage	**Fax:** (07) 548 1764	Kowhai Suite Single $50
15km N of Tauranga	**E:** walnuthomestay@netscape.net	Double $75
KO & LAB Curreen	**W:** www.bnb.co.nz/hosts/	Dinner $15
309 Plummers Point Road	walnutcottage.html	**Beds:** 1 Queen 1 Double
Omokoroa, RD 2		(2 bdrm)
Tauranga		**Bath:** 2 Ensuite

Omokoroa

Our home is situated in a quiet rural area, spectacular views of Tauranga Harbour and Mt Maunganui. We are 15 minutes north of Tauranga where there is a good selection of restaurants, also local dining facilities, alternatively you are welcome to dine with us. Our guest floor is sunny with views, separate covered entrance and private lounge with fridge and laundry facilities. Golf, bowls, horse riding, hot pools, bush walks, boat launching. 2km off State Highway 2. Look for B&B sign.

Highlands	**Tel:** (07) 552 5275	**Cost:** Double $75 Single $45
Homestay	**Fax:** (07) 552 5770	Dinner $20 by arrange
14km N of Tauranga	**W:** www.bnb.co.nz/hosts/	ment Visa/MC
Shirley & John Whiteman	highlands.html	**Beds:** 1 Queen 2 Single
89 Whakamarama Road		(2 bdrm)
RD 6		**Bath:** 1 Guests share
Tauranga		

Tauranga

Welcome. We are located close to town, with a golf course and licensed restaurants nearby and a park opposite. Twin room has every comfort and large private bathroom. The single guest room has own facilities and TV. You can enjoy our spacious lounge and sunny balcony, or take a short stroll to harbour edge. Your hostess Christine, is a miniaturist and doll maker and has travelled extensively and is enjoying retirement. Breakfast of your choice. Off street parking plus a garage. Will meet public transport.

B&B Homestay	**Tel:** (07) 576 8895	**Cost:** Double $70 Single $40
2km W of Tauranga	**E:** rossvale@xtra.co.nz	**Beds:** 1 Twin 1 Single
Christine Ross	**W:** www.bnb.co.nz/hosts/ross.html	(2 bdrms)
8A Vale Street		**Bath:** 2 Private
Bureta		
Tauranga		

Tauranga

Bolney Gate is a comfortable 4 level home overlooking a mature park. We have a secluded pool, Sky TV and an interesting cuisine. Tauranga has world renowned surf beaches - salt and fresh water fishing - scenic walks - rafting and jet water facilities. Rotorua is within easy reach - the thermal areas - Coromandel near at hand with a wealth to offer. Interests - history - current affairs - art - creative writing. Jack and I have travelled widely both in NZ and overseas. Off street parking and pick up facilities available.

Bolney Gate
B&B Homestay
5km E of Tauranga
J & J Ingram
20 Esmerelda St
Welcome Bay
Tauranga

Tel: (07) 544 0107
Fax: (07) 544 3228
W: www.bnb.co.nz/hosts/
bolneygate.html

Cost: Double $60 Single $35
  Child $20, under 10yrs
  $15, under 3 nil Visa/MC
Beds: 1 King/Twin 2 Queen
  2 Twin 2 Single (3 bdrm)
Bath: 1 Family share

Tauranga - Matua

Our home in the pleasant suburb of Matua is set in a garden of NZ native trees, shrubs and ferns, The guest wing is quiet and comfortable. Please use our lounge and enjoy the garden. Our home is smoke-free. Breakfast - see our menu of special choices. Can cater for food allergies. Close to harbour beaches and parks; seven minutes drive to Tauranga city centre and fifteen minutes to Mount Maunganui's Ocean Beach. Our interests include growing native plants, the performing arts and motorcycling.

Christiansen's B&B
B&B
6km N of Tauranga
Heather & John Christiansen
210 Levers Road
Matua
Tauranga

Tel: (07) 576 6835
Fax: (07) 576 6464
E:
christiansensband@clear.net.nz
W: www.bnb.co.nz/hosts/
christiansensbb.html

Cost: Double $90 Single $60
  Visa/MC
Beds: 1 Queen 2 Single
  (2 bdrm)
Bath: 1 Guests share

Tauranga - Oropi

We invite you to stay with us in our spacious home overlooking the countryside, sea, Tauranga city and Mt Maunganui. Our property is a sheltered 3 1/2 acres with trees, gardens and lawns. You may relax in quiet and privacy, enjoy the spa, or swim in our pool. both rooms have ensuite, electric blankets, TV, and comfortable chairs. Tea facility in guest area, laundry done overnight if required. We love to share our home and travel experiences with guests. Be sure of a warm welcome.

Grenofen
Farmstay Homestay
9km S of Tauranga
Jennie & Norm Reeve
Castles Road
Oropi, RD 3
Tauranga

Tel: (07) 543 3953
Fax: (07) 543 3951
E: n.reeve@wave.co.nz
W: www.bnb.co.nz/hosts/
grenofen.html

Cost: Double $100 Single $70
  Child by age Dinner $35
Beds: 1 King 2 Single (2 bdrm)
Bath: 2 Ensuite

Tauranga - Bethlehem

Hollies, an elegant sophisticated modern country house, acre of gardens. Large luxuriously appointed rooms, panoramic views of gardens and rolling hills. The spacious suite has super king (or twin) bed, ensuite, lounge & TV, kitchenette, alternative private entrance and balcony. Hairdryers, bathrobes and toiletries. Fresh flowers, chocolates and crisp linen and every attention to detail combine to ensure your stay is truly memorable. Complimentary tea/coffee. Landscaped gardens, swimming pool. Breakfast: home made bread, muffins, fresh fruit and tempting cooked dishes. Muffee our cat. Children by arrangement.

The Hollies	**Tel:** (07) 577 9678	**Cost:** Double $120-$250
Superior Inn	**Fax:** (07) 579 1678	Single $95-$165
6km NW of Tauranga	**E:** stay@hollies.co.nz	Dinner $40 PP Visa/MC
Shirley & Michael Creak	**W:** www.hollies.co.nz	**Beds:** 1 King/Twin 1 Queen
Westridge Drive		1 Twin 2 Single (3 bdrm)
Bethlehem, Tauranga 3001		**Bath:** 1 Ensuite 2 Private

Tauranga

Welcome to Longwood Homestead our modern spacious home set in a peaceful mandarin orchard with expansive views over Tauranga city, Mt Maunganui and Kaimai Ranges. Longwood Homestead features large guest bedrooms with garden oulooks. Sip a wine on the verandah before enjoying your home cooked dinner. Tea and coffee facilities are available. Our home is smoke free inside. See the sunrise over the hills and after a day visiting friends, family, golf course, race course, hot pools or any one of the many local attractions quietly enjoy the amazing sunset and city lights.

Longwood Homestead	**Tel:** (07) 543 4292	**Cost:** Double $100- 135 Single
B&B Homestay	**Fax:** (07) 544 6122	$80 Dinner $35pp by
10km SE of Tauranga	**Mob:** 025 220 4592	arrangement Visa/MC
Robyn and J Maguiness	**E:** longwood@voyager.co.nz	**Beds:** 2 Queen 2 Single
208 Pukemapu Road	**W:**	(3 bdrm)
RD 3, Oropi, Tauranga	www.longwoodhomestead.co.nz	**Bath:** 1 Ensuite 1 Guests share

Tauranga

Welcome to quality accommodation in our spacious well appointed home in a peaceful garden setting. Stroll 200 metres to the harbour beach to see spectacular estuary views. Enjoy a good nights sleep in tastefully furnished guest rooms. Tea,coffee and milo are available at any time. We have travelled extensively and are happy to help you plan visits to local places of interest. We look forward to meeting you, offering Kiwi hospitality and making your stay with us very special. Phone now for reservation and directions.

Matua Homestay	**Tel:** (07) 576 8083	**Cost:** Double $70 Single $40
Homestay	**Mob:** 025 915 566	Child $20
6km N of Tauranga	**E:** pa_seaton@clear.net.nz	**Beds:** 1 Double 2 Single
Peter & Anne Seaton	**W:** www.bnb.co.nz/hosts/	(2 bdrm)
34 Tainui Street	matuahomestay.html	**Bath:** 1 Guests share
Matua		
Tauranga		

Tauranga

Harbinger House is centrally located to hospital, conference centres, beaches and downtown shopping. Our upstairs has been renovated with your comfort a top priority, using quality furnishings and linen. The queen rooms have vanity units and private balconies. A guest phone and laundry facilities are available. Breakfast is a gourmet event, using local produce where possible. We offer complimentary pick up from public transport depots and have off street parking. Our house is smoke free inside and we have a cat called Bronson.

Harbinger House	**Tel:** (07) 578 8801	**Cost:** Double $75-$90
B&B Homestay	**Fax:** (07) 578 8801	Single $55-$70
3km N of Tauranga Central	**Mob:** 025 583 049	Child 1/2 price
Helen & Doug Fisher	**E:** d-h.fisher@xtra.co.nz	Dinner $25 Visa/MC
209 Fraser Street	**W:** www.harbinger.co.nz	**Beds:** 2 Queen 2 Single
Tauranga		(3 bdrm)
		Bath: 1 Guests share

Tauranga

We are a German couple and have been living in our dream house since 1997. Our guests are offered luxurious self-contained apartments, a garden like paradise with a beautiful swimming pool (10x5) for your relaxation. Enjoy our splendid breakfast and if you want to spoil yourself book a 3 course dinner or German coffee and cake. Lydia's hobby is cooking. In our 8000m2 garden you can play table tennis, Boccia also archery and shooting with an air rifle are possible. We are only a 10 minute drive from the most beautiful Mount Maunganui beaches.

Lutz and Lydia's Paradise	**Tel:** (07) 544 0219	**Cost:** Double $90-$130
Self-contained Homestay	**Fax:** (07) 544 0215	Single $70-$110
5km S of Tauranga	**Mob:** 025 628 7015	Dinner $25
Lutz & Lydia Heutmann	**E:** lutzh@ihug.co.nz	**Beds:** 2 Queen 1 Twin
98E Boscabel Drive	**W:** www.bnb.co.nz/hosts/	(3 bdrm)
Ohauiti, Tauranga	lutzandlydiasparadise.html	**Bath:** 3 Ensuite

Tauranga

Luxurious, comfortable one-level 'home away from home' on 3 1/2 acres growing tamarillos and avocados. We enjoy meeting people, have travelled extensively and our interests include Blackie our cat, sport, reading, gardening, good food and wine. We offer a 3 course dinner option, swimming and spa pools, tour information and local courtesy pickup. Tauranga, Mt Maunganui, cafes and restaurants are a ten minute drive. Make us your base for day trips to Lake Taupo, Rotorua, Waitomo Caves or Coromandel Peninsula. Go sightseeing - have fun - return and relax!

Birch Haven	**Tel:** (07) 544 2499	**Cost:** Double $80 Single $50
B&B Homestay	**Mob:** 025 414 289	Child $25 Dinner $25
10km E of Tauranga	**E:** george.mcconnell	**Beds:** 1 King/Twin 1 Queen
Judy & George McConnell	@paradise.net.nz	(2 bdrm)
R403 Welcome Bay Road	**W:** www.bnb.co.nz/hosts/	**Bath:** 1 Private 1 Family share
RD 5, Tauranga	birchhaven.html	

Tauranga

Welcome to our home within easy walking distance to the city's cafes, bars and restaurants. Guests may park inside, next to their room & ensuite with its own entry and court yard and are welcome to share our kitchen, lounge and laundry. A separate twin bedroom (upstairs) is available for your family but share your ensuite. Our home is pet and smoke free. We are across Devonport Road to Memorial Park which is on harbours edge. Our hobbies - motor caravaning and travel. Please, a phone call essential.

Tauranga B&B	**Tel:** (07) 577 0927	**Cost:** Double $85 Single $55
B&B	**Fax:** (07) 577 0954	Child $25
0.5km SW of Tauranga	**Mob:** 025 297 1349	**Beds:** 1 Queen (1 bdrm)
Jeanette & Buddy Craig	or 025 281 5649	**Bath:** 1 Ensuite
4 Ninth Avenue	**W:** www.bnb.co.nz/hosts/	
Tauranga	taurangabb.html	

Tauranga

We have a luxury full self contained one bedroom unit set in a cottage garden with your own private outdoor area. We are close to all amenities, walking distance to waters edge, memorial park, swimming pool, bowling greens, ten pin bowling and restaurants. Or just enjoy walking around the avenues. Continental or cooked breakfasts are our specialty with home made bread and local jams and honey. We have one pet, Penny small poodle.

Fraser Cottage	**Tel:** (07) 578 4233	**Cost:** Double $120 Single $100
B&B Self-contained	**Fax:** (07) 578 4907	Child $10
2km S of Tauranga	**E:** frasercottage@xtra.co.nz	Visa/MC Amex Diners
Ron & Noeleen Johnston	**W:** www.bnb.co.nz/hosts/	**Beds:** 1 Queen 1 Double
77 Fraser Street	frasercottage.html	(1 bdrm)
Tauranga		**Bath:** 1 Private

Tauranga

Come join us our comfortable, family Country home, just 15 minutes from downtown Tauranga.
Relax amongst the Bays' finest gardens, set on 5 acres with magnificent rural views.
Enjoy tennis, swimming in Summer, the putting green, walking or cycling.
Your room offers every facility to ensure your utmost in comfort. Restaurants, golf courses, beaches, wineries, shopping etc. all very close by.
Come, relax and have fun with us.

Floribunda	**Tel:** (07) 543 0454	**Cost:** Double $85 Single $65
Farmstay Homestay	**Fax:** (07) 543 0454	Dinner $25pp
12km S of Tauranga	**Mob:** 021 778 414	**Beds:** 1 Queen (1 bdrm)
John & Sue Speirs	**E:** s.phillips@clear.net.nz	**Bath:** 1 Private
70 Gargan Road	**W:** www.bnb.co.nz/hosts/	
RD 1,	floribunda.html	
Tauranga		

Tauranga

Relax in a completely refurbished 100 year old villa. This historic dwelling was originally the Tauriko Post Office and serviced river traders during the saw-milling era early last century. Rural property comprising 3 acres with house situated amongst giant redwood and oak trees. Your own lounge, bathroom (claw foot bath), verandahs and outdoor areas. Only 12 minutes to downtown Tauranga and over Harbour bridge to Mt Maunganui. Attractions: stroll to river, tramping, parks, wineries, beaches, restaurants. We have two cats and a dog. Smoking outside only.

Redwood Villa	**Tel:** (07) 543 4303	**Cost:** Double $75-$85
B&B	**Fax:** (07) 543 3403	Single $50 Dinner $20
10km SW of Tauranga	**Mob:** 025 296 5565	Full B/fast by arrangement
Mike & Dee Forsman	**E:** redwoodvilla@ihug.co.nz	**Beds:** 1 Queen 1 Double
17 Redwood Lane	**W:** redwoodvilla.co.nz	(2 bdrm)
Tauriko RD 1, Tauranga		**Bath:** 1 Ensuite 1 Private

Mt Maunganui

Welcome to our magnificent home by the sea. Choose from our self-contained suite, sleeping 5 guests (suitable for children) with private deck. 1 min to beach for those casual walks. Upstairs is our Queen ensuite with TV. Your continental breakfast includes eggs any style. International golf course 500 metres. The famous "Mount Walk" up or around with 360 degree views is breathtaking. 4kms are shops, hot salt water pools, and restaurants for your enjoyment. Sorry no pets. Off street parking. Look forward to having you stay.

Homestay on the Beach	**Tel:** (07) 575 4879	**Cost:** Double $130 Single $80
Self-contained Homestay	**Fax:** (07) 575 4828	Child negotiable
4km N of Mt Maunganui	**Mob:** 025 766 799	Suite Double $160
Bernie & Lolly Cotter	**E:** bernie.cotter@xtra.co.nz	$25 pp extra guests
85C Oceanbeach Road	**W:** www.bnb.co.nz/hosts/	**Beds:** 2 Queen 1 Single
Mt Maunganui	homestayonthebeachcotter.html	(2 bdrm)
		Bath: 1 Ensuite 1 Private

Mt Maunganui

The Irish Inn offers real hospitality at affordable prices, comfortable rooms with TV's, billiard/games room, tea/ coffee on tap. Breakfast is great, cereal, fruit, bacon & egg, toast, marmalade. We are situated close to downtown Mt MaungAnui featuring excellent restaurants, cafes, clubs, Blake Park sporting complex. Minutes away from the best beach in New Zealand and wonderful hot salt water pools sooooo relaxing. 'Cead Mile Failte' (A Hundred Thousand welcomes). Our pets Benson an important Pomeranium and Blackie our cate are an added attraction.

Fitzgeralds Irish Inn	**Tel:** (07) 575 4013	**Cost:** Double $80-$90
B&B Holiday Flats	**Fax:** (07) 575 4013	Single $55-$65
1km E of Mount Maunganui	**Mob:** 025 794 555	Visa BC
Edna & Bill Fitzgerald	**E:** fitzgeraldsinn@hotmail.com	**Beds:** 4 Double (4 bdrm)
463 Maunganui Road	**W:** www.bnb.co.nz/hosts/	**Bath:** 2 Guests share
Mt Maunganui	fitzgeraldsirishinn.html	

Mt Maunganui - Omanu Beach

You are assured of a warm welcome to our quiet and comfortable home just 60 seconds off one of the country's finest beaches. Hot salt water pools, golf, bowls and shopping are all close by. A twin bedded room with bathroom for guests is available and a 2 course home cooked dinner by prior arrangement. Homemade jams and preserves are served for breakfast. We are retired, travelled and would enjoy sharing our experiences with yours over supper each evening. A smoke, pet and child free home.

Omanu Homestay
Homestay
6km S of Mt Maunganui
Judy & David Hawkins
Please phone for directions

Tel: (07) 575 0677
E: jhawkins@zip.co.nz
W: www.bnb.co.nz/hosts/
hawkins.html

Cost: Double $70 Single $40
Dinner $15pp
Beds: 2 Single (1 bdrm)
Bath: 1 Private

Mt Maunganui

Welcome to our absolute oceanfront Paradise, where you can relax in beautiful surroundings at one of the country's finest beaches. We are close to great restaurants, excellent shopping, bowls, golf and hot salt pools. We have one twin and one queen-sized bedroom, guest bathroom, lounge with kitchen facilities, TV etc. This unit is available to rent, also, at a separate rate. Undercover, off-street parking, laundry facilities offered, smoke-free home. Your well travelled hostess and resident cat (Bella) look forward to meeting you.

Beachfront Homestay
Self-contained Homestay
8km E of Tauranga
Barbara Marsh
28A Sunbrae Grove
Mount Maunganui

Tel: (07) 575 5592
Fax: (07) 575 5592
Mob: 021 707 243
W: www.bnb.co.nz/hosts/
beachfronthomestaymtmaunganui.html

Cost: Double $100 Single $70
Visa/MC
Beds: 1 Queen 2 Single
(2 bdrm)
Bath: 1 Guests share

Mt Maunganui

A Golfer's paradise. Our comfortable, timbered, character home adjoins the 8th fairway of the Mount glf course, and is across the road from the wonderful ocean beach. Enjoy with us, interesting food, wine, art, music, conversation, and bonus golf lessons. John is a retired solicitor, teacher and former scratch golfer, and Pippa a registered nurse involved in natural health. Our leisurely dinners are fun occasions, and John's desserts legendary. We are well travelled both in New Zealand and abroad, and look forward to meeting you.

Fairways
Self-contained Homestay
3km S of Mt Maunganui
Philippa & John Davies
170 Ocean Beach Road
Mt. Maunganui

Tel: (07) 575 5325
Fax: (07) 578 2362
Mob: 025 679 2052
E: pipjohn@clear.net.nz
W: www.bnb.co.nz/hosts/
fairways.html

Cost: Double $90 Single $60
Dinner including wines
$35pp B/A Visa/MC
Beds: 1 Queen 1 Double
(2 bdrm)
Bath: 1 Ensuite 1 Family share

Mt Maunganui

Welcome to our modern home. Cross the road to the Ocean Beach, where you can enjoy swimming, surfing and beach walks. Enjoy stunning sea-views while dining at breakfast. Near Palm Beach Shopping Plaza and restaurants. Separate guest lounge with TV and tea-making facilities. Cathy is a primary school teacher and Graham semi-retired - your host. We are widely travelled and both enjoy meeting people. We share our home with two precious cats - Twinkle and Crystal. (Not suitable for children under five years.)

Pembroke House
Homestay
9km S of Mt Maunganui
Graham & Cathy Burgess
12 Santa Fe Key
Royal Palm Beach Estate
Papamoa

Tel: (07) 572 1000
E: PembrokeHouse@xtra.co.nz
W: www.bnb.co.nz/hosts/
pembrokehouse.html

Cost: Double $90-$95
Single $70-$75
Child $35 Visa/MC
Beds: 2 Queen 2 Single
(3 bdrm)
Bath: 2 Ensuite 1 Private

Mt Maunganui

Award winning home on the lakeside, with beautiful sunset views to the Papamoa hills and only 300 metres from safe surf beach and close to all amenities. Our spacious executive suite is fully self contained with spa bath, TV and complimentary tea making facilities. A separate guest lounge also has tea making facilities, TV and large deck for sunbathing. Courtesy pick up from airport, buses, information centres. Coffee and cake served on arrival. We offer luxury at an affordable price. Not suitable for small children.

Royal Palm Beach Waters
B&B
10km E of Mt Maunganui -
Tauranga
Val & Dick Waters
36 Palm Beach Boulevard
Royal Palm Beach
Papamoa/Mt Maunganui

Tel: (07) 575 8395
Fax: (07) 575 8395
Mob: 021 510 900
E: waters.royalpalms@xtra.co.nz
W: www.bnb.co.nz/hosts/
royalpalmbeachwaters.html

Cost: Double $95-$125
Single $75 Visa/MC
Beds: 2 Queen 2 Single
(3 bdrm)
Bath: 1 Ensuite 1 Guests share

Mt Maunganui

Marilou and Gerard welcome you to our home at Mount Maunganui, with the best beach in the Bay of Plenty, just across the road for swimming, surfing, sunbathing and beach walks. Hot water pools, golf course, shops and restaurants are all close at hand. The fully self-contained apartment has two bedrooms, a bathroom, kitchen, lounge with TV and laundry facilities. A double bedroom upstairs with own bathroom is available. No smoking. Off street parking and garaging is provided. There are two friendly resident cats.

Oceanbeach B&B
B&B Self-contained
3km S of Mt Maunganui
Marilou & Gerard Meyers
14 Oceanbeach Road
Mt Maunganui

Tel: (07) 574 5568
Mob: 025 218 5682
or 021 158 9036
W: www.bnb.co.nz/hosts/
oceanbeachbb.html

Cost: Double $80 Single $50
Child $15
Beds: 1 Queen 1 Double
2 Single (3 bdrm)
Bath: 2 Private

Mt Maunganui

We invite you to share the relaxing atmosphere of our beachfront home. Enjoy walking the beach, restful seaviews and ultimate "at home" comforts - fine linens - fresh flowers - robes - toiletries. Breakfast to suit, healthy or indulgent, al fresco on the deck if you wish. Dinner by prior arrangement. Off street parking and laundry facilities for guests. non-smokers preferred. Two minutes to Bayfair shopping centre and ten to Downtown Mount Maunganui, with hot saltwater pools and many tempting restaurants, cafes and shops. looking forward to welcoming you.

Beachfront Homestays	**Tel:** (07) 575 6501	**Cost:** Double $110 Single $70
Homestay	**Fax:** (07) 574 6501	Dinner by arrangement
5km S of Mt Maunganui	**Mob:** 025 604 2135	Visa/MC
Christine Mora	**E:** beachfront@clear.net.nz	**Beds:** 1 Queen 2 Single
3/323 Oceanbeach Road	**W:** www.bnb.co.nz/hosts/	(2 bdrm)
Mt Maunganui 3002	beachfronthomestays.html	**Bath:** 1 Guests share

Papamoa

Retired - Late 60's - Hosts for twelve years (mostly Dickson Road). Our hobbies are gardening, travel and entertaining. A high level of entertaining a high level of personal service in quiet surroundings will, we hope, make you feel relaxed and comfortable. 'Arrive as a guest, leave as a friend'. Free laundry - 10 mins. walk to beach - good restaurants nearby. Directions - from SH2 (Rotorua - Tauranga) turn left at Domain Rd signpost Papamoa the second left at BP s/station. Beachwater Drive is first left at Roundabout, Pedrosa Court first cul de sac on right. Markbeech first house.

Markbeech Homestay	**Tel:** (07) 572 3588	**Cost:** Queen $90, Twin $80,
Homestay	**Fax:** (07) 572 3588	Single $45 Children $1/_2$ price
12km E of Mt Maunganui	**Mob:** 025 318132	Dinner by arr. $20 Visa/MC
Joan and Jim Francis	**Tollfree:** 0800 168 791	**Beds:** 1 Queen (ensuite, self
Pedrosa Court	**E:** 2jaysfrancis@free.net.nz	contained, small kitchenette)
Beachwater Drive	**W:** www.bnb.co.nz/hosts/	2 Singles (2 bdrm)
Papamoa	markbeechhomestay.html	**Bath:** 1 Guests

Papamoa Beach

My beach front home is situated on the beach. Activities include swimming, fishing and excursions around the district. My home is two storeyed, with guest accommodation on the lower level, serviced by the ensuite and laundry combined. Continental or cooked breakfast, dinner on request. Children welcome, no pets, smoking outside please. Directions: Turn off State Highway 2 (Tauranga to Rotorua) at Wilsons Garden Centre. Proceed 2km to Roundabout at Papamoa Domain, turn right, 4km to Motiti Rd. Turn left and left into Taylor Road.

Papamoa Homestay	**Tel:** (07) 542 0279	**Cost:** Double $70 Single $40
B&B Homestay	**Fax:** (07) 542 0279	Child $20 under 10yrs free
20km Tauranga	**Mob:** 021 215 1523	Dinner $15
Genyth Harwood	**W:** www.bnb.co.nz/hosts/	**Beds:** 1 King 1 Double 2 Twin
8 Taylor Road	papamoahomestay.html	(3 bdrm)
Papamoa		**Bath:** 1 Ensuite 1 Guests share
Bay of Plenty		1 Family share

Papamoa Hills

Splendid new golf house using natural timbers, stone and a turf roof. Overlooking a forested sheep and beef farm plus panoramic views of the Bay of Plenty sea and Islands. A challenging 9 hole golf course- par 36, runs through a chestnut orchard. Clubs can be hired. Farm walks and bike trails through established native and exotic forests.

Adjacent to a famous Maori pa site/ Te Puke the kiwi-fruit capital/ golden sand beaches of Papamoa with shops and restaurants/ hot salt water pools of Mt Maunganui, and airport. Please phone for reservations.

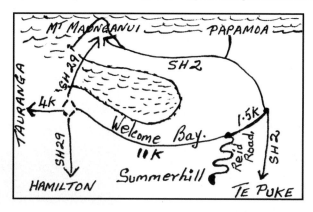

Summerhill
B&B Homestay Golf Course
13km W of Te Puke
Brent & Rachel
Reid Road
RD 7 Te Puke
Bay of Plenty

Tel: (07) 542 0077
Fax: (07) 542 0077
Mob: 025 286 3613
E: res@summerhill.co.nz
W: www.bnb.co.nz/hosts/
summerhill.html

Cost: Double $100-$150
Single $80-$100
Dinner By Arrangement
Beds: 2 Queen 4 Single
(4 bdrm)
Bath: 3 Ensuite 1 Guests share

Papamoa

Rose and Graeme welcome you to their home on three acres, with extensive gardens highlighted with objects of old plus ceramics and mosaics created by Rose. We are retired farmers who have travelled and enjoy meeting and entertaining in our relaxed country atmosphere. Only 2km to beach, Palm Beach Mall. Handy to golf, walks, hot pools and 12kms to Mt Maunganui or Tauranga. Come and relax with us. Directions: From SH2 (Rotorua-Tauranga) turn at Wilson Garden Centre. Signposted. "Papamoa". Proceed 150 mtrs. Turn right onto Tara Road. 1 km down.

Tara Homestay B&B	**Tel:** (07) 542 3785	**Cost:** Double $80 Single $50
B&B Homestay	**Fax:** (07) 542 3787	Child $15 under 12yrs
7km S of Bay Fair	**Mob:** 025 501 254	Dinner $20 - $25 Visa/MC
Rose & Graeme Wilson	**E:** GRwilson.Tarabb@actrix.co.nz	**Beds:** 2 Queen 2 Single
118 Tara Road	**W:** www.bnb.co.nz/hosts/	(3 bdrm)
Papamoa, RD 7	tarahomestaybb.html	**Bath:** 1 Ensuite 1 Guests share
Te Puke		

Te Puke

Lindenhof is an imposing building in the style of a Georgian country home. You are able to indulge in affordable luxury. Te Puke is the heart of Kiwifruit country. Close to town, semi rural. Tennis court, swimming pool. Languages spoken, English, Swiss German, German and French. Hobbies: vintage cars and spinning. No smoking in house. Not suitable for children. SH2 from Tauranga, Dunlop Rd turns right by Gas Centre (international B/B sign) 1 km. Up Dunlop Rd on left.

Lindenhof	**Tel:** (07) 573 4592	**Cost:** Double $90 Single $50
Homestay	**Fax:** (07) 573 9392	Dinner $20
2km NW of Te Puke	**E:** henryandsandra@xtra.co.nz	Visa/MC Amex
Sandra & Henry Sutter	**W:** www.bnb.co.nz/hosts/	**Beds:** 1 Double 4 Single
58 Dunlop Road	lindenhof.html	(3 bdrm)
Te Puke		**Bath:** 1 Ensuite 2 Private

Te Puke

Welcome to AOTEA VILLA built in 1910 and recently renovated. Quiet location, nestled between kiwi and avocado orchards. Enjoy our spa, swimming pool, or relax on our wide verandas, viewing the gardens or sunsets. Close to golf, beaches, tourists attractions, and only 40 minutes from Rotorua, Whakatane, 20 minutes from Mt. Maunganui, Tauranga. Gourmet meals by arrangement. Personality pet dog and cat. Well travelled hosts that will assist you with your interests in this area, to maximise an enjoyable stay. Visit our website www.aoteavilla.co.nz

Aotea Villa	**Tel:** 07 573 9433	**Cost:** Double $90 Single $70
Homestay	**Fax:** 07 573 9463	Child $30 Dinner by arr
4.5 km E of Te Puke	**Mob:** 025 821 842	Visa/MC
Leigh & Jerry Basinger	**E:** Leigh.Pool@xtra.co.nz	**Beds:** 1 Queen 2 Double 2 Twin
246 Te Matai Road	**W:** www.aoteavilla.co.nz	1 Single (4 bdrm)
Te Puke		**Bath:** 1 Ensuite 1 Guests share

Maketu Beach

So central to exciting tourist activities, shops and a
choice of beaches. So much to see and do. Located on
the water's edge in a multicultural village full of
ancient history. Breakfast with a local storyteller on
request. Cafes and restaurants near by, amazing
sunsets and night skies. Safe swimming and walks,
boat ramp and hunting, warm and cozy year round.
Kiwi home cooking, easy to find, pickups by
arrangement. Very relaxed. We searched the world
and settled here - come and see why! Great for all
seasons!

Blue Tides Beachfront B&B
Homestay Self-contained Unit
6km E of Te Puke
Patricia Haine
7 Te Awhe Road
Maketu Beach

Tel: (07) 533 2023
Fax: (07) 533 2023
Mob: 025 261 3077
Tollfree: 0800 359 191
E: info@bluetides.co.nz
W: www.bluetides.co.nz

Cost: Double $120 Single $75
Unit $120 Dinner $25-$35
Beds: 2 King/Twin 2 Queen
(4 bdrm)
Bath: 3 Ensuite 1 Private
1 Guests share

Pukehina Beach

Welcome to our Absolute Beachfront Home situated on the
Pacific Ocean. Your accommodation situated downstairs,
allowing you complete privacy, if you so wish, includes,
T.V. Lounge with Coffee/Tea, Fridge and Laundry facilities,
also available at separate rate. Enjoy magnificent views
from your own private Sundeck, including White Island
Volcano and occasional visits from the friendly Dolphins.
Golf Course 13 k's. 30-40 minute drive from Tauranga,
Mount Maunganui, Whakatane and Rotorua. 2 Licensed
Restaurants within 4k's, Surf Casting, Swimming walks or
relax and enjoy our Unique Paradise.

Homestay on the Beach
Homestay
21km N of Te Puke
Alison & Paul Carter
217 Pukehina Parade
Pukehina Beach, RD 9, Te Puke

Tel: (07) 533 3988
Fax: (07) 533 3988
Mob: 025 276 7305
E: p.a.carter@pukehina-beach.co.nz
W: www.homestays.net.nz/
pukehina.htm

Cost: Double $95 Single $65
Child 1/2 Price
Dinner $30 Unit $120
Visa/MC
Beds: 2 Double (2 bdrm)
Bath: 1 Guests share

Matata

Pohutukawa Farmhouse and Te Moemoea Cottage are set
in a picturesque location on the Pacific Coast Highway with
sea views to active volcano White Island. Sometimes
dolphins and whales pass by. We offer warm hospitality,
sharing our home and cottage with travellers. Have a
relaxing time on the beach and farm. The B&B is base for
our own tour company "Prinz Tours", specialised in guided
day tours and personalised intineraries New-Zealand-wide.
Dinners with ingredients from our organic garden and cattle
farm on request. We speak German.

Pohutukawa Farmhouse &
Te Moemoea Cottage
B&B Self-contained Farmstay
34km W of Whakatane
Susanne & Jorg Prinz
State Highway 2
RD 4, Whakatane

Tel: (07) 322 2182
Fax: (07) 322 2182
E:
pohutukawa@prinztours.co.nz
W: www.prinztours.co.nz/
bube.html

Cost: Double $95 Single $75
Dinner $25
S/C Cottage, $120-$150
sleeps 4 Visa/MC
Beds: 2 Queen 2 Twin (4 bdrm)
Bath: 2 Ensuite 1 Private

Whakatane

Whakatane is off the beaten tourist track, yet it is the centre for a wide range of activities. We can arrange sightseeing trips, including White Island. Relax in peaceful surroundings - watch the activities in our Red Barn Country Kitchen and Craftshop, which promotes 270 Bay of Plenty artisans. Two 50/50 sharemilkers manage our properties and milk over 400 cows. We grow citrus and breed black and coloured sheep. As "young oldies" we enjoy bowls, Lions Club, SWAP, genealogy, and organic gardening. Currently no domestic pets.

Leaburn Homestay
Homestay
7km W of Whakatane
Kathleen and Jim Law
237 Thornton Road
RD 4, Whakatane

Tel: (07) 308 7487
Fax: (07) 308 7487
E: kath.law@xtra.co.nz
W: www.bnb.co.nz/hosts/
leaburnhomestay.html

Cost: Double $70 Single $40
Dinner $25 Visa/MC
Beds: 1 Queen 2 Single
(2 bdrm)
Bath: 1 Guests share

Whakatane

We invite you to stay with us in our contemporary home which sits high on a hill commanding panoramic views. We farm deer organically and grow Hydrangeas for export. You will be the only guest so you have sole use of a quiet private wing. Your evening meal will be 'special', venison - lamb or fresh seafood with home-grown vegetables. We dive, fish, tramp, ski, golf and love to travel. We have a friendly chocolate Labrador and a Burmese cat. Laundry available.

Omataroa Deer Farm
Farmstay
18km S of Whakatane
Jill & John Needham
Paul Road
RD 2
Whakatane

Tel: (07) 322 8399
Fax: (07) 322 8399
Mob: 025 449 250
E: jill-needham@xtra.co.nz
W: www.bnb.co.nz/hosts/
needham.html

Cost: Double $80 Single $40
Dinner $25
Beds: 1 King 1 Queen (2 bdrm)
Bath: 1 Ensuite 1 Private

Whakatane

Enjoy warm and friendly hospitality in our comfortable home set in extensive gardens where the peace and tranquillity of rural life can be truly appreciated. Check out our kiwifruit orchard, feed the guinea fowl, doves and hens, who supply the breakfast eggs. Lois is the gardener (camellias and roses are her favourites) also collector of antiques, quiltmaker, and embroiderer and examples of her handiwork abound. Tony is the "background support force" and provides essential services such as cork pulling. Tea making in bedrooms. Children welcome.

Rakaunui
Farmstay
14km W of Whakatane
Lois & Tony Ranson
Western Drain Road
RD 3, Whakatane

Tel: (07) 304 9292
Fax: (07) 304 9292
Mob: 025 246 6077
E: ranson@wave.co.nz
W: www.bnb.co.nz/hosts/
rakaunui.html

Cost: Double $80 Single $50
Child $25 Dinner $25
Visa/MC
Beds: 1 Queen 1 Double
2 Single (3 bdrm)
Bath: 1 Ensuite 1 Private
1 Family share

Whakatane

Needing Time Out? Join Jeff and Karen in their quiet home and garden beside the Whakatane River. Enjoy scenic river walks, rest in their garden, or visit the vibrant, local, art, craft, or garden trail. Take a short drive to Ohope beach, Hot Pools, River or Sea activities. Our Interests are: family, roses, gardening, photography, walking our dog, model cars, pen and stamp collecting. We look forward to sharing time with our guests, as does our friendly cat. Campervans are welcome. Internet facility available.

Travellers Rest
Homestay
Whakatane Central
Karen & Jeff Winterson
28 Henderson Street
Whakatane

Tel: (07) 307 1015
Mob: 025 276 6449
E: travrest@wave.co.nz
W: www.bnb.co.nz/hosts/
travellersrest.html

Cost: Double $70 Single $35
Visa/MC
Beds: 1 King/Twin 2 Single
(2 bdrm)
Bath: 1 Guests share

Whakatane

Features & Attractions: *Beautiful cottage gardens * Quiet and Relaxing * Lovely Bush walks * Five minutes to beach *Active volcanic tours * Swim with dolphins * Quality food and wine * Wedding ceremonies. On the hilltop above the township, Briar Rose and Cottage are nestled in a peaceful cove of native bush. You can also enjoy our beautiful cottage garden specialising in old fashioned roses. Active volcano, White Island, deep sea fishing, boating, diving, dolphin excursions, hunting and fishing, jet boating, white water rafting, golf, Mt Tarawera and waterfall, Ohope beach, sun and surf.

Briar Rose
B&B Self-contained Homestay
Private Cottage
Annette & David Pamment
54 Waiewe Street
Whakatane

Tel: (07) 308 0314
Fax: (07) 308 0317
Mob: 025 942 589
E: Briarrosewhk@hotmail.com
W: www.bnb.co.nz/hosts/
briarrose.html

Cost: Double $80 Single $60
Child neg Dinner $25
Beds: 1 Queen 1 Double
1 Single (2 bdrm)
Bath: 1 Ensuite 1 Family share

Whakatane

Welcome. Enjoy country charm in our modern attractively appointed Homestay. Share the peace and tranquillity of our park like property with quail, tui, wild pigeon and doves. Practice, or learn croquet on our full size lawn. Relax in a spa and if you prefer privacy, your own lounge. Fishing! There is parking for your boat. Day trip and enjoy our fantastic deep water, or land base fishing. Sea, coast, bush river or mountain - it is all here. Please phone for directions. We will pick up if needed. See you soon.

Baker's
B&B Homestay Private
Cottage
10km S of Whakatane
Lynne & Bruce Baker
40 Butler Road
RD 2, Whakatane

Tel: (07) 307 0368
Fax: (07) 307 0368
Mob: 025 284 6996
E: bakers@world-net.co.nz
W: www.bnb.co.nz/hosts/
bakers.html

Cost: Double $100-$110
Single $65 Dinner $25 by
arrangement Visa/MC
Beds: 1 King/Twin 2 Queen
2 Single (4 bdrm)
Bath: 2 Ensuite 1 Private

Whakatane

Our restful property has superb ocean bush and rural views. With a private indoor entranceway the upstairs area is semi self contained exclusively for guests. Enjoy the views from the sunny balcony off your bedroom and lounge, which has TV, phone and internet facilities. Also fridge and tea/coffee making area. There is a separate toilet and bathroom (private if requested) Friendly relaxed hosts who enjoy travelling to remote areas, outdoor activities, fishing from our boat, gardening and coastguard interests. You are welcome to join us for refreshments and chat.

Crestwood Homestay
Homestay
1.5km S of Whakatane P.ost Office
Jan & Peter McKechnie
2 Crestwood Rise
Whakatane, Bay of Plenty

Tel: (07) 308 7554
Fax: (07) 308 7551
Mob: 025 624 6248
E: pandjmckechnie@xtra.co.nz
W: www.crestwood-homestay.co.nz

Cost: Double $80 Single $60
Dinner $25 Visa/MC
Beds: 1 Queen 2 Single
(2 bdrm)
Bath: 1 Guests share

Whakatane

Enjoy expansive sea and active volcano views from our B & B and Self Contained units. Set in 23 secluded acres of coastal kanuka with private access to sandy surf beach. Good surf casting/kontiki fishing. White Island tours, deep sea fishing, and other recreational activities arranged. Large and interesting succulent, cacti and bromeliad gardens with plants fro sale. Feed our friendly alpaca, goats and chickens. Sample our fresh vegetables, fruit and eggs organically produced on our property. Kanuka Forest Organic vineyard and winery next door. We are on Pacific Coast Highway.

Kanuka Cottage
B&B Farmstay
13km W of Whakatane
Carol & Ian Boyd
880 Thornton Road
RD 4
Whakatane

Tel: (07) 304 6001
Fax: (07) 304 6001
Mob: 021 883 684
E: kanuka1@xtra.co.nz
W: www.bnb.co.nz/hosts/ kanukacottage.html

Cost: Double $70-$90
Single $50 Child neg
Dinner $20 b/a
Visa/MC Amex Diners
Beds: 1 King/Twin 1 Queen
3 Single (2 bdrm)
Bath: 2 Ensuite

Ohope Beach

Homestay: Paradise on the beach - view White Island and enjoy our hospitality. Facilities available for disabled guests. Classic car enthusiasts - well travelled. Self contained unit 1 twin bedroom, 1 single bed with bed settee (2) if required. Tariff $30-$35 own bedding, $40-$45 supplied. Access to beach across road. Fishing, swimming, surfing, and bush walks.

Shiloah
B&B Self-contained Homestay
6km E of Whakatane
Pat & Brian Tolley
27 Westend
Ohope Beach

Tel: (07) 312 4401
Fax: (07) 312 4401
W: www.bnb.co.nz/hosts/ shiloah.html

Cost: Double $66-$80
Single $35-$45
Child 1/2 price
Dinner $18 - $25 by
arrangement S/C unit
Beds: 1 Queen 1 Twin 4 Single
(3 bdrm)
Bath: 2 Private 1 Guests share

White Island as seen from "The Rafters"
Ohope accommodation unit right on the Beach

Ohope Beach

Panoramic sea views: White, Whale islands, East Coast. Safe swimming. Many interesting walks. Golf, tennis, bowls, all within minutes. Licensed Chartered Club Restaurant opposite. Trips to volcanic White Island, fishing, jet boating, diving, swimming with dolphins arranged. Full cooking facilities; private entrance, sunken garden, BBQ. Complimentary: tea, coffee, biscuits, fruit, newspaper, personal laundry service. By special arrangement, dinner with Host and his Weimaraner dog, Gazelle, in Library - dining room, $30 - $42.00, includes pre dinner drinks and wines. Pat, interests: wines, golf, bowls, music, literature, History, tramping.

We have a friendly Weimaraner dog. Courtesy car available. House trained animals welcomed. Two restaurants and Oyster farm within 5 minutes drive.

I look forward to your company and assure you unique hospitality.

Directions: On reaching Ohope Beach turn right, proceed 2 km to 261a (beach-side) name "Rafters" on a brick letterbox with illuminated B&B sign.

The Rafters	**Tel:** (07) 312 4856	**Cost:** Double $80-$90
Self-contained	**Fax:** (07) 312 4856	Single $75-$80 Child $10
8km from Whakatane	**W:** www.bnb.co.nz/hosts/	Extra adult $20, limit 1
90km E from Rotorua	therafters.html	Dinner $30 - $42
Pat Rafter		**Beds:** 1 King 1 Single (2 bdrm)
261A Pohutukawa Ave		**Bath:** 1 Ensuite Hair Drier
Ohope Beach		

Ohope Beach

Base yourselves with us and "daytrip". We offer
luxury, multilevel accommodation, opposite a safe
beach, cafe and shops. Treat yourself to the special
"Blue Room" with private deck overlooking Pacific
Ocean, or the "Garden Room" opening onto a patio,
also with sea views, both equipped with fridge,
television, phone, as well as other special treats.
Interests: farming. Love: tennis and golf: gear
available. We promise you won't be disappointed,
we've been hosting for many years, and love spoiling.

Turneys Bed & Breakfast	**Tel:** (07) 312 5040	**Cost:** Double $120-$150
B&B	**Fax:** (07) 312 5040	Single $50
5km SE of Whakatane	**Mob:** 025 960 894	Dinner by arrangement
Marilyn & Em Turney	**Tollfree:** 0800 266 269	**Beds:** 1 King 1 Queen 2 Single
28 Pohutukawa Ave	**E:** turneys@xtra.co.nz	(3 bdrm)
Ohope Beach	**W:** www.bnb.co.nz/hosts/	**Bath:** 2 Ensuite 1 Private
	turneysbedbreakfast.html	

Ohope Beach

Stunning views and a warm welcome greet you at
Oceanspray Homestay - a beachfront property with views to
White Island, also East Cape. Our downstairs modern,
separate 3 bedroom unit exclusively for you. Enjoy
complimentary wine, home baking, home comforts of TV,
books, toys- children welcome! Comprehensive continental
breakfasts- homemade bread and home preserved fruits, 3
course dinners by arrangement of fish caught on the longline
by John, a keen kayaker. Frances enjoys cooking, gardening.
Tessa, our labrador, Benny the cat add to your memorable
stay.

Oceanspray Homestay	**Tel:** (07) 312 4112	**Cost:** Double $90-$110
B&B Homestay	**Mob:** 025 286 6824	Single $55-$70 Child neg
8km SE of Whakatane	**E:** frances@oceanspray.co.nz	Dinner $30pp b/a
Frances & John Galbraith	**W:** www.bnb.co.nz/hosts/	**Beds:** 2 Queen 2 Twin (3 bdrm)
283A Pohutukawa Avenue	oceansprayhomestay.html	**Bath:** 1 Private
Ohope, Bay of Plenty		

Opotiki

We provide two self contained accommodation options
located on our hobby farm. As well as pets and farm
animals we collect English classic cars and varied
memorabilia. Enjoy the beach and bird life, swim at nearby
sandy beach. Fish, ramble over the rocks, explore caves.
The two storied cottage features lead-light windows, native
timbers, large decks look out across the bay and native bush.
The mews has separate bedroom, large lounge, all on one
level. Looks out into our garden. Covered parking, home
made bread, preserves.

Coral's B&B	**Tel:** (07) 315 8052	**Cost:** Double $75-$115
Self-contained Farmstay	**Fax:** (07) 315 8052	Single $43-$63 Child $15
18km E of Opotiki	**Mob:** 021 299 9757	Dinner $30
Coral Parkinson	**Tollfree:** 0800 258 575	**Beds:** 1 Queen 1 Double
Morice's Bay	**E:** coralsb.b@wxc.net.nz	2 Single (2 bdrm)
Highway 35, RD 1, Opotiki	**W:** www.bnb.co.nz/hosts/	**Bath:** 2 Private
	coralsbb.html	

Opotiki

A welcome awaits you at Fantail Cottage any time of the
year. The panoramic view from the guest room and from
the spa overlooking Ohiwa Harbour, and the entrance, is
awesome. Meg and Mike have travelled extensively
overseas and enjoy cooking and entertaining. There is Pepe
the cat, and three chooks. We are located 34km from
Whakatane and 11km from Opotiki off SH2. A great place
to relax, swim, walk or fish. Directions: From Whakatane
turn left on SH2 at Waiotahi Bridge, following signs to
Ohiwa Camping ground. Turn left at fork, then right on to
318 Ohiwa Harbour Road.

Fantail Cottage	**Tel:** (07) 315 4981	**Cost:** Double $80 Single $45
Homestay	**Fax:** (07) 315 4981	Dinner $25
11km W of Opotiki	**E:** wendylyn@wave.co.nz	**Beds:** 1 Twin
Meg & Mike Collins	**W:** www.bnb.co.nz/hosts/	**Bath:** 1 Ensuite
318 Ohiwa Harbour Road	fantailcottage.html	
RD 2, Opotiki		

Opotiki - Tirohanga

Tirohanga Beach Holiday Home is an ideal get-away for all
seasons. Magnificent ocean view right from your bed!
Beautiful beach extends for miles in each direction.
Swimming, surfing, fishing, beach walking at your
doorsteps. Enjoy breathtaking sun-rises and sun-sets from
the large deck overlooking White and Whale Islands. We
offer 2 self-contained units, each with everything you need
to relax and enjoy your holiday, complete with cooking
facilities, barbecue and washing machine. Dinners by
arrangement. Try our authentic Russian cuisine - borsch
with hot pies! Weekly/monthly rates

Tirohanga Beach Holiday Home	**Tel:** (07) 315 8899	**Cost:** Double $90 Single $45
Self-contained	**Fax:** (07) 315 8896	Child $30 up to 10yrs
7km E of Opotiki	**E:** jaffarian@xtra.co.nz	Dinner $25 by arrangement
Natalie & Jeff Jaffarian	**W:**	Visa/MC
#787 State Highway 35E	www.beachholidayhomenewzealand.com/	**Beds:** 2 Dbl 1 Twin 3 Sgl (4 bdrm)
Opotiki		**Bath:** 2 Private

Opotiki - Maraenui

Nestled in bush on a secluded coastal farmlet near the
mouth of the Motu River, OARIKI FARMHOUSE offers
farmhouse accommodation, bed and breakfast, or a two
bedroom self contained cottage with kitchen. Our famlet
grows organic produce often we have fresh fish or mussels.
Our dog will take you on beach walks, and our cat escorts
you fishing! The perfect place to relax for a few days in
peaceful surroundings. Fishing, rafting, walking, riding, jet
boating, arranged. Some maps show Maraenui as Houpoto.
Directions are essential.

Oariki Farm House	**Tel:** (07) 325 2678	**Cost:** Double $100 Single $50
B&B Self-contained Farmstay	**Fax:** (07) 325 2678	Child $25 Dinner $30
40km E of Opotiki	**Mob:** 025 531 678	S/C Cottage $90 - $130
Chris Stone	**E:** oariki@clear.net.nz	Visa/MC
Maraenui Beach	**W:** www.bnb.co.nz/hosts/	**Beds:** 1 King 2 Queen
Box 486, Opotiki	oarikifarmhouse.html	1 Double 1 Single (3 bdrm)
		Bath: 1 En. 1 Priv. 1 Guests share

Opotiki - Wairata

Join us on our 1900 hectare hill country sheep, cattle, deer and goat farm in the heart of the scenic Waioeka Gorge. Numerous tracks to walk, glowworms and crystal clear Waioeka River at doorstep for trout fishing, eeling, swimming, kayaking. We can take guests on 4WD excursion or guided deer or pig hunting. Guest self-contained accommodation adjoins house we serve hearty home baked meals. We have 4 children, two of whom still live at home. We always welcome guests and look forward to meeting you. Directions: Please phone.

Wairata Station Farmstay
Farmstay
40km S of Opotiki
M & B Redpath
Private Bag 1070
Wairata
Opotiki

Tel: (07) 315 7761
Fax: (07) 315 7761
E: rl.redpath@xtra.co.nz
W: www.bnb.co.nz/hosts/
wairatastation.html

Cost: Double $80 Single $50
Child $25 Dinner $20
Beds: 1 Queen 4 Single
(2 bdrm)
Bath: 1 Private

Opotiki - Te Kaha

Set in 3 acres of gardens "our lodge" features ambience, comfort and tranquility without equal on "the coast". Purpose built in 1998, our guests tell us that we have something that is very special. From our visitor book; "the lodge is a dream. I could stay for life" Horst Kersten, Germany. "Our first homestay, wonderful experience, wonderful location" B&D Morrison, Gisborne. "So gracious and what wonderful food" J&C Daley, North Carolina USA. "on a par with paradise, great hosts and a magnificent location" A&S Goss, Napier.

Tui Lodge Garden Resort
B&B Inn
66 E of Opotiki
Joyce, Rex & Peter Carpenter
201 Copenhagen Road
Te Kaha
BOP 3093

Tel: (07) 325 2922
Fax: (07) 325 2922
W: www.bnb.co.nz/hosts/
tuilodgegardenresort.html

Cost: Double $95-$125
Single $75-$95 Child $25
Dinner $25pp Visa/MC
Beds: 3 Queen 4 Single
(6 bdrm)
Bath: 3 Ensuite 1 Private

Opotiki - Te Kaha

Welcome to Waikawa Bed & Breakfast. 200 metres down driveway off State Highway 35. Our dwelling is on the water's edge facing north in tranquil surroundings. The west views, spectacular seascapes and stunning sunsets with White Island guarding on the horizon. Our detached guest rooms have ensuites, TV, fridge, tea and coffee facilities. Stroll the 2 acre property and enjoy the farm yard animals. We also have a cat and small dog. We have fresh organic fruit and vegetables in season.

Waikawa B&B
B&B
1hr N of Opotiki
Bev & Kev Hamlin
7541 State Highway 35
RD 3
Opotiki

Tel: (07) 325 2070
Fax: (07) 325 2070
E: WAIKAWA.BnB@xtra.co.nz
W: www.bnb.co.nz/hosts/
waikawabb.html

Cost: Double $80-$85
Single $50
Child 1/2 price under 12
Dinner $25 Visa/MC
Beds: 1 King/Twin 1 Queen
(2 bdrm)
Bath: 2 Ensuite

Opotiki - Waihau Bay

Surrounded by unspoiled beauty we invite you to come and enjoy magnificent views, stunning sunsets, swim, go diving, kayaking (we have kayaks) or just walk along the sandy beach. You are most welcome to join Merv when he checks his craypots each morning and his catches are our cuisine specialty. Fishing trips, horse treks and guided cultural walks are also available. We have two self-contained units with disabled facilities, and a double room with ensuite. Our cat Whiskey, and dog Meg enjoy making new friends.

Waihau Bay Homestay
Self-contained Homestay
112km N of Opotiki
Noelene & Merv Topia
RD 3
Opotiki

Tel: (07) 325 3674
Fax: (07) 325 3679
Mob: 025 674 2157
Tollfree: 0800 240 170
E: n.topia@clear.net.nz
W: www.bnb.co.nz/hosts/
waihaubayhomestay.html

Cost: Double $80-$100
　　　Single $55-$75
　　　Child 1/2 price
　　　Dinner $25 Visa/MC
Beds: 1 King 1 Queen 2 Twin
　　　2 Single (4 bdrm)
Bath: 1 Ensuite 2 Private
　　　1 Guests share

Rotorua

Come rest awhile with us as we help you plan your itinerary and book your local tours. Explore our farm of 150 acres, running beef and deer, by foot or farm vehicle. Now our children have flown, Tigger, our trusty farm dog who lives in the garden is our chief helper. The views are magical. 360 degrees of lake, island, forest, city and farm land. Guest area has private entrance; lounge with tea, coffee making facilities, TV, fridge and laundry available. Two triple rooms, each with ensuite lead out to sunny private terraces where you are welcome to smoke.

Hunts Farm
Farmstay
4km SW of Rotorua
Maureen and John Hunt
363 Pukehangi Road
Rotorua

Tel: (07) 348 1352
W: www.bnb.co.nz/hosts/
hunt.html

Cost: Double $90 Single $60
　　　Child $20
Beds: 1 Queen 1 Twin 2 Single
　　　(2 bdrm)
Bath: 2 Ensuite

Rotorua

We invite you to make our spacious, modern home in its tranquil lake setting your base to explore Rotorua's many attractions. Free use of Canadian canoe. Home-hosts since 1988, interested in world and local affairs and environmental issues, we enjoy outdoor activities. Now retired, we have lived overseas and still travel extensively. Your patronage will ensure continued travel. A generous, healthy breakfast with many home-made goodies, will set you up for the day. While sharing it, we'll help you plan activities, happily arranging any local bookings.

Rotorua Lakeside Homestay
Homestay
2km Rotorua
Ursula and Lindsay Prince
3 Raukura Place
Rotorua

Tel: (07) 347 0140
Fax: (07) 347 0107
Tollfree: 0800 223 624
E: the-princes@xtra.co.nz
W: www.bnb.co.nz/hosts/
rotorualakesidehomestay.html

Cost: Double $85-$95
Beds: 1 King/Twin 1 Queen
　　　(2 bdrm)
Bath: 1 Ensuite 1 Private

Rotorua - Ngongotaha

Welcome to Deer Pine Lodge. Enjoy the panoramic views of Lake Rotorua and Mt Tarawera. We farm deer, our property surrounded with trees planted by the New Zealand Forest Research as experimental shelter belts on our accredited deer farm.

The nearby city of Rotorua is fast becoming New Zealand's most popular tourist destination offering all sorts of entertainment. We have a cat and a Boxer (Jake), very gentle. Our four children have grown up and left the nest. Our bed/breakfast units are private, own bathroom, TV, radio, fridge, microwave, electric blankets all beds, coffee/tea making facilities, heaters. Heaters and hair dryers also in all bathrooms.

Our two bedroom fully self contained units, designed by prominent Rotorua architect Gerald Stock, each having private balcony, carport, sundeck, ensuite, spacious lounge, kitchen, also laundry facilities, TV, radio, heater etc. Cot and highchair available. Security arms fitted on all windows, smoke detectors installed in all bedrooms and lounges, fire extinguisher installed in all kitchens.

Holding NZ certificate in food hygiene ensuring high standards of food preparation and serving - lodge has Qualmark 3 Star rating. Guests are free to do the conducted tour and observe the different species of deer and get first hand knowledge of all aspects of deer farming after breakfast. If interested please inform host on arrival. Three course meal of beef, lamb, or venison by prior arrangement, pre dinner drinks.

Hosts John and Betty, originally from Scotland have travelled extensively overseas and have many years experience in hosting look forward to your stay with us. Prefer guests to smoke outside. Budget accommodation available.

Deer Pine Lodge
Self-contained Farmstay
17km N of Rotorua
John Insch
PO Box 22
Ngongotaha
Rotorua

Tel: (07) 332 3458
Fax: (07) 332 3458
Mob: 025 261 9965
E: deerpine@xtra.co.nz
W: www.bnb.co.nz/hosts/
deerpinelodge.html

Cost: Double $85-$100
Single $70-$85
Child $20 - $25
Dinner $30 by arrange
ment Visa/MC
Beds: 3 King 1 Queen 4 Single
(5 bdrm)
Bath: 5 Ensuite

Rotorua - Ngakuru

Te Ana, a 569 acre dairy beef, sheep and deer property, offers peace and tranquility in a spacious rural garden setting affording magnificent views of lake, volcanically formed hills and lush farmland. A farm tour, by arrangement, introduces guests to our herd of red deer farmed for their meat (cervena) and velvet. Enjoy a leisurely stroll before joining hosts for a generous breakfast. Visit Waiotapu thermal, Waikite Valley mineral swimming pool, Rotorua and Taupo attractions. Cottage & Homestead Accommodation. Families are welcomed by Sam, our loyal Jack Russell.

Te Ana Farmstay
Farmstay Cottage &
Homestead Accomodation
32km S of Rotorua
Heather & Brian Oberer
Poutakataka Road
Ngakuru, RD 1, Rotorua

Tel: (07) 333 2720
Fax: (07) 333 2720
Mob: 025 828 151
E: teanafarmstay@xtra.co.nz
W: webnz.com/bbnz/teana.htm

Cost: Double $90-$120
Single $75 Child $35
Dinner by arrangement
Beds: 2 Queen 4 Single
(4 bdrm)
Bath: 2 Ensuite
1 Family share

Rotorua

MARVEL - at unsurpassed views of geysers, city, lakes and beyond. RELAX - in all day sun, on the deck, in the conservatory or in the privacy of our garden. INDULGE - in comfort, home cooked cuisine and the friendly folk who have been enjoying hosting for many years. Our interests are, golf, tramping, gardening, antiques and sharing our extensive local and national knowledge with you. Let us advise you on the "must see" list while in Rotorua and other highlights of our beautiful country. WELCOME!!

Serendipity
B&B Homestay
4km S of Rotorua
Kate & Brian Gore
3 Kerswell Terrace
Tihi-o-tonga
Rotorua

Tel: (07) 347 9385
Mob: 025 609 3268
E: b.gore@clear.net.nz
W: www.bnb.co.nz/hosts/
serendipityrotorua.html

Cost: Double $90 Single $60
Child $30 Dinner $25 by
arrangement Visa/MC
Beds: 1 Double 2 Twin
(2 bdrm)
Bath: 1 Private

Rotorua

Haeremai - Welcome to my comfortable home in the heart of the thermal area, minutes from the city centre yet quiet and private. Rotorua born and bred I am proud of my city and Maori heritage and enjoy sharing what knowledge I have with my guests. I am a teacher working part-time at a local college. For 10 years I have enjoyed being a B & B host and I look forward to many more visitors to my home and unique city. Directions - off Fenton Street.

Heather's Homestay
B&B Homestay
1.5km S of Rotorua
Heather Radford
5A Marguerita Street
Rotorua

Tel: (07) 349 4303
W: www.bnb.co.nz/hosts/
heathershomestay.html

Cost: Double $75 Single $45
Visa/MC Amex
Beds: 1 Double 1 Twin
(2 bdrm)
Bath: 2 Private

Rotorua - Ngongotaha

Waiteti Lakeside Lodge stands in what has to be the most idyllic location in the region. Nestled on the mouth of the Waiteti Trout Stream and the shores of Lake Rotorua the lodge offers superb panoramic views of lake, mountains and city.

Solidly built from cedar and local Hinuera stone this elegant and spacious home features an interior of exposed beams and warm wood panelling. From the dining room a native rimu staircase leads upstairs to the guests lounge where they can enjoy satellite TV, video, library, pool table and tea and coffee facilities in privacy.

There are five supremely comfortable double bedrooms, three with ensuite, two sharing a bathroom. The ensuite rooms have TV's and open onto balconies overlooking the lake.

The lodge has private off-road parking and although it is less than 10kms from the city there is no traffic noise so guests can enjoy peace and tranquillity as well as clean fresh air free form the infamous sulphur fumes of Rotorua.

Brian is a professional fishing guide and skippers his own charter boat. He enjoys taking guests trout fishing on Lake Rotorua, with 30 years fishing experience your success is virtually guaranteed or cruise to the sacred Mokoia Island and experience the history, culture, rare wildlife and natural spas. With the help of his expert guides he can offer a truly memorable trout fishing experience by 4WD, raft or take a helicopter into the pristine back country to fish the wilderness rivers and streams. If you are a "do-it-yourself" angler you can use one of the lodge's Canadian canoes or simply grab a rod and cast from the back lawn into the stream or lake.

Val and Brian have gained an unsurpassed reputation for providing excellent accommodation and hospitality in this unique location and are proud to be included in the "Superior Inns of New Zealand" brochure.

Directions: Take Highway 5 from Rotorua, straight on at the roundabout through Ngongotaha main town centre and across the railway line then 2nd turn right into Waiteti Road. At the end turn right into Arnold Street and the lodge is on the left at the end of the street next to the footbridge.

Waiteti Lakeside Lodge
Homestay Lakestay
10km N of Rotorua
Val & Brian Blewett
2 Arnold Street
Ngongotaha
Rotorua

Tel: (07) 357 2311
Fax: (07) 357 2311
Mob: 025 615 6923
E: waitetilodge@xtra.co.nz
W: www.waitetilodge.co.nz

Cost: Double $125-$185
Single $110-$170
Child $35 12 & over
Visa/MC
Beds: 4 Queen 2 Single
(5 bdrm)
Bath: 3 Ensuite 2 Guests share

Rotorua

Handy to airport our quiet rural retreat overlooking
Lake Rotorua will provide a welcome homely
atmosphere. Farm animals are horses, cows, sheep,
working dogs, chickens and goats. Horse riding and
trout fishing can be arranged. Our interests include
horse racing, fishing, gardening and travel. We can
arrange for a visit to a Maori Hangi and Concert. For
the latter you can be collected and returned home. Two
house pets: "Lucy" Fox Terrier, "Edie" the cat. Pet
lambs in spring. Children welcome.

Peppertree Farm
B&B Farmstay Homestay
10km E of Rotorua
Elma & Deane Balme
Cookson Road
RD 4, Rotorua

Tel: (07) 345 3718
Fax: (07) 345 3718
Mob: 025 776 468
E: peppertree.farm@xtra.co.nz
W: www.bnb.co.nz/hosts/
peppertreefarm.html

Cost: Double $90 Single $60
      Child 1/2 price Visa/MC
Beds: 1 Queen 2 Twin
      (3 bdrm)
Bath: 1 Ensuite 1 Guests share

Rotorua

The cottage, situated in its own garden area has one double
and one twin bedroom, lounge, kitchen, bathroom and
laundry. Room in the house has one double; one single bed;
ensuite; tea/coffee facilities; microwave; separate entrance
as well as access to hosts living area. Complete privacy or
be one of the family. Colleen is a Technical Institute tutor
and Ike is a keen fisherman and golfer with background of
farming and the paper industry. Two friendly little dogs will
welcome you. 24 hours notice if evening meal required.

Walker Homestay
B&B Self-contained Homestay
5km SE of Rotorua
Colleen & Isaac Walker
13 Glenfield Road
Owhata
Rotorua

Tel: (07) 345 3882
Fax: (07) 345 3856
Mob: 025 289 5003
E: colleen.walker@clear.net.nz
W: www.bnb.co.nz/hosts/
walkerhomestay.html

Cost: Double $65-$70 Single
      $35-$40 Child 1/2 price
      Dinner by arrangement
      Extra adult $15 Visa/MC
Beds: 2 Double 1 Twin
      1 Single (3 bdrm)
Bath: 1 Ensuite 1 Private

Rotorua

Retired farmers with years of hospitality involvement,
live 3km from city on Western outskirts. Interests
include meeting people, farming, international current
affairs. Brian a Rotorua Host Lions member, Judy's
interest extend to all aspects of homemaking and
gardening. Both well appointed comfy guest rooms
are equipped with electric blankets. The friendly front
door welcome and chatter over the meal table add up
to our motto "Home away from Home". Assistance
with sightseeing planning and transport to and from
tourist centre available.

West Brook
B&B Homestay
3km W of Rotorua
Judy & Brian Bain
378 Malfroy Road
Rotorua

Tel: (07) 347 8073
Fax: (07) 347 8073
W: www.bnb.co.nz/hosts/
westbrook.html

Cost: Double $70 Single $45
      Child under 12 half price
      Dinner $25
Beds: 4 Single (2 bdrm)
Bath: 1 Family share

Rotorua - Hamurana

Come and enjoy our deer farm situated close to
Rotorua's renowned tourist attractions. Guests are
welcome to a farm tour with opportunity to feed a few
friendly hinds and pet our outdoor dog. Our modern
smoke free home, with panoramic views over Rotorua
lake and city, has upstairs accommodation for guests
exclusive use. Rod is a keen trout fisherman, Dianne a
teacher. We enjoy meeting people.

Daniel Farmstay
Farmstay
20km NE of Rotorua
Rod & Dianne Daniel
Te Waerenga Road
RD 2
Rotorua

Tel: (07) 332 3560
Fax: (07) 332 3560
Mob: 025 775 341
W: www.bnb.co.nz/hosts/
danielfarmstay.html

Cost: Double $90 Dinner $25pp
by arrangement
Beds: 1 Queen 1 Double
3 Single (3 bdrm)
Bath: 1 Private 1 Guests share

Rotorua

RELAX at HIDEAWAY our friendly, homely, quiet haven,
your "home away from home". Double room with private
bathroom, fridge, tea making facilities. Separate wing with
2 single rooms and shared bathroom, one has fridge, tea
making facilities. Electric blankets and heaters, swimming
pool and indoor spa pool. Enjoy breakfast overlooking our
private garden with native birds. Interests, meeting people,
photography, video, computer graphics, walking, sailing,
health, education. We're happy to assist you plan your stay
in our unique area. Offstreet parking, inside smokefree.

Hideaway
B&B Homestay
1.5km W of Rotorua Central
Patricia & Ron Heydon
38 Corlett St
Rotorua

Tel: (07) 347 0944
Fax: (07) 347 0924
Mob: 021 273 2974
Tollfree: 0800 317 153
E: home.stay@clear.net.nz
W: www.bnb.co.nz/hosts/
hideaway.html

Cost: Double $80 Single $45
Child 1/2 price
Dinner $25 by arrange
ment Visa/MC
Beds: 1 Queen 2 Single
(3 bdrm)
Bath: 1 Private 1 Guests share

Rotorua

Anne and Don invite you to share their private rural
retreat, six minutes from city centre. Enjoy friendly
hospitality, share an entertaining evening meal, or relax
in your private suite, featuring panoramic views of the
lake, forest and city. Don can assist with personalised
tours and will take pride in showing you the splendour
of local forest walks and the glow worms. Anne's
garden is her passion, and with Foxy the resident
supervising cat, encourages guests to share their love of
Rotorua's best kept secret.

Kairuri Home Hosts
Homestay
6km E of Rotorua
Anne & Don Speedy
24 Mark Pl
Lynmore 3201, Rotorua

Tel: (07) 345 5385
Fax: (07) 345 7119
Mob: 025 929 254
E: dspeedy@clear.net.nz
W: www.babs.com.au/nz/
kairuri.htm

Cost: Double $135 Single $75
Dinner $35 - $45
Visa/MC/JCB
Beds: 1 King/Twin 1 Queen
(2 bdrm)
Bath: 1 Ensuite 1 Private

Rotorua - Ngongotaha

Welcome to our HOMESTAY/BED & BREAKFAST WITH THE MILLION DOLLAR VIEW and our two acre lifestyle block with the black sheep and friendly atmosphere where your comfort is our priority. Just 10 mins from Rotorua City, handy to major tourist attractions, and walking distance to Lake Rotorua and Waiteti Stream where you can fly fish and then smoke your catch in our smoker. We can arrange any other sightseeing you wish to do...be it Bungy Jumping or White Water Rafting or just taking a ramble through some of our beautiful bush and Redwood groves in the surrounding lake district..

Breakfast on scrumptious food in the conservatory while you enjoy the stunning 200 degree plus views of Lake Rotorua, Tarawera and Ngongotaha Mountains. You will have the choice of three bedrooms, king/twin, Queen or double, guaranteed to give you a restful nights sleep, all with comfortable innersprung mattresses, electric blankets, reading lights, shaver points & hairdryer....Bathrooms have full facilities and the ensuite has a jacuzzi. All bedrooms have a pleasant outlook over the garden.

Enjoy our company or the privacy of the guest lounge with it's peaceful lake and garden views. There are no sulphur fumes and traffic noises. The guest lounge has CTV with teletext, stereo/radio, books and magazines. In the conservatory there is tea/coffee making facilities, available 24 hours for your convenience. If you wish you can enjoy a drink on the sunny garden patio and listen to the bird life. Laundry is available Dinner is an option but prior notice please. We have secure off street parking. Our accommodation is smoke free. We have no pets.

Your hosts have been hosting for many years and enjoy the wonderful experience of meeting people from all over the world. Our interest includes, Lions, Music, Masonry, gardening, walking, yachting, trout fishing, surfcasting and boating. Alf is a retired commercial builder and we have travelled extensively to many places in the world.

Directions: to find the BED & BREAKFAST WITH THE MILLION DOLLAR VIEW, take highway 5 to Ngongotaha, thru the township, over railway line, turn second right into Waiteti Road, then 1st left into Leonard Road. We are 200 metres on left. Please phone/fax /email write for reservations. Relax in a HOME AWAY FROM HOME. We hope to meet you soon.

Alrae's Lake View B&B
B&B Homestay
10km N of Rotorua
Raema & Alf Owen
124 Leonard Road
PO Box 14
Ngongotaha

Tel: (07) 357 4913
Fax: (07) 357 4513
Mob: 025 275 0113
Tollfree: 0800 RAEMAS
E: alraes@xtra.co.nz
W: www.beds-n-leisure.com/
alraes.htm

Cost: Double $95-$140
Dinner $30 - $35
Visa/MC
Beds: 1 King/Twin 1 Queen
1 Double (3 bdrm)
Bath: 1 Ensuite 1 Private
1 Guests share

Rotorua

Welcome to Studio 21: make our home your home for a
refreshing stay. Our spacious studio unit opens on to a
private patio, cascading water garden and one minute
pathway to lake. Easy chairs, tea/coffee facilities, laundry.
Plane and bus pick up arranged. Knowledgeable guidance
for tourist attractions including mountain biking, fishing,
Maori culture, thermal sites, restaurants etc. Children with
well behaved parents welcomed by our Labrador Grace and
two cats. Tranquil safe location, full cooked breakfast of
your choice, REAL COFFEE. Please phone/fax for
directions and further details.

Studio 21
B&B Lakeside Retreat
8km E of Rotorua Central
Daphne & Terry Wood
21A Holden Avenue
Holdens Bay, Rotorua

Tel: (07) 345 5587
Fax: (07) 345 9621
Mob: 025 621 1730
W: www.bnb.co.nz/hosts/
studiorotorua.html

Cost: Double $90 Single $60
Child $20 Triple $120
Dinner by arr. Visa/MC
Beds: 1 Queen 1 Single 1 Fold-
away (all in studio unit)
Bath: 1 Private

Rotorua City

Our parkside "Innercity Homestay" is in the heart of
Rotorua, close to lake, main street, shopping and local
attractions. We offer a comfortable spacious home,
thermally heated (including an outdoor private thermal pool)
and with our calico cat "Mieko" assure you of a warm
welcome. Breakfast if of your choice, using home made
and fresh produce. Museum, gardens, thermal activity, lake
edge attractions etc are all within comfortable walking
distances. Laundry service, off street parking, and smokers -
balcony or garden area for your convenience.

Inner City Homestay
B&B Homestay
100m N of Tourism Centre
Susan & Irvine Munro
1126 Whakaue Street
Rotorua

Tel: (07) 348 8594
Fax: (07) 348 8594
Mob: 025 359 923
W: www.bnb.co.nz/hosts/
innercityhomestay.html=

Cost: Double $85 Single $50
Child $30
Beds: 1 Double 2 Single
(2 bdrm)
Bath: 1 Guests share

Rotorua

Lake edge home of professional fishing guide with the most
productive rainbow trout fishing at the front doorstep. You
can go fishing, charter a cruise with special hot pool charter
for guests or simply enjoy the tranquillity of the lakeside
lifestyle and be only 10 minutes from all the attractions of
Rotorua. Your accommodation has a separate entrance,
cooking facilities, Sky TV, electric blankets, tea and coffee,
own private ensuite and can be as self-contained or catered
for as you request. Join us and our Siamese and Burmese
cats to watch the sun set over Lake Rotorua.

Lake Edge Homestay &
Trout Fishing Charters
Self-contained Homestay
14km E of Rotorua
Glenda & Paul Norman
8 Parkcliff Road
RD 4, Rotorua

Tel: (07) 345 9328
Fax: (07) 345 9328
Mob: 025 758 750
E: lake.charters@xtra.co.nz
W: www.lured.co.nz

Cost: Double $85-$100
Single $65-$85
Dinner $25pp Visa/MC
Beds: 1 King 2 Single (2 bdrm)
Bath: 1 Ensuite

Rotorua - Ngongotaha

Welcome to our friendly and comfortable lodge on the shore of **Lake Rotorua**, where we have **panoramic** views of the lake and surrounding mountains. Our lodge is central to all major tourist attractions in the Rotorua area but far enough away to be **sulphur free**. The upper level of our two-storey home is exclusively for guests with three **ensuite bedrooms** equipped with everything you need for a comfortable stay including TV. The **guest lounge** opens onto a **conservatory** which overlooks the lake. It has Sky TV, video, library. The guest kitchen offers **complimentary** tea and coffee facilities and a fridge. A laundry service is available on request.

A full breakfast is served every morning while we help you plan your day using our **complimentary** map and knowledge of the region. Gordon is an experienced fisherman and will happily share his knowledge with you so you can try your luck for the **fighting trout** just metres from the lodge. We'll also cook your catch for you. Ample off street parking. Canoes, fishing rods, golf clubs free to guests.

Directions Take state highway 5 to Ngongotaha Drive through the village. After the railway line turn right into Wikaraka Street, left into Okana crescent then left into Operiana Street and the lodge is on the right.

Ngongotaha Lakeside Lodge	**Tel:** (07) 357 4020	**Cost:** Double $115-$150
B&B Homestay	**Fax:** (07) 357 4020	Single $80-$110
10km N of Rotorua	**Mob:** 025 200 7539	Children over 10 $25.
Ann & Gordon Thompson	**E:** lake.edge@xtra.co.nz	Dinner $40 by arrange
41 Operiana Street	**W:** www.bnb.co.nz/hosts/	ment Visa/MC
Ngongotaha	ngongotahalakesidelodge.html	**Beds:** 1 King 1 Queen 1 Twin
Rotorua		4 Single (3 bdrm)
		Bath: 3 Ensuite

Rotorua

"An Oasis In the City" (Scene Lifestyle magazine) Quiet, central, private. Thermally heated home and swimming pool, spa in winter. Relax in our tranquil gardens featuring waterfall, fish and native birdlife, yet be walking distance to city centre, thermal activities, forests and golf courses. Well travelled hosts who enjoy good food,wine and conversation. Our company, or time in the guest lounge with private patio. Dine with us or sample one of our many restaurants or Maori hangi/concerts. Off road parking, table tennis. Laundry, e-mail and fax available. Pet -Candy, a large and friendly tabby cat.

Thermal Stay Bed & Breakfast **Tel:** (07) 349 1605
B&B Homestay   **Fax:** (07) 349 1641
3km S of Rotorua   **Mob:** 025 377 122
Wendy & Rod Davenhill   **E:** davenhill@clear.net.nz
367 Old Taupo Road   **W:** www.bnb.co.nz/hosts/
Rotorua   thermalstaybedbreakfast.html

Cost: Double $95-$120
Single $65
Child under 12 yrs 1/2 price
Din $30pp by arr Visa/MC
Beds: 2 Queen 1 Twin
1 Single (3bdrm)
Bath: 2 Guests share 1 Fam. share

Rotorua

This is an ideal base to stay whilst visiting Rotorua. The architecturally designed cedar and brick home takes full advantage of the panoramic views of Lake Rotorua and surrounding countryside, away from the sulphur smells of Rotorua. All bedrooms have ensuites or private bathroom with heaters, toiletries, hair dryers and heated towel rails. Play tennis or relax in the heated jaccuzi, or go for walks to Hamurana Springs, or Redwood Forest. Five golf courses and fishing close by. There are friendly sheep and working dogs. Dinner is available. Discount for over two nights.

Panorama Country Homestay **Tel:** (07) 332 2618
B&B Farmstay Homestay   **Fax:** (07) 332 2618
15km N of Rotorua   **Mob:** 021 610 949
Dave Perry & Chris King   **E:** panorama@wave.co.nz
144 Fryer Road   **W:** www.bnb.co.nz/hosts/
Hamurana   panoramacountryhomestay.html
Rotorua

Cost: Double $135-$160
Single $100-$110 Child $50
Dinner $50 Visa/MC
Beds: 1 King/Twin 1 King
1 Queen 1 Double 1 Twin
1 Single (3 bdrm)
Bath: 2 Ens. 1 Private bathroom

Rotorua

"Dudley House" is a typical English Tudor style house built in the 1930's, with rimu doors and trims and matai polished floors. The house is tastefully and warmly decorated, with thermal heating. The dining room is adorned with military and police memorabilia. Non-smoking. Your hosts are happy to sit and chat about the numerous attractions around Rotorua, some within walking distance. Restaurants, cafes or bars, shops and banks are 5 minutes walk, also a 2 minute walk to lake front and village green. We welcome your inquiry.

Dudley House   **Tel:** (07) 347 9894
Guesthouse   **W:** www.bnb.co.nz/hosts/
Rotorua Central   dudleyhouse.html
Bobbie & Philip Seaman
1024 Rangiuru Street
Rotorua

Cost: Double $65-$70
Single $45
Beds: 1 Queen 1 Double
1 Twin 1 Single (4 bdrm)
Bath: 2 Guests share

"A UNIQUE PLACE TO STAY"

Rotorua - Ngongotaha

For the discerning, a place to unwind and rediscover the simple pleasures in life. Magnificent Deer & Ostrich farm retreat set amidst 35 acres of green pasture, only 15 minutes drive north from Rotorua city centre.

We can offer you the Governor's Suite, or one of our three beautifully appointed spacious guestrooms, complete with ensuite bathrooms. Each room is equipped with tea & coffee facilities, refrigerator, TV, video. Rooms are serviced daily and there are laundry facilities available

After a sumptuous breakfast, join Lloyd and our friendly dogs on our farm tour, try a game of pentanque, or just relax on your individual outdoor deck and enjoy the peace and tranquility of Clover Downs Estate.

There are many things to do and see in Rotorua. Visit our many cultural and scenic tourist attractions, go horse riding, play a round of golf , or try trout fishing with an experienced guide at one of the many lakes and rivers in the area.
Rotorua has some wonderful restaurants and cafes, or maybe enjoy a Maori hangi & concert. We have extensive overseas and New Zealand travel experience so let us help make your stay in our country relaxing, pleasant and memorable.

Kiwi Hosts, Member of Superior Inns, NZ Boutique Lodgings and Heritage and Character Inns of NZ.

Clover Downs Estate	**Tel:** (07) 332 2366	**Cost:** Double $175-$240
Countrystay	**Fax:** (07) 332 2367	Single $160-$225
17km N of Rotorua	**Mob:** 025 712 866	Child neg
Lyn Ferris	**E:** Reservations	Visa/MC Amex Diners
175 Jackson Road	@cloverdowns.co.nz	**Beds:** 3 King/Twin 1 King
RD 2	**W:** www.cloverdowns.co.nz	(4 bdrm)
Ngongotaha		**Bath:** 4 Ensuite

Rotorua

Welcome to our quiet, high quality country home. On our
small farm near Lake Rotorua, close to Lake Rotoiti and
Okataina, we have a dog, calves, sheep, chickens, rabbits,
bees, organic vegetables and fruit trees. Native bush drive to
clear trophy trout fishing lakes and bush walks, thermal area,
Maori culture, Hotpools, horseriding, skydiving, whitewater
rafting. Our hobbies are troutfishing from boat, and fly
fishing in lakes and rivers, hunting and shooting. We lived
in the USA, Canada, Indonesia, Mexico and Germany and
speak their languages. Please no smoking inside the house.

Eucalyptus Tree Country	**Tel:** (07) 345 5325	**Cost:** Double $80 Single $55
Homestay	**Fax:** (07) 345 5325	Dinner $25
B&B Country Homestay	**Mob:** 025 261 6142	**Beds:** 2 Queen 1 Double
12km NE of Rotorua	**E:** euc.countryhome@actrix.co.nz	(3 bdrm)
Manfred & Is Fischer	**W:** actrix.co.nz/users/	**Bath:** 1 Guests share
66 State Hwy 33, RD 4, Rotorua	euc.countryhome	1 Family share

Lake Rotorua

The Lake House is a home chosen to give guests the
best beach front location on Lake Rotorua. Enjoy good
food and good company and the beautiful peaceful
location. Wonderful lake views from all rooms,
comfortable beds and friendly attentive hosts will make
your stay memorable. 4 course dinner with NZ wines
by arrangement. Telephone, Email, laundry, parking,
kayaks. Directions: Holdens Bay is down Robinson
Avenue off Te Ngae Road (SH30). Cooper Avenue is
right off Robinson Avenue 200m on left.

The Lake House	**Tel:** (07) 345 3313	**Cost:** Double $110-$130
B&B Homestay	**Fax:** (07) 345 3310	Single $80-$100
7km NE of Rotorua	**Tollfree:** 0800 002 863	Child $35
Susan & Warwick Kay	**E:** SusanK@xtra.co.nz	Dinner $35 by arrangement
6 Cooper Avenue	**W:** www.babs.co.nz/lakehouse/	Visa/MC Amex Diners
Holdens Bay	index.html	**Beds:** 2 Queen 2 Single (3 bdrm)
Rotorua		**Bath:** 1 Ensuite 1 Private

Rotorua

Welcome to our elevated smoke free home with views over
Rotorua. We really enjoy home hosting, and our lifestyle
enables us to spend time (as required) with our guests.
Guest bedrooms/bathroom downstairs. Breakfast is served
upstairs in our spacious lounge. We offer free pickup from
bus, train or plane. Off street parking is available. Des has
many years experience with a national organisation
providing both local and NZ touring information. Doreen,
originally from South Wales, likes gardening and reading,
and enjoys meeting people.

The Towers Homestay	**Tel:** (07) 347 6254	**Cost:** Double $75 Single $45
B&B Homestay	**Tollfree:** 0800 261 040	Child $25, 12 & under
4km W of Rotorua City Centre	**E:** ddtowers@xtra.co.nz	Dinner $25 by arrange
Doreen & Des Towers	**W:** www.mist.co.uk/homestaynz/	ment Visa/MC
373 Malfroy Road		**Beds:** 1 Double 1 Twin
Rotorua	We host only one party	(2 bdrm)
	at a time.	**Bath:** 1 Private

Rotorua

We have a new home in a beautiful setting beside Lake
Rotoiti (Okere Arm). Within a short walking distance
there are bushwalks, waterfalls, river and lake fishing.
Each B&B is centrally heated with ensuite, comfortable new beds, TV, refrigerator, tea/coffee making
facilities. Smokefree inside, Boat mooring, BBQ and
laundry facilities available. We share convivial meals
with many guests. Our outdoor dog is small and
friendly. We are easy to find just one minute from
Highway 33. Please ring for directions.

B&B Homestay	**Tel:** (07) 362 4288	**Cost:** Double $100 Single $60
20km E of Rotorua	**Fax:** (07) 362 4288	Dinner $25pp Visa/MC
Laurice & Bill Unwin	**Mob:** 025 521 483	**Beds:** 1 King/Twin 2 Queen
155G Okere Road	**E:** tengae.physio@xtra.co.nz	(3 bdrm)
RD 4	**W:** www.bnb.co.nz/hosts/	**Bath:** 2 Ensuite 1 Private
Rotorua	unwin.html	

Rotorua

A peaceful country retreat, 10 minutes from Rotorua
and its many attractions. your stay in this magnificently restored Victorian style villa, which was
originally built in 1906 in Auckland and 90 years later
moved to this splendid site, will be a memorable one.
The views over rolling pasture to the lake and in the
distance Mount Tarawera are unforgettable. Country
Villa is an ideal base to stay for several days, with
Taupo and Tauranga only an hour away. Country Villa
is smoke free inside.

Country - Villa	**Tel:** (07) 357 5893	**Cost:** Double $175-$195
Countrystay	**Fax:** (07) 357 5890	Single $155-$175
10km N of Rotorua	**Mob:** 025 272 6807	Child Neg. Visa/MC
Anneke & John Van Der Maat	**E:** countryvilla@xtra.co.nz	**Beds:** 4 Queen 3 Single
351 Dalbeth Road	**W:** www.bnb.co.nz/hosts/	(5 bdrm)
RD 2	countryvilla.html	**Bath:** 3 Ensuite
Rotorua		1 Private

Rotorua

Anchorage Estate is a perfect base for visiting Rotorua's
attractions and exploring its thermal wonderland. The
purpose built home is set on six hectares of farmland with
sheep and miniature cattle, only 15 minutes from the city
centre. The two downstairs queen suites are spacious with
their own bathrooms, private entry, refrigerator and tea/
coffee/snack-making facilities. Each room has magnificent
views over the countryside to the lake and city beyond.
Evening meals are available. Heated spa pool/Jacuzzi on
site. Personalised Trout and Deep Sea fishing trips avail.

Anchorage Estate	**Tel:** (07) 332 2996	**Cost:** Double $150-$180
B&B Homestay	**Fax:** (07) 332 2997	Single $130-$150
10km N of Rotorua	**Mob:** 025 931 943	Dinner by arrangement
Ra & Leon Batchelor	**Tollfree:** 0800 267 455	Visa/MC Amex
48 Sharp Road	**E:** anchorage@xtra.co.nz	**Beds:** 3 King/Twin 2 Queen
RD 2, Rotorua	**W:** www.anchorage.co.nz	(5 bdrm)
		Bath: 4 Ensuite 1 Guests share

Rotorua

"Honfleur" is a French country-style home in quiet, semi-rural surroundings close to lakes and forest. We offer generous hospitality amid antique furnishings and a beautiful garden. Downstairs double bedroom with ensuite bathroom has a private entrance. Upstairs a twin bedroom has lake views and shares family bathroom (separate toilet). We are long-term Rotorua residents with sound local knowledge - retired medical professionals with friendly Labrador dog. Interests include travel, gardening, books, bridge, music, sport and Erica's embroidery. We offer a three course dinner (with wine) by arrangement.

Honfleur	**Tel:** (07) 345 6170	**Cost:** Double $100 Single $50
B&B Homestay	**Fax:** (07) 345 6170	Dinner $35 Visa/MC Amex
4km E of Rotorua	**Mob:** 025 233 9741	Not for young children.
Bryan & Erica Jew	**W:** www.bnb.co.nz/hosts/	**Beds:** 1 Double 2 Single
31 Walford Drive	honfleur.html	(2 bdrm)
Lynmore, Rotorua		**Bath:** 1 Ensuite 1 Family share

Rotorua

Welcome...bienvenue! Discover real character and warmth, nestled beside lovely forest walks, yet easily found 5 minutes drive from the centre. Leonie, ex-teacher, and Paul, scientist, delight in being New Zealanders - share our love of this remarkable area of lake, forest, volcano. Meet Paul's guide dog, Toby, a character in himself. Enjoy well-appointed rooms; relax in the guest lounge, patio, verandah, or beautiful garden- native trees a feature, Excellent breakfasts, great coffee (this couple enjoys food!). Smoke-free inside. Leonie parle francais.

Lynmore B&B Homestay	**Tel:** (07) 345 6303	**Cost:** Double $90 Single $70
B&B Homestay	**Fax:** (07) 345 6353	Visa/MC
4km E of Rotorua	**E:** kibble@xtra.co.nz	**Beds:** 1 Queen 1 Double
Leonie & Paul Kibblewhite	**W:** www.bnb.co.nz/hosts/	(2 bdrm)
2 Hilton Road	lynmorebbhomestay.html	**Bath:** 1 Ensuite 1 Private
Lynmore, Rotorua		

Rotorua - Lake Tarawera

Boatshed Bay is located on the shore of scenic Lake Tarawera with its sparking waters fringed by native bush at the foot of majestic Mount Tarawera. We offer boat charter, world renowned trout fishing, tramping (Mountain trek), bushwalks or just relax in peace and tranquillity only 15km from Rotorua. All facilities are available, including laundry, kitchen and nearby licensed restaurant "The Landing Cafe". We provide home style breakfast and meals on request. Your host Lorraine is well travelled and enjoys meeting people. My place is your place.

Boatshed Bay Lodge	**Tel:** (07) 362 8441	**Cost:** Double $95 Single $75
B&B Self-contained Homestay	**Fax:** (07) 362 8441	Child $25 Dinner $30
15 SE of Rotorua	**Mob:** 025 279 9269	S/C $75 Visa/MC
Lorraine van Praagh	**E:** boatshedbay@xtra.co.nz	**Beds:** 2 Queen 1 Double
94 Spencer Road	**W:** www.bnb.co.nz/hosts/	2 Single (2 bdrm)
Lake Tarawera, RD 5	boatshedbaylodge.html	**Bath:** 2 Ensuite
Rotorua		

Lake Rotorua

Kotare Lodge offers you absolute lake front with glorious views and lovely park like grounds. A tranquil, secluded setting, yet only 20 minutes from Rotorua's airport, restaurants and many tourist attractions. Your hosts have travelled widely and are very aware of the needs of our guests. Enjoy our warm, friendly hospitality, relax in the guest lounge, garden room, patios or garden. Beautifully appointed bedrooms assure you of privacy and a comfortable night's sleep. Delicious breakfasts, assistance in activity bookings plus on-site kayaking and sailing.

Kotare Lodge	**Tel:** (07) 332 2679	**Cost:** Double $130-$180
Homestay Lake Front B&B	**Fax:** (07) 332 2678	Single $90-$140 Visa/MC
20km N of Rotorua	**Mob:** 025 622 0629	**Beds:** 1 King/Twin 1 Queen
Murray & Kate Pollard	**E:** pollards@kotarelodge.co.nz	(2 bdrm)
1000J Hamurana Road	**W:** www.bnb.co.nz/hosts/	**Bath:** 1 Ensuite 1 Private
Hamurana	kotarelodge.html	
Rotorua		

Rotorua

Warm hospitality, great food and country comforts await you at Kahilani. Easily located, just minutes from Rotorua's attractions, but a feeling of world's away with the homestead beautifully sited in the midst of a 100 hectare (250 acre) Deer/Sheep farm, offering panoramic rural, forest and lake views. Upstairs guest suites, cool in summer, centrally heated in winter, provide all the facilities discerning travellers may expect. Classy comfort food is the House Specialty! Extensive gardens, Labradors (in compound) and two Tonkinese cats complete the picture.

Kahilani Farm	**Tel:** (07) 332 5662	**Cost:** Double $160-$175
B&B Luxury Farmstay	**Fax:** (07) 332 5662	Single $120-$135
15km NW of Rotorua	**Mob:** 025 990 690	Child 1/2 price Dinner
Yvonne & David Medlicott	**E:** kahilani@wave.co.nz	$35 - $75 Visa/MC Amex
691 Dansey Road	**W:** www.bnb.co.nz/hosts/	**Beds:** 1 King/Twin 2 Queen
RD 2, Rotorua	kahilanifarm.html	1 Single (4 bdrm)
		Bath: 1 Ensuite 1 Private

Rotorua - Lake Tarawera

Located at the magic Lake Tarawera renowned for its scenery and history we offer warm hospitality with a personal touch. Expect total privacy, magnificent lake views, luxurious and relaxing outdoor whirlpool, spacious bathroom with shower and bath, fitness area, stereo, TV, internet connection, lake beach 5 minutes on foot, sea 45 minutes by car, bush walks, fishing and hunting trips by arrangement, home-made bread, German cuisine on request, organic garden, German/English spoken, free pick-up from airport or city.

Lake Tarawera Rheinland	**Tel:** (07) 362 8838	**Cost:** Double $100-$120
Lodge	**Fax:** (07) 362 8838	Single $75-$85
B&B Homestay	**Mob:** 025 234 3024	Child 1/2 price
20km SE of Rotorua	**E:** tarawera@ihug.co.nz	Dinner $25
Gunter & Maria	**W:** www.bnb.co.nz/hosts/	**Beds:** 1 King/Twin 1 Queen
484 Spencer Road	rheinlandlodge.html	(2 bdrm)
RD 5, Rotorua		**Bath:** 1 Private 1 Family share

Rotorua - Hamurana

Relax in your own private country-style cottage which is fully serviced every day. Continental breakfast ingredients supplied in the cottage kitchen. Take a swim in the pool to cool down during the hot summer. If you have children, they will enjoy playing in our playground with our children. We have an outside dog and other farm animals on our property. Golf course and gardens 2km away and Lake Rotorua across the road. 10 minutes drive to city and some major tourist attractions.

Oaklane Cottage
Self-contained
15km N of Rotorua
Brigit & WillemNieuwboer
551 Hamurana Rd
Rotorua

Tel: (07) 332 3179
Fax: (07) 332 3179
Mob: 021 121 1971
E: oaklanecottage@xtra.co.nz
W: www.bnb.co.nz/hosts/
oaklane.html

Cost: Double $95 Single $85
Child $15 Visa/MC
Beds: 2 Single 1 Queen
(2 bdrm)
Bath: 1 Private

Rotorua - Lake Tarawera

"Bush Haven" is a 2 level Lockwood home nestled in 5 acres of attractive gardens and bush reserve with views across Otumutu Island and bay to the south western section of Lake Tarawera. The tourist flat is the ground floor. Hosts Rob and Marie and friendly pet Spaniels live in the upper level. There is a delightful 300 metre bush walk from the garden down to a secluded bay. Native flora and fauna in abundance. "Bush Haven" is quiet and peaceful away from the main settlement.

Bush Haven
B&B Self-contained Homestay
Tourist flat
23km SE of Rotorua
Rob & Marie Dollimore
588 Spencer Road
Lake Tarawera, Rotorua

Tel: (07) 362 8447
Fax: (07) 362 8447
W: www.bnb.co.nz/hosts/
bushhaven.html

Cost: Double $95-$125
Single $75
Dinner by arrangement
Beds: 1 Queen 2 Double
Bath: 1 Private 1 Guests share

Rotorua

"Rhodohill" is set in a mature 4 acre garden in picturesque Paradise Valley, 10km west of Rotorua. Its hillside setting, large trees and hundreds of rhododendrons, camellias etc and many native birds offer a relaxing retreat within easy distance of major tourist attractions, golf courses and cafes and restaurants. The renowned Ngongotaha trout stream flows through the valley. Modern, self-contained accommodation with own entrance, ensuite bathroom, fully equipped kitchen, dining room-lounge. Smoke free indoors. Our retired sheep dog "Max" enjoys escorting guests around the garden.

Rhodohill
B&B Self-contained
10km W of Rotorua
Ailsa & Dave Stewart
569 Paradise Valley Road
Rotorua

Tel: (07) 348 9010
Fax: (07) 348 9041
Mob: 025 672 4009
W: www.bnb.co.nz/hosts/
rhodohill.html

Cost: Double $80 Single $60
Visa/MC
Beds: 1 Queen (1 bdrm)
Bath: 1 Ensuite

Rotorua

Lakeview Country Homestay is a lakefront country-side home, nestled in a picturesque rural setting. By day or by night the panoramic views over Lake Rotorua, Mt Tarawera, Rotorua's steaming thermal area and the City beyond is simply stunning. A peaceful, relaxing area surrounded by friendly farm animals, free roaming chickens, a cat called Misty and a pet turkey that loves to be stroked. Guestrooms are well appointed, large picture windows capture the spectacular lake/rural views. Major tourist attractions and golf course are easily accessible from our home.

Arrive as a tourist
Leave as a friend

Lakeview Country Homestay	**Tel:** (07) 332 2445	**Cost:** Double $100-$140
B&B Farmstay Homestay	**Fax:** (07) 332 2445	Dinner $25 Visa/MC
20km N of Rotorua	**Mob:** 025 467 121	**Beds:** 1 King/Twin 1 Queen
Carol & Bernie Mason	**E:** lakeview@xtra.co.nz	1 Double (3 bdrm)
983 Hamurana Road	**W:** http://webnz.com/bbnz/	**Bath:** 1 Ensuite 1 Private
Rotorua RD 2	lakeview.htm	1 Guests share

Rotorua

Gywn, John and Smokey, the cat, offer you a warm friendly welcome to our comfortable, quiet, thermally heated home. Guests will enjoy relaxing in our genuine hot mineral pool. We serve a substantial breakfast. Complimentary tea and coffee always available. Laundry facilities. Ample off street parking. Our home is situated one block from Rotorua CBD, close to excellent restaurants and all attractions. We are happy to advise on and arrange tours either prior to or on your arrival.

Tresco	**Tel:** (07) 348 9611	**Cost:** Double $75-$85
B&B	**Fax:** (07) 348 9611	Single $50 Visa/MC
Rotorua Central	**Mob:** 025 450 674	**Beds:** 3 Queen 1 Twin 2 Single
Gwyn & John Hanson	**Tollfree:** 0800 TRESCO (873 726)	(6 bdrm)
3 Toko Street	**E:** trescorotorua@xtra.co.nz	**Bath:** 3 Ensuite 2 Guests share
Rotorua	**W:** www.bnb.co.nz/hosts/	
	tresco.html	

Kinloch

Nestled within private gardens in the picturesque lakeside village of Kinloch. Golf, fishing, watersports, (all five minute stroll), snow skiing, bush and mountain walks. The north facing guest wing with private entrance, includes lounge and sunny deck. Hearty breakfasts, wholesome dinners and warm welcomes assure guests of an enjoyable stay. Paul is a NZ Kennel Club judge, golf, music, travel and sports are family interests. We have two friendly dogs Sieger and Sparky. Laundry and delicious home baking always available. Comp. kayak and fishing tackle available.

Twynham at Kinloch	**Tel:** (07) 378 2862	**Cost:** Double $125 Single $95
B&B Country Village Accom-	**Fax:** (07) 378 2868	Dinner $45 Visa/MC
modation	**Mob:** 025 285 6001	**Beds:** 1 Queen 2 Single
15mins W of Taupo	**E:** twynham.bnb@xtra.co.nz	(2 bdrm)
Elizabeth & Paul Whitelock	**W:** www.bnb.co.nz/hosts/	**Bath:** 1 Ensuite 1 Private
84 Marina Terrace	twynham.html	
Kinloch, Taupo		

Kinloch

Trish & Tom's B&B is ideal for active people looking for a break in a friendly atmosphere set in parklike surroundings. Offstreet parking is right at your door. Hearty breakfasts are served with homemade bread and jams. Kinloch offers golf (complimentary clubs available), fishing, biking, tennis, sailing, rockclimbing, bushwalks. Tom is a keen fisherman and frequently sails and fishes the lake with guests. Trish and Tom love golf and can join you for a game. You can join us for a kiwi BBQ at days end.

Tom Sawyer's B&B	**Tel:** (07) 377 2551	**Cost:** Double $95 Single $50
B&B Self-contained	**Fax:** (07) 377 2551	Child under 5 free
20km W of Taupo	**Mob:** 025 764 739	Dinner $25 Visa/MC
Trish & Tom Sawyer	**E:** sawyer@reap.org.nz	**Beds:** 1 King/Twin 1 Queen
34 Angela Place	**W:** www.bnb.co.nz/hosts/	1 Single (2 bdrm)
Kinloch, Taupo	tomsawyers.html	**Bath:** 2 Private

Taupo

Bob and I have enjoyed hosting for over fifteen years, our Lakeview Homestay with beautiful mountains backdrop makes our guests' stay in Taupo very special. Our home is spacious, comfortable and relaxing. All Taupo's attractions are nearby, golf courses, thermal pools, Huka Falls and fishing. We are retired sheep and cattle farmers, Bob excels at golf and is in charge of cooked breakfasts. Home made jams and marmalade are my specialty. It is a pleasure to provide dinner by arrangement. Laundry facilities are always available. Off street parking.

Yeoman's Lakeview Homestay	**Tel:** (07) 377 0283	**Cost:** Double $100 Single $50
B&B Homestay	**Fax:** (07) 377 4683	Child $25
2km E of Taupo	**W:** www.bnb.co.nz/hosts/	Dinner $30 by arr.
Colleen & Bob Yeoman	yeomans.html	**Beds:** 1 Queen 3 Single
23 Rokino Road		(3 bdrm)
Taupo 2730		**Bath:** 1 Ensuite
		1 Guests share

Taupo

Taupo is great for holidays any season, swimming, fishing, tramping, skiing. Our modern warm house has wonderful lake views from lounge and deck. Quiet and comfortable guest bedrooms are downstairs with shared bathroom. Home made muesli, preserves, fresh cooked bread and muffins our breakfast specialty. Two minutes walk to lake and excellent restaurants. Self-contained cottage, 3 bedrooms, sleeps seven, open plan lounge, potbelly stove, linen and firewood supplied. Great for families. Interests include church, Probus, roses, WW2 memorabilia and adorable shitzu dog.

Hawai Homestay	**Tel:** (07) 377 3242	**Cost:** Double $80 Single $45
Self-contained Homestay	**Fax:** (07) 377 3242	Child $20 Dinner $20
3km S of Taupo	**Mob:** 025 234 0558	Marmite Cottage $55
Jeanette & Bryce Jones	**E:** jeanettej@xtra.co.nz	double Visa/MC
18 Hawai Street	**W:** www.bnb.co.nz/hosts/	**Beds:** 1 Queen 1 Twin (2 bdrm)
2 Mile Bay, Taupo	hawaihomestay.html	**Bath:** 1 Guests share

Taupo

Our one level home is located up a tree lined drive with
ample parking, nestled among trees. Superb views of town,
lake mountains and ranges. Retired sheep and cattle
farmers we have travelled widely with many tangible
reminders furnishing our home. Relax or enjoy trout
fishing, tramping, sightseeing or golf. Betty loves to cook
but Taupo abounds in good restaurants. Our cat assures you
of a warm welcome. This is not just a Bed and Breakfast
but a HOMESTAY! Directions: Lakefront Take Taharepa
Road to Hilltop shops turn left into Rokino road. No 30 is
on right after Waihora Street. (One loved cat)

Nolan's Homestay	**Tel:** (07) 377 0828	**Cost:** Double $90 Single $50
Homestay	**Fax:** (07) 377 0828	Child 1/2 price
2km S of Taupo	**Mob:** 025 244 9035	Dinner $25
Betty & Ned Nolan	**E:** nolans@beds-n-leisure.com	**Beds:** 2 Twin 4 Single (2 bdrm)
30 Rokino Road	**W:** www.bnb.co.nz/hosts/	**Bath:** 1 Ensuite 1 Private
Taupo	nolanshomestay.html	1 Family share

Taupo - Acacia Bay

VIEWS VIEWS. Our home is Scandinavian style with
wooden interior. Situated in a very quiet area and
minutes form the beach, we have magnificent,
uninterrupted views of Lake Taupo and The Ranges
from bedrooms and living room. We have travelled
extensively and Eric was previously a tea planter in
Indonesia, having lived in The Netherlands, Spain and
Italy. Directions: Turn down between 95 and 99
Wakeman Road. We are the last house on this short
road (200 metres).

Pariroa Homestay	**Tel:** (07) 378 3861	**Cost:** Double $75 Single $50
Homestay	**Fax:** (07) 378 3866	Child $30 Visa/MC
5km W of Taupo	**Mob:** 025 530 370	**Beds:** 1 Queen 2 Single
Joan & Eric Leersnijder	**E:** pariroa@xtra.co.nz	(2 bdrm)
77A Wakeman Road	**W:** www.mysite.xtra.co.nz/	**Bath:** 1 Guests share
Acacia Bay	~Pariroa	
Taupo		

Taupo

We are 100 yards from Waitahanui River - 200 yards
from beautiful Lake Taupo consisting of two cottages,
one we live in. The second a well equipped accommodation, with gas - electric fires, electric blankets for the
comfort of winter visitors, a deck for our summer
travellers to relax on. For interested fishermen, John is
a Trout fishing guide who can take you to some magic
places. Come visit Waitahanui, we'd love to meet you.
We have ample parking. Please phone for directions.

Riverway Cottages	**Tel:** (07) 378 8822	**Cost:** Double $75 Single $45
Self-contained	**Mob:** 025 278 1732	Child $20
14km S of Taupo	**W:** www.bnb.co.nz/hosts/	**Beds:** 1 Queen 1 Double
Joyce & John Johnson	riverwaycottages.html	1 Single (2 bdrm)
16 Peehi Manini Road		**Bath:** 1 Private
Waitahanui RD 2		
Taupo		

Taupo

We enjoy meeting people and making new friends and warmly welcome you to our spacious, attractively furnished home, close to restaurants and shops. We invite you to relax and wander in our garden and use the summer pool with courtyard. Raewyn & Neil are proud of their homestay business offering hospitality, use of lounge, laundry facilities, swimming pool, barbecue and large carpark. Pataka House is close to the thermal hot springs and on the doorstep of a world-famous lake. Courtesy car available.

Pataka House	**Tel:** (07) 378 5481	**Cost:** Double $100 Single $60
Self-contained Homestay	**Fax:** (07) 378 5461	Child $30 S/C $110
1km S of Taupo	**Mob:** 025 473 881	**Beds:** 2 Queen 4 Single
Raewyn & Neil Alexander	**W:** www.beds-n-leisure.com/	(4 bdrm)
8 Pataka Road	pataka/htm	**Bath:** 1 Ensuite 1 Private
Taupo		1 Guests share

Taupo

"Kooringa" is situated in sheltered Acacia Bay (2 mins walk to Lake), surrounded by native bush and gardens with magnificent views of Lake Taupo and Mt Tauhara. We are a retired professional couple, lived overseas and travelled extensively with our two sons. We are within easy distance of all major attractions. Your private guest suite includes lounge, Sky TV and deck. A generous breakfast with plenty of variety is served in the conservatory overlooking the Lake. Please phone, fax or email for bookings. Directions: www. kooringa.co.nz

Kooringa	**Tel:** (07) 378 8025	**Cost:** Double $110 Single $60
Lakestay	**Fax:** (07) 378 6085	Visa/MC
6km W of Taupo	**Mob:** 025 272 6343	**Beds:** 1 Queen 1 Double
Robin & John Mosley	**E:** kooringa@xtra.co.nz	1 Single (2 bdrm)
32 Ewing Grove	**W:** www.kooringa.co.nz	**Bath:** 1 Ensuite
Acacia Bay, Taupo		

Taupo

Nestled in a restful tree-lined street, a mere five minutes stroll form the Lake's edge and shopping centre "Lakeland Homestay" is a cheerful and cosy home that enjoys views of the lake and mountains. Keen gardeners, anglers and golfers Chris and Lesley work and play in an adventure oasis. For extra warmth on winter nights all beds have electric blankets, and laundry facilities are available. A courtesy car is available for coach travellers and there is off-street parking. Please phone for directions.

Lakeland Homestay	**Tel:** (07) 378 1952	**Cost:** Double $100 Single $60
Homestay	**Fax:** (07) 378 1912	Visa/MC
Taupo Central	**Mob:** 025 877 971	**Beds:** 1 Double 2 Single
Lesley, Chris & Pussycats	**E:** lakeland.bb@xtra.co.nz	(2 bdrm)
11 Williams Street	**W:** www.bnb.co.nz/hosts/	**Bath:** 1 Private 1 Family share
Taupo	lakelandhomestay.html	

J. B. Charters

Taupo - Acacia Bay
UNIQUE GENUINE LAKEFRONT LOCATION

PAEROA'S hosts Barbara and John welcome you to their spacious modern quality Homestay at sheltered ACACIA BAY, developed on three levels to capture the MAGNIFICENT UNINTERRUPTED, PANO-RAMIC VIEWS of world famous LAKE TAUPO and beyond.

The flower filled garden gently descends to the private beach, jetty where you can swim, relax. Use the rowboat or catch a FISHING CHARTER with John in his 30-ft cruiser. John has fished Lake Taupo and its rivers successfully for 35 years. We can cook your large RAINBOW TROUT for breakfast or smoke it for your lunch.

The house is large, comfortable and well appointed for your comfort and privacy with spacious lounge areas, sundecks, patios and outdoor seats in the garden to enjoy the abundant birdlife, flowers and Lake Views. The rooms have comfortable beds, TV, electric blankets and heaters, great views, ensuite bathrooms with heated towelrails and hairdriers - serviced daily. Laundry service is available. A large guest lounge for your use with tea and coffee facilities, TV, piano, books and comfort. Private decks off the rooms. Breakfasts are a specialty.

We are retired sheep and beef farmers enjoying living in our quiet peaceful and private home beside the beach, just minutes from the town centre, 3 golf courses, bush walks, restaurants, shops, boating, thermal hot springs, and all the many major attractions the area provides.

Plan to STAY SEVERAL DAYS and base your CENTRAL NORTH ISLAND visits to Napier, Rotorua, Tongariro National Park and ski-fields from here. There is so much to do in Taupo. Amongst your hosts' interests are travel, golf, gardening, fishing, entertaining and family. We have a detailed knowledge of the region and members of the NZ Assn Farm & Home Hosts.

Paeroa Lakeside Homestay	**Tel:** (07) 378 8449	**Cost:** Double $150-$200
B&B Homestay	**Fax:** (07) 378 8446	Single $150-$200
5km W of Taupo	**Mob:** 025 818 829	Child $75 Dinner $40
Barbara & John Bibby	**E:** bibby@reap.org.nz	Triple (2 Rooms) $225
21 Te Kopua Street	**W:** www.taupohomestay.com	Visa/MC
Acacia Bay, Taupo		**Beds:** 2 King 1 Queen 2 Single
		(3 bdrm)
		Bath: 3 Ensuite

Taupo

A few metres from the lakefront beach and a short stroll to town we are close to all local facilities and attractions. Hospitality is our priority. We enjoy sharing the ambience of our much admired home and garden with our guests. Bedrooms are comfortable and attractive with facilities to match - one party at a time. A widely travelled retired couple with numerous interests we are the recipients of the coveted National Travel Courtesy Award. Telephone for directions. Courtesy car available if required.

Tui Glen
Homestay
1km S of Taupo
Robbie & Stan Shearer
10 Pataka Road
Taupo

Tel: (07) 378 7007
Fax: (07) 378 2412
Mob: 025 239 2931
E: stanrob@ezysurf.co.nz
W: www.bnb.co.nz/hosts/
tuiglen.html

Cost: Double $100 Single $65
Dinner B/A Visa/MC
Beds: 1 King 2 Single (2 bdrm)
Bath: 1 Ensuite 1 Private

Taupo

Welcome to Ben Lomond. Jack and I have farmed here for 40 years and our comfortable family home is set in a mature garden. There is a self contained cottage in the garden or 2 bedrooms available in the house. We have interests in fishing, golf and the Equestrian world and are familiar with the attractions on the Central Plateau. Our pets include dogs and cats who wander in and out. Taupo restaurants are 15 minutes away or dine with us by arrangement.

Ben Lomond
Self-contained Homestay
15km W of Taupo
Mary & Jack Weston
1434 Poihipi Road
RD 1
Taupo

Tel: (07) 377 6033
Fax: (07) 377 6033
Mob: 025 774 080
E: benlomond@xtra.co.nz
W: www.bnb.co.nz/hosts/
benlomond.html

Cost: Double $90 Single $45
Child $22 Dinner $25 by
arrangement S/C price on
inquiry Visa/MC
Beds: 1 Queen 1 Twin (2 bdrm)
Bath: 1 Guests share

Taupo

We enjoy having guests in our spacious home overlooking farmland and bordering Taupo's Botanical gardens. We hope you will join us for dinner (maybe a barbecue in the summer) and complimentary wine in our pleasant dining room. There are many good restaurants in Taupo should you prefer that. Our launch "Bonita" is available for fishing or sight seeing on the beautiful lake - Dan is an excellent skipper. We (and our elderly cat Ginny) look forward to welcoming you to our warm, comfortable, home.

Homestay
3km SE of Taupo
Ann & Dan Hennebry
28 Greenwich Street
Taupo

Tel: (07) 378 9483
Mob: 025 297 4283
E: brie@xtra.co.nz
W: www.bnb.co.nz/hosts/
hennebry.html

Cost: Double $90 Single $60
Dinner $30
Beds: 1 King 1 Single (2 bdrm)
Bath: 1 Guests share

Taupo Countryside

Turn into our leafy driveway and relax in tranquil, rambling gardens. Accommodation options: 1: Enjoy bed & breakfast in our comfortable, centrally heated farmhouse. Delicious farm breakfasts. Homegrown produce and excellent cooking make dining recommended. 2: Settle into Bird Cottage which is self-contained and cosy, with delightful views. Perfect for two, will sleep 4/5. Firewood and linen provided. No meals included, but breakfast/dinner happily prepared by arrangement. Meet our gentle donkeys, coloured sheep, outdoor dog. Laundry facilities available for small charge.

South Claragh & Bird Cottage
Homestay & Self-contained
35km NW of Taupo
Lesley & Paul Hill
South Claragh
RD 1, Mangakino, Taupo

Tel: (07) 372 8848
Fax: (07) 372 8047
Mob: 025 620 7325
E: lhill@reap.org.nz
W: mysite.xtra.co.nz/
~aCountryHomestay

Cost: Dbl $100 Sgl $50-$65
Child 1/2 price Dinner $40pp
Bird Cottage $65 - $75
$20 extra person, Visa/MC
Beds: 1 Queen 1 Single (2 bdrm)
Bath: 2 Private

Taupo

Bramham is situated just two minutes walk form the Hot Beach of Lake Taupo and offers tremendous views of the lake and mountains to the south.   John and Julia, having spent 24 years in the RNZAF, including service with the USAF in Tucson Arizona, welcome you to our quiet, homely and peaceful atmosphere. Hearty breakfasts are our specialty. Local knowledge is our business. Bus terminal and airport service complimentary. Being non smokers our dogs, Bob and Daisy, ask you not to smoke in our home.

Bramham
B&B
2km S of Taupo
Julia & John Bates
7 Waipahihi Avenue
Taupo

Tel: (07) 378 0064
Fax: (07) 378 0065
Mob: 025 240 9643
E: info@bramham-bed-and-breakfast.com
W: www.bramham-bed-and-breakfast.com

Cost: Double $100-$110
Single $60-$70
Beds: 1 Double 2 Twin
1 Single (3 bdrm)
Bath: 2 Ensuite 1 Private

Taupo

If you want a quiet Homestay with panoramic views of lake and mountains, generous breakfasts and warm hospitality, this is the place for you. Upstairs guest rooms open onto a sheltered sundeck with extensive views of the lake and snow capped volcanoes. We also have a comfortable self-contained unit with its own garden entrance. All Taupo's famous attractions are nearby including Huka Falls and thermal pools. Laundry facilities are available. You will enjoy your stay in this lovely area. To avoid disappointment booking is recommended.

Catley's Homestay
Homestay
3km S of Taupo
Beverley & Tom Catley
55 Grace Crescent
Taupo

Tel: (07) 378 1403
Fax: (07) 378 1402
E: taupo@actrix.gen.nz
W: www.bnb.co.nz/hosts/catleyshomestay.html

Cost: Double $100 Single $70
Child $30 Dinner by
arrangement Visa/MC
Beds: 1 Queen 1 Double
2 Single (3 bdrm)
Bath: 1 Private 1 Family share

Taupo

Wend your way along a tree-lined drive to enter the tranquillity of our 11 acre rural retreat, just 12 minutes from Taupo, 45 minutes from Rotorua and central to tourist attractions. Our large home has billiard room with fridge for guest use, lounge with feature fireplace and covered verandah. The spacious, well appointed guest rooms, two with ensuite and balcony, overlook park-like grounds with colourful gardens, mature trees, grass tennis court and beyond pond and stream, friendly farm animals. Barbara speaks fluent German.

Minarapa
Homestay Rural Homestay
14km NW of Taupo
Barbara & Dermot Grainger
620 Oruanui Road
RD 1
Taupo

Tel: (07) 378 1931
Mob: 025 272 2367
E: minarapa@voyager.co.nz
W: www.minarapa.co.nz

Cost: Double $90-$115
Single $70-$85 Child $30
Dinner by arrangement
Visa/MC
Beds: 2 Queen 2 Single
(3 bdrm)
Bath: 2 Ensuite 1 Private

Taupo

With a view across Lake Taupo to Acacia Bay we are flanked by rhododendrons and a small park, enjoying peace and privacy in a residential area, 2km from the city centre. From our upstairs (lounge, bar dining area) we have enjoyed brilliant sunsets with our guests from all parts of the planet. We specialise in arranging your activities (boating to bungy) prior to or on arrival. We will meet you at local transport termimals if required. Please phone.

Gillies Lodge
B&B
Kay & Gerry English
77 Gillies Ave
Taupo

Tel: (07) 377 2377
Fax: (07) 377 2377
E: genglish@reap.org.nz
W: www.bnb.co.nz/hosts/
gillieslodge.html

Cost: Double $85 Single $65
Child under 12 free
Visa/MC Amex
Beds: 4 Double 12 Single
(9 bdrm)
Bath: 9 Ensuite

Taupo

You will get a warm welcome in our home. Stay two nights or more, and Jack will take you for a FREE cruise on Lake Taupo's replica steamboat "Ernest Kemp" (conditions apply). Breakfast is served in the main living room, and includes Bridget's home baked bread and home-made jams. (Cooked breakfast optional extra.) We are able to recommend and book local attractions. Off street parking available. We appreciate guests not smoking in the house. Please phone for directions.

Mountain Views Homestay
Homestay
2km S of Taupo
Jack & Bridget
17B Puriri Street
Taupo

Tel: (07) 378 6136
Fax: (07) 378 6134
Mob: 025 200 5437
E: mtviews@reap.org.nz
W: www.bnb.co.nz/hosts/
mountainviewshomestay.html

Cost: Double $70 Single $40
Child negotiable
Dinner by arrangement
Visa/MC
Beds: 1 Queen 1 Twin
(2 bdrm)
Bath: 1 Guests share

Taupo

Welcome to our completely private guest area which includes queen size bed, separate sitting room with fridge, log fire, TV and two single beds. Plus private bathroom, laundry facility, easy access to indoor thermal spa and outdoor salt pool. We invite you to join us for breakfast and enjoy the lake and mountain views. Georgia, our social Labrador, looks forward to your company. Armchair cricketers and active golfers especially welcome. We are happy to suggest 'what's hot and what's not' with local activities and eateries.

Above the Lake
B&B Self-contained Homestay
3km S of Taupo
Judi & Barry Thomson
32 Harvey Street
Taupo

Tel: (07) 378 4558
Fax: (07) 378 4071
Mob: 025 817 443
E: judi.thomson@xtra.co.nz
W: www.geocities.com/abovethelake

Cost: Double $95 Single $65
Visa/MC
Beds: 1 Queen (1 bdrm)
Bath: 1 Private

Taupo

Welcome to our dream: "Richlyn" warm, spacious, comfortable, smokefree. Eight park-like peaceful acres, views of mountain, lake, and countryside. Outdoor spa pool, gardens, places to walk and relax, two cats, two poodles, one lovebird. Richard and Lyn enjoy travelling, we provide what we expect, comfortable beds, great breakfasts and genuine friendship at "Richlyn", a home away from home for up to eight guests. Directions: From Taupo, up Napier Road 6 km, right into Caroline Drive, 2 km to Mark Wynd turn left, first driveway left.

Richlyn Homestay
Homestay Country Homestay
8km E of Taupo
Lyn & Richard James
1 Mark Wynd
Bonshaw Park, Taupo

Tel: (07) 378 8023
Fax: (07) 378 8023
Mob: 025 908 647
E: richlyn.james.taupo@xtra.co.nz
W: www.richlyn.co.nz

Cost: Double $140 Single $100
Child neg Visa/MC
Beds: 1 King 2 Queen 2 Single
(4 bdrm)
Bath: 1 Ensuite 1 Private

Taupo

Enjoy the warm hospitality and relaxed atmosphere in our sunny home, situated in a quiet cul-de-sac, just a stroll to the lake. Upstairs is exclusive to guests, with two double bedrooms offering panoramic views; both equipped with cable TV, refrigerators and tea/coffee facilities. One bedroom and guest lounge open onto a sunny balcony overlooking lake. Soak in our hot mineral pool in the garden - totally private except for our friendly cat. Home baking and delicious continental/countrystyle cooked breakfasts a speciality. Free E mail facilities. Telephone anytime.

Ambleside Homestay and Bed
& Breakfast
B&B Homestay
2km S of Taupo
Patricia & Russell Jensen
5 Te Hepera Street, Taupo

Tel: (07) 378 1888
Fax: (07) 378 1888
Mob: 025 836 888
E: scandic@xtra.co.nz
W: www.ambleside.co.nz

Cost: Double $110-$120
Single $100 Child $30
Visa/MC
Beds: 2 Queen (2 bdrm)
Bath: 1 Ensuite 1 Private

Taupo - Acacia Bay

Your hosts Bob and Marlene and Cleo our Burmese cat
extend a warm welcome to our large Lockwood home
with woodfire for winter and north facing sunny deck
from guest bedroom. Also magnificent view of Lake
Taupo from lounge and front deck. There are bush
walks and steps down to lake to swim in summer. We
are awaiting your arrival with anticipation of making
friends. You are welcome to smoke but not inside.
Please phone for directions.

Leece's Homestay
Homestay
6km W of Taupo
Marlene and Bob Leece
98 Wakeman Road
Acacia Bay
Taupo 2736

Tel: (07) 378 6099
W: www.bnb.co.nz/hosts/
leeceshomestay.html

Cost: Double $80 Single $50
Child neg
Beds: 1 King 1 Double 2 Single
(2 bdrm)
Bath: 1 Guests share

Taupo

Set amongst flower gardens on a hillside overlooking
picturesque farmland, with a scattering of animals
including our pet poodle and cat, we offer a warm
welcome, wonderful food, peace and tranquillity,
Fantails, Tuis, Bellbirds flitting from tree to tree. Close
to the many 'wonders' of Taupo we tempt you in home
comforts, breakfast to suit, healthy, indulgent or a little
of both. A private guest wing in the house or a separate
annex, join us let us spoil you. Dinner by arrangement.
Members NZAFHH Association.

Brackenhurst
Farmstay
19km N of Taupo
Margaret and Noel Marson
801 Oruanui Road
RD 1
Taupo

Tel: (07) 377 6451
Fax: (07) 377 6451
W: www.bnb.co.nz/hosts/
brackenhurst.html

Cost: Double $100 Single $60
Child $30
Dinner $35 by arrangement
Beds: 1 Queen 1 Double
3 Single (3 bdrm)
Bath: 2 Ensuite

Taupo

Absolute lakeside location with natural thermal spa and
unobstructed views of the lake to Mt Ruapehu. Close
to town and a menagerie of activities with a memorable
scenic walkway to restaurants. Friendly helpful hosts
in comfortable pleasant and interesting surroundings.
Small well-behaved dog. Stairs to your cosy room.
Children welcome. We appreciate you not smoking in
our home. We are members of NZAFHH and look
forward to hearing from you. Please phone for
directions. Inspections by appointment.

Lakeside Thermal Homestay
Homestay
2km S of Taupo
Terri McCallum
No 3, 227 Lake Terrace
Taupo

Tel: (07) 378 1171
Fax: (07) 378 1101
Mob: 021 120 4961
E: terri.max@xtra.co.nz
W: www.bnb.co.nz/hosts/
lakesidethermalhomestay.html

Cost: Double $100 Single $60-
$85 Child $15
Beds: 1 Queen 2 Double
(2 bdrm)
Bath: 1 Guests share

Taupo - Acacia Bay

Situated 5 minutes from Taupo township The Loft is nestled on a hillside overlooking LAKE TAUPO. Your hosts LINDA AND TODD welcome you into their world of luxury, fine food and romance. Their years of experience in the hospitality industry, make them a couple who excel in the art of entertainment.

Todd is an internationally travelled CHEF and he and Linda are both culinary masters. Their enthusiasm for good food and wine is something that spills over into everything that they do. Sumptuous breakfasts of homemade preserves, freshly squeezed orange juice, fresh baked muffins and croissants, smoked salmon scrambled egg and piping hot waffles are an experience not to be missed.

Arrange an evening meal at The Loft and you will be treated to a four course CANDLELIT BANQUET that will leave you with a lasting memory of New Zealand hospitality. The Loft boasts three very private Queen sized rooms with ensuite bathrooms. Their style is RUSTIC, ROMANTIC AND WARM where the attention to detail shows that your comfort takes top priority. The guest lounge with a large open fire welcomes you to relax, enjoy afternoon tea, or complimentary pre-dinner drinks and port while you chat about the Taupo region and your sight-seeing plans.

TROUT FISHING TRIPS & ADVENTURE TREKS can be arranged by your hosts along with a myriad of other more relaxing activities. Linda & Todd look forward to sharing their home and their company with you, assuring you of a warm welcome and a luxurious stay. Directions: www.theloftnz.com

The Loft
B&B
5km W of Taupo
Todd & Linda Gilchrist
3 Wakeman Road
Acacia Bay
Taupo

Tel: (07) 377 1040
Fax: (07) 377 1049
Mob: 025 851 347
E: the_loft@xtra.co.nz
W: www.theloftnz.com

Cost: Double $120-$170
Single $90 Child $75
Gourmet Dinners $55pp
Visa/MC
Beds: 3 Queen 1 Single
(3 bdrm)
Bath: 3 Ensuite

Taupo

3 course dinner includes wine. Breakfast includes fruit, farm eggs, bacon, sausages, home-made bread and conserves, coffee, English/herb tea. Our 461 acre farm grazes sheep, cattle, deer, goats and thoroughbred horses, which we breed and Jim trains and races. Judith, a NZAFHH member and food professional enjoys gardening, especially growing organic vegetables. We enjoy sharing our large comfortable home, garden, farm, welcome children (5-12 half price, under 5 negotiable). We appreciate you not smoking in our home. Directions: please phone.

Whitiora Farm
Farmstay
12km NW of Taupo
Judith & Jim McGrath
1281 Mapara Road
RD 1, Taupo

Tel: (07) 378 6491
Fax: (07) 378 6491
E: mcg.whitiora@xtra.co.nz
W: www.bnb.co.nz/hosts/
whitiorafarm.html

Cost: Double $100 Single $60
Child $25 Dinner $30,
Lunch $15
Beds: 1 Queen 4 Single
(3 bdrm)
Bath: 2 Family share

Taupo

A Warm and inviting new one bedroomself-contained cottage set in extensive park like gardens. Our farm has sweeping rural views and is 10 minutes easy drive from Taupo and 45 minutes from Rotorua. Enjoy home cooked cuisine, explore ou 10 acres and meet the family of alpacas. We look forward to welcoming you to our smoke free cottage and home.

Bellbird Ridge Farm
B&B Farmstay Homestay
13km N of Taupo
Mike & Lorraine Harrison
68 Tangye Road
RD 1
Taupo

Tel: +64 7 377 1996
Fax: +64 7 377 1996
Mob: 025 668 7754
E: lharrison@xtra.co.nz
W: www.bnb.co.nz/hosts/
bellbirdridge.html

Cost: Cottage ouble $120
Single $80
Dinner $30 by arr.
Beds: 1 Queen (1 bdrm)
Bath: 1 Ensuite

Taupo

We invite you to enjoy the tranquillity of our beautiful property beside Lake Taupo. Our luxury accommodation is smokefree, offers breakfast of your choice and has air conditioning and central heating. All rooms have lake views and a balcony or terrace. Totally relax beside the lake, in the lake (swimming), on the lake (boating, fishing) or around the lake, fishing in world famous trout rivers; walking trails; ski slopes; golf courses, natural thermal pools and unique volcanic countryside. Enjoy your break beside the lake.

Beside the Lake
B&B
5km S of Taupo
Irene & Roger Foote
8 Chad Street
Taupo

Tel: (07) 378 5847
Fax: (07) 378 5847
Mob: 025 804 683
E: foote.tpo@xtra.co.nz
W: www.bnb.co.nz/hosts/
besidethelake.html

Cost: Double $120 Single $100
Visa/MC
Beds: 2 King/Twin (2 bdrm)
Bath: 1Ensuite 1 Private

Taupo

The Haven offers hospitality, fine fare and the assurance we will make your stay a comfortable and welcoming one.

Situated in a quiet location, mere minutes from the town centre, you are invited to share the inviting luxuries that our well appointed, newly renovated home offers. The private guest lounge with gym equipment and pool table are at your disposal, as is a leisurely soak in the spa pool.

All guest rooms are spacious, private and have Queen size beds. The house is centrally heated to make the cooler season's stay a cosy one.

Breakfast can be light or a lavish, tasty affair, to set you on your way for the day to enjoy the many attractions the Taupo region has to offer. If you have not already done so, we will be happy to help with bookings, etc.

We are happy to cater in house 3 course dinners from $45pp. Lunches may be arranged where necessary. Digital Sky TV, video, email and internet facilities are all available. Laundry facilities are available on request. Good off street parking with a limited facility for lock-up.

Above all, we warmly welcome you to our home, and wish to make your stay a pleasurable one. User-friendly cat and small dog reside.

The Haven
B&B
3km S of Taupo
Katarina Shaw & Grant Whittaker
53 Chesham Ave
Taupo

Tel: (07) 378 3122
Fax: (07) 378 3122
Mob: 021 251 4280
E: sacrlett@voyager.co.nz
W: www.bnb.co.nz/hosts/ thehaven.html

Cost: Double $190-$270
Single $130-$180
Child $25 Dinner B/A
Visa/MC
Beds: 4 Queen (4 bdrm)
Bath: 2 Ensuite 1 Guests share

Taupo

You are invited to stay at my modern smoke-free homestay situated in a tranquil neighbourhood within walking distance of Hot Pools and Lake. Relax and enjoy Fairviews gardens. Be as private as you wish or socialise with hosts. Rooms are tastefully decorated and comfortable. Double room is large with private entrance, TV, fridge, tea/coffee facilities, robe and hairdryer. Generous breakfasts provided. Email facilities and laundry are available at small charge. My knowledge of region is extensive. Interests include theatre, antiques/collectables, travel, tramping.

Fairviews
Homestay Boutique Accommoda-
tion
2.5km S of Taupo
Brenda Watson
8 Fairview Terrace
Taupo

Tel: (07) 377 0773
E: fairviews@reap.org.nz
W: www.reap.org.nz/~fairviews

Cost: Double $100-$130
Single $85-$100
Child n/a Dinner n/a
Visa/MC
Beds: 1 Queen 2 Single
(2 bdrm)
Bath: 1 Ensuite 1 Private

Turangi

Welcome to our smoke-free home, with ENSUITE bathrooms for your comfort, in QUIET street, beside Tongariro RIVER walkway and fishing, handy to restaurants and town, with arranged transport to TONGARIRO NATIONAL PARK at your door. LAKE TAUPO and THERMAL baths 5 minutes drive. Upstairs QUEEN rooms with balconies, separated for PRIVACY by tea, coffee making area. Downstairs is twin suite, laundry and lounge where we'll share interests in flying, skiing, fishing, tramping, and maps, of our VOLCANIC area. Guest-shy cat. Cottage suitable for families.

The Andersons'
B&B Homestay &
Self-contained Cottage
1.5km NW of Turangi Central
Betty & Jack Anderson
3 Poto Street, Turangi

Tel: (07) 386 8272
Fax: (07) 386 8272
Mob: 025 628 0810
E: jbanderson@xtra.co.nz
W: www.bnb.co.nz/hosts/
anderson.html

Cost: Double $90 Single $55
Child by arrangement Dinner
$30pp by arrangement S/C
Cottage $70 - $120 Visa/MC
Beds: 2 Queen 1 Twin (3 bdrm)
Bath: 3 Ensuite

Turangi

Set in half-acre woodland garden, featuring rhododen-drons and native plants, which attracts many species of birds. Access through the garden gate to the Tongariro River and the major fishing pools. Perfect retreat for that restful break. 4 mins from an excellent golf course, 1/2 hour to the mountains. Our home and garden are adjacent, but allows utmost privacy to cottage. Full modern kitchen and laundry, all linen supplied. Full breakfast can be provisioned prior to arrival. Come, share this corner of nature's paradise with us.

Akepiro Cottage
Self-contained
53km S of Taupo
Jenny & John Wilcox
PO Box 256
Turangi

Tel: (07) 386 7384
Fax: (07) 386 6838
E: jennywilcox@xtra.co.nz
W: www.bnb.co.nz/hosts/
akepirocottage.html

Cost: Double $70 Single $50
Breakfast $10 Visa/MC
Beds: 2 Queen 2 Single
(2 bdrm)
Bath: 1 Private

Turangi

You open the back gate and there is the Island Pool. We can now offer 1 self contained unit with 2 bedrooms, kitchen, lounge and sun deck. 2 double rooms inside the lodge with ensuites. A spacious lounge with open fire is available along with Sky TV. Kerry, your guide has fished the area for 50 years and has been a guide for some 30 years. Suzanne, the other Simpson partner is your resident chef and is renowned for her trout sashimi. Please come and "enjoy".

Ika Fishing Lodge
B&B Self-contained Homestay
1km E of Turangi
Suzanne & Kerry Simpson
155 Taupahi Road
PO Box 259
Turangi

Tel: (07) 386 5538
Fax: (07) 386 5538
E: ikalodge@xtra.co.nz
W: www.ika.co.nz

Cost: Double $120-$160
Single $90-$120
Dinner $40pp
Visa/MC Amex Diners
Beds: 2 King/Twin 3 Queen
(4 bdrm)
Bath: 3 Ensuite

Turangi - Motuoapa

Stop and enjoy this outdoor Paradise. Just off SH1 (B & B Sign). Overlooking Lake Taupo, our two-storey home offers ground-floor self-contained accommodation with own entrance. Fully equipped Kitchen, Dining room, Lounge. Two cosy bedrooms (each with TV). Vehicle/Boat off-street parking. Minutes to Marina and World-renowned Lake/river fishing. Beautiful bush walks. 45 minutes to ski fields and Tongariro National Park. Our association with Tongariro/Taupo area spans over 30 years, through work and outdoor pursuits. Welcome to our Retreat.

Meredith House
B&B Homestay
10km N of Turangi
Frances & Ian Meredith
45 Kahotea Place
Motuoapa, RD 2
Turangi

Tel: (07) 386 5266
Fax: (07) 386 5270
E: meredith.house@xtra.co.nz
W: www.bnb.co.nz/hosts/
meredithhouse.html

Cost: Double $80 Single $50
Dinner $25 by arrangement
Self-contained $80 - $120
Breakfast $10. Visa/MC
Beds: 1 Queen 3 Single
(2 bdrm)
Bath: 1 Private

Turangi

On the banks of the Tongariro River in tranquil gardens this perfect hideaway cottage has a fully equipped kitchen, TV, potbelly and a host of other above average details to ensure your comfort. Enjoy breakfast at your leisure. Fish in world famous pools adjacent to our boundary, participate in the myriad outdoor activities offered in the area or relax with a book in our beautiful garden. We have travelled extensively and enjoy meeting people. We are enthusiastic gardeners, "helped" by our dachshunds, Minnie and D'Arcy.

River Birches
Self-contained
52km S of Taupo
Gill & Peter Osborne
21A Koura Street
Turangi

Tel: (07) 386 5348
Fax: (07) 386 5948
E: gillo@voyager.co.nz
W: www.bnb.co.nz/hosts/
riverbirches.html

Cost: Double $150 Single $95
Visa/MC
Beds: 1 King/Twin 2 Single
(2 bdrm)
Bath: 1 Private

Turangi

Welcome to Turangi and to our New Zealand colonial-style home. Relax and unwind in the unique beauty of the trout fishing capital of the world. Ensuite bedrooms open onto verandas, a log fire in the lounge in winter or coffee on the deck in summer. Explore the trout rivers, the mountains of Tongariro National Park, Lake Taupo and experience the activities available in this place for all seasons. We offer organic food, dinners by arrangement and hearty, always special breakfasts. Two friendly dogs live outdoors. Not suitable for children.

Founders Guest Lodge
B&B
54km S of Taupo
Peter & Chris Stewart
253 Taupahi Road, Turangi

Tel: (07) 386 8539
Fax: (07) 386 8534
E: founders@ihug.co.nz
W: www.founders.co.nz

Cost: Double $140 Single $80
    Dinner $35 Visa/MC
Beds: 1 King/Twin 3 Queen
    (4 bdrm)
Bath: 4 Ensuite

Turangi

Close to the world renowned Tongariro River we offer a charming and gracious residence in a quiet street. This unique setting has exceptional access to tramping, fly fishing, skiing, rafting or purely a retreat from life's hustle and bustle. Enjoy superior and spacious ensuite accommodation with TV and coffee/tea making facilities in a separate part of the house. Your Dutch/Canadian hosts have considerable international experience and can speak Dutch and French. Dinner by arrangement. Not suitable for young children or pets.

The Birches
Homestay
52km S of Taupo
Tineke & Peter Baldwin
13 Koura Street
Turangi

Tel: (07) 386 5140
Fax: (07) 386 5149
Mob: 021 149 6594
E: tineke.peter@xtra.co.nz
W: www.bnb.co.nz/hosts/
thebirches.html

Cost: Double $105 Single $90
    Dinner by arrangement
    Visa/MC
Beds: 1 Queen (1 bdrm)
Bath: 1 Ensuite

Turangi

Our home is on the banks of Lake Taupo in its beautiful southwest corner with wonderful views, excellent fishing, boating, swimming, lakeside and bush walks. Only 15 minutes to Turangi shops and restaurants, Tongariro river, trout hatchery, eco tours, thermal pools, golf. 40 minutes to Tongariro National Park and mountains. We offer a comfortable private smoke free suite with separate entry. Tea making facilities, fridge, microwave, TV, laundry available. We love this special place and with our friendly labrador look forward to sharing it with you.

Wills' Place
B&B
16km NW of Turangi
Jill & Brian Wills
145 Omori Road
Omori

Tel: (07) 386 7339
Fax: (07) 386 7339
Mob: 025 228 8960
E: willsplace@wave.co.nz
W: www.bnb.co.nz/hosts/
willsplace.html

Cost: Double $100 Single $60
    Dinner by arrangement
    Child neg
Beds: 1 Queen 2 Single
    (1 bdrm)
Bath: 1 Ensuite

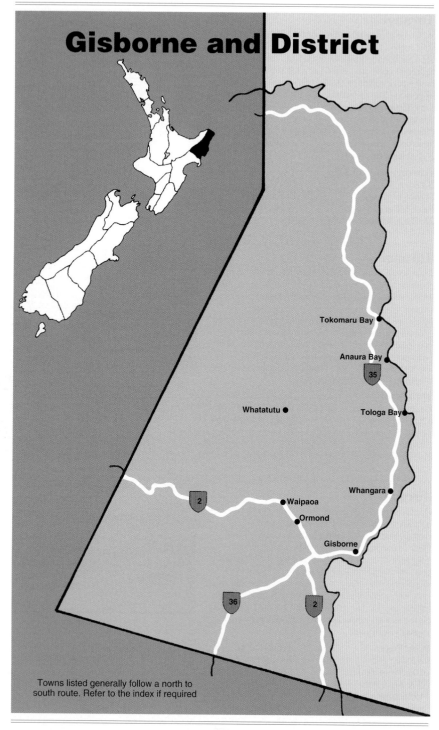

Gisborne and District

Tokomaru Bay

Anaura Bay

35

Whatatutu

Tologa Bay

Whangara

2

Waipaoa

Ormond

Gisborne

36

2

Towns listed generally follow a north to
south route. Refer to the index if required

Tokomaru Bay

Welcome to 'Rahiri' a gracious 100 year old homestead situated on Pauariki Station, 7km inland from Tokomaru Bay. We offer spacious relaxing accommodation for those wanting a break away from a busy stressful life. Situated amongst mature trees and gardens, with swimming pool, tennis court and wonderful views of Mt Hikurangi. Open fire places in one bedroom and other rooms. Flowers, antique furniture, Alfresco dining in summer. Dinner includes aperitifs, three course meal, wine included. Laundry facilities available.

Rahiri	**Tel:** (06) 864 5615	**Cost:** Double $275 Single $200
Farmstay Homestay	**Fax:** (06) 864 5817	price includes dinner, bed
7km W of Tokomaru Bay	**Mob:** 025 246 2619	and breakfast Visa/MC
Meg & Bill Busby	**Tollfree:** 0800 347 411	**Beds:** 1 King 1 Queen
263 Mata Road	**E:** Info@Rahiri.com	1 Double 2 Single
Tokomaru Bay	**W:** www.rahiri.com	(3 bdrm)
East Coast		**Bath:** 1 Ensuite 1 Guests share

Anaura Bay

Paradise - the best of both worlds - Breakfast with us at either our beachfront cottage in picturesque Anaura bay with glorious sunrises, white sand and backdrop of beautiful native bush, fishing and walkways or "Willowflat" our 200ha sheep, cattle and cropping farm,12km, with spacious home and grounds, 11-year old granddaughter and cat, an hour north of Gisborne. Village, Cashmere Company, fishing charters, hunting, golf course, walkways within 12km. Extra beds occasionally available. Self-contained Beachstay also available $150 per night, 2 couples. (Minimum 2 nights)

Anaura Beachstay or	**Tel:** (06) 862 6341	**Cost:** Double $80 Single $45
Willowflat Farmstay B&B	**Fax:** (06) 862 6371	Child Half price
B&B Self-contained	**E:** willowflat@xtra.co.nz	Dinner $25
Farmstay Beachstay	**W:** www.bnb.co.nz/hosts/	S/C Beachfront Cottage,
12km N of Tolaga Bay	anaurabeachstay.html	2 Doubles $150
June & Allan Hall		**Beds:** 1 Double (1 bdrm)
Tolaga Bay, Gisborne		**Bath:** 2 Family share

Anaura Bay

A peaceful haven we are happy to share with others. Our property covers 3.5 acres, sweeps down to a beautiful white sand beach and is bordered on one side by a native bush reserve. Views of sunrise and the bay from the loft bedroom and deck are sensational. Lots of quiet spots for time out and an outdoor shower and bath for the romantics. Bush walks. Fishing charters and marae visits by arrangement. All meals can be provided by arrangement.

Rangimarie	**Tel:** 021 633 372	**Cost:** Double $90 Single $60
B&B Self-contained Beachstay	**Fax:** (06) 868 9940	Visa/MC
75km N of Gisborne	**Mob:** 021 633 372	**Beds:** 1 King (1 bdrm)
Judy and David Newell	**E:** anaurastay@xtra.co.nz	**Bath:** 1 Private
930 Anaura Bay Road	**W:** www.bnb.co.nz/hosts/	
Anaura Bay	rangimarie.html	
East Coast		

Tolaga Bay

Papatahi Homestay is very easy to find being just 3km north of the Tolaga Bay township, on the Pacific Coast Highway. We have a comfortable, modern, sunny home set in a wonderful garden. Papatahi offers separate accommodation with ensuite. A golf course, fishing charters, the Tolaga Bay Cashmere Co and several magnificent beaches are all just minutes away. Daily farm activities are often of interest to our guests. Friendly farm pets and three children add to the experience! Great country meals and good wine are a speciality. Inspection will impress!

Papatahi
Self-contained Homestay
3km N of Tolaga Bay
Nicki & Bruce Jefferd
427 Main Road North
Tolaga Bay

Tel: (06) 862 6623
Fax: (06) 862 6623
Mob: 025 283 7178
E: b.n.jefferd@xtra.co.nz
W: www.bnb.co.nz/hosts/
papatahi.html

Cost: Double $85 Single $50
  Child 1/2 price
  Dinner $25
Beds: 1 Queen 1 Double
  (2 bdrm)
Bath: 1 Ensuite 1 Guests share

Whangara

Mataurangi is a 607 Ha Hill Country sheep and cattle station situated 14km up Panikau Rd, off SH35 between Tolaga Bay and Gisborne. You will stay in "The Roost"; a secluded, fully refurbished, self contained shepherds cottage. (Full kitchen facilities, BBQ, sundeck and small garden). While we may be slightly off the beaten track, we know you will enjoy the experience, and look forward to meeting you and sharing our corner of New Zealand. Please phone for detailed direction.

The Roost
Self-contained Farmstay
50km E of Gisborne
Nick Reed
Mataurangi Station
RD 3, Gisborne

Tel: (06) 862 2858
Fax: (06) 862 2857
Mob: 025 242 2449
Tollfree: 0800 398 411
E: mataurangi@extra.co.nz
W: www.bnb.co.nz/hosts/
theroost.html

Cost: Double $80 Single $50
  Child $25
Beds: 1 Double 1 Single
  (1 bdrm)
Bath: 1 Private

Whatatutu

Our Colonial Farmhouse, on a 4000 acre hill country station, is an easy 40 minute drive from Gisborne, off SH2 North. Enjoy hands-on farm experiences, learning about life on a sheep and cattle station; watch the shepherds riding horses, expertly handling stock with their sheepdogs. Walking, clay-bird shooting and hunting are all options, or choose to relax and enjoy the many facilities we have to offer including our pool and hot spa. Our two young sons take pleasure in showing guest their many pets. All meals available.

Te Hau Station
Farmstay
50km NE of Gisborne
Chris and Jenny Meban
332 Te Hau Road
Whatatutu
Eastland 3871

Tel: (06) 862 1822
Fax: (06) 862 1997
Mob: 025 844 574
E: tehaustn@xtra.co.nz
W: www.bnb.co.nz/hosts/
tehaustation.html

Cost: Double $95 Single $60
  Child 1/2 price
  Dinner $30 Visa/MC
Beds: 1 Queen 1 Double
  2 Single (3 bdrm)
Bath: 1 Guests share
  1 Family share

THE WILLOWS

Waipaoa

Our home is situated on a hill amid a park like garden with some wonderful trees planted by our forefathers. We enjoy the amenities available in the city and also the country life on our 440 acre property involving deer, cattle, sheep, grapes and cropping. This year we can now offer a double bedroom with a private bathroom. The bedroom has its own access so you can enjoy privacy if you so desire.

We enjoy meeting people and look forward to your visit. We welcome you to have dinner with us, or if you prefer only Bed & Breakfast. We would appreciate it if you could ring prior to your arrival.

Directions: We are situated 20km north of Gisborne on SH2 through to Opotiki and the Bay of Plenty. We have a sign "The Willows" at the end of our driveway above the letter box with the Number 1809 close by. A good landmark is the curved Kaiteratahi Bridge and we are 1km north of that. Our house is white with a black tiled roof situated on a hill overlooking the Waipaoa River.

The Willows	**Tel:** (06) 862 5605	**Cost:** Double $80 Single $50
Farmstay	**Fax:** (06) 862 5601	Child 10% discount
20km N of Gisborne	**Mob:** 025 837 365	Dinner $30
Rosemary & Graham Johnson	**W:** www.bnb.co.nz/hosts/	**Beds:** 2 Queen 2 Single
& Montgomerie the Labrador	thewillows.html	(3 bdrm)
Waipaoa, RD 1,		**Bath:** 1 Private 1 Guests share
Gisborne		

Ormond

Country living with style and comfort. Stay in our Villa Moderna guest house, or our home with private lounge/bathroom. Spend lazy afternoons in the sun sampling wine from our local wineries. During the chillier winter nights take a long soak in our indoor spa and watch the stars, set amongst the Chardonnay capital of NZ. Come relax with us and our cats and dogs on our kiwifruit orchard and sample the fruit. 5 min to restaurant bar/grill.   Sky, fax, internet, email available. Pets welcome.

Kiwifruit Orchard Stay	**Tel:** (06) 862 5688	**Cost:** Double $85 Single $55
Self-contained Homestay	**Fax:** (06) 862 5688	Child $20.00
Orchard Stay B&B	**Mob:** 025 412 876	Dinner $25.00
18km N of Gisborne	**Tollfree:** 0800 107 886	**Beds:** 2 Queen 1 Single
Jenny & Greig Foster	**E:** jdfoster@ihug.co.nz	(2 bdrm)
37 Bond Road RD1	**W:** www.bnb.co.nz/hosts/	**Bath:** 2 Private
Ormond	kiwifruitorchardstay.html	
Gisborne		

Gisborne

From our spacious home it is only a five minute stroll to the city centre, wharf complex, museum, rose gardens etc. Secure off-street parking available. We are happy to meet bus or plane. Guests have own TV lounge with tea and coffee making facilities etc. Sight seeing can be arranged at an agreed price. We also have a self-contained unit at $85 per night. Alec and I enjoy a game of bridge, and are also keen bowlers.

Thomson Homestay	**Tel:** (06) 868 9675	**Cost:** Double $70 Single $50
B&B Self-contained Homestay	**Fax:** (06) 868 9675	Dinner $20 S/C $85
Gisborne Central	**Mob:** 025 265 5350	**Beds:** 1 Queen 1 Double
Barbara & Alec Thomson	**Tollfree:** 0800 370 505	2 Twin 2 Single (3 bdrm)
16 Rawiri Street	**W:** www.bnb.co.nz/hosts/	**Bath:** 1 Guests share
Gisborne	thomsonhomestay.html	

Gisborne

Welcome to our home - the centre of farm and family life for 3 generations. We are surrounded by a large garden and 1,600 acres of sheep, beef and forestry. Our interests include travelling, cooking, reading and gardening. Breakfast is special and is served in the sunporch overlooking the bay. Join us for an evening meal and enjoy excellent homegrown produce, local wines and award winning cheese. Meet our two cats and Lewis the corgi. Laundry facilities available as is our tennis court.

Wairakaia Farmstay	**Tel:** (06) 862 8607	**Cost:** Double $120-$150
Farmstay	**Fax:** (06) 862 8607	Single $80 Child $30
25km S of Gisborne	**Mob:** 025 611 5778	Dinner $25 - $40 Visa/MC
Sarah & Rodney Faulkner	**Tollfree:** 0800 329 060	**Beds:** 1 King/Twin 1 Queen
1894 State Highway 2	**E:** wairakaia@xtra.co.nz	(2 bdrm)
Muriwai, Gisborne	**W:** www.bnb.co.nz/hosts/	**Bath:** 1 Ensuite 1 Private
	wairakaiafarmstay.html	

Gisborne

We live 5 minutes drive from the famous Eastwood Hill Arboretum. Eastwood Hill is internationally recognized comprising 65 hectares of numerous varieties of trees and shrubs, it is a rewarding experience at any time of the year. We have a 1000 acre hill country property, farming sheep and cattle. We offer our guests separate accommodation with ensuite just a few metres from the main house, giving them the privacy they may desire. Tennis court and pool which our guests are welcome to use. Freephone 0800 469 4401

Farmstay	**Tel:** (06) 867 1313	**Cost:** Double $85 Single $50
40km W of Gisborne	**Fax:** (06) 867 6311	Child 1/2 price
Sally & Andrew Jefferd	**Tollfree:** 0800 469 4401	Dinner $25
RD 2	**E:** jefferd@xtra.co.nz	**Beds:** 1 Queen 1 Double
Ngatapa	**W:** www.bnb.co.nz/hosts/	1 Twin (2 bdrm)
Gisborne	jefferd.html	**Bath:** 1 Ensuite 1 Private
		1 Family share

Gisborne

Absolute luxury and comfort. Beachfront bed and breakfast. Seaview is situated on the foreshore of Waikanae beach with unsurpassed panoramic views of Young Nicks head and beautiful Poverty Bay. Just 50 metres from front door to golden sand, and warm blue waters of Poverty Bay. Only two minutes drive to the city (easy walking distance) and visitor information centre. Relax and enjoy safe swimming and great surfing. Five minutes to international golf course and Olympic pool complex. We offer 2 double bedrooms and twin room. 2 private bathrooms. Internet facilities available.

Sea View	**Tel:** (06) 867 3879	**Cost:** Double $95 Single $70
B&B Homestay	**Fax:** (06) 867 5879	**Beds:** 2 Double 1 Twin
Gisborne Central	**Tollfree:** 0800 268 068	1 Single (3 bdrm)
Raewyn & Gary Robinson	**E:** raewyn@regaleggs.co.nz	**Bath:** 2 Private
68 Salisbury Road	**W:** www.bnb.co.nz/hosts/	
Gisborne	seaviewgisborne.html	

Gisborne

We welcome you to our home which is situated right on the beach front at Wainui. The steps from the lawn lead down to the beach, which is renowned for its lovely clean sand, surf, pleasant walking and good swimming. Gisborne can also offer a host of entertainment, including golf on one of the finest golf courses, charter fishing trips, wine trails, Eastwood Hill Arboretum, horse trekking etc, or you may wish to relax on the beach for the day with a light luncheon provided.

Beach Stay	**Tel:** (06) 868 8111	**Cost:** Double $80 Single $45
Beachstay	**Fax:** (06) 868 8162	Child $10 Dinner $25
5km NE of Gisborne	**Mob:** 025 794 929	Visa/MC
Peter & Dorothy Rouse	**W:** www.bnb.co.nz/hosts/	**Beds:** 1 Queen 2 Double
111 Wairere Road	beachstaygisborne.html	2 Single (2 bdrm)
Wainui Beach		**Bath:** 1 Ensuite 1 Private
Gisborne		

Gisborne

Welcome to our American-style character home, set amongst old English trees. We offer peaceful surroundings with off-street parking. An 8 min. walk along the riverbank will take you to the city centre, the "wharf" area, the museum and a variety of restaurants. Gavin is a well-known local artist and we have an art gallery on site. We have travelled overseas ourselves and enjoy meeting people in our comfortable user-friendly home.

Studio 4	**Tel:** (06) 868 1571	**Cost:** Double $80 Single $55
Homestay Gallery	**Fax:** (06) 868 1457	Dinner $25pp Visa/MC
Gisborne Central	**Mob:** 025 386 502	**Beds:** 1 Queen 3 Single
Judy & Gavin Smith	**Tollfree:** 0800 370 398	(2 bdrm)
4 Heta Road	**E:** Studioart@clear.net.nz	**Bath:** 1 Guests share
Gisborne	**W:** www.bnb.co.nz/hosts/	1 Family share
	studiogisborne.html	

Gisborne

We have a lovely old villa in a peaceful setting in an old established country garden, only 20 minutes from the city centre and beaches. We have a tennis court and swimming pool available in season. We enjoy meeting people and regard homestaying as a wonderful way of achieving this by sharing our home and hospitality with others. Come and enjoy the Ngatapa Valley with our famous 'Eastwoodhill Arboretum' 5 minutes away and also local crafts and furniture makers. Reservations by appointment only.

Manurere

Manurere	**Tel:** (06) 863 9852	**Cost:** Double $80 Single $50
Homestay	**Fax:** (06) 863 9842	Dinner $20 Visa/MC
24km W of Gisborne	**E:** john.sherratt@	**Beds:** 1 Queen 1 Single
Joanne & John Sherratt	xtra.co.nz	(1 bdrm)
RD 2, Ngatapa	**W:** www.bnb.co.nz/	**Bath:** 1 Ensuite
Gisborne	hosts/manurere.html	

Gisborne

Our home is 1/2 km off Highway 35 at the northern end of Wainui Beach. With beautiful sea and sunrise views, surrounded by farmland and our own young olive grove. Handy to bush and coastal walkways. We have travelled overseas and enjoy the company of others. Roger is a water colour artist with examples of his overseas and local works available for viewing or purchase. Horse trekking, fishing trips, country excursions by arrangements. We have one friendly small dog not allowed indoors.

Makarori Heights	**Tel:** (06) 867 0806	**Cost:** Double $80 Single $45
Homestay	**Fax:** (06) 868 7706	Dinner $20 Visa/MC
8km N of Gisborne	**Mob:** 021 250 4918	Diners
Roger & Morag Shanks	**W:** www.bnb.co.nz/hosts/	**Beds:** 1 Double 2 Single
36 Sirrah St	makaroriheights.html	(2 bdrm)
Wainui Beach		**Bath:** 1 Guests share
Gisborne		1 Family share

Gisborne

Our renovated Edwardian mansion is just 5 minutes walk to shopping and cafes. Guests are offered refreshments on arrival and a pre-dinner drink. Each spacious smoke-free guestroom features sumptuous beds, cotton robes and slippers, artworks, flowers, and turndowns. Breakfasts include fresh local produce, home-made preserves and baking, and daily changing cooked item. TV lounge, 24-hour guest tea/coffee making and refreshment area, ample off street parking. Dinner, complimentary airport transfers, trout-fishing guide all available by arrangement. Off-season and multiple-night discounts apply.

Cedar House	**Tel:** (06) 868 1902	**Cost:** Double $120-$180 Single
B&B	**Fax:** (06) 867 1932	$100-$160 Child $50
Gisborne Central	**E:** cedar.house@3dnz.co.nz	Dinner $40 b/a Triple extra
Derek & Carole Green	**W:** www.cedarhouse.co.nz	$50 Visa/MC Amex
4 Clifford Street		**Beds:** 4 King/Twin (4 bdrm)
Gisborne		**Bath:** 2 Ensuite 2 Private
		1 Guests share

Gisborne

Welcome to our tasteful retreat situated in our delightful gardens in a quiet location within easy walking distance of city. Relax around our pool and enjoy use of our BBQ. Sky TV in bedrooms. We play bowls and bridge and will gladly arrange for guests with free use of clubs and trolleys. We are Tuberous Begonia enthusiasts with lovely display in gardens, pots and baskets in season. We will gladly arrange tours. Cut lunches on request. Off street parking available.

Fox Street Retreat
B&B Homestay
1km E of Gisborne
Jan & Alan Saunders
103 Fox Street
Gisborne

Tel: (06) 868 8702
Fax: (06) 868 8702
Mob: 025 907 777
Tollfree: 0800 868 8702
E: jan.saunders@clear.net.nz
W: geocities.com/fox_street_retreat

Cost: Double $70 Single $50
    Child $25 Visa/MC
Beds: 1 Queen 1 Twin
    (2 bdrm)
Bath: 1 Family share

Gisborne

After retiring from working lives involving overseas and local travel we missed meeting new friends and contact with the world outside our Eastland haven – solution - we converted the family home and our Anaura Bay beach property to accommodate guests. Our daughter Marney is qualified in hotel management and keeps us in order as well as helping with hosting. Our home is on a quiet riverbank location 5 minutes by car from the city. We enjoy assisting our guests plan activities to suit individual interests.

Riverbank Homestay
B&B
Judy and David Newell
100 Oak Street
Gisborne

Tel: 021 633 372
Fax: (06) 868 9940
Mob: 021 633 372
E: anaurastay@xtra.co.nz
W: www.bnb.co.nz/hosts/riverbankhomestay.html

Cost: Double $75 Single $50
    Child $20.00 Studio $85
    Dinner $25.00 Visa/MC
Beds: 1Twin 1 Queen 1 Double
    (3 bdrm)
Bath: 1 Ensuite 1 Private
    1 Guests share

Gisborne

Your hosts, Paul and Pauline welcome you to Hide-A-Way Cottage. We have two friendly cats and six chooks. Hide-A-Way Cottage is situated on our mandarin orchard with a rural outlook overlooking the mandarin trees and surrounding vinyards to the hills. The cottage captures the sun from early morning to late evening. The cottage is very clean and tidy, private and peaceful, fully self-contained with ramps and bathroom set up for the disabled. By arrangement and for a small cost guests can share dinner with us.

Hide-A-Way Cottage
Self-contained
18km N of Gisborne
Paul and Pauline Manning
1354 Matawai Rd
Ormond RD 1
Gisborne

Tel: (06) 862 5456
Fax: (06) 862 5456
Mob: Paul: 021 151 1873
E: paulandpauline@xtra.co.nz
W: www.bnb.co.nz/hosts/user98.html

Cost: Double $85 Single $65
    Child $10 Dinner $20
    Visa/MC
Beds: 1 Double 3 Single
    (2 bdrm)
Bath: 1 Private

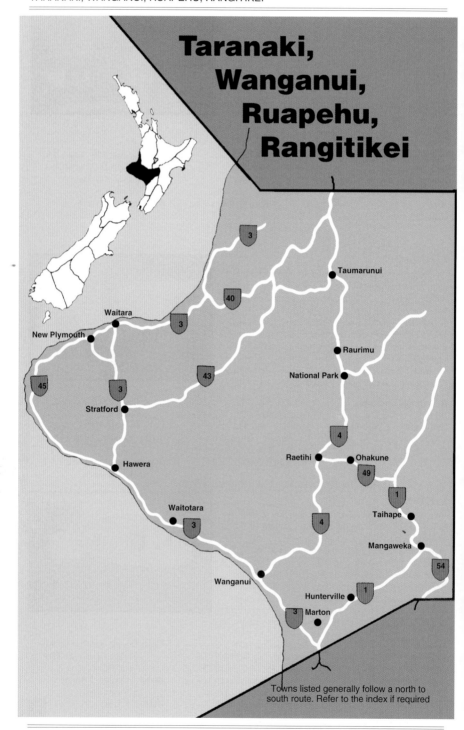

Taranaki, Wanganui, Ruapehu, Rangitikei

Towns listed generally follow a north to south route. Refer to the index if required

Waitara

Travel inland on Ngatimaru Road to our cosy brick home situated on a hill with panoramic views of Mt Egmont and the Waitara Valley farmlands. 20 minutes from New Plymouth. Visitors are welcome at our son's dairy farm, next door, to view farm activities and go for walks. Our children are now adults and as we are interested in farming, gardening, sports and travelling we have no pets. We look forward to meeting you. Directions: Please phone.

Farmstay
8km SE of Waitara
Anne & John Megaw
31 Tikorangi Road West
RD 43
Waitara

Tel: (06) 754 6768
W: www.bnb.co.nz/hosts/
megaw.html

Cost: Double $60 Single $40
  Dinner $15
Beds: 1 Double 2 Single
  (2 bdrm)
Bath: 1 Guests share

Waitara

Garden Homestay plus self-contained B&B cottage situated right on the main north-south Auckland/New Plymouth/ Wellington highway at historic Waitara. Large family house with guest homestay(ensuite) plus additional B&B cottage with separate bedroom,lounge/dining/kitchen area with separate bathroom/laundry/toilet. Fully equipped with TV/ music/library; all set in 18 acres of landscaped gardens, private lake and orchards. Close to 4 golf courses, local fishing, bush and mountain walks. Ten minutes from New Plymouth restaurants, twenty minutes from the mountain. We have an interesting array of animals, and pets are welcome.

Trenowth Gardens
B&B Self-contained Homestay
15kms N of New Plymouth
Sherril and Ken George
2 Armstrong Avenue
Waitara

Tel: (06) 754 7674
Fax: (06) 754 8884
Mob: 025 736 055
E: sherril@trenowth.co.nz
W: www.trenowth.com

Cost: Double $75 Single $55
  Child $15 Dinner $25pp
  Visa/MC
Beds: 2 Double 1 Single
  (2 bdrm)
Bath: 1 Ensuite 1 Private

New Plymouth

Relax and enjoy our rural views although we are only five minutes drive from the city while the well known "Tupare Gardens" are just next door. Each guest room has a queen and a single bed with an ensuite in the upstairs bedroom. We have a large garden, some sheep and a friendly dog called Bill who lives outside. Intersts, equestrian, sport, gardening. There is plenty of off street parking. Mangorei Road can be easily found when approaching New Plymouth from either north or south.

Blacksmiths Rest
Homestay
6km N of New Plymouth
Evelyn & Laurie Cockerill
481 Mangorei Road
New Plymouth

Tel: (06) 758 6090
Fax: (06) 758 6078
Mob: 025 678 8641
W: www.bnb.co.nz/hosts/
blacksmithsrest.html

Cost: Double $70 Single $45
  Dinner $20
Beds: 2 Queen 2 Single
  (2 bdrm)
Bath: 1 Ensuite 1 Private

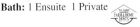

New Plymouth

My home is located in a peaceful and tranquil setting overlooking a bush clad walkway leading to the renowned Pukekura and Brooklands Parks and city centre. The guest wing consists of bathroom and toilet facilities, two bedrooms, one queen size and the other a twin room. I enjoy sharing my comfortable home with visitors from abroad and New Zealand travellers. I offer you a warm and friendly welcome and a relaxed stay in New Plymouth. I request please no smoking in the house.

Brooklands B&B
B&B Homestay
2km N of New Plymouth
Neal Spragg
39 Plympton Street
Brooklands
New Plymouth s

Tel: (06) 753 2265
Mob: 025 285 7602
E: brooklandsbb@freenet.co.nz
W: www.bnb.co.nz/hosts/
brooklandsbb.html

Cost: Double $65 Single $35
Beds: 1 Queen 2 Single
 (2 bdrm)
Bath: 1 Private

New Plymouth

Welcome to our city and home. Located in a quiet cul-de-sac, it is easily found from both Northern and Southern approaches of SH3, via Mangorei Road. We are an active retired couple who enjoy meeting new friends. Local attractions include coastal and riverside walks, parks, gardens, art galleries, museums, very popular aquatic centre, great surfing, big game fishing, mountain activities, and renowned Pukeiki Rhododendron Reserve. Complimentary tea/ coffee is always available. Guests are requested to please avoid smoking in the house.

B&B Homestay
4.5km NE of New Plymouth
A & E Howan
11 Tamati Place
Merrilands
New Plymouth

Tel: (06) 758 8932
E: ahowan@xtra.co.nz
W: www.bnb.co.nz/hosts/
howan.html

Cost: Double $60 Single $40
 Visa/MC
Beds: 1 Double 3 Single
 (3 bdrm)
Bath: 1 Guests share

New Plymouth

Ours is a peaceful place to spread out, relax and enjoy panoramic views over dairy farmland to the city, Mt Taranaki to the south and far away as Mt Ruapehu out east. Upstairs accommodation includes a self contained kitchen, microwave, large sunny lounge and TV. Laundry available. We share our home with two huggable cats, plus a poodle called Dixie. We have a friendly cattle dog Danny and sweet horse Millie nearby. Travelled, outdoor hosts, non smokers. "Come visit the West, experience the Best". Please phone for reservations.

Mountain Dew Farm
Farmstay
12km SW of New Plymouth
Marion & Geoff Rivers
1602 Carrington Road
RD 1, New Plymouth

Tel: (06) 753 5123
Mob: 025 267 0418
E: mlrivers@paradise.net.nz.
W: www.bnb.co.nz/hosts/
mountaindewfarm.html

Cost: Double $70 Single $45
 Dinner $20pp
Beds: 2 Queen 2 Single
 (2 bdrm)
Bath: 1 Private 1 Family share

New Plymouth

Balconies is nestled amongst lovely gardens in the heart of the city, just 5 min walk to New Plymouth's shopping centre. Our warm, comfortable 110-year old character home offers three tastefully decorated downstairs guest rooms, (with queen size beds, electric blankets and heaters), large guest share bathroom with claw-foot bath and guest lounge with tea and coffee making facilities. Laundry facilities courtesy transport and off-street parking available. Guest are requested not to smoke inside. We are within walking distance to many attractions, restaurants and parks.

Balconies	**Tel:** (06) 757 8866	**Cost:** Double $75 Single $55
B&B	**Fax:** (06) 757 8262	Child neg Visa/MC
500m W of City Central	**Mob:** 025 423 789	Amex Diners
Viv & Trevor Lewis	**E:** balconies@paradise.net.nz	**Beds:** 3 Queen 2 Single
161 Powderham Street	**W:** www.bnb.co.nz/hosts/	(3 bdrm)
New Plymouth	balconies.html	**Bath:** 1 Guests share

New Plymouth

Henwood House is a beautiful restored colonial homestead set in 2 acres of grounds, minutes from city. Spacious elegantly furnished guest bedrooms enjoy rural views. Guest lounge with open fire looks out over the garden. Delicious gourmet breakfasts served in the country kitchen, dining room or verandah. Guests tea and coffee facilities. Enjoy strolling in the garden with Basil our golden retriever or relax by the fire. Guests may smoke outdoors. Directions: 3.14km up Henwood Road off SH3 from Bell Block.

Henwood House	**Tel:** (06) 755 1212	**Cost:** Double $120-$150
B&B Inn	**Fax:** (06) 755 1212	Single $100
5km N of New Plymouth	**Mob:** 025 248 4051	Dinner $35 b/a
Lynne & Graeme Axten	**E:** henwood.house@xtra.co.nz	Visa/MC Amex
314 Henwood Road	**W:** www.bnb.co.nz/hosts/	**Beds:** 3 Queen 4 Single
RD 2	henwoodhouse.html	(5 bdrm)
New Plymouth		**Bath:** 3 Ensuite 1 Guests share

New Plymouth

"Kirkstall House" invites you to experience its old world beauty and comfort, in an atmosphere of easy hospitality and relaxed surroundings. "Kirkstall House" is one of surprise. Enjoy our superb mountain views, cosy open fire, and delightful garden leading down to the river. The sea, beaches, and walkways, restaurants and shops are all within easy walking distance. Lindy, a practising physiotherapist, and Ian, involved with tourism, are here to help you enjoy Taranakai to the utmost. We are smoke free and have four great cats.

Kirkstall House	**Tel:** (06) 758 3222	**Cost:** Double $80 Single $60
Homestay	**Fax:** (06) 758 3224	Ensuite room $75/95
New Plymouth Central	**Mob:** 025 973 908	Visa/MC
Ian Hay & Lindy MacDiarmid	**E:** kirkstall@xtra.co.nz	**Beds:** 1 Queen 1 Double
8 Baring Terrace	**W:** www.bnb.co.nz/hosts/	1 Twin (3 bdrm)
New Plymouth	kirkstallhouse.html	**Bath:** 1 Ensuite 2 Private

T'NAKI, W'NUI,
R'PEHU, R'TIKEI

New Plymouth - Omata

10 minutes from New Plymouth. Separate chalet with ensuite, queen bed, TV, and balcony overlooking bush and sea. Twin room with guest facilities in house. Your choice of breakfast (except kippers!). Dinner with wine, $30.00 per head, by arrangement. Enjoy bush or orchard walks, relax by our pool, or visit some of the nearby attractions: beautiful Mt Taranaki, some of the best surf in the world, famous gardens, art gallery, museum, historic sites and golf courses. Bookings: Please phone for reservations/directions. Dog and cat.

Rangitui	**Tel:** (06) 751 2979	**Cost:** Double $70-$90
B&B	**E:** twaghorn@clear.net.nz	Single $60-$80
5km S of New Plymouth	**W:** www.bnb.co.nz/hosts/	Dinner $30 Visa/MC
Therese & Tony Waghorn	rangituiorchard.html	**Beds:** 1 Queen 2 Single
Waireka Road		(2 bdrm)
RD 4 New Plymouth		**Bath:** 1 Ensuite 1 Private

New Plymouth

Ensuring your comfort and pleasure is important to us. We have lived in three continents and enjoy travelling. We love welcoming guests to Birdhaven and endeavouring to exceed your expectations. Share our tranquil, spacious, tastefully furnished home, secluded gardens and spectacular mountain view. Relax on the patios overlooking our beautiful native bush, woodlands and birdlife. Indulge in the complimentary refreshments and the special breakfast of seasonal and homemade temptations. A peaceful haven only five minutes from city. Cedric, our cat, is gregarious and well behaved.

Birdhaven	**Tel:** (06) 751 0432	**Cost:** Double $77-$85
Homestay Farmlet	**Fax:** (06) 751 3475	Single $54-$65
5km W of city central	**Tollfree:** 0800 306 449	Dinner b/a Visa/MC
Ann & John Butler	**E:** info@birdhaven.co.nz	**Beds:** 1 Queen 2 Single
26 Pararewa Drive	**W:** www.bnb.co.nz/hosts/	(2 bdrm)
New Plymouth	birdhaven.html	**Bath:** 1 Guests share

New Plymouth

Your hosts, Pat and Paul, two friendly people with a wealth of experience in the hospitality industry, invite you to a unique bed and breakfast in their beautifully appointed home with views from each room to Mount Egmont. These beautiful views make an impression which we will everlasting. Guests can choose their own privacy or socialise with us. We have a variety of animals, donkey, peacocks, pigs, ostrich and dogs. Ducks and geese enjoy the lake. Golf course 10 minute drive. Laundry available.

Oak Valley Manor	**Tel:** (06) 758 1501	**Cost:** Double $105 Single $75
Self-contained Farmstay	**Fax:** (06) 758 1052	Child $1 per year to 12yrs
3km S of New Plymouth	**Mob:** 025 420 325	Dinner $30 Pets welcome
Pat & Paul Ekdahl	**E:** kauri.holdings@xtra.co.nz	Visa/MC
248 Junction Road	**W:** www.bnb.co.nz/hosts/	**Beds:** 2 Queen 1 Single
RD 1	oakvalleymanor.html	(2 bdrm)
New Plymouth		**Bath:** 2 Ensuite

New Plymouth

Go to sleep with the sound of the waves...wake with
the birds. This modern, peaceful cottage, nestled
amongst landscaped gardens and lawns, offers
complete privacy. You may take a short bushwalk
down 100 steps to the beach, relax on the veranda
watching ever-changing sea views, or request a tour of
our small commercial flower business. There is a
comfortable sofabed in the lounge. The kitchen is fully
equipped. Subtract $7.50 pp if providing your own
breakfast. Our family dog may greet you.

Cottage by the Sea
Self-contained
25km N of New Plymouth
Nancy & Hugh Mills
66 Lower Turangi Road
RD 43
Waitara

Tel: (06) 754 7915
Fax: (06) 754 7915
E: nancy.mills@clear.net.nz
W: www.bnb.co.nz/hosts/
cottagebytheseanewplymouth.html

Cost: Double $95 Single $75
       Child neg. extra $25 pp
Beds: 1 Queen 1 Double
       (1 bdrm)
Bath: 1 Private

New Plymouth

Come and stay in our modern architecturally designed
award-winning home built with the privacy and
comfort of our guests in mind. With unique bush
views and a house designed to take full advantage of
the sun our guests can enjoy relaxing in the lounge or
the extensive tiled courtyards. The Grange is
centrally heated, security controlled and located
adjacent to the renowned Pukekura Park and Bowl of
Brooklands. The city is within a short 5 minute
walk.

The Grange
Homestay
Cathy Thurston & John Smith
The Grange
44B Victoria Road
New Plymouth Central

Tel: (06) 758 1540
Fax: (06) 758 1539
Mob: 025 333 497
E: cathyt@clear.net.nz
W: www.bnb.co.nz/hosts/
thegrange.html

Cost: Double $95 Single $70
       Dinner $25 by arrangement
       Visa/MC Amex
Beds: 1 King/Twin 1 Queen
       2 Single (2 bdrm)
Bath: 2 Ensuite

New Plymouth

Exclusive use of downstairs facility including off-
street parking, lounge, bedrooms, bathroom (spa bath,
super shower, laundry), ONE PARTY ONLY. Guests
share breakfast with us while enjoying the sights,
sounds, and feel of the garden, surf, and ocean. Buller
St. leads to a Beach/Park, 150 metres from our
gateway.Adjacent walkways access reserves, parks,
and central city (15 minutes approx). Guest's
Comment 2000, "A true taste of 'Southern Hospitality'
New Zealand style. We loved our stay, and hope to be
back another day. (A&L, Alabama, U.S.A.)

93 By the Sea
B&B
New Plymouth Central
Patricia & Bruce Robinson
93 Buller Street
New Plymouth

Tel: (06) 758 6555
Mob: 025 230 3887
E: pabron@xtra.co.nz
W: www.bnb.co.nz/hosts/
bythesea.html

Cost: Double $90 Single $70
       Dinner by arrangement
Beds: 1 King/Twin 1 Double
       (2 bdrm)
Bath: 1 Private

T'NAKI, W'NUI,
R'PEHU, R'TIKEI

New Plymouth

Lorraine and Herb invite you to our stunning Treehouse. Our guest accommodation is situated downstairs with all rooms opening on to our attractive garden, but please feel free to join us upstairs or lounge on our sunny deck anytime. We are just minutes from all amenities and beautiful Pukekura Park. Our home is smoke free but not really suitable for children or pets. Ample off street parking available. Lorraine, Herb and our friendly house cat, Sam, look forward to meeting you.

The Treehouse	**Tel:** (06) 757 4288	**Cost:** Double $80 Single $50
B&B	**E:** herbabel@xtra.co.nz	Dinner $25 by arrangement
1km S of Civic Centre	**W:** www.bnb.co.nz/hosts/	Visa/MC
Herbert & Lorraine Abel	thetreehouse.html	**Beds:** 1 Double 2 Twin (3 bdrm)
75 Morley Street		**Bath:** 1 Guests share
New Plymouth		

New Plymouth

Situated in scenic New Plymouth's port view. Moturoa suburb. Spacious upstairs open- plan studio, maximising the 300 degree views of harbour, mountains, city, countryside and sea. Handy to beaches, Marine Park, port and fishing. Guests may be as self contained as wished - lock up garage, separate entrance and mini-kitchen. Lounge with private balcony, dining-table, Sky TV and stereo. Extra bed(s) by arrangement. Shirley and Trevor bring their own wide travel experiences to their enthusiasm to ensure guests enjoyment -assisted by pet cat Missy!

Vineyard Holiday Flat	**Tel:** (06) 751 2992	**Cost:** Double $75 Single $50
B&B Self-contained	**Fax:** (06) 751 2995	Triple $100
Shirley & Trevor Knuckey	**Mob:** 025 622 3553	Dinner by arrangement
12 Scott St	**E:** shirley12vineyard@xtra.co.nz	Visa/MC
Moturoa	**W:** www.bnb.co.nz/hosts/	**Beds:** 1 Double 1 Twin
New Plymouth	vineyardholidayflat.html	**Bath:** 1 Ensuite

New Plymouth

Issey Manor offers 4 luxury sunny suites all with designer bathrooms, 2 having spa baths. All rooms have beautiful bedding, refreshments, work desks, data points & comfortable seating. An inner city location just 2 mins. stroll to the many cafes & restaurants, seaside promenade, Govett Brewster art gallery, Information Centre, Pukekura Park & Brooklands Bowl.
Enjoy our many books, artwork & collectables and relax on the enormous decking overlooking a tranquil bush & stream vista. For business or pleasure your comfort & privacy assured.

Issey Manor	**Tel:** (06) 758 2375	**Cost:** Double $100-$150
Guest House	**Fax:** (06) 758 2375	Single $80-$130 Child b/a
New Plymouth central	**Mob:** 025 248 6686	Winter & business rates
Carol & Lewis	**E:** issey.manor@actrix.co.nz	Visa/MC Amex Diners
32 Carrington Street	**W:** www.bnb.co.nz/hosts/	**Beds:** 1 King 3 Queen (4 bdrm)
New Plymouth	isseymanor.html	**Bath:** 4 Ensuite

Stratford

1900 "Upstairs Downstairs" comfort. Cooked/continental breakfast included. Free self catering kitchen, tea, coffee, biscuits. Homely or private. Own key. Optional separate lounge. Restaurants, taverns, shops nearby. Rooms are antique, romantic with TV, heaters, electric blankets, serviced daily. Gardens, BBQ, row boat, bush bath, river walks. 15 mins Mt Egmont skifields, climbing, tramping. Centrally located on edge of Stratford, easy distance to New Plymouth, museums, famous gardens, tourist attractions. We are semi retired farmers. Interests include gemstones travel, art. Welcome.

Stallard B&B	**Tel:** (06) 765 8324	**Cost:** Double $70 Single $40
B&B Farmstay	**Fax:** (06) 765 8324	Child $20
1/2km N of Stratford	**E:** stallardbb@infogen.net.nz	Family room sleeps 4 $95
Billieanne & Corb Stallard	**W:** www.bnb.co.nz/hosts/	Visa/MC Amex
SH 3	stallardb&b.html	**Beds:** 2 Double 2 Twin (4 bdrm)
Stratford Northern Boundry		**Bath:** 4 Ensuite 1 Guests share

Egmont National Park

Swiss style chalet surrounded with native gardens and bush. Spectacular views of Mount Egmont/Taranaki and Egmont National Park opposite our front gate. Five kilometers to Mountain House and its famed restaurant, further 3km to Stratford Plateau and skifields. Tramps, summit climbs, trout stream, gardens & museums nearby. Private helicopter summit flights. Pet sheep, pig, ducks etc. Kiwi Keith and Swiss Berta Anderson owned mountain lodges for 25 years, winning many awards. Keith is noted Taranaki artist specializing in mountain scenes.

Anderson's Alpine Lodge	**Tel:** (06) 765 6620	**Cost:** Double $115-$145
Farmstay Homestay	**Fax:** (06) 765 6100	Single $115 Dinner $30-$35
9km W of Stratford	**Mob:** 025 412 372	Visa/MC Amex Diners
Keith & Berta Anderson	**Tollfree:** 0800 668 682	**Beds:** 1 King/Twin 1 Queen
PO Box 303	**E:** mountainhouse@xtra.co.nz	1 Double 2 Single (3 bdrm)
Stratford	**W:** www.mountainhouse.co.nz	**Bath:** 3 Ensuite
Taranaki		

Stratford

"A beautiful & special place" (Guest's comment). A peaceful country retreat set in an extensive woodland & perennial garden surrounded by forest-clad gorges and streams, with wonderful birdlife. Our guest wing provides private, quality accommodation. Relax in the comfort of your suite (with woodburning fire), explore our intriguing 34-acre property or the delights of Taranaki. We love good food & wine. Share our dining table, dine privately in your suite, or self cater if you wish. Our two dogs, Sergeant & Pepper, share our home.

Sarsen House	**Tel:** (06) 762 8775	**Cost:** Double $120-$140
Country Retreat	**Fax:** (06) 762 8775	Single $100-$120 Dinner
15km NE of Stratford	**E:** tepopo@clear.net.nz	$25 - $35
Bruce & Lorri Ellis	**W:** www.tepopo.co.nz	Visa/MC Amex Diners
Te Popo Gardens, 636 Stanley Rd		**Beds:** 1 King/Twin 2 Queen (3 bdrm)
RD 24 Stratford		**Bath:** 3 Ensuite

Hawera

Originally built in 1875 our Kauri villa has been renovated to its former Victorian glory and is nestled amongst established grounds. Polished Kauri floors add a golden glow to the tastefully decorated rooms. Each bedroom is spacious and has views over the woodland garden and swimming pool. Breakfasts are served in the dining room, verandah or privately on the balcony of the master suite. Along with our twin daughters, and friendly American Cocker Spaniel, Linda and Steve assure you a memorable stay at Tairoa Lodge.

TAIROA LODGE
@ BED & BREAKFAST @

Tairoa Lodge	**Tel:** (06) 278 8603	**Cost:** Double $95-$110
B&B Inn	**Fax:** (06) 278 8603	Single $75-$90
1.5km S of Hawera Central	**Mob:** 025 243 5782	Dinner by arrangement
Linda & Steve Morrison	**E:** tairoa.lodge@xtra.co.nz	Visa/MC Amex Diners
Puawai Street	**W:** www.tairoa-lodge.co.nz	**Beds:** 2 Queen 1 Single (2 bdrm)
PO Box 117		**Bath:** 2 Ensuite
Hawera		

Hawera

A delightful new self contained cottage set in a private serene country garden. Lovely rural outlook on 10 acre farmlet. Feel free to wander through the garden, play tennis, petanque or swim in the pool. Great restaurants and cafes nearby, with delivery services available. Local attractions include beaches, Mt Egmont, beautiful gardens, Dairylands in the Kiwi Dairies Complex, Tawhiti Museum, Lake Rotorangi and historic Turuturu Mokai. We both play bridge and golf. We look forward to meeting you and trust your stay is very relaxing.

Self-contained Homestay	**Tel:** (06) 278 6414	**Cost:** Double $70 Single $60
2km N of Hawera	**Fax:** (06) 278 2028	Visa/MC
Jill & Gary Dunlop	**Mob:** 025 517 404	**Beds:** 1 Queen (1 bdrm)
28A Arthur Street	**E:** gjdunlop@netsource.co.nz	**Bath:** 1 Ensuite 1 Private
Hawera	**W:** www.bnb.co.nz/hosts/ dunlop.html	

Hawera

Welcome to our home, named after the old English Linden trees growing at the entranceway. We are situated on SH3, directly opposite King Edward Park and Hawera's aquatic centre, and are in close proximity to Hawera's amenities, restaurants and local attractions. The mountain, intensive dairy farming, trout streams, parks, gardens, beaches, golf courses, museums and local industry offer a variety of activities. We trust ours will be a home away from home as you enjoy the loveliness of South Taranaki.

Linden Park	**Tel:** (06) 278 5421	**Cost:** Double $75 Single $55
B&B	**Fax:** (06) 278 5421	Visa/MC
Douglas & Merilyn Tippett	**Mob:** 025 281 6216	**Beds:** 2 Queen 1 Double
69 Waihi Road	**W:** www.bnb.co.nz/hosts/ lindenpark.html	(3 bdrm)
Hawera		**Bath:** 1 Guests share

Waitotara - Wanganui

We have a 500 acre sheep and cattle farm and live in a comfortable home, set in an attractive garden with a swimming pool and tennis court. Also in the garden is an antique shop selling Devonshire teas. 100 mts from the house is a 4 acre park and lake, aviaries and a collection hand fed pet farm animals. We welcome guests to have dinner with us. Self-contained accommodation is available in the park.

Ashley Park
Self-contained Farmstay
29km W of Wanganui
Barry Pearce & Wendy Bowman
State Highway 3
Box 36, Waitotara
Wanganui

Tel: (06) 346 5917
Fax: (06) 346 5861
E: ashley_park@xtra.co.nz
W: www.bnb.co.nz/hosts/
ashleypark.html

Cost: Double $70-$90
Single $40 Dinner $25
Visa/MC Amex Diners
Beds: 1 Queen 4 Single
(3 bdrm)
Bath: 1 Ensuite 1 Guests share

Wanganui

My home is a modern Lockwood set amongst mature trees, three kilometres from the centre of Wanganui on the main Wanganui./New Plymouth Highway. I have travelled extensively overseas and enjoy meeting and conversing with people from all countries. My many interests include sport, tramping, gardening, bridge, travel and fishing. Wanganui has many attractions including excellent sporting facilities, museums an art gallery and the scenic Wanganui river which offers everything from paddle steam cruises to kayaking to jetboating to the famous Bridge to Nowhere.

Homestay
3km W of Wanganui
Janet Dick
156 Great North Road
Wanganui

Tel: (06) 345 8951
Mob: 025 235 2733
E: janetdick@infogen.co.nz
W: www.bnb.co.nz/hosts/
dick.html

Cost: Double $60
Single $40
Beds: 2 Single (1 bdrm)
Bath: 1 Private

Wanganui

Farmstay overlooking the Whanganui River - en route to the Bridge to Nowhere - sheep, cattle and deer farming. Pottery and macadamia nuts and cat. Enjoy a country picnic and/or walk. Other activities along the river can be arranged: canoeing, jet boat rides, horse riding, mountain bike riding, Marae visit and farm activities according to season.

Operiki Farmstay
Farmstay
45km N of Wanganui
Trissa & Peter McIntyre
3302 River Rd
Operiki, RD 6
Wanganui

Tel: (06) 342 8159
W: www.bnb.co.nz/hosts/
operikifarmstay.html

Cost: Single $35 Child $15
Dinner $20 Visa/MC
Beds: 1 Double 2 Single
(2 bdrm)
Bath: 1 Family share

Wanganui

Welcome to Bradgate, a gracious 2 storey home. With its beautiful entrance hall and carved rimu staircase which reflects the original character and gracefulness of the house. 25 years ago my husband and I came to New Zealand. We owned Shangri-La Restaurant by Virginia Lake. After 20 years we retired and decided to welcome guests into our beautiful old home. We share my Mother's dog Bounce and have a grown up family. I play golf, enjoy gardening and meeting people. Non-smoking house, Dinner by arrangement.

Bradgate	**Tel:** (06) 345 3634	**Cost:** Double $70-$75
B&B Homestay	**Fax:** (06) 345 3634	Single $40-$50
5min walk Wanganui Centre	**W:** www.bnb.co.nz/hosts/	Dinner $25
Frances	bradgate.html	**Beds:** 2 Queen 1 Double
7 Sómme Parade		2 Single (3 bdrm)
Wanganui		**Bath:** 1 Guests share

Wanganui

Our homestead, built 1895, has been restored to retain its "olde worlde charm". Guest rooms are on the ground floor and a laundry and equipped self service kitchen are available. Friendly atmosphere and all home comforts. If you choose to stay with us we will ensure that your visit to Wanganui is well worth the journey. We request that you do not smoke inside the building and step over our cat, Casper, whose habit it is to sleep on the front door mat.

Riverside Inn	**Tel:** (06) 347 2529	**Cost:** Double $80 Single $50
Guesthouse	**Fax:** (06) 347 2529	Visa/MC
10min walk Wanganui Centre	**W:** www.bnb.co.nz/hosts/	**Beds:** 4 Double 8 Single
Joy & Philip Gedye	riversideinn.html	(8 bdrm)
2 Plymouth Street		**Bath:** 3 Guests share
Wanganui		

Wanganui

"Kembali" is a modern, sunny, centrally heated home at the end of a quiet cul-de-sac. Guest bedrooms and guest lounge are upstairs overlooking gardens and wetlands. Available tea/coffee facilities, off street parking, laundry. Our children have left home, our cat is middle aged, so a restful stay is assured. Interests include travel, gardening, reading and people. Historic Wanganui offers pretty walks, cultural museum, art gallery, craft shops, river activities - including canoeing, jet boating, historic paddle steamer. No smoking inside. Not suitable for children.

Kembali	**Tel:** (06) 347 1727	**Cost:** Double $65 Single $45
B&B Homestay	**Mob:** 025 270 1879	Visa/MC
2km NW of Wanganui	**E:** wespalmer@xtra.co.nz	**Beds:** 1 Queen 1 Twin (2 bdrm)
Wes & Marylyn Palmer	**W:** www.bnb.co.nz/hosts/	**Bath:** 1 Private
26 Taranaki Street	kembali.html	
St Johns Hill		
Wanganui		

Wanganui

Come as strangers, leave as friends when you stay at Omaka, a 1000 hectare mixed farm beside the historic and scenic Whanganui River bounding the Whanganui National Park. Stay in our comfortable home with spectacular bush views, join in farm activities, enjoy three hour canoe trips, horseride, swim, walk our bush and farm tracks. John's hobbies include running and trout fishing; Ann's books, herbs, gardening and cooking. We enjoy people and have travelled extensively. We have two cats and a sheep dog.

Omaka Homestay	**Tel:** (06) 342 5597	**Cost:** Single $35
Farmstay	**E:** omakaholiday@xtra.co.nz	Child half price
30km NE of Wanganui	**W:** www.bnb.co.nz/hosts/	Dinner $20
Ann & John Handley	omakahomestay.html	Campervans $10
1622 River Road		**Beds:** 1 Twin (1 bdrm)
RD 6		**Bath:** 1 Family share
Whanganui		

Wanganui

Misty Valley is a small organic farm at 3.7 hectares. We prefer to use our own produce whenever possible. There are farm animals for you to meet including our Brittany's George and Harley and cats Alice and Calico, who all live outside. Our two grandchildren visit us regularly and children will be made very welcome. We are non-smoking, but have pleasant deck areas for those who do. Our famous river and historical city offer plenty of activities for the whole family to enjoy.

Misty Valley Farmstay	**Tel:** (06) 342 5767	**Cost:** Double $70 Single $35
Farmstay	**E:** linda.garry.wadsworth@xtra.co.nz	Child $20 Dinner $30
20km NE of Wanganui	**W:** www.bnb.co.nz/hosts/	Visa/MC
Linda & Garry Wadsworth	mistyvalley.html	**Beds:** 2 Double 2 Twin
RD 5		(2 bdrm)
97 Parihauhau Road		**Bath:** 1 Guests share
Wanganui		

Wanganui

Come and experience tranquil rural environments. Your hosts, a border collie and two nurses, Brenda & Judi, establishing a lifestyle farm. Enjoy bush, farmlands, get close to nature and our Kunekune pigs, coloured sheep, chickens and ducks. Soak up the sun in hammocks enjoying sea views from extensive gardens. Canoe the duckpond. Enjoy homegrown vegetables, free range eggs. Children welcome. The perfect base to explore the Whanganui River City, two National Parks, local beaches, botanical gardens. Picnics on request. Discount for two or more nights.

Chestnut Farm	**Tel:** (06) 342 9998	**Cost:** Double $60 Single $40
Homestay	**Fax:** (06) 342 9998	Child $20 Dinner $20
20km N of Wanganui	**Mob:** 025 856 036	Visa/MC
Brenda Wilson	**E:** chestnutfarm@paradise.net.nz	**Beds:** 1 Queen 1 Twin
1690 State Highway 3 North	**W:** www.bnb.co.nz/hosts/	(2 bdrm)
RD4	chestnutfarm.html	**Bath:** 1 Guests share
Maxwell		

Taumarunui

Welcome to Orangi, it's your home away from home, spacious, quiet and private. Comfortable rooms with electric blankets and duvets. Toby 13 and Jana 12 and our friendly cats enjoy the company of other children. Our outside foxy will greet you on arrival. Go trout fishing, or walk along the river bank. We look forward to enjoying your company in our friendly and casual home. Join us for a good country meal, and the kettle is always on. Laundry available.

Orangi Farmstay	Tel: (07) 896 6035	Cost: Double $70 Single $40
Farmstay	Fax: (07) 896 6035	Child 1/2 price Dinner $15
10km E of Taumarunui	W: www.bnb.co.nz/hosts/	Campervans $20
Gayle & Dave Richardson	orangifarmstay.html	Beds: 1 Queen 3 Single
Orangi Road		(2 bdrm)
RD 4		Bath: 1 Family share
Taumarunui		

Raurimu

Our new home overlooks the Piopiotea Stream and a magnificent stand of native bush. We are 5 mins from National Park Village, gateway to Tongario and Wanganui National Parks. The Whakapapa ski area is a 25 min drive. We can organise any of the many adventure activities offered in the Ruapehu and Taupo Districts. Our luxury suits feature a queen bed, a bed settee, casual chairs, dresser and writing bureau. The bunk room sleeps 6, ideal for larger families. Our cosy cottage is self catering.

Spiral Gardens	Tel: (07) 892 2997	Cost: Double $95 Single $30
B&B Homestay Self-contained	Fax: (07) 892 2997	Child $20 Dinner B/A
Cottage	Mob: 025 753 482	Self Contained cottage $85
7km N of National Park	E: spiralgardens@xtra.co.nz	+ $15 Single Visa/MC
Phil & Margaret Hawthorne	W: www.bnb.co.nz/hosts/	Beds: 2 Queen 1 Double 4
Raurimu Road	spiralgardens.html	Single (3 bdrm)
Raurimu		Bath: 3 Ensuite

National Park

Welcome to Mountain Heights, a family run accommodation business offering bed and breakfast in the lodge or self catering adjacent to the lodge. Situated near World Heritage Tongariro National Park where there is an abundance of activities including the Tongariro Crossing, mountain biking, canoeing, skiing, fishing and hunting. We can help ou organise activities. Lodge facilities include a hot spa, comfortable, centrally heated rooms, woderful breakfasts. Our self contained units sleep 2-6 and have private bathroom, TV and kitchens. A warm welcome awaits you.

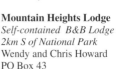

Mountain Heights Lodge	Tel: (07) 892 2833	Cost: Double $90-$140
Self-contained B&B Lodge	Fax: (07) 892 2833	Single $60 Child $30
2km S of National Park	E: mountainheights@xtra.co.nz	Dinner by arrangement
Wendy and Chris Howard	W: www.mountainheights.co.nz	S/C $70 - $120 Visa/MC
PO Box 43		Beds: 1 Queen 2 Double
National Park		2 Twin (5 bdrm)
		Bath: 4 Ensuite 1 Guests share

Raetihi

If you enjoy exploring away from the beaten track then drive the historic River Road between Raetihi and Wanganui. Our 1,000 acre hill country farm, running sheep and beef, is situated only 6km from Raetihi and ideal as a stopover. Handy too to the Tongario and Whanganui National Parks for bushwalks, jet boat rides, skiing, trout fishing. Perhaps a farm tour with son Nick. Our home is comfortable and warm set in a spacious garden. Interests include travel, photography and family. We have 2 cats.

Farmstay Homestay	**Tel:** (06) 385 4581	**Cost:** Double $80 Single $50
6km SW of Raetihi	**Fax:** (06) 385 4581	Child 1/2 price
Sonia Robb	**E:** ken.sonia@xtra.co.nz	Dinner $25pp
Pipiriki Road	**W:** www.bnb.co.nz/hosts/	**Beds:** 1 Queen 2 Single
RD 4	robb.html	(2 bdrm)
Raetihi		**Bath:** 1 Ensuite 1 Family share

Raetihi

A unique opportunity to stay in a modern authentic log home sited high on seven acres on the edge of town. Completely private accommodation, with own bathroom. All sleeping on mezzanine, your own lounge with wood fire, snooker table, TV/video, stereo and dining area, opening onto large verandah, with swimming pool and spa available. Panoramic views of Mts. Ruapehu, Ngauruhoe and Tongariro. Tongariro National Park and Turoa Skifield is half hour scenic drive.

Log Lodge	**Tel:** (06) 385 4135	**Cost:** Double $95
B&B Self-contained Homestay	**Fax:** (06) 385 4835	Single $50
0.5km N of Raetihi	**E:** Lamb.Log-Lodge@Xtra.co.nz	Child $40
Jan & Bob Lamb	**W:** www.bnb.co.nz/hosts/	Visa/MC Amex Diners
5 Ranfurly Terrace	loglodge.html	**Beds:** 2 Double 4 Single
Raetihi		**Bath:** 2 Private

Ohakune

We farm sheep, Bull Beef and run a Boarding Kennel in a beautiful peaceful valley with magnificent views of Mt Ruapehu. Tongariro National Park for skiing, walking, photography. Excellent 18 hole golf course, great fishing locally. We are members of Ducks Unlimited a conservation group and our local wine club. Have 2 Labradors and 1 large cat. We offer dinner traditional farm house (Diane, a cook book author), or breakfast with excellent home made jams. Take Raetihi Road, at Hotel/BP Service Station Corner. 4kms to Smiths Road. Last house 2kms.

Mitredale	**Tel:** (06) 385 8016	**Cost:** Double $80 Single $50
Farmstay Homestay	**Fax:** (06) 385 8016	Dinner $25pp Visa/MC
6km W of Ohakune	**Mob:** 025 531 916	**Beds:** 1 Double 2 Single
Audrey & Diane Pritt	**W:** www.bnb.co.nz/hosts/	(2 bdrm)
Smiths Road RD Ohakune	mitredale.html	**Bath:** 1 Family share

T'NAKI, W'NUI, R'PEHU, R'TIKEI

Ohakune

Enjoy spectacular views of volcanic Mt Ruapehu while relaxing in our tranquil 3 acre garden. Kohinoor (a gem of rare beauty) is an ideal base from where you can ski Turoa or Whakapapa skifields. Tramp in the world famous Tongariro World Heritage Park and enjoy golf, trout fishing and kiwi encounters. We are just 1 km from Ohakune with its cafes, restaurants and apres ski activities. Our interests include gardening, photography, trout fishing, skiing and giving genuine kiwi hospitality. We request no smoking.

Kohinoor	**Tel:** (06) 385 8026	**Cost:** Double $80-$120
Homestay	**Mob:** 025 620 5326	Single $45 Child $35
1km SW of Ohakune	**E:** kohinoor@xtra.co.nz	Dinner $25
Nita & Bruce Wilde	**W:** www.bnb.co.nz/hosts/	**Beds:** 2 Double 2 Single
1011 Raetihi Road	kohinoor.html	(3 bdrm)
Ohakune		**Bath:** 1 Ensuite 1 Private
		1 Family share

Taihape

A warm welcome awaits you at the top of the hill in Taihape, where panoramic views of the mountains, ranges and surrounding countryside, add to the tranquil surroundings. 3/4 acre has been landscaped with shrubs. Hydroponics and orchid houses are found along with chrysanthemums in season. Meals, if desired, are with hosts, using produce from the garden where possible. Comfortable beds with electric blankets. Rafting, Bungy Jumping and farm visits can be arranged. 1 hour to Ruapehu, Lake Taupo and 2 1/2-3 hours to Wellington and Rotorua.

Korirata Homestay	**Tel:** (06) 388 0315	**Cost:** Double $70 Single $40
B&B Homestay	**Fax:** (06) 388 0315	Child 1/2 price under 12yrs
1km N of Taihape	**E:** korirata@xtra.co.nz	Dinner B/A Visa/MC
Pat & Noel Gilbert	**W:** www.bnb.co.nz/hosts/	**Beds:** 4 Single (2 bdrm)
25 Pukeko Street	koriratahomestay.html	**Bath:** 1 Guests share
Taihape		

Taihape

Situated on State Highway One, 10 km north of Taihape and 20 km south of Waiouru, we offer comfortable accommodation in our spacious farm homestead. A separate guest lounge is available with tea and coffee making facilities. The farm is home for stud Romney sheep, Angus cattle, deer, farmdogs and two resident cats. 'Harmony' is an ideal stop over - halfway between Rotorua and Wellington. Turoa Skifield is an hour away. Taihape offers good shops and restaurants and is central to a host of outdoor adventures.

Harmony	**Tel:** (06) 388 1117	**Cost:** Double $75 Single $40
B&B Homestay	**Fax:** (06) 388 1117	Dinner B/A
10km N of Taihape	**Mob:** 025 297 5957	Visa/MC
Christine & John Tarrant	**E:** harmonybandb@xtra.co.nz	**Beds:** 1 Double 2 Single
RD 5	**W:** www.bnb.co.nz/hosts/	(2 bdrm)
Taihape	harmony.html	**Bath:** 1 Guests share

Taihape/Rangitikei

We are very lucky to have a piece of New Zealand's natural beauty. Tarata is nestled in bush in the remote Mokai Valley where the picturesque Rangitikei River meets the rugged Ruahine Ranges. With the Ruahines towering above us, stunning views, farm pets and unique trout fishing right at our doorstep, it is the perfect environment to bring up our three children.

Stephen offers guided fishing and rafting trips for all ages. Raft through the gentle crystal clear waters of the magnificent Rangitikei River, vertical papa gorges and stunning scenery you will never forget.

Our spacious home and garden allow guests private space to unwind. Whether it is by the pool on a hot summers day with a book or spending a cosy winters night in front of our open fire with a good wine. There is something special for the whole family and our spotlight safari and farm tour are free for all our guests.

Location, Location, Location. Our new "River Retreat" has a fully self-contained kitchen, lounge, bathroom and two bedrooms (wheelchair friendly). Soak in the spa-bath with "million dollar views" of the river or relax on the large decking amidst native birds and trees. Peace, privacy and tranquillity at its best! We will even deliver a candle light dinner to your door if you prefer.

Approved pets welcome.

We think Tarata is truly a magic place and we would love sharing it with you.

Directions: Tarata Fishaway is 26 scenic kms from Taihape. Turn off state highway one, 6km south of Taihape at the Bungy and Ohotu sign spots. Follow the Bungy and Tarata Fishaway signs (14km) to the Bungy bridge. We are 6 kms past here.

"Compliance for Commercial Rafting"

Features and Attractions

- Homestead Accommodation
- River Retreat
- Fisherman's Cottage
- Honeymoon Suite
- Spotlight Safaris
- Clay bird Shooting
- Bush Walks/4WD Treks
- Farm Tours

- Trout Fishing
- Rafting
- Camp Outs
- Swimming Pool
- "Magic" Carpet
- Flying Fox
- Miniature Horse
- "Mini" Golf

Tarata Fishaway
Self-contained/Farmstay/
Homestay/Fishingstay/Retreat
26km Taihape
Stephen & Trudi Mattock
Mokai Road
RD 3 Taihape

Tel: (06) 388 0354
Fax: (06) 388 0954
Mobile: 025 227 4986
E: fishaway@xtra.co.nz
W: www.tarata.co.nz

Cost: Double $80-$140
Single $40-$75 Child half
Dinner $25pp Visa/MC
Beds: 1 King/Twin 3 Queen
1 Double 4 Single (5 bdrm)
Bath: 1 Ensuite 2 Guests share
Spa bath

TNAKI, W'NUI, R'PEHU, R'TIKEI

Mangaweka

Mairenui Rural Retreat offers three accommodation options and meals are available at the Homestead for guests in the self contained houses. On the farm there is a concrete tennis court, a full size petanque court, a croquet lawn and river swimming. There is also a trout stream for catch and release fishing only. Locally there are the renowned Rangitikei gardens, river adventure, historic home tours and four scenic golf courses. Sue, David and Matt, Benji the cocker spaniel and cats Norman & Nicky welcome guests of all nationalities. French and German are spoken here (except by the animals!).

The Homestead

The Homestead offers quality in house accommodation for up to four people. One heritage-style double room with a small sitting area and a slate floored ensuite bathroom with sunken bath, toiletries, hairdryer and its own verandah. The twin room is larger with shower / toilet and also its own verandah.

B&B Farmstay
Cost: Double $120-$190
     Single $85-$100
     Dinner $30 Visa/MC
Beds: 1 Double 1 Twin (2 bdrm)
Bath: 2 Ensuite

The Retreat

A 1977 Comeskey designed open plan, three and a half storey building set in a stand of 700 year old native trees. A semi circular living room leads up to a brick paved kitchen which is fully equipped with electric oven, microwave and a wood burning stove. Double-hung doors lead through to a tiled breakfast conservatory. The bathroom and toilet are brick paved and the bricked central circular stair tower leads to the first storey double bedrooms and the twin room which is up a vertical ladder. A "seventies" experience! Meals available at Homestead.

Self-contained farmstay
Cost: Double $100 Single $50
     min.$100, max. $200
     Visa/MC
Beds: 2 Double 1 Twin (3bdrm)
Bath: 1 Guests share

The Colonial Villa

A restored hundred year old dwelling with polished wooden floors, a wind up gramophone, a small pool table, two open fires and a wood stove. There's a refrigerator, stove, some electric blankets and heaters. The beds have duvets and blankets, there is a separate shower and the bath is an original claw foot beauty! Verandahs on two sides of the house provide plenty of room for relaxing on the comfortable seats in the sun. Meals available at Homestead.

Self-contained Farmstay
Cost: Double $60 Single $30
     min $60.00, max $200.00
     Visa/MC
Beds: 3 Double 2 Twin (5 bdrm)
Bath: 2 Guests share

Tel: (06) 382 5564
Fax: (06) 382 5885
Mob: (025) 517 545
E: mairenui@xtra.co.nz
W: www.mairenui.co.nz

12km E of Mangaweka
Sue , David and Matt Sweet
Ruahine Road,
Mangaweka 5456

Hunterville

We are fifth generation farmers on Richmond Station, a 1200 acre sheep/cattle hill country farm. Our spacious home is in a tranquil setting of 100 year old trees and garden with swimming pool. You will enjoy our large family room, cosy lounge with open fire, great farm walks and beautiful views. Central to private gardens and river activities. We are midway Rotorua/Wellington, just off SH1 near Hunterville on scenic SH54. We are featured in "50 Great New Zealand Farmstays". Group lunches a specialty. Two outdoor cats.

Vennell's Farmstay
Farmstay
10km NE of Hunterville
Oriel & Phil Vennell
Mangapipi Road
Rewa, RD 10

Tel: (06) 328 6780
Fax: (06) 328 6780
Mob: 025 407 164
Tollfree: 0800 220 172 Pin
W: www.bnb.co.nz/hosts/
vennellsfarmstay.html

Cost: Double $100 Single $50
Child neg Dinner $30
Beds: 1 King/Twin 1 Queen
1 Twin 4 Single
(3 bdrm)
Bath: 2 Private

Hunterville

Otamaire is a lovely 50 year old farm house set in well established lawns, trees and rose gardens. Fully equipped for guests with all modern appointments. Four generations of the family have farmed the surrounding farms and there are two secluded lakes for trout fishing, swimming, rowing or observing wildfowl. Horses and pets are welcome. Guests can self cater or extra charges apply for meals and house keeping services which can be provided. Farm tours, chidren's farm activities, walks and horse treks are available, again extra charges apply.

Otamaire
B&B Self-contained or fully
catered Farmstay
D & V Duncan
R. D. 2
Hunterville

Tel: (06) 322 8484
Fax: (06) 322 8484
Mob: 025 447 966
E: otamaire@dlc.co.nz
W: www.bnb.co.nz/hosts/
otamaire.html

Cost: Double $120 base plus
$30 extra person Visa/MC
Beds: 1 King 1 Queen
1 Double 6 Single
(7 bdrm)
Bath: 3 Bathrooms

Most of our B&Bs will accept credit cards.

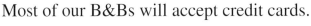

Marton

145 year colonial homestead in peaceful setting amongst native bush and gardens. 1000 acres with sheep, cattle and cropping paddocks. Great opportunities for interesting walks. Centre of garden and heritage home tours. Near Palmerston North and Wanganui. Homely atmosphere with cosy log fire and traditional farm meal. Ample verandahs and gardens to relax. Directions: From Marton township turn at Westpac Bank roundabout to Wanganui for 3 kms. Turn right at Fern Flats Road, then turn left to Waimutu Road. Farm at end of Howie Road through trees. 1 family cat, friendly and placid.

Tataramoa
Farmstay
9km NW of Marton
Janice & Des Gower
Howie Road
RD 2 Marton

Tel: (06) 327 8778
W: www.bnb.co.nz/hosts/
tataramoa.html

Cost: Double $90 Single $45
    Dinner $20
Beds: 1 Double 6 Single
    (4 bdrm)
Bath: 2 Guests share

Marton

Ridgewood is a lovingly restored and furnished historic homestead with olde world charm and commands one of the best vistas in the Rangitikei. Private native bush at the back door teams with birdlife. Mature rhododendrons and camellias fringe the large garden and tennis court. We are home to Cape Baron Geese, free ranging pure bred land and water fowl, 3 shy cats and 1 friendly dog. For a relaxing weekend away , an adventure holiday or a peaceful retreat. Let our warm hospitality welcome you. Bookings recommended

Ridgewood Farm
B&B Farmstay
5km N of Marton
Gay & Jarrah Greenough
Rural #5990, Snellgrove Road
RD 2 Marton

Tel: (06) 327 8887
Fax: (06) 327 8767
Mob: 025 467 057
E: gayg@rangitikei.co.nz
W: www.rangitikei.co,nz/
ridgew.html

Cost: Double $120 Single $70
    Child 1/2 price under 12yrs
    Dinner by arrangement
Beds: 2 Double 2 Twin
    (4 bdrm)
Bath: 1 Private 1 Guests share

To get the feel of a place
stay more than one night.

T'NAKI, W'NUI, R'PEHU, R'TIKEI

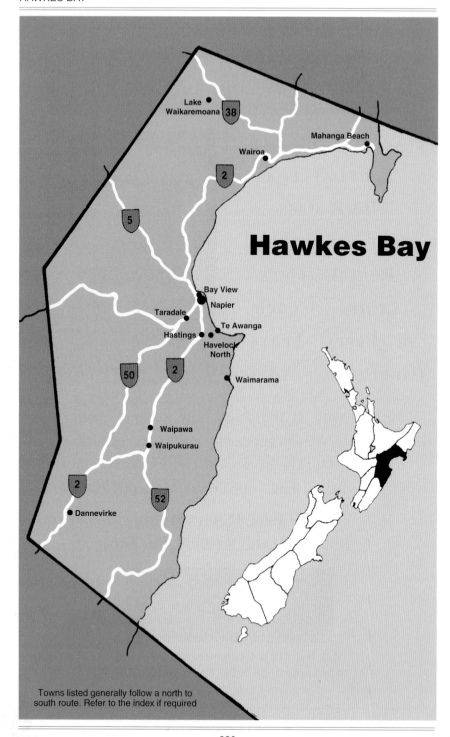

Hawkes Bay

Lake Waikaremoana **38**

Mahanga Beach

Wairoa **2**

5

Bay View
Napier
Taradale
Te Awanga
Hastings
Havelock North
50 **2**
Waimarama

Waipawa
Waipukurau

2
52
Dannevirke

Towns listed generally follow a north to
south route. Refer to the index if required

Mahanga Beach

"Reomoana" - The voice of the sea. Pacific Ocean front farm at beautiful Mahia Peninsula.
The spacious, rustic home with cathedral ceilings, hand-crafted furniture overlooks the Pacific with
breathtaking views. Enjoy the miles of white sandy beaches, go swimming, surfing or fishing.
A painter's paradise. Attractions in the area include: Morere Hot Springs, Mahia Reserve and Golf Course.
Horse rising and fishing charters by arrangement. 6km to 'Sunset Point Restaurant'.
Outside pets: Golden Labrador and cat. Also self-contained cottage in avocado orchard, ideal for families.

Reomoana
Self-contained Farmstay
50km N of Wairoa
Louise Schick
RD 8 Nuhaka Hawkes Bay

Tel: (06) 837 5898
Fax: (06) 837 5990
E: louiseschick@hotmail.com
W: www.bnb.co.nz/hosts/
reomoana.html

Cost: Double $100 Single $60
Dinner $30 Cottage $100
Visa/MC
Beds: 2 Double 1 Single
(3 bdrm)
Bath: 1 Ensuite 1 Private

Please let your hosts know
if you have to cancel.
They will have spent time preparing for you.

Waikaremoana

Lake Waikaremoana is a spectacular and unique Native Forest wilderness area on the Eastern boundary of Te Urewera National Park. Our homestay, set in the picturesque village of Tuai, is the ideal base for a hiking, fly-fishing, or boating holiday.

Tuai Village, the gateway to Waikaremoana, nestles around Lake Whakamarino (Tuai Lake) - part of the Wakaremoana Hydro Electricity Scheme.

We are 10 minutes drive from the Panekiri Bluff entrance to the lake Waikaremoana Track one of New Zealand's "Great Walks". The house, although 70 years old, has been modernised for open living and is extremely comfortable.

From the verandah you look out to Tuai Lake, observe native birdlife in the well developed reserve of mature trees across the road and watch the mist swirling from the forest-clad slopes of the Ngamoko Range.

Homecooking of an exceptional standard, using local and organic produce from garden and district, results in glowing references in my Visitor's Book. As we love to share the peace and unspoilt beauty of our surroundings, let us assist you to explore this awesome area. Sometimes I can even accompany you.

A fishing dinghy is available for guest's use. Also picnic meals, BBQ's and laundry services, by arrangement. Meals are at times to suit your activities, cars can be left at the house and minded by Dusky, the cat, while you walk the tracks. Please ring for directions as Tuai Hydro village is 1km off Highway 38. We look forward to welcoming you to our relaxed lifestyle at Tuai Village. Winter specials May to Sept.

Waikaremoana Homestay	**Tel:** (06) 837 3701	**Cost:** Double $80 Single $50
Homestay	**Fax:** (06) 837 3709	Dinner $25 Visa/MC
50km W of Wairoa	**E:** ykarestay@xtra.co.nz	**Beds:** 1 King/Twin 1 Queen
Judy Doyle	**W:** www.bnb.co.nz/hosts/	(2 bdrm)
RD 5	doylewaikaremoana.html	**Bath:** 1 Family share
Wairoa	or	
Hawkes Bay 4192	**W:** website www.lake.co.nz	

Bay View - Napier

We moved with our pets to the quiet end of an unspoiled
fishing beach by the Esk river, attracted by the beauty and
position away from the traffic noise, while only 15 minutes
from the main attractions. Nearby are vineyards, gardens,
walks and a full range of restaurants north of Napier.
Kilbirnie is near the Taupo Road intersection with the
Pacific Highway to Gisborne with off road parking.
Upstairs, guest rooms have restful views of the Pacific
Ocean one side, vineyards on the other, private bathrooms,
excellent showers, abundant hot water, comfortable firm
beds.

We are retired farmers with time to share good company,
fresh imaginative food, real coffee, fresh juice and books,
and invite you to enjoy our hospitality in modern surroundings.

We have 10 years home hosting experience and are non-
smokers.

Directions: From Taupo first left after intersection Highway
2/5 Franklin Road to Le Quesne, proceed to far end
beachfront. From Napier first right after Bay View "Mobil"
Station.

Kilbirnie	**Tel:** (06) 836 6929	**Cost:** Double $70-$80
Homestay Beach	**Mob:** 025 234 7363	Single $60
12km N of Napier	**E:** jill.johng@xtra.co.nz	Child not suitable
Jill & John Grant	**W:** www.bnb.co.nz/hosts/	Dinner $25pp B/A
84 Le Quesne Road	kilbirnie.html	**Beds:** 1 Queen 1 Double
Bay View, Napier		(2 bdrm)
		Bath: 1 Ensuite 1 Private

HAWKES BAY

The View

Bay View - Napier

In the heart of a thriving WINE REGION overlooking the picturesque Esk Valley nestles "THE GRANGE" our delightfully modern FARMSTAY and superior SELF-CONTAINED LODGE. Private, spacious accommodation in relaxing peaceful surrounds with spectacular rural, coastal and city views. Feel the comforts of home as we tempt you with our farm produce, baking, and preserves.

We're an outgoing family of five who really enjoy the company of guests. Hospitality is guaranteed! Experience our farm life with Roslyn, Drew (farm dog), and Sparkie (cat) - Milk a goat or bottle feed a lamb - seasonal. Don, a third-generation WINEMAKER combines 25 years knowledge with tasting at our Wishart Estate WINERY. Try hand plunging the reds at Vintage.

Explore the World's ART DECO capital NAPIER 12 MINUTES drive away and Hawkes Bay's many regional attractions within 30 minutes. Unwind on the deck to the soothing chorus of native birds in the surrounding gardens and trees and at day's end spend some time romancing over our wonderful night sky. Taupo (Kinloch) holiday home and email access available.

Share our home or retreat in the lodge. "Our Place Is Your Place". 1km off SH5 at Eskdale or 2km off SH2 at BayView.

The Farm

Inside the Lodge

The Winery

The Grange	Tel: (06) 836 6666	Cost: S/C Lodge Double $75
B&B Farmstay &	Fax: (06) 836 6456	Single $60 Extras $20pp
Self-contained Lodge	Mob: 025 281 5738	Breakfast provisions optional
12km N of Napier	E: stay_at_the_grange@xtra.co.nz	Dinner $30 Visa/MC
Roslyn & Don Bird	W: www.thegrangelodge.com	Beds: 1 King/Twin
263 Hill Road	Cost: Farmstay B&B	1 Double 2 Single (2 bdrm)
Eskdale	Double $75 Single $60	Bath: 2 Private
Hawkes Bay	Beds: 1King/Twin (1 bdrm)	

Bay View

Jim, Christine and Sarcha (Jack Russell) will welcome you
to their new beachfront home with breathtaking views of
Hawkes Bay and walking distance to local wineries. Guests
are offered self contained accommodation and own entrance
on ground floor. Jim a local stock agent and Christine works
at a local winery both enjoy meeting people and their
interests are fishing and the outdoor life. Surfcasting and
Kontiki fishing available. Beachfront homestay is just 5
mins from the Napier Taupo turn off and 12 minutes from
Napiers Marine Parade & Cafes.

Beachfront Homestay
Self-contained
12km N of Napier
Christine & Jim Howard
Box 184
Bay View
Napier

Tel: (06) 836 6530
Fax: (06) 836 6531
Mob: 021 159 0162
E: j-howard@clear.net.nz
W: www.bnb.co.nz/hosts/
beachfronthomestaybayview.html

Cost: Double $80 Single $50
Child $10 Dinner $25
Visa/MC Amex Diners
Beds: 1 Queen 2 Single
(2 bdrm)
Bath: 1 Private

Napier

Welcome to our comfortable new home, next door to
where we have home hosted for 10 years. Quiet area
10-15 minutes walk from art deco city centre. Guest
suite opens out side to patio. Lounge, tea making,
fridge, TV. Bedroom with Queen and single beds,
ensuitebathroom. Double bed setee for group of 4.
Walled garden being established with petanque court.
Able to meet public transport. Directions: Port end
Marine Parade, Coote Road, right into Thompson
Road, and left into Cobden Road opposite water tower.

Spence Homestay
Homestay
1km N of Napier
Kay & Stewart Spence
17 Cobden Road
Napier

Tel: (06) 835 9454
Fax: (06) 835 9454
Mob: 025 235 9828
E: ksspence@actrix.gen.nz
W: www.bnb.co.nz/hosts/
spence.html

Cost: Double $110 Single $80
Visa/MC
Beds: 1 Queen 1 Single
(1 bdrm)
Bath: 1 Ensuite

Napier

We welcome you to our modern home with a spectacular sea view, large garden and sunny hill location.
We're a fifteen minute walk to shops and restaurants at
historic Port Ahuriri or our Art Deco City Centre.
Private bath and shower. Laundry facilities at nominal
charge. No smoking inside please. Pick-up service at
no charge. Our interests are travel, gardening, the arts
and local history (we're both involved in preserving
our Art Deco architecture). We enjoy hosting,
conversation and laughter. Please phone or write first.

A Room With a View
Homestay
1.3km NW of Napier
Helen & Robert McGregor
9 Milton Tce
Napier

Tel: (06) 835 7434
Fax: (06) 835 1912
E: roomwithview
@artdeconapier.com
W: www.bnb.co.nz/hosts/
mcgregor.html

Cost: Double $80 Single $50
Visa/MC
Beds: 1 Double (1 bdrm)
Bath: 1 Private

Napier

If you require quiet accommodation just minutes from the city centre, our comfortable, smoke free home provides peace in restful surroundings. Relax on wide decks overlooking our garden, or enjoy the spectacular sea views. Explore nearby historic places and the Botanical Gardens. Your own lounge with tea/coffee making; laundry and off street parking available. We have travelled extensively and welcome the opportunity of meeting visitors. Our interests are travel, music, bowls and embroidery. We will happily meet you at the travel depots.

Hillcrest	**Tel:** (06) 835 1812	**Cost:** Double $75 Single $50
Homestay	**E:** lyons@inhb.co.nz	Visa/MC
Napier Central	**W:** www.bnb.co.nz/hosts/	**Beds:** 1 Double 2 Single
Nancy & Noel Lyons	hillcrestnapier.html	(2 bdrm)
4 George St		**Bath:** 1 Guests share
Hospital Hill Napier		

Napier City

We welcome you to our beautiful old home situated above Napier city, with outstanding views over Hawke Bay. A three minute walk takes you to the Art Deco buildings, cafes and shops. Parking on site. Laundry facilities available. Your double room has a queen size bed and adjoining toilet and hand basin. Also tea making facilities. Weather permitting, breakfast may be served on the veranda or in the garden, in the morning sun. We have a cat.

Madeira Bed & Breakfast	**Tel:** (06) 835 5185	**Cost:** Double $75 Single $50
B&B	**E:** julieball@clear.net.nz	**Beds:** 1 Queen (1 bdrm)
Julie & Eric Ball	**W:** www.bnb.co.nz/hosts/	**Bath:** 1 Family share
6 Madeira Road	madeirabedbreakfast.html	
Napier		

Napier

Set in tranquil gardens, we invite guests to share the warmth and comfort of our home. Our large rooms offer heating, refreshment facilities, colour television, and electric blankets. A mobility ensuite and wheelchair access is available for guests convenience. Also a laundry. Your day with us begins with a scrumptious breakfast and a chat to help plan your day's activities. Relax in our sparkling pool or indoor spa. Our dogs Tess and Hogan and cat Tabitha wait to welcome you.

Kerry Lodge	**Tel:** (06) 844 9630	**Cost:** Double $85-$90
B&B	**Fax:** (06) 844 1450	Single $60 Child $40
Jenny & Bill Hoffman	**Mob:** 025 932 874	Visa/MC
7 Forward Street	**E:** kerrylodge@xtra.co.nz	**Beds:** 1 King 1 Queen 2 Twin
Greenmeadows	**W:** www.bnb.co.nz/hosts/	(3 bdrm)
Napier	kerrylodge.html	**Bath:** 1 Ensuite 1 Guests share

Napier

Peaceful, private, 15 minutes walk to Bluff Hill lookout or city. A large sunny terrace with spa pool, flower garden and lily pond with pleasant views over the sea and northern coastline. Our home with spacious living areas, rimu timber floors and comfortable furnishings is warm and friendly. Bedrooms have electric blankets, heating and writing desk. Home grown fruits and vegetables are a speciality and local wine with dinner. We have travelled extensively, enjoy theatre, the outdoors and Digby our Jack Russell dog. Email& laundry service available.Good off street parking.

Treeways
Homestay
City Location
Cheryl & Maurie Keeling
1 Lighthouse Road
Bluff Hill Napier

Tel: (06) 835 6567
Fax: (06) 835 6567
E: mckeeling@clear.net.nz
W: www.bnb.co.nz/hosts/
treeways.html

Cost: Double $105 Single $75
Dinner $25 B/A
Beds: 1 King/Twin 1 Queen
(2 bdrm)
Bath: 2 Ensuite

Napier

Ruth & Don welcome you to our modern smoke free home with its rural outlook and sunny attractive patio. The garden studio with ensuite and tea making facilities has its own entrance. We are situated on the outskirts of Napier City, the Art Deco City of the World, and in close proximity to wineries and many other tourist attractions. We both have a background in teaching, with interests in travel, gardening and photography.

Snug Harbour
Self-contained Homestay
5km S of Napier
Ruth & Don McLeod
147 Harold Holt Avenue
Napier

Tel: (06) 843 2521
Fax: (06) 843 2520
E: donmcld@clear.net.nz
W: www.bnb.co.nz/hosts/
snugharbour.html

Cost: Double $70-$80
Single $45 Dinner $25 B/A
Visa/MC
Beds: 1 Queen 1 Twin 1 Single
(3 bdrm)
Bath: 1 Ensuite
1 Family share

Napier

Stunning views, comfort and complete privacy. Our downstairs area is for guests' use only, and offers twin bedroom, double bedsettee in guest lounge, and private bathroom, providing accommodation for up to 4 in one group. Tea/coffee making facilities, TV, fridge. Laundry and off-street parking available. A three minute drive takes you to the heart of our famous Art Deco City. Noted Hawke's Bay wineries/restaurants, popular craft outlets, Hastings City, and access to start of tours to gannet colony are all within a 30-minute drive.

Ourhome
B&B Homestay
Napier Hill
N & N Hamlin
4 Hospital Terrace
Napier

Tel: (06) 835 7358
Fax: (06) 835 7355
Mob: 025 852 304
E: ourhomeb&b@xtra.co.nz
W: www.bnb.co.nz/hosts/ourhome.html

Cost: Double $80 Single $50
Beds: 2 Single (1 bdrm)
Bath: 1 Private

Napier

Superior accommodation for the discerning traveller! This beautiful historic homestead takes its name from original owner, James Stanibridge Large Esquire. Constructed in 1858, one of Napier's earliest landmarks has now been fully restored as a boutique guest establishment. Its setting is breathtaking - cascading gardens, magnificent views of the Pacific Ocean, idyllic isolation, yet only a few minutes walk to central Napier. Delicious breakfasts are served in the stunning conservatory or on the balcony, each with captivating views and sounds of birdlife, waterfall and breaking waves.

The "Large" House
Boutique Guest Establishment
Napier Central
John Lucas & Judith Collins
4 Hadfield Terrace
Napier

Tel: (06) 835 0000
Fax: (06) 835 2244
Mob: 025 245 2870
E: large@xtra.co.nz
W: www.bnb.co.nz/hosts/thelargehouse.html

Cost: Double $225 Single $175
Twin $250
Visa/MC Amex Diners
Beds: 1 Super King/Twin 1 King
1 Queen (3 bdrm)
Bath: 2 Ensuite 1 Private

Napier

On the hill over-looking a gorgeous Mediterranean garden and sea views, the historic Coach-house is tastefully renovated and totally self-contained. It contains 2 bedrooms , open plan kitchen, dining, living rooms, bathroom and separate loo. The fridge will be full of a variety of breakfast supplies including "treats", TV and radio included and fresh flowers in all rooms. The sunny deck has a table and chairs and gas barbecue. Off-street parking and easy access plus peace and privacy complete the picture.

The Coach House
Self-contained
1km N of Napier
Jan Chalmers
9 Gladstone Road
Napier

Tel: (06) 835 6126
Mob: 025 657 3263
W: www.bnb.co.nz/hosts/thecoachhouse.html

Cost: Double $100 Single $100
Child $25 - babies free
Dinner $20 4 people $160
Beds: 1 Queen 2 Single
(2 bdrm)
Bath: 1 Private

Napier

The name says it all! You will score our home more
than 10 for Comfort, Convenience, Conviviality.
Comfort: Spacious, sunny, warm, rooms with TV, tea
making facilities, electric blankets, good linen.
Convenience: Quality new home with wonderful
views. Easy stroll to city, cafes, and tourist attractions.
Off-street parking. Conviviality: Our aim is to assist
you to make your stay enjoyable. A selection of
specialty breakfast choices is offered. We have a dog
and a cat. Please no smoking indoors. We look
forward to meeting you.

No 11
B&B Homestay
0.5 E of Napier Central
Phyllida & Bryan Isles
11 Sealy Road
Napier Hill Napier

Tel: (06) 834 4372
Mob: 025 246 3968
E: phyllbry@xtra.co.nz
W: www.bnb.co.nz/hosts/
nonapier.html

Cost: Double $100 Single $65
Beds: 1 Queen 2 Single/King
(2 bdrm)
Bath: 1 Guests share

Napier

Inglenook is situated on the hill in a garden setting
overlooking city and sea and only five minutes stroll to
shops and restaurants. Inglenook offers privacy and a
quiet restful atmosphere. It is immaculately presented
and serviced. Guest suites are self contained with their
own separate entrances and keys. A special breakfast
including fruit is served to guests at a pre-arranged
time outdoors or in guests rooms as required. Tea/
coffee making facilities available in each suite. You
are welcome to make further enquiries.

Inglenook
B&B Self-contained
Napier Central
Phyl Olsen
3 Cameron Terrace
Napier

Tel: (06) 834 2922
Mob: 025 414 992
W: www.bnb.co.nz/hosts/
inglenook.html

Cost: Double $95 Single $60
Child $20
Beds: 2 Double 2 Twin
(4 bdrm)
Bath: 4 Ensuite

Napier

Blue Water Lodge is on the beach front opposite the
Aquarium on Napier's popular Marine Parade. Close
to all local tourist attractions and within walking
distance to the city centre, information centre, family
restaurants, RSA and Cosmopolitan Club. Owner
operated.

Blue Water Lodge Ltd
Guesthouse
471 Marine Parade
Napier

Tel: (06) 835 8929
Fax: (06) 835 8929
Mob: 025 500 192
E: bobbrown@voyager.co.nz
W: www.bnb.co.nz/hosts/
bluewaterlodgeltd.html

Cost: Double $70-$80
Single $40 Child $10
under 14 yrs
Visa/MC Amex Diners
Beds: 6 Double 9 Single
(9 bdrm)
Bath: 1 Ensuite 2 Guests share

Taradale - Napier

Relax on the deck as trees filter the afternoon sun. Savour Ann's homemade preserves and eggs benedict. Put the world to rights as we discuss the follies of presidents and kings. Laugh (or cry) as Peter tries to converse in German and French. Our loves are family, entertaining and education. Our interests are history, art, computers and golf. A short walk takes you to Taradale shops, restaurants and wineries. Tourist attractions and golf courses are within easy driving distance.

Greenwood Bed and Breakfast
Homestay
8km SW of Napier
Ann & Peter Green
62 Avondale Road
Taradale
Napier

Tel: (06) 845 1246
Fax: (06) 845 1247
Mob: 025 795 403
E: greenwood@clear.net.nz
W: www.bnb.co.nz/hosts/
greenwoodbedandbreakfast.html

Cost: Double $90 Single $60
Dinner $25 Visa/MC
Beds: 2 Queen 2 Single
(3 bdrm)
Bath: 3 Ensuite

Taradale - Napier

Comfortable, quiet apartment in the heart of our foremost wine producing area. Superb day and night views over Napier and local rural scenes. 10 minutes drive to the Art Deco capital of the world. 2km to Taradale village. Safe off-street parking. Top quality restaurants and wineries nearby. We are a friendly couple who have enjoyed B&B overseas and like meeting people. Our interests are travel, theatre, good food and wine. Bella, our cat, keeps to herself. Handy to E.I.T and golf course.

Otatara Heights
B&B Self-contained
10km W of Napier
Roy & Sandra Holderness
57 Churchill Drive
Taradale Napier

Tel: (06) 844 8855
Fax: (06) 844 8855
E: sandroy@xtra.co.nz
W: www.bnb.co.nz/hosts/
otataraheights.html

Cost: Double $85 Visa/MC
Beds: 1 Queen 1 Double
(1 bdrm)
Bath: 1 Private

Taradale - Napier

Built in 1997, "279" offers elegant spacious accommodation in a unique setting amongst mature trees and picturesque gardens. Breakfast at your leisure in formal dining room or alfresco on the patio. There is one family cat and your hosts strive to offer excellent hospitality in a friendly relaxed atmosphere to Domestic and International visitors. "279" is adjacent to Mission and Church Road Wineries, a short stroll to a craft gallery, pottery, award winning "Missionview" Gardens, and within a 20 minute drive of the many Hawkes Bay activities. Member NZAFHH.

'279' Church Road
B&B Homestay
7.5km SW of Napier
Sandy Edginton
279 Church Road
Taradale Napier

Tel: (06) 844 7814
Fax: (06) 844 7814
Mob: 025 265 6760
E: sandy.279@homestaynapier.co.nz
W: www.homestaynapier.co.nz

Cost: Double $90 Single $60
Dinner by arrangement
Visa/MC
Beds: 1 Double 1 Twin
(2 bdrm)
Bath: 1 Guests share

Napier

Come and share our 1920's smokefree home, garden and pool situated above the lovely Art Deco city of Napier. Our rooms are large and sunny. A five minute stroll will have you amongst the Art Deco buildings and the renowned Marine Parade, or relax poolside and enjoy our garden. We offer home cooked goodies using fresh produce from Hawkes Bay. Our interests include food, wine, classic cars, art deco and good company. Shiraz our cat shares our home. We offer laundry facilities and have bikes available. Phone for easy directions.

Cameron Close
Homestay
Napier Central
Joy & Graeme Thomas
33 Cameron Road
Napier

Tel: (06) 835 5180
Fax: (06) 835 4115
Mob: 021 683 551
E: BESCO@xtra.co.nz
W: www.bnb.co.nz/hosts/
cameronclose.html

Cost: Double $75 Single $50
Dinner $30
Beds: 2 Double 1 Single
(3 bdrm)
Bath: 1 Guests share

Napier

Lesleigh's homestay is conveniently located close to Napier City Centre, with Art Deco architecture, superb restaurants, cafes, fruit orchards and premier wineries. Nearby is the Onekawa Aquatic Centre and Gym. Lesley, Dick and Czar the cat welcome guests to their friendly, homely environment. Having extensively travelled throughout New Zealand we offer our knowledge to you. Guests have their own lounge, with pool table, TV, fridge, coffee/tea making facilities and use of the large outdoor deck. We will endeavour to make your stay an enjoyable experience.

Lesleigh's
B&B Homestay
2km S of Napier
Lesley Clark
4 Gallipoli Road
Onekawa, Napier

Tel: (06) 843 4528
Fax: (06) 843 4528
E: GASPdesigns@xtra.co.nz
W: www.bnb.co.nz/hosts/
lesleighs.html

Cost: Double $75 Single $55
Visa/MC
Beds: 1 Double 2 Twin
(3 bdrm)
Bath: 1 Guest share

Our B&Bs range from homely to luxurious,
but you can always be assured
of superior hospitality.

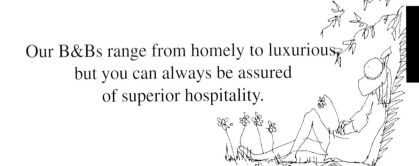

Napier

Our Picturesque 1870 Villa has been completely restored and fully furnished in the Art Deco Style. To which we brought our enthusiastic interest, together with artistic talent from America, to live in Napier - "The Art Deco City".

Situated on Bluff Hill... you may start your day enjoying breakfast in the spacious Conservatory while watching the Ocean sunrise. Then relax after days end with a glass of local wine and watch the Harbour sunset from the surrounding Verandah or elegant Dining Room.

We offer stylish bedrooms with ensuite or private bath, custom-comfort beds, fine quality linens and European down duvets. We also offer a "romantic" King bedroom with an ensuite that includes a deluxe jet spa tub with a separate double steam shower and adjoining private garden verandah.

All rooms have central heating and air conditioning with accessible porches for outdoor smoking. Both E-mail and facsimilie available upon request. Our interests include applical art, decorative antiques, conversational entertaining and sporty activities. German is well understood.

Directions: Marine Parade left on Coote Road (at Centennial Gardens) - Right turn onto Thompson Road - follow up around and remain left - Left turn onto Cobden Road (#11).

Cobden Villa Bed & Breakfast
B&B
1KM Napier City Centre
Amy and Cornel Walewski
11 Cobden Road
Bluff Hill Napier

Tel: (06) 835 9065
Fax: (06) 833 6979
Mob: 025 286 1789
E: info@cobdenvilla.com
W: www.cobdenvilla.com

Cost: Double $185-$365
Single $160 Visa/MC
Beds: 1 King 2 Queen
2 King Singles (4 bdrm)
Bath: 3 Ensuite 1 Private

Napier

Napier - Ahuriri. B&B cost: (full) Double $150, Single $85. Beds: Twin, Bath Private, TV, Studio with Patio. New townhouse on seafront. Easy walking distance to a variety of restaurants and cafes. Local Art Deco interests. Handy to all Hawkes Bay attractions and airport. Meet and greet service if required, tea making facilities available. Non smoking, secure parking.

Quayside
B&B
Ailsa Robertshawe
31 Nelson Quay
Ahuriri
Napier

Tel: (06) 835 0269
E: NelsonQuay@xtra.co.nz
W: www.bnb.co.nz/hosts/
quayside.html

Cost: Double $150
Single $85
Visa/MC
Beds: 1 Twin (1 bdrm)
Bath: 1 Private

Napier - Hastings

Copperfields: A small orchard between the Art Deco cities of Napier/Hastings. Wineries, craft trails, golf courses and tourist attractions are readily accessible. Pam and Richard are interested in weaving, crafts, furniture restoration and antiques. Non-smokers. We have a labrador dog and a pet pig. Guests stay in "Glen Cottage" large self contained accommodation attached to our house (own entrance) enabling guests to be totally private. Guests are welcome to join us for breakfast or dinner (three courses). Family rates negotiable. Dogs welcome (conditions apply).

Copperfields
Self-contained Homestay
btw Napier/ Hastings
Pam & Richard Marshall
Copperfields
Pakowhai Road Napier

Tel: (06) 876 9710
Fax: (06) 876 9710
Mob: 021 256 7590
E: rich.pam@clear.net.nz
W: www.bnb.co.nz/hosts/
copperfields.html

Cost: Double $95 Single $70
Child neg Dinner $25 pp
Visa/MC
Beds: 1 Double 3 Single
(2 bdrm)
Bath: 1 Private 1 Family share

Just as we have a variety of B&Bs
you will also discover
a variety of breakfasts,
and they will always be generous.

Napier - Hastings

Our home is situated in Charlton Road Te Awanga which is approximately twenty minutes form both Napier and Hastings and right next door to the gannets at Cape Kidnappers and one of Hawkes Bay leading winery restaurants. With us you can enjoy space, tranquillity, and fine hospitality while receiving every assistance to make your stay in our area as interesting and enjoyable as possible. We have two Jack Russel dogs. Directions: Charlton Road is the first road on your right after passing through Te Awanga village.

Farmstay Homestay
15km E of Napier/Hastings
Bill and Heather Shaw
Charlton Road
RD 2
Hastings

Tel: (06) 875 0177
Fax: (06) 875 0525
W: www.bnb.co.nz/hosts/
shaw.html

Cost: Double $100
Single $100
Dinner by arrangement
Beds: 4 Single (2 bdrm)
Bath: 1 Ensuite 1 Family share

Napier - Hastings

Experience a genuine farmstay, delicious home produce and food, trout fishing and friendly rural hospitality at our historic homestead and farm. Our family and pet Foxy Becky enjoy meeting people and catering for individuals or families interested in the outdoor life (two nights recommended) on our large sheep, beef and deer farm, and organic apple and pear orchard. Enrich your stay by experiencing outdoor activities at our backdoor including, guided farm tours, trout fishing, hunting , bush and farm walks, jet boating and extensive mountain hikes.

Waiwhenua Farmstay
Farmstay Homestay
50km W of Hastings - Napier
Kirsty Hill & Family
808 River Road
RD 9 Hastings

Tel: (06) 874 2435
Fax: (06) 874 2465
Mob: 025 759 369
E: kirsty.hill@xtra.co.nz
W: www.bnb.co.nz/hosts/
waiwhenuafarmstay.html

Cost: Double $100 Single $50
Child $40 Dinner $25
Campervan welcome
Beds: 2 Queen 3 Single
(2 bdrm)
Bath: 1 Private

Napier - Hastings

Riverbank house is set on 1 1/2 acres of tranquil gardens by the Clive River. We have 2 well appointed cottages suit all types of travellers. We have a large swimming pool and a spa. Laundry and BBQ facilities are available on request. Our family consists of 3 children, one is in London and the other two are at home. We have all sorts of pets ranging from cats to miniature horses. We have all done lots of travelling and look forward to making you welcome. Pets are welcome. Breakfasts are great!

Self-contained Cottage
1.5km N of Clive
Kerry & Jan McKinnie
PO Box 38
Clive
Hastings North

Tel: (06) 870 0759
Fax: (06) 870 0528
Mob: 025 211 0464
E: ker.jan@xtra.co.nz
W: www.bnb.co.nz/hosts/
mckinnie.html

Cost: Double $75 Single $50
Dinner B/A Visa/MC
Beds: 1 Queen 1 Double
4 Single (3 bdrm)
Bath: 3 Ensuite

Napier - Hastings

Situated on the Wine Trail, "Silverford" - one of Hawkes Bay's most gracious Homesteads - is spaciously set in 17 acres of farmland, established trees and gardens. Drive through our half a kilometre long gorgeous Oak lined avenue to the sweeping lawns, bright flower gardens and ponds surrounding our elegant home designed by Natusch at the turn of the century.

We are relaxed and friendly and offer a warm ambience in private, comfortable and tranquil surroundings - a romantic haven with tastefully furnished bedrooms, charming guest sitting room and a courtyard to dream in.

Silverford is an idyllic welcoming haven for a private, peaceful and cosy stay whilst at the same time being close to all the amenities and attractions that Hawkes Bay has to offer. Good restaurants close by. Friendly deer, cow, pigeons, ducks and dogs. Central Heating. Swimming Pool.

We are smokefree and regret the property is unsuitable for children. Some French and German spoken.

Silverford
Homestay
18km W of Napier
Chris & William Orme-Wright
Puketapu
Hawkes Bay

Tel: (06) 844 5600
Fax: (06) 844 4423
E: homestay@paradise.net.nz
W: www.silverford.co.nz

Cost: Double $145-$165
Single $115
Visa/MC Amex
Beds: 1 King 1 Queen
1 Double (3 bdrm)
Bath: 1 Ensuite 1 Guests share

Hastings - Havelock North

We welcome you to our new home. In rural surroundings only five minutes to Havelock North. Hastings and Napier approximately fifteen minutes. We are gardeners and golfers and what better place to be than Hawkes Bay with four excellent golf courses, superb gardens and many wineries. Our four children have gone but we have two friendly black cats. There is a queen bed with guests' own bathroom in the house. An outside unit has two single beds, shower, toilet and tea making facilities. No smoking inside please.

B&B Self-contained Homestay
2.5km SE of Havelock North
Jill & Jock Taylor
134 Kopanga Road
Havelock North

Tel: (06) 877 8797
Fax: (06) 8 77 2335
E: jilljock@paradise.net.nz
W: www.bnb.co.nz/hosts/
taylor.html

Cost: Double $75 Single $45
Dinner $15 by arrangement
Beds: 1 Queen 2 Single
(2 bdrm)
Bath: 2 Private

Hastings - Havelock North

20 minutes from Hastings, Havelock North or Waipawa, enjoy the beautiful Hawkes Bay. We are handy to the many attractions Hawkes Bay has to offer. Gannets - wineries - art deco - golf courses - Splash Planet - a local trout river (guide available) or just relax in peace and space. Dinner (featuring local produce) available on request. If interesetd and weather permits a farm tour in 4WD.

Farmstay Homestay
16km S of Havelock North
Ros Phillips
Wharehau
RD 11 Hastings

Tel: (06) 877 4111
Fax: (06) 877 4111
W: www.bnb.co.nz/hosts/
phillips.html

Cost: Single $40 Child 1/2 price
Dinner $25 Beach Bach
Beds: 1 Queen 2 Twin
1 Single (4 bdrm)
Bath: 1 Guests share
1 Family share

Hastings City

Enjoy our peaceful garden back section, away form all traffic noises, yet central to Hastings City. Our Siamese cat says "Hi". Nearby are parks, golf courses, wineries, orchards and the best icecream ever. Short trips take you to spectacular views, Cape Kidnapper's Gannet colony, or Napier's Art Deco. Activities include ballooning, Clydesdale wagon ride, hot pools, wine trails, or relaxing having coffee on our deck. Directions: From Wellington, take the Napier/ Stratford Lodge route, left off main highway at Paki Paki. From Taupo ring. No smoking please.

McConchie Homestay
Homestay
Hastings Central
Barbara & Keta McConchie
115A Frederick Street
Hastings

Tel: (06) 878 4576
Mob: 025 610 2902
E: barbaramcconchie@xtra.co.nz
W: www.bnb.co.nz/hosts/
mcconchie.html

Cost: Double $80 Single $45
Child $15 Dinner $20
Visa/MC
Beds: 1 Queen 2 Single
(2 bdrm)
Bath: 1 Guests share

Hastings

We look forward to giving you a warm welcome to the
Hawkes Bay which offers a wide variety of attractions,
in particular wineries and the Art Deco buildings of
Napier. We are close to the Ngaruroro River for good
trout fishing during the season and within easy reach
of a variety of other rivers and lakes. Guided fishing is
offered by Peter. Our accommodation has a small
kitchen and living room. Non smoking and not
suitable for children. Owners have two dogs. Ring for
directions.

B&B Self-contained
9km W of Hastings
Anne & Peter Wilkinson
Box 2116
Hastings

Tel: (06) 879 9357
Fax: (06) 879 9357
Mob: 025 216 3785
E: ph-aawilkinson@clear.net.nz
W: www.bnb.co.nz/hosts/
wilkinson.html

Cost: Double $85 Single $70
Visa/MC
Beds: 2 Single (1 bdrm)
Bath: 1 Private

Hastings

Our home is set in half acre of cottage garden on the
Hastings boundary close to Havelock North. Swimming pool and tennis court for the energetic and a spa
bath to relax in at night Hastings city centre is five
minutes by car and Havelock North 2 minutes. 'Splash
Planet', with its many water features and hot pools is
only two minutes away. We look forward to your
company and can assure you of a comfortable and
relaxing stay. Non smoking and not suitable for small
children or pets.

Woodbine Cottage
Homestay
2.5km Hastings
Ngaire & Jim Shand
1279 Louie Street
Hastings

Tel: (06) 876 9388
Fax: (06) 876 9666
Mob: 025 529 522
E: nshand@xtra.co.nz
W: www.bnb.co.nz/hosts/
woodbinecottage.html

Cost: Double $100 Single $55
Dinner $25pp B/A
Visa/MC
Beds: 1 Double 1 Twin
(2 bdrm)
Bath: 1 Guests share

Hastings

We welcome you to our home situated in a quiet rural
setting. "Raureka" is an apple orchard 3 kms from
town, close to restaurants, golf courses and wineries.
We have an attractive detached room with a queen size
bed, ensuite, TV and tea & coffee making facilities.
Guests are welcome to use our pool and tennis court set
in an attractive garden with a view out to 100 year old
oak trees. We offer you a relaxed, quiet, friendly stay.
Smoking outside only.

Raureka
B&B Self-contained
3km S of Hastings
Tim & Rosemary Ormond
26 Wellwood Road
RD 5 Hastings

Tel: (06) 878 9715
Fax: (06) 878 9715
E: r.t.ormond@xtra.co.nz
W: www.bnb.co.nz/hosts/
raureka.html

Cost: Double $80
Single $65
Beds: 1 Queen (1 bdrm)
Bath: 1 Ensuite

Hastings

A warm welcome awaits you at Bramble Hedge, set on 2 acres half-way between Napier and Hastings. The house, designed by John Scott, is comfortable and well appointed with a delightful ambience. We have an outdoor spa set in private gardens for summertime use and two lounges both with wood fires for the colder months. Ample off-street parking available. We have no children living at home, only one cat. Property not suitable for children. Our interests include gardening, growing palms and following motor sports. (We ask guests not to smoke in the house)

Bramble Hedge	**Tel:** (06) 870 1070	**Cost:** Double $85 Single $60
B&B Homestay	**Fax:** (06) 870 1075	Visa/MC
5km N of Hastings	**Mob:** 021 509 441	**Beds:** 1 Queen 2 Twin
Grace and Roger Terry	**E:** bramblehedge@xtra.co.nz	(2 bdrm)
527 State Highway 2	**W:** www.bnb.co.nz/hosts/	**Bath:** 1 Private 1 Guests share
RD 2 Hastings	bramblehedge.html	

Hastings

Welcome to Hawkes Bay, the premier food and wine region of New Zealand. Stitch-Hill invites you to relax in the quiet countryside surrounded with panoramic views. Our prime location is just minutes from the city centres, wineries and attractions. In our comfortable smoke-free home we offer the very best hospitality. Your requirements our challenge. Your choice of room, twin with ensuite, queen bed with ensuite. Stroll in our gardens or around our acres, enjoy fishing and tramping. Unsuitable for children and pets.

Stitch-Hill Farm	**Tel:** (06) 879 9456	**Cost:** Double $75 Single $45
B&B Farmstay	**Fax:** (06) 879 9806	Dinner $20 B/A
12km W of Hastings, 12km SW	**E:** cjtrask@xtra.co.nz	**Beds:** 1 Queen 1 Twin
Taradale	**W:** www.bnb.co.nz/hosts/	(2 bdrm)
Charles Trask	stitchhill.html	**Bath:** 2 Ensuite
170 Taihape Road		
RD 9 Hastings		

Hastings - Kereru

GLOW-WORMS AND GORGES. Welcome to our 1100 acre sheep, cattle, and forestry property, extensively planted in diverse tree species, with 100 acres of protected native bush. "Longview" offers panoramic views of Hawkes Bay, from the coast to the ranges (Homestead at 1500ft) and is situated on the Ngaruroro section of the Awarua Heritage Trail. Visit our special glow-worm grottoes, in our network of gorges. Camp, tramp, fish and picnic (on, or off farm) join in daily activities, or just relax. Pets - Missy a small dog.

Longview	**Tel:** (06) 876 0918	**Cost:** Double $90 Single $45
Farmstay + Self-contained	**Fax:** (06) 876 0918	Child $25 Dinner $15
40km W of Hastings	**Mob:** 025 265 5580	Visa/MC
David & Ngaire Bryant	**Tollfree:** 0800 349 697	**Beds:** 1 Double 5 Single
1202 Salisbury Road	**W:** homepages.ihug.co.nz/~bryr/	(3 bdrm)
RD 1 Hastings		**Bath:** 1 Private 1 Guests share

Hastings

Set high on 15 acres, planted with 2000 trees, Wharenikau overlooks Hawkes Bay's world-renowned vineyards and the picturesque Ngaruroro river. Newly built, Wharenikau represents John and Anne's desire to offer guests exceptional accommodation, food and wine. We serve a gourmet three course dinner with premium Hawkes Bay wines. Architecturally designed to enjoy the magnificent views, peace and tranquillity, Wharenikau is ideally suited for people who want to relax in style and is therefore not suitable for children. Privacy is afforded to guests by way of a separate cottage. Pets by arrangement with the owners' 3 dogs.

Wharenikau	**Tel:** (06) 879 5899	**Cost:** Double $100-$120
Self-contained Homestay	**Fax:** (06) 879 5896	Dinner $130 per couple
9km N of Hastings	**Mob:** 025 381 477	Visa/MC
John & Anne Porter	**E:** john.porter@leather.co.nz	**Beds:** 1 King 1 Queen 1 Twin
172 Taihape Road	**W:** www.bnb.co.nz/hosts/	(3 bdrm)
R. D. 9, Owaka Hastings	wharenikau.html	**Bath:** 1 Private 1 Guests share

Hastings

Welcome to Hastings. We have something special to offer, with 6 recently built self-contained 1 & 2 bedroom cottages. Each of our cottages is individually located within the 1 ha block of land and every cottage contains 2 bedrooms, a modern kitchen that includes a fridge, microwave, electric fry pan and gas hobs. Several Bar-B-Ques are also available for the outdoor enthusiasts. A grass tennis court, children's play and petanque area is also available for our guests. There are 2 golf courses located minutes up the road. Our tariff includes a continental breakfast. Our family includes Mark 13 and Sarah 6 and our Golden Labrador named Bess. We look forward to meeting you and making your stay, an enjoyable one.

Cottages Hawkes Bay	**Tel:** (06) 876 4104	**Cost:** Double $80-$100
Self-contained	**Fax:** (06) 876 4104	Single $60 Children neg.
2km S of Hastings	**Mob:** 025 491 526	Visa/MC/eftpos
John & Rose Roil	**E:** cottageshb.co.nz	**Beds:** 6 Queen 12 Single
15 Irongate Road Hastings	**W:** www.cottageshb.co.nz	**Bath:** 6 Private

Havelock North - Hastings

Relax in our century old home in large gardens and lawns on 25 acres of horticulture land. We enjoy meeting people. After 14 years of hosting we have made many new friends. Our aim is to provide a pleasant and memorable stay. Good firm beds, electric blankets, meals are generous. Interest include tramping, caravaning, bushwalks, fishing, gardening and genealogy. Dianne has certificate in Homestay management. Lovely boutique shops and cafes in Havelock North. Handy to wineries. Napier art Deco city 25 mins. No smoking inside please.

PeakView Farm	**Tel:** (06) 877 7408	**Cost:** Double $70 Single $45
Farmstay Homestay	**Fax:** (06) 877 7410	Child 1/2 price Dinner $25
1km N of Havelock North	**W:** www.bnb.co.nz/hosts/	Visa/MC
Dianne & Keith Taylor	peakviewfarm.html	**Beds:** 1 Double 2 Single
92 Middle Road		(2 bdrm)
Havelock North		**Bath:** 1 Family share

Havelock North

Our comfortable family home is set in ten acres next to the
Tukituki River by Te Mata Peak five minutes from
Havelock North. We have a number of friendly animals,
four dogs, kunekune pigs, coloured sheep, horses and cats.
You are welcome to swim in the pool or play tennis on the
grass court. Our other interests include theatre, music,
spinning, horse riding and flying. Dinner served with local
wine is a pleasant time to get to know one another. We
appreciate no smoking indoors.

Overcliff
Farmstay Homestay
4km E of Havelock North
Joan & Nigel Sutton
Waimarama Rd
RD 12
Havelock North

Tel: (06) 877 6852
Fax: (06) 877 6852
E: jn.partners@clear.net.nz
W: www.bnb.co.nz/hosts/
overcliff.html

Cost: Double $90 Single $65
Dinner $25 Visa/MC
Beds: 1 Double 3 Single
(3 bdrm)
Bath: 1 Private

Havelock North

In a quiet picturesque garden at the end of a lavender lined lane,
WELDON offers comfort and quality with romantic olde
worlde charm. Accommodation is offered in spacious
elegantly appointed bedrooms, furnished with period and
antique furniture. TV & tea/coffee are provided in each room.
Fresh flowers, fine linen and fluffy towels reflect the luxury of
fine accommodation. Breakfast of fresh local fruits & gourmet
cooked options is served outdoors among the roses in summer
or in the dining room during winter. Two toy poodles (James
and Thomas) will greet you enthusiastically!

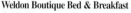

Weldon Boutique Bed & Breakfast
B&B Homestay Boutique
1km N of Havelock North
Pracilla Hay
98 Te Mata Road
Havelock North Hawkes Bay

Tel: (06) 877 7551
Fax: (06) 877 7051
Mob: 025 303 569
Tollfree: 0800 206 499
E: pracilla@weldon.co.nz
W: www.weldon.co.nz

Cost: Double $110-$120
Single $80-$90 Dinner $30
$130 - $140 Queen Visa/MC
Beds: 1 Queen 2 Double 1 Twin
1 Single (5 bdrm)
Bath: 2 Private 1 Guests share

Havelock North

Belvedere is a large 2 storeyed home set in half an acre
of well kept lawns and gardens. The elegant rooms
have balconies with great views. It is a short walk to
Havelock North village where there are a great variety
of shops and restaurants. Hawkes Bay is a well known
tourist resort with something for everyone. Having
travelled extensively within New Zealand and
Overseas we have enjoyed the hospitality of many
Homestays and are pleased to be able to offer the same
in return. Not suitable for children under 12yrs.

Belvedere
Homestay
5km E of Hastings
Shirley & Mervyn Pethybridge
51 Lucknow Road
Havelock North

Tel: (06) 877 4551
Fax: (06) 877 4550
E: pethybridge@actrix.gen.nz
W: www.bnb.co.nz/hosts/
belvedere.html

Cost: Double $70 Single $45
Dinner $20 by arrangement
Beds: 1 Queen 1 Double
1 Twin (3 bdrm)
Bath: 1 Ensuite 1 Private

Havelock North

Offering a unique Bed & Breakfast experience in a lovingly restored 1910 villa. Take a peek into the museum of early pioneer farming displayed in the century old stables or marvel at the simplicity of early stationary motors. Feed the hand reared deer or arrange a ride in a classic 1951 Sunbeam Talbot motor car. We are located in the heart of the Te Mata wine region only minutes from the pictureque village of Havelock North. Non smoking and not suitable for children under 12 years.

Totara Stables
B&B Homestay
5 km N of Havelock North
John W. Hayes & Sharon A. Bellaart
324 Te Mata - Mangateretere Road
Havelock North
RD 2, Hastings

Tel: (06) 877 8882
Fax: (06) 877 8891
Mob: 025 863 910
E: totarastables@xtra.co.nz
W: welcome.to/totarastables

Cost: Double $85-$95
Single $65 Visa/MC
Beds: 1 King/Twin 1 Queen
1 Twin (3 bdrm)
Bath: 1 Ensuite 1 Private

Havelock North

I live on a small life style block. Very central to Hastings and Havelock North with golf, wineries and many other attractions all within short distance. I have farm animals including 2 farm dogs. I am happy to share my home - you will be very welcome.

Garda
6km W of Havelock North &
6km S Hastings
Fay Hanna
84 Longlands Rd E
PO Box 8305
Havelock North

Tel: (06) 878 2444
Fax: (06) 873 5017
E: ecmb@xtra.co.nz
W: www.bnb.co.nz/hosts/
garda.html

Cost: Double $100 Single $100
Dinner available
3 course with HB wine
Beds: (2 bdrm)
Bath: Share

Havelock North

Poona is a picturesque arts and crafts style house in the heart of the wine country on the slopes of Te Mata Peak. Only minutes from restaurants, village markets and art deco architecture. Suite comprises Queen bedroom, private bathroom and sitting room with TV, tea making facilities and fridge. Complimentary delicacies. Comfortably furnished with antiques. Breakfast of seasonal local produce served on our terrace overlooking pretty gardens with old brick paving or in the dining room with open fire, fresh flowers and one cat, Cleo. Non smoking.

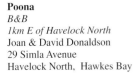

Poona
B&B
1km E of Havelock North
Joan & David Donaldson
29 Simla Avenue
Havelock North, Hawkes Bay

Tel: (06) 877 1706
Fax: (06) 877 1709
Mob: 025 748 218
W: www.bnb.co.nz/hosts/
poona.html

Cost: Double $90 Single $70
Visa/MC Amex
Beds: 1 Queen (1 bdrm)
Bath: 1 Private

Te Awanga

Merriwee was built in 1908 and is set in an apricot orchard just a stroll from Te Awanga beach. It is close to Napier/ Hastings and Havelock North, with Cape Kidnappers and wineries nearby. The home is spacious, with quality furnishings, open fires and sea views across to Napier. French doors access bedrooms to verandahs and garden. The main guest area is self contained with sitting room ensuite and kitchen. There is a swimming pool and pentanque court. Terrier "Mags" and two cats reside. Gordon Road is the first on the right as you enter Te Awanga Village.

Merriwee Homestay	**Tel:** (06) 875 0111	**Cost:** Double $100-$150
Homestay	**Fax:** (06) 875 0111	Single $80 Dinner B/A
12km E of Napier/Hastimgs	**Mob:** 021 214 5023	**Beds:** 1 King 1 Queen
Jeanne Richards	**E:** merriwee@xtra.co.nz	1 Double 1 Twin (4 bdrm)
29 Gordon Road	**W:** www.merriwee.co.nz	**Bath:** 1 Ensuite 2 Private
Te Awanga		
Hawkes Bay		

Waimarama Beach

Lovely beach for surfing, swimming, diving, boating, fishing etc. Bushwalks and golf course nearby. Situated only 5 minutes walk from beach with lovely views of sea, local park and farmland. Nearest town is Havelock North - 20 minutes drive, with Napier 40 minutes. We have 2 double rooms available, a spa pool and separate toilet and bathroom for guests. Cooked breakfast is offered and dinner is available if required. Please phone for reservations 06-874 6795. No smoking inside please. Pets: 2 cats, 1 dog.

Homestay	**Tel:** (06) 874 6795	**Cost:** Double $70 Single $45
34km SE of Hastings	**E:** rwebb@xtra.co.nz	Dinner $20
Rita & Murray Webb	**W:** www.bnb.co.nz/hosts/	**Beds:** 2 Double (2 bdrm)
68 Harper Road	webb.html	**Bath:** 1 Guests share
Waimarama		
Hawkes Bay		

Waipawa

Come and enjoy an evening or two at "Haowhenua" with a farming family in a spacious and comfortable old country home set in park like surrounds with lovely gardens and swimming pool, and share your adventures with us. We have two cats and a labrador and only 2km off State Highway 2 and in close proximity to all of Hawkes Bay's attractions. No smoking inside. Please phone for directions.

Haowhenua	**Tel:** (06) 857 8241	**Cost:** Double $100 Single $75
Farmstay Country Home	**Fax:** (06) 857 8261	Child 1/2 price
2km E of Waipawa	**Mob:** 025 2684 854	Dinner $25pp Visa/MC
Caroline & David Jefferd	**E:** d.jefferd@xtra.co.nz	**Beds:** 1 Queen (1 bdrm)
77 Pourerere Road	**W:** www.bnb.co.nz/hosts/	**Bath:** 1 Ensuite
RD 1	haowhenua.html	
Waipawa 4170		

Waipawa

A warm welcome awaits you at Corgarff, our very sunny and comfortable home, set in 13 acres amongst lovely old Trees. We have a flock of Texel sheep and a Birman Cat 'Mollie'. Our guest wing has a separate entrance and also a small private sitting room with TV. Our facilities are very suitable for wheelchair or disabled persons. Children under 12 half price. Three hours easy run to Ferry in Wellington. 4 challenging golf courses within easy reach. 5 safe sandy beaches. Hastings and top NZ Wineries less than 30 minutes. First class rivers for trout fishing. Directions: Please phone

Corgarff Homestay	**Tel:** (06) 857 7828	**Cost:** Double $90 Single $50
Homestay	**Fax:** (06) 857 7055	Child $25 Dinner $20
2km N of Waipawa	**W:** www.bnb.co.nz/hosts/	Visa/MC
Judy & Neil McHardy	corgarffhomestay.html	**Beds:** 2 King/Twin 3 Single
104 Great North Road		(3 bdrm)
Waipawa Hawkes Bay		**Bath:** 1 Ensuite 1 Guests share
		1 Family share

Waipukurau

Hinerangi Station is an 1800 acre sheep, cattle and deer farm set in the rolling hills of Central Hawkes Bay. Our spacious 1920 homestead was designed by Louis Hay of Napier Art Deco fame. It has a full size billiard table and there is a tennis court and swimming pool in the garden. Guests have their own private entrance."The Cookhouse",a recently renovated 100 yr old cottage offers self contained accomodation for couples and families.We have one terrier and a cat.

Hinerangi Station	**Tel:** (06) 855 8273	**Cost:** Double $100-$120
Self-contained Farmstay	**Fax:** (06) 855 8273	Single $80 Child $30
20km S of Waipukurau	**E:** carovond@amcom.co.nz	Dinner $30pp
Caroline & Dan von Dadelszen	**W:** www.bnb.co.nz/hosts/	$110 Double $40 each
615 Hinerangi Road	hinerangistation.html	extra person S/C cottage
RD 1		**Beds:** 2 Queen 1 Double
Waipukurau		5 Single (4 bdrm)
		Bath: 2 Guests share

Waipukurau

Mynthurst, genuine working sheep and cattle farm 560 acres. Guests from NZ and overseas welcomed for 17 years. The homestead is large, warm and comfortable. Observe farm activities, enjoy swimming, trout fishing, golf, tennis, wineries. Dinner available on request, using finest local produce. Whether travelling North or South, visiting beautiful Hawkes Bay, you'll find Mynthurst the perfect retreat. 1/2 hour from Hastings SH2. Booking avoids disappointment. Phone for directions. No smoking. Children welcome. Two Cats. Expect Excellence. Farm tour included. Superb Environment.

Mynthurst	**Tel:** (06) 857 8093	**Cost:** Double $150 Single $85
Farmstay	**Fax:** (06) 857 8093	Child $25 Dinner $35pp
9km W of Waipukurau	**Mob:** 025 232 2458	**Beds:** 1 King/Twin 1 Double
Annabelle & David Hamilton	**E:** mynthurst@xtra.co.nz	1 Single (3 bdrm)
912 Lindsay Rd	**W:** www.bnb.co.nz/hosts/	Extra space for children
RD 3 Waipukurau	mynthurst.html	**Bath:** 1 Ensuite 1 Private

Waipukurau

Are you looking for a memorable Hawkes Bay experience?

Retreat to a beautiful historic homestead nestled in the heart of Hawkes Bay, Wine Country. Unwind with uninterrupted farm views from the gracious verandah. Experience farming first hand or wander through the extensive gardens with solar heated swimming pool, pathways and a pond where birdlife prevails.

Breakfast may be enjoyed in the private dining room or on the verandah, weather providing. Other sumptuous meals may be arranged by request. Gourmet lamb is Judy's speciality, complimented with fresh produce from the kitchen garden or grown locally. Scenic flights or farm tours are available with Donald if you wish to encouter Hawkes Bay from a different perspective. Enjoy a touch of our Scottish heritage with Mac, the Scottish terrier.

Situated just five minutes from Waipukurau, Mangatarata is one of Hawkes Bay's most historic sheep stations. The second to be established in the entire province (1851) and is still a working farm of 2,500 acres.

The 1897 homestead and established gardens create unforgettable ambience. The garden was featured in a national magazine in Nov 2000. Farm walks, good fishing, golfing, and Hawkes Bay's excellent wineries nearby.

Visit Art Deco Napier, fly with Donald in a Tiger Moth, or take a picnic to one of the local beaches. Judy and Donald are members of the Hawkes Bay Wine Country Food Group.

Mangatarata Country Estate
Farmstay
7km E of Waipukurau
Judy & Donald Macdonald
415 Mangatarata Road
RD 5
Waipukurau

Tel: (06) 858 8275
Fax: (06) 858 8270
Mob: 021 480 769
Tollfree: 0800 858 857
E: mangatarata@xtra.co.nz
W: www.hawkesbaynz.com/pages/
mangataratacountryestate

Cost: Double $150-$160
　　　　Single $85 Dinner $35pp
Beds: 2 Queen 1 Double
　　　　3 Single (3 bdrm)
Bath: 1 Private 1 Guests share

Waipukurau

Historic fully restored "Airlie Mount", built in 1870, is situated in the exact centre of Waipukurau, a few steps away from shops and restaurants - yet it's an island of tranquillity, surrounded by cottage gardens and native bush. The comfortable (non-smoking) homestead offers verandahs, billiard room and swimming pool. The guest rooms are very private, have their own bathrooms, TV and outside courtyards. Your hosts have travelled extensively and have two children and a Labrador who all enjoy meeting new guests. Historic Homestead walks arranged.

Airlie Mount
Homestay
Waipukurau Central
Aart & Rashida van Saarloos
South Service Lane, off
Porangahau Road
PO Box 368 Waipukurau

Tel: (06) 858 7601
Fax: (06) 858 7609
Mob: 025 249 9726
E: salos@xtra.co.nz
W: www.bnb.co.nz/hosts/
airliemount.html

Cost: Double $90 Single $60
Child $30, 12 & under
Beds: 2 Queen 1 Single (2 bdrm)
Bath: 2 Ensuite

Dannevirke - Tararua

Fully equipped one-bedroomed cottage, comfortable sofa bed in the lounge and a loft with 2 singles. Indulge in a hot bath under the stars, in the intimate cottage garden, complete with seats and brazier. In the homestead garden enjoy the 7 circuit labyrinth, the bush walk through mature natives, a swim in the pool, a game of petanque or badminton, or simply rest on one of the many seats found throughout this large 'open' garden. Working dairy farm - large dog and donkeys. Tourism Tararua Award Winner 2001.

Gardenstone Cottage
B&B Self-contained Farmstay
5km E of Dannevirke
Lyn & Mike Charlton
Otope Road
RD 5 Dannevirke

Tel: (06) 374 8259
Mob: 025 205 4418
E: charlton@voyager.co.nz
W: www.bnb.co.nz/hosts/
gardenstonecottage.html

Cost: Double $90 Single $60
Child $15 Dinner $25
extra guests $20 Visa/MC
Beds: 1 Queen 1 Double
2 Single (1 bdrm)
Bath: 1 Private

If you are unsure about anything
ask your hosts.
They are your own personal
travel agent and guide.

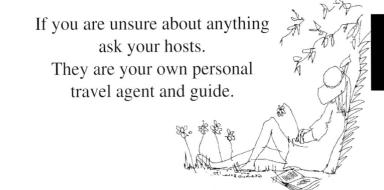

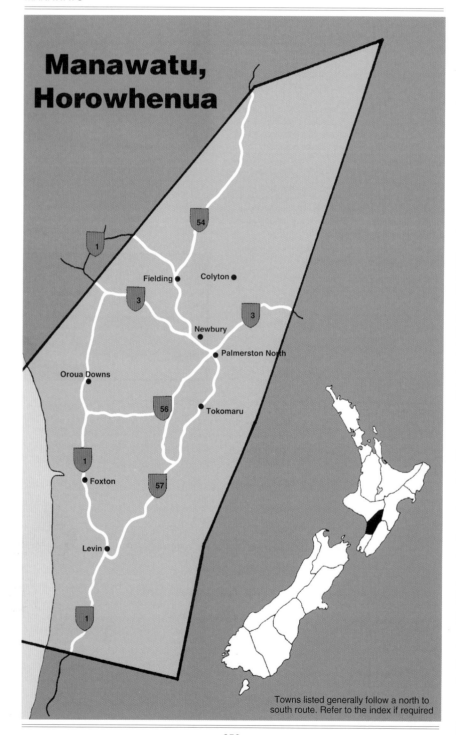

Manawatu, Horowhenua

Fielding ●   Colyton ●

Newbury ●

Palmerston North ●

Oroua Downs ●

56   ● Tokomaru

● Foxton

Levin ●

Towns listed generally follow a north to
south route. Refer to the index if required

Colyton - Feilding

Toos,John, Edmund (8yrs), Julius (7yrs) and Guido (7yrs) look forward to giving you a warm welcome to "Hiamoe" and during your stay, it is our aim that you experience a home away from home. We are the 3rd generation, farming our sheep, cattle and deer property and live in a 100-year-old colonial home. We have many interests and as Holland is Toos original homeland we are quite accustomed to travel and hosting visitors of all nationalities. There is a pool and central heating.

Hiamoe	**Tel:** (06) 328 7713	**Cost:** Double $70 Single $40
Farmstay	**Fax:** (06) 328 7787	Child $20 Preschool free
16km E of Feilding	**E:** johnhiamoe@clear.net.nz.	Dinner $15
John & Toos Cousins	**W:** www.bnb.co.nz/hosts/	**Beds:** 1 Queen 1 Double
Waiata	hiamoe.html	1 Single (2 bdrm)
Colyton Feilding		**Bath:** 1 Ensuite

Feilding

A comfortable and sunny family home where guests should feel free to wander and use the facilities as family members. No pets thank you. A choice of breakfast timed to your travel arrangements. Feilding is the centre of a prosperous farming area with many places of natural beauty within reach. Easy access to East Coast and only 15 minutes from Palmerston North, Feilding has an interesting shopping area and several good restaurants. Please phone for directions.

Feilding Homestay	**Tel:** (06) 323 4409	**Cost:** Double $65-$75
B&B Homestay	**Fax:** (06) 323 4745	Single $45 Child 1/2 price
1.3km E of Feilding	**W:** www.bnb.co.nz/hosts/	**Beds:** 1 Double 2 Single
Beryl Walker	feildinghomestay.html	(2 bdrm)
5 Wellington Street		**Bath:** 1 Ensuite 1 Guests share
Feilding		

Feilding

Enjoy a break in friendly Feilding, ten times winner of New Zealand's Most Beautiful Town Award. You are assured of a warm welcome and an enjoyable stay in a comfortable smoke free home set in an attractive garden. We are within easy walking distance of the town centre, pool complex and parks and off street parking is available for your vehicle. The main bedroom also has a separate outside entrance for your convenience. Our interests are music, gardening, cooking, travel and meeting people.

Avoca Homestay	**Tel:** (06) 323 4699	**Cost:** Double $75 Single $45
Homestay	**Fax:** (06) 323 4061	Dinner $20 by arrangement
Feilding Central	**W:** www.bnb.co.nz/hosts/	**Beds:** 1 Queen 2 Single
Margaret Hickmott	avocahomestay.html	(2 bdrm)
12 Freyberg Street		**Bath:** 1 Ensuite 1 Family share
Feilding		

Palmerston North - Newbury

Quiet country surroundings, only minutes from Palmerston North. 'Grinton' has early family connections with Yorkshire, England. Large character home set in attractive garden settings offers a comfortable stay, warm, cosy fires in the winter, and pleasant indoor/outdoor areas in the summer. We enjoy the stimulation of our guests who may share our interest of travel, music, grandchildren, golf, trout fishing, bread making. A convenient location for attending UCOL & Massey graduations, Central District field days, Manfield or just a retreat form city life.

Grinton Farmstay - Homestay	**Tel:** (06) 354 8961	**Cost:** Double $80 Single $50
Self/C Farmstay Homestay	**Fax:** (06) 354 8961	Child 1/2 price Dinner $25
8km N of Palmerston North	**W:** www.bnb.co.nz/hosts/	S/C $90 Visa/MC
Keith & Margaret Morriss	grintonfarmstayhomestay.html	**Beds:** 2 Queen 1 Single (2bdrm)
RD 5 Palmerston North		**Bath:** 1 Ensuite 1 Private
		1 Guests share

Palmerston North - Hokowhitu

A warm welcome awaits you in our comfortable home. We are a retired, non-smoking couple with varied interests: meeting people, travel, cooking and golf. Our home is close to Massey University and the Manawatu Golf Club. There are some interesting walkways nearby, and two minutes will take you to the Hokowhitu Village (Post Office, Pharmacy, Restaurants etc). Jillian is a Kiwi Host, assuring you of great hospitality. laundry facilities and covered off-street parking are available.We are happy to meet public transport.

Glenfyne	**Tel:** (06) 358 1626	**Cost:** Double $70
Homestay	**Fax:** (06) 358 1626	Single $45
Palmerston North Central	**E:** glenfyne@inspire.net.nz	Visa/MC
Jillian & Alex McRobert	**W:** www.bnb.co.nz/hosts/	**Beds:** 1 Double 2 Single
413 Albert Street	glenfyne.html	(2 bdrm)
Hokowhitu		**Bath:** 1 Guests share
Palmerston North		

Palmerston North

Our fully restored 1930's home in a mature garden with historic trees is only 10 minutes walk from the CBD and numerous restaurants and a few minutes by car or bus from Massey University. Our self contained cottage in the style of a New England Barn is very popular, and, like the house, furnished with antiques and decorated in the country style. We host children only by arrangement. Our delightful pomeranian Bobby"the fluffy doorbell" will announce your arrival.

The Gables	**Tel:** (06) 358 3209	**Cost:** Double $80-$110
B&B Self-contained	**Fax:** (06) 358 3209	Single $50-$80 Dinner $20
Palmerston North Central	**E:** Thegables.pn.nz@xtra.co.nz	Visa/MC Amex Diners
Monica & Paul Stichbury	**W:** www.bnb.co.nz/hosts/	**Beds:** 3 Queen 1 Single
179 Fitzherbert Avenue	thegables.html	(4 bdrm)
Palmerston North		**Bath:** 1 Private
		2 Guests share

Palmerston North

Lynn and David offer you a warm welcome to Karaka House. We are a friendly couple who enjoy meeting people in the relaxed atmosphere of our home which is within an easy walk of the city centre, restaurants and theatres. The College of Education, Polytech and Massey are within easy reach. The tiled front entrance opens to a wide hall with a rimu staircase leading to the large sunny bedrooms which have been designed with your comfort in mind. We look forward to meeting you. We have a pet cat.

Karaka House	**Tel:** (06) 358 8684	**Cost:** Double $90
Homestay	**Fax:** (06) 358 8685	Single $65
1km N of City Central	**Mob:** 025 245 2765	**Beds:** 2 Queen 2 Single
Lynn & David Whitburn	**E:** dave_lynn@xtra.co.nz	(3 bdrm)
473 College Street	**W:** www.bnb.co.nz/hosts/	**Bath:** 1 Guests share
Palmerston North	karakahouse.html	

Palmerston North - Rongotea

Kay, Warren and Libby (6yo) welcome you to "Andellen", a lovely large 90 year old farm villa set on 42 acres with extensive lawn, garden and orchard. We offer guests the opportunity to relax in a lovely tranquil country setting. Seasonal farm activities available. Children very welcome. Beach 10 minutes away. We have a pet cat and dog. Directions: Situated 11 kms South of Sanson or 11 kms North of Himitangi intersection. Off State Highway 1, into Kaimatarau Road and travel across first intersection. Next gate on LEFT - Farm no. 221. Our name is on the gate.

Andellen	**Tel:** (06) 324 8359	**Cost:** Double $85 Single $45
Farmstay	**Fax:** (06) 324 8359	Child 1/2 price
20km W of Palmerston North	**Mob:** 021 324 8359	Dinner $25pp Visa/MC
Kay and Warren Nitschke	**E:** nitschkek@agriquality.co.nz	**Beds:** 1 Queen 2 Single (2 bdrm)
RD 3 Palmerston North	**W:** www.bnb.co.nz/hosts/	**Bath:** 1 Ensuite 1 Family share
	andellen.html	

Palmerston North

A warm friendly welcome awaits you at our 1906 spacious, beautifully restored villa. Unique features are the magnificent stained glasswork in the front entry door and the heptagonal turret where guests can join us for dinner. We offer 2 bedrooms, one with ensuite, one with separate bathroom and each with own lounge/dining area with TV, fridge, tea and coffee making facilities. Situated close to UCOL, hospitals, golf courses, university and airport. Laundry facilities and off street parking. Local tours available if required. Non smoking.

Miranui Homestay	**Tel:** (06) 355 1772	**Cost:** Double $85
Homestay	**Fax:** (06) 355 1772	Single $60
1.2km N of Palmerston North	**Mob:** 025 285 3643	Dinner $25 Visa/MC
Robyn and Grant Powell	**E:** miranui@xtra.co.nz	**Beds:** 2 Queen (2 bdrm)
148 Russell Street	**W:** www.bnb.co.nz/hosts/	**Bath:** 1 Ensuite 1 Private
Palmerston North	miranuihomestay.html	

Palmerston North

Welcome to Clairemont. We are a rural spot within the city boundary, plenty of trees and a quite extensive garden. On our 1 1/4 acres we keep a few sheep, silky bantams, and our little dog Toby. We are handy to river walks, golf course, and shops are a few minutes away. We have a cosy, spacious family home we would like to share with you. Our interests are walking, gardening, model engineering and barbershop singing. Good off street parking provided, no smoking in house.

Clairemont	**Tel:** (06) 357 5508	**Cost:** Double $70
B&B	**Fax:** (06) 357 5501	Single $45
3.5km E of Palmerston North	**W:** www.bnb.co.nz/hosts/	**Beds:** 1 Double 1 Twin
Joy & Dick Archer	clairemont.html	(2 bdrm)
10 James Line		**Bath:** 1 Guests share
RD 10 Palmerston North		

Palmerston North

A warm welcome awaits you at our home in Moonshine Valley. We offer a private and peaceful stay in a rural-residential area. Situated only eight minutes drive to the Square, four minutes to Massey University and closer to the International Pacific College. Guests share a lounge/dining room with refreshments always available. The bathroom includes a bath and shower. Interesting walkways and gardens are nearby, or just relax on the terrace and enjoy the panoramic city, rural and mountain views with our cat Sophie.

Panorama B&B	**Tel:** (06) 354 8816	**Cost:** Double $70
B&B	**Fax:** (06) 356 2757	Single $50
4km E of Palmerston North	**E:** sawers@voyager.co.nz	Visa/MC
Claire & Bill Sawers	**W:** www.voyager.co.nz/-sawers/	**Beds:** 1 Double 1 Twin
30 Moonshine Valley Road		(2 bdrm)
RD1, Aokautere Palmerston North		**Bath:** 1 Guests share

Palmerston North

"Experience inner city life in style." Treat yourself in a luxurious purpose built (September 2000) executive house nestled between tennis court and orchard. Five minutes walk to restaurants and CBD. Guests enjoy full house facilities self-catering, featuring indoor/outdoor living with private courtyards. All bedrooms have ensuite access. Off street parking - smoke free environment, sky digital - spa pool. Located next to Aorangi Hospital - Bookings essential. Suitable for corporate short term accommodation. M/B House of the Year 2001.

The Palm & Oaks	**Tel:** (06) 359 0755	**Cost:** Double $155-$250
Self-contained Luxury Accom-	**Fax:** (06) 359 0756	Single $125-$155 Child n/a
modation	**Mob:** 025 232 7863	Visa/MC
Palmerston North Central	**E:** enquiries	**Beds:** 3 Queen 2 Single (4 bdrm)
Heather & Mike Rogers	@thepalm-oaks.co.nz	**Bath:** 1 Ensuite 1 Private
183 Grey Street Palmerston North	**W:** www.thepalm-oaks.co.nz	1 Guests share

Palmerston North - Whakarongo

Only 10 minutes from Palmerston North our home offers
separate upstairs accommodation with a guest lounge
downstairs. Along with our two small dogs, pet sheep and
pigs we enjoy meeting people and sharing our home and
fifteen acres of undulating land on a quiet country road. We
also have a self contained studio unit away from the house.
Situated amongst mature trees the property has sweeping
views of the Tararua Ranges. TV in all rooms. We are able
to meet public transport.

Glenlea Lodge
Self-contained Farmstay
Homestay
9km NE of Palmerston North
Neil & Gael McKechnie
158 Henderson Line
RD 10 Palmerston North

Tel: (06) 357 8733
Fax: (06) 357 8736
E: Glenlea@infogen.net.nz
W: www.bnb.co.nz/hosts/
glenlea.html

Cost: Double $95 Single $65
Child 1/2 price
Dinner $20 B/A Visa/MC
Beds: 2 King/Twin 1 Queen
1 Double (3 bdrm)
Bath: 1 Private 1 Guests share

Palmerston North

Enjoy mature trees and gardens from the balcony of this
secluded, inner city lodge. Creatively designed to replicate a
coach house in keeping with our traditional 1920's
homestead, "The Lodge" is self contained, peaceful, stylish
and spacious. Cosy seating around the gas fire, aged timber,
rustic fittings and fine linen give you a sophisticated but
casual experience. We are a professional couple who have
travelled extensively. "The Lodge" has the privacy, comfort
and point-of-difference we expect ourselves. Our adult
children live overseas.

Plum Tree Lodge
Self-contained
Robyn & Robert Anderson
97 Russell Street
Palmerston North

Tel: (06) 358 7813
Mob: 025 273 5113
E: plumtreelodge@xtra.co.nz
W: www.bnb.co.nz/hosts/
plumtreelodge.html

Cost: Double $105
Single $95
Visa/MC
Beds: 1 Queen (1 bdrm)
Bath: 1 Ensuite

Tokomaru

Looking for something unique - then Hi-Da-Way lodge
extends a warm welcome. The fully self contained
rustic cabin is set in a peaceful garden setting
surrounded by trees and has its own spa, TV, video and
fridge/freezer. Guests may enjoy volley ball, shared
swimming pool, BBQ or just meander around our 6.5
hectare property. Situated just 10 mins from Massey
University and 1 1/2 hours from Wellington off State
Highway 57. We have two boys still at home and two
pet dogs who enjoy meeting people. Treat yourself.

MANAWATU

Hi-Da-Way Lodge
Self-contained
19km S of Palmerston North
Sue & Trevor Palmer
21 Albert Road
RD 4 Palmerston North

Tel: (06) 329 8731
Fax: (06) 329 8732
Mob: 021 119 4443
W: www.bnb.co.nz/hosts/
hidawaylodge.html

Cost: Double $90
Single $65
Child $20 Dinner B/A
Beds: 1 Double (1 bdrm)
Bath: 1 Private

Oroua Downs

Bev and Ian invite you to share their spacious 2 storey, smoke free home nestled amongst 1 1/2 acres of tree-lined gardens. Enjoy the opportunity to relax and leisurely walk with our 2 cats amongst the garden listening to the bird song. We also operate a Building and Wooden Toy manufacturing business. Directions: turn off at Bed & Breakfast sign on State Highway 1, 14km north of Foxton and 16km south of Sanson. Travel 2 km down Omanuka Road.

Oroua Downs Farmstay	**Tel:** (06) 329 9859	**Cost:** Double $70
Farmstay	**Fax:** (06) 329 9859	Single $40
14km N of Foxton	**Mob:** 025 986 023	Child $20 Dinner $20pp
Bev & Ian Wilson	**E:** getwilsons@xtra.co.nz	**Beds:** 1 Double 3 Single
Omanuka Road	**W:** www.bnb.co.nz/hosts/	(3 bdrm)
RD 11 Foxton	orouadownsfarmstay.html	**Bath:** 1 Guests share

Foxton

Karnak Stud, mini farm, is an ideal quiet stopover 1 1/2 hour from Wellington. Perfect for children to meet friendly farm dog Meg, cat Mousie, thoroughbred horses, and Big Ben our beautiful Clydesdale horse- the star! Relaxing, excellent meals, organic farmhouse food. Table tennis, darts, children's toys, guests' library. Stroll through our sixteen acres of pasture and woodland. Follow Farmstay arrow on State Highway One for 1 km up Purcell Street, over white bridge, next on left. One night just isn't long enough! See animal friends on website.

Karnak Stud	**Tel:** (06) 363 7764	**Cost:** Double $80 Single $45
Farmstay	**Fax:** (06) 363 8941	Child under 6 free
1km E of Foxton	**W:** www.bnb.co.nz/hosts/	Dinner $25 Visa/MC
Margaret Barbour	karnakstud.html	**Beds:** 1 Double 1 Twin
Ridge Road		1 Single (2 bdrm)
Foxton		**Bath:** 1 Ensuite 1 Private

Levin

"Every picture tells a story" - Two acres of native bush, English trees and lots of birdlife and butterflies. Tranquillity and security. Our bedrooms all have a lovely outlook onto the garden, a good night's sleep on very comfortable beds, with all those extras. Home cooked eats on arrival and many more surprises when you stay at the Fantails (organic food a speciality). We also offer Retreat cottages (they sleep 2-4 people). Wheelchair friendly and smoke free. Laundry facilities available. Directions, please phone. Courtesy coach available.

Fantails	**Tel:** (06) 368 9011	**Cost:** Double $90-$120
B&B Self-contained Cottages	**Fax:** (06) 368 9279	Single $60-$80 Dinner $35
5min Levin	**Mob:** 021 469 606	S/C Cottages $100 - $140
Heather Watson	**E:** fantails@xtra.co.nz	Visa/MC Amex
40 MacArthur Street	**W:** www.fantails.co.nz	**Beds:** 1 King 1 Queen 1 Twin
Levin		4 Single (4 bdrm)
		Bath: 3 Ensuite 1 Private

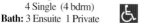

Levin

A pastoral retreat 4 minutes from town centre. Comfortable distance for ferry and air travel. Our home is spacious, ranch-style with warm aspect, situated in 1 acre of lawns and gardens. Tastefully appointed guest rooms 'picture postcard views', delicious breakfasts. Beverley has many years experience in hospitality business. Peter is a JCI Senator. We breed coloured sheep, enjoy entertaining and Beau our cat. Turn east off SH1 at Post Office into Queen Street East. We are 3.4 km on left. Sign at gate.

Lynn Beau Ley	**Tel:** (06) 368 0310	**Cost:** Double $80 Single $45
Farmstay	**Fax:** (06) 368 0310	Dinner $20 B/A Visa/MC
3.4km E of Levin	**Mob:** 025 274 4564	**Beds:** 1 Double 2 Single
Beverley & Peter Lynn	**W:** www.bnb.co.nz/hosts/	(2 bdrm)
Queen Street East	lynnbeauley.html	**Bath:** 1 Ensuite 1 Private
RD 1 Levin		

Levin

A convenient tranquil retreat to break your journey, being only 1.5 hours drive from Wellington and two minutes drive from SH1. We offer quality beds with electric blankets, in a comfortable attractive decorated room. You will enjoy a delicious breakfast. We enjoy meeting people, are keen travellers and look forward to offering you warm and generous hospitality in our smoke-free home, shared by Princess, a good natured wheaten dog. Directions: Please phone.

The Walnut Tree Cottage	**Tel:** (06) 368 1513	**Cost:** Double $75
B&B	**Mob:** 025 238 3934	Single $45
1km N of Levin	**W:** www.bnb.co.nz/hosts/	Visa/MC
Marilyn Kerr	thewalnuttreecottage.html	**Beds:** 2 Single (1 bdrm)
38 Kawiu Road		**Bath:** 1 Ensuite
Levin		

Levin

Buttercup Acres is a small tranquil rural property at the foothills of the Tararua Ranges. We specialise in breeding Miniature Horses and Alpaca's. Our home is surrounded by 3 acres of gardens and a large pond. In the evenings you can relax in the lounge. Learn to spin or weave in our weaving studio or view the stars through our telescope. Our model railway will fascinate visitors. Free laundry facilities available. Directions: At Ohau turn into Muhunoa East Road. 5km to Florida Road.

Buttercup Acres	**Tel:** (06) 368 0557	**Cost:** Double $90
Farmstay	**Fax:** (06) 368 0557	Single $45
9km SE of Levin	**W:** www.bnb.co.nz/hosts/	Dinner $20 Visa/MC
Ivan & Pat Keating	buttercupacres.html	**Beds:** 1 Double 2 Single
55 Florida Road		(2 bdrm)
RD 20 Levin		**Bath:** 1 Ensuite 1 Private

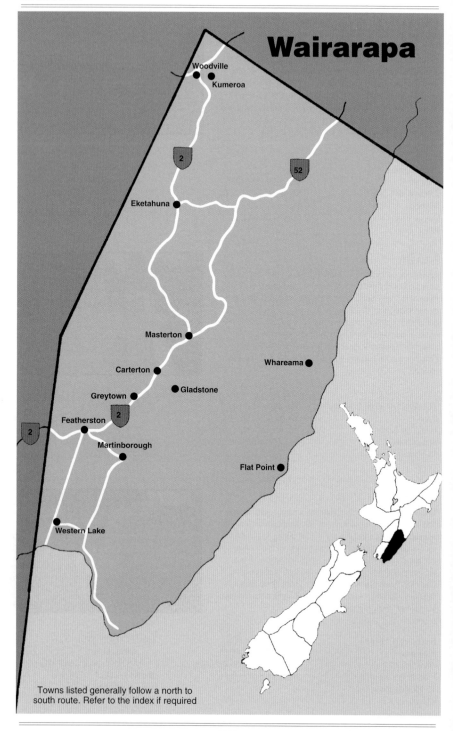

Wairarapa

Woodville
Kumeroa

2

52

Eketahuna

Masterton

Carterton

Whareama

Greytown

Gladstone

Featherston

2

2

Martinborough

Flat Point

Western Lake

Towns listed generally follow a north to
south route. Refer to the index if required

Woodville

Hill country farm beside Manawatu River renowned for its fishing. The family have fled the nest. Farming activities may be in progress and tourists may like to become involved. The self contained double bed unit has its own toilet and handbasin otherwise guests share bathroom facilities. If approaching via Pahiatua, ring for directions and avoid Woodville. Travellers on SH2 turn down Hopelands Road, cross high bridge over river, turn right towards Pahiatua, fourth house is where "welcome" is on the mat.

B&B Self-contained Farmstay
13km NE of Woodville
Chris & Jo Coats
370 River Road
Hopelands, RD 1
Woodville

Tel: (06) 376 4521
E: jo.coats@clear.net.nz
W: www.bnb.co.nz/hosts/
coats.html

Cost: Double $80 Single $40
Child $20 Dinner $20
Beds: 1 Double 2 Single
(2 bdrm)
Bath: 1 Family share

Kumeroa

Relax ... relax ... rejuvenate in our historic 1914 homestead set on 80 acres overlooking the Ruahine Ranges. Be enchanted by the Edwardian elegance of wood panelling, stained glass, art nouveau plasterwork and period furnishings. Walk in native bush, listen to the tuis or relax in our spacious guest sitting room and sunny library. Hunt for antiques down in Woodville or fish in the Manawatu. Dine on local produce with an emphasis on fish and organic cuisine. Our hot-water radiator system ensures comfort all year.

Otawa Lodge
Historic Lodge
18km NE of Woodville
Del and Sue Trew
132 Otawhao Road
Kumeroa, R D 1 Woodville

Tel: (06) 376 4603
Fax: (06) 376 5042
Mob: 025 230 1327
E: OTAWA.LODGE@xtra.co.nz
W: www.bnb.co.nz/hosts/
otawalodge.html

Cost: Double $130-$165
Single $90-$110 Child Neg
Dinner $40 - $60 Visa/MC
Beds: 1 King/Twin
1 Queen (2 bdrm)
Bath: 1 Guests share

Eketahuna

Guests have their own wing with a large upstairs lounge, tea coffee facilities, TV and pool table. Our interests, gardening, golf, wildlife and conservation, meeting and talking to our guests from all parts of the world. Meet Tyson and Pershey, our two pet cats. Enjoy, farm tours and walks on our 1200 acre sheep/beef property, trout fishing and kayaking, renowned Mt Bruce National Wildlife Centre, Golf at our local 18 hole course, friendly honest hospitality. $1^1/_2$ hours to Wellington, 45 minutes to Palmerston North. Situated State Highway 2.

Mount Donald Farmstay
B&B Farmstay
5km N of Eketahuna
Lynne & Jim Sutherland
Mount Donald
Newman, RD 4 Eketahuna

Tel: (06) 375-8315
Fax: (06) 375 8391
E: mountdonald@xtra.co.nz
W: www.bnb.co.nz/hosts/
mountdonaldfarmstay.html

Cost: Double $100 Single $60
Dinner $25 Visa/MC
Beds: 1 Queen 2 Single
(2 bdrm)
Bath: 1 Ensuite 1 Private

Masterton

Comfortable modern house and fully equipped s/c flat in quiet secluded country garden with mountain views, 1km from bypass. Flat has one bedroom with double and single, two divan beds in living area. Self cater or breakfast in our warm dining room. Half hour drive to wildlife centre or Martinborough vineyards. 1 1/2 hour drive to Picton Ferry. Convenient for show grounds, schools, restaurants and tramping. We have been hosting since 1970 and still enjoy it. Meeting people, travel, reading, gardening, farming, tramping. Baby facilities available. One outside cat. Smoke free.

Harefield
B&B Self-contained Farmstay
3km W of Masterton
Marian Ahearn
147 Upper Plain Road
Masterton

Tel: (06) 377 4070
W: www.bnb.co.nz/hosts/
harefield.html

Cost: Double $80 Single $45
Child 1/2 price
Dinner $20 B/A
S/C Flat for 2 $55
Beds: 1 Double 1 Single (1 bdrm)
Bath: 1 Private

Masterton

A warm welcome awaits you at 'Tidsfordriv' - a 64 acre farmlet - 7 kms off the main bypass route. A comfortable modern home set in park like surroundings with large gardens, ponds and many species of wetland birds. Enjoy bird watching with ease. Glenys has home-hosted for 14 years and invites you to join her for dinner. Conservation, gardening and travel are her interests. A Labrador dog is the family pet. Local Wairarapa attractions - National Wildlife Centre, gardens, vineyards, Tararua Forest Park.

Tidsfordriv
Rural Homestay
10km W of Masterton
Glenys Hansen
4 Cootes Road
RD 8, Matahiwi
Masterton

Tel: (06) 378 9967
Fax: (06) 378 9957
E: ghansen@contact.net.nz
W: www.bnb.co.nz/hosts/
tidsfordriv.html

Cost: Double $75 Single $40
Child 1/2 price
Dinner $20 B/A Visa/MC
Beds: 1 Double 2 Single
(2 bdrm)
Bath: 1 Private

Masterton

Victoria House is a two storey house built pre 1886, renovated to retain the character of the period. The peaceful nature of the furnishings and outdoor area create a quiet, relaxing atmosphere, great for a "get away from it" weekend. We are also only a three minute walk from the town centre and Masterton's excellant restaurants. Being "wine friendly" hosts we enjoy discussing wines and freely offer advice on the Wairararapa's growing wine industry. Cooked breakfast available on request at extra cost.

Victoria House
B&B Guesthouse
Central Masterton
Marion and Sara Monks and
Mike Parker
15 Victoria Street
Masterton

Tel: (06) 377 0186
Fax: (06) 377 0186
E: parker.monks@xtra.co.nz
W: www.bnb.co.nz/hosts/
victoriahouse.html

Cost: Double $65
Single $42
Twin $65 Visa/MC
Beds: 3 Double 1 Twin
2 Single (6 bdrm)
Bath: 2 Guests share

Masterton - Whareama

(Close to Riversdale, Castlepoint beaches)

Les, Carol, Barney the Labrador, Dougal the cat, offer you a warm friendly welcome to "Alderford". Tastefully decorated warm cottage room away from main homestead. Cosy double bed, TV, fridge, tea, coffee, home-made biscuits. Delicious country meals with home-made jams, bottled fruits, fresh veges, free range eggs. "Alderford" is a 200 acre sheep, cattle, deer farm. 10 minutes to Riversdale beach with lovely 9 hole golf course, 10 minutes to Tinui pub, 25 minutes to the picturesque Castlepoint beach, canoe trips in area. "Alderford" 30 minutes drive from Masterton.

Alderford Farmstays
B&B Self-contained Farmstay
40km E of Masterton
Carol & Les Ross
RD 12
Masterton

Tel: (06) 372 3705
W: www.bnb.co.nz/hosts/
alderford.html

Cost: Double $75 Single $45
Dinner $25pp. 3 course
Cooked breakfast $7.50pp
Visa/MC
Beds: 1 Double (1 bdrm)
Bath: 1 Ensuite

Masterton

LLandaff Country Residence is a large elegant historic 1880 homestead, now a boutique B&B, with beautiful original NZ timbers throughout, wood paneled rooms, polished floors, spacious bedrooms, old pull-handle toilets, a "coffin" bath, open fireplaces, and a cosy wood-burning kitchen stove. Explore the historic out-buildings, soak up the peaceful country atmosphere, relax in the majestic garden beneath 120 old trees, or wander the farm and feed the animals. Enquire about our LLandaff Carriage, and Llandaff Gourmet Weekenders.

LLandaff Country Residence
B&B Self-contained
5km W of Masterton
Elizabeth Tennet
Upper Plain Road
RD 8 Masterston

Tel: (06) 378 6628
Fax: (06) 378 6612
E: llandaff@xtra.co.nz
W: www.wairarapa.co.nz/
llandaff

Cost: Double $100-$120
Single $70 Child $25
Dinner $30 Visa/MC
Beds: 2 Queen 2 Twin
1 Single (4 bdrm)
Bath: 1 Ensuite 2 Guests share

Masterton

Down a country lane, amongst apple orchards, discover our tranquil French Provencal farmhouse with its stream, water fowl, and petanque court. Our children have departed, leaving us with a cat, two small dogs and cattle on our small farm. Guest lounge and bathroom with bath and shower. Open fire and central heating. Enjoy farmhouse cooking with fresh vegetables from our large country garden. We can also provide barbecues and picnic lunches. We are a well travelled couple who enjoy helping guests discover the unspoilt Wairarapa.

Mas des Saules
Homestay
1km E of Masterton
Mary & Steve Blakemore
9A Pokohiwi Road
Homebush Masterton

Tel: (06) 377 2577
Fax: (06) 377 2578
Mob: (025) 620 8728
E: mas-des-saules@wise.net.nz
W: www.bnb.co.nz/hosts/
masdessaules.html

Cost: Double $95 Single $55
Child $40 Dinner $25
Visa/MC
Beds: 1 Queen 1 Double (2 bdrm)
Bath: 1 Guests share

Masterton

Try an experience that's a little different! Our colonial style homestead is set in an operating apple orchard and has a separate guest wing with lounge and two bedrooms with ensuites. You are welcome to share dinner or a country breakfast with us and enjoy the ambience of stanley range based cooking along with relaxing by the open fire or on the deck. There are orchard walks and a garden haven. Watch the daily orchard activities and pick some fruit in season. Ask us about the Model A tourer courtesy car.

Apple Source Orchard Stay	**Tel:** (06) 377 0820	**Cost:** Double $100 Single $60
Farmstay	**Fax:** (06) 370 9401	Child 1/2 price Dinner $25
2km E of Masterton	**Mob:** 021 667 092	**Beds:** 2 Queen 1 Single
Niel & Raewyn Groombridge	**E:** raeg@voyager.co.nz	(2 bdrm)
Te Ore Ore	**W:** www.bnb.co.nz/hosts/	**Bath:** 2 Ensuite
RD 6 Masterton	applesource.html	

Masterton

Looking for a warm Wairarapa welcome and superb mountain views? Relax in our spacious home with private guest lounge, log fire and tea making facilities. Enjoy a hearty dinner with your hosts, or privately, in smokefree comfort. Loop Line is the Wairarapa's "nouveau vin" and olive grove area, and Taravista is ideally situated for excursions to the seaside, Mount Bruce, Museums, Golf Courses and fishing/hunting adventures. Walk to a winery, river or playground or, drive five minutes to Masterton's shops, restaurants etc.

Taravista	**Tel:** (06) 377 2987	**Cost:** Double $80 Single $50
B&B	**Fax:** (06) 377 2987	Child $15 Dinner $25
7km N of Masterton	**Mob:** 025 285 8709	**Beds:** 1 Double 1 Twin
Pam & Ray Ward	**E:** pam.ray.ward@xtra.co.nz	(2 bdrm)
49 Loop Line	**W:** www.bnb.co.nz/hosts/	**Bath:** 1 Private
RD 1 Masterton	taravista.html	

Masterton

A marvellous old two storied self contained home built in 1893. Right in the centre of town within easy reach of great dining, bars,parks etc. Four double bedrooms each with a queen sized bed, two bathrooms, parlour, dining room and well appointed modern kitchen, off-street parking for up to four cars. Old style with luxury appointments. This is a Historic Places Trust listed home - a delight to stay in. A delicious breakfast is included on a self help basis.

Natusch Town House	**Tel:** 06 378 9252	**Cost:** Double $150
B&B Self-contained	**Fax:** 06 378 9330	Single $40 per extra
Masterton Central	**Mob:** 025 363 732	person
Anne Bohm	**E:** anne@natusch.co.nz	**Beds:** 4 Queen (4 bdrm)
55 Lincoln Road	**W:** www.natusch.co.nz	**Bath:** 2 bathrooms
Masterton		

Flat Point Coast

Come experience the ultimate retreat! We are a Kiwi/
Canadian couple with 2 boys under 5, on an 1880 acre
sheep/cattle station. Our self contained luxury
accommodation consists of a renovated 3 bedroom, 2
bathroom farm cottage and 2 Queen sized suites, newly
built in traditional New Zealand style. Each with
cooking facilities, fireplace, electric blankets and sea
views. Enjoy walking the beach, through our extensive
gardens, exploring the farm or just curl up with a book.
DOC walkway to Seal Colony is nearby.

Caledonia Coastal Farmstay
Self-contained Farmstay
65km E of Masterton
Wenda & Paul Kerr
RD 3 Masterton

Tel: (06) 372 7553
Fax: (06) 372 7553
E: wendakerr@xtra.co.nz
W: www.sendme.to/caledonia

Cost: Double $125-$150
Single $75 Child $10
Beds: 4 Queen 2 Single (5 bdrm)
Bath: 1 Ensuite 2 Private
1 Guests share

Carterton

Our 100 acre farm offers tranquillity, comfort, variety -
borders the Waiohine River, under the Tararua Ranges.
Spacious home with fire, spa bath and oak furniture. Port-a-
cot available. The farm has Santa Gertrudis cattle, Koura
(fresh water Crayfish), kune kune pig, sheep, dogs, cats,
hens, goats and daughter Elese (8). Enjoy farmland, river
flats, native bush, wetlands, trout fishing, swimming, rafting
and the forest park for tramping/hunting. Also small self-
contained cottage, near the farmhouse - Single bedroom,
shower, kitchen and double bed in living area.

Waiohine Farm
B&B Self-contained Farmstay
15km W of Greytown
Jenni & Trevor Berthold
Waiohine Gorge Road -
fire no 21 RD 1 Carterton

Tel: (06) 379 6716
Fax: (06) 379 6716
Mob: 025 523 839
Tollfree: 0800 387 437
E: mail@waiohine.co.nz
W: www.waiohine.co.nz

Cost: Double $80 Single $50
Child $30 Dinner $20
S/C Unit $60
Visa/MC Amex Diners
Beds: 2 Double 2 Single (3 bdrm)
Bath: 2 Private

Carterton

A warm and friendly welcome awaits you at Portland
House, a 125 year old refurbished villa and home to
Birmans Missy and George. You can rest, relax and
enjoy the country air of the Wairarapa in our peaceful
surroundings and comfortable home. We are just off
the main highway (SH2) and within 5 to 10 minutes
drive to Masterton, the cafes in Greytown, the
vineyards in Martinborough, the scenic Waiohine
Gorge, the Tararua Forest Park and many wonderful
Wairarapa Gardens. Smoking outside only please.

Portland House
B&B
3km S of Carterton
Judy Betts
Portland Road
State Highway 2 Carterton

Tel: (06) 379 8809
Mob: 025 602 8358
E: portlandhouse@paradise.net.nz
W: www.bnb.co.nz/hosts/
portlandhouse.html

Cost: Double $80 Single $50
Dinner B/A Visa/MC
Beds: 1 Double 1 Twin
(2 bdrm)
Bath: 1 Private 1 Family share

Carterton

Homecroft is surrounded by our country garden and farmland yet handy to the vineyards, crafts, antiques, and golf courses of the Wairarapa. Wellington and the inter-island ferry 90 minutes away. Guest accommodation has own entrance in a separate wing of the house with small lounge, the sunny bedrooms open onto a deck overlooking the garden. Enjoy a leisurely breakfast in our dining room and perhaps meet our two cats. We look forward to meeting you, looking after you and making your stay an enjoyable experience.

Homecroft	**Tel:** (06) 379 5959	**Cost:** Double $80
B&B	**E:** homecroft@xtra.co.nz	Single $50
1km N of Carterton	**W:** www.bnb.co.nz/hosts/	Dinner $25
Christine & Neil Stewart	homecroft.html	**Beds:** 1 Queen 1 Twin
Somerset Road		(2 bdrm)
RD 2 Carterton		**Bath:** 1 Guests share

Gladstone

Experience the peace and tranquility of Hinana Cottage, a delightfully restored 1930's bungalow nestling in the Gladstone hills, with spectacular views of the Tararuas and Wairarapa Valley. Handy to Masterton, Carterton and Greytown; an easy 25 minutes from Martinborough, Hinana Cottage is ideally situated for the exploration of Wairarapa's vineyards, walkways, caves and rivers. Simply relax in the spa pool, or by the open fire and enjoy Hinana's native timber floors, ornate plaster ceilings, fine china and beautiful linen - all reminders of a bygone era.

Hinana Cottage	**Tel:** (06) 372 7667	**Cost:** Double $120
B&B Homestay	**Fax:** (06) 372 7657	Single $60
22km E of Carterton	**Mob:** 025 998 928	Dinner $38pp Visa/MC
Louise (and George & Jessa, the	**E:** hinanacottage@xtra.co.nz	**Beds:** 1 Queen 1 Double
Schnauzers) Walker	**W:** www.bnb.co.nz/hosts/	(2 bdrm)
Fire No 15 Admiral Road,	hinanacottage.html	**Bath:** 1 Ensuite 1 Family share
RD 3 Masterton		

Gladstone

Country hospitality awaits in our homestead (1870s circa) on our 200 acre sheep and cattle stud. Queen bedroom opens on a sunny verandah, elegant private sitting room with open fire. Delicious hearty breakfasts and homemade panforte with coffee. Foxy Ollie and two cats share our home. Experience Caveland's beauty and explore glowworm caves, walks, sheep mustering demos, mountain biking and grass tennis. Horse riding by arrangement. Central to Gladstone's attractions, gardens, vineyards, ostrich and cheese farms. Close to homestead, peaceful hideaway for two in simple, self contained "whare". Open fire.

Cavelands Homestay	**Tel:** (06) 372 7733	**Cost:** Double $110 Single $80
B&B S/C Farmstay	**Fax:** (06) 372 7773	Dinner $35 B/A S.C $70
15km SE of Masterton	**Mob:** 025 365 738	Visa/MC
Belinda & Rod Cranswick	**E:** cranswick@wise.net.nz	**Beds:** 1 King 1 Queen
Fire No 10, Cavelands Road	**W:** www.bnb.co.nz/hosts/	1 Twin (2 bdrm)
RD 4 Masterton	cavelands.html	**Bath:** 1 Private

Greytown - The Ambers

Built in the 1800's The Ambers exudes the ambience of its era. The house is nestled in two acres of gardens with many beautiful old trees.

Our guest wing is separate enough to provide privacy or the intimate atmosphere you desire without feeling isolated from us. We offer guests secluded verandahs, a spa pool for those starry summer nights, lounge with open fire for winter.

The Cherub Room has a queen bed and private bathroom. The Vintage Room has a king bed with ensuite bathroom. If two couples wish to share a bathroom we also have our Oak Aged Room with double bed.

Breakfast includes homemade muffins and fresh fruit in season.

We are within walking distance of Greytown's Main Street with unique wooden Victorian architecture, cafes, and ten minutes drive to Martinborough's vineyards.

If you desire the ultimate privacy or a 'romantic getaway' we offer a "Blissful" cottage set in its own private garden featuring lovely old trees. Country Bliss Cottage has two double bedrooms, with own amenities including fire and bath.

The Ambers	**Tel:** (06) 304 8588	**Cost:** Double $90-$110
B&B Homestay	**Fax:** (06) 304 8590	Single $65 Child $25
80km N of Wellington	**Mob:** 025 994 394	Visa/MC
Marilla & Steve Davis	**E:** ambershomestay@xtra.co.nz	**Beds:** 1 King 1 Queen
78 Kuratawhiti Street	**W:** www.ambershomestay.co.nz	1 Double (3 bdrm)
Greytown		**Bath:** 1 Ensuite 1 Private
		1 Guests share

Greytown

Spacious relaxed accommodation. The house is designed for space, comfort and warmth. We are situated just minutes away from Greytown's cafes, restaurants and village shops and ten minutes from Martinborough's vineyards and golf course. Facilities include queen bedroom with ensuite. Twin bedroom and queen bedroom with shared bathroom. Lounge, satellite TV, continental breakfast at your leisure. Outdoor areas with pool and barbecue.

Southey Manor	**Tel:** (06) 304 9367	**Cost:** Double $80-$90
B&B	**Fax:** (06) 304 9789	Single $45
Greytown Central	**Mob:** 025 424 035	**Beds:** 2 Queen 2 Single
Gavin Southey	**W:** www.bnb.co.nz/hosts/	(3 bdrm)
182 West St	southeymanor.html	**Bath:** 1 Ensuite
Greytown		1 Guests share

Greytown

A top category award winner in 'New Zealand House of the Year', Westwood has been designed to blend with its picturesque surroundings - nine acres of magnificent trees, with mountain views, a tranquil stream and formal Herb Garden. Just a short stroll to historic Greytown's cafes and specialty shops. Enjoy stylish comfort with an old fashioned ambience in your spacious ensuite room with private entrance, verandah, tea/coffee making facilities and SKY television. Breakfast poolside in summer or fireside in winter. Experience country hospitality at its best!

Westwood House	**Tel:** (06) 304 8510	**Cost:** Double $125-$150
B&B Homestay	**Fax:** (06) 304 8610	Single $90-$125 Visa/MC
Jill & Peter Kemp	**Mob:** 025 530 154	**Beds:** 3 King/Twin
PO Box 34	**E:** westwood.kemp@xtra.co.nz	1 Single (4 bdrm)
82 West Street	**W:**www.westwood.greytown.co.nz	**Bath:** 2 Ensuite 1 Guests share
Greytown		

Greytown

Kuratawhiti, built in 1892, is one of South Wairarapa's finest historic properties, set in an acre of mature trees and gardens. A short walk to Greytown village, it is the ideal place for a relaxing retreat or as a base to explore the Wairarapa region. We are a young family with children; families are welcome and we offer babysitting. We have travelled extensively, love reading, music and meeting new people. Enjoy our outdoor spa, designer bed linen, fine wine, gourmet breakfasts and dinner.

Kuratawhiti	**Tel:** (06) 304 9942	**Cost:** Double $120-$150
B&B Homestay	**Fax:** (06) 304 9942	Single $90-$120 Child $30
Greytown central	**Mob:** 021 484 018	Dinner $40 Visa/MC
Mary & Geoff Major	**E:** info@kuratawhiti.co.nz	**Beds:** 1 King/Twin
40 Kuratawhiti Street	**W:** www.kuratawhiti.co.nz	2 Queen (3 bdrm)
Greytown		**Bath:** 1 Ensuite
		1 Private/Guests share

Featherston

Judi Adams and her Burmese cats welcome you. We enjoy meeting people and providing friendly hospitality. Our interests include travelling (Spanish is spoken), gardening, books, music, collecting and cross-stitch. Our home is set in a secluded garden containing native, exotic and rare plants. We offer warm, luxury accommodation with off street parking. For breakfast enjoy home made treats including home preserved fruit and fresh juice. During the day explore beautiful Wairarapa or relax in comfort. In the evening dine at a local restaurant or by prior arrangement join me for an evening meal. Picnic hampers are available (additional charge). Smoking outdoors only please.

Woodland Holt Bed &	**Tel:** (06) 308 9927	**Cost:** Double $100-$120
Breakfast	**Mob:** 025 291 2774	Single $60-$65
B&B	**E:** woodland-holt@xtra.co.nz	Dinner $35 Amex
Judi Adams	**W:** www.bnb.co.nz/hosts/	**Beds:** 1 Queen 1 Double
47 Watt Street Featherston	woodlandholtbedbreakfast.html	2 Single (4 bdrm)
		Bath: 1 Ensuite 1 Guests share

Martinborough

Quality Country Stays. "GLENDOON" (photo). Distinctive country comfort. Tranquil setting, rest, picnic, feed the doves. All amenities. Laundry, farmhouse kitchen, woodburners, open fire, sleeps 6-8. Described as sweet seclusion. "STONEMEAD COTTAGE". Cozy, comfortable, two bedroom cottage. EACH is non share, with kitchen and pantry, TV, music system, bedding, firewood, clawfoot bath, BBQ, shower, farm walks, protected bush, front verandah, lovely valley views, established garden, and picturesque trees. Handy to Wellington (where Glendoon offers accommodation), Martinborough Wineries, shops and restaurants, country pub, and trout waters.

Glendoon, StoneMead Cottage	**Tel:** (06) 372 7779	**Cost:** Double $120 Single $120
S/C Farmstay Cottage	**Fax:** (06) 372 7599	Child $20 Extras $50
14km NE of Martinborough	**Mob:** 025 776 968	**Beds:** 1 Queen 1 Double
Norman Campbell	**E:** norman@gawith.co.nz	2 Single (3 bdrm)
PO Box 98 Longbush Valley Road	**W:** www.glendoon.co.nz	**Bath:** 2 Private
Martinborough		

Martinborough

Our characterful eighty year old Californian bungalow offers gracious accommodation. Our spacious, wood-burner heated guest lounge provides a relaxed setting for sampling winemaker Chris' wonderful products. Our guest wing has its own entrance, bathroom (large bath and roomy shower) and separate wc. Both bedrooms enjoy afternoon sun and garden views. Breakfast features freshly baked croissants, home preserved local fruits and conserves. Creative cook Polly enjoys matching delicious dishes (often local game) with Chris' great wines. Our pets include multitalented cats, chickens and kunekune piggies.

Oak House	**Tel:** (06) 306 9198	**Cost:** Double $100 Single $50
B&B Homestay	**Fax:** (06) 306 8198	Child & Dinner by
1km NW of Martinborough	**E:** chrispolly.oakhouse@xtra.co.nz	arrangement
Polly & Chris Buring	**W:** www.bnb.co.nz/hosts/	**Beds:** 1 Queen 2 Single
45 Kitchener Street	oakhouse.html	(2 bdrm)
Martinborough		**Bath:** 1 Guests share

Martinborough - Wairarapa

Well travelled hosts Karin Beatson and John Cooper offer you a friendly and relaxed stay in their 1905 houses "Harrington" and "Cologne", lovingly restored as boutique accommodation, to ensure your year-round comfort.

Furnishing includes some antiques and an interesting collection of New Zealand paintings and crafts. Polished matai floors, high ceilings and individually decorated, spacious bedrooms with ensuites feature. In the living areas, french doors open onto verandahs, with tables overlooking the garden with its cottage plantings, natives, fruits trees and herbs. Woodburners provide winter warmth. Great home cooking includes speciality country breakfasts using local products, homemade breads and preserves. (Dinners and functions by arrangement).

"Heriot Cottage" is a one-bedroomed self-contained comfortable colonial garden cottage featuring an original clawfoot bath, and a verandah to sip wine. "Rothesay" is a three bedroomed Lockwood house and can sleep eight. It's good for self-catering groups and families. It has great outdoor spaces and large trees, and boasts Martinborough's smallest unnamed vineyard.

All Beatson's of Martinborough places are just five minutes walk from Martinborough Square with its cafes, restaurants and speciality shops. Close to vineyards.

Beatson's of Martinborough
B&B Self-contained Homestay
Martinborough Central
John Cooper & Karin Beatson
9A Cologne Street
Martinborough
Wairarapa

Tel: (06) 306 8242
Fax: (06) 306 8243
Mob: 025 499 827
E: beatsons@wise.net.nz
W: www.bnb.co.nz/hosts/
beatson.html

Cost: Double $120150
Single $100
Dinner by arrangement
Visa/MC
Beds: 2 King/Twin 4 Queen
(6 bdrm)
Bath: 6 Ensuite

Martinborough

Our home nestles in over three acres of landscaped gardens which includes a Camellia Walk, Woodlands, Sunken Rose Garden, Orchard and Pond area, and we are surrounded by Vineyards. Both our guestrooms have french doors opening onto a sunny deck with private access. Guests are welcome to relax with us and our small spoilt dog and cat in our large cosy (woodburner heated) lounge. Breakfast includes fresh croissants, homemade jams, jellies and preserved fruit. Cooked breakfast on request and dinner by arrangement.

Ross Glyn
Homestay gardens
1km SW of Martinborough
Kenneth & Odette Trigg
1 Grey Street
Martinborough

Tel: (06) 306 9967
Fax: (06) 306 8267
E: rossglyn1@hotmail,com
W: www.bnb.co.nz/hosts/
rossglyn.html

Cost: Double $90 Single $50
Dinner $25+ Diners
Beds: 1 Double 2 Single
(2 bdrm)
Bath: 1 Private 1 Guests share

Martinborough

Set amidst an extensive garden, Shadyvale has beautiful views across 44 acres of farmland. Enjoy a stroll around the property, a game of golf or a walk to the vineyards. Relax around the pool in summer or curl up by your own fire in the winter. All rooms open onto the spacious verandah and the wood stove provides central heating throughout the house. Breakfast is served in the dining room or on the verandah. Tea and coffee facilities in bedroom and lounge. Unsuitable for pets or children.

Shadyvale
B&B Farmstay Homestay
3km E of Martinborough
Robyn & Peter Taylor
PO Box 160
Martinborough

Tel: (06) 306 9374
Fax: (06) 306 9374
Mob: 025 291 7711
E: huntervale@wise.net.nz
W: www.bnb.co.nz/hosts/
shadyvale.html

Cost: Double $120
Single $90
Visa/MC
Beds: 1 Queen 1 Double
(2 bdrm)
Bath: 1 Ensuite 1 Private

Martinborough

Nestled in a pretty valley 5 minutes drive east of Martinborough we are close to the golf course and vineyards. The spacious and comfortable guest wing has its own entrance, with a lounge/library looking over our olive grove which leads down to the trout stream on our boundary. Have a hearty breakfast with farm fresh eggs in our farmhouse kitchen or on the deck on a lovely Wairarapa morning. Sheryll and John, farm dog Ben, cats Mac and TK warmly welcome you.

Alder Hey
B&B Country B&B
4km E of Martinborough
Sheryll & John Lett
Hinakura Road
RD 4   Martinborough

Tel: (06) 306 9599
Fax: (06) 306 9598
Mob: 025 247 5012
E: bnb@alderhey.co.nz
W: www.alderhey.co.nz

Cost: Double $100-$120
Single $80 Visa/MC
Beds: 2 Queen 1 Twin
(2 bdrm)
Bath: 1 Ensuite 1 Private

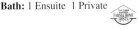

Martinborough

The"Martinborough Retreat" is only five minutes walk from the Square, close to vineyards cafes/restaurants, golf course, tennis courts etc. Contemporary, spacious, fully furnished, character, two storey home (open plan), el fresco dining on large deck with outdoor furniture and gas barbecue. All facilities, TV/Video, radio/CD, microwave, dishwasher, washing machine, gas heater, and wood burner. Large flat grassed area with fruit trees. Ideal for self-catering family or group. Futons in lounge and mezzanine (plus 2 foldaway beds) - sleep 6 - 12.

Martinborough Retreat
Self-contained
Martinborough Central
John & Jenny Simpson
79 Dublin Street
Martinborough

Tel: (04) 476 9154
Fax: (04) 473 7717
Mob: 025 760 115
E: jns@sievwrights.co.nz
W: www.bnb.co.nz/hosts/
martinboroughretreat.html

Cost: Double $140 Child $20
Additional adults $40
Beds: 1 Queen, 1 Double, 1 Twin
+ single & 2 futons + 2
foldaway beds (3 bdrm)
Bath: 1 Ensuite 1 Private

Martinborough

In the heart of the wine district, a beautifully restored Presbyterian Manse, built in 1876, has been transformed into a boutique homestay. Spacious relaxed accommodation in quiet, peaceful setting. One twin plus four Queensize bedrooms all with their own ensuites. All day sun. Off street parking and open fireplace. Amenities include spa pool, petanque and billiards. Enjoy breakfast or wine overlooking vineyard. Walking distance to Martinborough Square with a selection of excellent restaurants. Close to vineyards, antique and craft shops, adventure quad bikes and golf courses.

The Old Manse
Homestay
1km Martinborough
Sandra & John Hargrave
Cnr Grey & Roberts Streets
Martinborough

Tel: (06) 306 8599
Fax: (06) 306 8540
Mob: 025 399 229
Tollfree: 0800 399 229
E: info@oldmanse.co.nz
W: www.oldmanse.co.nz

Cost: Double $130-$150
Visa/MC Amex
Beds: 5 Queen (5 bdrm)
Bath: 5 Ensuite

Palliser Bay - Western Lake

We enjoy welcoming guests to our award winning contemporary home which overlooks the dramatically scenic Palliser Bay. The house is designed for space, comfort and warmth and to take advantage of the spectacular views. We also have a sauna. We offer delicious meals of fresh healthy food. We have walking tracks through our 20 hectares of native bush and there is good tramping, mountain biking, fishing, beach and bush walking close to Tarawai. Smoking outdoors only please. 24 hour Internet access available, laundry service available.

Tarawai
Homestay Rural
35km S of Martinborough
Maria Wallace & Ron Allan
Western Lake Road
Palliser Bay

Tel: (06) 307 7660
Fax: (06) 307 7661
Mob: 025 218 5889
E: tarawai@xtra.co.nz
W: www.bnb.co.nz/hosts/
tarawai.html

Cost: Double $150-$190
Visa/MC
Beds: 2 King/Twin 1 Queen
(3 bdrm)
Bath: 3 Ensuite

Martinborough Rural

We, Irwin and Kay, offer you a warm friendly welcome
and invite you to stay with us at 'Waituna'. Our eighty
five year old farm homestead is luxuriously appointed
with handpainted wallpapers and friezes, original
artworks and private sunny verandahs to each of its two
guest areas.

Set in five acre gardens with superb views of the
countryside, choose to play petanque, ride the
mountain bikes or relax by the fire.

The daily tariff of $295 Double includes afternoon tea
on arrival, four course dinner and all beverages, an
extensive cooked breakfast selection and your picnic
lunch to enjoy later in the day. 'Waituna Cottage',
Your cottage in the country! Enjoy fresh flowers and
home made cookies. Choose from self catering in the
well equipped cottage kitchen, the luxury of breakfast
in the Homestead conservatory or the full package of
'Homestead Treats'.

Waituna Homestead & Cottage
B&B Self-contained Farmstay
Homestay Country Lodge
30km S of Martinborough or
Featherston
Kay & Irwin Luttrell
East - West Access Road
RD 3 Featherston

Tel: (06) 307 7743
Fax: (06) 307 7753
E: waituna.homestead@xtra.co.nz
W: www.bnb.co.nz/hosts/
waitunahomestead&cottage.html

Cost: Double $130-$295
(special package).
Single $100
Dinner at cottage B/A
Visa/MC Amex Diners
Beds: Homestead: 1 King/Twin,
2 Queen (3 bdrms),
Cottage: 2 Queen + 1 set
bunks + Single (3 bdrms).
Bath: 1 Ensuite 2 Private

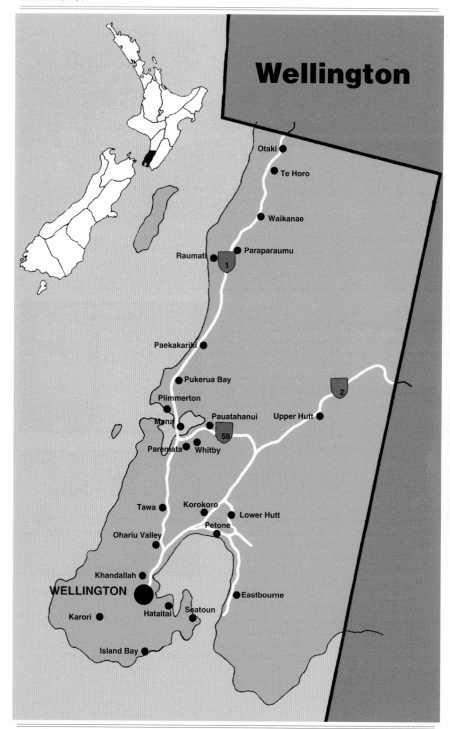

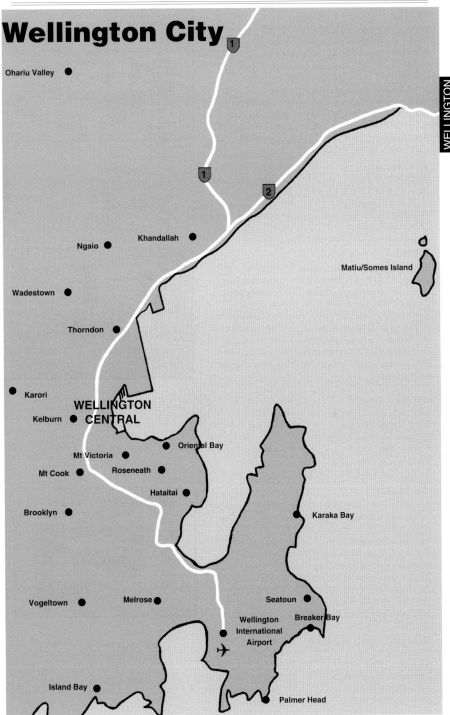

Wellington City

Otaki

Waitohu Lodge, your "QUALITY AWARD' winning homestay is ideally located and easy to find.Only 50 mins drive to Wellington City and the Picton ferry and 20 mins to Paraparaumu Golf Course. Set back from the highway in trees and gardens we offer you quality smokefree accommodation and friendly country hospitality. Enjoy comfortable beds, garden views, spabath and showers, guest lounge with television, books and complimentary tea/coffee, delicious breakfasts. Keith taught Geography, Mary paints, we enjoy people, travel, wines, homegrown produce and Burmese cat Raj. WELCOME.

Waitohu Lodge	**Tel:** (06) 364 5389	**Cost:** Double $75-$95
B&B and Art Studio	**Fax:** (06) 364 5350	Single $60 Child $30
72km N of Wellington City	**Tollfree:** 0800 364 239	Visa/MC
Mary & Keith Oldham	**E:** waitohulodge@xtra.co.nz	**Beds:** 1 Queen 4 Single
294 Main Highway	**W:** www.bnb.co.nz/hosts/	(3 bdrm)
Otaki Wellington	waitohulodge.html	**Bath:** 1 Private 1 Guests share

Otaki

Ballantrae, a 2 acre garden, approx 3 km from SH 1 and 1 km from Otaki Beach. Featuring native trees, ephemeral stream, 200 roses, home orchard, doves and bantams. Lynne and Christine warmly welcome you to our comfortable s/c unit with garden views and your own entrance with secure onsite parking. A cooked breakfast is served including home-made bread, preserves and free range eggs. Tea/coffee making facilities available. Neva and Crystal, our two friendly dogs, share our smoke free environment.

Ballantrae Garden	**Tel:** (06) 364 6158	**Cost:** Double $80
B&B S/C Gardenstay	**Fax:** (06) 364 0158	Single $55
74km N of Wellington	**E:** eathorne@ihug.co.nz	Visa/MC
Lynne & Christine Eathorne	**W:** www.bnb.co.nz/hosts/	**Beds:** 1 Double (1 bdrm)
117 Rangiuru Road	ballantraegarden.html	**Bath:** 1 Ensuite 1 Private
Otaki Beach Otaki 5560		

Te Horo

Nestled in a pleasant garden and surrounded by our small angora and cattle farm, Shepreth has a special feel. Our home is tranquil and spacious, the guest lounge and bedrooms open directly onto the garden, and you can relax in the spa! Meals are generous and delicious; dinners available by arrangement. You'll be close to the beach and Kapiti Coast's many attractions, and just fifty minutes from Wellington and the Inter-Island ferry. You'll find us easily! We have a cat called Gruffyd. You will be very welcome at Shepreth. Please phone for directions.

Shepreth Country Homestay	**Tel:** (06) 364 2130	**Cost:** Double $90-$110
Homestay	**Fax:** (06) 364 2134	Single $55-$65
6.5km N of Waikanae	**Mob:** 025 441 088	Dinner $30 B/A Visa/MC
Lorraine & Warren Birch	**E:** shepreth@xtra.co.nz	**Beds:** 1 Queen 1 Double
38 Te Hapua Road	**W:** www.bnb.co.nz/hosts/	2 Twin (3 bdrm)
Te Horo, RD 1 Otaki	shepreth.html	**Bath:** 2 Private

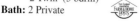

Te Horo

Let us pamper you in our purpose built luxurious Country Lodge. Set next to five acres of native bush with a rural outlook, Te Horo Lodge offers a relaxing, tranquil environment. The three bedrooms downstairs open out to a veranda and expansive lawns. The upstairs "master-suite" has a lounge area with intimate bush views. The decor and furnishings throughout consist of strong vibrant colours. The feature fireplace anchors our stunning lounge. It is crafted by a local stone artist and is perfect for those cold winter nights. The dining-room has a striking recycled timber table.

Te Horo Lodge also offers a "picture perfect" pool area. It includes a secluded in-ground swimming pool and luxury spa pool. The pool area is surrounded by manicured lawns and gardens.
It features a gazebo - our summer dining room - an ideal spot to linger over a scrumptious BBQ dinner.

Te Horo Lodge is not suitable for children. For the comfort of our guests the Lodge is smokefree. There are no pets. A generous cooked country breakfast is provided, including fruit locally grown. The Kapiti region has some fine restaurants or you are most welcome to dine with me at the Lodge by prior arrangement.

Te Horo Lodge is an ideal escape from the pressures of the city, whether you are looking at just relaxing or exploring this unique part of the countryside. You can wander around our ten acre property, including a walk through our native bush.

Local attractions include: Golf courses, the "World Class" Southwards Car Museum, Kapiti Cheeses, gardens, nature reserve, bushwalks, arts and crafts and our rugged West Coast beaches. For the more active try: Fly by Wire, local kayaking, rafting, abseiling or take a tour to Kapiti Island.
We will be happy to assist you in planning your local activities.

How to find us: Te Horo Lodge is located just 3 km off State Highway 1, turn across the railway opposite the Te Horo Store, onto School Road, then left into Arcus Road. You'll find us at the end of the road.

Te Horo Lodge
Homestay Country
65km N of Wellington
Craig Garner
PO Box 43
Te Horo

Tel: (06) 364 3393
Fax: (06) 364 3323
Mob: 025 306 009
Tollfree: 0800 483 467
E: TeHoro.Lodge@xtra.co.nz
W: www.bnb.co.nz/hosts/
tehorolodge.html

Cost: Double $185-$210
Single $135-$150
Child n/a Dinner $45 B/A
Visa/MC Amex Diners
Beds: 3 King/Twin 1 Queen
1 Single (4 bdrm)
Bath: 4 Ensuite

Te Horo

Roz and Jon invite you to share their spacious two storey, smoke free home, nestled among the mature native totara, matai and titoki trees of Cottle Bush. Join us and our friendly dogs for a relaxing stay in a secluded rural atmosphere, not far from local attractions and ammenities and only an hour from Wellington. When you wake,enjoy your choice of cooked or continental breakfast. In the evening dine at a local restaurant or join us for dinner. Please make contact prior to arrival by letter, phone or e-mail.

Cottle Bush	**Tel:** (06) 364 3566	**Cost:** Double $90-$120
B&B Homestay	**Mob:** 021 254 3501	Single $65-$80 Dinner $30
3km S of Otaki	**E:** jonandroz@msn.com	**Beds:** 2 Queen 1 Twin (3 bdrm)
Jon Allan & Roz White	**W:** www.bnb.co.nz/hosts/	**Bath:** 1 Ensuite 1 Guests share
990a State Highway 1	cottlebush.html	
Te Horo 5560		

Waikanae Beach

Pauline and Allan invite you to enjoy the relaxing comfort of their sunny open plan home, with panoramic views of Kapiti Island and the Tararua Ranges. We have direct access to a sandy beach. An ideal place to break your journey. Guest laundry, tea and coffee making facilities are available at all times. Local attractions include Lindale Tourist Centre, Southwards Car Museum, Nga Manu Nature Reserve, a golf course and Kapiti Island Reserve - visits need to be booked. Our interests include music and crafts. Directions: Please phone.

Waikanae Beach Homestay	**Tel:** (04) 293 6532	**Cost:** Double $90 Single $50
B&B Homestay	**Fax:** (04) 293 6543	Child $20, under 8 $10
5km W of Waikanae	**Mob:** 025 300 785	Visa/MC
Pauline & Allan Jones	**E:** albeach@paradise.net.nz	**Beds:** 2 Queen 1 Single
115 Tutere Street	**W:** www.bnb.co.nz/hosts/	(2 bdrm)
Waikanae	joneswaikanaebeach.html	**Bath:** 1 Ensuite 1 Private

Waikanae Beach

Konini Cottage, set in our one acre grounds, borders the golf links and is only a 300 metre stroll to a glorious beach. The 'Lockwood' cottage is self contained with a fully equipped kitchen to enable self-catering, open plan living areas and laundry facilities. If you choose to have breakfast you may either join us in our home or have it served to you in the privacy of the cottage. Bob, a cabinetmaker, works from his home workshop and Maggie's interest is the garden.

Konini Cottage	**Tel:** (04) 904 6610	**Cost:** Double $80 Child $10
Self-contained	**Fax:** (04) 904 6610	$20 extra person Visa/MC
5km W of Waikanae	**E:** konini@paradise.net.nz	Optional breakfast (full)
Maggie & Bob Smith	**W:** www.bnb.co.nz/hosts/	$15pp
26 Konini Crescent	koninicottage.html	**Beds:** 1 Double 2 Single
Waikanae Beach		(2 bdrm)
		Bath: 1 Private

Waikanae

Two delightful self contained accommodation sites with. Country patch studio with its own entrance and deck has a queen bed with ensuite and twin beds on the mezzanine floor of the kitchen lounge. Country patch cottage has an open fire and a large verandah with magic views. it is wheelchair accessible and the two bedroom (each with ensuite) have king beds that unzip to twin. We warmly invite you to share our patch of the country with Kate (16), Simon (14) and Holly our labrador.

Country Patch	**Tel:** (04) 293 5165	**Cost:** Double $90-$160
Self-contained	**Fax:** (04) 293 5164	Single $70-$130 Child $25
1km E of Waikanae	**Mob:** 025 578 421	Visa/MC
Sue & Brian Wilson	**E:** countrypatch@actrix.co.nz	**Beds:** 2 King/Twin 1 Queen
18 Kea Street	**W:** www.bnb.co.nz/hosts/	2 Single (3 bdrm)
Waikanae	countrypatch.html	**Bath:** 3 Ensuite

Waikanae

We invite you to share the informal lifestyle in our warm spacious home set in park like surroundings on your next holiday. We are an active retired couple who enjoy welcoming new friends and helping them to take advantage of the attractions of the Kapiti Coast and New Zealand. Alternatively if you feel like peace and tranquillity this will suit you too as we host only one party at a time. Buffy, our beagle cross dog shares our smoke free home. Directions: Please phone, write or fax.

Millrest	**Tel:** (04) 904 2424	**Cost:** Double $90
Homestay	**Fax:** (04) 904 2424	Single $65
58km N of Wellington	**E:** topdog@paradise.net.nz	Dinner $20
Colleen & Gordon Butchers	**W:** www.bnb.co.nz/hosts/	**Beds:** 1 Queen 1 Twin (2 bdrm)
57 Park Avenue	millrest.html	**Bath:** 1 Private
Waikanae Kapiti Coast		

Waikanae

Hear the dawn chorus - the birds are here only you are missing. Discover hospitality and tranquillity beyond expectation, either in the deluxe one bedroom cottage (with kitchen) or traditional homestay. The 2 1/2 acre garden, lily pond, and untouched bush provide a peaceful environment in which to relax before tomorrow's travel. Kapiti's many attractions provide plenty to see and do. We have no pets or children at home and enjoy good wine, travelling and entertaining. We prefer guests do not smoke inside. Unsuitable for children. Laundry available.

"The place to stay in Kapiti"

Sudbury Homestay and Garden	**Tel:** (04) 902 8530	**Cost:** Double $100-$120
Self-contained Homestay	**Fax:** (04) 902 8531	Single $80-$100
Glenys and Brian Daw	**Mob:** 021 129 6970	Dinner B/A Visa/MC
39 Manu Grove	**E:** sudbury@paradise.net.nz	**Beds:** 2 Queen (2 bdrm)
Waikanae 6010	**W:** www.bnb.co.nz/hosts/	**Bath:** 1 Ensuite
	sudbury.html	1 Guests share

Waikanae

Birdsong, the sound of the river and complete privacy.
Peace and quiet with a scrumptious breakfast and
comfortable accommodation. Riverstone has five
hectares of paddocks and garden with river walks and
local pottery and cafe. Waikanae, Raumati and
Paraparaumu have a variety of cafes, shops, boutiques, Lindale farm park, the Southward Car
museum, Nga Manu bird sanctuary, golf courses and
beautiful beaches. Pick up from train or bus.
Laundry facilities. Smoke free. No pets.

RiverStone
Self-contained Rural Homestay
6km E of Waikanae
Paul & Eppie Murton
111 Ngatiawa Road
Waikanae

Tel: (04) 293 1936
Fax: (04) 293 1936
E: riverstone@paradise.net.nz
W: www.bnb.co.nz/hosts/
riverstone.html

Cost: Double $100
　　　Single $70
　　　Child $45 Visa/MC
Beds: 1 Queen 1 Single
　　　(2 bdrm)
Bath: 1 Private

Waikanae Beach

Julie a Yorkshire girl and Lancashire husband, offer visitors
a warm, northern welcome, into their unique comfy home,
which overlooks the 11th fairway". If you "LOVE GOLF"
or want a relaxing holiday near a safe sandy beach,
"HERE!" is the place to stay. Our interests include GOLF,
swimming, tennis, tramping, bowls and snooker, situated
locally. Outdoor heated pool 5 minutes drive away.
Facilities available: tea/coffee, soft drinks, games, darts,
music, books, jigsaws, TV and laundry room. We are non
smokers and have two friendly dogs.

11th Fairway Homestay
B&B Homestay
5km W of Waikanae
Julie Entwistle
4 Atua Street
Waikanae Beach

Tel: (04) 293 2234
Mob: 025 611 5761
W: www.bnb.co.nz/hosts/
thfairwayhomestay.html

Cost: Double $90 Single $50
　　　Child $30
　　　Dinner $25pp by arrangement
　　　Campervans $30 Visa/MC
Beds: 1 King 1 Queen
　　　4 Single (4 bdrm)
Bath: 2 Guests share

Waikanae

*EXQUISITE ACCOMMODATION *2 ACRES SECLUDED
GARDENS *SWIMMING POOL & PRIVATE SPA ROOM
*NATIVE BIRDS AND FOREST WALK *TENNIS AND
PETANQUE *PRIVATE IDYLLIC PARADISE Wake to
birdsong from your beautifully decorated romantic bedroom in
the upstairs guest wing. Enjoy quality linens, bathrobes,
handmade quilts, fresh flowers, fine china. Two lounges (log
fires), plus guest's sitting room with breathtaking garden vistas,
and complimentary refreshments. Indulgent breakfasts, elegantly
served, include seasonal fruits and homemade specialties. Visit
Erica's art quilt studio/gallery. Unsuitable children under 10yrs.
Restaurants, beach and golf nearby. ENJOY!

HURUNUI HOMESTEAD
B&B Homestay
58km N of Wellington
Erica & Geoff Lineham
15 Hurunui Street Waikanae

Tel: (04) 902 8571
Fax: (04) 902 8572
E: hurunui@lineham.co.nz
W: www.hurunui.lineham.co.nz

Cost: Double $130-$150
　　　Single $100-$120 Visa/MC
Beds: 2 Queen 1 Single
　　　(3 bdrm)
Bath: 1 Ensuite 1 Private

Waikanae

Our property features a 10-acre English-style garden backed by native bush and bordered by the Waikanae River. The self-contained B&B unit is located directly behind the main homestead and occupies the attic area above a 3-car garage. It is very spacious with dormer windows and barndoors overlooking an area planted with daffodils and deciduous trees. The room has two beds, a kitchenette, living and dining areas. A private bathroom is downstairs. Guests are welcome to play tennis, croquet and petanque or swim in the private swimming hole of the Waikanae River. Please ring for directions.

Burnard Gardens
B&B Self-contained
3km E of Waikanae
Mary & Robert Burnard
236 Reikorangi Road Waikanae

Tel: (04) 293 3371
Fax: (04) 293 3378
Mob: 025 222 5675
E: mary@burnardgardens.co.nz
W: www.burnardgardens.co.nz

Cost: Double $100-$120
Single $80-$100 Child $10
Beds: 1 Queen 1 Single
(1 bdrm)
Bath: 1 Private

Paraparaumu

Our 1950's beach house has hill and island views and is situated two blocks back from Marine Parade. Shops, golf course, airport, cafes and excellent restaurants are 1-2km walk away. Off-street parking is provided and we will meet bus or train. Jude is, with prior notice, pleased to provide meals for those on special diets. We love walking, food, music, and Citroens. Non smokers preferred. We have a cat. Directions: Watch for yellow letterbox on seaward corner of Bluegum and Rua Roads.

Homestay
60km N of Wellington
Jude & Vic Young
72 Bluegum Road
Paraparaumu

Tel: (04) 902 0199
Fax: (04) 902 0199
W: www.bnb.co.nz/hosts/
youngparaparaumu.html

Cost: Double $75 Single $45
Child 1/2 price Dinner $20
Beds: 1 Double 1 Single
(2 bdrm)
Bath: 1 Private 1 Family share

Paraparaumu

Our self-contained accommodation is peaceful and sunny. A view across small lake, full with wildlife. Beach, shopping centre and excellent restaurants close by. Sunny lounge with t.v., books and games; well equipped kitchen, bathroom and laundry facilities. Information about indoor and outdoor attractions available. No dogs please and guests are asked not to smoke indoors. Tariff: accommodation only. Continental breakfast optional $5 pp. Please phone or fax for bookings and directions. We look forward meeting you.

M & S Homestay
Self-contained
55km N of Wellington
Sytske & Marius Kruiniger
60A Ratanui Road
Paraparaumu

Tel: (04) 297 3447 or
Tel: (04) 2998098
Fax: (04) 297 3447
W: www.bnb.co.nz/hosts/
mshomestay.html

Cost: Double $65 Single $50
Child $5 under 5yrs extra
persons $10 Visa/MC
Beds: 1 Queen 2 Single
(2 bdrm)
Bath: 1 Private

Paraparaumu Beach

Enjoy warm friendly hospitality in the relaxing atmosphere of our modern new home. Peaceful surroundings next to river estuary and beach. Wonderful views of sea, lake and hills. Lovely coastal and river walks. Tourist attractions include trips to Kapiti Island Bird Sanctuary. Paraparaumu Beach world ranking Golf Course six minutes drive. South Island Ferry Terminal 45 minutes away. We are newly retired non smokers who enjoy meeting people. We love our NZ scenery and bush walking. Ernie paints landscapes. Enquiries welcome.

Beachstay	**Tel:** (04) 902 6466	**Cost:** Double $75 Single $50
Homestay	**Fax:** (04) 902 6466	Child $20 Dinner $25B/A
5.5km N of Paraparaumu	**Mob:** 025 232 5106	Visa/MC
Ernie & Rhoda Stevenson	**W:** www.bnb.co.nz/hosts/	**Beds:** 1 Double 2 Single
17 Takahe Drive Kotuku Park	beachstayparaparaumu.html	(2 bdrm)
Paraparaumu Beach 6010		**Bath:** 1 Private

Paraparaumu

Your well travelled hosts welcome you to their sunny modern home situated in a quiet cul de sac in Paraparaumu Beach, Kapiti. Centrally situated and five minutes from the main tourist attractions of an international golf course, Southwards Vintage Car museum, Lindale farm complex and the beach. Bush walks, bird sanctuaries and restaurants etc., are close by.Boat trips to Kapiti island nature reserve can be arranged. The interisland ferry terminal in Wellington is just 45 minutes away. We request no smoking indoors.

B&B	**Tel:** (04) 904 2022	**Cost:** Double $75 Single $45
4km N of Paraparaumu Centre	**E:** thelancasters@zfree.co.nz	Dinner $25 by arrangement
Elaine & Don Lancaster	**W:** www.bnb.co.nz/hosts/	Visa/MC
33 College Drive	lancaster.html	**Beds:** 2 Single (1 bdrm)
Paraparaumu Beach		**Bath:** 1 Private

Paraparaumu Beach

Relax in the comfort of our "Golf Road Homestay". Situated adjacent to NZ's famous links course, ranked 79th in the world. Our home is a short walk to beach, shops and restaurants. A must for visitors is a charter boat trip that goes over to Kapiti Island Nature Reserve (bookings are essential). A guest lounge is available with TV, telephone, tea and coffee making facilities. Depending on the weather, you could enjoy your continental breakfast on our deck. We have two cats. Non smokers please.

Golf Road Homestay	**Tel:** (04) 902 0029	**Cost:** Double $120 Single $80
B&B Homestay	**Fax:** (04) 970 7553	Dinner B/A Visa/MC
1.5km W of Paraparaumu	**E:** golfhomestay@hotmail.com	**Beds:** 1 Queen 1 Double
Lyn & Arty Seiringer	**W:** www.golfroad-homestay.co.nz	1 Twin (3 bdrm)
47 Golf Road		**Bath:** 2 Ensuite
Paraparaumu Beach		1 Guests share

Paraparaumu Beach

Welcome to our spacious home by the beach where you may swim, fish or wander on the sand. Stroll to nearby villages and enjoy the restaurants, cafes and shops. Watch the sunset over the sea; enjoy a soak in the spa; play golf. Laugh at the antics of Snapper, our apricot cat and little Josie, our dog. Catch the train to Wellington, the capital city and explore without parking worries. We would love to tell you about nearby attractions. We look forward to meeting you.

B&B Self-contained
1km S of Paraparaumu Beach
shops
Val & Geoff Brannan
137 Seaview Road
Paraparaumu Beach

Tel: (04) 298 1798
Mob: 025 616 2345
E: v.g.brannan@xtra.co.nz
W: www.bnb.co.nz/hosts/
brannan.html

Cost: Double $80-$120
Single $50-$100 Child neg
Beds: 2 Queen 1 Double
(3 bdrm)
Bath: 1 Ensuite 1 Family share

Raumati Beach

A magical beachside retreat. Literally 20 footsteps to the beach, private cottage opens onto a beautiful view which can be enjoyed from the comfort and serenity of your room. Very short stroll to local amenities, restaurants, etc. Two rooms make it ideal for a getaway, family stay or two couples. Fully equipped kitchenette if self-catering preferred. Laundry and internet facilities also available. We have two children and a dog and cat and we all look forward to sharing our piece of paradise with you.

Kapiti Beach Bed & Breakfast
Self-contained
5km SW of Paraparaumu
Brent and Sylvia Henderson
15 Matatua Road
Raumati Beach
Kapiti Coast - Wellington

Tel: (04) 902 1388
Fax: (04) 902 1388
Mob: 025 628 6005
E: brenth@clear.net.nz
W: kapiti-beach.co.nz

Cost: Double $135 Single $120
Child $10 Long term
negotiable Visa/MC
Beds: 2 Queen (2 bdrm)
Bath: 1 Private

Paekakariki

Relax and enjoy the sound of the sea, fabulous views and direct beach access. Spacious accommodation upstairs includes a queen and/or twin room, private bathroom and guest lounge,with outstanding views from Kapiti Island to the South Island. We host one party at a time. Continental breakfast provided. Have a relaxing spa; enjoy beach activities (surf-casting gear available); walk to local cafes/ restaurants; or explore the Kapiti Coast. 30 minutes from Wellington. Laundry facilities available. Our interests include sports, literature, entertaining, and travelling. KHHA Members

Killara Homestay
Homestay
10km S of Paraparaumu
Carole & Don Boddie
70 Ames Street
Paekakariki

Tel: (04) 905 5544
Fax: (04) 905 5533
Mob: 025 944 551
E: killara@paradise.net.nz
W: www.killarahomestay.co.nz

Cost: Double $120
Single $90
Visa/MC Amex
Beds: 1 Queen 1 Twin (2 bdrm)
Bath: 1 Private

Pukerua Bay

Come share our warm, sunny refurbished smokefree home. Relax in the conservatory - enjoy the views. We have two friendly cats - Tabitha & Sienna. Pukerua Bay, home of creative people, has an interesting safe for swimming beach about 15 mins walk. Railway station closeby. I'm a keen spinner - spinning wheel/fibre available to use. Variety of restaurants & cafes 5-15 mins drive. Most special diets catered for, lunches arranged. Smokers seat undercover; off-street parking; laundry facilities; garaging for bikes; powerpoint small campervans; cot & highchair available.

Sheena's Homestay	**Tel:** (04) 239 9947	**Cost:** Double $70 Single $45
Homestay	**Fax:** (04) 239 9942	Child $20 Dinner $18 B/A
32 km N of Wellington	**Mob:** 025 602 1503	Visa/MC Amex
Sheena Taylor	**E:** homestay@sheenas.co.nz	**Beds:** 1 Double 1 Twin
2 Gray Street	**W:** www.bnb.co.nz/hosts/	(2 bdrm)
Pukerua Bay 6010 Kapiti Coast	sheenashomestay.html	**Bath:** 1 Family share

Plimmerton

We extend a warm welcome with: * Million dollar views of beach, sea and South Island * Easy access off State Highway 1, off street parking * Modern home with sun and views from every room * Private spacious guest bedroom with queen-size bed * own bathroom with bath and shower * Dinner by prior request * Catch up on your e-mail or laundry * Friendly hosts who have travelled extensively * Direct route to Interisland Ferries * Close proximity to local railway station

131 Homestay	**Tel:** (04) 233 9444	**Cost:** Double $110
Homestay	**Fax:** (04) 233 9515	Single $90
27km N of Wellington	**Mob:** 025 461 495	Dinner B/A Visa/MC
Joan & Denis Sawkins	**E:** sawkins@xtra.co.nz	**Beds:** 1 Queen (1 bdrm)
131 Pope Street	**W:** www.bnb.co.nz/hosts/	**Bath:** 1 Private
Plimmerton Wellington	homestay.html	

Plimmerton

Stay at Aquavilla in the centre of picturesque Plimmerton with its cafes and seaside atmosphere, 20 minutes to Wellington City & Ferry terminal, close to State Highway 1 and Plimmerton Station, 50m from best beach in Wellington. Superior, architecturally designed accommodation with your own bedroom, kitchenette, bathroom, lounge and courtyard. We have travelled extensively overseas and throughout New Zealand. We love art, photography and the outdoors. Carolyn is an Artist photographer and her scrumptious breakfasts are memorable. Ours is a smoke free home.

Aquavilla	**Tel:** (04) 233 1146	**Cost:** Double $120 Single $100
Self-contained	**Mob:** 025 231 0141	Child neg Extra adults neg
6km N of Porirua	**E:** carolyn.wallace@paradise.net.nz	Visa/MC
Graham & Carolyn Wallace	**W:** www.bnb.co.nz/hosts/	**Beds:** 1 Queen 1 Single
16 Steyne Ave	aquavilla.html	(1 bdrm)
Plimmerton		**Bath:** 1 Private

Plimmerton

We are a professional couple who would love to share our 90 year old beachside house with you. Our guest accommodation is in a private wing with its own entrance from a charming courtyard and features a private lounge, bedroom and ensuite. Enjoy a drink on the verandah by the waters edge, relax on the beach at our front gate or even take the plunge into the sea from our steps if the tide is in. Feel free to use our canoe and if you fancy a bike ride we can provide those also. At our back door is Plimmerton village with no less than 6 dining establishments and 2 minutes walk to train station. We have a cat and a friendly back Labrador and children are welcome. Directions: Please phone or directions

Beachside	**Tel:** (04) 233 9469	**Cost:** Double $90 Single $70
20 mins N of Wellington	**Fax:** (04) 233 9427	Child $30 Visa/MC
Brian & Mary Wesley-Smith	**Mob:** 021 620 782	**Beds:** 1 Double (1 bdrm)
9 Beach Road	**E:** wesley-smith@xtra.co.nz	**Bath:** 1 Ensuite
Plimmerton	**W:** www.bnb.co.nz/hosts/user11.html	

Paremata

Bayview Homestay is large, modern, sunny home situated two minutes from Paremata Bridge on State Highway 1, and enjoys spectacular views across Paremata Harbour and out to sea. Join us for dinner. Jocelyn is a professional caterer and will provide meals to your taste. Our interests include gardening, music, sport, travel, food and wine. Off street parking. Two minutes to trains. For further information please view our website.

Bayview	**Tel:** (04) 233 2575	**Cost:** Double $95 Single $60
Homestay	**Fax:** (04) 233 9414	Dinner $30 - $40 Visa/MC
20km N of Wellington	**Mob:** 025 218 5633	**Beds:** 1 Double 1 Single
Jocelyn Jackson	**E:** relax@bayview.co.nz	(2 bdrm)
43 Bayview Road	**W:** www.bayview.co.nz	**Bath:** 1 Private
Paremata Wellington		

Paremata

We extend a warm welcome to our guests. Enjoy the tranquil, peaceful setting of 'Penryn Cove' surrounded by native bush reserve, set on the edge of a peninsula overlooking the Pauatahanui inlet and bird sanctuary. Easy access onto inlet walkway will provide you with some relaxing recreation. We have travelled extensively, enjoy meeting and sharing with fellow travellers. Easy walking distance cafes, restaurants, shops, rail. Private spacious guest area with magical views, private deck. Directions: 2 minutes from State Highway 1. Please phone for directions.

Penryn Cove	**Tel:** (04) 233 8265	**Cost:** Double $110-$120
Homestay	**Fax:** (04) 233 8265	Single $70 Child Neg.
26km N of Wellington	**Mob:** 025 815 525	Dinner B/A Visa/MC
Eleanor & John Clark	**E:** JWClark@xtra.co.nz	**Beds:** 2 Queen (2 bdrm)
32 Penryn Drive	**W:** www.bnb.co.nz/hosts/	**Bath:** 1 Private
Paremata Wellington	penryncove.html	1 Guests share

Mana

Dream away the evenings on one of the many decks whilst listening to good music and watching the sun set over the South Island. Modern, sunny three level home, with off street parking. Situated just 2 minutes walk from cafes, restaurants, yacht club, train station, sandy beaches and beautiful Pauatahanui Inlet. Wellington CBD just 20 minutes by car or train and Porirua city 4 kilometres. Host is well travelled and enjoys art, theatre and entertaining. Large comfortable bedroom with ensuite bathroom, queen bed, electric blankets, lounge chairs, tea and coffee anytime, TV, internet line. Fax facility available.

Le Solaire	**Tel:** (04) 233 8407	**Cost:** Double $110
B&B	**Fax:** (04) 233 8450	Single $80
13km N of Wellington	**Mob:** 025 439 822	Child free Visa/MC
Irene Denford	**E:** irene.denford@xtra.co.nz	**Beds:** 1 Queen (1 bdrm)
16A Mana View Road	**W:** www.bnb.co.nz/hosts/	**Bath:** 1 Ensuite
Mana, Wellington	lesolaire.html	

Whitby

Our home is situated in a quiet cul-de-sac street, with large decks overlooking garden and bush. As we are on our own with our two pet cats, we would really enjoy the company of New Zealand and overseas visitors. Having travelled and lived overseas we are always interested in other peoples experiences. We are ten minutes by car to Paremata train station and main highway, 25 minutes to Wellington city. We assure you of a warm welcome and memorable stay. House smoke free.

Oldfields	**Tel:** (04) 234 1002	**Cost:** Double $85
Homestay	**Mob:** 021 254 0869	Single $55
10km NE of Porirua	**E:** oldfields@paradise.net.nz	Dinner $25
Elaine & John Oldfield	**W:** www.bnb.co.nz/hosts/	**Beds:** 2 Queen (2 bdrm)
22 Musket Lane	oldfield.html	**Bath:** 1 Guests share
Whitby Wellington		

Pauatahanui

Looking for something special away from city noise? Stay near but not in the City. "Braebyre", one of Wellington's fine countryhomes, is easily found on state Highway 58 - the Northern Gateway. Two luxury studio suites nestle in the large landscaped gardens surrounding "Braebyre", on a mohair goat farm. The guest wing (with separate entrance) includes a lounge with table tennis, log fire and indoor spa pool. Evening dinner with your hosts, featuring homegrown produce, is available on request. Laundry $5.

Braebyre Rural Homestay	**Tel:** (04) 235 9311	**Cost:** Double $100-$160
Homestay Self-contained Suites	**Fax:** (04) 235 9345	Single $90-$150 Child neg
25km N of Wellington	**Tollfree:** 0800 36 93 11	Dinner $40 Visa/MC
Jenny & Randall Shaw	**E:** braebyre@paradise.net.nz	**Beds:** 1 King/Twin 1 King
Flightys Rd Pauatahanui, RD 1	**W:** www.braebyrehomestay.co.nz	1 Queen 1 Double
Porirua		1 Twin (5 bdrm)
		Bath: 3 Ensuite 1 Guests share

Tawa

Our comfortable family home is in a quiet street in Tawa. We have a separate toilet, shower and spa bath. Freshly ground coffee a speciality, with breakfast of your choice. Jeannette's interests are: Ikebana, Japanese, German languages, porcelain painting, knitting, dressmaking, playing tennis, learning to play golf and the piano and gardening. Alf's interests are: Amateur radio, woodwork, Toastmasters international - and being allowed to help in the garden. We are both members of LIONS INTERNATIONAL.

Tawa Homestay	**Tel:** (04) 232 5989	**Cost:** Double $75 Single $40
Homestay	**Fax:** (04) 232 5987	Dinner $20pp Visa/MC
15km N of Wellington	**W:** www.bnb.co.nz/hosts/	**Beds:** 1 Queen 1 Single
Jeannette & Alf Levick	tawahomestay.html	(2 bdrm)
17 Mascot Street		**Bath:** 1 Family share
Tawa Wellington		

Tawa

No. 3 is situated in a quiet street 7 minutes by car and rail to Porirua City and 15 minutes from Wellington and the InterIsland Ferry Terminal. Our house is wheelchair friendly and we have an extra bedroom downstairs with single bed or cot if required at reduced rate of $15. Spa, laundry facilities also available. Safe off-street parking. Tawa is close to beaches, ten-pin bowling, swimming pool and fine walks. Our house is "smokefree". Dinner by arrangement. Please phone for directions.

Homestay	**Tel:** (04) 232 5547	**Cost:** Double $70
15km N of Wellington	**Fax:** (04) 232 5547	Single $40
Joy & Bill Chaplin	**Mob:** 025 349 078	Dinner B/A
3 Kiwi Place	**E:** chapta@xtra.co.nz	**Beds:** 1 Double 1 Single
Tawa Wellington	**W:** www.bnb.co.nz/hosts/	(2 bdrm)
	chaplin.html	**Bath:** 1 Guests share

Tawa

We are a retired couple. Together we welcome you to stay with us. We are 15kms from Wellington city. A five minute walk to the suburban rail station with half hourly service into the city (15 minutes) and north to the Kapiti Coast. Alternatively you can drive north to the Coast, enjoying sea and rural views before sampling tourist attractions in this area. We are happy to provide transport to and from the Inter Island ferry. We are a smoke free household. Laundry facilities available.

B&B Homestay	**Tel:** (04) 232 7664	**Cost:** Double $75
15km NW of Wellington	**W:** www.bnb.co.nz/hosts/	Single $40
Jocelyn & David Perry	perry.html	Child $20 Dinner $20pp B/A
5 Fyvie Avenue		**Beds:** 1 Double 3 Single (3 bdrm)
Linden		**Bath:** 1 Guests share
Tawa		1 Family share

Upper Hutt - Te Marua

Our home is situated in a secluded bush setting. Guests may relax on one of our private decks or read books from our extensive library. For the more energetic there are bush walks, bike trails, trout fishing, swimming and a golf course within walking distance. The guest wing has a kitchenette and television. Lloyd is a landscape photographer with over 30 years experience photographing New Zealand. Sheryl is a teacher. Travel, tramping, skiing, photography, music and meeting people are interests we enjoy.

Te Marua Homestay	**Tel:** (04) 526 7851	**Cost:** Double $80 Single $45
Homestay	**Fax:** (04) 526 7866	Dinner $25pp b/a
7.4km N of Upper Hutt	**Mob:** 025 501 679	Visa/MC Amex Diners
Sheryl & Lloyd Homer	**Tollfree:** 0800 110 851	**Beds:** 1 Queen 1 Double (2 bdrm)
108A Plateau Road	**E:** sheryl.lloyd@clear.net.nz	**Bath:** 1 Private
Te Marua Upper Hutt	**W:** www.bnb.co.nz/hosts/homer.html	

Upper Hutt

Executive Timout/Homestay. Escape from the stress of City Life just approx 40 minutes from Wellington off SH2. Close to Upper Hutt - Restaurants, Cinema, Golf, Racecourse, leisure Centre (swimming), Bush Walks etc. We are near the confluence of the Hutt and Akatarawa Rivers which is noted for its fishing. 13km to Staglands. Country setting, relax and listen to the New Zealand Tuis and watch the fantails or Wood Pigeons, or just simply relax and read. Comfortable and warm and friendly hospitality, Good New Zealand style food.

Tranquillity Homestay	**Tel:** (04) 526 6948	**Cost:** Double $90
Homestay	**Fax:** (04) 526 6968	Single $45-$55
Elaine & Alan	**Mob:** 025 405 962	Dinner 20 B/A Visa/MC
136 Akatarawa Road	**Tollfree:** 0800 270 787	**Beds:** 1 Queen 2 Single (3 bdrm)
Birchville	**E:** tranquility@xtra.co.nz	**Bath:** 1 Ensuite 2 Family share
Upper Hutt	**W:** www.bnb.co.nz/hosts/	
	tranquillity.html	

Stay more than one night
to get the feel of a place

Upper Hutt

Our spacious Swiss Chalet style home, has a Douglas Fir theme, and is set at the end of Colletts Road on 67 acres of elevated farmland.

A quiet location, with enchanting views, overlooking the north end of the Mangaroa Valley. We breed pedigree Hereford cattle, and also keep coloured sheep, goats, poultry, bees, a collie dog and a cat.

It is an ideal out of town stopover, when travelling to or from the Wellington Ferry, or just want to get away for a change. Our travels have taken us to many countries, and now we are semi retired, particularly enjoy meeting people from around the world. The farm, garden, and handcrafts along with our local Church keep us active.

Further to Bed and Breakfast,you may wish to join us for a three course evening meal, which usually consists of produce from our farm, garden or orchard, all grown without artificial fertilizer.

Please contact us for reservations at earliest convenience. We are 6 kms from SH2.

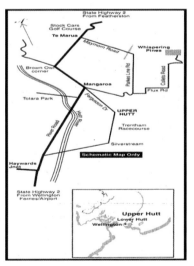

Whispering Pines
B&B Farmstay
8km NE of Upper Hutt
Ruth & Graham Ockwell
207 Colletts Road
RD 1, Mangaroa
Upper Hutt

Tel: (04) 526 7785
Fax: (04) 526 7785
Mob: 025 233 0999
E: whisperingpines@xtra.co.nz
W: www.bnb.co.nz/hosts/
whisperingpines.html

Cost: Double $100 Single $60
Child neg Dinner $25
Visa/MC
Beds: 2 King/Twin 1 Queen
1 Single (3 bdrm)
Bath: 1 Ensuite 1 Guests share

Lower Hutt - Korokoro

Just off State Highway 2, very quiet area, a warm,
welcome awaits. Our Terrier/Cross dogs Prince and
Ben love guests. View Wellington's magnificent
harbour relaxing over a meal in or out doors. Maurice
is a fingerprint expert with the New Zealand Police
and Virginia enjoys the time spent with guests.
Laundry free if staying 2 consecutive nights. 10-13
minutes to Picton Ferry, handy to many restaurants.
Of street parking. Telephone for directions.

Western Rise	**Tel:** (04) 589 1872	**Cost:** Double $85-$100
Homestay	**Fax:** (04) 589 1873	Single $55-$66
12km N of Wellington	**Mob:** 025 438 316	Dinner $15 Visa/MC
Virginia & Maurice Gibbens	**W:** www.bnb.co.nz/hosts/	**Beds:** 1 Queen 2 Single
10 Stanhope Grove	westernrise.html	(2 bdrm)
Korokoro		**Bath:** 1 Guests share
Lower Hutt		

Lower Hutt

Our home is situated plumb in the centre of Woburn, a picturesque
and quiet central city suburb of Lower Hutt, known for its
generous sized houses and beautiful gardens. Within walking
distance of the Lower Hutt downtown, 15 minutes drive from
central Wellington and its Railway Station and Ferry terminals;
Airport 25 minutes; 3 minutes walk to Woburn Rail Station.
Separate lounge and TV. Love to entertain and share hearty Kiwi
style cooking with good New Zealand wine. Laundry facilities.
Directions: Please phone, fax, email or write. Transfer transport
available. High speed and dial up Internet connections
available.

Judy & Bob's Place	**Tel:** (04) 971 1192	**Cost:** Single $50 Dinner $25
Homestay	**Fax:** (04) 971 6192	Visa/MC Amex Diners
Judy & Bob Vine	**Mob:** 021 510 682	**Beds:** 1 Queen 2 Single
11 Ngaio Crescent	**E:** bob.vine@paradise.net.nz	(2 bdrm)
Lower Hutt	**W:** www.bnb.co.nz/hosts/	**Bath:** 1 Guests share
	judybobsplace.html	

Hutt City

Our comfortable house is situated in the Eastern Hills of
Hutt City. The idyllic surroundings make this a great place
to enjoy a quiet, peaceful holiday. We are within easy reach
of four golf courses, city centre, cinemas, good restaurants
and a host of other entertainment. Wellington is 15 minutes
by train, or 20 minutes by car on SH1. Our interests
include: meeting people, walking and tramping, theatre,
sports, travel, and dining out. We have a self contained
apartment with bedroom (double), bathroom, large lounge
and fully equipped kitchen. We prefer no smoking in the
house. Please phone for directions.

Casa Bianca	**Tel:** (04) 569 7859	**Cost:** Double $90
Self-contained	**Fax:** (04) 569 7859	Single $65
Jo & Dave Comparini	**E:** compo@voyager.co.nz	**Beds:** 1 King 1 Single
10 Damian Grove	**W:** www.bnb.co.nz/hosts/	(1 bdrm)
Hutt City	casabianca.html	**Bath:** 1 Private

Lower Hutt

Our 70-year-old cottage has been fully refurbished while retaining its original charm. It is 15 minutes from the Ferry terminal and the Stadium, and 20 minutes from the Museum of NZ, "Te Papa". Our home is centrally heated and the sunny guest bedroom looks over our secluded garden. The beds have electric blankets and down duvets. Vegetarians are catered for, laundry facilities are available and we have ample offstreet parking. Our main interests are travel, music, gardening, shows and NZ wines.

Dungarvin
Homestay
2km SE of Lower Hutt
Beryl & Trevor Cudby
25 Hinau St
Woburn Lower Hutt

Tel: (04) 569 2125
Fax: (04) 569 2126
E: t.b.cudby@clear.net.nz
W: www.bnb.co.nz/hosts/
dungarvin.html

Cost: Double $90 Single $70
Dinner $30 B/A
Visa/MC
Beds: 2 Single (1 bdrm)
Bath: 1 Private

Lower Hutt

Relax in the comfort of our cosy home which is just a five minute walk to the Hutt City Centre. Originally built in 1910 the house has been fully renovated. We have travelled extensively Overseas and in NZ. Interests include Travel, Gardening, Sports and live Theatre. As well as TV in Guest room there's Coffee and Tea-making facilities. Breakfast will be served in our Dining room at your convenience. Unsuitable for children. We look forward to welcoming you into our smoke-free home which we share with Scuffin our cat.

Rose Cottage
B&B Homestay
0.5km SE of Lower Hutt Central
Maureen & Gordon Gellen
70A Hautana St
Lower Hutt Wellington

Tel: (04) 566 7755
Fax: (04) 566 0777
Mob: 021 481 732
E: g.gellen,100406.1025@
compuserve.com
W: www.bnb.co.nz/hosts/
rosecottagelowerhutt.html

Cost: Double $95 Single $60
Dinner $30 B/A Visa/MC
Beds: 1 Queen 1 Single
(2 bdrm)
Bath: 1 Ensuite 1 Family share

Lower Hutt

Our modern spacious, split level home is in a tranquil haven.We have a secluded property situated beneath the Eastern Hills Scenic Reserve. We are 15 minutes from the Ferry terminal and 20 minutes from "Te Papa" the Museum of N.Z. Come and relax in our peaceful surroundings.We are smokefree.Secure parking.Own T.V & Tea/coffee facilities. Directions.Please phone,fax,email or write. We look forward to welcoming you into our home.

Tyndall House
Homestay
2km E of Lower Hutt
Paulene & Nigel Lyne
6/2 Tyndall Street
Lower Hutt 6009

Tel: (04) 569 1958
Fax: (04) 569 1952
Mob: 025 851 901
E: tyndallhouse@xtra.co.nz
W: www.bnb.co.nz/hosts/
tyndallhouse.html

Cost: Double $110-$115
Single $70 Dinner $30
Visa/MC
Beds: 2 Queen (2 bdrm)
Bath: 2 Private

Lower Hutt - Korokoro

Stay at the closest vineyard to the capital. An Edwardian-styled homestead overlooking Wellington Harbour, built at the turn of the century [2000!] based upon the MacDonald family home in Scotland. Built for views and comfort: guest living-room with woodburner; chairs, TV, writing-desk, hand-basin in guest bedrooms. Free Internet access, NZ toll calls after 7pm, laundry service, Petone Station pickup – see Devenport's website for more details. Alasdair, Christopher, Marlene and two cocker spaniels, welcome you to a comfortable stay in Wellington on our vineyard estate.

Devenport Estate
B&B Vineyard Accommodation
12km N of Wellington
Alasdair, Christopher, Marlene
1 Korokoro Road
Korokoro Lower Hutt

Tel: (04) 586 6868
Fax: (04) 586 6869
Mob: 025 274 0394
E: devenport_estate@hotmail.com
W: http://homepages.paradise.net.
nz/devenpor

Cost: Double $100 Single $80
Visa/MC
Beds: 1 Queen 2 Single
(2 bdrm)
Bath: 1 Guest share
$120 for private use

Petone - Korokoro

Our natural bush environment and spectacular harbour views are only 20 mins train or drive from Wellington and handy to Petone's ethnic restaurants. Here you can enjoy your own private ground floor space including sitting room with tea making facilities and parking outside. Upstairs, Kate and Barry look forward to your company. Our interests are conservation, gardening, bee-keeping and computers. We offer a healthy, nourishing breakfast with new laid eggs, home grown honey, freshly baked bread and home made muesli.

B&B Homestay
2km W of Petone
Kate and Barry Malcolm
29 Singers Road
Korokoro
Petone

Tel: (04) 566 6010
E: barrym@actrix.co.nz
W: www.bnb.co.nz/hosts/
malcolm.html

Cost: Double $80
Single $55
Child $30 Visa/MC
Beds: 1 Twin (1 bdrm)
Bath: 1 Private

Petone

We have a 97 year old home by the beach. We are two minutes from a Museum on beach, shop and bus route to the city. A restaurant is nearby. We are ten minutes from Picton Ferries. Off street parking available. Children are very welcome. Reg is a keen amateur ornithologist and goes to the Chatham Islands with an expedition trying to find the nestling place of the Taiko - a rare sea bird, on endangered list. Other interests are Genealogy and conservation. Laundry facilities are available.

Homestay
3km S of Lower Hutt
Anne & Reg Cotter
1 Bolton Street
Petone
Wellington

Tel: (04) 568 6960
Fax: (04) 568 6956
W: www.bnb.co.nz/hosts/
cotter.html

Cost: Double $60 Single $30
Child 1/2 price over 10yrs
Dinner $15 Visa/MC
Beds: 1 Double 2 Single
(2 bdrm)
Bath: 1 Family share

Petone - Korokoro

We have a large garden including a croquet lawn and Bush reserve, in a very quiet locality yet only 12 minutes to Wellington and Ferries. Easy to find. We came from England to New Zealand in 1957 and enjoy travel. Jim is a desultory woodworker with a background in machinery. Bridget teaches and is a weaver/feltmaker, working and selling from home. We enjoy visual arts, theatre, cinema, music, books and the outdoors. Your food will be home-cooked and mainly organic as we prefer an environmentally friendly lifestyle.

Korokoro Homestay	**Tel:** (04) 589 1678	**Cost:** Double $90
Homestay	**Fax:** (04) 589 2678	Single $50
2km W of Petone	**Mob:** 025 260 4948	Child & Dinner
Bridget & Jim Austin	**E:** jaustin@clear.net.nz	by arrangement Visa/MC
100 Korokoro Road	**W:** www.bnb.co.nz/hosts/	**Beds:** 1 Queen 1 Twin (2 bdrm)
Korokoro Petone	korokorohomestay.html	**Bath:** 1 Guests share

Eastbourne

Come and enjoy the peace and tranquillity of the Eastern Bays. You will be hosted in a beautifully restored 1920's settler cottage nestled amongst native bush and looking towards the Kaikoura mountains of the South Island. My love of cordon-bleu cooking and the pleasure of the table are satisfied through the use of my country kitchen and dining room. Other attractions: Outdoor spa and a Devon Rex cat. Eastbourne is a small seaside village across the harbour from Wellington city with a range of attractions.

Bush House	**Tel:** (04) 568 5250	**Cost:** Double $90
Homestay	**Fax:** (04) 568 5250	Single $60
3km N of Eastbourne	**Mob:** 025 654 5433	Dinner by arrangemet
Belinda Cattermole	**W:** www.bnb.co.nz/hosts/	**Beds:** 1 Double 1 Single
12 Waitohu Rd	bushhouse.html	(2 bdrm)
York Bay, Eastbourne		**Bath:** 1 Private 1 Family share
Wellington		

Eastbourne

Nestled between beach & bush. 20 minutes by car to Wellington. Public transport (bus and ferry) conveniently availably. Steps to the house give a panoramic view. Garage parking for one guest car. Interests: Barry & Bev retired, passionate about our two Belgian Shepherd dogs. Barry: former sales consultant, has 40 years as judge, works these dogs in obedience and agility trials. Bev: former counsellor and school dental nurse, now kennel maid, also interested in sculpture, glass painting and Seniornet (computers). Vegetarian, dinners by prior arrangement.

York Bay B&B	**Tel:** (04) 568 7104	**Cost:** Double $75-$90
B&B Homestay	**Fax:** (04) 568 7104	Single $60-$70 Child $50
10 S of Lower Hutt	**Mob:** 021 118 4191	Dinner $35 Visa/MC
Barry Monaghan & Bev Laybourn	**E:** bevlaybourn@xtra.co.nz	**Beds:** 1 King/Twin (1 bdrm)
15 Marine Drive	**W:** www.bnb.co.nz/hosts/	**Bath:** 1 Private
York Bay, Eastbourne, Wellington	yorkbaybb.html	

Eastbourne

Secluded, romantic retreat nestled in native bush above Wellington harbour. Enjoy a scenic ride in our private cablecar or wander up through ferns and beech trees. Stylish, spacious guest apartment comprises bedroom, lounge with divan, kitchenette, bath/shower/toilet. Wake to the songs of the bellbird; breakfast on your private garden patio; relax indoors with books, games, TV, radio. Sea views, guest phone/computer port. Laundry available. Stroll to picturesque beach, restaurants, charming village, bus/ferry to Central Wellington. CBD 20 minutes (ferry, car).

Treetops	**Tel:** (04) 562 7692	**Cost:** Double $95-$120
B&B Self-contained	**Fax:** (04) 562 7690	Single $95-$115
12km E of Wellington	**Mob:** 025 616 9826	$20 extra person. Visa/MC
Robyn & Roger Cooper	**E:** treetopsbnb@xtra.co.nz	**Beds:** 1 Queen (1 bdrm)
7 Huia Road	**W:** mysite.xtra.co.nz/~treetops	1 Double divan in lounge
Days Bay Eastbourne		**Bath:** 1 Private

Eastbourne

Enjoy our hospitality. Welcome to our special home. Warm, restful, peaceful, yet close to Wellington and Hutt Cities, transport, restaurants and art galleries. Play tennis on our court, stroll to the beach, walk in the bush, sail on our 28 foot yacht, or relax under a sun umbrella on the deck. Native birds abound. Our sunny, elegant bedrooms have garden views, TV, tea/coffee and central heating. We have two daughters, Isabella 18 and Kirsty 12, a cat and many interests. Laundry. Non-smoking indoors. From SH2 follow Petone signs then Eastbourne.

Lowry Bay Homestay	**Tel:** (04) 568 4407	**Cost:** Double $100-$130
B&B Homestay	**Fax:** (04) 568 2474	Single $80-$110
17km E of Wellington	**Tollfree:** 0508 266 546	Child Neg Visa/MC
Pam & Forde Clarke	**E:** forde.clarke@xtra.co.nz	**Beds:** 1 King 1 Queen 1 Single
35 Cheviot Road	**W:** www.bnb.co.nz/hosts/	(2 bdrm)
Lowry Bay, Eastbourne, Wellington	lowrybayhomestay.html	**Bath:** 1 Private

Eastbourne

Jennifer, Ken and our friendly cat Tuppence look forward to giving you a warm welcome to our home. It is nestled amongst native bush by the beach. Share with us the magical views of Wellington harbour and the city. You may wish to join us on a deck in summer, or in front of a cosy fire in winter. As non-smokers we appreciate no smoking inside. At any time we would be pleased to assist you with your stay. We hope to make your stay a memorable one. Please phone, fax or email us for directions.

Jennifer & Ken's Homestay	**Tel:** +64 4 568 4817	**Cost:** Double $75-$95
B&B Homestay	**Fax:** +64 4 568 4817	Single $60-$70 Child &
17km NE of Wellington	**Mob:** +64 25 500 670	Dinner B/A Visa/MC
Jennifer & Ken	**Tollfree:** 0800 390 385	**Beds:** 1 Double 1 Single (2 bdrm)
Marine Drive	**E:** kjackson@pop.ihug.co.nz	**Bath:** 1 Private
Sorrento Bay Eastbourne	**W:** www.bnb.co.nz/hosts/	
	jenniferkenshomestay.html	

Eastbourne

Located in quiet, leafy Lowry Bay, 3 minutes walk from the beach, The Gatehouse is part of a larger property built in 1929 by well-known architect Natusch and based on another home in Cornwall, England. The Gatehouse was formerly a coach-house until transformation in 2001 and is completely detached from the main house.

The Gatehouse offers a lounge with open fire, sofa-bed for extra guests, stereo, TV, telephone and full kitchen with tea/coffee making provisions. The bathroom has a large tiled and pebbled shower, toilet and hand-basin, heated towel-rail, beach towels and bathrobes. Upstairs overlooking the formal parterre garden and pond is the airy bedroom with super-king or twin beds, crisp cotton bed linen and feather duvets. We have lots of books, magazines and board-games available in the reading nook off the bedroom.

Breakfast is served in The Gatehouse at a time convenient to our guests.

We are 5 minutes drive from Eastbourne village, which offers galleries, gift shops, cafes and restaurants. There are also some lovely walks through native bush and along the Bays.

We are 20 minutes from Wellington and 30 minutes from the airport. Buses depart for the city at the end of the street, or you can board the ferry from Days Bay and enjoy Wellington's harbour. Transfers to and from the airport by arrangement.

Laundry service. Fax available. Off street parking. Cot, highchair and baby-sitting available.
We have four children, Bianca 12, Elliot 10, Renee 7 and Lily 3. We also have two cats and two rabbits. For your comfort we are smoke free.

The Gatehouse	**Tel:** (04) 568 7600	**Cost:** Double $195
B&B S/C Premium B&B	**Mob:** 021 527 600	Child $12.50 under 12
18km NE of Wellington	**E:** lisa@thegatehouse.co.nz	Extra Guest $25 Visa/MC
Lisa & Philip Andrew	**W:** www.bnb.co.nz/hosts/	**Beds:** 1 King/Twin (1 bdrm)
57 Cheviot Road	thegatehouse.html	**Bath:** 1 Private
Lowry Bay, Wellington		

Eastbourne

You are invited to share in the peace and tranquillity of our bush clad home overlooking Wellington Harbour. We offer cosy well appointed bedrooms with doors opening out onto a balcony. Enjoy the unique village atmosphere of Eastbourne with its restaurants, galleries, gift shops, and beach or take the harbour ferry to Wellington. Our interests are the arts, theatre and music. Wendy, Doug, our retriever cross Rosy and two cuddly cats look foward to greeting you, be assured of a warm welcome and an enjoyable stay.

Frinton by the Sea
B&B Homestay
17km E of Wellington
Wendy & Doug Stephenson
55 Rona Street
Eastbourne, Wellington

Tel: (04) 562 7540
Fax: (04) 562 7860
Mob: 025 417 365
E: frinton@voyager.co.nz
W: www.bnb.co.nz/hosts/
frintonbythesea.html

Cost: Double $90-$115
Single $70-$95
Child not suitable
Dinner on request Visa/MC
Beds: 2 Queen 1 Double (3 bdrm)
Bath: 1 Ensuite 1 Private
1 Family share

Ohariu Valley - Wellington

As the name suggests Mill Cottage is the cosy and intimate home of Bev and Cliff. We would like to invite you to experience a stay on a sheep and cattle station, 3200 acres within the Wellington city boundary. Papanui Station has Colonial Knob 1500ft at the north, Boom Rock to the south sea level, offers some most rugged coastline of New Zealand, along with great views of Cook Strait and South Island Mountains. We offer you an extreme location unique home hospitality and surroundings.

Papanui Station Farm Stay
B&B Farmstay
12km NW of Johnsonville
Bev & Cliff Inglis
Boom Rock Rd, Ohariu Valley
RD, Johnsonville
Wellington

Tel: (04) 478 8926
Mob: 025 283 0635
W: www.bnb.co.nz/hosts/
papanuistationfarmstay.html

Cost: Double $76
Single $38
Dinner $25
Beds: 1 Double 1 Twin
(2 bdrm)
Bath: 1 Guests share

Khandallah - Wellington

We are a couple who enjoy relaxing and meeting people and our particular interests are travel, sport, food, wine, and the Arts. We have a small tabby cat called Amy. Our family of 3 girls have left home, and while we both work, we are able to take time off to show guests our beautiful harbour city. Khandallah is a hillside suburb handy to all the attractions of the capital, with a village atmosphere and a ten minute bus or train ride to town. Very close to the ferry terminal. We look forward to making your stay an enjoyable one. Local Pub/Cafe within easy walking distance. Please phone and we will arrange to pick you up.

Homestay
6km N of Wellington
Genevieve and Peter Young
10A Izard Road
Khandallah Wellington

Tel: (04) 479 5036
Fax: (04) 479 5037
W: www.bnb.co.nz/hosts/
youngkhandallah.html

Cost: Double $80
Single $50
Beds: 5 Single (3 bdrm)
Bath: 1 Guestshare

Khandallah - Wellington

This is a lovely, sunny and warm open plan home with glorious harbour and city views. A quiet easily accessible street just ten minutes from the city and five minutes from the ferry. We are close to the Khandallah Village and the local "Posties Whistle" pub. Excellent food, wine and bar service. We are a non-smoking household. Another family member is an aristocratic white cat called Dali. We enjoy sharing our home with our guests.

Homestay	**Tel:** (04) 479 1180	**Cost:** Double $100
7km N of Wellington	**Fax:** (04) 479 2717	Single $70
Sue & Ted Clothier	**W:** www.bnb.co.nz/hosts/	Visa/MC Amex Diners
22 Lohia Street	clothier.html	**Beds:** 1 Twin (1 bdrm)
Khandallah		**Bath:** 1 Ensuite
Wellington		

Khandallah - Wellington

A large home filled with antiques and New Zealand art. Lovely garden with heated pool and tennis court, guests welcome to use. We enjoy golf and can arrange a game. Lovely bush walks nearby. Walk to local pub for dinner. The bedroom includes TV, tea/coffee, home baking, electric blankets, heating. Laundry facilities available. Breakfasts continental or full, with homemade jams, muffins and preserved fruit. Children at university, Buffy the cat at home. We love sports, Wellington and meeting pepole. Phone or e-mail for directions.

Khandallah Bed & Breakfast	**Tel:** (04) 479 5578	**Cost:** Double $150
B&B	**E:** fairhall@paradise.net.nz	Single $120
7km N of Wellington Central	**W:** www.bnb.co.nz/hosts/	Visa/MC
Tim & Margaret Fairhall	fairhall.html	**Beds:** 1 Twin 1 Queen
50 Clark Street		(2 bdrm)
Khandallah Wellington		**Bath:** 1 Ensuite 1 Private

Ngaio - Wellington

Our unconventional family home is in Ngaio, 5 mins to ferry terminal, 10 mins to CBD. We offer: views, sun, off street parking, quiet surroundings, 2 mins bush walk to local train station, dinner by arrangement, homely atmosphere. Children welcome. Our 2 self contained units are adjacent to our property, 1 double, 1 twin, each unit can sleep up to 4 persons. Equipped kitchen, laundry facilities, phone, Cable TV, perfect for relocating or immigrating. All accommodation is smoke free. Phone, fax, email, write for bookings.

Ngaio Homestay	**Tel:** (04) 479 5325	**Cost:** Double $95-$120
B&B Self-contained Homestay	**Fax:** (04) 479 4325	Single $75-$100 Child neg
7km NW of Wellington	**E:** jennifer.timmings@clear.net.nz	Dinner $25pp S/C $120
Jennifer & Brian Timmings	**W:** www.bnb.co.nz/hosts/	Visa/MC
56 Fox St	ngaiohomestay.html	**Beds:** 3 Double 2 Twin
Ngaio Wellington		2 Single (5 bdrm)
		Bath: 3 Ensuite 1 Private
		1 Family share

Karori - Wellington

Welcome to our home in the suburbs, easy to find from motorway or ferry terminal. Telephone and we will meet you at ferry, train, bus or air terminals. Join us for pre-dinner drinks, dine with us, or eat out at the local pub/cafe or licenced restaurant. We are close to the city on three bus routes. Make use of our laundry, large garden, spacious home, email/internet facilities. Meet Charlie our border collie dog and Honey the cat.

Campbell Homestay	**Tel:** (04) 476 6110	**Cost:** Double $85
Homestay	**Fax:** (04) 476 6593	Single $50
5km W of Wellington	**Mob:** 025 535 080	Child 1/2 price
Murray & Elaine Campbell	**E:** ctool@ihug.co.nz	Dinner $25 Visa/MC
83 Campbell Street	**W:** www.bnb.co.nz/hosts/	**Beds:** 1 Queen 1 Twin 3 Single
Karori	campbellhomestay.html	(3 bdrm)
Wellington		**Bath:** 1 Guests share

Wadestown - Wellington

A short walk to Otari Native Botanic Gardens and bus from door to central city 10 minutes. Own bathroom, separate lounge if preferred, electric blankets and heaters. Share the fireside in the evening with the host and Persian cat or attend some of the varied activities in the 'Cultural Capital'. Gardening, embroidery, playing the cello and mahjong are some of the interests the host enjoys. Visitors can be collected form the ferry etc. Parking on the street. Phone for directions.

Homestay	**Tel:** (04) 499 6602	**Cost:** Single $60
5km W of Wellingtom	**Fax:** (04) 473 7332	Visa/MC
Julie Foley	**Mob:** 025 203 2228	**Beds:** 1 Twin 1 Single (2 bdrm)
72 Wilton Road	**W:** www.bnb.co.nz/hosts/	**Bath:** 1 Guests share
Wadestown	foley.html	
Wellington		

Kelburn - Wellington Central

"Rawhiti", meaning sunrise, is a charming 1905 two-storeyed home with magnificent views overlooking city and harbour. With only a 2 minute walk to the top of the cable car taking you directly into city centre, provides easy access to city and tourist attractions, plus Victoria University and the beautiful Botanic Gardens for a leisurely stroll into city. Both bedrooms with their windows on harbour and city, have comfortable beds, quality linen and complimentary coffee/tea, mineral water. A full gourmet breakfast is offered. Good library and parking available. Request: No smoking indoors.

'Rawhiti'	**Tel:** (04) 934 4859	**Cost:** Double $125-$200
Boutique B&B	**Fax:** (04) 972 4859	Single $125-$200 Visa/MC
1km W of Wellington Central	**Mob:** 025 276 8240	**Beds:** 1 King 1 Double
Annabel Leask	**E:** rawhiti@paradise.net.nz	(2 bdrm)
40 Rawhiti Terrace	**W:** www.bnb.co.nz/hosts/	**Bath:** 1 Ensuite 1 Family share
Kelburn Wellington	rawhiti.html	

Kelburn - Wellington Central

Nestled on a private section amongst native trees, Ruby House offers guests a perfect balance of luxury, privacy and location.

This villa style guesthouse boasts three spacious, beautifully appointed rooms that provide the essential ingredients for a luxurious stay in the capital city - firm comfortable beds, antique furniture, private ensuite bathrooms, private telephone and modem lines.

The self contained rooms have been purpose built for maximum privacy, and entry is via security keypad at the front door.

Guests may request a country style bathroom with claw foot bath and French doors opening on a courtyard, a sunny loft bedroom or an elegant room with sash hung windows and stained glass.

A fourth self contained room with private entrance is also available in the base of the owner's house. Ruby House has all the elements of a secluded executive holiday retreat - yet it is just around the corner from Victoria University and only a short stroll from Wellington's CBD and the shopping plus entertainment precincts.

Ruby House is only 2 minutes walk to the Cable Car - which takes you directly into Lambton Quay (main street). Non-smoking/children welcome by arrangement/secure car parking/please phone for directions.
www.rubyhouse.co.nz

Ruby House
Boutique B&B
1km W of Wellington Central
Elizabeth Barbalich
35 Rawhiti Terrace
14B Kelburn Parade
Wellington

Tel: (04) 934 7930
Fax: (04) 934 7935
Mob: 021 483 980
E: elizabeth@rubyhouse.co.nz
W: www.rubyhouse.co.nz

Cost: Double $165 Child $30
Long term, weekly rates,
House rates avaliable.
Children neg
Visa/MC Amex Diners
Beds: 1 King/Twin 2 King
1 Queen (4 bdrm)
Bath: 4 Ensuite

Wellington Central

Elegant, historic English house in a commanding position, enjoying panoramic views of city and harbour. 2 minutes walk to the CBD or short stroll to the cable car. Across the road from Botanical Gardens and charming Thorndon. Fully restored, this Georgian home is relaxed and inviting. All guests rooms with ensuites, or private bathroom and stunning sea views. Facilities include private guest lounge, television, music, tea and coffee facilities, library, laundry, terrace and garden. Secure off-street parking.

29 Salamanca B&B
B&B
1km W of Wellington Central
Sandra & Keith Brown
29 Salamanca Road
Kelburn, Wellington

Tel: (04) 473 1800
Fax: (04) 473 1800
Mob: 025 516 363
E: belle.holdings@xtra.co.nz
W: www.bnb.co.nz/hosts/
salamanca.html

Cost: Double $150 $180 $250
Single $100 Visa/MC
Beds: 4 Queen 1 Double
(5 bdrm)
Bath: 3 Ensuite 2 Private

Kelburn - Wellington Central

Our modern hillside home overlooks a native bush reserve. Just 5 minutes drive from central Wellington, the motorway and Inter-Island Ferry terminal, we are within easy walking distance of several excellent restaurants and cafés. The Cable Car, Botanic Gardens, and Karori Wildlife Sanctuary are also a short walk. Join us for a delicious continental breakfast, including waffles and maple syrup. Tea/coffee-making facilities. TV in rooms. E-mail access. Courtesy car from/to ferry. Smokefree home. We have a small fox terrier named Patsy.

Rangiora B&B
B&B
2KM W of City Central
Lesley and Malcolm Shaw
177 Glenmore Street
Kelburn Wellington 6005

Tel: (04) 475 9888
E: rangiora.bnb@xtra.co.nz
W: www.bnb.co.nz/hosts/
rangiora.html

Cost: Double $100
Single $90
Visa/MC
Beds: 1 Queen 1 Double
(2 bdrm)
Bath: 1 Guests share

Wellington Central

'Talavera', a no share apartment, situated on the upper level of an inner city villa, with its own entrance and staircase, offers wonderful city/harbour views, comfort and privacy; is close to all amenities, with the Cable Car nearby. Quality beds with cotton linen. Bathroom - deep claw foot bath with shower over - heated towel rail and toiletries. Spacious living area with Sky TV. Breakfast downstairs with hosts. Freshly squeezed juice, fruits, honey granola, variety omelettes, croissants, breads, espresso coffee.Garage parking available. Adult children welcome.

Talavera
B&B Serviced Apartment
0.5km W of Wellington Central
Bobbie Littlejohn
7 Talavera Terrace
Wellington Central

Tel: (04) 471 0555
Fax: (04) 471 0551
W: www.bnb.co.nz/hosts/
talavera.html

Cost: Double $150 Single $135
$35 extra person
Visa/MC
Beds: 1 Queen 2 Single
(2 bdrm)
Bath: 1 Private

Thorndon - Wellington Central

Located in Wellington's most historic part of town Thorndon "Eight Parliament Street" a serviced/self-contained B&B is in walking distance to most of the Capital's attractions: The cable car, Botanical Gardens, Te Papa, Parliament Buildings, Cafes and Restaurants. The traveller will find a home away from home with stylish interior (NZ Artwork), relaxing features (sunny courtyard, quiet location), convenient details (espresso machine, fax, video, and laundry service) and a delicious breakfast for all taste buds. Whole house rental available, no smoking premises, children over 12 years welcome.

Eight Parliament Street	**Tel:** (04) 499 0808	**Cost:** Double $155
B&B Self-contained	**Fax:** (04) 479 6705	Single $120
0.5km N of Wellington	**Mob:** 025 280 6739	$270 house rate Visa/MC
Christine Grasenack - Voelker	**E:** Christine@boutique-bb.co.nz	**Beds:** 3 Queen (3 bdrm)
8 Parliament Street	**W:** www.boutique-bb.co.nz	**Bath:** 1 Ensuite 1 Private
Thorndon, Wellington		

Thorndon - Wellington Central

A stylish private, studio with great views of Wellington Harbour. The setting is a magnificent restored Victorian home surrounded by bush. Thorndon Views is a ten-minute walk to the CBD, close to the Inter-island Ferry. Bush walks on your doorstep lead to breathtaking vistas of the harbour. Facilities include ensuite bathroom with warm towels and hairdryer, cooking facilities, cable TV, spa and Internet access. Healthy continental breakfast with a selection of breads, croissants, freshly brewed coffee, fresh fruit and yogurt.

Thorndon Views	**Tel:** (04) 938 0783	**Cost:** Double $115
B&B Self-contained	**Fax:** (04) 938 0784	Single $90
1km W of Wellington Central	**Mob:** 025 284 7996	Child $15
Janelle & David	**E:** janelle@xtra.co.nz	**Beds:** 1 Queen 1 Double
37 Newman Terrace	**W:** mysite.xtra.co.nz/	(1 bdrm)
Thorndon Wellington	~thorndonviews	**Bath:** 1 Private

Oriental Bay - Wellington Central

Oriental Bay is perhaps the finest location in Wellington. No 11 has an intimate view of the city and is an easy stroll to Te Papa: the Museum of New Zealand, the City Art Gallery, all the major theatres and cinemas, great restaurants and cafes. Virginia has extensive knowledge of what's going on, and where to go. The accommodation is in a comfortable room for two, with bathroom adjacent, electric blankets and tea & coffee facilities. Breakfast will be an occasion. Cat in residence.

No 11	**Tel:** (04) 801 9290	**Cost:** Double $120
B&B	**Fax:** (04) 801 9295	Single $95
0.75km N of Wellington	**W:** www.bnb.co.nz/hosts/	Visa/MC
Virginia Barton-Chapple	noorientalbay.html	**Beds:** 1 King/Twin (1 bdrm)
11 Hay Street		**Bath:** 1 Guests share
Oriental Bay Wellington		

Mt Victoria - Wellington Central

Our comfortable, gracious, Victorian home is five minutes from Courtenay Place, with its cafes, theatres, galleries, and even closer to Te Papa our National Museum and lovely Oriental Bay. Our large guest room upstairs with veranda alongside, includes comfortable chairs, tables, TV, tea making facilities and robes. MacFarlane Street is quiet in contrast to all the excitement of Courtenay place. We have interests in the arts, architecture and all that our beautiful harbour city offers. Enjoy super breakfasts, help in planning sightseeing, and Fiji our non-obtrusive cat.

The Cherry Tree	**Tel:** (04) 801 5080	**Cost:** Double $130
Homestay	**Fax:** (04) 801 5252	Single $100
Margaret & Frits Bergman	**Mob:** 025 200 1592	**Beds:** 1 Queen 1 Single
9 Macfarlane Street	**W:** www.bnb.co.nz/hosts/	(1 bdrm)
Mt Victoria	thecherrytree.html	**Bath:** 1 Private
Wellington		

Mt Victoria - Wellington Central

WELCOME TO VILLA VITTORIO. Centrally located close by Courtenay Place. Short walk to restaurants, theatres, shopping, conference centres, Te Papa Museum, Parliament and Stadium. Guest bedroom with TV, tea and coffee facilities. Adjoining sitting room with balcony overlooking city. Bathroom with shower and bath. Breakfast served in Italian styled dining room or outside in courtyard. We enjoy having guests, having travelled extensively ourselves. Transport and gourmet dinner by arrangement. Garaging and laundry at small charge. No children or pets. Direction: Phone, fax, email or write.

Villa Vittorio	**Tel:** (04) 801 5761	**Cost:** Double $130-$160
B&B Homestay	**Fax:** (04) 801 5762	Single $110-$125
0.5km E of Central Wellington	**Mob:** 025 321 267	Dinner from $40
Annette & Logan Russell	**E:** l&a@villavittorio.co.nz	Visa/MC Amex Diners
6 Hawker Street	**W:** www.villavittorio.co.nz	**Beds:** 1 Double (1 bdrm)
Mt Victoria Wellington		**Bath:** 1 Private

Mt Victoria - Wellington Central

Dream Catcher is a renovated spacious Victorian house in central, picturesque historic Mount Victoria, only 5 minutes stroll from Wellington's day/night vibrant attractions. Quality accommodations available: 1) "VIP Suite" - private livingroom, double bedroom and ensuite. 2) "Upstairs" - a self contained 2nd storey includes two bedrooms, guests shared bathroom, deck, verandah, living/kitchen, sun, and city views. Taly, John, their teenage daughter and two cats, keen travellers themselves, welcome the city visitor to enjoy the relaxed comfort of home, and the fresh generous breakfasts in the main kitchen or the back garden.

Dream Catcher - Arts &	**Tel:** (04) 801 9363	**Cost:** Double $110-$130
Accommodation	**Mob:** 021 210 6762	Single $90-$110 Child $40
B&B Homestay	**W:** www.bnb.co.nz/hosts/	Visa/MC
Wellington Central	dreamcatcher.html	**Beds:** 1 Queen 2 Double 2 Single
Taly & John Hoekman		(3 bdrm)
56 Pirie Street		**Bath:** 1 Ensuite 1 Guests share
Mt Victoria Wellington		

Mt Victoria - Wellington Central

Our comfortable self- contained studio is relaxing and private. We are a few minutes by foot to Courtenay Place (Wellington's restaurant, cafe and theatre district) and Te Papa. Our studio has an ensuite, TV and external access so you can come and go at your own leisure. Breakfast, you can make in your own time at the kitchenette while browsing through the provided paper. Laundry facilites are available. Andrew works in the banking industry and Kate looks after our young child. Our studio is smoke free.

Austin Street B&B
Self-contained
Wellington Central
Andrew & Kate Chapman
103 Austin Street
Mt Victoria Wellington

Tel: (04) 385 8384
Fax: (04) 385 8374
Mob: 021 385 833
W: www.bnb.co.nz/hosts/
austinstreetbb.html

Cost: Double $125
    Single $125
    Visa/MC
Beds: 1 Queen (1 bdrm)
Bath: 1 Ensuite

Mt Victoria - Wellington Central

We welcome you to share Scarborough House, our modern centrally-heated home in a quiet, sunny Mt Vic street with views over the city, close to Courtenay Place with its many restaurants and night life, Te Papa Museum, Westpac Stadium and the waterfront. Option of king, queen or twin accommodation. Tea/coffee, hairdryer, bathrobes,Sky TV; garaging and laundry available. Our interests include travel, skiing, golf and many of the activities our magnificent city offers. Children over 12 welcome; we are smokefree.

Scarborough House
B&B Homestay
Wellington Central
Sue Hiles & Miles Davidson
36 Scarborough Tce
Mt Victoria Wellington

Tel: 0064 4 801 8534
Fax: 0064 4 801 8536
Mob: 025 501 346
E: info@scarborough-house.co.nz
W: www.scarborough-
house.co.nz

Cost: Double $125-$140
    Single $120 Child $50
    Visa/MC
Beds: 1 King/Twin 1 Queen
    (2 bdrm)
Bath: 1 Private

Mt Cook - Wellington Central

Welcome to our home. It has character, charm, central heating and has great city and harbour views. Guest accommodation is private, comfortable, sunny and spacious. Tea/coffee/laundry facilities available. Excellent location with only 5 minute strolls to the centre of the city and all its attractions. Ten minutes to Te Papa, The Stadium, Ferry terminals and Wellington Hospital. Massey University just across the road. Off street parking. Bus stop almost at the door. Please use our sheltered courtyard for outdoor living and smoking. French and German spoken.

Homestay
Wellington Central
Roy & Gwen Carré
2 Wallace Street
Mt Cook Wellington

Tel: (04) 384 3828
Fax: (04) 385 7949
E: homestay@hotmail.com
W: www.bnb.co.nz/hosts/carr.html

Cost: Double $110-$130
    Single $100
Beds: 1 Queen 1 Double
    1 Twin (3 bdrm)
Bath: 1 Guests share
    1 Family share

Roseneath - Wellington

This boutique guesthouse is 5 minutes drive from Wellington city, 10 minutes drive from the airport and on the No. 14 bus route. The house offers comfortable hospitality and elegance. Each bedroom opens on to a wide deck, offering expansive views of Wellington harbour. Pleasantly decorated rooms feature quality beds and linen. There is a choice of a double bedroom and/or share twin room, separate guest's bathroom with shower and spa bath. Harbourview is situated in a peaceful setting close to the city, catering for Businesspeople, Tourists and Honeymooners.

Harbourview Homestay
B&B Homestay
3km E of Wellington
Hilda & Geoff Stedman
125 Te Anau Road
Roseneath Wellington

Tel: (04) 386 1043
Tollfree: 0800 0800 78
E: hildastedman@clear.net.nz
W: www.bnb.co.nz/hosts/
harbourviewhomestayandbb.html

Cost: Double $110-$120
Single $75-$90
Dinner $35 Visa/MC
Beds: 1 Double 2 Single
(2 bdrm)
Bath: 2 Private

Roseneath - Wellington

Our grand colonial home sits in a prime location overlooking the harbour and city, and captures all day sun. Walk along the sparkling waterfront to the CBD or Te Papa Museum, visit art galleries, shops or enjoy the local restaurants and cafes. If you want solitude, your room is large enough to lounge in all day! Fully furnished rooms include lounge chairs, desk, TV, stereo, tea and coffee facilities. Guests facilities also include large lounge with log fire, minstrel's gallery, sheltered garden, verandah, off-street parking. Meals/snack by arrangement.

70 The Crescent Homestay
B&B Homestay
1km E of Wellington central
Janice George & Tony Owen
70 The Crescent
Roseneath Wellington

Tel: (04) 385 0001
Fax: (04) 385 0003
E: belle.holdings@xtra.co.nz
W: www.bnb.co.nz/hosts/
70thecrescent.html

Cost: Double $120 $140 $160
Single $95 Visa/MC
Beds: 1 Queen 3 Double
1 Single (5 bdrm)
Bath: 1 Ensuite 1 Guests share
1 Private

Hataitai - Wellington

Hataitai ('breath of the ocean') is a popular suburb midway between the Airport and central Wellington. City attractions are 5-10 minutes by bus or car. Our comfortable family home of 60 years is a welcome retreat for guests. The studio is fully equipped, including cable television and phone. Long term rates available. We share a range of cultural interests; have travelled widely, and will be glad to help you make the most of your visit to Wellington. Smoke free inside. Not suitable for young children.

Top O' T'ill
B&B Self-contained Homestay
3km E of Wellington CBD
Cathryn & Dennis Riley
2 Waitoa Rd
Hataitai Wellington 6003

Tel: (04) 386 2718
Fax: (04) 386 2719
Mob: 025 495 410
E: top.o.hill@xtra.co.nz
W: www.bnb.co.nz/hosts/
topotill.html

Cost: Double $85-$120
Single $55-$110
Visa/MC
Beds: 2 Queen 1 Twin
1 Single (4 bdrm)
Bath: 2 Ensuite 1 Private
1 Guests share

Hataitai - Wellington

Matai House takes its name from its surroundings. Matai, translated from Maori, means "gaze out to sea".

Built in 1913, this fine two storey villa is conveniently located in the Eastern inner suburb of Hataitai, between the airport and city. A quiet residential area with great sea views and a small garden of New Zealand native plants. City bus is just a 300m walk. Off-street car parking available.

The purpose-built guest suites are refurbished in harmony with the era of the home and have French doors opening onto a large deck overlooking the garden and sea views and access a lounge with private entrance. Each room is tastefully decorated, heavenly king sized beds, with a thick pillow-top mattress, crisp linen, goose down covers and plump pillows. Each rooms own bathroom features hairdryer, toiletries, bathrobes and heated towel rails. Tea and coffee making facilities, fridge, laundry and ironing facilities. Fresh flowers.

Breakfast includes espresso coffee, homemade muesli, fruit and cooked options at a time to suit. Enjoy an open fire in winter.

Telephone, fax, e-mail facilities available.

<u>Features and Attractions:</u>
- Extensive sea views
- City 4 mins, airport 5 mins
- Ferry 8 mins drive
- Delicious full breakfast
- Espresso coffee
- 20 channel cable TV
- Suites adjoin guest lounge

<u>Guest comments:</u>
"Very beautiful accommodation. Really enjoyed the room and view, as well as all the nice little extras. We appreciated the wonderful hospitality."
Mark & Jessica, Waipahu, Hawaii USA

"Thank you Raema and Rex for a delightful visit. Our stay with you has been one the highlights of our tour of New Zealand" Jon & Linda, Oakland, California, USA

<u>Directions:</u>   On State Highway One follow the airport signs until exiting Mt Victoria tunnel (2nd Tunnel), drive ahead into Hataitai, turn left & then right into Waitoa Road. Drive up Waitoa & second left into Matai Road. From airport on Highway One turn right at first lights into Evans Bay Parade, 2nd left into Rata Road, left & left again into Matai Road.

Matai House	**Tel:** (04) 934 6985	**Cost:** Double $170
B&B	**Fax:** (04) 934 6987	Single $150
3km E of Central Wellington	**E:** matai@paradise.net.nz	Visa/MC Amex Diners
Raema & Rex Collins	**W:** www.bnb.co.nz/hosts/	**Beds:** 2 King (2 bdrm)
41 Matai Road	mataihouse.html	**Bath:** 2 Ensuite
Hataitai		
Wellington 6003		

Melrose - Wellington

Large sunny home with spectacular scenery and beautiful
views over Wellington, Cook Strait and Mountains. New
tastefully decorated, private entrance, 1 Bedroom, self
contained, double flat with private balcony, T.V, tiled
Conservatory, fridge and microwave. Surf or swim at our
safe local beach. Close to hospitals. We are interested in
food, wine, travel, relaxing and meeting people. Willy is a
nurse, enjoys cooking, gardening and speaks Dutch. Kerry
has travelled and has a background with animals, is retired
and enjoys bowling. No children at home.

Buckley Homestay
B&B Self-contained Homestay
8 km S of Wellington Central
Kerry and Willy Muller
51 Buckley Road
Melrose Wellington

Tel: (04) 934 7151
Mob: 025 607 1853
E: kandwmuller@paradise.net.nz
W: www.bnb.co.nz/hosts/
buckley.html

Cost: Double $95
Dinner B/A
Visa/MC
Beds: 1 Double (1 bdrm)
Bath: 1 Private

Brooklyn (city end) - Wellington

Stay at 'Karepa' our sunny, spacious home overlooking city, harbour and mountains. The secluded rear
garden adjoins native bush. Private guest rooms have
TV, and tea/coffee facilities. City 5 minutes, ferry 10
and airport 15. Residents of 18 years, ex UK, we
have travelled widely, play golf and tennis, and enjoy
Wellington's many attractions. Ann gardens and Tom
watches from his deckchair. On-site parking. Bus at
door. Laundry facilities. Sorry, no smokers or pets.
Please phone/fax for directions.

Karepa
Homestay
3km SW of Wellington City Centre
Ann and Tom Hodgson
56 Karepa Street
Brooklyn Wellington

Tel: (04) 384 4193
Fax: (04) 384 4180
Mob: 025 KAREPA
E: golf@xtra.co.nz
W: www.holidayletting.co.nz/
karepa

Cost: Double $100-$135
Single $80-$110 Child $25
Dinner $30 B/A Visa/MC
Beds: 2 King 1 Double 1 Single
(3 bdrm)
Bath: 1 Ensuite 1 Guests share

Brooklyn - Wellington

Our elegant and spacious character home overlooking
city, harbour and mountains is situated only minutes
strolling from Wellington Art and Cultural centres;
where you can enjoy shopping, galleries, Te Papa
museum, cinemas and the city's many restaurants.
You will enjoy your room which is luxurious and
comfortable and offers spectacular harbour views
from the bay windows.

Our home has been exquisitely decorated with art,
Persian rugs and tapestries from all over the world.
Feel free to visit our New Zealand wine library,
situated in the cellar of the house.

Our guests are served a lovely breakfast, presented in
the sunny breakfast room, having a choice of
continental and cooked breakfasts.

Dinner by appointment only and prepared by our mad
Italian chef. You find us well travelled and conversant
on langauges and many topics of interest.

Tuscany
Homestay
3km S of Wellington Central
Natasha May
11 Heaton Terrace
Brooklyn
Wellington

Tel: (04) 381 3788
E: vlads@paradise.net.nz
W: www.bnb.co.nz/hosts/
heatonsquare.html

Cost: Double $130
    Dinner from $40
    Visa/MC Amex Diners
Beds: 1 King/Twin 1 Queen
    (3 bdrm)
Bath: 2 Private

Brooklyn City Side - Wellington

Choose personal hospitality, city centre 5 minutes - travellers
and business visitors welcome. Striking new architecturally
designed home with stunning harbour and bush vistas. Relax
or work in warm peaceful surroundings. City and bush
walks, transport handy. Drive-on parking; well-equipped
private guest-room; luxury bathroom (shower and double
bath); own deck. Guidance available on restaurant selection
and local attractions - our interests include travel, visual and
performing arts, architecture, art glass, deco design, ceramics.
Rail/road/ferry/air-terminal pick-ups, laundry, room service,
internet.

Quintessential Wellington	**Tel:** +64 4 380 1982	**Cost:** Double $120
B&B Homestay	**Fax:** +64 4 380 1985	Single $100
2.5km S of Wellington central	**Mob:** 025 243 5674	Dinner B/A Visa/MC
Georgie Jones	**E:** georgie.jones@xtra.co.nz	**Beds:** 1 Queen 1 Single
2A Coolidge Street	**W:** www.bnb.co.nz/hosts/	(1 bdrm)
Brooklyn Wellington	quintessentialwellington.html	**Bath:** 1 Private

Vogeltown - Wellington

Vogeltown is a quiet suburb 10-15 minutes from airport and
ferry. The city's many attractions are easily reached by bus
or car. Two comfortable twin rooms share a guest bathroom
and look out onto a private, sunny deck. Originally from
northern England, I've lived in Wellington for many years
and enjoy sharing my home and knowledge of the city with
visitors. I've travelled extensively around NZ and tramped
most of the major tracks. The house is smoke-free. Well-
behaved children and pets welcome. Laundry facilities.

Vogeltown Homestay	**Tel:** (04) 934 2004	**Cost:** Double $80
Homestay	**Fax:** (04) 934 2004	Single $45
3km S of Wellington Central	**E:** valerie.tait@paradise.net.nz	Visa/MC
Valerie Tait	**W:** www.bnb.co.nz/hosts/	**Beds:** 4 Single (2 bdrm)
14 Krull Street	vogeltownhomestay.html	**Bath:** 1 Guests share
Vogeltown Wellington		

Breaker Bay - Wellington

Just 12 minutes from the city and 5 minutes from the
airport, Breaker Bay Homestay offers you a coastal retreat
in a friendly community. The view is stunning, looking over
the entrance to Wellington Harbour and watching the ships.
We are delighted to welcome visitors, as do our 3 cats, in
their own inimitable ways. Just relax, walk or explore
Wellington's many attractions – restaurants, Te Papa, art
gallerys, shopping, sporting facilities. We offer you
breakfast of your choice and can provide dinner if required.
Smokefree.

Breaker Bay Homestay	**Tel:** (04) 972 3043	**Cost:** Double $100-$120
Homestay	**Fax:** (04) 972 3046	Single $80-$100 Visa/MC
10km SE of City Central	**Mob:** 025 455 624	**Beds:** 1 King/Twin 1 Queen
Sheridan & Graham Evans	**E:** breakerbay@paradise.net.nz	(2 bdrm)
115 Breaker Bay Road	**W:** www.bnb.co.nz/hosts/	**Bath:** 1 Guests share
Seatoun	breakerbay.html	

Karaka Bay - Wellington

Edgewater is situated on the seafront at Karaka Bay, Seatoun.

Only 10 minutes from Wellington City and Airport. Featuring expansive ocean views, this mediterranean-style home offers 4 airy guest bedrooms with peaked cedar ceilings beneath seperate roofs.

Stella serves fresh fruits, homemade breads, pancakes and egg dishes for breakfast in the dining room or alfresco on the guest balcony in the morning sun. Dinner is also offered, specialising in premium quality meats, seafood and game.

As ex-owner/chef of an award winning Wellington Restaurant, Stella's motto is "fresh is best".

We have a tabby cat and a small scruffy dog. Please phone, fax or email for directions.

Edge Water Boutique Homestay
Homestay
5km S of Wellington
Stella & Colin Lovering
459 Karaka Bay Rd
Seatoun
Wellington

Tel: (04) 388 4446
Fax: (04) 388 4446
Mob: (021) 613 357
E: edgewaterwellington@xtra.co.nz
W: www.edgewaterwellington.co.nz

Cost: Double $160-$250
Single $140-$220
Dinner $60 wines extra
Off Peak rates apply
Visa/MC Amex
Beds: 1 King/Twin 2 King
1 Queen (4 bdrm)
Bath: 4 Ensuite

Seatoun - Wellington

Although handy to Wellington Airport (3 kms away) our modern home is located in a quiet seaside village. A warm welcome awaits you in a home away from home. Choice of restaurants nearby. Flat off street parking. Laundry facilities available. Directions: Entering Wellington from the north follow the signs to the Airport then the signs to Seatoun. Monro Street is the second street on the left after the shops. From the Airport first turn right then as above. Bus stop one minute, frequent service.

Francesca's
B&B Homestay
9km S of Wellington
Frances Drewell
10 Monro Street
Seatoun Wellington

Tel: (04) 388 6719
Fax: (04) 388 6719
W: www.bnb.co.nz/hosts/
francescas.html

Cost: Double $80 Single $50
    Child $25 Dinner $25 B/A
    Visa/MC
Beds: 1 Double 2 Single
    (2 bdrm)
Bath: 1 Guests share

Palmer Head - Wellington

Relax in my lovely sunny home and enjoy the magic views of Wellington - South Island to Inner Harbour. I'm only 5 mins from the airport and 10 mins to the city, and for the energetic a golf course, aquatic centre, and walking tracks are nearby. Enjoy at your leisure a continental breakfast (cooked on request) on the deck. I would be delighted to have you as my guest and welcome house trained kids and dogs. Smoke free inside, centrally heated. Laundry facilities if required.

Birkhall House
B&B
6km S of Wellington
Jocelyn Scown
14 Birkhall Grove
Palmer Head
Wellington 6003

Tel: (04) 388 2881
Fax: (04) 388 2833
Mob: 025 762 870
E:jocelyn.scown@nz.towerlimited.com
W: www.bnb.co.nz/hosts/
birkhallhouse.html

Cost: Double $85-$110
Beds: 1 King 2 Single (2 bdrm)
Bath: 1 Guests share

Island Bay - Wellington

Island Bay - 10 minutes city centre, 10 minutes airport, 20 minutes ferry terminal. The Lighthouse is on the South coast and has views of the island, fishing boats in the bay, the beach and rocks, the far coastline, the open sea, the shipping and, on a clear day, the South Island. There are local shops and restaurants. The Lighthouse has a kitchen and bathroom on the first floor, the bedroom/sitting room on the middle floor and the lookout/bedroom on the top. Romantic.

The Lighthouse
B&B Self-contained
Bruce Stokell
326 The Esplanade
Island Bay
Wellington

Tel: (04) 472 4177
Fax: (04) 472 4177
Mob: 025 425 555
E: bruce@sportwork.co.nz
W: www.bnb.co.nz/hosts/
thelighthouse.html

Cost: Double $150-$180
Beds: 1 Double (2 bdrm)
Bath: 1 Private

GERALD BULL '91.

Island Bay - Wellington

We live in an eleven year old Lockwood house, at the end of High Street in a very private section. Our land goes three quarters of the way up the hill and above that is Town Belt.

Wonderful views, overlooking the Cook Strait with its Ferries, Cargo and Fishing boats on the move day and night. We see planes landing or taking off (depending on wind direction) but the airport is round a corner and we get no noise from it.

We only let two of our rooms and each has its own private bathroom, just outside the bedroom door. TV in rooms. A warm, comfortable smokefree home with warm clean comfortable beds and two warm owners who enjoy meeting people.

We do our best to provide good, old fashioned Homestay, without charging the earth!

We have two lovely Moggies.

Regrets we cannot accept bookings from guests arriving from Australia on the midnight arrivals or guests leaving on the 6 AM departures.

Directions: From State Highway 1 or 2 take the Aotea Quay turnoff. (From the Ferry take the City exit). Follow the main road which bears slightly to the left until you come to a T junction (Oriental Parade). Turn right in to Kent Terrace and get in the right hand lane before going round the Basin Reserve (cricket ground) and in to Adelaide Road. Keep going straight, up the hill and the road becomes The Parade. Keep going until you reach the sea and then turn right into Beach Street. Left and left again in to High Street and up the private road at the end. From Wellington Airport: Take the rear exit (past the cargo warehouses) and turn right. Follow the coast road for ten minutes and Beach Street is on the right. For the Navigator we live at - Lat. S.41.20.54   Long E.174.45.54. Not suitable for children under 14. Full Breakfast 7.30 AM onwards.

Island Bay Homestay
Homestay
Wellington
Theresa & Jack Stokes
52 High Street
Island Bay
Wellington 6002

Tel: (04) 970 3353
Fax: (04) 970 3353
Tollfree: 0800 335 383
E: tandjstokes@paradise.net.nz
W: www.bnb.co.nz/hosts/
islandbayhomestay.html

Cost: Double $70
Single $45
Beds: 2 Double (2 bdrm)
Bath: 2 Private

Chatham Islands

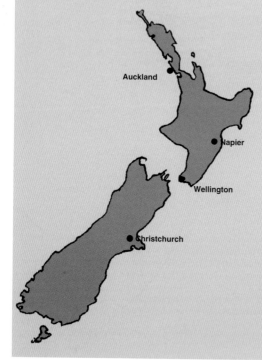

Chatham Islands

Chatham Islands

Relax in our natural wood home which is situated in eighty acres of bush on lagoon edge with mown walkways throughout. The lagoon is ideal for swimming and fishing and has nice sandy beaches. Farm activities and kayaks available.

Guests may meal with family or in separate dining room. Bedrooms are separated from main house by covered swimming pool and home gym area. We are a non smoking household; so request guests to refrain from doing so in our home. We have two cats and a host of domestic farm animals.

Farmstay
Pat & Wendy Smith
PO Box 63
Te Matarae
Chatham Islands

Tel: (03) 305 0144
Fax: (03) 305 0144
W: www.bnb.co.nz/hosts/
smithchathamislands.html

Cost: Double $85
    Single $73 Dinner $25
Beds: 2 Queen 2 Single
    (3 bdrm)
Bath: 2 Ensuite 1 Family share

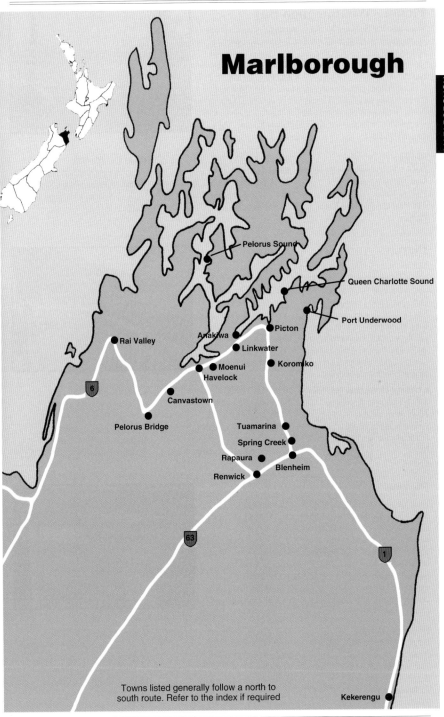

Marlborough

Pelorus Sound

Queen Charlotte Sound

Port Underwood

Rai Valley

Anakiwa

Picton

Linkwater

Moenui

Koromiko

Havelock

Canvastown

Pelorus Bridge

Tuamarina

Spring Creek

Rapaura

Blenheim

Renwick

Kekerengu

Towns listed generally follow a north to
south route. Refer to the index if required

Picton - Whatamango Bay

Welcome to "Seaview". Set in peaceful surroundings, 10 minutes by road from the Ferry Terminal, our apartments are comfortable and private with extensive views over Queen Charlotte Sound. A short walk to the beach. Relax, fish, or take the 1 km stroll to the historic Maori pits. A cafe/bar is close by. Join us in the morning when a full breakfast is served. Directions: Follow Waikawa road from the round-a-bout in the middle of Picton for approximately 8 kms. Sign at bottom of drive.

Seaview
B&B Self-contained Homestay
9km NE of Picton
Pam & John
424 Port Underwood Road
Picton

Tel: (03) 573 7783
Fax: (03) 573 7783
E: pamjohn@xtra.co.nz
W: www.bnb.co.nz/hosts/
seaviewpicton.html

Cost: Double $80
Single $40 Dinner $25
Beds: 1 Queen 1 Double
2 Single (3 bdrm)
Bath: 3 Private

Picton - Anakiwa

Our home at the head of Queen Charlotte Sound has a magnificent view, this tranquil and peaceful area is noted for bush walks, bird life, boating and kayaking. Our warm and comfortable self-contained guest area has twin bedroom, sunny lounge, private bathroom and fully equipped kitchen. Ross is a wood turner and Leslie a potter, both are happy to demonstrate their skills and their Gallery is open every day. Jack Russell terrier, Lofty, enjoys fishing trips in the motor launch as much as his owners do.

Crafters Homestay &Gallery
Self-contained Homestay
22km W of Picton
Leslie & Ross Close
Anakiwa Road
RD 1
Picton

Tel: (03) 574 2547
Fax: (03) 574 2547
Mob: 025 231 2245
E: crafters@actrix.gen.nz
W: www.bnb.co.nz/hosts/
craftershomestaygallery.html

Cost: Double $85
Single $50
Dinner $25 B/A
Visa/MC Amex
Beds: 2 Single (1 bdrm)
Bath: 1 Private

Picton

Built in 1860 and surrounded by a sprawling garden that is situated in the heart of Picton, yet very secluded and peaceful. Scandinavian creativity and NZ hospitality is blended into a colourful and vibrant home with a difference. As Birgite is a Masterweaver, House of Glenora incorporates the International Weaving School, studio and gallery. The large bedrooms offer extensive living areas, wide sunny verandas and patios are decorated with a stunning mixture of antiques and contemporary pieces.

House of Glenora
B&B Homestay Historic
Homestay
Picton Central
Birgite Armstrong
22 Broadway
Picton

Tel: (03) 573 6966
Fax: (03) 573 7735
Mob: 025 229 0594
E: glenora.house@clear.net.nz
W: www.glenora.co.nz

Cost: Double $95-$130
Single $60-$85 Visa/MC
Beds: 3 Queen 3 Double
3 Single (6 bdrm)
Bath: 2 Ensuite 1 Private
1 Guests share

Picton

'RETREAT INN' is an ideal spot to 'recharge' the travel weary! Nestled on a hillside, surrounded by natural vegetation (& native birds), it is quiet & restful ..... & only 1km from the quaint waterside village of Picton. Cosy guest bedrooms are upstairs, facing the sun.....very comfortable beds all have electric blankets. Breakfast at 'Retreat Inn' is special. Transport provided locally. Laundry facilities. Flat off-street parking. Sorry, no smoking indoors. Come see us, our two cute cats...& little bantam hens!

Retreat Inn
B&B Homestay
Picton Central
Alison & Geoff
20 Lincoln Street
Picton

Tel: (03) 573 8160
Fax: (03) 573 7799
E: elliott.orchard@xtra.co.nz
W: www.bnb.co.nz/hosts/
retreatinn.html

Cost: Double $90
Single $60
Dinner B/A Visa/MC
Beds: 1 Queen 2 Single
(2 bdrm)
Bath: 2 Guests share

Picton

Situated on the hills overlooking Picton, Grandvue offers panoramic views of Queen Charlotte Sound. At the end of a cul-de-sac Grandvue is a haven in a secluded garden, five minutes walk to town and its assortment of restaurants. Accommodation is a comfortable , warm self contained apartment with TV, video, and access to a barbecue. Feast on panoramic views from our upstairs conservatory, while enjoying a delicious and satisfying breakfast. A portable cot and highchair are available. Courtesy transport available.

Grandvue
B&B Self-contained
Picton Central
Rosalie & Russell Mathews
19 Otago Street
Picton

Tel: (03) 573 8553
Fax: (03) 573 8556
E: grandvue-mathews
@clear.net.nz
W: www.bnb.co.nz/hosts/
grandvue.html

Cost: Double $80
Single $60
Child $15 Visa/MC
Beds: 1 Queen (1 bdrm)
Bath: 1 Ensuite

Picton

We would like to invite you in our sunny spacious home in Picton, where we have a breathtaking view over the town and harbour, with a 5 minute walk to the shops and restaurants. Enjoy a "cuppa" on the balcony, watching the ferry and activities on the water. The bedrooms have coffee and tea facilities, TV, fridge, electric blankets. A warm welcome awaits you at "Panorama View" including a generous breakfast. Looking forward to meeting you. Courtesy car available.

Panorama View
B&B Homestay
Picton Central
Din & Colin Trimbach
21 Otago street
Picton

Tel: (03) 573 6362
Fax: (03) 573 6362
Mob: 025 267 0522
E: panoramaview@paradise.net.nz
W: www.bnb.co.nz/hosts/
panoramaview.html

Cost: Double $80
Single $55
Beds: 1 Double 2 Single
(2 bdrm)
Bath: 1 Ensuite 1 Private

Picton

We offer you a warm friendly atmosphere at Rivenhall, one of Picton's older more gracious homes, situated at the top of Wellington Street, overlooking the town, a four minute walk from Picton centre and easy walking to the ferry. Nan will provide the breakfast of your choice (evening meal upon request). Laundry facilities available. Marlborough Sounds tours leave from the bottom of Wellington Street. And of course just ring for directions or to have us pick you up from the ferry, bus, train or aircraft.

Rivenhall	**Tel:** (03) 573 7692	**Cost:** Double $80
B&B Homestay	**Fax:** (03) 573 7692	Single $55
200m S of Picton	**E:** laurenson_nan_malcolm	Dinner $25pp B/A
Nan & Malcolm Laurenson	@xtra.co.nz	Child $15 Visa/MC
118 Wellington Street	**W:** www.bnb.co.nz/hosts/	**Beds:** 1 Queen (1 bdrm)
Picton	rivenhall.html	**Bath:** 1 Private

Picton

Lyn and Eddie welcome you to a relaxed atmosphere at Echo Lodge. Breakfast is our speciality. Come and experience our home-made bread, jams, omelettes and treats. Comfortable bedrooms with ensuites, tea-coffee making facilities, ensure a good nights sleep. 5 min walk to shops, restaurants, ferries, busses and bush walks. A cosy wood fire for those chilly nights. Courtesy car available treat yourself to an aromatherapy facial or foot massage, massage includes neck, shoulders, hands and feet cost $40

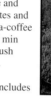

Echo Lodge	**Tel:** (03) 573 6367	**Cost:** Double $75
B&B	**Fax:** (03) 573 6387	Single $55
800m S of Picton	**W:** www.bnb.co.nz/hosts/	**Beds:** 1 Double 2 Single
Lyn & Eddie Thoroughgood	echolodge.html	(2 bdrm)
5 Rutland Street		**Bath:** 2 Ensuite
Picton		

Picton - Kenepuru Sound

The Nikaus is a sheep & cattle farm situated in Waitaria Bay, Kenepuru Sound, 2 hours drive from Blenheim or Picton. We offer friendly personal service in our comfortable spacious home. A swimming pool is available for guests use. We have two dogs Sam (corgie) and Minny (Jack Russel x). Other animals include the farm dogs, donkeys, pet wild pigs. "Miss Piggy", turkeys, hens and peacocks. Good hearty country meals, home grown produce, home made ice-cream a speciality thanks to 'Muggies' our friendly hose cow. A non-smoking household.

The Nikaus	**Tel:** (03) 573 4432	**Cost:** Double $75
B&B Farmstay	**Fax:** (03) 573 4432	Single $45
80km NE of Havelock	**Mob:** 025 544 712	Dinner $25 Visa/MC
Alison & Robin Bowron	**W:** www.bnb.co.nz/hosts/	**Beds:** 1 Double 2 Single
Waitaria Bay	thenikaus.html	(2 bdrm)
RD 2		**Bath:** 1 Guests share
Picton		

Picton

The White House in Pictons main street offers affordable luxury - just ask any previous guest - in a friendly, quiet, warm home environment. It nestles on a sunny 1/4 acre, surrounded by mature trees and gardens, and is just a minutes walk to Picton's fabulous cafes and restaurants for your evening meal.

Located conveniently in the middle of town, this delightful 70 year old home is filled with Gwen's porcelain doll collection and numerous 'old worlde' touches. It has been immaculately maintained throughout with all refurbishments reflecting the era in which it was built.

Guest bedrooms are upstairs, all of which have quality beds to ensure a good nights sleep. Also on the same floor is the guest lounge which affords panoramic views over Picton to the harbour and hills beyond. However, if they prefer, guests are most welcome to share the downstairs lounge with their host.

Gwen's long association with the hospitality industry has made her aware that some of the things people miss when travelling is being able to pop into the kitchen and make a pot of tea or a cup of coffee when they like. White House guests are invited to do just that.

The laundry facilities are also available for guests. We look forward to making our guests' Picton visit an enjoyable and memorable one.

And while The White House is a non-smoking residence, guests are most welcome to smoke on the front verandah or the back deck areas. We regret our home is unsuitable for children.

The White House
Homestay
Picton Central
Gwen Stevenson
114 High Street
Picton

Tel: (03) 573 6767
Fax: (03) 573 8871
W: www.bnb.co.nz/hosts/
thewhitehousepicton.html

Cost: Double $60
Single $40 Twin $60
Beds: 2 Double 3 Single
(4 bdrm)
Bath: 2 Guests share

Picton

Couples, families and singles are welcome in our brand new, spacious home, designed for your comfort and convenience. It's just a few minutes walk from the centre of town and all leisure activities. Our three guest rooms - one double ensuite, one twin, one queen and single beds - can be adapted to your needs. We provide a cot and highchair and offer a laundry service and courtesy pick-up. We're keen lawn bowlers, and we share our home with two friendly cats, Bijou and Toby.

Palm Haven	**Tel:** (03) 573 5644	**Cost:** Double $65-$80
B&B Homestay	**Fax:** (03) 573 5645	Single $45 Child $25
Picton central	**Mob:** 025 275 0860	Dinner $25
Dae & Peter Robertson	**E:** palmhaven@xtra.co.nz	**Beds:** 2 Queen 3 Single
15A Otago Street	**W:** www.bnb.co.nz/hosts/	(3 bdrm)
Picton	palmhaven.html	**Bath:** 1 Ensuite
		1 Guests share

Picton

We welcome you to our property which is within easy walking distance of all activities in Picton. Accommodation is self contained with TV, tea/coffee making facilities. We provide a full breakfast with freshly brewed coffee and tea. Safe off street parking, laundry facilities, courtesy transport to ferry, train and bus. Mila enjoys embroidery, sewing and art, Steve enjoys most sport. We also speak French. We are a non smoking household, however you may smoke on the deck or veranda.

Bridgend Cottage	**Tel:** (03) 573 6734	**Cost:** Double $85-$100
B&B Self-contained Homestay	**Fax:** (03) 573 8323	Single $60 Child $20
Picton Central	**E:** stevejb@voyager.co.nz	Group $120 - $150
Mila & Steve Burke	**W:** www.bnb.co.nz/hosts/	Dinner $25 Visa/MC
36 York Street	bridgendcottage.html	**Beds:** 1 King/Twin 1 Double
Picton		2 Single (3 bdrm)
		Bath: 2 Ensuite

Picton - Queen Charlotte Sounds

Ngakuta Bay Homestay is on the scenic Queen Charlotte Drive set in an acre of bush, the Homestay is built of NZ beach with large verandahs giving magnificent views over Ngakuta Bay. Each room has French doors onto the verandah with fridge, complimentary tea & coffee. Large lounge area with Sky TV. Also available from the Homestay are sailing dinghys, windsurfers and kayaks. The Bay has landscaped recreational area with safe swimming and barbecue facilities making it an ideal holiday resort for water sports, walking and fishing.

Ngakuta Bay Homestay	**Tel:** (03) 573 8853	**Cost:** Double $100-$120
Self-contained Homestay	**Fax:** (03) 573 8353	Single $80 Dinner $35 B/A
11km S of Picton	**Mob:** 025 237 3300	S/C unit $100 - $150
Eve & Scott Dawson	**E:** ngakutabayhouse@xtra,co.nz	Weekly rates from $500
Manuka Drive	**W:** www.picton.co.nz/ngakuta	**Beds:** 2 Double 2 Twin (4 bdrm)
RD 1, Ngakuta Bay		**Bath:** 2 Ensuite 2 Private

Picton - Queen Charlotte Sounds

Nestled amongst the native ferns overlooking Queen Charlotte Sounds. Relax in our luxurious spacious rooms with ensuite. Our private guest wing includes lounge, kitchenette and barbeque area. Guests may choose to self-cater or home cooked meals are available by arrangement. Listen to the birds sing. Walk with us to view the glow-worms or enjoy our beautiful native garden. Swim at the beach only 100 metres away or enjoy a spot of fishing. Drop off and pick up by arrangement. Only 10 minutes away Queen Charlotte Track.

Tanglewood	**Tel:** (03) 574 2080	**Cost:** Double $95-$105
B&B Self-contained Homestay	**Fax:** (03) 574 2044	Single $70 Dinner $35
16km W of Picton	**Mob:** 025 814 388	S/C Unit $150 Visa/MC
Stephen and Linda Hearn	**E:** tanglewood.hearn@xtra.co.nz	**Beds:** 2 King/Twin (2 bdrm)
Queen Charlotte Drive	**W:** www.bnb.co.nz/hosts/	**Bath:** 2 Ensuite
The Grove, RD 1, Picton	tanglewoodpicton.html	

Picton - Ngakuta Bay

A warm welcome awaits you at Bayswater B&B in Ngakuta Bay, situated 11km from Picton and 24km from Havelock on Queen Charlotte Drive in the beautiful Marlborough Sounds. Our modern home has a self-contained apartment with 2 double bedrooms, ensuite and private bathroom, kitchen, lounge, dining and laundry. Spectacular views over surrounding bush and Ngakuta Bay from your own private balcony. We offer continental breakfast or self catering. Complimentary transport available. Suitable for longer stays. Come relax with us in our little piece of paradise.

Bayswater	**Tel:** (03) 573 5966	**Cost:** Double $80
B&B Self-contained Homestay	**Fax:** (03) 573 5966	Single $45
11km W of Picton	**W:** www.bnb.co.nz/hosts/	**Beds:** 1 Queen 1 Twin
Paul & Judy Mann	bayswater.html	(2 bdrm)
25 Manuka Drive, Ngakuta Bay		**Bath:** 1 Ensuite 1 Private
Queen Charlotte Drive, Picton		

Port Underwood Sound

Oyster Bay Lodge has an uninterrupted view over the Bay in a charming historical part of Marlbourgh Sounds. We share this delightful spot with our lovely Bichon Frise Tammy. Lynnette is an avid patchwork and quilter, while Jim is a semi-retired bulider. Directions - follow Port Underwood Drive east from Picton, through Waikawa Bay, Whatamonga Bay, over the hill, don't turn off, the next Bay on your right is Oyster Bay and we're on the far side of the Bay.

Oyster Bay Lodge	**Tel:** (03) 579 9644	**Cost:** Double $85
B&B Homestay	**Fax:** (03) 579 9644	Single $55
20km E of Picton	**Mob:** 025 316 630	Dinner $25
Jim & Lynnette Mark	**W:** www.bnb.co.nz/hosts/	**Beds:** 2 Double 1 Single
Oyster Bay	oysterbaylodge.html	(2 bdrm)
PO Box 146		**Bath:** 1 Guests share
Picton		

Picton

Adrienne & Bill and their 2 black Labradors invite you
to stay in one of Picton's finest historic homes. Once a
convent, this 1880's restored 2 storeyed villa is steeped
in history and charm and retains its original character.
Guest rooms have a view of Picton harbour and open
out onto a sunny veranda. We are centrally located
within walking distance to the foreshore and an array
of cafes and restaurants. Courtesy vehicle, hiking trails
and tour guiding, massage and aromatherapy baths
available.

St Catherine's
Bed & Breakfast
Picton, New Zealand.
Phone/Fax: (64) 03 573 8580 ~ Mobile 025 502 090 ~ Email: abxn@xtra.co.nz

St Catherine's	**Tel:** (03) 573 8580	**Cost:** Double $95-$120
B&B	**Fax:** (03) 573 8580	Single $50 Child $40
Picton Central	**Mob:** 025 502 090	Visa/MC
Adrienne & Bill Crossen	**E:** abxn@xtra.co.nz	**Beds:** 2 Double 1 Twin
123 Wellington Street	**W:** www.bnb.co.nz/hosts/	1 Single (4 bdrm)
Picton	stcatherines.html	**Bath:** 1 Private 1 Guests share

Picton

A warm welcome awaits you at our completely
refurbished self contained cottage, set in a peaceful
location within walking distance of town. We are
surrounded by beautiful bush and delightful walkways.
Enjoy a delicious breakfast - panoramic views from the
dining room, the ambience (including a cosy fire in the
winter), or just relax on the sundeck. A fully equipped
kitchen, off-street parking, laundry facilities and
courtesy transport are available for your convenience.
We look forward to meeting you.

Lincoln Cottage	**Tel:** (03) 573 5285	**Cost:** Double $80-$100
B&B Self-contained	**Fax:** (03) 573 5285	Single $65 Visa/MC
Picton Central	**Mob:** 021 658 140	**Beds:** 2 Queen 2 Twin (4 bdrm)
Laurel & Bruce Sisson	**E:** lincolncottage@xtra.co.nz	**Bath:** 2 Ensuite 1 Guests share
19 Lincoln Street	**W:** www.bnb.co.nz/hosts/	
Picton	lincolncottage.html	

Picton - Whatamango Bay

Welcome to Whatamango Lodge, situated at the head of Whatamango Bay, looking out towards Queen Charlotte Sound. We invite you to share our modern, waterfront home and enjoy total peace and tranquility. Relax on your own private balcony and watch the magnificent birdlife. Take a stroll around the beach or swim in the crystal clear water. There are also numerous bush walks. You may like to use our dinghy or fish off the rocks.

Kayaks are available to paddle round the bay. We are situated 10 mins on a sealed road from Picton. Follow the Port Underwood Road from Waikawa to Whatamango Bay, turn left into McCormicks Rd, waterfront location, no 17. A courtesy car is also available for transport to or from the ferry.

Guest accommodation comprises
1. A self contained unit (sleeps 4), Queen sized bedroom, lounge (sofa bed), full kitchen facilities, large deck.
2. Queen sized bedroom with ensuite. Use of spacious lounge and balcony. Laundry facilities available.

Dinner is available by arrangement and features traditional New Zealand cuisine, served with complimentary wine. For breakfast choose either a full country style cooked breakfast, or a light continental breakfast, or if you prefer a delectable combination of both. We are a non-smoking household. Not suitable for children.

Whatamango Lodge
B&B Self-contained Homestay
10km E of Picton
Ralph and Wendy Cass
17 McCormicks Road
Whatamango Bay
Picton

Tel: (03) 573 5110
Fax: (03) 573 5110
E: whatamango-lodge
@paradise.net.nz
W: www.picton.co.nz/
whatamango

Cost: Double $90-$120
Single $70 Dinner $30
Visa/MC
Beds: 2 Queen (2 bdrm)
Bath: 2 Ensuite

Tirimoana House

Picton - Queen Charlotte Sound

We have been here over a year and have completely renovated our house and self contained flat. We are proud of our end results and invite you to come and share them with us. Delight in our stunning, uninterrupted views of Queen Charlotte Sound from all rooms.

We have a swing seat where you can listen to the fountain, watch the black swans and yachts out in the Sounds, marvel as the fantails flutter past and listen to the tuis and the bellbirds. If you fancy a swim we have a wonderful swimming pool. Once again, with those uninterrupted views, you can relax in the hammock, sit under the sun umbrella or laze on the grass. There is also a private spa pool room, with extra boosters for those big, massaging bubbles.

Our lounge and dining area is restful and welcoming. The new Queen size bedrooms have their own ensuites and the "Sunrise Suite" has a SuperKing/Twin size bed, armchairs, Juliet balcony and it's own private bathroom with spa bath, separate shower and toilet. You have tea/coffee making facilities so you can lie in bed with a morning cuppa, and look straight down the Sounds.

The flat has its own private deck under the shade of a kowhai tree and those views, fantails and tuis again!

We can prepare delicious evening meals, if you have special dietary requirements, or dislikes, we will help in any way we are able. When you finally have to depart you won't leave hungry, our breakfasts are hearty and fulsome!

We, along with our very friendly German Short Haired Pointer, Digby, look forward to meeting you with a welcoming cuppa and home made "Goody".

Tirimoana House
B&B Self-contained Homestay
22km W of Picton
Stephanie & Peter Bonser
257 Anakiwa Road
RD 1
Picton

Tel: (03) 574 2627
Fax: (03) 574 2627
E: tirimoana.bonser@xtra.co.nz
W: www.truenz.co.nz/tirimoana

Cost: Double $95-$140
Single $70 Dinner $30
S/C Flat $95, $15 pp extra
Visa/MC/Eftpos
Beds: 1 King/Twin 2 Queen
2 Double 2 Single (4 bdrm)
Bath: 3 Ensuite 1 Private

Picton - Karaka Point

Karaka Point Lodge, 8km from InterIsland Ferries, is tasteful boutique/luxury accommodation. Bedrooms and living area open onto spacious decks and have exceptional, tranquil marine views. Beautiful cat, secure rooms, best beds, air-conditioning, generous yummy meals (dinner by arrangement only, includes top wines). Guest computer, outdoor furniture and spa in secluded area. Spa under the stars! Perfect for relaxation. 5 minutes walk to beach via historic Maori site. Enjoy some of the numerous walking, water and wine based activities One night is not enough!

Karaka Point Lodge	**Tel:** (03) 573 7700	**Cost:** Double $110-$175
B&B Homestay	**Fax:** (03) 573 5444	Single $95-$160
8km E of Picton	**Mob:** 025 614 3878	Dinner $55pp B/A
Juliet & Brian Kirke	**E:** jb@karakapointlodge.co.nz	Visa/MC
312 Port Underwood Road	**W:** www.karakapointlodge.co.nz	**Beds:** 1 King 1 Queen (2 bdrm)
Picton - Havelock		**Bath:** 1 Ensuite 1 Private

Moenui Bay - Havelock - Pelorus Sound

Come and share our tranquil sounds setting. Enjoy warm hospitality and lovely seaviews. Moenui Bay just 10 minutes from Havelock, 40 minutes from Picton along scenic Queen Charlotte Drive is a good base for local walkways, mailboat, watertaxi and kayaking trips or visiting vineyards. Brian an educator, wine and American football buff is a keen fisherman. Susan enjoys crafts, painting, gardening and practicing her culinary skills using Marlborough's fine produce. Lucy, Mindy and Charlie are the resident cats. Please no smoking inside. Longer visits welcomed.

The Devonshires	**Tel:** (03) 574 2930	**Cost:** Double $75-$85 Single $50
B&B Homestay	**Fax:** (03) 574 2930	Dinner $25 - $30 B/A
32km W of Picton	**Mob:** 025 463 118	Not suitable for Children
Brian & Susan Devonshire	**E:** devs.1@xtra.co.nz	Visa/MC
Moenui Bay, Queen Charlotte Dr.	**W:** www.bnb.co.nz/hosts/	**Beds:** 1 Queen 2 Twin (2 bdrm)
RD 1, Picton - near Havelock	thedevonshires.html	**Bath:** 1 Guests share

Ensuite and private bathrooms are for your use exclusively

Guests share bathroom means you

will be sharing with other guests

Family share means you will be sharing with the family

Tuamarina

We invite you to stay in our nice affordable spacious two bedroom flat. It has its own entrance from lovely gardens. There's a clean modern open plan fully equipped kitchen dining (with TV) & laundry, which is sometimes shared with other guests. All rooms have comfortable quality beds with electric blankets. We are 18km south of Picton ferry terminal at Tuamarina on the popular wine trails. Close to beaches, golf course and fishing. Panda a friendly corgi loves to greet guests and play ball. Meals by prior arrangement or restaurant 5 minutes by car.

The White House
B&B Homestay
10km N of Blenheim
Bev & Hugh Emslie
1866 State Highway 1
Tuamarina

Tel: (03) 570 5353
Fax: (03) 570 5353
E: bevswhitehouseb-b
   @xtra.co.nz
W: www.bnb.co.nz/hosts/
   thewhitehousetuamarina.html

Cost: Double $70-$80 Single $40
   Child $20 Dinner $20
Beds: 1 Queen 2 Twin 2 Single
   (3 bdrm)
Bath: 1 Guests share
   1 Family share

Blenheim

Welcome to our small farm in Blenheim for quality accommodation in our spacious home with excellent beds. Bacon, eggs and tomatoes from our farm make a delicious breakfast. Our executive suite has a "Bechstein" piano. Tree ferns and gardens surround a large swimming pool. Spacious lawns with rhododendrons, roses and trees. We are close to Gourmet restaurants and have a selection of their menus. Marlborough has beautiful parks, wine trails, and scenic Marlborough sounds. Laundry available and courtesy phone call for next homestay. Happy Holidays.

Rhododendron Lodge
Farmstay
1.5km S of Blenheim
Audrey & Charlie Chambers
St Andrews, RD 4
State Highway 1, Blenheim

Tel: (03) 578 1145
Fax: (03) 578 1145
W: www.bnb.co.nz/hosts/
   rhododendronlodge.html

Cost: Double $80 Single $60
   Suite $100 10% discount
   3 days or more
Beds: 2 Queen 2 Single
   (3 bdrm)
Bath: 1 Ensuite 1 Private

Blenheim

Welcome to our warm, spacious, non-smoking home in a quiet suburb with outdoor pool, off-street parking, and no pets. All beds have quality mattresses, electric blankets and wool underlays. Interests: Rex's (retired airline pilot) - are aviation oriented - models, microlights, homebuilts and gliding. Builds miniature steam locomotives, has 1930 Model A soft top tourer vintage car and enjoys barbershop singing. Adrienne's - cooking, spinning, woolcraft. Let us share these hobbies, plus our caring personal attention, complimentary beverages and all the comforts of home with you.

Hillsview
Homestay
3km S of Blenheim
Adrienne & Rex Handley
Please Phone

Tel: (03) 578 9562
Fax: (03) 578 9562
Mob: 025 627 6727
E: aidrex@xtra.co.nz
W: www.bnb.co.nz/hosts/
   hillsview.html

Cost: Double $75-$80 Single $50
   10% discount if pre-booked
   the night before. Dinner B/A
Beds: 1 King/Twin 1 Double
   2 Twin 1 Single (4 bdrm)
Bath: 2 Private

Blenheim

As keen travellers ourselves, we'd like to be sensitive to your needs, and warmly welcome you to our clean, comfortable accommodation,spacious living,guest lounge and proximity to Marlborough's diverse attractions.Although within the town boundary,we still offer a peaceful,rural aspect where we grow export flowers, fresh vegetables and can treat you to homemade jams/preserves at our table.Best of both worlds.Directions: Highway 6 from Blenheim. First left after Shell Service Station,right hand side, opposite last street light.

Mirfield	**Tel:** (03) 578 8220	**Cost:** Double $65-$70 Single $40
B&B Homestay	**Fax:** (03) 578 8220	Child $15 under 12yrs
2km W of Blenheim	**Tollfree:** 0800 395 720	Dinner $17.50 B/A Visa/MC
Pam & Charles Hamilton	**Mob:** 025 284 5912	**Beds:** 2 Queen 2 Single
24 Severne Street	**E:** lifes4living@xtra.co.nz	(3 bdrm)
Blenheim	**W:** www.bnb.co.nz/hosts/	**Bath:** 2 Private 1 Family share
	mirfield.html	

Blenheim

We're 8kms from Blenheim on a Hill Country property running Beef Cattle. Our home is in a quiet valley with spacious grounds (350 roses) and native birds. Marlborough is a major grape growing area plus horticulture, agriculture and livestock farming. Marlborough Sounds nearby. Good trout fishing rivers, skifield 1 1/2 hours drive. Blenheim has golf courses, croquet greens and tennis courts set in beautiful gardens. We enjoy taking guests for a look around farm. Horse trekking 5 mins drive. No pets. Laundry available. Directions: Please phone.

Maxwell Pass Farmstay	**Tel:** (03) 578 1941	**Cost:** Double $80 Single $45
Farmstay	**Fax:** (03) 578 1941	Child 1/2 price
8km S of Blenheim	**W:** www.bnb.co.nz/hosts/	Dinner by arrangement
Jean & John Leslie	maxwellpassfarmstay.html	**Beds:** 1 Double 3 Single
Maxwell Pass		(3 bdrm)
PO Box 269, Blenheim		**Bath:** 1 Private 1 Family share

Blenheim

Our large home is surrounded by vineyards and within walking distance of the Wairau River and several wineries. In our home there are three upstairs bedrooms and a guest lounge which opens onto a swimming pool courtyard. The self-catering house has two bedrooms and is fully equipped for longer stays. We are widely travelled and some interests are bird watching, trout fishing, woodworking and cards. Evening meals, by prior arrangement, are served with our own wines. Unsuitable for children.

Thainstone	**Tel:** (03) 572 8823	**Cost:** Double $100 Single $60
Self-contained Vineyard	**Fax:** (03) 572 8623	S/C House $100 - $150
Homestay	**Mob:** 021 283 1484	Dinner $25 Visa/MC Amex
12km NW of Blenheim	**E:** thainsto@voyager.co.nz	**Beds:** 1 King 2 Queen 1 Double
Vivienne & Jim Murray	**W:** www.bnb.co.nz/hosts/	1 Twin 1 Single (5 bdrm)
120 Giffords Road	thainstone.html	**Bath:** 1 Ensuite 1 Private
RD 3, Blenheim		1 Guests share

Blenheim

"A very special place our own mini resort" guests' remarks who keep coming back!! Nestled amongst beautiful park-like gardens, mature trees in a country locality, we offer excellent accommodation. Secluded large heated swimming pool, spa, top tennis court. On the doorstep of Marlborough's Exciting Wine Region, Superb Vineyard, Restaurants, Trout Rivers. We provide "In House" B&B accommodation, own ensuite, or modern high standard self-contained units. Cook in or dine out. Situated on Rapaura Road Spring Creek turn off. Courtesy vehicle for Airport or Ferry pickups.

Chardonnay Lodge
B&B Self-contained Homestay
6min N of Blenheim
George and Ellenor Mayo
1048 Rapaura Road
RD 3, Blenheim

Tel: (03) 570 5194
Fax: (03) 570 5194
E: chardonnaylodge@xtra.co.nz
W: www.bnb.co.nz/hosts/
chardonnaylodge.html

Cost: SC Units Doube $95.
Room in house with ensuite
Double $89.
Extra beds by arr. $20 pp.
Continental Breakfasts $9 pp.
Other meals by arr.

Blenheim

Your hosts Neil and Lyn and their Labrador "Rusty" welcome you to their 14 ha property 15 km west of Blenheim, in the Brancott Valley beside Marlborough's famous wine trail. We overlook vineyards, olives and deer. A full breakfast is provided. Dinner is additional by arrangement. Our interests are pottery, almond growing and organic gardening. Directions: See Marlborough wine trail maps.

The Sentinel
Country Retreat
15km W of Blenheim
Lyn & Neil Berry
Wrekin Road, off Brancott Road
Fairhall
Blenheim

Tel: (03) 572 9143
Fax: (03) 572 9143
E: TheSentinel@xtra.co.nz
W: www.bnb.co.nz/hosts/
thesentinel.html

Cost: Double $120
Single $100
Dinner $35 incl. wine
Visa/MC Amex Diners
Beds: 2 Queen 2 Single
(2 bdrm)
Bath: 2 Ensuite

Blenheim

Our self-contained unit can accommodate one couple or a single. Features include your own entrance, queensize bed, mini kitchen, bathroom - large bath, shower and separate toilet. Use of our laundry can be made upon request. Two cats and a bird live with us. We have off-street parking and are within ten minutes walk from central Blenheim. Please phone before 8 am or after 4.30 pm during the working week. If no response, Jennie can be contacted via her cell-phone. Fax us anytime.

Beaver B&B
Self-contained Homestay
Blenheim Central
Jen & Russell Hopkins
60 Beaver Road
Blenheim

Tel: (03) 578 8401
Fax: (03) 578 8401
Mob: 021 626 151
Mob: 021 626 151
E: jhopkins@voyager.co.nz
W: www.bnb.co.nz/hosts/
beaverbb.html

Cost: Double $80
Single $50
Visa/MC
Beds: 1 Queen (1 bdrm)
Bath: 1 Ensuite

Blenheim

Set among 150 year old trees Wycoller is architectually designed to blend into its surroundings and is a ten minute walk to Blenheim. A separate guest wing with all amenities including tea/coffee making facilities. Private patio from both rooms to enjoy lawns and gardens. Marlborough offers golf courses, Sounds cruises, dolphins, walking tracks, art trails, wine trails, excellent diversity of restaurants in Blenheim and vineyards. Modern elegance, tranquillity and exceptional location give Wycoller a special feel. Welcome to the McCormicks, Please phone first.

Wycoller Homestay	**Tel:** (03) 578 8522	**Cost:** Double $85-$95
Homestay	**W:** www.bnb.co.nz/hosts/	Single $65-$75
Valerie & Terry McCormick	wycollerhomestay.html	**Beds:** 1 Double 1 Twin
Blenheim Central		(2 bdrm)
106A Maxwell Road, Blenheim		**Bath:** 1 Ensuite 1 Private

Blenheim

Welcome to our home 2kms from the town centre. Guests can join us in our spacious sunny living areas. We both enjoy all TV sports and our other interests include wood turning, handcrafts and the Lions organisation. Blenheim is an ideal place to visit Picton, Nelson, whale watch and the many wineries, parks and craft shops in the area . We have two cats Snookie and Cuddles. Smoking is not encouraged. Just phone to be picked up at airport, train or bus. Dinner on request.

Philmar	**Tel:** (03) 577 7788	**Cost:** Double $70-$80
B&B Homestay	**Fax:** (03) 577 7788	Single $50 Dinner $20pp
2km N of Blenheim	**W:** www.bnb.co.nz/hosts/	**Beds:** 2 Queen 1 Twin
Wynnis & Lex Phillips	philmar.html	(3 bdrm)
63 Colemans Road		**Bath:** 1 Ensuite 1 Guests share
Blenheim		

Blenheim

Our new stone and cedar home is surrounded by gardens and 18 acres of Sauvignon Blanc vines. Close by are some of NZ's most outstanding wineries. We have the space, comfort and privacy to make your stay memorable. Share an interesting fresh breakfast with us in the "Pavilion" overlooking the swimming pool. We enjoy travel, skiing, books, music, gardening and good food. There are many fine restaurants locally or you may prefer to dine with us. We have a friendly Burmese cat and are non smokers.

Stonehaven	**Tel:** (03) 572 9730	**Cost:** Double $150-$160
Homestay Vineyard Homestay	**Fax:** (03) 572 9730	Single $90 Dinner B/A
9km SW of Blenheim	**Mob:** 021 442 433	Visa/MC
Jocelyn & David Wilson	**E:** dgwilson@voyager.co.nz	**Beds:** 1 King 1 Queen
414 Rapaura Road	**W:** www.bnb.co.nz/hosts/	1 Single (3 bdrm)
RD 3	stonehavenblenheim.html	**Bath:** 2 Ensuite 1 Private
Blenheim		

Blenheim - Spring Creek

Charmwood is located in beautiful wine & olive growing countryside within easy reach of the town, airport, seaport and recreational Marlborough. Charmwood facilities include tranquil gardens, asphalt tennis court and swimming pool. In the colder months enjoy bubbling away in the spa or relaxing beside our cosy fire. We share our home with Murdoch the cat who also enjoys the rural tranquility that Charmwood provides. Start the day with our Country Fare breakfast where we would be happy to help you plan your itinerary.

Charmwood Rural Retreat	**Tel:** (03) 570 5409	**Cost:** Double $100-$145
B&B Farmstay Homestay	**Fax:** (03) 570 5110	Single $90 Visa/MC
6km N of Blenheim	**Mob:** 025 847 403	**Beds:** 2 Queen 2 Single
Linda & Peter Gibson	**E:** charmwood@xtra.co.nz	(3 bdrm)
158 Murrays Road	**W:** charmwood.co.nz	**Bath:** 2 Ensuite 1 Private
RD 3, Blenheim		

Blenheim

Black Birch Lodge is ideally situated for exploring Marlborough's wine trail. Your hosts have been involved in the wine industry since 1981 both as growers and David as editor of Winepress. Most Marlborough wineries are only a matter of minutes away, the closest being the prestigious Herzog Winery and Restaurant situated at the bottom of Black Birch's vineyard. Other features include tennis court, pool, bikes, library, laundry, wine trail advice, vineyard walks and trout fishing in nearby Wairau River. We have a small friendly dog, "Ci-Ni".

Black Birch Lodge	**Tel:** (03) 572 8876	**Cost:** Double $100-$140
B&B Homestay Vineyard	**Fax:** (03) 572 8806	Single $70-$85
Homestay	**E:** barnsley@ihug.co.nz	Child 1/2 price
12km W of Blenheim	**W:** www.bnb.co.nz/hosts/	Dinner $35 B/A Visa/MC
Margaret & David Barnsley	blackbirchlodge.html	**Beds:** 2 Queen 3 Single
Jeffries Road		(3 bdrm)
RD 3, Blenheim		**Bath:** 2 Ensuite

Blenheim

Brian, a renowned NZ artist, and Kathy, a keen gardener, welcome you to their spacious, sunny, modern home & art gallery. T.V. in all bedrooms (smokefree). Guests can enjoy magnificent panoramic views over Blenheim and nearby vineyards, or explore terraced gardens of roses, rhododendrons, camellias, perennials, deciduous trees etc. We can arrange tours to wineries, gardens, ski-field, golf courses etc. Laundry facilities available for small charge. Our interests include gardening, music, travel, fishing, skiing, art and meeting people from all over the world.

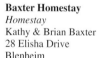

Baxter Homestay	**Tel:** (03) 578 3753	**Cost:** Double $90-$130
Homestay	**Fax:** (03) 578 3796	Dinner from $25 Visa/MC
Kathy & Brian Baxter	**E:** baxterart@xtra.co.nz	**Beds:** 2 King/Twin 1 Double
28 Elisha Drive	**W:** mysite.xtra.co.nz/~baxterart	(3 bdrm)
Blenheim		**Bath:** 2 Private 1 Guests share

Blenheim

Pauline and Peter invite you to stay at our 8 acre olive grove and vineyard, which is located conveniently on SH1 on the northern boundary of Blenheim.
We offer 4 double bedrooms with ensuites plus bedroom and bathroom appliances. Our home is designed especially with homestay guests in mind. Spacious guest lounges (with televisions) opening onto large balconies, offer panoramic views of the plains ranges and river.

After a day of sightseeing and enjoying the delights of the "Gourmet Province", cool off in the swimming pool, relax in the spa, take a stroll in Pauline's gardens the olive grove/vineyard. Some courtesy transport is available for evening dining.

We offer continental and cooked breakfast and meals as requested. A former restaurateur and butcher, peter's breakfasts are legendary. Evening meals may consist of meats and fresh grown vegetables or fish caught by Peter from the Marlborough Sounds, rivers and lakes. If you feel like dining out, Marlborough's finest Italian Restaurant (Best pasta in the world - "Cuisine"), the Whitehaven winery and cafe and local bar and bistro are within 5 minutes walking distance.

We are happy to share our extensive local knowledge and contacts which will enable you to personalise and optimise your stay in the "Gourmet Province"/ Free laundry facilities. Directions: On Blenheim's north boundary definitely 100 metres north of narrow concrete bridge, on state highway 1, turn into multi signed entrance shared by the Research Centre. Then immediately turn left into gravel drive and follow to house.

Grove Bank
B&B Homestay Family
Blenheim Central
Pauline & Peter Pickering
2652 State Highway 1
Grovetown
Blenheim

Tel: (03) 578 8407
Fax: (03) 578 8407
Tollfree: 0800 422 632
E: grovebank@xtra.co.nz
W: www.home.xtra.co.nz/hosts/grovebank/index.htm

Cost: Double $70-$85
Single $50-$55
Dinner $20 - $35
Groups $75 -$150 Visa/MC
Beds: 2 King/Twin 3 Queen
2 Single (5 bdrm)
Bath: 3 Ensuite 2 Private

Blenheim

Only 5km south of Blenheim on SH1, you will find Windmill Farm, a spacious and modern home in close proximity to the golf driving range and to Montana Winery. Comfortably appointed spacious twin bedroom with private ensuite and one double bedroom with private bathroom and spa. We have travelled to many countries overseas and aim to make our guests feel welcome and relaxed. We are non smokers who enjoy gardens, travel and meeting people. We welcome you to our home. Please phone first.

Windmill Farm	**Tel:** (03) 577 7853	**Cost:** Double $80
Farmstay	**Fax:** (03) 577 7853	Single $50
5km S of Blenheim	**W:** www.bnb.co.nz/hosts/	**Beds:** 1 Double 2 Twin
Millie Amos	windmillfarm.html	(2 bdrm)
3516 Main Road		**Bath:** 1 Ensuite 1 Private
Riverlands, Blenheim		

Blenheim Central

"A very special world within your walls" a visitor signed our friendship quilt. The gracious home features unique decor of maps, charts, photos and art. Guests' quiet spacious rooms have TVs, tea/coffee/cookies, Lizzie's cherry port and comfortable chairs. Warm, informal hosts provide memorable breakfasts and links with aviators, quilters, golfers, artists, olivers and vineyards. Three minutes stroll to shops, cinema, galleries, churches, sports complex, pool and restaurants. Off-street parking, courtesy bikes, laundry, garden hot tub. Find us on Henry St between High St and Maxwell Rd.

Henry Maxwell's Central B&B	**Tel:** (03) 578 8086	**Cost:** Double $90-$120
B&B	**Fax:** (03) 578 8089	Single $65 Visa/MC Amex
100m W of Blenheim	**Tollfree:** 0800 436 796	**Beds:** 2 Queen 1 Double 4 Twin
Ken & Christy Rolfe	**E:** stay@henrymaxwells.co.nz	2 Single (4 bdrm)
28 Henry Street, Blenheim	**W:** www.henrymaxwells.co.nz	**Bath:** 2 Ensuite 1 Private
		1 Guests share

Blenheim

Welcome to Marlborough. We invite you to stay at Maxwell House, a grand old Victorian residence. Built in 1880 our home has been elegantly restored and is classified with the Historic Places Trust. Our large guest rooms are individually appointed with ensuite, lounge area, television and tea and coffee making facilities. Breakfast will be a memorable experience, served around the original 1880's Kauri table. Set on a large established property Maxwell House is an easy ten minute walk to the town centre. Non Smoking.

Maxwell House	**Tel:** (03) 577 7545	**Cost:** Double $115
Homestay	**Fax:** (03) 577 7545	Single $90
Blenheim Central	**Mob:** 025 234 9977	Visa/MC
John and Barbara Ryan	**W:** www.bnb.co.nz/hosts/	**Beds:** 1 Queen 1 Twin (2 bdrm)
82 Maxwell Road	maxwellhouse.html	**Bath:** 2 Ensuite
Blenheim		

Blenheim

Enjoy your stay at our luxurious and exceptionally
spacious two storey home located in rural Blenheim.
Only 2km form the town centre, Green Gables is set
in a tranquil, one acre landscaped garden and offers
quiet, luxurious surroundings, although close to State
Highway 1 and to town.

Guest accommodation comprises of three large
bedrooms, all with en suite bathrooms. Two of our
rooms have queen - sized beds and the third has a
double bed. All rooms are fully equipped with
electric blankets, radio clocks, hair dryers and room
heating and two rooms have glass doors that open
onto private balconies affording panoramic views of
Blenheim. An adjoining guest lounge has a small
library and television set and there are additional TV
sets in the queen rooms. Coffee and tea making
facilities are available and you are invited to use the
laundry, fax and email facilities if required.

For breakfast choose either a full, country-style cooked breakfast or a light continental breakfast or if
you prefer a delectable combination of both, served with delicious home-made jams and preserves.
Dinner is available by arrangement and features traditional New Zealand cuisine served with a
complimentary drink.

We are horticulturists and grow fresh vegetables and cut flowers. Bruce our friendly cocker spaniel
would love to play ball with you and our ginger cat Sharky is visitor friendly and lives outside.
Green Gables backs onto the picturesque Opawa river. In season this gentle river offers trout fishing,
eeling and whitebaiting. A small rowing boat is available for your use at no extra charge.
As an additional courtesy üwe would be pleased to help you with the on -booking of your B&B
accommodation. Let us phone ahead for you and you'll make valuable savings on your phone card.

Directions: On SH1, 1/2 km south of Blenheim town, gate number 3011. 20 minutes form Picton
ferry. Green Gables sign at drive entrance.

Green Gables
B&B Homestay Country
Homestay
1.5km S of Blenheim
Raelene and Bill Rainbird
RD 4 Gate 3011
Blenheim

Tel: (03) 577 9205
Fax: (03) 577 9206
Tollfree: 0800 273 050
Mob: 025 547 520
E: linknz@voyager.co.nz
W: www.bnb.co.nz/hosts/
greengables.html

Cost: Double $85-$100
    Single $40-$60
    Continental Cooked
    Breakfast $5 extra
    Dinner $25 Visa/MC
Beds: 2 Queen 2 Double
    (3 bdrm)
Bath: 3 Ensuite

Blenheim

Two totally self-contained cottages set amongst 1.5 acres of Chardonnay grapes and an acre of garden. Only 5 minutes drive from Blenheim town but in a rural setting. One cottage has wheelchair access and a wheelchair friendly bathroom. The cottages and setting are ideal for families, with plenty of space to play. A cot is available if needed. Well behaved pets are welcome by prior arrangement. Well-appointed kennel or inside basket available. Continental breakfast is available on request for $5 per person.

Na Clachan Cottages	**Tel:** (03) 578 8881	**Cost:** Double $65
Self-contained	**Fax:** (03) 578 8881	Single $45
3km E of Blenheim	**Mob:** 025 260 7212	Families $85
Wendy Mein	**E:** helen.r@xtra.co.nz	**Beds:** 1 Double 2 Single
47 Rowberrys Road	**W:** mysite.xtra.co.nz/	(2 bdrm)
RD 3, Blenheim	~NaClachan/index.html	**Bath:** 1 Private 1 Guests share

Blenheim - Rapaura

Situated in the heart of the wine region, Tamar is one of Marlborough's oldest vineyards. Our newly built cottage is a romantic retreat with breathtaking views through the vines to the Richmond Ranges. Luxuriate in an ornately carved four poster bed under a feather down duvet, then enjoy a gourmet breakfast before taking a leisurely stroll to nearby wineries and restaurants. Or let us help organise your wine trail, skifield, or Marlborough Sounds experience. Our secluded, smoke free cottage is self-contained and a warm welcome and memorable stay is assured.

Tamar Vineyard	**Tel:** (03) 572 8408	**Cost:** Double $140-$160
B&B Self-contained Self-	**Fax:** (03) 572 8405	Single $120 Child neg
contained Vineyard Cottage	**Tollfree:** 0800 429 922	Visa/MC
15km SW of Blenheim	**E:** tamar.vineyard@xtra.co.nz	**Beds:** 1 Queen 1 Single
Clive & Yvonne Dasler	**W:** www.bnb.co.nz/hosts/	(1 bdrm)
67 Rapaura Road	tamarvineyard.html	**Bath:** 1 Private
RD 3, Blenheim		

Blenheim

Set in 3/4 acre of parklike gardens, 3 mins drive to Blenheim and 10 mins to Picton. Our home is very popular with guests for its spaciousness and homely atmosphere. Orchard View is an ideal base for exploring the many wineries, craft shops and walk-ways. We are very relaxed and encourage our guests to be also. Full breakfast supplied. Meals by arrange-ment. Own guests lounge with refreshments, TV, stereo. Also there is plenty of parking space. We have a cat called Oscar.

Orchard View	**Tel:** (03) 578 5444	**Cost:** Double $85-$110 Single $60
B&B Homestay	**Fax:** (03) 578 5444	Dinner $25 B/A
2km N of Blenheim	**Tollfree:** 0800 006 903	Ensuite $110
Lynley & John McGinn	**Mob:** 021 295 7031	Visa/MC Diners
20 Nolans Road, Grovetown	**W:** www.bnb.co.nz/hosts/	**Beds:** 2 Queen 1 Double
Blenheim, Marlborough	orchardview.html	2 Single (3 bdrm)
New Zealand		**Bath:** 1 Ensuite 1 Family share

Rapaura - Blenheim

Our new self-contained, double storey accommodation has views across the garden and vineyard to the Richmond Ranges. The living area includes a kitchenette, TV and wood-burner. We are at the heart of the Marlborough wine region and close to the Marlborough Sounds, renowned for its mussel industry. After many years spent abroad in Africa, we and our two teenage sons look forward to welcoming you to this special corner of New Zealand.

Twiga
Self-contained Vinestay
8km N of Blenheim
Andy & Kris Bibby
35 Selmes Road
Rapaura, RD 3
Blenheim

Tel: (03) 570 5706
Fax: (03) 570 5726
Tollfree: 0800 284 670
Mob: 021 899 926
E: twiga@agrimech.co.nz
W: www.twiga.co.nz

Cost: Double $175
Single $100
Twin $150 Visa/MC
Beds: 1 Queen 1 Twin (2 bdrm)
Bath: 2 Ensuite

Blenheim

Karere House enjoys a rural aspect, offering modern elegant accommodation in the heart of the Marlborough wine district. Three luxuriously appointed guest bedrooms, with terraces and outstanding views. Walk or cruise the Marlborough Sounds, wine tasting, arts and crafts, whale watching at Kaikoura, just a few of the local amenities. On your return enjoy a glass of wine followed by one of Maggie's (Cordon Bleu qualified) dinners. Heated swimming pool and petanque available. Welcome to Karere House, we look forward to meeting you.

Karere House
B&B
2km W of Blenheim
David & Maggie Cleveland
6 Karere Place
Springlands
Blenheim

Tel: (03) 579 1159
Fax: (03) 579 1160
E: david@karerehouse.co.nz
W: www.accommodation
marlborough.co.nz

Cost: Double $150-$170
Single $115-$130
Unsuitable for children
Dinner $60 Visa/MC
Beds: 1 King/Twin 1 King
1 Queen (3 bdrm)
Bath: 1 Ensuite 1 Private

Blenheim

We welcome you to our new home built on the slopes of Wither Hills situated to the South side of Blenheim having panoramic views of town, Richmond ranges and Cook Strait in the distance. Offering Queen and Twin rooms with electric blankets and heating. Complimetary spa available. Bathroom and toilet are separate and private. Our interests comprise boating, vintage cars, flying and enjoying Marlborough's fantastic waterways and wineries which you can share by arrangement. Local pickup available on request. Dinner by arrangement.

Richmond View
Homestay
3km Blenheim
Allan & Jan Graham
25 Elmwood Avenue
Blenheim

Tel: (03) 578 8001
Fax: (03) 578 8001
Mob: 025 458 074
E: a.w.graham@xtra.co.nz
W: www.bnb.co.nz/hosts/
richmondview.html

Cost: Double $80
Single $60
Dinner $30 pp
Beds: 1 Queen 1 Twin
(2 bdrm)
Bath: 1 Private 1 Guests share

Renwick

Waterfall Lodge - self-contained, vineyard setting. 2 beds.
Queen, 2 single. Kitchen facilities, dining, lounge area, gas
bbq. Main house - Queen room, private bathroom. Both
offer unique mud-brick construction and offer rustic charm
combined with stylish furnishings. Breakfast hamper with
full provisions daily. Ideal base for winery visits, golf,
Sounds cruising, walking, Trout fishing. Blenheim Town
10 mins drive. Solar heated indoor pool. LeGrys &
Mudhouse wines available, complimentary tasting and tray
of nibbles to welcome you. We have a Springer Spaniel,
Pippin.

LeGrys Vineyard
Self-contained Homestay
Vineyard Lodge
15km W of Blenheim
Jennifer & John Joslin
PO Box 65, Renwick, Marlborough

Tel: (03) 572 9490
Fax: (03) 572 9491
Mob: 021 313 208
E: legrys@voyager.co.nz
W: www.legrys.co.nz

Cost: Double $140
S/C $190 + $40, max 4
Visa/MC
Beds: 2 Queen 2 Single
(3 bdrm)
Bath: 2 Private

Renwick

Our colonial style home is set in 1/2 acre of lovely
private grounds in the heart of vineyard country. We
overlook orchards and out to the Richmond Range. In
summer relax under the trees with refreshments - by a
glowing fire in winter. Visit our quaint local English
country pub - dine at village or vineyard restaurants.
We are within 'stroll & taste' distance of a number of
prestigious vineyards. We have farmed, sailed, and
thoroughly enjoy all our varied guests. A warm
welcome definitely awaits you at "Devonia".

Devonia
Homestay
10km W of Blenheim
Maurie & Marg Beuth
2A Nelson Place, Renwick
Marlborough 7352

Tel: (03) 572 9593
Fax: (03) 572 7293
W: www.bnb.co.nz/hosts/
devonia.html

Cost: Double $80-$90
Single $65 Visa/MC
Beds: 1 Queen 2 Single
(2 bdrm)
Bath: 2 Private

Havelock

Our home is a gracious 1930's Villa, designed for space
and comfort, only 40 minutes from the Interisland
Ferry. We have travelled widely abroad and have
family here and overseas. We are members of the
Lions club and we have a friendly West Highland
Terrier who loves to greet our guests. Havelock is only
20 minutes from the Marlborough wine trail and a hub
for many outdoor activities both on and off the water.
Several excellent restaurants are within easy walking
distance of our home.

Carnlough
B&B
40km E of Picton
Reg & Margaret Williams
101 Main Road
Havelock, Marlborough

Tel: (03) 574 1444
E: Paregma@clear.net.nz
W: www.bnb.co.nz/hosts/
carnlough.html

Cost: Double $80-$90
Single $80 Child $20
Visa/MC
Beds: 1 Queen (1 bdrm)
Bath: 1 Ensuite

Canvastown

We are down to earth people, our home is lodge style with country atmosphere. You will be accommodated in the guest wing but share meals and conversation in our dining room and lounge. Consider more than one night's stay as fishing and hunting are only minutes away. Walking and tramping tracks are prolific or cruise the fabulous sounds in comfort. Fishing and hunting parties must book forward. We love traditional Kiwi tucker and wines and encourage you to share evening meals with us. Welcome to Woodchester.

Woodchester
Homestay
50km W of Nelson
Wayne & Marilyn Te Amo
84 Te Hora Pa Road
Canvastown

Tel: (03) 574 1123
Fax: (03) 574 1123
Mob: 025 224 4765
E: mariltynt@xtra.co.nz
W: www.bnb.co.nz/hosts/woodchester.html

Cost: Double $70-$90
Single $50 Child $20
Dinner $30 incl wine
Visa/MC
Beds: 1 Queen 1 Double
2 Twin (3 bdrm)
Bath: 1 Guests share

Pelorus Bridge

We wish to invite you to our beautiful Fraemos Lodge. We are situated 45 minutes from Nelson and Blenheim on State Highway 6 in the midst of 1 1/2 acre of untouched natural South Island native forest with prolific bird life. We are 1 1/2km from Pelorus Bridge Scenic Reserve, which is one of the finest reserves in New Zealand. As we have our own private dwelling, the guests have the run of the house with excellent cooking facilities. Entire house available. Bitte kommen Sie uns besuchen.

Lord Lionel
Self-contained Guest House
45mins Blenheim/Nelson
Lionel & Monika Neilands
SH6 Pelorus
RD 2, Rai Valley, Marlborough

Tel: (03) 574 2770
Fax: (03) 574 2770
W: www.bnb.co.nz/hosts/lordlionel.html

Cost: Double $80
Single $50
Child 1/2 price Visa/MC
Beds: 1 King 3 Double
2 Single (6 bdrm)
Bath: 1 Private 2 Guests share

Rai Valley

Dear Guests. We invite you to have soul time on our 125 acre hill side property. Guests will enjoy total privacy and comfort of their own chalet with kitchen and bathroom. The chalets are environmentally friendly built, and are painted inside with beeswax. Great for allergy sufferers. Excellent rainbow and brown trout fishing only 5 minutes form the lodge. Alternatively you may relax on the terrace and enjoy the flower garden. Foot reflexology massages available on request. Iris and Helmut speak Swiss German and French.

Bulford Lodge
B&B Self-contained
Farmstay Chalets
71km S of Nelson
H Spiess & I Grossenbacher
Bulford Road, RD 2, Rai Valley
Marlborough

Tel: (03) 571 6049
Fax: (03) 571 6049
Mob: 025 201 9074
W: www.bnb.co.nz/hosts/bulfordlodge.html

Cost: Double $93-$118
Single $89
Beds: 2 Queen 1 Double
4 Single (3 bdrm)
Bath: 2 Private

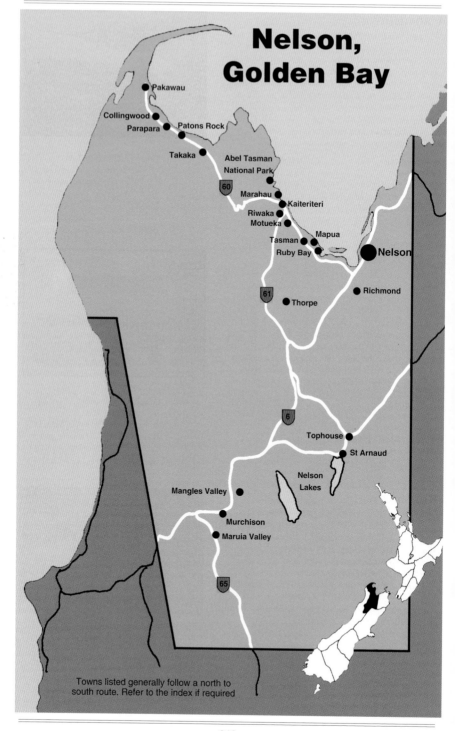

Nelson, Golden Bay

Towns listed generally follow a north to south route. Refer to the index if required

Nelson

Make SERENDIPITY your "fortunate discovery" while in Nelson. Our beautiful Victorian (1880's) Villa has been tastefully redecorated over recent years to offer the best of both eras. The spacious, sunny, upstairs bedrooms give stunning views across Nelson City or Tasman Bay towards the setting sun and Abel Tasman National Park. All the beds are firm but comfortable, have electric blankets and feather duvets. Each bedroom has TV, heating, tea & coffee making facilities, hairdryers and fresh flowers.

The hilltop, garden setting offers a quiet retreat for the traveller. We take a maximum of two groups at a time. Relax and enjoy a pre-dinner drink in your own guest lounge. You are very welcome to make use of our laundry free of charge. We also offer access to Internet and E-mail so that you can keep in touch with home or work. There is ample off-street parking.

Nelson has many good cafes and award winning restaurants, however, by prior arrangement you may join us for a three-course dinner with local wine or perhaps a lighter meal. We invite you to relax by, or swim in, the salt-water pool in warmer weather and make use of the spa on those cooler evenings.

We know our country well and delight in meeting fellow travellers from overseas or around New Zealand while sharing a leisurely, and scrumptious cooked or continental breakfast. Sherry enjoys gardening, cooking and sewing while Warwick is an engineer whose interests include renovation, photography and computing. We both enjoy art, music, travel, films and shows. We request that guests do not smoke in the house- Boris the cat doesn't like it.

Serendipity
B&B Homestay
2km W of Nelson
Sheridan & Warwick Bishop
95 Queens Road
Nelson

Tel: (03) 548 2133
Mob: 021 420 165
E: enquiries@serendipity.co.nz
W: www.serendipity.co.nz

Cost: Double $145-$160
Single $100 Child $55
Dinner $35 by arr.
Lighter meal $25 Visa/MC
Beds: 2 Queen 1 Twin (3 bdrm)
Bath: 1 Ensuite 1 Private

Nelson

Quiet, spacious, sunny; we invite you to enjoy the charm and character of our faithfully restored 1893 villa. Features include English oak panelling, stained glass windows, NZ native timbers and wide verandahs overlooking the garden. Your choice of 5 well appointed guestrooms with ensuite bathrooms, colonial furnishings, memorabilia & fresh flowers from the garden. Guest sitting room with library, open fire, refreshments, a congenial atmosphere and friendly hosts ensure relaxation and enjoyment. Delicious homebaked Californian breakfasts a highlight, all within 5 minutes walk of city centre!

California House Inn	**Tel:** (03) 548 4173	**Cost:** Double $160-$210
B&B Heritage Inn	**Fax:** (03) 548 4173	Single $130-$160
Nelson Central	**E:** info@californiahouse.co.nz	Visa/MC
Neil & Shelley Johnstone	**W:** www.californiahouse.co.nz	**Beds:** 4 Queen 1 Double
29 Collingwood St		1 Twin 5 Single (5 bdrm)
Nelson		**Bath:** 5 Ensuite

Nelson

Our home is above the harbour entrance. Huge windows capture spectacular r views of beautiful Tasman Bay, Haulashore Island, Tahunanui Beach, across the sea to Abel Tasman National Park and mountains. Observe from the bedrooms, dining room and decks, ships and pleasure craft cruising by as they enter and leave the harbour. If you can tear yourself away from our magnificent view, within walking distance along the waterfront there are excellent cafes and restaurants. From Judy,David and Puss a warm welcome and thank you for not smoking inside.

Harbour View Homestay

Harbour View Homestay	**Tel:** (03) 548 8567	**Cost:** Double $115-$125
Homestay	**Fax:** (03) 548 8667	Single $85-$110 Visa/MC
2km SW of Nelson	**Mob:** 025 247 4445	Full breakfast $5pp extra
Judy Black	**W:** www.bnb.co.nz/hosts/	**Beds:** 2 Queen 2 Single
11 Fifeshire Crescent	harbourviewhomestaynelson.html	(3 bdrm)
Nelson		**Bath:** 2 Ensuite 1 Private

Nelson

Five minutes from Nelson City centre we give you a warm welcome to our comfortable home in a safe quiet neighbourhood with superb views over Tasman Bay and out to the Tasman mountains. Our guest accommodation is almost self-contained and is well equipped with a fridge, TV, tea and coffee making facilities and a microwave. Laundry facilities are available for your use. Our interests include our large collection of books which you are welcome to use, sea fishing, education and canine obedience with our schnauzer dog.

B&B Homestay	**Tel:** (03) 545 1671	**Cost:** Double $65 Single $45
6km N of Nelson	**Fax:** (03) 545 1671	Child neg Dinner $30
Mike Cooper & Lennane Kent	**E:** cooperkent@actrix.gen.nz	with prior notice Visa/MC
4 Seaton St	**W:** www.bnb.co.nz/hosts/	**Beds:** 1 Double 2 Single
Nelson	kent.html	(2 bdrm)
		Bath: 2 Ensuite

Nelson

Behind a high laurel hedge you will discover
BOROGOVE, our century-old heritage home.
Characteristic high ceilings, period furniture and
antiques contribute to its unique charm. Bedrooms are
elegantly decorated and have en-suite bathrooms.
Relaxing arm-chairs, tea/coffee, heaters, electric
blankets, reading-lights and TV ensure your comfort.
Generous cooked breakfasts are served in our Victorian
dining-room. It is a 3 minute walk to the Visitors'
Centre, the shops and restaurants. Abel Tasman bus
will collect at door. Off-street parking.

Borogove	**Tel:** (03) 548 9442	**Cost:** Double $95
B&B	**Fax:** (03) 548 9443	Single $75
Nelson Central	**Tollfree:** 0800 379 308	**Beds:** 2 Queen 1 Single
Judy & Bill Hiener	**E:** hihiener@xtra.co.nz	(3 bdrm)
27 Grove Street	**W:** www.bnb.co.nz/hosts/	**Bath:** 3 Ensuite
Nelson	borogove.html	

Nelson

The two smokefree units in our large home offer comfort,
privacy and offstreet parking in a central location. Unit 1,
which is larger, is in a private garden setting. A ranchslider
opens on to a deck with outdoor furniture. It has an Electric
Stove, Microwave, TV, Auto Washing Machine & Phone. 2
beds in a private 'Sunroom' could sleep additional family
members. Unit 2 has a balcony with seating to enjoy sea
and mountain views. It has a Microwave, TV & Phone. We
have 2 Tonkinese cats.

Arapiki	**Tel:** (03) 547 3741	**Cost:** Double $65-$75
B&B	**Fax:** (03) 547 3742	Single $55-$60 Visa/MC
Self-contained Homestay Units	**E:** arapiki@tasman.net	Optional continental
5km SW of Nelson	**W:** www.ts.co.nz/brochures/	breakfast $7.50pp
Kay & Geoff Gudsell	arapiki	**Beds:** 1 Queen 1 Double
21 Arapiki Road		1 Single (2 bdrm)
Stoke, Nelson		**Bath:** 2 Ensuite

Nelson

In a quiet street surrounded by gardens and mature
trees, we offer quality accommodation for only one
group of guests at a time giving them exclusive use of
all facilities. These include a comfortable lounge with
TV, video and complimentary teas and coffee. There is
a comprehensive selection of local information so that
you can plan your stay, and we are always available to
help you with ideas, expecially if time is limited. If
allowed, our friendly Golden Labrador loves the
opportunity to socialise with guests.

Tarata Homestay

*When you want a home
away from home*

Tarata Homestay	**Tel:** (03) 547 3426	**Cost:** Double $80
B&B Homestay	**Fax:** (03) 547 3640	Single $60
6km S of Nelson	**Tollfree:** 0800 107 308	Child $20 Visa/MC
John & Mercia Hoskin	**E:** hosts@taratahomestay.co.nz	**Beds:** 1 Queen 2 Single
5 Tarata Street	**W:** www.taratahomestay.co.nz	(2 bdrm)
Stoke, Nelson		**Bath:** 1 Private

Nelson

Many of our guests have told us we have some of the finest views of any Bed & Breakfast in New Zealand. High on a ridge overlooking the whole of Nelson City, beautiful Tasman Bay, mountains and harbour entrance. Drive downtown in three minutes, or try our new walkway from the top of Quebec Road to the valley below. Breakfast is special, our own Muesli made with Beech honey and cinnamon, homemade yoghurt, breads, muffins and scones. Taste our local Pomeroy's fruit or spiced teas, or Sheridan's special blend of coffee beans. Waffles are our specialities, try a Vanilla and Cinnamon one, topped with

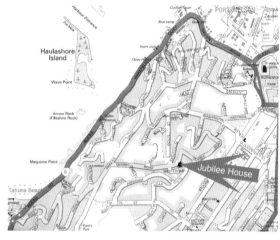

seasonal fruit and real Canadian maple syrup. You might like to go savoury with salami, tasty bacon and Bratwurst sausage. We can serve something traditional or different, or cater for your special diet, with adequate notice. As Nelson leads the rest of the country in sunshine hours stay a while in this beautiful region. You may even get to see one of our spectacular sunsets. We are happy to help or advise you on places of interest and things to do, or on the many great restaurants and cafes we have in our City. We provide a smoke free environment, courtesy pick-up from the airport, visitor centre or bus depot, and offer off street parking. KJ our Devon Rex cat may grace you with his presence; he is none allegenic as his coat is wool.

Jubilee House	**Tel:** (03) 548 8511	**Cost:** Double $90
Homestay	**Fax:** (03) 548 8511	Single $60
2km W of Nelson Central	**Mob:** 025 487 767	Visa/MC
Patsy & Sheridan Parris	**E:** jubilee.house@actrix.co.nz	**Beds:** 2 Double 2 Single
107 Quebec Road	**W:** www.bnb.co.nz/hosts/	(4 bdrm)
Nelson	jubileehouse.html	**Bath:** 1 Guests share

Nelson

Sunset Waterfront B&B provides wonderful panoramic sea and mountain views of Tasman Bay. Ideally situated to walk to quality seafood restaurants. Stroll along the promenade to enjoy the sunset or take an evening walk along the beach. 10 minutes drive from the airport and bus station. Quiet and secluded location. We provide comfortable bedrooms with ensuites, TV, fridge, and sea views. One room for optional self catering. Freshly brewed coffee and local fresh produce provided. Off street parking. Regretfully no children under 12. Pet, Bono our Golden Retriever. Come enjoy our paradise!

Sunset Waterfront B&B	**Tel:** (03) 548 3431	**Cost:** Double $120-$130
B&B Self-contained	**Fax:** (03) 548 3743	Single $105
2.5km S of Nelson	**Mob:** 025 363 300	Visa/MC
Bernie Kirk & Louis Balshaw	**E:** waterfrontnelson@xtra.co.nz	**Beds:** 2 Queen 1 Twin 1 Single
455 Rock Road, Nelson	**W:** www.bnb.co.nz/hosts/	(2 bdrm)
	sunsetwaterfrontbb.html	**Bath:** 2 Ensuite

Nelson

"Walmer" is a spacious, sunny house opposite the harbour entrance and is close to the sea, beach, city and three seaside restaurants. Splendid views of the harbour and bay are gained from your upstairs apartment which has a sunroom, lounge, double bedroom, single bedroom, bathroom and kitchen all for your exclusive use. You may be independent by self-catering using your own kitchen and private entrance or choose to use the B&B option. There are two Labrador dogs. House unsuitable for children.

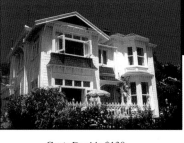

Walmer	**Tel:** (03) 548 3858	**Cost:** Double $130
B&B Apartment	**Fax:** (03) 548 3857	Single $90
2km W of Nelson	**E:** bob.hart@xtra.co.nz	Visa/MC
Bob & Janet Hart	**W:** www.walmer.co.nz	**Beds:** 1 Queen 1 Single
7 Richardson Street		(2 bdrm)
Nelson		**Bath:** 1 Private

Nelson

Welcome to Muritai Manor, a unique Edwardian home in a semi-rural setting with superb views across Tasman Bay. Five luxury ensuite bedrooms furnished with antiques, TVs, refreshments, hairdryers, bathrobes, flowers, & toiletries; with electric blankets on all the beds. Enjoy gourmet breakfasts in the guest dining room. Open fires in both lounge & dining room in winter. Large solar heated swimming pool & spa in established garden with mature trees. Jess Gennie & Dande are the friendly canine family members. Your hosts - Jan & Stan.

Muritai Manor	**Tel:** (03) 545 1189	**Cost:** Double $165-$190 Single
B&B Self-contained	**Fax:** (03) 545 0740	$130-$155 Child by arr.
7km N of Nelson	**Mob:** 025 370 622	Dinner by arrangement
Jan & Stan Holt	**Tollfree:** 0800 260 662	Visa/MC Amex
48 Wakapuaka Road	**E:** muritai.manor@xtra.co.nz	**Beds:** 2 King/Twin 1 King
Wakapuaka, RD 1	**W:** www.muritaimanor.co.nz	2 Queen 5 Single (5 bdrm)
Nelson		**Bath:** 5 Ensuite

Nelson

Experience the peace and charm of yesteryear in our fully restored c1880's B&B, one of Nelson's original family homes. Situated beside the beautiful Maitai River, The Sussex has retained all the original character and romantic ambience of the era. It is only minutes walk from central Nelson's award winning restaurants and cafes, the Queens Gardens, Suter Art Gallery and Botanical Hill (The Centre Of NZ) and many good walks, river and bush.

The five sunny bedrooms all have TV's and are spacious and charmingly furnished. All rooms have access to the verandahs and complimentary tea & coffee facilities are provided. This is a musician's house and travelling musicians can enjoy the use of our instruments, including guitars, fiddles, mandolins, player piano, double bass and more.

Breakfast includes lots of fresh and preserved fruits, homemade muffins baked fresh every morning, hot croissants, homemade yoghurts, cheeses & salamis and a large variety of cereals, bagels, rolls, breads and crumpets. The Sussex provides a smoke free environment and all foods, to the best of our knowledge, are free from genetically modified ingredients.

We regret that we are not suited to children.

OTHER FACILITIES INCLUDE: Email/ Internet station; fax; courtesy phone; laundry facilities; separate lounge for guest entertaining; complimentary port; tea & coffee facilities; very sociable cat (Riley); bread to feed the ducks.

The Sussex Bed &	**Tel:** (03) 548 9972	**Cost:** Double $120-$150
Breakfast Hotel	**Fax:** (03) 548 9975	Single $100-$130
Historic Bed & Breakfast Hotel	**Mob:** (025) 784 846	Visa/MC Amex Diners
500m E of Nelson Central	**Tollfree:** 0800 868 687	**Beds:** 5 Queen 2 Twin
Carol & Stephen Rose	**E:** reservations@sussex.co.nz	2 Single (5 bdrm)
238 Bridge Street	**W:** www.sussex.co.nz	**Bath:** 4 Ensuite 1 Private
Nelson		

Nelson

Brooklands is a spacious, luxurious 4 level home with
superb sea views. Guests have exclusive use of 2 levels.
The large bathroom has a spa bath for two. One bedroom
has a private balcony. There are spacious indoor/outdoor
living areas. We enjoy sports, running, travel and outdoors.
Lorraine makes dolls and bears and enjoys crafts, gardening
and cooking. We are close to Nelson's attractions - beaches,
crafts, wine trails, national parks, lakes and mountains. We
enjoy making new friends. Smoke free. Courtesy transport
available.

Brooklands	**Tel:** (03) 545 1423	**Cost:** Double $90-$100
B&B Homestay	**E:** bsignal@paradise.net.nz	Single $60 Child By arr.
2km E of Nelson	**W:** www.bnb.co.nz/hosts/	Dinner $25 Visa/MC
Lorraine & Barry Signal	brooklands.html	**Beds:** 1 Queen 1 Double
106 Brooklands Rd		2 Single (3 bdrm)
Atawhai, Nelson		**Bath:** 1 Ensuite 1 Guests share

Nelson Central

Welcome to our home on the banks of the Maitai River.
Our large bedrooms, with ensuite bathrooms, are
serviced daily with fresh flowers, complimentary
basket of fruit and contain TV, microwave, fridge, tea/
coffee making facilities, and toaster. Breakfast is self-
service. We are very close to Queen's Gardens, Suter
Art Gallery and the Botanical Hill, where after an easy
walk to the centre of New Zealand, you experience
wonderful views over Tasman Bay and Nelson
township. Courtesy car to airport or bus depot. No
smoking inside please.

Sunflower Cottage	**Tel:** (03) 548 1588	**Cost:** Double $95
B&B	**Fax:** (03) 548 1588	Single $65
0.8km E of Nelson	**E:** sunflower@netaccess.co.nz	Dinner $25
Marion & Chris Burton	**W:**	**Beds:** 2 King/Twin 2 Twin
70 Tasman Street	www.sunfloweraccommodation.co.nz	2 Single (2 bdrm)
Nelson		**Bath:** 2 Ensuite

Nelson

Overlooking the Maitai River, Brook Stream and Centre
of New Zealand this elegantly restored 1885 Victorian,
offers spacious and luxuriously appointed rooms. Each
has its own character and charm with antique furnishings, comfortable beds and modern amenities. Enjoy
afternoon tea or cappuccino in the cozy guest lounge,
sunroom or garden and chat with Tim about his classic
MG's. Janet, a cook by profession, makes breakfast to
order, healthy or indulgent, cooked or continental. This
Canadian/New Zealand ambiance is enhanced by their
lively fox terrier.

The Baywick Inn	**Tel:** (03) 545 6514	**Cost:** Double $120-$145
B&B	**Fax:** (03) 545 6517	Single $95-$105
Nelson Central	**Mob:** 025 545 823	Dinner $40pp Visa/MC
Tim Bayley & Janet Southwick	**E:** baywicks@iconz.co.nz	**Beds:** 3 Queen 1 Single
51 Domett Street	**W:** www.bnb.co.nz/hosts/	(3 bdrm)
Nelson	thebaywickinn.html	**Bath:** 2 Ensuite 1 Private

Nelson Central

Step back in time and enjoy the experience of staying in our sympathetically restored 100 year old home, cleverly combining modern convenience with the ambience & style of yesteryear. We are 5 minutes walk into Nelson City with it's wonderful cafes, interesting shops and very close to Nelson's main iconz - Suter Art Gallery, Queens Gardens, Nelson School of Music, NMIT (Polytech), Maitai River Walks, heated Riverside Pool Centre of NZ, Founders Park, Miyazu Japanese Gardens, Christchurch Cathedral, main churches, Info Centres & Bus Station.

Our home is on one level. Each comfortable bedroom contains quality beds & furniture, electric blankets, hair dryers, heaters, iron/ironing board, clock radio, T.V, fresh flowers and sweet treats. Guest have exclusive use of the sunny lounge with pantry & fridge for any time refreshments, verandahs and courtyards both sunny & shady.

All rooms are furnished with antiques & interesting furniture, memorabilia and original art. This all makes your stay at Grove Villa an added bonus to your Nelson visit.

Our breakfasts are special, homemade breads, muesli, jams, marmalades, preserves, yoghurt, seasonal fresh fruit and NZ cheeses.

Our guest book testifies to the enjoyment of great breakfasts, ground coffee & many tea choices.

We are happy to help you with sightseeing choices however we will also respect your privacy and encourage you to treat Grove Villa as your home away from home.

If you are interested in gardens you will delighted by the lovely garden setting, roses, lavenders, cherry trees - plus the largest & oldest cycad revoluta in the South Island. Registered as a notable tree this cycad is an excellent example of the primitive life form of prehistoric times.

We have no pets or family. Happy for you to smoke on the verandah.

Because there is so much for you to enjoy in this region we offer a discount for 3 plus nights stay. We want you to experience "jewels" like Abel Tasman National Park (we are ticketing agents), Tahunanui Beach - safest in the country, golf courses, fishing rivers, wonderful wineries, superb arts & crafts, fabulous fresh food. All theses things and more are here in the acclaimed Sunshine Capital of NZ.

Grove Villa	**Tel:** (03) 548 8895	**Cost:** Double $85-$140 Single
B&B	**Fax:** (03) 548 8856	$75-$115 Child over 10years
400m Nelson Central	**Tollfree:** 0800 488 900	Dinner by arr. Visa/MC
Lynne Harrison-Greening	**E:** lynne@grovevilla.co.nz	**Beds:** 1 King/Twin 2 Qn 1
36 Grove Street	**W:** www.grovevilla.co.nz	Dbl 2 Twin 2 Sgl (6 bdrm)
Nelson		**Bath:** 3 Ens 1 Priv 1 Guests share

Nelson - Tahunanui

Our quiet hillside home, nestled in 1/2 acre of gardens, enjoys panoramic 180 degrees views - including Tasman Bay and Tahunanui Beach, with the distant mountain backdrop affording us glorious sunsets. The guest rooms are situated at the south western wing of the house offering own access, tea/coffee facilities and outdoor spa. We invite you to enjoy a drink and chat on our large deck before going on to the fabulous waterfront restaurants just minutes away. A social family - including one son & kitten. Phone for directions.

Somerset House
B&B
3km SW of Nelson
Nicki & Richard Harden
33 Chamberlain Street
Tahunanui, Nelson

Tel: (03) 548 5998
Fax: (03) 548 5436
E: R.Harden@xtra.co.nz
W: www.bnb.co.nz/hosts/ somersethouse.html

Cost: Double $110
Single $75
Child Neg Visa/MC
Beds: 1 Queen 1 Single
(2 bdrm)
Bath: 1 Ensuite

Nelson

Our home is situated overlooking Tahunanui Beach, Haulashore Island and Nelson waterfront with amazing daytime mountain views and magnificent sunsets. Enjoy a wine out on the deck or relax in the spa. Excellent restaurants and cafes within walking distance, stroll to the beach or a 5 minute drive to the city. Golf course, tennis courts and airport nearby. Both rooms have ensuite/private bathrooms, quality beds, electric blankets, fridge, TV, tea & coffee making facilities, heaters, iron, hairdryers. Laundry available.

Beach Front B&B
B&B
3km S of Nelson
Peter & Oriel Phillips
581 Rocks Road
Nelson

Tel: (03) 548 5299
Fax: (03) 548 5299
Mob: 025 216 5237
W: www.bnb.co.nz/hosts/ beachfrontbb.html

Cost: Double $90
Single $65
Visa/MC
Beds: 1 Queen 1 Double
(2 bdrm)
Bath: 1 Ensuite 1 Private

There are tips about enjoying B&Bs on page 5

Nelson

Experience tranquil garden setting with waterfall and private seating areas, only three blocks to city centre. All rooms have television, telephones, writing desks, hairdryers, curling irons, heated towel racks and cotton bed linens. Fax and email facilities available for business purposes. Large dining room, separate guest lounge with amenities. Extensively decorated with local arts and crafts. Walk to galleries, cinema, restaurants, shopping, churches, and exercise facility. Maitai River walks, Grampian Trails, trail to centre of New Zealand within five minutes walking distance from Villa. No pets, no children under 12.

Shelbourne Villa	**Tel:** (03) 545 9059	**Cost:** Double $195-$250
B&B	**Fax:** (03) 546 7248	Visa/MC Amex Diners
Nelson Central	**Mob:** 025 423 0238	**Beds:** 4 King (4 bdrm)
Leon & Joyce Riebel	**E:** beds@shelbournevilla.co.nz	**Bath:** 4 Ensuite
21 Shelbourne Street	**W:** www.shelbournevilla.co.nz	
Nelson		

Nelson

Imagine beautiful sunsets and magnificent views of Mount Arthur Range and Tasman Bay. Private rear garden filled with flowers for you to enjoy breakfast and evening drinks or just relax in. Situated 5 minutes drive to fine restaurants and cafes, at Tahunanui Beach and Nelson City. In our home you will find a warm and friendly atmosphere, good comfortable beds, electric blankets, TV, tea/coffee making facilities plus dressing gowns, hairdryers etc. Most of all great hospitality. Don't imagine, come relax and enjoy.

Cherry Trees	**Tel:** (03) 547 3735	**Cost:** Double $85-$90
B&B	**Fax:** (03) 547 0135	Single $65-$70 Visa/MC
5km S of Nelson	**Mob:** 025 266 7579	**Beds:** 1 Double 1 Twin
Ann & John Connor	**W:** www.bnb.co.nz/hosts/	(2 bdrm)
537 Waimea Road	cherrytrees.html	**Bath:** 1 Guests share
Nelson		

Nelson

Enjoy the unique experience of historic South Street, a cul de sac of preserved circa 1860 cottages in the heart of Nelson City. In the peaceful beautiful grounds of Baxter's Cottage are two individual garden cottage studio's offering privacy and independence with en suite bathrooms, very comfortable beds, TV & CD stereo, fridge,tea/coffee facilities. Character, charm and warm hospitality are assured. A delicious breakfast is served, either alfresco in the garden, or in Baxter's dining room. Stroll in minutes to all Nelson City has to offer. Smoke free.

Baxters Cottage	**Tel:** (03) 545 6001	**Cost:** Double $110
B&B Self-contained	**Fax:** (03) 545 6409	Single $100
Nelson Central	**Mob:** 021 117 4726	**Beds:** 1 Queen 1 Twin
Eva & Bruce Batty	**E:** baxcott@ihug.co.nz	(2 bdrm)
14 South Street	**W:** www.bnb.co.nz/hosts/	**Bath:** 2 Ensuite
Nelson	baxterscottage.html	

Nelson

Enjoy your spacious private suite in our Heritage Villa, only ten minutes riverside walk from Nelson's city centre. Your master bedroom includes ensuite bathroom and walk in wardrobe. Your adjoining rooms include a large lounge with additional double innersprung sofabed, log fire, Sky TV, fridge, kettle, toaster etc. and sunroom with cane setting and private entrance. Email/internet/fax facilities and off-street parking available. Children are welcome. We have two daughters aged seven and five and a cat called Chocolate.

Peppertree B&B	**Tel:** (03) 546 9881	**Cost:** Double $90
B&B	**Fax:** (03) 546 9881	Child $15
Nelson Central	**E:** c.sygrove@clear.net.nz	Dinner $20 by arrangement
Richard Savill & Carolyn	**W:** www.bnb.co.nz/hosts/	Visa/MC
Sygrove	peppertreebb.html	**Beds:** 1 Queen (1 bdrm)
31 Seymour Ave		**Bath:** 1 Ensuite
Nelson		

Nelson - Tahunanui

Welcome to our friendly atmosphere at Parkside. In our large modern bedrooms and separate guest lounge there are TV, fridge, tea/coffee facilities. Close to restaurants, golf course, sporting grounds, beach and airport. Shopping from Nelson City is only 8 mins drive. Have your breakfast in private or join us on our sunny deck. You can be sure of a warm friendly stay in our smoke free home with our two daughters aged 14 and 6 and friendly cat Mickey. There is secure garaging for all guests.

Parkside Bed & Breakfast	**Tel:** (03) 548 6629	**Cost:** Double $110
B&B	**Fax:** (03) 548 6621	Single $75
8km W of Nelson City	**Mob:** 025 217 7811	Visa/MC
Brent & Diane Williams	**E:** parkside.nelson@xtra.co.nz	**Beds:** 3 Queen 2 Single
16 Centennial Road	**W:** www.bnb.co.nz/hosts/	(3 bdrm)
Tahunanui	parkside.html	**Bath:** 2 Ensuite 1 Private
Nelson		

Nelson - Stoke

Modern, sunny and comfortable house with peacefull garden area. Situated in a quiet cul-de-sac off the Main Road. Ideally situated to visit Abel Tasman National Park and Nelson Lakes. Warm and friendly Japanese hosts. We serve either delicious Japanese breakfast or continental breakfast with home baked breads. Fresh vegetable salad and fruits are also included. Complimentary coffee and tea,home-made biscuits, fruits at all times. Children $5 for 3-5years old, $15 under 12. Sorry no pets. Non smoking inside the house.

Sakura Bed & Breakfast	**Tel:** (03) 547 0229	**Cost:** Double $120
B&B	**Fax:** (03) 547 0229	Single $60
7KM SW of Nelson city centre	**Mob:** 021 547 022	**Beds:** 1 Double (1 bdrm)
Fumio & Sayuri Noguchi	**E:** fumio.noguchi@paradise.net.nz	**Bath:** 1 Ensuite 1 Family share
604 Main Road	**W:** www.sakura-nelson-nz.com	
Stoke, Nelson		

Nelson

At Brougham Gardens B&B you are assured of a warm welcome and comfortable stay. Our 1930s two-storey bungalow is in the heart of Nelson, opposite historic Melrose House and Gardens, with the Grampians as our backdrop. Nelson City centre is a five-minute walk through the Cathedral gardens. Our home is set in lovely bush and mature trees, wake up to bird song! Enjoy a swim during the summer months in our heated pool, or relax in the spa all year round after a busy day exploring all that Nelson has to offer: sunshine, golden beaches, arts and crafts, restaurants and cafes.

The Abel Tasman National Park is close enough to enjoy a scenic cruise, kayaking, or tramping. Or you may prefer to visit the Nelson Lakes or Kahurangi National Park. Spend a day exploring boutique wineries art studio or potteries, on your own or with a guided tour. With our local knowledge we are able to help you plan your holiday so you get the best of Nelson.

Our three guest rooms are downstairs and all have quality king/twin beds, electric blankets, down duvets, cotton linen, bathrobes, toiletries, hair-driers, fresh flowers, and homemade chocolate. Two with ensuites and one private bathroom. Relax in comfort in the guest lounge or garden room, where tea and coffee making facilities and home baking are yours to enjoy. Breakfast may be served on the verandah, the garden room or in the library.

A three-course dinner, including local wine, is available by prior arrangement, or you may prefer to use the guest barbecue, which is there for your enjoyment. Our gourmet picnic hampers will delight you, and are available on request. Other facilities include laundry, off-street parking, Sky TV, Email, fax and Internet.

No smoking in the house please.

Brougham Gardens
B&B
Nelson City
Judith Nicholas
23 Brougham Street
Nelson

Tel: (03) 545 9049
Fax: (03) 545 9038
E:broughamgardensbnd@xtra.co.nz
W: www.bnb.co.nz/hosts/
broughamgardens.html

Cost: Double $160-$210
Single $120
Dinner $25 B/A Visa/MC
Beds: 3 King/Twin (3 bdrm)
Bath: 2 Ensuite
1 Private

Nelson

Welcome to our Mediterranean-style home. Enjoy the comfort and privacy of our charmingly decorated rooms. They each catch their fair share of our Nelson sunshine, have private bath and entrance, and are equipped with kitchen facilities, fridge/freezer, microwave, hair dryer, TV, radio, phone and heating.

Our honeymoon studio apartment also features a double bath and - like all the upstairs rooms - a spacious balcony with panoramic views of the Mt Arthur mountain range in the distance. All rooms are smokefree and serviced daily.

BEACHSIDE VILLAS is in easy walking distance from a safe swimming beach and local restaurants and only a one hour drive from three National Parks. Our beautiful gardens, the courtyard and our large swimming pool also invite you to just relax and have a break.

A delicious continental breakfast is served at your room, alfresco on the balcony/patio or in the courtyard. On request we serve home-made German and Swiss style bread.

We also offer laundry service, access to the Internet, information and booking service for local activities and off-street parking. A courtesy car is available to and from the bus depots and the airport. Special off season tariffs are available. We speak German.

Beachside Villas
B&B Self-contained
6km W of Nelson
Andrea & Gerhard Merschdorf
71 Golf road
Tahunanui
Nelson 7001

Tel: (03) 548 5041
Fax: (03) 548 5078
Tollfree: 0800 623 023
E: enquiries@beachsidevillas.co.nz
W: www.beachsidevillas.co.nz

Cost: Double $119-$158
Single $109-$148
Child $20
Visa/MC Amex Diners
Beds: 6 King 1 Twin 1 Single
(6 bdrm)
Bath: 5 Ensuite 1 Private

Nelson

100 metres from the Visitor Information Centre right in the heart of Nelson City is the Mikonui. This delightful old house built in the 1920's is constructed of New Zealand native timbers milled from the Mikonui Forest area in South Westland. The lovely Rimu staircase leads to 3 tastefully appointed bedrooms all with ensuites. Downstairs the old laundry has been transformed into a lovely dining room where guests can enjoy tea and coffee at any time, and where a tempting continental or cooked breakfast is served each morning.

Mikonui	**Tel:** (03) 548 3623	**Cost:** Double $100
B&B	**Tollfree:** 0800 4 MIKONUI	Single $70
Nelson Central	**E:** bess.osborne@xtra.co.nz	**Beds:** 1 Queen 1 Double 1 Twin
Elizabeth Osborne	**W:** www.bnb.co.nz/hosts/	(3 bdrm)
7 Grove Street	mikonui.html	**Bath:** 3 Ensuite
Nelson		

Nelson - Brightwater

Welcome to our 20 acre mini-farm and pinot-noir vineyard. We are 20 minutes drive south of Nelson, centrally sited to the region's many attractions and only 10 minutes drive to the nearest cafe, bars and restaurants. Experience the feeling of tranquility that surrounds our comfortable home. Meet our friendly pets which include a NZ wild pony, wild sheep and be entertained by our two little Belgium Barge dogs. Go fo a magic beach ride on our special horse Rocco. Enjoy a farm style or continental breakfast. Smoke free home.

Teapot Valley Farmstay & Vineyard	**Tel:** (03) 542 3570	**Cost:** Double $95
Farmstay	**Fax:** (03) 542 3570	Single $75
17km S of Nelson	**Mob:** 025 974 168	Dinner B/A Visa/MC
Liz & Roy Brown	**E:** rcb#clear.net.nz	**Beds:** 1 Queen 1 Single
Bell Road	**W:** www.bnb.co.nz/hosts/	(2 bdrm)
Teapot Valley	teapotfarmstayvineyard.html	**Bath:** 1 Private 1 Guests share
Brightwater, Nelson		

Richmond

A welcome with drinks poolside in summer, fireside in winter awaits you when you stay in our peaceful home where birdsongs greet you from surrounding bush. We are on the route to Golden Bay, Abel Tasman Park Region but just 15 minutes from Nelson. We travel frequently overseas so appreciate travellers' needs. With firm comfortable beds, good laundry, dinner with local food, wine, and with travellers tales your stay with us will be memorable. Our other interests are music, reading, bridge and 'Coco' our friendly Dalmation.

Hunterville	**Tel:** (03) 544 5852	**Cost:** Double $80 Single $50
Homestay	**Fax:** (03) 544 5852	Child 1/2 price
0.5km E of Richmond	**Tollfree:** 0800 372 220	Dinner $20
Cecile & Alan Strang	**W:** www.bnb.co.nz/hosts/	**Beds:** 1 King 1 Twin 1 Single
30 Hunter Avenue	hunterville.html	(3 bdrm)
Richmond, Nelson		**Bath:** 1 Private 1 Family share

Richmond

Bayview is a modern, spacious home built on the hills above Richmond township, with spectacular views of Tasman Bay and mountain ranges.

We offer rooms that are quiet, private and immaculately furnished with your complete comfort in mind. A large guest bathroom has shower and spa bath. The lounge opens onto a sheltered deck where you can relax, enjoy a drink or sit and chat. The self-contained suite with private entrance, off-street parking, kitchen, bathroom/laundry, lounge area and Queen bed offers privacy and all home comforts.

We have two miniature Schnauzer dogs, a variety of birds in a large aviary, tend our colourful garden and enjoy meeting people from new Zealand and overseas.

By car Bayview is 15 minutes from Nelson, 2 minutes from Richmond and award-winning restaurants, close to National parks, beaches, vineyards and crafts.

Be assured of warm, friendly hospitality and a happy stay in our smokefree home.

Bay View	**Tel:** (03) 544 6541	**Cost:** Double $80-$100
B&B Self-contained	**Fax:** (03) 544 6541	Single $65
10km S of Nelson	**Mob:** 025 623 0252	Dinner by arrangement
Janice & Ray O'Loughlin	**E:** bayview@ts.co.nz	Visa/MC
37 Kihilla Road	**W:** www.bnb.co.nz/hosts/	**Beds:** 1 King 2 Queen (3 bdrm)
Richmond	bayviewrichmond.html	**Bath:** 1 Ensuite 1 Guests share

Richmond

We are a couple who like meeting people. Near by are lovely gardens, crafts, such as Pottery, Glass Blowing, Dried Flowers and Wood Turning. Beaches at Tahuna and Rabbit Island are only 10 minutes away by car. We are situated in an area very central for travellers going South, North or to Golden Bay and Tasman area. Buses and planes met. Enjoy Kiwi hospitality in Richmond. Directions: Above round-about in Queen Street turn into Wasbourn Drive, Farnham Drive and Rochfort Drive.

Anderson Homestay	**Tel:** (03) 544 2175	**Cost:** Double $60 Single $35
Homestay	**Fax:** (03) 544 2175	Child $15 Dinner $12.50
0.5km E of Richmond	**Mob:** 025 440 530	Visa/MC
Jean & Jack Anderson	**W:** www.bnb.co.nz/hosts/	**Beds:** 1 Double 2 Single
46 Rochfort Drive	andersonhomestay.html	(2 bdrm)
Richmond		**Bath:** 1 Guests share
Nelson		

Richmond

We are situated on a kiwifruit and apple orchard on State Highway 6, 2km south of Richmond. A lengthy driveway ensures quiet surroundings in a lovely garden setting, with a pool. We are centrally situated, placing Nelson's many attractions within easy reach. We will happily provide information about these and make arrangements as required. Complimentary tea or coffee is offered to guests upon arrival and dinner may be provided by arrangement. A phonecall before arrival would be appreciated. Ours is a non smoking home.

Nicholls Country Homestay B&B	**Tel:** (03) 544 8026	**Cost:** Double $75 Single $40
Country Homestay B&B	**Fax:** (03) 544 8026	Dinner $12.50
2km S of Richmond	**Mob:** 021 256 1359	**Beds:** 1 Queen 1 Double
Alison & Murray Nicholls	**E:** m_a.nicholls@xtra.co.nz	2 Single (3 bdrm)
87 Main Road, Hope, Nelson	**W:** www.bnb.co.nz/hosts/	**Bath:** 1 Guests share
	nicholls.html	1 Family share

Richmond

Call us out of this world if you will, but with just two intimate guest rooms, Althorpe provides warm old fashioned fuss and care that defines the art of hospitality. Guests are afforded the quiet luxury of relaxing lounge rooms, spacious gardens featuring spa and swimming pool. Whether travelling on or exploring our diverse region you will find our tasty gourmet breakfast a delightful starter to the day. Bob, Jenny and our cat Tackles look forward to welcoming you to our smoke-free home.

Althorpe	**Tel:** (03) 544 8117	**Cost:** Double $120-$140
B&B	**Fax:** (03) 544 8117	Single $100-$110
0.5km S of Richmond	**Tollfree:** 0800 ALTHORPE	Child by arrangement
Jenny & Bob Worley	**E:** rworley@voyager.co.nz	Dinner $40 by arr.
13 Dorset Street	**W:** www.bnb.co.nz/hosts/	Visa/MC
Richmond	althorpe.html	**Beds:** 1 King/Twin 1 Double
Nelson		(2 bdrm)
		Bath: 1 Ensuite 1 Private

Richmond

If you are looking for something special and restful away from city noise yet conveniently located to Nelson City and Abel Tasman National Park then Chester Le House beckons. Our lovely modern home has rural and sea views with safe walkways for evening strolls just a few steps away. Evening dinner featuring fine NZ wines or a typical Kiwi barbecue is available on request. Our out-door living area is relaxing and welcoming for a memorable evening of New Zealand hospitality. Our guest rooms are spacious combining charm with modern facilities.

Chester Le House
B&B Self-contained Homestay
10km W of Nelson
Noelene & Michael Smith
39 Washbourn Drive
Richmond
Nelson

Tel: (03) 544 7279
Fax: (03) 544 7279
Mob: 025 213 5335
E: n.smith@xtra.co.nz
W: www.bnb.co.nz/hosts/
chesterlehouse.html

Cost: Double $85 Single $50
Dinner $25 by arr.
Flat $90 Visa/MC
Beds: 1 Queen 4 Single
(3 bdrm)
Bath: 1 Ensuite 1 Guests share
1 Family share

Richmond

Bob and Joanne Souch welcome you to their peaceful home only 2 minutes from Richmond (15 minutes drive south of Nelson) - excellent base for exploring National Parks, beaches, arts/crafts, skifields etc. Relax in the garden, beside the swimming pool or in our large TV/Guest lounge. Tea/coffee facilities, home baking and memorable breakfasts. Our family pets are Zoe (the cat) and Gemma (friendly border collie). As local antique shop owners we know the area well.

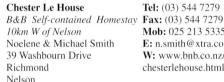

Antiquarian Guest House
B&B Guesthouse
1km E of Richmond
Robert & Joanne Souch
12A Surrey Road
Richmond
Nelson

Tel: (03) 544 0253
Fax: (03) 544 0253
Mob: 025 417 504
W: www.bnb.co.nz/hosts/
antiquarian.html

Cost: Double $95
Single $75
Visa/MC
Beds: 1 King 1 Queen 1 Twin
(3 bdrm)
Bath: 1 Ensuite 1 Guests share

Richmond

A warm welcome to our home centrally located to explore the Nelson region. 2km from Highway 6, in a quiet grove neighbouring the country. Our modern house is elevated to catch the sun and views. For your comfort the bedrooms, recently furnished, have superior beds. Breakfast includes a continental selection and/or a cooked breakfast. Join us for dinner, by prior arrangement, and relax with us in the lounge over coffee. Our aim is to provide a home away from home and to offer tasty meals.

Idesia
B&B Homestay
1km E of Richmond
Jenny & Barry McKee
14 Idesia Grove
Richmond
Nelson

Tel: (03) 544 0409
Fax: (03) 544 0402
Mob: 025 604 0869
Tollfree: 0800 361 845
E: idesian@xtra.co.nz
W: www.bnb.co.nz/hosts/
idesia.html

Cost: Double $85-$95
Dinner $25 by arr.
Visa/MC
Beds: 1 King/Twin 1 Queen
2 Single (3 bdrm)
Bath: 1 Ensuite 1 Private

Richmond

Enjoy the stunning rural and sea views from this country cottage on the hill, set in its own private grounds, wonderful gardens with large herbal garden and boutique jam factory. Located 20 mins from Nelson and 10 mins from Richmond on the wine trail. Excellent cafes and restaurants minutes away. Trout fishing a short drive away. The cottage has a full kitchen, bathroom and laundry for privacy and independence. The bedroom is very comfortable with a queen bed. There is a TV and video.

Bentwood Barn	**Tel:** (03) 544 4800	**Cost:** Double $120
Self-contained Homestay	**Fax:** (03) 544 4800	Single $120
20km W of Nelson	**Mob:** 025 887 752	Child $20 Visa/MC
Sue & Les Stephens	**E:** bentwoodbarn@clear.net.nz	**Beds:** 1 Queen 1 Single
Moutere Highway	**W:** www.bnb.co.nz/hosts/	(2 bdrm)
RD 1, Richmond	bentwoodbarn.html	**Bath:** 1 Private
Nelson		

Thorpe

You are offered a peaceful, rural retreat with international hosts (Dutch and North American). Our two children (7 & 9) are real "Kiwis". The homestead is surrounded by rolling hills, forests and situated along the Dove River. We have a variety of trees, chickens, pigs, sheep, and an outdoor cat and dog. Note: Our main business is 'Tailored Travel', personalized New Zealand Custom Tours (2-6 pax), tailored to your specific requirements and dates.

Rerenga Farm	**Tel:** (03) 543 3825	**Cost:** Double $95 Single $75
Homestay Rural Homestay	**Fax:** (03) 543 3640	Dinner $30 Visa/MC
55km W of Nelson	**Mob:** 025 243 1284	**Beds:** 1 Queen (1 bdrm)
Robert & Joan Panzer	**E:** Robert@Customtours.co.nz	**Bath:** 1 Ensuite
Thorpe	**W:** www.customtours.co.nz	
RD 2, Wakefield		
Nelson		

Mapua

Our home is situated on the edge of the Waimea Inlet amid 2 acres of gardens and bush. The guest wing is upstairs and comprises 2 guest rooms with ensuites. Adjoining, is a guest lounge with fridge, tea/coffee etc. Special breakfasts, dinner by arrangement, award winning Cafes and Restaurants 10 minutes. Children welcome. Martha our aged spaniel and beautiful cat Carlos complete the family. Our personal attention is assured in a relaxed and informal atmosphere.

Atholwood Country Accommo-dation	**Tel:** (03) 540 2925	**Cost:** Double $145-$165
	Fax: (03) 540 3258	Single $120-$145
Country Accomodation	**Mob:** 025 310 309	Child by arr. Dinner $40
10km N of Richmond	**E:** atholwood@xtra.co.nz	by arr. Visa/MC
Robyn & Grahame Williams	**W:** www.bnb.co.nz/hosts/	**Beds:** 2 Queen 1 Single
Bronte Road East	atholwood.html	(2 bdrm)
off Coastal Highway 60 .		**Bath:** 2 Ensuite
near Mapua		

Mapua - Nelson

1915 ambience and charm, gourmet food, peace and quiet, genuine hospitality. You'll find it all at Hartridge, set in picturesque coastal Mapua, ideally located between Nelson city and Abel Tasman. Upstairs, sunny, spacious, private guest rooms, wonderful views, every comfort. Breakfast in the drawing room furnished with antiques and inherited art, or on the sunny verandah amongst ferns and passion flower. Good coffee, fresh baking daily, strawberries, juicy omelettes, special dishes. Mature gardens, roses, native birds, walk to cafes/beach, superb local activities, 1939 Morgan, friendly terrier 'Gentleman Jack'.

Hartridge
B&B
Coastal Village Accommodation
14km NW of Richmond
Sue & Dennis Brillard
103 Aranui Road, Mapua, Nelson

Tel: (03) 540 2079
Fax: (03) 540 2079
E: hartridge@mapua.gen.nz
W: www.hartridge.co.nz

Cost: Double $175 Single $140
Dinner $45 Visa/MC
Beds: 1 King/Twin 1 Queen
(2 bdrm)
Bath: 2 Ensuite\

Mapua Village

Enjoy the dress-circle off street location of our sunny elevated site overlooking "Waimea-Estuary" with it's natural peaceful vista and busy birdlife. An easy stroll to Mapua Village and choice of beachfront licensed restaurants(smoked-fish speciality). Enjoy swimming in the warm Estuary tidal-waters, especially after a day exploring the nearby "Able Tasman" famous scenic walkways. Mapua jet-boat rides offer wild life tours of "Waimea Estuary" with opportunity of a Ornithologist on board.A comfortable night is assured and our guest rooms having quality Queen-size beds, their own ensuites, TV etc.

Mapua Sea View B&B
B&B Homestay
30km W of Nelson
Murray & Diana Brown
40 Langford Drive
Mapua, Nelson

Tel: (03) 540 2006
Fax: (03) 540 2006
Mob: 025 839 634
E: mapua.bb@paradise.net.nz
W: www.mapua.co.nz

Cost: Double $80-$99
Single $70 Dinner $25pp
Visa/MC
Beds: 2 Queen (2 bdrm)
Bath: 2 Ensuite

Mapua

Soak up the stunning views from our heated swimming pool or spa. Set in 4 acres. Kimeret Place offers tranquility in relaxed but stylish surroundings. Our accommodation includes king/queen bedded rooms with en-suite or private facilities, a self-contained cottage, and Luxury suites with sitting areas, balconies and sumptuous bathrooms. An ideal base to explore the Abel Tasman National Park and the numerous local wineries and crafts. Dog-lovers may wish to meet our 2 black Labradors, who will give you a special welcome of their own.

Kimeret Place Coastal B&B
B&B with Self contained
cottage
4km S of Mapua
Clare & Peter Jones
Bronte Road East
RD 1, Upper Moutere, Nelson

Tel: (03) 540 2727
Fax: (03) 540 2726
E: inquiries@kimeretplace.co.nz
W: www.kimeretplace.co.nz

Cost: Double $110-$140
Single $85-$95
2 Bdrm Cottage & Luxury
Suites $170 - $250 Visa/MC
Beds: 3 King/Twin 2 Queen
(5 bdrm)
Bath: 4 Ensuite 1 Private

Ruby Bay

Beach front accommodation, double room with own bathroom and toilet. Lovely walks on beach and reserve, cafes, Tavern, wineries, restaurants, in close vicinity. Fifteen minutes from Richmond & Motueka. Beaches, Rabbit Island, Kaiteriteri, Tahuna in close proximity. Near gateway to Abel Tasman National Park. Plenty of places to see, or 2 minutes to the beach with no maddening crowds. We want guests to feel at home and have their privacy. A continental and full cooked breakfast is served, and cups of coffee, tea and biscuits available. Birman cat and Labrador Sally will greet you outside.

Broadsea B&B	**Tel:** (03) 540 3511	**Cost:** Double $100
B&B	**Fax:** (03) 540 3511	Single $90
20km W of Nelson	**E:** broadsea42@hotmail.com	**Beds:** 1 Queen (1 bdrm)
Rae & John Robinson	**W:** www.bnb.co.nz/hosts/	**Bath:** 1 Ensuite 1 Private
42 Broadsea Avenue	broadseabb.html	
Ruby Bay, Nelson		

Tasman

Enjoy sea views and a peaceful rural outlook from this comfortable room. Own private entrance and courtyard, carport, antique furniture. Wheelchair friendly. Private beach access with picnic/barbecue area beside beach. Farm/beach walks. Continental breakfast basket delivered to room in evening. Hosts can provide transport. 30 minutes to Abel Tasman Track. Friendly farm dog. Golf, restaurants, gallery, pottery, jet-boating, aquarium, winery - all 5 minutes away. Directions: On S.H.60 Coastal route Nelson to Motueka. 2 1/2km south of Tasman, 5km north of Mapua.

Te Pari	**Tel:** (03) 526 6887	**Cost:** Double $130
B&B	**Fax:** (03) 526 6887	Single $100
10km S of Motueka	**Mob:** 025 388 896	Visa/MC
Biddy & Gerald Karsten	**E:** gb.karsten@xtra.co.nz	**Beds:** 1 King/Twin (1 bdrm)
Permin Road	**W:** www.bnb.co.nz/hosts/	**Bath:** 1 Ensuite
Tasman, Nelson	tepari.html	

You can order
The Australian Bed & Breakfast Book.
Contact Moonshine Press,
PO Box 1, Brooklyn,
NSW 2083, Australia
or visit
www.bbbook.com.au.

Tasman

Secluded, private, our sunny comfortable farmhouse has magnificent views of Tasman Bay and the Kahurangi National Park. Exercise in the saltwater swimming pool or relax in the perfumed flower garden and catch up on writing postcards. Compete on the petanque court, then collapse in a hammock and enjoy the native birds: tuis, bellbirds, fantails, wood pigeons and more. Stroll through the paddock to the beach (5 minutes) or simply enjoy a complimentary glass of wine or our own cider. Tough decision!

Perfect to recover from the pleasures of long distance driving. Spacious guest rooms with ensuites, cotton bed linen, comfortable chairs, TV, CD, refrigerator, coffee/tea facilities, home baking, fresh fruit and flowers. Delicious breakfasts of fruits, conserves, home made bagels, breads, croissants and full English-style are usually served al fresco on the grape and hop clad deck as Nelson's weather is usually glorious.

We are centrally situated off Highway 60, between Nelson and Motueka, enabling travellers to explore the best of the province, Abel Tasman and Kahurangi National Parks and Golden Bay. Beautiful, safe, swimming beaches and walks are nearby as are three golf courses, trout fishing rivers, award-winning wineries, arts and great restaurants in nearby Mapua. Nelson Airport half hour. Picton ferry two hours.

Will's Cottage with king/twin, queen bedrooms, sitting room, dining/kitchenette, bathroom and verandah to enjoy the setting sun over the ranges. Breakfast at the house or hamper at cottage. One party booking. The Pondsiders Stylish but relaxed, self-contained 2 x 1 and 1 x 2 bedrooms, ensuites, living/kitchen galley. Marian and Mike offer sound local knowledge and warm hospitality. Dinner is available by arrangement. Special winter tariff available.

Aporo Orchard	**Tel:** (03) 526 6858	**Cost:** Double $150 Single $130
B&B Lodge	**Fax:** (03) 526 6258	Dinner $40
8km S of Motueka	**Mob:** 025 240 3757	Will's Cottage $40 extra
Marian & Mike Day	**E:** marian@aporo.co.nz	person Summer Houses
Permin Road Tasman	**W:** www.aporo.co.nz	Visa/MC
RD 1, Upper Moutere		**Beds:** 6 King/Twin 2 Queen
Nelson		(5 bdrm)
		Bath: 4 Ensuite 2 Guests share

Tasman

Kina Colada - a healthy cocktail for body and soul! Our Mediterranean home offers more than just charming suites with excellent sea and mountain views plus scrumptious breakfasts! Spend all or part of your holidays amid uniquely beautiful surroundings on our 8 ha property adjoining estuary and Tasman Bay, directly above Kina Beach.

Located on lovely and tranquil Kina Peninsula with its own golf course we are in the centre of many activities. Our area offers something exciting to every seeker! After a good night's sleep in our great European beds let your eyes do the walking from Abel Tasman to Kahurangi National Park, Rainbow Skifield, Richmond Ranges to the Marlborough Sounds. Nearby you find famous beaches with a variety of watersports, excellent fishing, inviting vineyards, arts and crafts.

Is your understanding of the true 'dolce vita" more like total relaxation? Perfect - enjoy quiet days on the peninsula! After a yummy breakfast take a long walk on the beach or relax in the sauna with a book and your favourite music from our library! Our stunning pool invites you to float for ages! The cosy suites are equipped with stylish ensuites, tea making facilities, fridge, TV, phone and private balcony. Meals can be served by prior arrangement in the Mediterranean courtyard, the charming guest lounge with fireplace or ... by the pool in romantic setting.

For recharging your batteries we recommend the traditional German "Cure" spa treatments in our in-house clinic; enjoy the lasting effects of Moor-mud, Marine body wraps, medical baths, oxygen therapy, and massages. We welcome children above 10 years; exceptions during off-seasons can be arranged. During the last 14 years we have been working with tourists and patients in a German Spa Resort, and we enjoy to spoil you with our experience!

Our children are 13 and 23 years; a friendly family dog lives with us. Tariff includes great breakfast, tea and coffees, sauna and pick-up service from Motueka or Nelson airport. Special winter tariff available! All rooms are smoke-free.

Kina Colada	**Tel:** (03) 526 6700	**Cost:** Double $135-$185
Holiday & Health Retreat	**Fax:** (03) 526 6770	Single $100-$140
7km Motueka	**E:** kina@voyager.co.nz	Dinner $35
Susanne & Francesco Oldofredi	**W:** www.bnb.co.nz/hosts/	**Beds:** 3 King 2 Single (3 bdrm)
Kina Peninsula Road	kinacolada.html	**Bath:** 3 Ensuite
RD 1		
Upper Moutere/Tasman		

Motueka Valley

Peace and tranquility , trout fishing haven, beautiful 4 acre bush and garden setting, native birds, house pets, sheep, chickens, ducks and donkeys, weaving and woolcraft studio, all abound at Doone Cottage, which we have enjoyed sharing with guests for over 20 years. 100yr old home, comfortably furnished cottage style, overlooking Motueka Valley and Mt Arthur Range. Guest rooms - 2 in-house & private Garden Chalet. Countrystyle meals, free range eggs home made breads, etc. Access 3 National Parks, beaches, mountains, horsetreking, 5 trout rivers (guiding available).

Doone Cottage Country Homestay
B&B Homestay
28km S of Motueka
Glen & Stan Davenport
2455 Motueka Valley Highway
RD 1, Motueka

Tel: (03) 526 8740
Fax: (03) 526 8740
E: doone-cottage@xtra.co.nz
W: www.doonecottage.co.nz

Cost: Double $130-$175
Single $110-$155
Dinner by arr. Visa/MC
Beds: 2 King/Twin 1 Queen
(3 bdrm)
Bath: 3 Ensuite

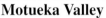

Motueka Valley

Beside the Motueka River and close to 3 National Parks, trout fishing, scenic walks, river rafting, sea kayaking, horse trekking etc. Borrow our inner tubes and float down the river. We have a friendly dog, cat, ducks, gold fish and goat. Our house is owner built with lots of natural timber and country charm. Meals for your wants and needs from our organic fruit, veges and meat. Directions: 10km south from Motueka on 61, cross the Motueka River on Alexander Bluff Bridge. Turn left and go 15 km.

The Kahurangi Brown Trout
Homestay
25km S of Motueka
David Davies & Heather
Lindsay
Westbank Road
Pokororo, RD 1, Motueka

Tel: (03) 526 8736
Fax: (03) 526 8736
Tollfree: 0800 460 421
E: enquiries@kbtrout.co.nz
W: www.kbtrout.co.nz

Cost: Double $95-$125
Single $75-$105
Child $25
Dinner $18 - $35 Visa/MC
Beds: 2 King/Twin 1 Single
(2 bdrm)
Bath: 2 Ensuite

Motueka Valley

Experience the uniqueness of the Nelson Back Country. Surrounded by rivers and mountains, River Island Lodge offers stylish, self contained accommodation with a relaxed country feel. Fish for trout, swim in clear river pools, go horse trekking or kayaking or relax and enjoy the remote, rural atmosphere. Our farming family includes two school age children, farm dogs, horses, cattle and hens. Prepare your favourite meals in your own well equipped kitchen or have delicious meals prepared for you. Perfectly located to enjoy Nelson's wine and craft trails and national parks.

River Island Lodge
Self-contained Farmstay
34km S of Motueka
Alistair Webber & Carol
Mckeever
Baton Valley Road
Woodstock, RD 1, Motueka

Tel: (03) 543 3844
Fax: (03) 543 3802
E: relax@riverislandlodge.co.nz
W: www.riverislandlodge.co.nz

Cost: Double $140
Single $110
Dinner $25 Visa/MC
Beds: 4 Queen 4 Single
(4 bdrm)
Bath: 4 Ensuite

Motueka Valley

Your hosts Alan and Veronica offer B&B Farmstay and separate cottage accommodation on our 35 acre organic property complete with unique Dexter cows and Native Bush Covenanted area. Perfectly situated for anglers, close to 3 National Parks and art/craft/garden trails. Mountain View Cottage is completely self-contained while our homestead offers spacious bedroom with own ensuite, tea/coffee & TV facilities. Meals are cooked on our wood-fired range and breakfast comprises choice of homemade muesli, bread, yoghurt, pancakes and organic eggs. Mitzi the cat completes the picture.

Mountain View Cottage/Dexter Tel: (03) 526 8857
Farmstay   **E:** ajandvhall@xtra.co.nz
Self-contained Farmstay   **W:** www.bnb.co.nz/hosts/
18km S of Motueka   mountainviewcottage.html
A & V Hall
Waiwhero Road, RD 1, Motueka

Cost: Double $85-$95
Single $50-$60 Dinner $20
Cottage $85 -$95 Visa/MC
Beds: 1 King/Twin 1 Double
(2 bdrm)
Bath: 1 Ensuite 1 Private

Motueka River Valley

Situated along scenic Motueka Valley Highway, Singing Trout River Cottage in Ngatimoti offers a restful stay in a beautiful cottage garden setting. Relax in the hammock or feed the tame eels.   Bordering the Motueka River, guests have access to swimming holes, trout fishing areas and leisure walks. Other area attractions include: horse riding, Kahurangi National Park, canoeing, numerous craft outlets and, across the swinging bridge, Tuesday twilight bowls at the quaint Ngatimoti Bowling Green! Country hospitality and a relaxing stay are guaranteed at Singingtrout. Children welcome.

Singing Trout   **Tel:** (03) 526 8288
B&B   **Fax:** (03) 526 8288
15km SW of Motueka   **E:** jklaus@xtra.co.nz
Judy Klaus   **W:** www.bnb.co.nz/hosts/
Greenhill Road   klaus.html
Ngatimoti, R D 1, Motueka

Cost: Double $80 Single $60
Child $20 under 12 years
Dinner $15-20
Beds: 1 Double 1 Twin
(2 bdrm)
Bath: 1 Guests share

Motueka

Our house, shared with one cat, is on a quiet road across from a beach with safe swimming, beautiful walks and an estuary for bird watching. Off-street parking. Guest annex comprises lounge, bathroom, two bedrooms and a private courtyard. Tea/coffee making. No smoking inside. We have travelled widely and we enjoy meeting guests from near or far away. DIRECTIONS: At the southern roundabout in High Street turn into Wharf Road, continue straight into Everett Street. At the end turn left into North Street.

The Blue House   **Tel:** (03) 528 6296
B&B   **Mob:** 021 263 0259
2km SE of Motueka   **W:** www.bnb.co.nz/hosts/
Gail & Doug Bayne   thebluehouse.html
15 North Street
Motueka

Cost: Double $70 Single $40
Child Age + $2, over 12
adult price
Dinner $15 by arr. Visa/MC
Beds: 1 Double 2 Single
(2 bdrm)
Bath: 1 Guests share 1Fam.share

Motueka

Enjoy a unique and quality experience: attention to detail is our forte'. Stay in the light and spacious home of   John R Gatenby - one of New Zealand's leading landscape artists. Indulge in Carol's sumptuous breakfasts on the sun-drenched patio overlooking two acres of private garden and a bird sanctuary. At day's end return from Abel Tasman or Kahurangi National Parks to a warm welcome from Abbi, the outdoor Golden Labrador and enjoy a glass of locally produced wine with your kiwi hosts in the peace and tranquillity of their stylish home.

NELSON, GOLDEN BAY

Copper Beech Gallery	**Tel:** (03) 528 7456	**Cost:** Double $180
An Artists Home	**Fax:** (03) 528 7456	Single $150
1km E of Motueka	**Mob:** 021 256 0053	Visa/MC/BC
Carol & John Gatenby	**E:** copper.beech.gallery@xtra.co.nz	**Beds:** 1 Queen 2 Single
240 Thorp Street	**W:** www.bnb.co.nz/hosts/	(2 bdrm)
Motueka	copperbeechgallery.html	**Bath:** 2 Ensuite

Motueka

Hi, welcome to Rosewood your home from home where a warm and friendly atmosphere awaits you. A 4 minute walk to the centre of Motueka. Our rooms are clean and comfortable. The upstairs room has an adjacent lounge with TV and offers magnificent views of the bush-clad mountains. A delicious breakfast is provided. There is a spa available, notice is required. Our interests include travel, gardening, golf, and fishing. Love to see you as will Jasper our cat. "Rosewood", gateway to the beautiful Abel Tasman.

Rosewood	**Tel:** (03) 528 6750	**Cost:** Double $85
B&B	**Fax:** (03) 528 6718	Single $50
0.5km S of Motueka	**Mob:** 021 251 0131	Child 1/2 price Visa/MC
Barbara & Jerry Leary	**E:** Barbara.Leary.Rosewood	**Beds:** 1 Double 2 Single
48 Woodlands Avenue	@xtra.co.nz	(2 bdrm)
Motueka	**W:** accommodation-new-	**Bath:** 1 Private
	zealand.co.nz/rosewood	1 Family share

Motueka

Ashley Troubadour used to be a nunnery. Nowadays it is an Adventure Base for the Abel Tasman National Park and all other outdoor pursuits available in this area. You name it, we've got it, and John and Coral Horton, your friendly Ashley Troubadour hosts will gladly arrange all bookings etc. to make your stay a pleasure. Laundry facilities, security room, ample off-street parking all available for your peace of mind. Our ensuite rooms are near-new and fully self contained in quiet garden setting.

Ashley Troubadour	**Tel:** (03) 528 7318	**Cost:** Double $75 Single $52
B&B Self-contained	**Fax:** (03) 528 7318	Child $10 S/C $85 - $110
1km S of Motueka	**Tollfree:** 0800 222 046	Visa/MC Amex
Coral & John Horton	**W:** www.bnb.co.nz/hosts/	**Beds:** 2 Queen 2 Double
430 High St	ashleytroubadour.html	2 Single (4 bdrm)
Motueka		**Bath:** 2 Ensuite
		2 Guests share

Motueka

At the Tri-angle Inn you will find; a dazzling array of baked and locally grown delights for breakfast, large, comfortable beds, guest pantry with tea, coffee and juice, large colourful private suites with television, refrigerators, private ensuites and entrance. Set in one acre of garden with wonderful views of Mt Arthur and only 5 min walk from restaurants and cafes. Our family, which includes Liam our son and 2 dogs, actively participate in the multitude of recreational facilities available. Daniel is also a part-time local trout guide. Regrettably not suitable for children under 10.

Tri-angle Inn	**Tel:** (03) 528 7756	**Cost:** Double $125
B&B	**Mob:** 025 484 778	Single $75
Motueka Central	**E:** Daniel.hdt@xtra.co.nz	Child $35 Visa/MC
Lesley & Daniel Jackson	**W:** www.triangle-inn.co.nz	**Beds:** 2 King 4 Single (3 bdrm)
142 Thorp Street		**Bath:** 2 Ensuite
Motueka		

Motueka

"Affordable Luxury". Welcome, to our (smoke-free) modern home, with unsurpassed seaviews over Tasman Bay. Guest TV lounge (tea/coffee facility) and three bedrooms have native bush, lagoon, and seaviews - "breathtaking" scenery! A large sundeck, for your relaxation, leads to a natural rock garden. Just five minutes to Kaiteriteri Beach, gateway to Abel Tasman National Park, where you can enjoy beaches, kayaking, and scenic cruises. Jake, our friendly Golden Labrador will greet you. Directions: 2.65 kms from Cook Corner - Riwaka - Kaiteriteri Road.

Bracken Hill B&B	**Tel:** (03) 528 9629	**Cost:** Double $95-$105
B&B Not Suitable for Children	**Fax:** (03) 528 9629	Single $90 Visa/MC
10km N of Motueka	**E:** gracet@actrix.co.nz	**Beds:** 2 Queen 2 Twin (4 bdrm)
Grace & Tom Turner	**W:** www.bnb.co.nz/hosts/	**Bath:** 2 Ensuite 1 Guests share
265 Riwaka Kaiteriteri Road	brackenhillbb.html	
RD 2, Motueka		
Nelson		

Motueka

Children are welcome to our home set on two acres of land with a swimming pool. We are 1.4 km to shopping centre and 1.2 km to 18 hole golf course. Each bedroom has own ensuite, coffee making facilities and fridge. A guest lounge is upstairs. Motueka is the stop-over place for visitors to explore Abel Tasman and Kahurangi National Parks. Golden Bay and Kaiteriteri golden sands beach is 10km away. Major is the friendly cat.

B&B Homestay	**Tel:** (03) 528 9385	**Cost:** Double $60-$80
1.4km E of Motueka	**Fax:** (03) 528 9385	Single $40 Child $15
Rebecca & Ian Williams	**Mob:** 025 480 466	Dinner by arrangement
184 Thorp Street	**W:** www.bnb.co.nz/hosts/	**Beds:** 2 Queen 2 Single
Motueka	williams.html	(2 bdrm)
		Bath: 2 Ensuite

Motueka

We are a couple recently moved form the North of Italy to the South of New Zealand, much travelled and keen on tramping and mountaineering.

Our beautiful garden faces the Moutere River Estuary: you will enjoy our breakfast (traditional English and Italian specialities including organic home-made bread and jams) overlooking a super tidal view of the estuary and of the Kahurangi National Park mountain range. You will appreciate our Mediterranean atmosphere in the heart of New Zealand nature, among native trees and lovely singing birds. Depending on the season, you will have the chance to see the spectacular White Herons and Royal Spoonbills feeding in the estuary.

PLAN a longer holiday in this Region and PROFIT by Sandro's experience in Geology, Mountaineering and Outdoor (Registered Instructor) and Italian Language Teaching: BOOK with us as extra geological and botanical guided walks along the tracks of the surrounding National Parks, Rock-climbing and Ice-climbing by special arrangements or Cultural weeks including Italian Cooking Classes, Entertaining with slides about Italy, and, on request, Italian Language lessons for beginners and advanced.

Our house is close to the beach: you can have a jog or a quiet walk along the Quay, safe wind-surfing and swimming just across the road. The 18 hole golf course is 15 min. walking. The Ensuite bedroom is small and cosy and includes a private driveway and ground-floor entrance.

On request we prepare delicious recipes of our Italian Cuisine, famous all around the world, using fresh herbs from our garden. You can enjoy dinner with us, overlooking wonderful sunsets beyond the mountains. Coffee, tea, laundry facilities. Secure off-street parking. Links with kayaking and trout fishing companies for booking tours. BENVENUTI TUTTI GLI AMICI ITALIANI.

Directions: From Nelson, at the Southern roundabout in High street, turn right towards Port Motueka, then turn left into Trewavas Street. From the West Coast, at the Clock Tower in High Street, go straight and then turn right into Trewavas Street. Look for our sign.

Grey Heron B&B - Airone	**Tel:** (03) 528 0472	**Cost:** Double $70-$110
Cinerino	**Fax:** (03) 528 0473	Single $45-$75
B&B Homestay	**Mob:** 021 266 0345	Dinner $30
2km S of Motueka	**E:** sandro@greyheron.co.nz	Budget Twin $60
Sandro Lionello & Laura Totis	**W:** www.greyheron.co.nz	**Beds:** 1 King 2 Queen
110 Trewavas Street		2 Single (4 bdrm)
Motueka 7161		**Bath:** 1 Ensuite 1 Guests share

Motueka

Enjoy the serenity and rustic charm of the Riwaka estuary while using us as your base to explore Abel Tasman National Park, Kaiteriteri and Golden Bay. Our luxury apartment has a FULLY EQUIPPED MODERN KITCHEN and LAUNDRY, large living area, and a patio with barbecue. We offer delicious continental breakfasts or you may self -cater. Directions: Take Kaiteriteri Road from Motueka, across the Motueka River Bridge. Take 1st right into Lodders Lane, left into School Road, right into Green Tree Road.

Sea Haven
B&B Self-contained
5km N of Motueka
Barbara & Tim Robson
43 Green Tree Road
Riwaka, RD 3
Motueka

Tel: (03) 528 8892
Mob: 025 207 7836
E: seahaven@ihug.co.nz
W: www.bnb.co.nz/hosts/
seahaven.html

Cost: Double $90
Single $70
Child $15 Visa/MC
Beds: 2 Double 1 Single
(2 bdrm)
Bath: 1 Private

Motueka

Guest's room with ensuite and private entrance has views through our olive trees to the estuary. Full breakfast, on deck or in family dining room. Swimming pool, craft gallery, Sky TV, internet and laundry facilities. 500 metres to The Sea Kayak Company and we also offer advice/make bookings on Abel Tasman National Park, tramping, sightseeing, wine trails, restaurants, beaches, crafts and activities. We are a non-smoking family with two teenagers, a friendly spaniel and cat. Across from coastal highway into Motueka, left turn at roundabout.

Estuary
B&B
2km S of Motueka
Eric & Bonnie Stretton
543 High St South
Motueka

Tel: (03) 528 6391
E: b.stretton@xtra.co.nz
W: www.bnb.co.nz/hosts/
estuary.html

Cost: Double $95
Single $75
Beds: 1 Queen (1 bdrm)
Bath: 1 Ensuite

Motueka

Character home - 100 year old villa set amongst beautiful trees which are home to many birds, including Tuis and Fantails. Guest bedrooms are spacious and quiet with comfortable beds and views of the garden. You are welcome to use our kitchen and laundry and access your emails. An ideal base while you enjoy the many attractions in this region. For business people, an alternative to motels. We guarantee a homely and relaxing stay. We have a 14 year old son, Liam and a small dog, Rocky.

Time Out
B&B
2km S of Motueka
Valerie Rae & Ian McLauchlan
41 King Edward Street
Motueka 7161

Tel: (03) 528 4696
Tollfree: 0800 005 097
E: rae.mclauchlan@xtra.co.nz
W: www.bnb.co.nz/hosts/
timeout.html

Cost: Double $75-$80
Single $60 Visa/MC
Beds: 1 Queen 1 Twin
(2 bdrm)
Bath: 1 Guests share

Motueka

Welcome to our sunny home "on 18 hole golf course", beside the sea. Listen to the native birds fantail and tui. View sunsets from the deck. Close to restaurants. National Parks and golden beaches nearby, your choice of the many activities the region has to offer. Then sleep well in our comfortable beds. Generous flexitime breakfast is served in hosts' dining room or alfresco. Breakfast option is available for self-cater apartment (extra). Complimentary laundry, tea, coffee making facilities. BBQ avail.

Golf View Chalet
B&B Self Contained Apartment
0.5km E of Motueka
Kathleen & Neil Holder
20A Teece Drive
Motueka

Tel: (03) 528 8353
Mob: 025 234 8471
E: info@GolfViewChalet.co.nz
W: www.GolfViewChalet.co.nz

Cost: Double/Twin $75-$85
　　　Single $50-$55 Child $15
　　　Apartment $85 Double
　　　$10 extra adult
Beds: 1 Queen 1 Double
　　　2 Single (2 bdrm)
　　　Apartment 2 bedrooms
Bath: 1 Ensuite 2 Private

Motueka

Behind our cottage, we offer a self contained studio, set amidst fruit trees, flowers and fragrant herbs on our 1/2 acre ORGANIC property. Our large, friendly, obedient New Foundland-cross dog is very popular with our guests. Town is 10 minutes walk, although our place is tranquil with a rural feel. Our local beach is 25 minutes walk and is wonderful for bird-watchers. At Rowan Cottage, you will find the perfect blend of hospitality and privacy. Children are welcome.

Rowan Cottage
B&B Self-contained
Trish McGee & Renee Alleyne
27 Fearon Street
Motueka

Tel: (03) 528 6492
E: trish-renee@clear.net.nz
W: www.rowancottage.net

Cost: Double $120 for 1 night
　　　$110 for 2 or more nights
　　　Discounts for longer stays
　　　Single $100 per night
Beds: 1 King 1 Twin 1 Single
　　　(2 bdrm)
Bath: 1 Ensuite 1 Private

Riwaka Valley

Kaiweka Farm is situated in the north branch of the Riwaka Valley adjacent to the scenic reserve at the Riwaka River source. We are close to the Abel Tasman National Park, Kaiteriteri Beach and beautiful walks. We offer accommodation in a modern self contained flat, sleeps four with day bed, fully equipped with fridge, TV, microwave. Laundry, phone, fax, available. We have four children and enjoy the company of our dogs and two cats. Smoking outside please.

Kaiweka Farm
Self-contained
15km NW of Motueka
Reginald & Pauline Dysart
RD 3
Riwaka Valley
Motueka

Tel: (03) 528 9267
Fax: (03) 528 9267
Mob: 025 605 2753
E: rdysart@ihug.co.nz
W: www.bnb.co.nz/hosts/
kaiwekafarm.html

Cost: Double $75
　　　Single $65
　　　Child $10 Dinner by arr.
　　　Visa/MC
Beds: 1 Double 1 Single
　　　(1 bdrm)
Bath: 1 Private

Kaiteriteri

We welcome you to Paradise. Kaiteriteri Beach, the gateway to the Abel Tasman National Park with the most beautiful coastline in New Zealand and the sunniest weather.

Here we can offer you Bed and Breakfast at its very best. Your rooms are large and beautifully furnished with extensive views of the Bay. You have a comfortable sitting area, outside terrace, ensuite with heated towel rail and hair dryer, fridge, tea/coffee making facilities, radio and TV. Laundry, phone, fax and email are available. You are welcome to share our living area, terraces, extensive collection of books, or be as private as you wish.

A full breakfast is served at your convenience, on your terrace or in the dining room. Dinner, of fresh New Zealand fish, meat and produce is available by prior arrangement. There are 2 restaurants, seasonal , within walking distance and a variety of cafes and hotels within 5-10 minutes drive.

From Bayview you can enjoy coastal and bush walks, see plenty of birdlife, or relax and swim at one of three beautiful beaches. Stay an extra day and explore the Able Tasman National Park. We can book your trip by launch, water-taxi or kayak. They all operate from Kaiteriteri Beach. There is excellent trout fishing in the Riwaka River, 5 minutes away. Visit craft people and wineries, take a day trip over the Takaka Hill to Golden Bay.

Our location is quiet and peaceful . Turn off 4kms along the Kaiteriteri Road at the Blue B&B sign on Cederman Drive corner. Our name is on the gate. Map on homepage.

What our guests say!

Everything has a Touch of Class
Wonderful stay in fabulous home, thanks for hospitality
Absolutely delightful. Wonderful views and hospitality
Wonderful place, excellent hospitality enjoyed our stay & time in Abel Tasman immensely .
Our best stay in every way. Many many thanks.

Bayview
B&B
16km N of Motueka
Aileen & Tim Rich
Kaiteriteri Heights
RD 2
Motueka

Tel: (03) 527 8090
Fax: (03) 527 8090
Mob: 025 545 835
E: kaiteri.bayview@xtra.co.nz
W: bayviewbandb.webnz.co.nz

Cost: Double $120-$135
    Dinner by arrangement
    Visa/MC
Beds: 1 King/Twin 1 King
    1 Twin (2 bdrm)
Bath: 2 Ensuite

Kaiteriteri

Jackie and Tig welcome you to our peaceful and ideally located coastal property just 5 minutes to Kaiteriteri beach and handy to Abel Tasman and Kahurangi National Parks. Nearby attractions include sea kayaking, water taxi trips, beach and bush walks, golden sands and safe swimming beaches. Set against a large area of private native bush with abundant birdlife we offer panoramic views of Tasman Bay with breathtaking sunrises and sunsets. Guest lounge with tea/coffee making facilities. Bar and restaurant 4 minutes.

Seaview B&B	**Tel:** (03) 528 9341	**Cost:** Double $90
B&B	**Fax:** (03) 528 9341	Single $60
9km N of Motueka	**W:** www.bnb.co.nz/hosts/	Visa/MC
Jackie & Tig McNab	seaviewbb.html	**Beds:** 2 Queen 1 Single
259 Riwaka-Kaiteriteri Road		(2 bdrm)
RD 2		**Bath:** 1 Guests share
Motueka		

Kaiteriteri

We live 3 minutes walk from the golden sands of Kaiteriteri Beach with wonderful sea views. Full breakfast includes fresh home baked bread or muffins. Being ex-sheep farmers our interests are varied, and include golf, music, travel, walking, conversation and reading. The Abel Tasman National Park is right here with all the associated activities of kayaking, walking and boat trips, plus restaurants, wineries and craft shopping. Email access is offered and even a piano to play! We have no pets and are non-smokers, but guests are welcome to smoke outside.

Everton	**Tel:** (03) 527 8301	**Cost:** Double $90
B&B	**Fax:** (03) 527 8301	Single $80
13 km N of Motueka	**Mob:** 025 505 944	Visa/MC
Martin & Diane Everton	**E:** everton@xtra.co.nz	**Beds:** 1 Queen 1 Twin
Kotare Place	**W:** www.bnb.co.nz/hosts/	(2 bdrm)
Little Kaiteriteri	everton.html	**Bath:** 1 Guests share
RD 2 Motueka		

Marahau - Motueka

Great views, hospitality, peaceful garden setting are yours at Abel Tasman Stables accommodation. Closest ensuite facility to Abel Tasman National park. Guests comments include "I know now that hospitality is not just a word" TH Germany. "Wonderful place, friendly hospitality. The best things for really special holidays. We leave a piece of our hearts" P&M Italy. "The creme-de-la-creme of our holiday. What a view" MN & JW England. Homestay bed & breakfast or self-contained options. Dinner by arrangement $25. Cafe close by.

Abel Tasman Stables	**Tel:** (03) 527 8181	**Cost:** Double $95 - $105
Self-contained Motels	**Fax:** (03) 527 8181	Single $60 Dinner $25 by
B&B Homestay	**E:** abel.tasman.stables.accom	arr. Visa/MC
18km NW of Motueka	@xtra.co.nz	**Beds:** 3 Queen 1 Double
George Bloomfield	**W:** www.abeltasmanstables.co.nz	4 Single (6 bdrm)
Marahau Valley Road		**Bath:** 3 Ensuite 1 Private
RD 2, Motueka		1 Family share

Abel Tasman National Park

Wake to the sound of waves breaking on the beach below in this new architect designed home with magnificent sea views overlooking Tasman Bay. Each room has panoramic sea views, ensuite, fridge, tea/coffee making facilities, TV, hair dryer, heated towel rails, comfortable seating.

Breakfast can be served in either the guest lounge or on your own private terrace. We are only minutes away from two beaches, bush walks and five minutes drive to start of Abel Tasman Track. Photos of the view are taken from guest balcony.

Directions: Go past Kaiteriteri Beach towards Marahau for 4km. Turn right onto Tokongawa Drive and go right to the top.

Twin Views
B&B
17km NW of Motueka
Ellenor & Les King
Tokongawa Drive
Split Apple Rock, RD 2, Motueka

Tel: (03) 527 8475
Fax: (03) 527 8479
Mob: 025 318 937
E: twinviews@xtra.co.nz
W: www.bnb.co.nz/hosts/
twinviews.html

Cost: Double $125 Single $90
  Visa/MC
Beds: 1 King/Twin 1 Queen
  (2 bdrm)
Bath: 2 Ensuite

Marahau - Abel Tasman Nat. Park

Sandspit is set in the Split Apple Rock sanctuary overlooking Marahau and the tranquil waters of Abel Tasman National Park. Sit on the deck and enjoy our freshly prepared breakfast while looking out over the bay. Take a leisurely, stroll to Split Apple Beach or a dip in the pool. Swimming pool, private entrance, TV, fridge, tea/coffee and home baking. Internet access. Directions: On the Marahau - Kaiteriteri Road, take the Tokongawa Drive turnoff. 0.6km up Tokongawa Drive turn left into Lady Barkly Grove. Sandspit is 100m on your left.

Sandspit	**Tel:** (03) 527 8388	**Cost:** Double $130
B&B, 17km NW of Motueka	**Fax:** (03) 527 8388	Single $100
Paul & Marieann Kennedy	**Mob:** 025 240 4370	Dinner by arrangement
Lady Barkly Grove off	**E:** kennedy.keenan@xtra.co.nz	**Beds:** 2 Queen (2 bdrm)
Tokongawa Drive	**W:** www.bnb.co.nz/hosts/	**Bath:** 2 Ensuite
Split Apple Rock, RD 2	sandspit.html	
Motueka		

Takaka Hill - Motueka

Two modern well equipped cottages. The cottages are exclusively yours, with wonderful sea views and very private. A good selection for breakfast is supplied at the cottage but made by yourselves. Both the cottages are comfortable with sitting room, kitchen, laundry, bathroom, telephone, TV, electric blankets, microwave. Our 4000 acre sheep and cattle farm is set high on the unique marble mountain and offers guests a chance to stay on a working hill country cattle farm. Children are welcome and enjoy feeding and handling our pet sheep, goats, pig and chickens.

Kairuru Farmstay	**Tel:** (03) 528 8091	**Cost:** Double $150 Single $130
Self-contained Farmstay	**Fax:** (03) 528 8091	Dinner by arrangement
17km NW of Motueka	**Mob:** 025 337 457	Self Catering $110
Wendy & David Henderson	**Tollfree:** 0800 524 787	Visa/MC
Kairuru, State Highway 60	**E:** kairuru@xtra.co.nz	**Beds:** 2 King/Twin 2 Queen
Takaka Hill, Motueka	**W:** www.kairurufamstay.co.nz	1 Twin (5 bdrm)
		Bath: 2 Private

Takaka

Farmstay: A "Bay Beauty"awake to the sound of the sea below and enjoy with us a hearty breakfast.Our lovely home has "simply magic"views,pretty gardens and is very peaceful"above the rest"surrounded by our 200 acre dairy farm Villas Four new,spacious,deluxe self contained units,own attached carports.2 bedrooms. Peaceful rural setting a few minutes walk to the beach.Central location."Simply the Best" Your kiwi hosts David & Vicki invite you to be our guests.

Patondale	**Tel:** (03) 525 8262	**Cost:** Double $100
Self-contained Farmstay	**Fax:** (03) 525 8262	Single $70
4villas(motel)	**Mob:** 025 936 891	Child $20 $110dbl. Villas
10km W of Takaka	**Tollfree:** Res.0800306697	Visa/MC
Vicki & David James	**E:** patondale@xtra.co.nz	**Beds:** 4 King 1 Queen
Patons Rock	**W:** www.bnb.co.nz/hosts/	10 Single (10 bdrm)
RD 2	patondale.html	**Bath:** 5 Private
Takaka		

Takaka

Rose cottage, much loved home of Phil and Margaret situated in the beautiful Takaka valley, in 2 1/2 acres of garden amongst 300 year old Totara trees, is ideally situated to explore Golden Bay's many attractions. Our 3 self contained units have full kitchens, private sun decks and quality furniture made by Phil in his craft workshop. The 12 metre indoor solar-heated swimming pool is available to our guests. Our interests are travel, photography, gardening, arts and crafts and helping to make our guests' stay a memorable one.

Rose Cottage
B&B Self-contained
5km S of Takaka
Margaret & Phil Baker
Hamama Road
RD 1, Takaka

Tel: (03) 525 9048
Fax: (03) 525 9114
W: www.bnb.co.nz/hosts/
rosecottage.html

Cost: Double $70-$80
Single $50-$55
Self contained units $85 -
$105 SC Visa/MC
Beds: 1 Queen 2 Single (2 bdrm)
Bath: 1 Guests share

Takaka

A relaxed 'home away form home' atmosphere, happy echoes from the past in furnishings and character. A large secluded, tranquil garden, to enjoy afternoon tea, picnic, barbecue. Your Haven. 'Home' goodies and orchard fruits compliment the traditional English breakfast, served in sunny conservatory or outside on terrace overlooking rose garden. Central to all tourist attractions, 10 minutes stroll to shops and cafes. Courtesy vehicle. Our aim is friendly personal service and hospitality endeavouring to make your stay a memorable one. Looking forward to meeting you.

Haven House
Homestay
Takaka Township
Pam Peacock
177 Commercial Street
Takaka
Golden Bay

Tel: (03) 525 9554
Fax: (03) 525 8720
W: www.bnb.co.nz/hosts/
havenhouse.html

Cost: Double $85 Single $55
Child neg Dinner $20 by
arr. Triple $105 Visa/MC
Beds: 1 Queen 1 Twin 2 Single
(3 bdrm)
Bath: 1 Guests share
1 Family share

Takaka

You are welcome to our spacious home in a peaceful rural setting close to Takaka. Views of Kahurangi National Park are spectacular. Pam loves cooking evening meals, including special diets, using home grown produce. Breakfasts include home made bread, muesli, yoghurt and preserves. We enjoy assisting visitors make the most of their visit. We are near beaches and national parks. We have many New Zealand books. No children at home, or pets. Non smokers preferred. We offer guided walks in the ABEL TASMAN and KAHURANGI national parks.

Croxfords Homestay
Homestay
2km S of Takaka
Pam & John Croxford
Dodson Road
RD 1, Takaka
Golden Bay

Tel: (03) 525 7177
Fax: (03) 525 7177
Tollfree: 0800 26 41 56
E: CROXFORDS@xtra.co.nz
W: www.kahurangiwalks.co.nz

Cost: Double $100
Single $70
Child $10 Dinner $25
Visa/MC
Beds: 1 Double 3 Single
(2 bdrm)
Bath: 2 Ensuite

Takaka - Pohara

Bay Vista House is set on a hillside above Pohara beach. These tastefully furnished rooms are all ensuited with TV, arm chairs, and your own fabulous view. Tea & Coffee is available at all times in the guests separate entrance area. Come and enjoy the beauty and peacefulness of both our National parks, the Able Tasman & Kahurangi or maybe you would prefer to lay back in our garden spa, watching the sunset over the bay. We regret our accommodation is not suitable for children under 12 years old.

Bay Vista House
Boutique B&B
10km W of Takaka
Van & Desrae Johnson
Paradise Way
Pohara

Tel: 03 525 9772
Fax: (03) 525 9772
E: bayvistahouse@xtra.co.nz
W: www.bayvistahouse.co.nz

Cost: Double $140-$185
Single $95-$145
Dinner $40 by arr.
Visa/MC
Beds: 1 King 2 Queen (3 bdrm)
Bath: 3 Ensuite

Patons Rock Beach - Takaka

Lie in bed and watch the tide come and go, or the moon reflecting on the water. Your room is right on the beach and has all the luxuries (including fridge, TV, CD stereo) needed for a relaxing, memorable seaside break. Our very special breakfasts are served in the privacy of your room or terrace. Patons Rock is a beautiful, sheltered north-facing beach, great for swimming, walking and beach-coming, or just sitting in the sun. This is truly a magical place. We live with two beautiful cats. Smoking outside please.

The Beach House
B&B
10km NW of Takaka
Lesley & Murray McIver
Patons Rock Beach
RD 2, Golden Bay

Tel: (03) 525 8133
Fax: (03) 525 7533
Mob: 025 302 729
Tollfree: 0800 426 555
E: m.l.mciver@xtra.co.nz
W: www.bnb.co.nz/hosts/
thebeachhouse.html

Cost: Double $120-$140
Single $100-$120
Beds: 1 King/Twin (1 bdrm)
Bath: 1 Ensuite

Parapara

Hakea Hill House at Parapara has views from its hilltop of all Golden Bay. The two story house is modern and spacious. Two guest rooms have large balconies; the third for children has four bunk beds and a cot. American and New Zealand electric outlets are installed. Television, tea or coffee, and telephone lines are available in rooms. Vic is a practicing physician with an interest in astronomy. Liza is a quilter and cares for three outdoor dogs. Please contact us personally for reservations and directions.

Hakea Hill House
B&B
20km NW of Takaka
Vic & Liza Eastman
PO Box 35
Collingwood 7171

Tel: (03) 524 8487
Fax: (03) 524 8487
E: vic.eastman@clear.net.nz
W: www.bnb.co.nz/hosts/
hakeahillhouse.html

Cost: Double $120
Single $80
Child $40 Dinner by arr.
Visa/MC
Beds: 2 Double 6 Single
(3 bdrm)
Bath: 1 Guests share

Collingwood

The drive form Collingwood takes guests off the beaten track to the untouched wilderness of Westhaven. Here, the panoramic views are captured by the north-facing dining and living room with 280 degree facing over the ocean. Set on a 1000 acre peninsula, Westhaven includes private beaches, rainforest with thousands of native nikau palms, caves, eye catching rock formations and over 40 llamas for guests to feed and have pleasure with a variety of international dinner menus can cater for all tastes. Pick up avail.

Westhaven Retreat	**Tel:** (03) 524 8354	**Cost:** Dbl $130-$180 Sgl $110-$140 Dinner. $40 2brm Cottage $140 dbl, $10 extra person Visa/MC
Retreat	**Fax:** (03) 524 8354	
40km Collingwood	**Mob:** 025 220 3941	
Bruno & Monika Stompe	**E:** Westhaven.Retreat@xtra.co.nz	
Te Hapu	**W:** www.westhavenretreat.com	**Beds:** 3 King/Twin 1 Qn 1 Twin (5 bdrm)
RD		
Collingwood		**Bath:** 2 Ens 1 Priv 1 Guests share 1 Fam share

Collingwood

Skara Brae, the original police residence in Collingwood built in 1908, has been tastefully renovated over the years. Our historic home is in a quiet, peaceful garden setting. Join us in the house for bed and breakfast or our two self contained units. Either way you will experience a warm welcoming atmosphere and individual attention. We are a minute away from the excellent Courthouse Cafe and local tavern bistro bar and it is a short stroll to the beach. Farewell Spit trips depart close by.

Skara Brae Garden Motels & Bed and Breakfast	**Tel:** (03) 524 8464	**Cost:** Double $110 Single $80 2 Self contained Units $85 Visa/MC
B&B Self-contained	**Fax:** (03) 524 8474	
25km N of Takaka	**Mob:** 025 626 6018	
Joanne & Pax Northover	**E:** skarabrae@xtra.co.nz	**Beds:** 2 Queen 1 Double 1 Twin 2 Single (4 bdrm)
Elizabeth St, Collingwood	**W:** www.accommodation collingwood.co.nz	**Bath:** 1 Ensuite 3 Private

Collingwood

A warm welcome to Win's Bed & Breakfast. 100km onto a sheep and cattle farm with mountain range in back ground, close to walking tracks and beach. 3km from Collingwood where there are 2 excellent cafes and a tavern bistro bar also bookings for Farewell Spit trips. I have 1 cat Bibbee.

Win's B&B	**Tel:** (03) 524 8381	**Cost:** Double $60 Single $35 Dinner by arrangement
B&B	**W:** www.bnb.co.nz/hosts/ wins.html	
3km SE of Collingwood, 25km Takaka		**Beds:** 1 Queen 1 Double 2 Twin (4 bdrm)
Heather Margaret Win		
State Highway 60		**Bath:** 1 Guests share 1 Family share
at start of Plain Road		

Pakawau Beach - Collingwood

We are the northern most homestay in the South Island, 9km from Farewell Spit. We offer self-contained accommodation from $70 per night. The Farewell Spit Tours will pick you up from our gate. You only have to walk a few metres through our garden to a safe swimming beach. Local seafoods available, eg. whitebait, scallops, or you can walk across the road to a licensed cafe. We are non smokers, have two cats and look forward to sharing our lifestyle with you.

Pakawau Homestay
Self-contained Homestay
12km N of Collingwood
Val & Graham Williams
Pakawau Beach
RD, Collingwood

Tel: (03) 524 8168
Fax: (03) 524 8168
W: www.bnb.co.nz/hosts/
pakawauhomestay.html

Cost: Double $80
Single $70
Dinner $20 S/C $70
Beds: 1 Double 1 Single
(1 bdrm)
Bath: 1 Private 1 Family share

St Arnaud

Our much admired timbered home, warm and private, is amidst native forest with a 5 minute walk to Lake Rotoiti (one of NZ's most beautiful unspoiled Lakes), Nelson Lakes National Park. The home affords lovely views of surrounding forests and mountains. Native birds abound. A paradise for those interested in nature. Choose a prolonged stay to hike a variety of tracks or relax in this beautiful environment. Restaurant nearby. In St Arnaud 400 mtrs via Bridge Street to Holland Street/Lake Road intersection is our sign.

St Arnaud House
B&B
100km S of Nelson
Jill & Colin Clarke
Postal Agency
Nelson 7150

Tel: (03) 521 1028
Fax: (03) 521 1028
E: c-clarke@st-arnaud.co.nz
W: www.bnb.co.nz/hosts/
starnaudhouse.html

Cost: Double $125
Single $80
Visa/MC
Beds: 3 Queen 2 Single
(3 bdrm)
Bath: 2 Ensuite 1 Private

Nelson Lakes

We invite you to enjoy the luxury and comfort of our spacious home, just 4km east of St Arnaud, Lake Rotoiti and Nelson Lakes National Park - a year around adventure playground. Relax in our comfortable lounge, enjoy coffee or tea and cookies and the magnificent views from every window. There is garaging for your vehicle and laundry facilities for your use. Enjoy our delicious meals and friendly relaxed atmosphere. We are a non smoking household with one cat. Directions: State Highway 63 - 200 meters towards St Arnaud from the Nelson intersection.

Nelson Lakes Homestay
Homestay
85km S of Nelson
Merv & Gay Patch
RD 2
State Highway 63
Nelson

Tel: (03) 521 1191
Fax: (03) 521 1191
Mob: 021 261 8529
E: Home@Tasman.net
W: www.bnb.co.nz/hosts/
nelsonlakeshomestay.html

Cost: Double $95
Single $60
Dinner $25pp by arr.
Visa/MC
Beds: 2 King/Twin 1 Queen
(2 bdrm)
Bath: 2 Ensuite

Tophouse - Nelson Lakes

We, Gladys and Mac Hollick together with our two cats, invite you to share our unique home with huge open fires, lovely setting and homely atmosphere. Tophouse, a cob (mud) building, dating from the 1880's when it was a hotel, and reopened in 1989 as a Farm Guest House, has that 'good old days' feel about it.

Situated on a 300 ha (730 acre) picturesque high country farm running cattle, with much native bush and an abundance of bird life also a unique 9 hole golf course. A popular holiday spot for its peace and beauty, bush walks, fishing and in the winter serves the two local ski fields. Tophouse is only 9km from St Arnaud, gateway to Nelson Lakes National Park.

A typical farmhouse dinner is taken with family and since the fire's going 'real' toast for breakfast. Cottages are 2 bedroom, fully self contained including kitchen, with great views of the surrounding mountains.

Directions: Just off State Highway 63 between Blenheim and Murchison and 9km from St Arnaud is Tophouse, that's us. The area took its name from the building. If travelling from Nelson, leave State Highway 6 at Belgrove and travel towards St Arnaud, we're signposted from the main road and looking forward to your visit. Come, see and feel the living history of this unique place.

Tophouse	**Tel:** (03) 521 1848	**Cost:** Double $80
Self-contained Farmstay	**Fax:** (03) 521 1848	Single $40
9km N of St Arnaud	**Tollfree:** 0800 867 468	Child $20 Dinner $20
Gladys & Mac Hollick	**E:** tophouse@clear.net.nz	Visa/MC
Nelson Lakes	**W:** www.tophouse.co.nz	**Beds:** 1 Queen 5 Double
RD 2		19 Single (13 bdrm)
Nelson		**Bath:** 4 Private 2 Guests share

Mangles Valley

Welcome to our hill-country sheep and beef farm in beautiful Mangles Valley. Visitors appreciate the beauty and relaxed lifestyle. Excellent trout fishing. Golf course (clubs available), horse trekking, white water rafting, beautiful bush walks all nearby. We are still farming, love meeting and welcoming people to our home and garden. Involved in community affairs, Lions, Rural Women, ITC SPELD teaching. Breakfast includes muesli, fruit, local honey, homemade marmalade. Farm eggs if wanted. Comfortable self contained cottage (kitchen) for longer stay or overnight privacy. TV, wood burner. Dinner by arr.

Green Hills Farm	**Tel:** (03) 523 9067	**Cost:** Double $80 Single $50
Self-contained Farmstay Cottage	**W:** www.bnb.co.nz/hosts/	Dinner $25pp
5km N of Murchison	greenhillsfarm.html	S/C Cottage $80
Margaret & Henry Rouse		**Beds:** 2 Single
Green Hills Farm		1 Double bed settee
Mangles Valley, Murchison		**Bath:** 1 Private

Murchison

Kia-ora! Welcome to the great outdoors. Warm Kiwi hospitality is assured. Our uniquely crafted home is set on 3 acres, secluded and quiet, surrounded by mature trees and overlooking the Buller River. Dine with us or walk to local restaurants. Mike is a professional fishing guide and Noela manages the Information Centre. Friendly pets include 2 dogs and 2 cows. Enjoy a hearty breakfast of healthy homemade fare. Spend your days fishing, rafting, kayaking, golfing, horse trekking, hunting, bush walking, jet boating, etc. Reservations not essential but recommended.

Coch-Y-Bondhu Lodge	**Tel:** (03) 523 9196	**Cost:** Double $100-$115
B&B Self-contained Homestay	**Fax:** (03) 523 9196	Single $75 S/C cottage $100
0.5km N of Murchison	**Mob:** 025 221 0681	Dinner By Arr. Visa/MC
Mike & Noela Buchanan	**E:** cochybondhu@xtra.co.nz	**Beds:** 2 Queen 1 Double
15 Grey Street	**W:** www.homestays.net.nz/	1 Twin 1 Single (5 bdrm)
Murchison 7191	cochybondhu.htm	**Bath:** 2 Ensuite 1 Private
		1 Guests share 1 Fam. share

Maruia Valley

To experience something different visit Awapiriti nestled beside the Maruia River in the beautiful Maruia Valley. Share our comfortable Homestead with its warm glow of native timber, log fires and colonial decor, providing the ultimate in comfort and relaxation. Smell the roses and breathe the clean, country air, take a farm walk and talk to the animals - elk/deer, bison, cattle, sheep and enjoy a romantic candle light dinner with your hosts. Just 3hrs approx from Picton/Christchurch/Hokitika, Awapiriti is a haven for adults, unsuitable for children.

Awapiriti Farmstay	**Tel:** (03) 523 9466	**Cost:** Double $105-$110
Farmstay	**Fax:** (03) 523 9777	Single $95 Child n/a
David & Irene Free	**Mob:** 025 220 4466	Dinner by arr. Visa/MC
Private Bag	**W:** www.bnb.co.nz/hosts/	**Beds:** 1 Queen 1 Double
Highway 65	awapiritifarmstay.html	2 Single (3 bdrm)
Murchison		**Bath:** 2 Ensuite 1 Private

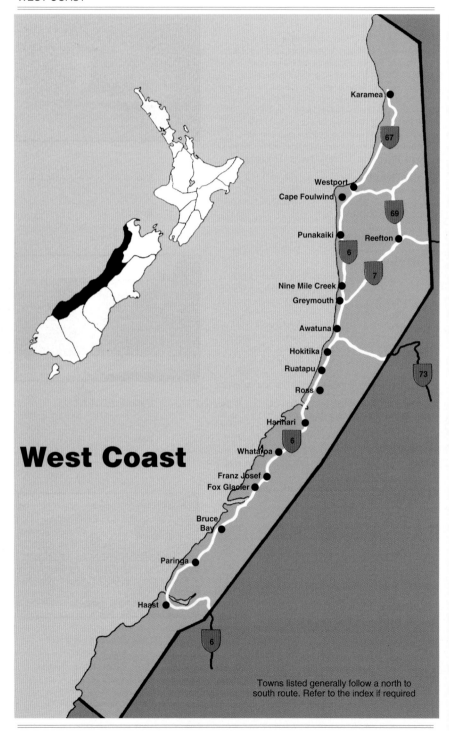

West Coast

Towns listed generally follow a north to
south route. Refer to the index if required

Karamea

Our home is 2 mins walk from a deserted sandy beach. Come as far north as you can on the West Coast and relax for a few days. Enjoy our garden, wonderful views and watch the native birds. We have a dairy farm milking 330 cows. Breakfasts are generous, dinners include farm grown meat, organic vegetables, and home made desserts, with complimentary wine. For the more adventurous, try 4 wheel bike or horse riding, hunting, fishing, bird watching. Karamea offers the spectacular limestone caves, arches and scenic short walks.

Beachfront Farmstay	**Tel:** (03) 782 6762	**Cost:** Double $110-$130
Farmstay	**Fax:** (03) 782 6762	Single $90 Child neg
84km N of Westport	**Mob:** 025 222 1755	Dinner $35 Visa/MC
Dianne & Russell Anderson	**E:** farmstay@xtra.co.nz	**Beds:** 1 King 1 Queen
Karamea	**W:** www.bnb.co.nz/hosts/	1 Single (3 bdrm)
RD 1, Westport	beachfrontfarmstay.html	**Bath:** 2 Ensuite 1 Family share

Karamea

Since relinquishing their dairy farm to daughter Caroline and son-in-law Bevan, Rosalie and Peter has purpose built on the property accommodation that neatly bridges the gap between motel and farm stay. Both are happy to share their extensive knowledge of their district, its people and environment and introduce guests to the many short walks that Karamea offers. Each quality suite is self contained and has a private lounge that overlooks the farm to Kahurangi National Park beyond. A small mob of deer and alpaca graze nearby.

Bridge Farm	**Tel:** (03) 782 6955	**Cost:** Double $85-$95
Self-contained Farmstay	**Fax:** (03) 782 6748	Child $10 Visa/MC
0.5km Karamea	**Tollfree:** 0800 KARAMEA	**Beds:** 4 Queen 8 Single
Rosalie & Peter Sampson	**E:** Enquires@karameamotels.co.nz	(8 bdrm)
Bridge Street	**W:** karameamotels.co.nz	**Bath:** 6 Private
Karamea, RD 1		
Westport		

Westport

The Lodge is a peaceful retreat overlooking the Buller River. On the main road form Picton and Nelson to the West Coast. The suites are private, tastefully decorated with ensuites. Rooms open onto a large verandah and look out onto part of the garden and lawn. The garden is also featured in the NZ Gardens to Visit. Lunch and dinner by arrangement. Laundry facilities. Smoking outside only. Unsuitable for pets. We have one small very friendly dog. Reservations are recommended. Ample parking. Children by arrangement.

River View Lodge	**Tel:** (03) 789 6037	**Cost:** Double $145-$174
Boutique Country Lodge	**Fax:** (03) 789 6037	Single $106-$124
7km SE of Westport	**Mob:** 025 249 1286	Dinner $35 B/A Visa/MC
Noeline Biddulph	**Tollfree:** 0800 18 46 56	**Beds:** 3 Queen 1 Twin
State Highway 6	**E:** info@rurallodge.co.nz	(4 bdrm)
Lower Buller Gorge	**W:** www.rurallodge.co.nz	**Bath:** 4 Ensuite
PO Box 229, Westport		

Westport - Cape Foulwind

Enjoy our peaceful rural home, magnificent views of Tasman Sea, rugged coastline beaches, great swimming, surfing, fishing, walking. Within 5 minutes walk popular seal colony walkway, Bay House Restaurant and Star Tavern, or play a round of golf at Carters Beach Golf links. Other local attractions include Coaltown Museum, horse riding, underworld and white water rafting, bush walks, Punakiki National Park. We are keen gardeners and enjoy all sports and have a Jack Russell dog and a cat. All laundry facilities and off street parking available.

Steeples Homestay
B&B Homestay
11km S of Westport
Pauline & Bruce Cargill
Lighthouse Road
Cape Foulwind, RD 2
Westport

Tel: (03) 789 7876
Mob: 025 291 7665
E: Steepleshomestay@xtra.co.nz
W: www.bnb.co.nz/hosts/
steepleshomestay.html

Cost: Double $80
　Single $40
　Child $15 Visa/MC
Beds: 2 Queen 2 Single
　(3 bdrm)
Bath: 2 Private

Westport

Ann and Bill would like to welcome you to Chrystal Lodge. Our home, built on 20 acres is beside a beach ideal for walking, surfing, fishing or swimming. The self-contained units have a fully equipped kitchen/lounge with en-suite bathrooms off the bedrooms. Breakfast is optional in units. Our garden setting has ample off-street parking. Free guest laundry. Continental breakfast includes croissants and muffins. We have two cats. Smoking outside please. Off season rates. Directions: Turn right at the Post Office, continue down Brougham Street, turn left at Derby Street until at beach.

Chrystal Lodge
Self-contained Homestay
2km N of Westport
Ann & Bill Blythe
PO Box 128
Westport

Tel: (03) 789 8617
Fax: (03) 789 8617
Tollfree: 0800 259 953
E: chrystal@clear.net.nz
W: www.bnb.co.nz/hosts/
chrystallodge.html

Cost: Double $80 Single $50
　Child 1/2 price
　S/C Double $75 Visa/MC
Beds: 1 Queen 1 Double
　5 Single (4 bdrm)
Bath: 2 Ensuite 1 Guests share

Westport

Peace in Paradise - this is Havenlee, offering tranquil, central location 300 metres from town centre. Born and bred West Coasters - hospitality is part of our heritage. Share our modern, spacious home set amongst native and exotic trees and shrubs. With breathtaking scenery, Westport is sited between the Kahurangi and Paparoa National Parks. Close by are Tauranga Bay Seal Colony and Punakaiki Pancake Rocks. Enjoy a continental-plus breakfast, warm, comfortable beds, full laundry facilities, local knowledge in a friendly, relaxed smokefree environment.

Havenlee Homestay
Homestay
Westport Central
Jan & Ian Stevenson
76 Queen Street
Westport

Tel: (03) 789 8543
Fax: (03) 789 8502
Mob: 025 627 2702
Tollfree: 0800 673 619
E: havenlee76@hotmail.com
W: www.webnz.com/bbnz/
havenlee.htm

Cost: Double $85
　Single $60
　Child neg Visa/MC
Beds: 1 Queen 1 Double
　1 Twin (3 bdrm)
Bath: 1 Guests share suite

Westport - Cape Foulwind

A stay at our tranquil new home offers stunning cliff top views of the Tasman Sea, Steeples, and glorious sunsets. Short walk to secluded beach with blow-holes, lighthouse, seal colony walkway and country pub which has great meals and take-aways. 4kms to beautiful Tauranga Bay and award winning restaurant. Enjoy a spa bath, complimentary tea/coffee and laundry.....and "Murphy, the Beagle". Whitebait meals by arrangement. Directions: Turn first right past "Star Tavern" then right at beach car park.

Clifftop Homestay	**Tel:** (03) 789 5472	**Cost:** Double $80-$90
Homestay	**W:** www.bnb.co.nz/hosts/	Single $60 Child $15
11km W of Westport	clifftophomestay.html	Full breakfast by arr.
Paddy & Gail Alexander		Twin Bed/Sit $90
Clifftop Lane		**Beds:** 1 Double 1 Twin
Cape Foulwind, RD 2		(2 bdrm)
Westport		**Bath:** 1 Private 1 Family share

Westport

We offer you quality accommodation in 1907 villa with original pressed steel ceilings and decor. Two of our three bedrooms are ensuite, one with spa-bath and one with shower. Comfortable guest lounge available with open fire and TV. We hope you will take the opportunity to dine in our pleasant dining room (all tastes catered for). We have two friendly Jack Russet dogs. Basic laundry free. Facilities for smokers. Directions: Entering Wesport on Palmerston Street turn right at Mill Street then left into Derby Street.

Derby Street Bed & Breakfast	**Tel:** (03) 789 7757	**Cost:** Double $70
B&B	**Mob:** 025 238 2661	Single $55
Westport Central	**E:** derbyst@xtra.co.nz	Dinner $15
J & R Ferguson	**W:** www.bnb.co.nz/hosts/	**Beds:** 1 Queen 2 Double
118 Derby Street	derbystreetbedbreakfast.html	2 Single (3 bdrm)
Westport		**Bath:** 2 Ensuite 1 Private

Westport - Cape Foulwind

Enjoy the soothing tranquillity of amazing sea views from your bedroom/patio. Walk the impressive Cape Foulwind Walkway with its seals and captivating coastline, ending at the magic Bay House Restaurant overlooking Tauranga Bay. Numerous outdoor activities and attractions nearby. Helen and Derek can take you out on the farm shifting cattle or walking through native rainforest. Let "Poppy" our fox terrier take you beachwalking below the cliffs. Kayaks, mountain bikes available. Short walk to friendly country pub. Smokefree inside.

Lighthouse Homestay	**Tel:** (03) 789 7942	**Cost:** Double $80-$90
(formerly The Cape House)	**Fax:** (03) 789 7942	Single $60
B&B Farmstay Homestay	**Mob:** 025 857 583	**Beds:** 2 Queen 1 Double
10km W of Westport	**Tollfree:** 0800 227 322	2 Single (3 bdrm)
Derek Parsons & Helen Jenkins	**E:** derek.parsons@xtra.co.nz	**Bath:** 1 Ensuite 1 Guests share
32 Lighthouse Road	**W:** www.westcoast.org.nz/	
Cape Foulwind, Westport	tourism/accommodation/	
	lighthouse/lighthouse.html	

Westport

3 large bedrooms, 2 with ensuites, 1 with private facilities. All bedrooms have TVs and tea/coffee facilities. Bathrooms have a hair dryer, heated towel rail and toiletries.

Sunny balconies and relax in a sheltered private conservatory or one of the two guest lounges. New Zealand Heritage Home, with outstanding historic significance to the West Coast creared by leadlighting masterpieces, fireplaces and antique furniture.

Short stroll to all town amenities including Victoria Square and heated swimming pool. Whole home is available for rental for those who prefer privacy.

See website for more details, www.archerhouse.co.nz.

DIRECTIONS: From Greymouth & airport, cross bridge over Buller River into main street of Westport (Palmerston St). Turn right into Wakefield St. Archer House on left, on right-hand corner of Queen St.

Archer House	**Tel:** (03) 789 8778	**Cost:** Double $120-$150
B&B	**Fax:** (03) 789 8763	Single $110-$140
Kerrie Fairhall	**Mob:** 025 260 3677	Visa/MC Amex
75 Queen Street	**E:** accom@archerhouse.co.nz	**Beds:** 3 Queen 2 Single
Westport	**W:** www.archerhouse.co.nz	(3 bdrm)
		Bath: 2 Ensuite 1 Private

Westport

Being retired hoteliers born and bred in the Buller we welcome you to enjoy the hospitality we offer in a peaceful quiet cul de sac. Your large sunny room has total privacy self contained except for stove, own entrance and patio. There are tea making facilities, fridge, toaster, hairdrier, television, telephone, radio. Sky TV available. Off street parking. Airport 1km away. Use of laundry. Complimentary bicycles and golf clubs. Courtesy car available.

Bellaville	**Tel:** (03) 789 8457	**Cost:** Double $80
B&B Self-contained	**Mob:** 025 6131 689	Single $50
3km S of Westport	**E:** fairhalls@xtra.co.nz	**Beds:** 1 Queen 1 Single
Marlene & Ross Burrow	**W:** www.bnb.co.nz/hosts/	(1 bdrm)
4 Martin Place	bellaville.html	**Bath:** 1 Ensuite
Carters Beach		
Westport		

Reefton

Toni and Ian invite you to experience "Quartz Lodge" nestled within Victoria Forest Park and in the heart of the West Coast quartz gold/coal mining country. Let this be your home away from home- but with all the extras. Huge picture windows in every room offer best views in town. Guests only entrance, lounge/dining area. Luxurious bedsrooms serviced daily. Country style breakfast, tea/coffee facilities, laundry service and phone/fax. Evening meals available- arriving late? not a problem. Your comfort is our priority.

Quartz Lodge	**Tel:** (03) 732 8383	**Cost:** Double $60-$95
B&B	**Fax:** (03) 732 8083	Single $40-$70
Toni and Ian Walker	**Mob:** 025 619 4520	Dinner $20 - $35 Visa/MC
78 Sheil Street	**Tollfree:** 0800 302 725	**Beds:** 1 King 1 Queen 1 Twin
Reefton	**E:** quartz_lodge@hotmail.com	2 Single (3 bdrm)
West Coast		**Bath:** 1 Ensuite 1 Private
		1 Guests share

Reefton

Built in 1887 from native timbers for a local barrister. This historical Edwardian home has been carefully renovated to add light and space without losing its olde world charm. Elegantly decorated the house features open fires, original furniture, brassware and NZ artwork. Nestled in Historic Gold/Coal mining country between native beech forests and the Inangahua River, Reef Cottage is unrivalled as the finest accommodation in Reefton. For more information on activities, travel plans etc. or to view our facilities stop by anytime or use our freephone number above.

Historic Reef Cottage	**Tel:** (03) 732 8440	**Cost:** Double $60-$140
B&B and Cafe	**Fax:** (03) 732 8440	Single $49-$110
Reefton Central	**Mob:** 025 262 3855	Dinner $10 - $35
Susan & Ronnie Standfield	**Tollfree:** 0800 770 440	Visa/MC Amex Diners
51-55 Broadway	**E:** reefton@clear.net.nz	**Beds:** 1 King/Twin 1 Queen 2
Reefton	**W:** www.bnb.co.nz/hosts/	Double (4 bdrm)
	historicreefcottage.html	**Bath:** 2 Ensuite 2 Private

Punakaiki

We are a semi-retired couple who welcome you to share our home and surrounds. We have recently built "The Rocks Homestay" in a unique wilderness setting at Punakaiki (midway between Greymouth and Westport) within view of the famous Blowholes and Pancake Rocks. Guests enjoy exclusive panoramas encompassing the Tasman Sea coast and the limestone cliffs and rainforest of the Paparoa National Park. Sunsets are magnificent.

We offer warm hospitality in our modern and comfortable home. Two of our bedrooms have private conservatories. Amenities include heated towel rails, laundry service, hair dryers, email and an extensive library of New Zealand books. Breakfast includes a range of cereals, muesli, fresh yoghurt, fresh-baked muffins, toast and spreads; other menus can be arranged.

We provide home-cooked evening meals and wine by prior arrangement. We are associated with Green Kiwi Nature and Heritage tours and can organise eco-tours of the superb rainforest and dramatic landscapes of the West Coast. We invite people to share our interests in photography and the outdoors, and we can help plan a wide variety of other activities.

Also available: - new self-catering house in rainforest surrounds. Both premises and their surrounds are Smoke free. No pets.

Directions: Turn off SH 6 at the Hartmount Place blue bed sign, 3 km North of Punakaiki Visitors Centre. Drive 400 metres towards the Coast.

The Rocks	**Tel:** (03) 731 1141	**Cost:** Double $110-$155
B&B Homestay	**Fax:** (03) 731 1142	Single $80-$95
45km N of Greymouth	**Mob:** 025 204 9833	Child $40 - $60
Peg & Kevin Piper	**Tollfree:** 0800 272 164	S/C House $100 - $150
No 3 Hartmount Place Extension	**E:** therocks@minidata.co.nz	Dinner $30 - $45 Visa/MC
PO Box 16	**W:** www.minidata.co.nz/	**Beds:** 2 Queen 2 Single (3 bdrm)
Punakaiki	therocks/	**Bath:** 23 Ensuite

Punakaiki

Peace, tranquillity and a warm welcome awaits you at
Mahers Creek B&B. Nestled amongst 10 acres of
native bush overlooking the rose garden with a
panoramic sea view, you can unwind from a weary trip.
The unit is detached from the house and has its own
private decking with table, chairs & sun umbrella.
There are four restaurants within 10 mins driving
distance. We are semi retired dairy farmers and we live
here with our 2 Labradors and 3 cats.

Maher's Creek B&B	**Tel:** (03) 731 1001	**Cost:** Double $110
B&B Self-contained	**Fax:** (03) 731 1001	Single $75
8km S of Punakaiki	**W:** www.bnb.co.nz/hosts/	Visa/MC
Jen & Dermot Hahn	maherscreekbb.html	**Beds:** 1 Queen (1 bdrm)
RD 1		**Bath:** 1 Private
Runanga		
Westland		

Nine Mile Beach

Dramatic location, stunning views and sunsets are yours
from this absolute beachfront cottage 15 min north
Greymouth. The bushed landscape provides healthy sea air
and quality water for the refurbished holiday cottage with
new facilities. Our home adjoins. We are wildlife
enthusiasts so please excuse the little blue penguins who
choose to visit us. Heaps of adventures await you at the
Blow Holes Punakaiki 20 mins north. Breakfast always
included. Full kitchen and laundry . Children enjoyed and
welcome.

Tasman Beach B&B	**Tel:** (03) 762 7117	**Cost:** Double $95
Self-contained	**Fax:** (03) 762 7161	Single $75
15km N of Greymouth	**W:** www.bnb.co.nz/hosts/	Child $10
Jill Cotton	tasmanbeachbb.html	**Beds:** 1 Queen 1 Twin (2 bdrm)
9 Mile Coast Road		**Bath:** 1 Private
RD 1, Runanga		
Highway 6, Westland		

Nine Mile Creek

One of the West Coast's most spectacularly located B&B's,
with stunning views over the ocean. Private beach access
allows you to fossick for jade and beautiful stones. All
rooms are "en-suite" with TV and hot beverage making
facilities. A gourmet dinner is available, with 24 hours
notice, includes NZ wines and is constantly accompanied by
the crashing waves! The Breakers is a wonderful base to
visit the Pancake Rocks, the Paparoa National Park and the
best stretch of coastline in NZ. Sorry unsuitable for children

The Breakers	**Tel:** (03) 762 7743	**Cost:** Double $135-$185
B&B Homestay	**Fax:** (03) 762 7733	Dinner $55 Visa/MC
14km N of Greymouth	**Tollfree:** 0800 350 590	**Beds:** 3 Queen 1 Twin 1 Single
Frank & Barbara Ash	**E:** stay@breakers.co.nz	(3 bdrm)
PO Box 188	**W:** www.breakers.co.nz	**Bath:** 3 Ensuite
Greymouth		
Westland		

Greymouth

Ardwyn House is three minutes walk from the town centre in a quiet garden setting offering sea, river and town views. The house was built in the 1920's and is a fine example of an imposing residence with fine woodwork and leadlight windows, whilst being a comfortable and friendly home. Greymouths ideally situated for travellers touring the West Coast being central with good choice of restaurants. We offer a courtesy car service to and from local travel centres and also provide off street parking.

Ardwyn House	**Tel:** (03) 768 6107	**Cost:** Double $75-$80
Homestay	**Fax:** (03) 768 5177	Single $50
Greymouth Central	**Mob:** 025 376 027	Child 1/2 price Visa/MC
Mary Owen	**E:** ardwyhouse@hotmail.com	**Beds:** 2 Queen 3 Single
48 Chapel Street	**W:** www.bnb.co.nz/hosts/	(3 bdrm)
Greymouth	ardwynhouse.html	**Bath:** 1 Guests share

Greymouth

Tony and I offer warm hospitality in our lovely home overlooking the Tasman Sea and south to Mount Cook and Tasman. We have hosted for many years so you can be assured of a relaxed stay in this quiet street only five minutes walk from the beach. There is much to do and see, lakes and rivers, wonderful bush and coastline walks. Trout fishing and golf. Or just laze on the deck and watch the sun go down. Phone for direction please.

Homestay	**Tel:** (03) 768 4348	**Cost:** Double $80
4km S of Greymouth	**Fax:** (03) 768 4348	Single $50
Tony & Ib Pupich	**E:** jembo@actrix.co.nz	**Beds:** 1 King/Twin (1 bdrm)
5 Stanton Crescent	**W:** www.bnb.co.nz/hosts/	**Bath:** 1 Private
Greymouth	pupich.html	

Greymouth

Oak lodge is in a rural setting and was built in 1901 initially an old farmhouse and is surrounded with gardens. Many varities of Rhodddendrons and Azaleas. Beautiful in the Spring.The 20 acre hobby farm supports sheep and Scottish Belted Galloway Cows. For our guest use a swimming pool and tennis court is available. We are centrally situated to visit Shantytown, replica of a gold mining town and the Paparoa National Park where the pancake rocks are (Punakiki)We have a grey tabby cat called lucky.

Oak Lodge	**Tel:** (03) 768 6832	**Cost:** Double $100-$140
B&B Homestay	**Fax:** (03) 768 4362	Single $90 Visa/MC
3km N of Greymouth	**Tollfree:** 0800 351 000	**Beds:** 2 Double 1 Twin 2 Single
Zelda Anderson	**E:** NZH_OAK.LODGE	(3 bdrm)
Coal Creek	@xtra.co.nz	**Bath:** 3 Ensuite
State Highway 6	**W:** www.oaklodge.co.nz	
Greymouth		

Greymouth

Experience amazing seaview and incredible sunsets from twin-terraces modern, luxurious, classic home - 3 mins walk beach. Ensuite or private bathroom. Blowholes/Pancake Rocks, rainforest bush walks, and free glowwarm cave all within 35 mins drive radius. Excellent eating establishments 6 mins away. Pam enjoys people, collects antiques, fine china and enjoys everything associated with food. Awake to chorus of native bird nestling in towering Pohutukawa trees and shrubs. Pam has been home hosting for 7 years and offers wonderful West Coast hospitality to everyone. Smoking outside.

Paroa Homestay	**Tel:** (03) 762 6769	**Cost:** Double $99-$110
Homestay	**Fax:** (03) 762 6765	Single $75-$79
6km S of Greymouth	**Mob:** 025 208 7293	Child $30 Visa/MC
Pam Sutherland	**E:** paroahomestay@hotmail.com	**Beds:** 1 King/Twin 1 Super King
345 Main South Road	**W:** www.bnb.co.nz/hosts/	1 Double (3 bdrm)
Greymouth	paroahomestay.html	**Bath:** 1 Ensuite 1 Private 1 Guests

Greymouth

What a view! What a quiet location. Our home is set in native bush overlooking the sea. From our downstairs rooms you step out to the large deck where you can enjoy the bush and beautiful sunsets. Spa pool available ($5pp). Our animals, dog "Lady", cat "Misty" enjoy visitors company. Allison enjoys gardening, hospitality, playing bridge while Glen enjoys large jigsaws. Cable/Sky TV is available as is laundry facilities Transport to scenic spots (moderate charge).Level access and off street parking. Complimentary pick up from train/bus.

Maryglen Homestay	**Tel:** (03) 768 0706	**Cost:** Double $85-$105
Homestay	**Fax:** (03) 768 0599	Single $65-$75 Child neg
2.5km S of Greymouth	**Mob:** 025 380 479	Dinner $20 Visa/MC
Allison & Glen Palmer	**Tollfree:** 0800 627 945	**Beds:** 2 King/Twin 1 Queen
20 Weenink Road	**E:** mary@bandb.co.nz	1 Single (3 bdrm)
Karoro	**W:** www.bnb.co.nz/hosts/	**Bath:** 2 Ensuite
Greymouth	maryglenhomestay.html	1 Family share

Greymouth

Rosewood is one of Greymouth's finest old restored homes, a few minutes walk from restaurants. Rooms feature quality king and queen beds. Laundry service available (charge), and courtesy transport. Excellent home from which to visit the Punakaiki rock formations and Glaciers, as well as the recreational opportunities in our region. Margaret is a trained social worker, while Ian operates a personalised tour service. A polite 12 year old Trent, and a friendly cat 'Mischief' add to the experience. A smoke free home with off street parking.

Rosewood	**Tel:** (03) 768 4674	**Cost:** Double $95-$120
B&B	**Fax:** (03) 768 4694	Single $65-$90
1km S of Greymouth	**Tollfree:** 0800 185 748	Child $20 Visa/MC
Ian & Margaret	**E:** rosewoodnz@xtra.co.nz	**Beds:** 1 King 3 Queen 1 Twin
20 High St	**W:** www.bnb.co.nz/hosts/	2 Single (5 bdrm)
Greymouth	rosewoodgreymouth.html	**Bath:** 3 Ensuite 1 Private 1 Guests

Hokitika Central

Frances and Brian welcome you to 'catch your breath and breakfast' staying in our centrally situated, character home in the heritage area of Hokitika. Located opposite the information centre and museum, Teichelmann's is a short walk away from interesting craft galleries, shops, restaurants and cafes. Stroll on the beach in the evening and experience a West Coast sunset... the wild, romantic West Coast at its best. We look forward to your visit.

Teichelmann's B&B Lodge	**Tel:** (03) 755 8232	**Cost:** Double $110-$130
B&B	**Fax:** (03) 755 8239	Single $100
Hokitika	**Tollfree:** 0800 743 742	Visa/MC Amex Diners
Frances Flanagan and Brian Ward	**E:** teichel@xtra.co.nz	**Beds:** 3 King 2 Double
20 Hamilton Street	**W:** www.teichelmanns.co.nz	2 Twin 4 Single
Hokitika		(6 bdrm)
		Bath: 5 Ensuite 1 Private

Hokitika

Welcome to Rossendale where warm Kiwi hospitality awaits you. We are a retired couple who have travelled extensively both within NZ and overseas and enjoy meeting people. Our spacious home is situated in a quiet area 1 km from the centre of town on the banks of the Hokitika River with full view of the Southern Alps and off street parking. Hokitika is centrally situated for visits to the glaciers, pancake rocks, beaches, alps, bush walks and glow worm dell. Children welcome. We will meet plane or coach.

Rossendale	**Tel:** (03) 755 6620	**Cost:** Double $80
Homestay	**Fax:** (03) 755 6620	Single $50
Hokitika Central	**Mob:** 025 220 3525	Dinner $20pp B/A
Vi & Arthur Haworth	**E:** rossendale.homestay	**Beds:** 1 Queen 2 Single
Rossendale	@xtra.co.nz	(2 bdrm)
234 Gibson Quay	**W:** www.bnb.co.nz/hosts/	**Bath:** 1 Guests share
Hokitika	rossendale.html	

Hokitika

We are fourth generation West Coasters from South Westland and with our grey cat Tui have been home-hosting for 15 years. Our interests are West Coast history, gold prospecting, whitebating, rugby and we play bowls and social golf. Our home is your home. Hokitika has it all - restaurants, water world, jade carving studios, glass blowers, gold, paua, wood and craft galleries. The glow worm dell is within walking distance. Directions: Turn inland off State Highway 6 at Airport sign (Tudor Street), third house on your left.

McCarthy Homestay	**Tel:** (03) 755 7599	**Cost:** Double $80-$100
Homestay	**W:** www.bnb.co.nz/hosts/	Single $50
1km N of Hokitika Central	mccarthyhomestay.html	**Beds:** 1 Double 2 Single
Berna & Brian McCarthy		(2 bdrm)
70 Tudor St		**Bath:** 1 Private 1 Guests share
Hokitika, Westland		

Hokitika - Awatuna

Our views are SPECTACULAR, 120 feet above sea-level, just a walk to the beach and surrounded by native bush. We offer FREE evening trips to nearby glow-worm dells and their historic abandoned mines and should you stay a day or two, fishing or gold panning. Animals: Goats, sheep, cows, and a dog. (No inside animals). John's work and interests: Conservation, growing lilies and fishing. Helen's: genealogy, and chatting with overseas guests. Hot spa for relaxation or freshening outdoor swimming pool. Children welcome.

Gold and Green	**Tel:** (03) 755 7070	**Cost:** Double $80 Single $60
Farmstay Homestay	**Fax:** (03) 755 7070	Child $20
Countrystay	**E:** gold&green@xtra.co.nz	**Beds:** 1 Queen 1 Double 1 Twin
15km N of Hokitika	**W:** www.bnb.co.nz/hosts/	1 Single (4 bdrm)
Helen & John Hadland	goldandgreen.html	**Bath:** 1 Guests share
Awatuna, RD 2		1 Family share
Hokitika, Westland		

Hokitika

Our spacious rimu-timber featured home offers quiet rooms and wonderful views of Hokitika, Tasman Sea, Mounts Cook and Tasman. Complimentary night tour to glow-worms. Chris (Property Consultant, Rotarian)enjoys travel, golf and fishing; Dianne (Reading Teacher) enjoys travel, handcrafts, ceramic dolls and cooking. We love to chat with guests about travel experiences. Cat and dog live outside. Meet us by turning into Tudor Street towards the airport from main highway; take first left into Bonar Drive and next two left turns up to Whitcombe Terrace.

Terrace View Homestays	**Tel:** (03) 755 7357	**Cost:** Double $85
B&B Homestay	**Fax:** (03) 755 8760	Single $60
0.5km N of Hokitika	**Mob:** 025 371 254	Dinner B/A Visa/MC
Dianne & Chris Ward	**Tollfree:** 0800 261 949	**Beds:** 1 Queen 2 Single
24 Whitcombe Terrace	**E:** c.ward@minidata.co.nz	(2 bdrm)
Hokitika	**W:** www.bnb.co.nz/hosts/	**Bath:** 1 Guests share
	terraceviewhomestays.html	

Hokitika

Our comfortable home is on a terrace overlooking Hokitika with unsurpassed views of the Southern Alps, Tasman Sea and brilliant sunsets. The guest rooms have a private entrance and are connected by a small sitting room with TV. You are welcomed with home baking, tea/coffee making facilities available. We invite you to join us for a drink in the evening. Jon, a 4th generation Coaster has abundant local knowledge. From main highway turn into Tudor Street, signed Airport. Left into Bonar Drive and up the hill into cul-de-sac.

Alpine Vista Homestay	**Tel:** (03) 755 8732	**Cost:** Double $95
Homestay	**Fax:** (03) 755 8732	Visa/MC
1km N of Hokitika	**Mob:** 025 202 2401	**Beds:** 2 Queen (2 bdrm)
Rayleine & Jon Olson	**E:** jolson@minidata.co.nz	**Bath:** 1 Ensuite
38 Bonar Drive	**W:** www.bnb.co.nz/hosts/	
Hokitika	alpinevista.html	

Hokitika

Prospect House is situated on the outskirts of Hokitika on an ancient river terrace property of some 10 acres. This lovely colonial style family home commands sweeping views of the Southern Alps, has beautiful gardens and trees and is owned by a caring, friendly family.

Our guest books are full of accolades as to the space and luxurious comfort of our home and the friendliness of the host family.All say that they wish they had arranged their trip so that they could stay longer.

This spacious home features native rimu timbers, central heating, large deck and BBQ facilities, piped music throughout and full office facilities too. The main suite contains a King size double bed and full ensuite plus tea and coffee making facilities as well. Adjoining this is a separate bedroom with a double and single bed. The second suite has a Queen size bed and ensuite. Breakfast can be either continental or a full cooked breakfast.

Our interests vary from the garden to music, current affairs, sport flying and yes .... catering for guests. We can arrange scenic flights for you to the Glaciers or to the historic goldtown port of Okarito or to other interesting destinations. We can also assist to arrange other adventures for you. We have three dogs, a Westie, a Scotty and a Lab. We also have two cats.

To find us, if travelling from North turn left into Hampden Street, continue on for 3KM without turning again.

Prospect House
Homestay Semi-rural B&B
4km E of Hokitika
Danielle & Lindsay Smith
Blue Spur
RD 2
Hokitika

Tel: (03) 755 8043
Fax: (03) 755 6787
Mob: 025 221 2779
Tollfree: 0800 377 969
E: prospect@minidata.co.nz
W: www.bnb.co.nz/hosts/
prospecthouse.html

Cost: Double $160
Dinner B/A
Visa/MC
Beds: 1 King 1 Queen
1 Double 1 Single
(3 bdrm)
Bath: 2 Ensuite 1 Private

Hokitika

Welcome to Montezuma by the sea. So named after a ship that was wrecked here in 1865. Alison a Queenslander, Russell a genuine West Coaster. Enjoy a walk along the beach, watch the sunset, visit the nearby Glow Worm Dell and take time out to enjoy our West Coast hospitality. Directions: When travelling to Hokitika from North take first turn to your right (Richards Drive). Our house is the last on the street. From South turn left at the last street out of town.

Montezuma
Homestay
1km N of Hokitika
Russell & Alison Alldridge
261 Revell Street
Hokitika, Westland

Tel: (03) 755 7025
W: www.bnb.co.nz/hosts/
montezuma.html

Cost: Double $80
Single $55
Beds: 2 Queen 2 Single
(2 bdrm)
Bath: 1 Ensuite 1 Guests share

Hokitika

Tom and Alison welcome you to their lifestyle property, situated just minutes south of Hokitika. Our large home, which we share with 2 cats, is modern, sunny and warm, and has a large garden. Nearby we have the beach, excellent golf-links, an old gold mine, river, and of course Hokitika, with all its attractions. Directions: Travel south 2kms from south end of Hokitika Bridge on SH6, turn right - second drive on right. North-bound traffic - look for sign 1km north of Golf-links.

Meadowbank
Rural Homestay
3km S of Hokitika
Tom & Alison Muir
Takutai
RD 3, Hokitika

Tel: (03) 755 6723
W: www.bnb.co.nz/hosts/
meadowbank.html

Cost: Double $75 Single $50
Child 1/2 price
Dinner B/A
Beds: 1 Double 2 Single
(2 bdrm)
Bath: 1 Guests share

Hokitika

Fully furnished apartment - double bedroom, sunroom, lounge TV shower and laundry, own entrance plus internal access to house. Twin room in main house - share bathroom Relax in a friendly, homely atmosphere and enjoy panoramic views of the Southern Alps, Mount Cook and the Tasman Sea. We are retired farmers, have travelled extensively and enjoy meeting people from other countries. Directions: When travelling form Greymouth take first two left turns. We are at the end of Bonar Drive.

Karnbach
B&B Homestay
1km N of Hokitika
Errol & Bill Amberger
41 Bonar Drive
Hokitika

Tel: (03) 755 7102
W: www.bnb.co.nz/hosts/
amberger.html

Cost: Double $85
Single $50
Apartment $85
Beds: 1 Double 1 Twin
(1 bdrm)
Bath: 1 Private 1 Family share

Hokitika

Our visitors book has interesting entries:
John and Jane Adamson from the UK, 'Thank you for the Best B & B and guided tours we ever had'.
Roy and Mary Watts from the UK, 'Outstanding in all respects, great conducted tours'

We converted our 6500 square foot family home into a lodge in 1999 located on a 40 acre section our home provides complete quiet and privacy. The native Kahikatea trees that surround the lodge are unique.

Bruce is a tennis nut, a born and bred fourth generation Coaster and entrepreneur, he will delight you with his local knowledge and loves to take guests on guided tours which are complementary. Most of our guests allow us to chauffeur them to the local restaurant in the evening, pick them up take them to the glowworm dwell and other local sights.

Hokitika is the centre of the West Coast, most guests base themselves here for visits to the glaciers and the Punakaiki Pancake rocks, allow two nights.

Craidenlie Lodge
B&B
2km E of Hokitika
Bruce & Jenny Smith
Blue Spur
Hokitika

Tel: (03) 755 5063
Fax: (03) 755 8497
Tollfree: 0800 361 361
E: bruce@craidenlielodge.co.nz
W: www.craidenlielodge.co.nz

Cost: Double $160
Single $160
Visa/MC Amex Diners
Beds: 7 Queen 1 Twin
(8 bdrm)
Bath: 4 Ensuite 1 Private
1 Guests share

Hokitika

Self contained unit: queen bedroom and triple room with spacious living/dining area, full kitchen, laundry and wheelchair friendly bathroom. Landscaped private outdoor areas on a quiet, peaceful rear section. Homestay: (Located next door) Queen room with new private ensuite, own entrance, Tea /Coffee facilities. Twin room with host share bathroom. Hosts: Paul is a secondary teacher. Linda is an itinerant hairdresser. Our interests include travel, tramping and kayaking. We have a very friendly cat and may still have a very elderly German Shepherd.

Larry's Rest
B&B Self-contained Homestay
0.9 E of Hokitika
Linda & Paul Hewson
188 Rolleston Street
Hokitika

Tel: (03) 755 7636
Mobile: 021 220 3295
E: info@larrysrest.co.nz
W: www.larrysrest.co.nz

Cost: Double $100 Single $90
  Child $ Dinner $
  Visa/MC
Beds: 2 Queen 2 Twin (4 bdrm)
Bath: 1 Ensuite 1 Private
  1 Family share

Ruatapu

We offer you a warm and relaxed stay in our comfortable home. Magnificent views of the Tasman Sea and the Southern Alps are seen from the main living areas. We are close to Lake Mahinapua, the beach and Golf Links with the opportunity to experience the Westland bush sunsets and sunrises. We run sheep and cattle and grow pine trees on our hobby farm. We have two farm dogs (Sam and Jock) and we share our home with two cats Sammy and Sooty and our house dog Jed.

Berwick's Hill
B&B Country Stay
14km S of Hokitika
Eileen & Roger Berwick
Ruatapu-Ross Road
State Highway 6
RD 3, Hokitika

Tel: (03) 755 7876
Fax: (03) 755 7876
Mob: 025 673 7387
E: berwicks@xtra.co.nz
W: www.bnb.co.nz/hosts/
berwickshill.html

Cost: Double $90-$100
  Single $50-$60
  Dinner $25 B/A Visa/MC
Beds: 1 Queen 2 Single
  (2 bdrm)
Bath: 1 Ensuite 1 Private

Ross

We offer a cosy self contained Cottage next to our home with cooking facilities. A twenty minute drive form Hokitika and 1 1/2 hours to the Glaciers which makes an ideal stop over. Have your meals at your leisure or join us in our home. Allow time to explore our gold fields, beautiful walkways and glow worms. Dahlia Cottage is the second house on your right travelling from north. We look forward to meeting you and will make your stay a memorable one. Children welcome.

Dahlia Cottage
Self-contained Homestay
15km N of Hokitika
Dianne Johnston
47 Aylmer Street
Ross, Westland

Tel: (03) 755 4160
Fax: (03) 755 4160
Mob: 025 296 5934
W: www.bnb.co.nz/hosts/
dahliacottage.html

Cost: Double $70
  Single $40
Beds: 1 Queen 3 Single
  (3 bdrm)
Bath: 1 Private

Harihari

"A real tonic for weary travellers - food, facilities excellent. Hosting Incomparable" (RJ USA). "Absolutely Superb - Hosts, food, room - best stay in 5 weeks in NZ (GH UK) "This will be our 5th 4 night stay, it doesn't come any better than Wapiti Park" (I&B UK) Hosts Grant and Beverleigh invite you to discover the unique experience of staying at Wapiti Park Homestead, South Westlands premier hosted accommodation for the discerning traveller. Enjoy a special combination of elegance and warm hospitality. Relax in complete comfort and affordable luxury.

Set in tranquil surroundings, the modern colonial style lodge is set on the site of the original 1st Hari Hari accommodation house, coaching stop and post office and overlooks its own small farm which specialises in the breeding of Wapiti (Rocky mountain Elk).

The 6pm farm tour enables one to handfeed the Wapiti, meet the farm pet "Vicki" and learn about the elk velvet antler extract and its major health benefits. Enjoy spacious indoor/outdoor areas; large bedrooms with superior comfort beds and either ensuites or private facilities; 2 lounges and a trophy games room; a well stocked bar fridge; and our renowned "All you can eat" Country style dinners. Special diets can be catered for by prior arrangement.

Our location on state highway 6 makes us the ideal stopover between the Nelson/Christchurch - Wanaka/Queenstown areas. However to explore this scenic wonderland of rainforest glaciers, lakes and National Parks; to pursue the challenges of our renowned brown trout fishery, to hunt or to simply catch your breath and relax, you really need at least a 2 night stay. Guided hunting and fishing available and other activities arranged on request.

Unsuitable for children. No smoking indoors. Direct booking discounts available. Advance booking recommended. Spoil Yourself!

Wapiti Park Homestead	**Tel:** (03) 753 3074	**Cost:** Double $125-$245
Farmstay Country Lodge	**Fax:** (03) 753 3074	Single $100-$185
0.5km S of Hari Hari	**Tollfree:** 0800 WAPITI	Dinner $40 Visa/MC
Bev & Grant Muir	**E:** wapitipark@xtra.co.nz	**Beds:** 2 King 2 Queen 1 Twin
RD 1	**W:** www.countrylodge.co.nz	5 Single (5 bdrm)
Hari Hari 7953		**Bath:** 3 Ensuite 2 Private

Whataroa

Matai Lodge rests in the tranquil valley 20 minutes north of Franz Josef Glacier in the small farming community of Whataroa. Enjoy a walk across our 400 acre farm and experience the lush tropical landscape that is unique to this part of New Zealand. Listen to the vast array of native birds that call this valley home.

Enjoy our spacious home that has been specifically designed for guests with three rooms available. Two comfortable king-size beds or two warm single beds will give you a good nights sleep. Take in the expansive views of the Southern Alps sunsets from our conservatory or lounge.

Inside you'll enjoy fine New Zealand home cooking morning and night in a relaxed atmosphere. Outside our sheep, cows and loveable "working" dog Tess are always ready to visitors. Share your tales from your home, as we will help you discover ours with local advice and activity bookings available. Our motto is "A Stranger is a Friend we have yet to Meet".

If you are looking for activities, you will need at least 2 days to see the Glaciers, walk in the World Heritage Park, Kayak on the Okarito Lagon, Horse trek in this natural scenic valley, or fish in the isolated rivers and lakes. Glenice and Jim play golf at the scenic golf course in Whataroa (green fees $7.00 per day) golf clubs for hire. From November to February a jet boat trip to the White Heron bird sanctuary is spectacular.

Glenice has travelled to Japan many times teaching felting, weaving and spinning. She has enjoyed learning Japanese customs and language and being hosted by many friends there. Glenice and Jim look forward to sharing their home and knowledge of this tranquil scenic paradise.

Driving Time from Matai Lodge to - Christchurch 5 hours, Picton 6 hours, Nelson 6 hours, Queenstown 6 hours, Wanaka 4 hours, Greymouth 2 hours, Whataroa 3km from State Highway 6. Also available: Tel/Fax, Email, Sky TV, Laundry.

Matai Lodge	**Tel:** (03) 753 4156	**Cost:** Double $140
Farmstay	**Tollfree:** 0800 787 235	Single $80
35km N of Franz Josef	**Fax:** (03) 753 4156	Dinner $35pp
Glenice & Jim Purcell	**Mob:** 021 155 2506	**Beds:** 1 King/Twin 1 King
Whataroa	**E:** jpurcell@xtra.co.nz	2 Single (3 bdrm)
South Westland	**W:** www.bnb.co.nz/hosts/	**Bath:** 1 Ensuite 1 Private
	matailodgewhataroa.html	

Whataroa

Heading to the glaciers? Stay a night or two at Sleepy Hollow, your Ideal base in glacier country. We are just 20 minutes drive North of the Franz Josef Glacier!! Here you can relax, away from the sometimes hectic pace of travel and take time to unwind whilst admiring the breathtaking scenery of dramatic mountain views.

The homestead accommodation is on the top floor with guest share bathroom. Each beautifully decorated bedroom has queen sized beds, big fluffy towels, tea/coffee facilities, heater, electric blankets and television, enabling you to relax in privacy if you wish, or feel free to pop downstairs for a chat, but be warned! the jolly and relaxing atmosphere at Sleepy Hollow is contagious. The self contained unit is a real little gem and excellent for guests with children, with your own bathroom, lounge, dining & kitchen area, microwave, electric frypan and television, this is your own little home away from home.

Telephone, fax, email and laundry are available. Our 400 acre dairy farm milks 220 friesian cows, we have lot\'s of horses and some sheep. Mint Sauce our pet sheep loves being fed a slice or two of bread and along with her friends is eagerly awaiting your arrival. We have 2 farm dogs Trev and Buff.

A short bush walk takes you to the farm lane where you can view and feed our peacocks, pheasants, ducks etc in the bird enclosure or take a leisurely stroll over the farm. The area has lots to offer; South Westland Horse Treks are available here for all riding abilities from the complete learner to the experienced rider "an awesome experience" are just some of the comments we recieve on the rides. See brochure for more treking details. Breathtaking views of the glacier are to be had via a helicopter or fixed wing ski-plane flight both of which we are happy to provide details or make reservations for you. At Okarito (20 mins drive) you can kayak on the Lagoon, take some excellent walks & view beautiful sunsets on the beach.

Whataroa has a population of around 250 people, it has a 9 hole golf course, excellent fishing,Jet boat tours to New Zealand's only White Heron Colony, Gold prospecting on the Whataroa riverbed & Paintball. Casual evening meals are available in the Village. Nearest banks, Hokitika and Wanaka. Credit cards are welcome. We look forward to sharing our slice of paradise and some laughter with you!!
Distances: Picton-Whataroa: 6 hours. Hokitika-Whataroa: 1.5 hours. Whataroa-Wanaka: 4.5 hours. Whataroa-Queenstown: 6 hours. Christchurch - Whataroa: 5 hours

Sleepy Hollow
B&B Self-contained Farmstay
Horse Trekking
35km N of Franz Josef
Carolyn & Colin Dodunski
State Highway 6
Whataroa

Tel: (03) 753 4139
Fax: (03) 753 4079
Mob: 021 575 243
Tollfree: 0800 575 243
E: hollow@xtra.co.nz
W: www.bnb.co.nz/hosts/
sleepyhollow.html

Cost: Double $100-$110
    Single $60 Dinner n/a
    Visa/MC Amex Diners
Beds: 4 Queen 2 Single
    · (4 bdrm)
Bath: 1 Ensuite 1 Guests share

Whataroa - South Westland

If you're wanting to escape the crowds in the busy
tourist centres then we are an ideal place for you to
stay. Just a short 35 minute drive north of Franz Josef
Glacier. We are situated on our farm at the foot of Mt
Adam surrounded by farmlands and beautiful native
bush. Our lodge is just newly established and offers
comfortable accommodation and a fully licensed
restaurant. You can stroll along the river bank and farm
tracks meeting our variety of animals along the way.

Mt Adam Lodge
B&B Farmstay
13km N of Whataroa/70 mins
south of Hokitika
Elsa & Mac MacRae
State Highway 6
Whataroa

Tel: (03) 753 4030
Fax: (03) 753 4264
Tollfree: 0800 675 137
E: mtadamlodge@paradise.net
W: www.KeyWest.co.nz/
mtadamlodge

Cost: Double $85-$110
Single $70-$80
Visa/MC
Beds: 2 Queen 1 Double
4 Twin (7 bdrm)
Bath: 5 Ensuite
2 Guests share

Franz Josef Glacier

Rusty built our house from local material in true pioneering
spirit during 1998. Knightswood is surrounded by
spectacular scenery, nestled in native bush which attracts
prolific tuneful native birdlife. Both rooms offer breathtaking views of the Southern Alps. Jackie is a paediatric nurse
from England, Rusty a local helicopter pilot and keen deer
farmer. Over 200 deer run on the 250 acre farm. We, with
our daughter Amy, look forward to helping you discover the
magical qualities of the West Coast. Smoking outside only.

Knightswood B&B
B&B Farmstay
3km S of Franz Josef Glacier
Jackie & Russel Knight
PO Box 70
State Highway 6
Franz Josef

Tel: (03) 752 0059
Fax: (03) 752 0061
E: knightswood@xtra.co.nz
W: www.knightswood.co.nz

Cost: Double $120-$150
Single $100-$125
Child on request Visa/MC
Beds: 2 King/Twin (2 bdrm)
Bath: 2 Ensuite

Franz Josef Glacier

Managers Chanel, Dale and cat Tati, invite you to come
experience West Coast hospitality in the privacy of our self-
contained unit. Separate from the house, our room is
surrounded with gardens, farmland, rainforest, native birds
and excellent views of the mountains. Chanel, has 5 year
experience in the hospitality business and looks forward to
welcoming you to Glacier country. Partner Dale works at
the Alpine Adventure Centre and is able to assist with
bookings on Helicopter flights, Glacier walks, Fishing, etc.

Franz Josef Glacier B&B
Self-contained
3km N of Franz Josef
Marie & Glenn Coburn
Stoney Creek
State Highway 6
Franz Josef Glacier

Tel: (03) 752 0171
Fax: (03) 752 0171
E: green-family@actrix.gen.nz
W: www.bnb.co.nz/hosts/
franzjosefglacierbb.html

Cost: Double $100-$140
Single $95-$120
Dinner by arrangement
Visa/MC
Beds: 1 Queen (1 bdrm)
Bath: 1 Ensuite

WEST COAST

Franz Josef Glacier

Gerard and Bernie invite you to share their character home. Located on "The Glacier Highway", Holly Homestead (formerly Hollywood House) offers the peace and quiet of the country with the convenience of the township nearby. We happily provide local information and bookings for various activities for you to enjoy our magnificent region. There's plenty to do! Relax in our comfortable guest lounge after your adventures. Spectacular view from breakfast table, clouds permitting! Reservations recommended November to March (inclusive). Not suitable for children under 12 years.

Holly Homestead
B&B Homestay
1.5km N of Franz Josef
Gerard & Bernie Oudemans
State Highway 6
Franz Josef Glacier

Tel: (03) 752 0299
Fax: (03) 752 0298
E: hollyhomestead@xtra.co.nz
W: www.bnb.co.nz/hosts/
hollyhomestead.html

Cost: Double $98-$150
Single $75-$135
Visa/MC
Beds: 1 King/Twin 2 Queen
1 Twin (4 bdrm)
Bath: 1 Ensuite 1 Guests share

Fox Glacier

Kevin, Noeleen and Chancey our friendly Corgi, welcome you to our 2,800 acre beef/sheep farm. Our spacious 100yr old home, built for Kevin's grandparents has fine stained glass windows. Our ensuited rooms have great beds plus hairdryers. Homemade yoghurt, marmalade, jams and scones. Beautiful native forest-clad mountains surround on three sides and we view Mt Cook. A rural retreat within walking distance of village facilities, Matheson (Mirror Lake) & Glacier nearby. Directions: On Cook Flat Road, 5th house on right (350m back) before Church.

The Homestead
B&B Farmstay
0.5km W of Fox Glacier
Noeleen & Kevin Williams
PO Box 25
Cook Flat Road, Fox Glacier

Tel: (03) 751 0835
Fax: (03) 751 0805
W: www.bnb.co.nz/hosts/
thehomestead.html

Cost: Double $100-$145
Cooked Breakfast $5pp
Beds: 1 King/Twin 2 Queen
(3 bdrm)
Bath: 2 Ensuite 1 Private

The most suitable time to arrive
is late afternoon,
and to leave is before 10 in the morning.

Fox Glacier

Welcome to Fox Glacier. Reflection Lodge is situated 1/2 km down the Cook Flat Rd on your left, which is on the way to Lake Matheson- renowned for its famous picture postcard views.

Our home is surrounded by lovely gardens and offers panoramic views of New Zealands two highest mountains reflecting in our own private lake, directly opposite the dining room.

We enjoy meeting and talking to people from away and we endevour to make your stay an enjoyable moment. We are more than happy to assist in any way with local activities- eg.helicopter flights, helihikes and scenic walks to name a few. We look forward to seeing you and sharing our wonderful piece of paradise. Smoke free.

For bookings- free phone 0800 166 960.

Reflection Lodge
Homestay
Fox Glacier Central
Raelene Tuck
PO Box 46
Cook Flat Road
Fox Glacier

Tel: (03) 751 0707
Fax: (03) 751 0707
Tollfree: 0800 166 960
W: www.bnb.co.nz/hosts/
reflectionlodge.html

Cost: Double $110-$130
Child $35
Twin $100 - $110
Beds: 1 Queen 2 Single
(2 bdrm)
Bath: 1 Ensuite 1 Family share

Fox Glacier

Fox Glacier lodge is in the heart of Fox Glacier Village. The recently completed solid timber lodge is warm, clean and modern. Bathrooms are ensuite, two have double spa-baths. Breakfast room is stocked for self-serve continental, available at any time. Short stroll to cafes, restaurants. Lodge is smoke free. Reservations recommended. Attractions: glow worm grotto (on site), Fox Glacier, Lake Matheson, Mt Cook views, scenic flights, heli-hikes, bush walks. Directions: Our home/office is opposite BP. The Lodge is beyond, nestled within a slice of Heaven. Welcome!

Fox Glacier Lodge
B&B Self-contained Lodge
160km S of Hokitika
F & L Buckton
Box 22, Fox Glacier

Tel: (03) 751-0888
Fax: (03) 751 0888
Tollfree: 0800 36 98 00
W: www.bnb.co.nz/hosts/ foxglacierlodge.html

Cost: Double $98-$180
Unsuitable for children
Visa/MC
Beds: 1 King 5 Queen (6 bdrm)
Bath: 6 Ensuite

Fox Glacier

Relax in the comfort and warmth of our renovated two-story home. Our upstairs living area is lined with local timbers and enjoys 360-degree views of the glacier valley, mountains, farms and the township. We're the closest homestay to the glacier and 2 minutes walk to all eating and tourist facilities. After a comfortable, quiet night's sleep, you can wear yourself out on the glacier and surrounding walks. We offer a special cooked breakfast. We have one cat and one dog.

Roaring Billy Lodge
Homestay
160km S of Hokitika
Billy & Kathy
PO Box 16
21 State Highway 6
Fox Glacier

Tel: (03) 751 0815
Fax: (03) 751 0815
Tollfree: 0800 352 121
E: billy@xtra.co.nz
W: www.bnb.co.nz/hosts/ roaringbillylodge.html

Cost: Double $85-$95
Single $70-$75
Visa/MC
Beds: 1 Double 2 Single
(2 bdrm)
Bath: 1 Guests share

Fox Glacier

Eunice and Michael are third generation farming and tourism family. We have three grown children, 1 dog (Ruff), 1 cat (Black Cat). Our grandparents were founders of the Fox Glacier Hotel. We are a couple who enjoy meeting people and would like to share the joys of living in our little paradise (rain and all). Our home is surrounded by a large garden and have views of the mountains and Mt Cook. A five minute walk from township.

Fox Glacier Homestay
Homestay
Eunice & Michael Sullivan
64 Cook Flat Road
Fox Glacier

Tel: (03) 751 0817
Fax: (03) 751 0817
E: euni@xtra.co.nz
W: www.bnb.co.nz/hosts/
foxglacier.html

Cost: Double $80-$100
Single $60-$80
Beds: 2 Double 1 Single
(3 bdrm)
Bath: 1 Family share

Fox Glacier

Our family welcomes you to Mountain View homestay. Set on 10 acres of farmland surrounded by bush clad hills with spectacular views of Mt Cook and Mt Tasman. Situated 2km from Fox Village our 3 year old country home has it all, peaceful surroundings and friendly hospitality. We have extensive knowledge of the area and can organise Glacier flights and walks. We are just 2 minutes drive to restaurants and cafes. We have 2 school age children Harry 7 and Katie 5, 1 cat, 1 toy poodle and 2 horses. Children welcome. Smoke free.

Mountain View
B&B Self-contained Homestay
2km W of Fox Glacier
Julene & Phil Silcock
Williams Drive
Fox Glacier

Tel: (03) 751 0770
Fax: (03) 751 0744
W: www.bnb.co.nz/hosts/
user104.html

Cost: Double $100-$120
Single $80
Beds: 1 King/Twin 1 Double
1 Single (3 bdrm)
Bath: 3 Ensuite

Ensuite and private bathrooms are for your use exclusively
Guests share bathroom means you will be sharing with other guests
Family share means you will be sharing with the family

Bruce Bay

Welcome to Mulvaney Farmstays!

We run a beef farm consisting mainly of Hereford and Limosin cattle.

Our house was built in the 1920's by my Great Uncle Jack Mulvaney, for his bride to be but she never arrived. Jack Mulvaney was of Irish descent, just as the rest of his family was who settled in this valley 130 years ago. So he lived here by himself until 1971 raising Hereford cattle.

We have now lived her for 20 years with our children (who are all grown up and studying away from home). The house has been fully renovated with the farm also having been mostly redeveloped.

We are close to Bruce Bay and walking down the beach in the late afternoon after a long day of travelling can be very therapeutic. We are also near rivers and lakes which are also very scenic and great for trout fishing, or you can choose to go for short walks around our farm which are enjoyable, especially in the summer time. We are only 30 minutes from Fox Glacier and can arrange helicopter flights or glacier walks.

If you are heading south we can also arrange a jet boat ride on the spectacular Haast River. Malai, your hostess offers a choice of Thai or European dinners if you wish to have one (bookings preferred).

We have two cats and a dog and when you arrive you will be greeted by our friendly dog Monty.

Directions: 30 minutes south of Fox Glacier, 50 minutes north of Haast. 1 kilometre off SH6 on Condons Road - well sign posted.

Mulvawey Farmstay
Farmstay
50km S of Fox Glacier
Peter & Malai Millar
PO Box 117
Bruce Bay
South Westland

Tel: (03) 751 0865
Fax: (03) 751 0865
Tollfree: 0800 393 297
E: mulvaney@xtra.co.nz
W: www.bnb.co.nz/hosts/
millar.html

Cost: Double $80-$85
Single $60
Child n/a
Dinner $25
Beds: 1 Queen 1 Double 1 Twin
(3 bdrm)
Bath: 1 Guests share
1 Family share

Paringa

We run a 4th generation working beef farm, with a few sheep. We enjoy meeting people and have travelled to America, England, Kenya, Australia and some parts of Europe. Our farm is nestled beneath the bush clad foothills of the Southern Alps, close to Lake Paringa and the Paringa River. Our interests include hunting, jet boating, fishing, spinning, knitting and reading. We have one house cat and a small dog. Directions: 70 kms south of Fox Glacier, 50 kms north of Haast, four hours from Queenstown on State Highway 6.

Condon Farmstays
Farmstay Homestay
70km S of Fox Glacier
Glynis & Tony Condon
NZ Post Ltd
Lake Paringa, South Westland

Tel: (03) 751 0895
Fax: (03) 751 0001
Mob: 025 647 4965
E: condonfarms@xtra.co.nz
W: www.bnb.co.nz/hosts/
condonfarmstays.html

Cost: Double $80
Single $45 Child $20
Dinner $25by arrangement
Beds: 1 Double 4 Single
(3 bdrm)
Bath: 1 Family share

Haast

Okuru Beach gives you the opportunity to stay in a unique part of our country, in a friendly relaxed environment. Enjoy coastal beaches with driftwood, shells and penguins in season. Walk in the rainforest and view the native birds. We and our friendly Labrador dog enjoy sharing our comfortable home and local knowledge. Dinner served with prior notice. Our interests are our handcraft shop, photography, fishing, shooting and tramping. Also available - Seaview Cottage, self-contained sleeps 4 persons. Directions - turn into Jacksons Bay Road, drive 14km turn into Okuru.

Okuru Beach
B&B Self-contained Homestay
16km S of Haast
Marian & Derek Beynon
PO Box 59
Haast
South Westland

Tel: (03) 750 0719
Fax: (03) 750 0722
E: okurubeach@xtra.co.nz
W: www.okurubeach.co.nz

Cost: Double $70-$75 S.C $80
Single $45 Child $20
Dinner $20 Visa/MC
Beds: 3 Double 4 Single
(5 bdrm)
Bath: 1 Ensuite 1 Private
1 Guests share

WEST COAST

The best part about a homestay is
that you share the family's living area.

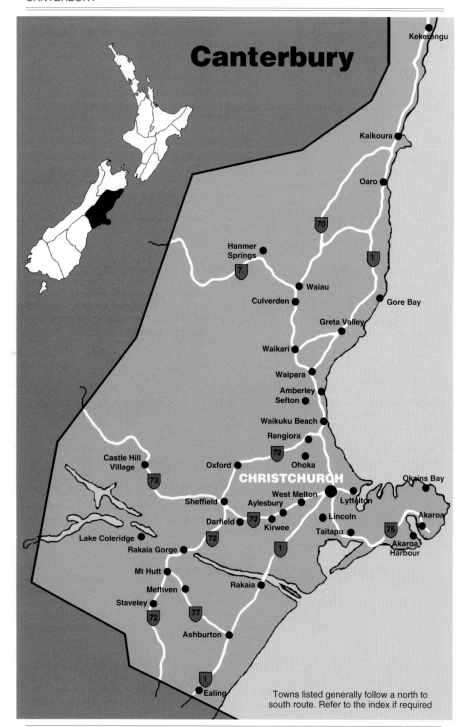

Canterbury

Kekerengu

Kaikoura

Oaro

70

Hanmer Springs

7

Waiau

Culverden

Gore Bay

Greta Valley

Waikari

Waipara

1

Amberley
Sefton

Waikuku Beach

Rangiora

72

Castle Hill Village

Oxford

Ohoka

CHRISTCHURCH

Okains Bay

73

Sheffield

West Melton
Aylesbury

Lyttelton

Akaroa

Darfield

73

Kirwee

Lincoln

75

Lake Coleridge

72

Taitapu

Akaroa Harbour

Rakaia Gorge

Mt Hutt

1

Methven

Rakaia

Staveley

72

77

Ashburton

1

Ealing

Towns listed generally follow a north to
south route. Refer to the index if required

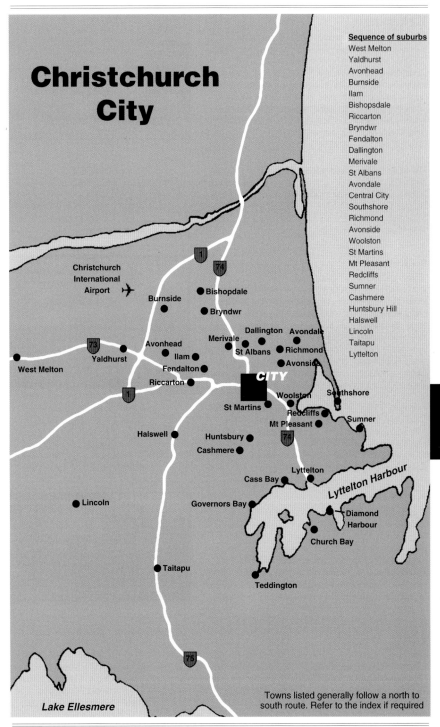

Christchurch City

Sequence of suburbs
West Melton
Yaldhurst
Avonhead
Burnside
Ilam
Bishopsdale
Riccarton
Bryndwr
Fendalton
Dallington
Merivale
St Albans
Avondale
Central City
Southshore
Richmond
Avonside
Woolston
St Martins
Mt Pleasant
Redcliffs
Sumner
Cashmere
Huntsbury Hill
Halswell
Lincoln
Taitapu
Lyttelton

CANTERBURY

Christchurch International Airport

Burnside

● Bishopdale

● Bryndwr

Dallington
Merivale
Avonhead
● St Albans Avondale
● Ilam ● Richmond
Fendalton ● Avonside

West Melton

Yaldhurst

Riccarton ●

CITY

St Martins ● Woolston Southshore

Halswell ● Redcliffs

Huntsbury ● Mt Pleasant ● Sumner

Cashmere ●

Lyttelton

Cass Bay ● *Lyttelton Harbour*

● Lincoln

Governors Bay ● Diamond Harbour

Church Bay

● Taitapu

Teddington

Lake Ellesmere

Towns listed generally follow a north to south route. Refer to the index if required

Kekerengu

Private and secluded Woodside cottage is nestled amongst
trees overlooking the rugged Kaikoura Coast. Situated near
State Highway 1, 60km between Kaikoura and Blenheim, an
ideal location for Marlborough Wineries or Kaikoura Whales.
Enjoy a scrumptious farm breakfast beside the open fire before
tackling a beach walk to seals, Woodside Gorge, fishing or
rafting (by arrangement), golf,or dinner at "The Store" cafe.
We also offer full kitchen facilities, BBQ, comfortable beds,
cotton sheets, real coffee, homemade biscuits. Directions -
please phone. Children Welcome. Pets by arrangement.

Woodside Cottage Country Retreat **Tel:** (03) 575 6819
Self-contained   **Fax:** (03) 575 6419
60km S of Blenheim or Kaikoura **Mob:** 025 349 951
Nick & Jock Clouston   **E:** woodsidecottage@xtra.co.nz
Main South Road   **W:** www.woodsidecottage.co.nz
Kekerengu Marlborough

Cost: Double $135
Single $90
Visa/MC
Beds: 1 King/Twin 1 Queen
1 Twin (3 bdrm)
Bath: 1 Private

Kekerengu

'Ellerton' is a magnificent Country Homestead nestled
in expansive gardens that overlook the Pacific Ocean
ensuring you a private stay of peace and tranquility. A
self-contained home with Master King Bedroom,
Super King Room, Twin Room and an adjacent annex
allows us to cater for larger groups. Complimentary
continental breakfast hamper provided. It is perfectly
situated for whale, dolphin and seal watching, bush
walks, surf fishing or fishing trips, wineries and garden
visits. Single party bookings only.

Ellerton   **Tel:** (03) 575 8673
B&B Self-contained   **Fax:** (03) 575 8672
65km S of Blenheim   **Tollfree:** 0800 004 173
Sharon Macdonald   **E:** ellerton@clear.net.nz
Ellerton/Valhalla Road   **W:** www.ellerton.co.nz
Kekerengu Marlborough

Cost: Double $200 Visa/MC
Beds: 1 Super King/Twin
1 King 1 Twin
Annexe - 1 Queen
1 Twin 1 Single (6 bdrm)
Bath: 1 Ensuite 2 Guests share

Kaikoura

Our spacious family home on Kaikoura Peninsula has
splendid mountain and sea views, is exceptionally quiet.
Only five minutes from township just off main highway
south. We book local activities and happily meet bus/train.
Laundry facilities and constant tea/coffee available.
Traditional breakfast with home baked bread, muesli, home
preserves, available early as required for whale watching etc.
Margaret, your friendly host enjoys gardening, golf, bowls,
her amusing Burmese cat and especially warmly welcoming
guests into her home. "Let Our Home be Your Home".

Bay-View   **Tel:** (03) 319 5480
Homestay   **Fax:** (03) 319 7480
130km S of Blenheim   **E:** MSBSDH@xtra.co.nz
Margaret Woodill   **W:** www.bnb.co.nz/hosts/
296 Scarborough Street   bayviewkaikoura.html
Kaikoura

Cost: Queen Ensuite $80 Double
and Twin $75   Single $45
Child $15 Dinner $25
Beds: 1 Queen 1 Double 1 Twin
1 Single (4 bdrm)
Bath: 1 Ensuite 1 Guests share
1 Family share

Kaikoura - Oaro

We are retired farmers, living on 48 acres close to the sea. Two cats share our home. We look north along the coast to Kaikoura Peninsula. Our home has one guest room with twin beds, self contained unit has two bedrooms, sleeps four. Enjoy coastal walk to Haumuri Bluff with bird-watching, fossil hunting etc. Drive to Kaikoura alongside rocky coastline. This is a mild climate and we grow citrus and sub-tropical fruit - mainly feijoas. Join us for dinner - fresh vegies, our own preserves and homemade ice cream!!

Waitane Homestay	**Tel:** (03) 319 5494	**Cost:** Double $70 Single $40
Homestay S/Cont. B&B	**Fax:** (03) 319 5524	Child $20
22km S of Kaikoura	**E:** waitane@xtra.co.nz	Dinner $15 by arrangement
Kathleen & Peter King	**W:** www.bnb.co.nz/hosts/	Visa/MC
Oaro RD 2 Kaikoura	waitane.html	**Beds:** 1 Double 4 Single (3 bdrm)
		Bath: 2 Private

Kaikoura

We are a friendly active retired couple who enjoy meeting new people and sharing the delights of our home on the beachfront. The view from our balcony is breathtaking, giving an unobstructed panorama of sea and mountains. We have guest TV lounge and games room. There is a swimming beach opposite, with children's play area and BBQ. Kaikoura has many tourist attractions, we are happy to help with bookings. Our home is centrally located, being a short walk to restaurants, galleries and scenic attractions.

Bevron	**Tel:** (03) 319 5432	**Cost:** Double $90 Single $80
B&B	**Fax:** (03) 319 5432	Child 1/2 price
Kaikoura Central	**E:** bevronhouse@hotmail.com	**Beds:** 2 Double 2 Single
Bev & Ron Barr	**W:** www.bnb.co.nz/hosts/	(2 bdrm)
196 Esplanade	bevron.html	**Bath:** 2 Ensuite
Kaikoura		

Kaikoura

Experience the atmosphere in our preserved convent buit in 1911. Your hosts offer personal sevice in a quiet and peaceful environment. For breakfast enjoy homemade yoghurt, muesli, breads, croissants and French Brioche. In the evenings the chef's passion for French cooking will ovelwhelm you. Our friendly dogs welcome you. Laundry facilities availiable. Fully licensed. Bicycles and courtesy car complimentary. Spanish/French spoken. Directions: The North edge of town, turn west off SH1 down Mill Road fro 1.5kms.

Old Convent	**Tel:** (03) 319 6603	**Cost:** Double $130 Single $75
B&B Inn	**Fax:** (03) 319 6690	Child $30 Dinner $50pp
3.6km N of Kaikoura	**Mob:** 025 353 954	Family Suites $205
W & M Launay	**Tollfree:** 0800 365 603	Visa/MC Amex
Mt Fyffe Road	**E:** o.convent@xtra.co.nz	**Beds:** 3 King/Twin 3 Queen
Kaikoura	**W:** www.thecoldconvent.co.nz	6 Double 3 Twin 2 Single
		(17 bdrm)
		Bath: 14 Ensuite 2 Private

Kaikoura

You will enjoy a relaxed and peaceful stay in a beautiful rural setting near the magnificent Kaikoura mountains. Relax on our deck and enjoy Alison's colourful garden which completes the panoramic view.

Ian's Great, Great, Uncle Jim, left "Ardara", Ireland in 1876. He bought our land here in Kaikoura in 1883 and milked cows. He established an orchard and planted macrocarpa trees for shelter. One macrocarpa tree was milled and used to build the cottage which was designed and built by Ian in 1998.

The cottage has an upstairs bedroom with a queen and two single beds. Downstairs there is a bedroom with a queen bed, a bathroom with a shower, and a lounge, kitchen, dining room. The deck is private with a great view of the mountains. It has been very popular with groups, families and honeymoon couples.

The house has ensuite bathrooms with queen beds, TV, fridge, settee and coffee/tea facilities. You have your own private entrance and you can come and go as you please. We offer laundry facilities, off street parking, courtesy car from bus/train.

Bookings for local tourist attractions, restaurants and farm tours can be arranged. Ian's brother Murray, has Donegal House, an Irish Garden Bar and Restaurant, which is within walking distance. Ian is a retired teacher and Alison a librarian. Our hobbies are tennis, golf, designing and building houses, gardening, handcrafts, spinning and we like to travel. No smoking indoors please. We look forward to your company.

Directions: Driving north, 4km from Kaikoura on S.H.1, turn left, 1.5km along Schoolhouse Road.

Apartment Peterborough No 12

Our one bedroom upmarket apartment is in central Christchurch and within walking distance to all amenities such as the Arts Centre, Museum, Casino and Hagley Park. The third level apartment is in a quiet area and looks out onto a large grassed courtyard. View the clock tower from the terrace. Double queen bed, sofa bed, television, video, etc.

Tariff: $110 per night or $560 per week serviced.
For more information: http://ardaralodge.com/flat.htm

Ardara Lodge	**Tel:** (03) 319 5736	**Cost:** House, Double $90-$95
B&B Self-contained	**Fax:** (03) 319 5732	Single $60-$65
5km N of Kaikoura	**Tollfree:** 0800 22 61 64	Cottage: Double $120-$130,
Alison & Ian Boyd	**E:** aemboyd@xtra.co.nz	4 persons $180 -$200 Visa/MC
233 Schoolhouse Road	**W:** www.ardaralodge.com	**Beds:** 6 Queen 2 Twin 3 Single
RD1 Kaikoura		(6 bdrm)
		Bath: 5 Ensuite

Kaikoura

Welcome to Kaikoura (Kai = food   Koura = Crayfish). My name is Roger and I'm the fourth generation "Boyd" to live and farm "Carrickfin". It is an ancient Irish name from where my Great Gran father emigrated. Dongal is still the home of the "Boyds". He bought and settled this land in 1867 for 100 gold sovereigns which he got prospecting.

The Lodge is built on 100 acres adjoining the Kairkoura township. It is a large and spacious place with an open fire and a guests' bar. It was built well back from the road amidst two acres of lawns and shrubs to give complete privacy and security.

There are breathtaking views from all rooms looking directly at the "Seaward Kaikouras" a spectacular mountain range which rises to 8,500ft. These mountains are home to a unique and variety of wild life.

As well as fattening heifers I am a professional Wool Classer by trade and have worked in shearing sheds throughout the South Island high Country.

Our sea and coastline is also unique for the Whales, Dolphins, Seals and many ocean going birds including the Wandering Albatros. It is one place in the world where Whales are found all the year round. I am 3km from Whale Watch, Dolphin Encounter and some of the best seafood restaurants in the South Island.

Directions: At the north end of town turn west into Mill Road and I am up on the left. Big Irish Breakfast (Easy to find - hard to leave).

Carrickfin Lodge
B&B Lodge
3km N of Kaikoura
Roger Boyd
Mill Road Kaikoura

Tel: (03) 319 5165
Fax: (03) 319 5162
Tollfree: 0800 265 963
W: www.bnb.co.nz/hosts/
carrickfinlodge.html

Cost: Double $85-$90
Single $60
Child Not Suitable
Beds: 5 Queen 5 Single
(6 bdrm)
Bath: 6 Ensuite

Kaikoura

We proudly offer two luxurious upstairs self contained units with private entrance and carparking facilities, designed and furnished to guarantee your holiday with us will be comfortable and enjoyable. The sea and mountain views from your balcony,are unbeatable in Kaikoura. Relax, soak up the sun, and eat your delicious Continental Breakfast within this very unique environment, only 5 minutes walk to the Beach, Town Centre, Shops and Restaurants. Our two cats, like us, are friendly and welcoming. Experience genuine Kiwi hospitality. See you soon.

Churchill Park Lodge	**Tel:** (03) 319 5526	**Cost:** Double $85
B&B Self-contained	**Fax:** (03) 319 5526	Single $65
130km S of Blenheim	**Tollfree:** 0800 363 690	Child $15 Visa/MC
Moira & Stan Paul	**E:** cplodge@ihug.co.nz	**Beds:** 1 Queen 1 Double
34 Churchill Street	**W:** www.bnb.co.nz/hosts/	1 Single (2 bdrm)
Kaikoura Marlborough	churchillparklodge.html	**Bath:** 2 Ensuite

Kaikoura

We are a semi retired couple who have moved form Southland and would like to welcome you to Austin Heights on the Kaikoura Peninsular. Our home is set in 1/2 acre of gardens and lawns offering lovely views of mountains and sea. The house is comfortable and modern and is situated on Austin Street which is the second turn left off Scarbrough Street off the main Highway South of town. We have two cats and are a non smoking household. Courtesy transport available.

Austin Heights	**Tel:** (03) 319 5836	**Cost:** Double $65
B&B Self-contained Homestay	**Fax:** (03) 319 6836	Single $40
130km S of Blenheim	**W:** www.bnb.co.nz/hosts/	Queen Ensuite $100
Val & Ian Johnson	austinheights.html	Visa/MC
19 Austin Street		**Beds:** 1 Queen 1 Double
Kaikoura		2 Single (3 bdrm)
		Bath: 1 Ensuite 1 Family share

Kaikoura

Dear Traveller, we offer you something special something different come away from the crowd and enjoy real NZ hospitality. Our luxury unit is fully self contained and caters for a group of one to four people. Large upstairs lounge with pool table. Our farm is 500 hectares and has sheep, cattle and goats. Pet lambs for the children. Enjoy our native birds, hear a Moorpork at night. Our price includes continental breakfast other meals on request. Farm tours and sheep shearing by arrangement. Looking forward to your visit.

Clematis Grove Lodge	**Tel:** (03) 319 5264	**Cost:** Double $85 Single $55
B&B Self-contained Farmstay	**Fax:** (03) 319 5278	Child 1/2 price Dinner $25
20km N of Kaikoura	**E:** clematisgrove@xtra.co.nz	Visa/MC
Margaret & Ken Hamilton	**W:** www.bnb.co.nz/hosts/	**Beds:** 1 King 1 Double
Blue Duck Valley	clematisgrovelodge.html	2 Single (2 bdrm)
RD 1 Kaikoura		**Bath:** 1 Private 1 Family share

Kaikoura

"One Hundred Thousand Welcomes" - "Donegal House", the little Irish Pub in the country, brimming with warmth and hospitality, open fires and accordion music. Set on an historical dairy farm which has been farmed by the Boyd family since their arrival from Donegal, Ireland in 1865, "Donegal House" offers, accommodation, full bar facilities and a public licensed restaurant.

The a-la-carte menu, specialising in Kaikoura's famous crayfish and seafood, plus locally farmed beef. NZ beers, Kilkenny and Guinness are on tap along with a good selection of Marlborough wines. Two spring fed lakes, home to Chinook salmon, Mute and Black Swans, Blue Teal, Paradise and Mallard ducks, are feature in the extensive lawns and gardens which surround "Donegal House". The towering Kaikoura Mountains make a perfect backdrop to this unique setting.

The Restaurant and Bar facilities at "Donegal House" have become a very popular place for visitors staying at the nearby Carrick-finn Lodge, Ardara Lodge, The Old Convent and Dylans Country Stay, to meet the Kaikoura locals and enjoy the rural hospitality in a unique Irish atmosphere.

We book whale watching, dolphin and seal swimming and hors trekking etc. "Even if you're not Irish-this is the place for you!" "A home away from home!"

Directions: Driving North 4kms from Kaikoura on SH1 turn left at Large transit signs, 1.6km along Schoolhouse Road.

Donegal House
B&B Farmstay Licenced Rest &
Accomodation
5km N of Kaikoura
Mimi & Murray Boyd
Schoolhouse Road
Kaikoura

Tel: (03) 319 5083
Fax: (03) 319 05083
E: donegalhouse@xtra.co.nz
W: www.donegalhouse.co.nz

Cost: Double $100
     Single $75
     Child $15
     Dinner $22.50 Visa/MC
Beds: 12 Queen 2 Single
     (10 bdrm)
Bath: 10 Ensuite

Kaikoura

It's big, it's blue and what a view. Sea and mountains fill the windows. Don't settle for less because it is Kaikoura's location that makes it unique. Nikau is just minutes walk to the main street where you can enjoy crayfish and seafood meals. At Nikau you can send your email from the desk overlooking the colourful garden, enjoy a special breakfast at the 4.2m table - once the council's - and chat to Judith who has travelled widely and grew up nearby. (Tea, coffee, laundry available.)

Nikau-the inn with the view	**Tel:** (03) 319 6973	**Cost:** Double $75-$90
B&B Guesthouse	**Fax:** (03) 319 6973	Single $60-$70
130km S of Blenheim	**E:** jhughey@xtra.co.nz	Visa/MC
Judith Hughey	**W:** www.bnb.co.nz/hosts/	**Beds:** 2 Queen 2 Double 3 Twin
53 Deal Street	nikau.html	6 Single (6 bdrm)
Kaikoura		**Bath:** 5 Ensuite 1 Private

Kaikoura - Peketa

A warm welcome awaits you at Coastal Retreat, where hospitality is our speciality. Nestled between mountains, river and sea, waiting to be explored. Cooked breakfast with delicious homemade spreads. Enjoy a variety of walks, golf, fishing, surfing and horse treks on our doorstep. Explore kaikoura or simply relax in our garden and enjoy the views. Don't miss the unique experience of soaking under the stars in our heated outdoor baths. Join us afterwards, or retreat to your cosy room. Tea/Coffee, laundry and email facilities available.

Coastal Retreat	**Tel:** (03) 319 6960	**Cost:** Single $55 DinnerB/A
Homestay	**Fax:** (03) 319 6964	$80 ensuite $70 Queen
8km S of Kaikoura	**E:** eileen.thomas@xtra.co.nz	share bath Visa/MC
Eileen & Kim	**W:** www.bnb.co.nz/hosts/	**Beds:** 2 Queen 1 Twin
1 Bullens Road	coastalretreat.html	(3 bdrm)
Peketa, RD 2 Kaikoura		**Bath:** 1 Ensuite 1 Family share

Kaikoura

We are retired dairy farmers, being fourth generation Kaikourians and having extensive knowledge of the area and surrounding districts. Our 1930's restored home and large garden are just minutes walk from the township, beach, Whale Watch etc and command incredible views of the Pacific Ocean and seaward Kaikouras. We enjoy meeting people and helping arrange visits to tourist attractions. Partake of our true country breakfast and other home-made treats. Other meals available. Courtesy car at all times.

Bendamere	**Tel:** (03) 319 5830	**Cost:** Double $70-$90
B&B Self-contained Homestay	**Fax:** (03) 319 7337	Single $50-$60
Ellen & Peter Smith	**W:** www.bnb.co.nz/hosts/	Child $15
37 Adelphi Tce	bendamere.html	**Beds:** 1 Queen 1 Double
Kaikoura		1 Twin (3 bdrm)
		Bath: 2 Ensuite 1 Private

Waiau

Conveniently situated midway between Kaikoura and Hanmer Springs on the "Alpine Pacific Triangle" (SH70), Mason Hills Station offers a real New Zealand rural experience: * Fourth generation New Zealanders. * Commercial Sheep and Beef Hill Country Station. * Large character Homestead in a genuine alpine setting. * 21 kms north of Waiau, 1km south of Mt Lyford ski field turn off. * 4WD Farm Tour encompassing spectacular Alpine to Pacific views available as an extra. Averil, Robert and Gracie the Labrador look forward to welcoming you.

Mason Hills	**Tel:** (03) 315 6611	**Cost:** Double $100
Farmstay Homestay	**Fax:** (03) 315 6611	Single $60
21km N of Waiau	**Mob:** 025 285 1333	Dinner $25 Visa/MC
Averil & Robert Leckey	**Tollfree:** 0800 101 961	**Beds:** 1 Queen 2 Single
Inland Kaikoura Road	**E:** mason_hills@xtra.co.nz	(2 bdrm)
Waiau, RD North Canterbury	**W:** www.bnb.co.nz/hosts/	**Bath:** 1 Ensuite 1 Private
	masonhills.html	

Waiau

If you like fresh air, clean green living, home baked food and home grown veggies. That is us. We enjoy people. Around Waiau we have trout and salmon fishing, jet boating, golfing, skiing and just 30 minutes to Hot Pools and horse trekking. One hour to wineries and whalewatch. Our home is set in half an acre of gardens which we share with our 2 cats. Waiau is one hour south of Kaikoura, 30 minutes from Hanmer Springs and ninety minutes north of Christchurch.

Waiau B&B	**Tel:** (03) 315 6356	**Cost:** Double $75
B&B	**Fax:** (03) 315 6356	Single $45
Waiau Central	**Mob:** 025 268 3024	Child $25 Dinner $25
Sally & Vern McAllister	**E:** vernandsally@xtra.co.nz	Visa/MC
32 Lyndon Street	**W:** www.bnb.co.nz/hosts/	**Beds:** 1 Queen 1 Twin (2 bdrm)
Waiau 8275 North Canterbury	waiaubb.html	**Bath:** 1 Family share

Hanmer Springs

Close to the thrills of Hanmer Springs lies our peaceful home at the foot of the mountains. New guest rooms have been tastefully decorated to make your stay special. There is a grand piano and an extensive CD collection. Our large garden has a swimming pool. As retired restaurateurs we know how to pamper you. We travelled widely and speak Dutch and German. An elderly Labrador and a young Jack Russell are part of our non-smoking household. Come as a stranger. Leave as a friend!

Mira Monte	**Tel:** (03) 315 7604	**Cost:** Double $100-$120
Country Homestay	**Fax:** (03) 315 7604	Single $85
5km SW of Hanmer Springs	**Mob:** 021 264 5809	Dinner $35 Visa/MC
Anna & Theo van de Wiel	**E:** vdwiel@xtra.co.nz	**Beds:** 2 King 1 Single
324 Woodbank Road	**W:** www.bnb.co.nz/hosts/	(2 bdrm)
Hanmer Springs	miramonte.html	**Bath:** 2 Ensuite

Hanmer Springs

Cheltenham House offers luxury accommodation, 200 metres from Hanmer Springs unique Thermal Pools. We renovated this 1930's villa with the travellers comfort paramount. Spacious, sunny suites have superior quality bedding, tea/coffee facilities, TV, hairdryers and comfortable seating and dining areas. Socialise in the evening with a glass of wine in the original billiard room. In the morning, enjoy a substantial breakfast at your leisure, in the privacy of your own suite. Together with our gentle Labrador, we offer a friendly relaxed environment.

Cheltenham House	**Tel:** (03) 315 7545	**Cost:** Double $130-$140
B&B Self-contained	**Fax:** (03) 315 7645	Single $110 Visa/MC
Maree & Len Earl	**E:** cheltenham@xtra.co.nz	**Beds:** 6 Queen 2 Single
13 Cheltenham Street	**W:** www.cheltenham.co.nz	(6 bdrm)
Hanmer Springs		**Bath:** 5 Ensuite 1 Private

Hanmer Springs

We offer a warm welcome, comfy beds, and a friendly breakfast dining room. Glenalvon, one of the original "guest houses" in Hanmer Springs has a guest room with ensuite and another with private facilities. Nestled behind are 8 spacious luxury suites all with ensuite bathrooms and Sky TV, breakfast is optional and extra in the suites. Set in a cottage garden setting on the main street just a two minute stroll to the Thermal Springs, village centre and adjacent to a restaurant. Call us or pop in and we will show you around.

Glenalvon Lodge	**Tel:** (03) 315 7475	**Cost:** Double $80-$89 Single $65
B&B Luxury Suites	**Fax:** (03) 315 7361	Child $20 Suites $85 - $125
130km N of Christchurch	**Tollfree:** 0800 45 36 25	Visa/MC Amex Diners
Trish & John Burrin	**E:** glenalvon@xtra.co.nz	**Beds:** 6 Queen 6 Double
29 Amuri Avenue	**W:** www.glenalvon.co.nz	7 Single (10 bdrm)
Hanmer Springs		**Bath:** 9 Ensuite 1 Private

Hanmer Springs

Hanmer View is surrounded by beautiful forest and adjoins Conical Hill track. Breathtaking alpine views. Purpose built to ensure guests enjoy a quiet, relaxing stay in warm, spacious luxury rooms. Each individually decorated room has ensuite, TV, wool duvets and hand made quilts. Tea, coffee and cake is always available and your hosts, Will and Helen delight in serving you a generous scrumptious breakfast. No-one goes away hungry. Short stroll to village, thermal pools and tourist attractions. See letterbox sign, on right, end Oregon Heights.

Hanmer View	**Tel:** (03) 315 7947	**Cost:** Double $110-$150
B&B	**Fax:** (03) 315 7958	Single $80-$120
Hanmer Springs	**Reservations:** 0800 92 0800	Dinner B/A Visa/MC
Will & Helen Lawson	**E:** hanmerview@xtra.co.nz	**Beds:** 1 King/Twin 1 Queen
8 Oregon Heights	**W:** www.hanmerview.co.nz	1 Double (3 bdrm)
Hanmer Springs		**Bath:** 3 Ensuite

Albergo Hanmer

True Hospitality without compromise!

Hanmer Springs

WE ARE PASSIONATE ABOUT BREAKFASTS
AND OUR EUROPEAN & PACIFIC RIM/NZ
CUISINE! Renowned 3 course gourmet breakfast,
served in the sunny conservatory...with the wafting
smell of freshly baked swiss miniloaves and Italian
roasted coffee. Dine by candle light: prime NZ beef
medallions, baby lamb, venison tenderloins, enveloped
with Italian and Asian entrees and Swiss surprise
desserts.

Guests comments: 'As for the breakfast...words fail me!
The best and tastiest we have had in any of the five
continents' *Michael and Shirley Hicks, Dunstable UK.*
'World class hospitality...our 3rd visit, which we
enjoyed every bit as much as the previous ones. Many
thanks!' *Dr N &J Grenfell, Christchurch, NZ,* "Thank
you for creating such an artistic, stimulating, get-
comfortable environment' *Bob Streeter, Fort Colins
USA.*

Set in a magic mountain arena, Albergo Hanmer offers
PEACE, PRIVACY and ALL DAY SUN, yet only 2
mins drive from the Thermal Pools and 18 hole golf.

The interior styling is modern European, creating a
fresh, light and comfortable feel (u/floor heating).
Unwind under a wonderful hot shower (high pressure),
or in the double spa, then relax in the private guest
lounge. Check out our new 2-room designer suite.
Dedicated hosts, Bascha & Beat Blattner, are a young
couple (NZ & Swiss origins) with 15 years experience
in hospitality & tourism. Bascha's background is in
Fashion, Teaching & Communications (NLP). Beat is a
Tourism Expert & Desktop Publisher. We speak
English, Swiss, German, French, Spanish and Italian.
Come and view our seahorse memorabilia. **We can
arrange your golfing, hunting & fishing tours.**

Swiss brunch-style breakfast

Start your day with:
Fruit Juice, fresh fruit platter
& home-made yoghurt, Swiss
Birchermuesli or Bascha's low-fat
muesli & other cereal selection.

Choose a hot main:
served with Béat's Swiss crunchy miniloaf.

Eggs Benedict on Salmon & fresh Hollandaise
Traditional French Omelettes
Spanish Fritatta with sage & apple
French Crêpes with lemon & maple syrup
Full English Breakfast
French Toast with Bacon & Banana
Freshly brewed italian coffee or teas

Special diets catered for!

Directions: At junction before main village, 300m past
Shell Garage, take ARGELINS ROAD (Centre branch),
go past Hanmer Golf Club, take first road on left
RIPPINGALE RD (no exit). Albergo Hanmer is 900m
down at the very end of this country lane.

Albergo Hanmer	**Tel:** (03) 315 7428	**Cost:** Double $120-$220
B&B	**Fax:** (03) 315 7428	Single $100
130km N of Christchurch	**Tollfree:** 0800 342 313	Dinner by prior arrangement
Bascha & Beat Blattner	**E:** albergohanmer@hotmail.com	Visa/MC
88 Rippingale Road	**W:** www.albergohanmer.com	**Beds:** 2 Super King/Twin
Hanmer Springs	Check our website for specials	1 King (3 bdrm)
		Bath: 3 Ensuite (spa)

Hanmer Springs

Alpenrose is situated in a quiet tree-lined street, within a mature garden setting with beautiful views to the surrounding mountains and garden, with all day sun. We are very private and quiet, yet we are only 200m walk to the thermal swimming reserve and main shopping area. Both our rooms are large with ensuite (one with a spa bath), TV and tea and coffee facilities. Our breakfast are delicious from a good selection. My aim is to provide you with a stay with unbeatable hospitality and cuisine.

Alpenrose	**Tel:** (03) 315 7679	**Cost:** Double $120-$140
B&B	**Fax:** (03) 315 7679	Single $100-$120
200m Hanmer Village	**Mob:** 025 859 938	Visa/MC
Sheryl Dennis	**E:** alpenrose@xtra.co.nz	**Beds:** 1 King/Twin 1 Queen
21 Cheltenham St	**W:** www.alpenrose.co.nz	1 Single (2 bdrm)
Hanmer Springs		**Bath:** 2 Ensuite

Culverden

Welcome to 'Ballindalloch' a 2090 acre irrigated farm 3km south of Culverdon. We milk 1100 cows in 2 floating rotary dairies, a concept unique to New Zealand. We also have a Corriedale sheep stud. Our home is set amongst lawns and gardens with a swimming pool. Panoramic views of the hills and mountains surround us. Our home is centrally heated in winter and has a log fire. We are just over 1 hour north of Christchurch and Hanmer Springs 1/2 hour to the north.

Ballindalloch	**Tel:** (03) 315 8220	**Cost:** Double $105
Farmstay	**Fax:** (03) 315 8220	Single $55
3km S of Culverden	**Mob:** 025 373 184	Child $30 Dinner $30
Diane & Dougal Norrie	**W:** www.bnb.co.nz/hosts/	**Beds:** 1 Queen 2 Single
Culverden	ballindalloch.html	(2 bdrm)
North Canterbury		**Bath:** 1 Guests share

Gore Bay

Welcome to paradise. Enjoy panoramic sea views, warm beds and other home comforts at our beach-front property, plus the native bush walk at the rear. The bay also offers coastal walks, safe swimming, surfing, fishing, lovely gardens and a little history and the spectacular Cathedral Cliffs. Gore Bay is one hour drive from Kaikoura or Hanmer and one and a half hours north of Christchurch and is on a sealed road. We are a retired couple and enjoy gardening, sport, art, travel and good company.

Gore Bay B&B	**Tel:** (03) 319 8535	**Cost:** Double $75-$90
B&B	**E:** gorebay.bnb@xtra.co.nz	Single $50 Visa/MC
8km E of Cheviot	**W:** www.bnb.co.nz/hosts/	**Beds:** 1 Double 2 Twin
Peter & Valerie McClatchy	gorebaybb.html	(2 bdrm)
6 Cathedral Road		**Bath:** 1 Ensuite 1 Family share
Gore Bay, Cheviot RD 3		
North Canterbury 8271		

Waikari - Waipara

Waituna is a sheep farm halfway between Christchurch and Hanmer Springs and about 1 hour from Christchurch Airport. The large Homestead is listed with The Historic Places Trust, (the Limestone part built in 1879). Waituna is 15 mins from the Waipara wineries and close to golf courses, fishing rivers and horse treks. Hanmer has thermal pools, bungy jumping and jet boating. We lived in Ireland till 1972, (David is English) and enjoy sports, travelling and meeting people. We look forward to welcoming you to our gracious old home.

Waituna
Farmstay Historic Home
5km N of Waikari
Joanna & David Cameron
PO Box 7
Waikari North Canterbury

Tel: (03) 314 4575
Fax: (03) 314 4575
E: waituna.waikari@xtra.co.nz
W: www.bnb.co.nz/hosts/
waituna.html

Cost: Double $120-$130
Single $60
Dinner $40 B/A Visa/MC
Beds: 1 King/Twin 1 Queen
4 Single (4 bdrm)
Bath: 1 Ensuite 1 Private
1 Guests share

Waipara

Situated on the northern edge of Waipara village, Winery Cottage offers you the ideal location to experience the many attractions that make our area unique. Base yourself in a cosy cottage with warm, spacious bedrooms and your very own modern ensuite bathroom. In the morning take a relaxed hearty breakfast with freshly baked breads, home-made muesli, fruit juice, hot porridge and filling cooked breakfast. Evening meal available upon request. Within walking distance, the Weka Pass Railway will take you on a steam train excursion. Smoke Free. Not suitable for children.

Winery Cottage
B&B
10km N of Amberley
Julian Ball
RD 3 Amberley
North Canterbury

Tel: (03) 314 6909
Fax: (03) 314 6909
E: winery.cottage@xtra.co.nz
W: www.winery.cottage.co.nz

Cost: Double $110
Dinner $40
Visa/MC
Beds: 2 Queen (2 bdrm)
Bath: 2 Ensuite

Amberley

Our drive goes off SH1 and so we are conveniently en route to and from the inter-island ferry, just 48km north of Christchurch and 100km south of the Kaikoura whales, and easy to find. The house is surrounded by an English style garden with swimming pool, and close to the Waipara wineries, beach and attractive golf course. We breed ostriches which we are pleased to show visitors, have travelled extensively and lived abroad, and now share our lives with a Newfoundland and a Labrador, two geriatric donkeys and Rupert the cat!

Bredon Downs Homestay
Farmstay Homestay
1km S of Amberley
Bob & Veronica Lucy
Bredon Downs Amberley,
RD 1 North Canterbury

Tel: (03) 314 9356
Fax: (03) 314 8994
Mob: 025 224 4061
E: lucy.lucy@xtra.co.nz
W: www.bnb.co.nz/hosts/
bredondownshomestay.html

Cost: Double $100-$110
Single $60
Dinner $30 B/A Visa/MC
Beds: 1 Queen 1 Twin 1 Single
(3 bdrm)
Bath: 1 Ensuite 1 Private

Waikuku Beach

Do you prefer to stay in a rural area but within easy reach of city and airport? Our home is just off the main highway, 30 minutes drive north from Christchurch. We have quiet, peaceful and warm accommodation with a large tranquil garden and comfortable fireside lounge, and just a short walk from the beach. Enjoy a continental breakfast with a fresh fruit platter. We enjoy tramping, theatre and travel, and offer a very friendly service. Our Labrador dog, Zeus, lives outside.

Homestay	**Tel:** (03) 312 2292	**Cost:** Double $70
10km E of Rangiora	**Fax:** (03) 312 2235	Single $40
Pauline & Graeme Barr	**E:** barrgp@paradise.net.nz	Visa/MC
74 Waikuku Beach Road	**W:** www.bnb.co.nz/hosts/	**Beds:** 1 Double 2 Single
Waikuku Beach	barr.html	(2 bdrm)
North Canterbury		**Bath:** 1 Private 1 Family share

Rangiora

Nestled on the northern side of Rangiora township on Highway 72, heading towards Oxford 30 minutes from Christchurch, roughly 1 hour to Mt Hutt. Walking distance to cafes and restaurants. Malcolm and I invite you to share our enchanting English style home for some Kiwi hospitality. Off street parking available. Warm comfortable beds, electric blankets, quality linen, and a hearty home style continental or cooked breakfast. Bedrooms overlook the garden with views of surrounding countryside. Meet Lucy our Foxy and Ralph our elderly cat. Email facilities available.

Willow Glen	**Tel:** (03) 313 9940	**Cost:** Double $80
B&B	**Fax:** (03) 313 9946	Single $50
30km N of Christchurch	**Mob:** 025 984 893	**Beds:** 1 Queen 1 Double
Glenda & Malcolm Ross	**E:** rosshighway@xtra.co.nz	(2 bdrm)
419 High Street Rangiora	**W:** www.geocities.co/	**Bath:** 1 Guests share
	willowglennz	

Oxford

Our house is 80 years old and has a spacious garden - warm and sunny. We are a contented married couple with a family of three grown-up sons. We retired from Dunedin to live in Oxford - a charming, restful town and a friendly community. Oxford offers scenic walks, horse treks, homecrafts, pottery and home spun hand-knitted garments, bowls, tennis, squash, restaurant, golf and bridge club handy. High Street is off the Main Road - left - sign outside the gate.

Country Life	**Tel:** (03) 312 4167	**Cost:** Double $60-$70
B&B Self-contained Homestay	**W:** www.bnb.co.nz/hosts/	Single $35-$40
60km W of Christchurch	countrylife.html	Dinner $20 B/A
Helen & Norton Dunn		**Beds:** 3 Double (3 bdrm)
137 High Street		**Bath:** 1 Ensuite 1 Family share
Oxford		
North Canterbury		

Oxford

'Glenariff' is a character home (circa 1886) operated as a Devonshire tea rooms set in a large country garden with mature trees. Oxford is a friendly country town with most leisure activities catered for. It will be our pleasure to welcome you to our home to relax and share our hospitality. A leisurely breakfast, candle light dinner or perhaps Devonshire tea served on the verandah. We have a pet cat and are smoke free. Directions: High Street is off Main Street - sign on gate.

Glenariff
Homestay
Oxford Central
Beth & John Minns
136 High Street
Oxford Canterbury

Tel: (03) 312 4678
W: www.bnb.co.nz/hosts/
glenariff.html

Cost: Double $70
Single $35
Child $15 Dinner $20 B/A
Beds: 1 Double 2 Single (2 bdrm)
Bath: 1 Guests share

Oxford

Welcome to our farm. A home away from home. Views of the Southern Alps, local mountains with walks through native bush and birds. Oxford offers most sports, horse riding, jet boating, golf, fishing. Come experience a working farm, cattle, sheep, three farm dogs or spend time enjoying the countryside. Our welcome includes tea, coffee and delicious home baking. Evening meals include local meat and produce. Situated 3.7 km west of Oxford. Look for sign on Main Road. 40 min from Christchurch. No smoking.

Twin Bridge Farmstays
Farmstay
3.7km W of Oxford
Anne & Don Manera
345 Woodside Road
Cooper Creek, Oxford
North Canterbury

Tel: (03) 312 4964
W: www.bnb.co.nz/hosts/
twinbridgefarmstays.html

Cost: Double $80
Single $45
Child $30 Dinner $20
under 5 free
Beds: 1 Double 1 Twin
1 Single (3 bdrm)
Bath: 1 Family share

Oxford

Nestled at the top of our drive in a peaceful, rural setting with the Oxford foothills as a backdrop we invite you to share our lovely home. Luxurious upstairs guest accommodation with separate entrance. Queen apartment has own lounge while both guest areas have TV, tea/coffee making facilities. Inground swimming pool, laundry, fax/internet facilities available. On Inland Scenic Route 72, the gateway to rest of South Island. Christchurch 45 mins away. Delicious menu breakfasts, lunch and dinners available. Your warm welcome includes our dog Chantel, home baking and that inviting cup of coffee/tea.

Hielan' House
Homestay
40mins from Christchurch Airport
Shirley & John Farrell
74 Bush Road
Oxford North Canterbury

Tel: (03) 312 4382
Fax: (03) 312 4382
Mob: 025 359 435
Tollfree: 0800 279 382
E: meg29@ihug.co.nz
W: www.bnb.co.nz/hosts/
hielanhouse.html

Cost: Double $95-$110
Single $60
Dinner B/A Visa/MC
Beds: 1 King/Twin 1 Queen
(2 bdrm)
Bath: 1 Ensuite 1 Private

Oxford

Spectacular Gorge and Mountain views/Brand new purpose built home in Spanish and Australian design/Dinner by arrangement/ Christchurch Airport 35 mins/Waimakariri Lodge is situated on Route 72, 12km south of Oxford, and very easy to find. A farmstay with panoramic views, of gorge and mountains. Home made mueslis, warm hospitality, home gym, relaxing private spa, 40 mins to ski fields, trout fishing, 18 hole golf course adjacent to our property - golf clubs available, a scenic tour can be arranged in our Vintage car, picnic lunch provided. If you long for a quite peaceful location then this is the place for you.

Waimakariri Lodge	**Tel:** (03) 312 3662	**Cost:** Double $130
Farmstay	**Fax:** (03) 312 3662	Single $90
35km E of Christchurch	**Mob:** 025 371 096	Dinner $30 B/A
Ian & Sharon Moore	**E:** sharonian@xtra.co.nz	**Beds:** 2 Queen 1 Twin
45 Depot Gorge Road	**W:** www.bnb.co.nz/hosts/	(3 bdrm)
RD 1 Oxford	waimakariri.html	**Bath:** 2 Ensuite 1 Private

West Melton

We have a 50 hectare property where we farm sheep and grow lavender. Close to all amenities, in a quiet rural setting with magnificent views of the mountains. Countless day trips can be taken from our home. We have enjoyed entertaining folk from different parts of the world and look forward to meeting and caring for many more. Relax with us and enjoy a farmhouse dinner. Begin or end a memorable holiday with us. 15 minutes from Christchurch Airport. Smoke free home. Friendly cat.

Hopesgate	**Tel:** (03) 347 8330	**Cost:** Double $80
B&B Farmstay	**Fax:** (03) 347 8330	Single $60
25km W of Christchurch	**Mob:** 025 311 234	Dinner $20 Visa/MC
Yvonne & Robert Overton	**E:** robove@free.net.nz	**Beds:** 1 Queen 2 Single
Hoskyns Road	**W:** www.bnb.co.nz/hosts/	(2 bdrm)
RD 5 Christchurch	hopesgate.html	**Bath:** 1 Guests share

West Coast Road - Christchurch

Gwenda and Peter invite you to come and enjoy the ambience of our warm and spacious home set in a large garden with magnificent views of the Southern Alps. Our home is situated on 7.5 acres where we farm ostriches and various other farm animals. We are ideally located just 7 minutes from the airport and 10 minutes from the city. A full sized tennis court is available for guests use

GP's Place	**Tel:** (03) 342 9196	**Cost:** Double $90
B&B	**Fax:** (03) 342 4196	Single $45
10km W of Christchurch	**Mob:** 021 158 6208	Dinner $25
Gwenda & Peter Bickley	**E:** gpsplace@hotmail.com	**Beds:** 1 Queen 1 Twin
164 Old West Coast Road	**W:** gpsplace.ttributes.com	(2 bdrm)
RD 6 Christchurch		**Bath:** 1 Private

Yaldhurst - Christchurch

Relax, enjoy the best of both worlds in a lovely rural setting just 20 minutes to the city centre. You are welcome to wander in our spacious gardens, feed the ducks and breathe our clear country air. We offer an Airport pickup only 10 minutes away, as is the Antarctic Centre. We are on the direct route to the West Coast and to many ski fields. Close by are several vineyards and golf courses. You are assured of a very warm welcome at Cherry Grove.

Cherry Grove	**Tel:** (03) 342 8629	**Cost:** Double $80-$90
B&B Homestay	**Fax:** (03) 342 4321	Single $65
10km W of Christchurch	**E:** cherrygrove@netaccess.co.nz	**Beds:** 1 Queen 1 Twin
Jan & Kirwan Berry	**W:** users.netaccess.co.nz/	(2 bdrm)
431 Old West Coast Road	cherrygrove/	**Bath:** 1 Ensuite 1 Private
RD 6 Christchurch		

Yaldhurst - Christchurch

Located close to Airport with easy access to key attractions. Be assured of professional, attentive hosting in a friendly environment. Enjoy our property which has a tennis court, swimming pool, spa and sauna available. We are able to accommodate couples travelling together as a group. Have knowledge of Maori history and culture. We are centrally heated. On bus route to City. On route to ski fields and West Coast Highway. Hosts Sue and Stuart, New Zealanders who have travelled and have a wide variety of interests.

Gladsome Lodge	**Tel:** (03) 342 7414	**Cost:** Double $75-$85 Single $55
Homestay	**Fax:** (03) 342 3414	Child neg Dinner $20
5km W of Christchurch Central	**Mob:** 025 299 1684	Visa/MC Amex Diners
Stuart & Sue Barr	**Tollfree:** 0800 222 617	**Beds:** 2 Queen 2 Double 2 Twin
314 Yaldhurst Road	**E:** sue@gladsomelodge.com	2 Single (5 bdrm)
Christchurch 4	**W:** www.bnb.co.nz/hosts/	**Bath:** 1 Ensuite 3 Guests share
	gladsomelodge.html	

Avonhead - Christchurch

Come visit with us in our warm comfortable home which is situated close to Airport (4km), City Centre (9km) and well served by regular buses or with free pick up for sight seeing trips. Guest bedrooms are bright and have comfortable firm beds. Tea, coffee and homemade cookies are always available. We serve a delightful selection of breakfast dishes including homemade bread, muffins and jams. Our home is a smoke free zone and we share it with two Burmese cats.

Fleur Lodge	**Tel:** (03) 342 5473	**Cost:** Double $85
Homestay	**Fax:** (03) 342 5475	Single $65 Dinner $25
10km W of Christchurch	**W:** www.bnb.co.nz/hosts/	**Beds:** 1 Double 1 Twin
Beverley & Harry Sweney	fleurlodge.html	(2 bdrm)
67 Toorak Ave		**Bath:** 1 Guests share
Avonhead Christchurch		1 Family share

Avonhead - Christchurch

Situated 2 minutes from Christchurch Airport "Russley 302"
is an ideal first or last night stay. We are recently retired
sheep farmers living in a rural setting farming, black/
coloured sheep. Wool from these sheep form the basis of
Sally's involvement in the handcraft industry. Brian's
interests include Rotary & sport. Our modern home offers
electric blankets, hairdryers, refrigerators, tea/coffee, laundry
facilities. We have enjoyed many years of farm hosting and
invite you to share this experience with us.

Russley 302	**Tel:** (03) 358 6543	**Cost:** Double $100
B&B	**Fax:** (03) 358 6553	Single $55-$70
10lkm W of City Centre	**Mob:** 025 224 3752	Visa/MC
Sally & Brian Carpenter	**E:** carpsrussley302@clear.net.nz	**Beds:** 1 Queen 1 Twin
302 Russley Road	**W:** www.bnb.co.nz/hosts/	1 Single (3 bdrm)
Avonhead	russley.html	**Bath:** 1 Ensuite 1 Private
Christchurch 8004		1 Family share

Avonhead - Christchurch

Ash Croft is a purpose built quality self-contained accommodation
for the visitor to Christchurch. In a quiet residential area Ash Croft
offers privacy and comfort with enclosed gardens and off-street
parking. Fully equipped modern facilities, comfortable
furnishings, spa bath, shower and separate toilet. Facilities include
telephone, TV, VCR, video and book library, games for children.
Laundry with washing machine and dryer. Portacot and highchair
available. Wheelchair accessible. Breakfast hampers available on
request. Easy access to airport, city centre, local shopping malls
and restaurants. Open Jan. 2002

Ash Croft	**Tel:** (03) 342 3416	**Cost:** Double $85 - $110
Self-contained	**Fax:** (03) 342 3416	$10 each extra person
10 min W of Christchurch central	**E:** ash.croft@paradise.net.nz	Special breakfast $10pp
Sky & Raewyn Williams	**W:** homepages.paradise.net.nz/	Child under 5 free Visa/MC
6 Fovant Street	ash_croft/	**Beds:** 1 Queen 1 Double
Avonhead Christchurch		1 Twin (3 bdrm)
		Bath: 1 Private

Burnside - Christchurch

Welcome to our comfortable, modern home in quiet
street, 5 minutes from the Airport and 15 minutes to
city centre. Be greeted with fresh flowers and sweets
in your bedroom. Relax in a garden setting with tea or
coffee and freshly baked muffins. A retired couple, we
have travelled in New Zealand and overseas. Our
interests include sport, walks, gardening, local history
and our friendly cat. We enjoy sharing our home with
guests and look forward to meeting you.

Burnside Bed & Breakfast	**Tel:** (03) 358 7671	**Cost:** Double $80
B&B	**Fax:** (03) 358 7761	Single $50
8km NW of Christchurch	**E:** elaine.neil.roberts@xtra.co.nz	**Beds:** 1 Queen 1 Twin
Elaine & Neil Roberts	**W:** www.bnb.co.nz/hosts/	(2 bdrm)
31 O'Connor Place	burnside.html	**Bath:** 1 Guests share
Burnside Christchurch		

Ilam - Christchurch

Our home is in the beautiful suburb of Ilam, ideally situated close to Christchurch Airport (7 mins by car), the Railway Station (10 mins), and the central City with its many attractions (10mins). We are adjacent to the city bus route. Guests are welcome to use our Laundry. We have a wide range of interests which include, our four adult children, Sport, Travel, Politics, and Gardening. We are able to provide conversational English classes for speakers of other languages (fee would apply).

Anne & Tony Fogarty Homestay	**Tel:** (03) 358 2762	**Cost:** Double $75
Homestay	**Fax:** (03) 358 2767	Single $45
7.5km E of Christchurch	**E:** tony.fogarty@xtra.co.nz	Dinner $25 by arrangement
Anne & Tony Fogarty	**W:** www.bnb.co.nz/hosts/	Visa/MC
7 Westmont Street	annetonyfogartyhomestay.html	**Beds:** 4 Single (2 bdrm)
Ilam Christchurch 8004		**Bath:** 1 Guests share

Bishopdale - Harewood

Our large colonial home is situated on a quiet private rear section amidst a tranquil 1/2 acre garden setting. Only 5 minutes from airport and 10 minutes to city centre. Bus at gate. Our spacious well appointed rooms include tea/coffee making facilities, TV, fridge. Our family comprises of a daughter, son and pet Golden Retriever. We have many interests, have travelled extensively and are happy to help with your travel plans. Internet and fax. Off street parking. Nearby attractions include Antarctic Centre and Orana Wildlife Park. Rental car available,

Highsted Homestead	**Tel:** (03) 359 6486	**Cost:** Double $100
Homestay	**Fax:** (03) 359 6490	Single $60
7.5km N of Christchurch Centre	**Mob:** 025 676 4625	Child $30 Visa/MC
Peter & Sherryn	**E:** h.h@xtra.co.nz	**Beds:** 2 Queen 1 Single
132B Highsted Road	**W:** www.bnb.co.nz/hosts/	(2 bdrm)
Christchurch	highstedhomestay.html	**Bath:** 1 Guests share

FAIRLEIGH GARDEN

Bishopdale - Christchurch

Dear Travellers,
We are staying at **Fairleigh Garden Guest House** and we just have to tell you about this wonderful place. A piece of 'country' so close to the airport and to the city, berry fields and sheep grazing just next door.

Garden views from every window and the smell of homebaking greets you in the mornings.

The breakfast table is laden with fresh fruits, juices, homemade breads, muffins, jams and the omelettes are something special.

It's just perfect! Valerie and Allan have helped us with what to do and where to go.

Day trips to Akaroa, Hamner Springs, Kaikoura, Mt Hutt Ski Fields, 15 golf courses in 15 minutes. Restaurants, shops, arts, crafts, gardens and NZ wildlife. The list could go on for ever.

The warmth and friendliness is great, a real home away from home. We are coming back for 2 more nights in the fabulous honeymoon suite before we fly out in 3 weeks. Do contact Valerie and Allan, they will be happy to meet you at the airport. True New Zealand hospitality. Don't miss it - We love it. See you soon - P.S. The beds are firm and - oh! so comfortable! and you will meet Zambie and Santa - two lovable black cats!

* Situated 800m off Highway One

Fairleigh Garden
B&B Homestay
Allan & Valerie Carleton
411 Sawyers Arms Road
Harewood

Tel: (03) 359 3538
Fax: (03) 359 3548
Mob: 025 224 3746
Tollfree: 0800 611 411
E: fairleighgardenbb@xtra.co.nz
W: www.bnb.co.nz/hosts/
fairleighgarden.html

Cost: Double $135-$165
Single $110-$145
Visa/MC Amex
Beds: 1 King/Twin 2 Queen
(3 bdrm)
Bath: 3 Ensuite
Honeymoon suite
dble spa bath

Riccarton - Christchurch

Our home is a comfortable, modern two storied townhouse in a quiet street near the University. Facilities for guests are two spacious upstairs twin bedrooms, a bathroom and separate toilet. The laundry is available for guest use. We are a pet and smoke free home. We offer a pick up service from the airport, railway station or city centre. Keith enjoys the outdoors and Caroline is a part time tourist guide and is interested in local history and embroidery and we both frequently travel locally and overseas.

Riccarton Homestay
Homestay
4km W of Christchurch City
Caroline & Keith Curry
70A Puriri Street
Riccarton
Christchurch

Tel: (03) 348 4081
Fax: (03) 348 4081
E: curryc@xtra.co.nz
W: www.bnb.co.nz/hosts/
riccartonhomestay.html

Cost: Double $80
Single $50
Visa/MC
Beds: 4 Single (2 bdrm)
Bath: 1 Guests share

Bryndwr - Christchurch

You are welcome to share my comfortable home and private garden, make tea or coffee and use laundry facilities. I have travelled in Europe, India, China etc and I enjoy meeting people. You are assured of comfortable beds and no waiting for the bathroom. I'm ten minutes from both Airport and City Centre, main highways are easily accessible. The Wairaiki Road-City bus is four minutes away. Various restaurants are closeby or you are welcome to bring home take-aways.

Allisford
B&B Homestay
5km N of Christchurch City
Peggy Crawford
1/61 Aorangi Road
Christchurch

Tel: (03) 351 7742
Fax: (03) 351 6451
Mob: 025 229 2486
E: saint@clear.net.nz
W: www.bnb.co.nz/hosts/
allisford.html

Cost: Double $80
Single $50
Beds: 2 Single (1 bdrm)
Bath: 1 Family share

CANTERBURY

Bryndwr - Christchurch

We warmly welcome you to our spacious and comfortable home set in quiet attractive gardens. The en-suite room opens onto a balcony overlooking a secluded outdoor swimming pool. A sun room/TV room is ideal as a second (private) lounge. Tea/coffee, juice, home baking always available. Generous breakfasts. Delicious dinners can be pre-arranged. We have both travelled, have wide ranges of interest and enjoy talking to people. If needed, we are happy to help with travel plans. Courtesy pick-up, off street parking and laundry facilities are available.

Bryndwr Homestay
B&B Homestay
5km NW of Christchurch Central
Patricia & Win Clancey
89A Aorangi Road
Bryndwr Christchurch

Tel: (03) 351 6092
Fax: (03) 351 6092
E: wclancey@xtra.co.nz
W: www.bnb.co.nz/hosts/
bryndwrbb.html

Cost: Double $100-$110
Single $80-$85
Child & Dinner B/A
Visa/MC
Beds: 1 Queen 2 Single
(2 bdrm)
Bath: 1 Ensuite 1 Family share

Bryndwr - Christchurch

Welcome to share our comfortable family home with relaxing
outdoor garden area. Located in the Northwest corner of
Christchurch 5 kilometres from the Airport off Wairakei Road or
via Memorial Avenue, left onto Ilam Road, past Aqualand and onto
Aorangi Road. Easy walking distances to local area shops and
restaurants. Welcome to bring home takeaways. Complimentary
tea or coffee any time. Laundry and ironing facilities available.
Short 3 minutes walk to Bus route, only 10 minutes ride to the City
Centre, passing Botanical Gardens, Museum and Art Centre.
Inspection welcomed. Feel free to ring if you have any questions,
we may be able to help.

Bryndwr B&B	**Tel:** (03) 351 6299	**Cost:** Double $85
B&B	**E:** eroom.b@xtra.co.nz	Single $65
NW of Christchurch	**W:** www.bnb.co.nz/hosts/	**Beds:** 1 Double (2 bdrm)
Brian & Kathy Moore	bryndwrbb2.html	**Bath:** 1 Guests share
108 Aorangi Road Christchurch		

Fendalton - Christchurch

Reccommended by Frommers Guide to NZ and the Rough
Guide. Come and stay in a warm friendly family house in
one of Christchurch's central and most prestigious garden
suburbs within walking distance of town. You are welcome
to share the sunny "grapevine roofed" conservatory, and eat
the grapes if they are ripe. After a large breakfast(which
may include waffles, pancakes etc) we walk down to the
bottom of garden to feed the wild ducks down there. Or you
can borrow one of the canoes and padde up our little stream.
My other web site is www.fendaltonhouse.co.nz

Fendalton House	**Tel:** (03) 355 4298	**Cost:** Double $145-$175
Homestay	**Fax:** (03) 355 0959	Single $135-$165
1.5 km NW of Christchurch	**Tollfree:** 0800 374 298	Visa/MC
Pam Rattray	**E:** fendaltonhouse@xtra.co.nz	**Beds:** 1 Super King/Twin 1 King
50 Clifford Ave	**W:** www.fendaltonhouse.co.nz	1 Queen 1 Single (3 bdrm)
Fendalton Christchurch 1		**Bath:** 3 Ensuite

Fendalton - Christchurch

Ambience on Avon in a private, picturesque garden
on the Avon. We enjoy welcoming guests into our
home with its elegant comfortable understated
furnishings, guest lounge with a large open fire, TV.
Enjoy complimentary coffee, tea, home baked
cookies under the large elm tree or down at the river
garden with friendly ducks, birds; or relax in our
special leather therapeutic chairs in our family room
opening into the garden. Art, comfortable beds, fine
linen, electric blankets, room heaters and all modern
conveniences for a relaxing friendly stay.

Ambience on Avon	**Tel:** (03) 348 4537	**Cost:** Double $120-$135
Homestay	**Fax:** (03) 348 4837	Single $90-$110
10 min City Centre	**Mob:** 025 333 627	Visa/MC Amex Diners
Lawson & Helen Little	**E:** lawsonh@amcom.co.nz	**Beds:** 1 Queen 1 Double
9 Kotare Street	**W:** www.ambience-on-avon.co.nz	(2 bdrm)
Fendalton Christchurch		**Bath:** 2 Private

Dallington - Christchurch

Peace, tranquillity and a cottage garden on the banks
of the river Avon. Self-contained detached double
accommodation is warm and cosy and includes fridge,
microwave, extra single couch-bed, and a private
garden. Tea/coffee, home baking, and laundry service
always available. Scenic river walks, or borrow our
dinghy and row. 6 minutes drive to city centre.
Buses stop nearby. Courtesy pick-up available, or
phone for directions. Both of us, and our 2 cats and
bearded collie look forward to meeting you.

Killarney	**Tel:** (03) 381 7449	**Cost:** Double $85
B&B Self-contained	**Fax:** (03) 381 7449	Single $60
4km NE of Christchurch	**Mob:** 025 235 2409	Child neg Dinner $20 B/A
Lynne & Russell Haigh	**E:** haigh.killarney@xtra.co.nz	**Beds:** 2 Double (2 bdrm)
27 Dallington Terrace	**W:** www.bnb.co.nz/hosts/	**Bath:** 1 Ensuite 1 Private
Dallington Christchurch	killarney.html	1 Family share

Merivale - Christchurch

Built in 1901 "Villa Victoria" is situated in one of Christchurch's
quiet historic suburbs just minutes from city activities.
Authentically restored by owner Kate it reflects the elegance and
charm of yesteryear. Furnishings are appropriate to Victoria/
Edwardian era with lace curtains/bedspreads, brass/iron bed,
antiques and collectables. This tranquil haven has been designed
to be a home away from home, small and intimate with
personalised hospitality. Delectable breakfasts a specialty using
fresh local produce served at guests convenience. Off street
parking. No pets or children.

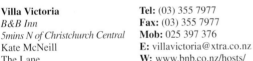

Villa Victoria	**Tel:** (03) 355 7977	**Cost:** Double $160
B&B Inn	**Fax:** (03) 355 7977	Single $110
5mins N of Christchurch Central	**Mob:** 025 397 376	Visa/MC
Kate McNeill	**E:** villavictoria@xtra.co.nz	**Beds:** 2 Double 1 Single
The Lane	**W:** www.bnb.co.nz/hosts/	(3 bdrm)
27 Holly Road Christchurch 1	villavictoria.html	**Bath:** 3 Ensuite

Merivale - Christchurch

Native timbers and leadlight windows are used
throughout this spacious 1920's English Colonial and
Historic Places listed home, just 15 mins walk to the
city centre and 15 mins drive to airport and rail
stations. Enjoy a full breakfast in our dining room,
complimentary tea and coffee throughout the day and
Merivales finest restaurants a short 5 mins stroll
away.Relax in the luxury of a bygone era, see our
website for details. Miniture Dashound Max and
Summer the cat respect your privacy.

Elm Tree House	**Tel:** (03) 355 9731	**Cost:** Double $145-$235
B&B	**Fax:** (03) 355 9753	Single $125-$195
5km N of Christchurch Central	**Mob:** 025 232 5058	Dinner $40 Visa/MC Amex
Karen & Allan Scott	**E:** elmtreeb.b@clear.net.nz	**Beds:** 2 King/Twin 3 King
236 Papanui Road	**W:** www.elmtreehouse.co.nz	3 Queen 6 Single (6 bdrm)
Merivale Christchurch		**Bath:** 6 Ensuite

Merivale - Christchurch

Kay and Brian invite you to their modern sunny townhouse. Situated in Merivale one of Christchurch's most beautiful suburbs. Only a short stroll to exclusive Merivale shopping and many top cafes, Hagley Park, Arts Centre, Museum, Botanical Gardens and Casino. After an enjoyable day exploring our wonderful city relax in our courtyard garden or inside by the fire. Bedrooms comfortably appointed with electric blankets and heaters. Tea, coffee, laundry and ironing facilities available. Along with pets Jake and Max we look forward to welcoming you.

Leinster Homestay B&B	**Tel:** (03) 355 6176	**Cost:** Double $110
B&B Homestay	**Fax:** (03) 355 6176	Single $80
2km N of Christchurch	**Mob:** 025 330 771	Child neg Visa/MC
Kay and Brian Smith	**E:** brian.kay@xtra.co.nz	**Beds:** 1 Queen 1 Double
34B Leinster Road	**W:** www.bnb.co.nz/hosts/	1 Single (2 bdrm)
Merivale Christchurch	leinsterhomestaybb.html	**Bath:** 1 Ensuite 1 Private

Merivale - Christchurch

A warm welcome awaits you at Melrose, a charming character home (1910) located in a small quiet street, just off Papanui Road only minutes away from the city and all the shops, restaurants and cafes of Merivale. Our house is spacious, we offer large rooms with tea and coffee making facilities and a private dining room/ lounge. We have many interests and having travelled extensively, are keen to accommodate your needs. Our family comprises of two daughters and a boxer Milly. Off street parking. Children are welcome.

Melrose	**Tel:** (03) 355 1929	**Cost:** Double $95
B&B	**Fax:** (03) 355 1927	Single $60
3min Christchurch	**Mob:** 025 647 5564	Child $35 Dinner B/A
Elaine & David Baxter	**E:** BaxterMelrose@xtra.co.nz	Visa/MC
39 Holly Road	**W:** www.selwyn.co.nz/melrose	**Beds:** 3 Queen (3 bdrm)
Merivale Christchurch		**Bath:** 2 Guests share

Merivale - Christchurch

Welcome to Mop Top Cottage. Self contained boutique accommodation adjacent to St Andrews College. Local shops, cafes, bars very close. 1km from Merivale. Christchurch's premier shopping centre (designer shops, cafes, bars) 3km from Central city and Information Centre. Thoughtfully prepared, plentiful breakfast served in apartment's own kitchen. Self-catering option if preferred. telephone, fax, private spa and barbecue area. greatly admired private garden. Off street parking/ garaging. Scenic drive in Porsche 911 Cabriolet by arrangement. Persian cats and King Charles spaniel secure in back garden.

Mop Top Cottage	**Tel:** (03) 355 9346	**Cost:** Double $100-$150
B&B Self-contained	**Fax:** (03) 355 9846	Single $85-$125 Child $15
1 km N of Merivale	**Mob:** 021 559 346	Dinner B/A Visa/MC
Carolyn Read	**E:** moptop.cottage@clear.net.nz	**Beds:** 1 Queen 1 Double
69 Normans Road	**W:** www.bnb.co.nz/hosts/	2 Single (2 bdrm)
Merivale Christchurch	moptop.html	**Bath:** 1 Ensuite 1 Private
		1 Family share

St Albans - Christchurch

Our home is startlingly alive and furnished with strong but tasteful interior colours. We are in a quiet street, easy walking distance from the city centre and tourist amenities. Both rooms are well appointed. The spacious queen suite has comfortable arm chairs and overlooks a lovely courtyard. Tea, coffee and biscuits are always available. Excellent breakfast menu. Pick-up transport, use of laundry, a high chair and cot are available. No resident children or pets, and no smoking indoors. Please contact us in advance.

Barrich House	**Tel:** (03) 365 3985	**Cost:** Double $80-$120
B&B Homestay	**Fax:** (03) 365 3467	Single $50-$80
1km N of Christchurch Central	**Mob:** 025 659 5787	Child neg
Barbara & Richard Harman	**E:** r.harman@ext.canterbury.ac.nz	**Beds:** 1 Queen 1 Twin
82 Caledonian Road	**W:** www.bnb.co.nz/hosts/	(2 bdrm)
St Albans Christchurch 8001	barrichhouse.html	**Bath:** 1 Ensuite 1 Family share

Avondale - Christchurch

Watch the sun rise over the river, enjoy views of the Port Hills or catch glimpses of the Southern Alps. Picturesque Hulverstone Lodge is an ideal base for year-round holidays. Delightful walks take you to QEII Park or New Brighton's sandy beach, pier and restaurants. Frequent buses offer a fast, friendly ride to the city. Hulverstone Lodge provides convenient access to all parts of Christchurch, yet offers a tranquil riverside haven. We, and our cat, look forward to sharing it with you. Complimentary pickup available.

Hulverstone Lodge	**Tel:** (03) 388 6505	**Cost:** Double $80-$120
B&B	**Fax:** (03) 388 6025	Single $60-$90
8km NE of Christchurch Central	**Tollfree:** 0800 388 6505	Visa/MC
Diane & Ian Ross	**Mob:** 025 433 830	**Beds:** 3 King/Twin
18 Hulverstone Drive	**E:** hulverstone@caverock.net.nz	1 Single (4 bdrm)
Avondale Christchurch	**W:** www.bnb.co.nz/hosts/	**Bath:** 1 Ensuite 1 Private
	hulverstonelodge.html	1 Guests share

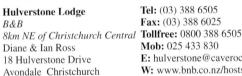

Most of our B&Bs will accept credit cards.

Christchurch City

Looking for Bed & Breakfast accommodation in Christchurch, then try "The Windsor".
Built at the turn of the century this inner city residence is located on the Tourist Tram Route and
is within 5-10 minutes walk of the City Centre, Restaurants, Banks, Town Hall, Convention
Centre, Casino, Art Centre, Museum and Botanical Gardens.
Guests are greeted on arrival by our pet dachshund "Miss Winnie" and shown around our
charming colonial style home. Often described as "Traditional" this family operated
Bed and Breakfast Hotel prides itself on the standard of accommodation that it
offers. The nicely furnished non-smoking bedrooms are all individually heated
and decorated with a small posy of flowers and a watercolour by local artist
Denise McCulloch.
The shared bathroom facilities have been conveniently appointed with
bathrobes provided, giving warmth and comfort in the Bed and Breakfast
tradition.
Such things as "Hotties" and "Brollies" add charm to the style of accommodation offered, as does our 1928 Studebaker sedan.
Our generous morning breakfast (included in the tariff) offers Fruit Juice, Fresh
Fruits, Yogurt and Cereals followed by Bacon and Eggs, Sausages, Tomatoes, Toast
and Marmalade, and is served in the dining room each morning between 6.30 and
9.00 am. The complimentary Tea and Coffee making facilities allow guests to
help themselves at their own convenience and we serve "Supper" (Tea, Coffee
and Biscuits) each evening in the lounge at 9.00 pm.
As part of our service the Hotel offers Laundry Facilities, off Street Parking
for the motorist and bicycle and baggage storage.

QUOTE THIS BOOK FOR 10% DISCOUNT

Windsor B&B Hotel
Private Hotel
Christchurch Central
Carol Healey & Don Evans
52 Armagh Street
Christchurch 1

Tel: (03) 366 1503
Fax: (03) 366 9796
Tollfree: 0800 366 1503
E: reservations@windsorhotel.co.nz
W: www.windsorhotel.co.nz

Cost: Double $98
Single $66
Triple $120
Family Rooms on request
Visa/MC Amex Diners
Beds: (40 bdrm)
Bath: 24 Guests share

Christchurch City

'Cead Mile Failte' (One hundred thousand welcomes) Turret House is a gracious superior Bed & Breakfast accommodation located in downtown Christchurch.

It is within easy walking distance of Cathedral Square, the Botanical Gardens, Museum, Art Gallery, the Arts Centre and Hagley Park 18 hole golf course. Also Casino, new Convention Centre, Town Hall.

Built around 1900 this historic residence is one of only three in the area protected by the New Zealand Historic Places Trust. It has been restored to capture the original character and charm. Situated within the grounds is one of Christchurch's best examples of our native kauri tree.

Attractively decorated bedrooms with heaters and electric blankets combine comfort and old world elegance, with private bathrooms, some with bath and shower, all offering a totally relaxed and comfortable environment.

Tea, coffee and biscuits available 24 hrs. Cots and highchairs are also available. Family room sleeps 4. If you're looking for a place to stay where the accommodation is superior and the atmosphere friendly - experience Turret House.

Non smoking policy. Just 15 minutes from Christchurch Airport.

Situated on the corner of Bealey Ave and Durham Street. (Off-street parking).

Turret House
B&B
Justine & Paddy Dougherty
435 Durham Street North
Christchurch

Tel: (03) 365 3900
Fax: (03) 365 5601
Tollfree: 0800 48 87 73
E: turretb.bchch@xtra.co.nz
W: www.turrethouse.co.nz

Cost: Double $95-$130
Single $65-$95
Child $20
Visa/MC Amex Diners
Beds: 2 King/Twin 4 Queen
1 Twin 1 Single (8 bdrm)
Bath: 8 Ensuite

Christchurch City

Listed in FODOR'S as "pick of the B&B accommodation in Christchurch".

If you like quality accommodation in a relaxed and quiet atmosphere, still just minutes walking away from the centre of an exciting city: this is the place to stay.

Our house is a restored Edwardian residence that reflects the grace and style of the period with some fine carved Kauri and Rimu features.

It is ideally situated on the banks of the Avon River in a tranquil setting surrounded by an old English garden with mature trees.

Guest rooms are elegant, combining modern facilities with colonial furnishings. All rooms have ensuite/private facilities, colour TV and heating, balconies provide a superb river view. Tea and coffee making facilities are available at all times.

Breakfast is a house specialty with a wide choice of cooked and continental fare.

In the Edwardian townhouse next door there are two very spacious (90m2) apartments for a very private stay. Guests find antiques and quality furniture, a fully equipped kitchen, television, private telephone and a lovely formal yard which backs onto the city park.

For full breakfast we invite guests into the lodge or if requested supply a self service breakfast in the apartment.

Kayaks, bicycles and golf clubs are available for guests to use. As experienced travellers and tour operators we'll be happy to provide you with all the information that will make your stay in Christchurch and New Zealand the information that will make your stay in Christchurch and New Zealand unforgettable.

German, Spanish, Dutch, French is spoken.

For cancellations 48 hours prior to arrival we charge the full amount of one night.

Directions: RIVERVIEW LODGE is located on the corner of Cambridge Terrace and Churchill Street. Take Salisbury (one way) Street to the end and follow the river.

Riverview Lodge
B&B Self-contained Homestay
Christchurch Central
Ernst Wipperfuerth
361 Cambridge Terrace
Christchurch 1

Tel: (03) 365 2860
Fax: (03) 365 2845
E: riverview.lodge@xtra.co.nz
W: www.bnb.co.nz/hosts/
riverviewlodge.html

Cost: Double $150-$185
　　　Single $90-$130
　　　S/C suites $195 Visa/MC
Beds: 3 Queen 1 Double
　　　1 Twin 1 Single (5 bdrm)
Bath: 4 Ensuite 1 Private

Christchurch City

Croydon House is a charming, small Hotel offering fine Accommodation in the Heart of New Zealand's Garden City. All Bedrooms are tastefully refurbished with private or ensuite bathroom. Start your day with our scrumptious buffet and indulge yourself in a deliciously cooked breakfast prepared especially for you. Explore the city's major attractions, great restaurants, conference venues and the famous Botanical Gardens are within easy walking distance. We provide Internet access. For more information visit our Home Page on the Internet with on-line booking form.

Croydon House
B&B Hotel
Nita & Siegfried Herbst
63 Armagh Street
Christchurch

Tel: (03) 366 5111
Fax: (03) 377 6110
Tollfree: 0800 276 936
E: welcome@croydon.co.nz
W: www.croydon.co.nz

Cost: Double $120-$135
Single $85-$99
Dinner B/A Visa/MC
Beds: 1 King 2 Queen 5 Double
4 Twin (11 bdrm)
Bath: 9 Ensuite 2 Private

Christchurch City

At The Grange Guesthouse you will enjoy your visit in this tastefully "refurbished" Victorian mansion with wood panelling and a beautiful wooden feature staircase, you can relax in the guest lounge or in the garden. The Grange Guesthouse is situated within walking distance to most of Christchurch's favourite spots including; Cathedral Square, the Arts Centre, Art Gallery and Museum also the Botanic Gardens, Hagley Park and Mona Vale. During your stay at The Grange you will be treated to comfortable accommodation, complimentary tea and coffee, off-street parking, laundry service and sightseeing tours arranged.

The Grange Guest House
B&B
Christchurch Central
Marie & Paul Simpson
56 Armagh Street
Christchurch

Tel: (03) 366 2850
Fax: (03) 374 2470
Mob: 021 366 608
Tollfree: 0800 93 2850
E: reservations@thegrange.co.nz
W: www.bnb.co.nz/hosts/
thegrangeguesthouse.html

Cost: Double $115-$125
Single $95 Child $15 under
12yrs Share Bath $85 - $98
Visa/MC Amex Diners
Beds: 2 King 3 Queen 3 Double
2 Twin (6 bdrm)
Bath: 6 Ensuite 1 Guests share

Christchurch City

Hambledon is a unique heritage mansion with beautiful walled gardens, giving a Country House atmosphere in the inner city. Lovely character suites furnished with family antiques including four poster bed, crisp linen, flowers, comfortable seating, TV, telephone, tea and coffee facilities and ensuite bathrooms. Enjoy the delicious gourmet breakfast in the magnificent dining room and later relax in the elegant guest lounge, conservatory or on the wisteria covered verandah. A stroll from restaurants, Hagley Park and Arts Centre. Off Street Parking. Guest Laundry. A member of Superior Inns, and Heritage Inns.

Hambledon
Self-contained B&B Inn
Christchurch Central
Jo & Calvin Floyd
103 Bealey Avenue Christchurch

Tel: (03) 379 0723
Fax: (03) 379 0758
E: hambledon@clear.net.nz
W: www.hambledon.co.nz

Cost: Double $185-$280
Single $165-$250
Visa/MC Amex Diners
Beds: 3 King 5 Queen 5 Single
(8 bdrm)
Bath: 8 Ensuite

Christchurch City

Eliza's is a superb gracious Victorian mansion, built in 1860, and lovingly restored. The original architectural gems including a magnificent entrance foyer, coloured lead light windows and banquet room are complimented with comfortable furnishings, antiques and collectables.

The bedrooms, all different, each with their own charm, are decorated in country cottage style with comfortable beds and most with their own en-suite.

The tariff includes continental buffet breakfast. Eliza's is a very comfortable and restful place to stay where you can relax and enjoy the convivial atmosphere. We offer complimentary tea, coffee, hot chocolate anytime, a cosy lounge to meet new friends and an olde-English style restaurant and bar.

We are a short pleasant drive from the airport and conveniently situated 10-15 mins level walk to Art centre, Botanical gardens, Art galleries, City centre, golf course, museums, restaurants. Eliza's is set well back from the street with magnificent trees, courtyard gardens and off street parking.

We look forward to sharing the delights of Eliza's with you.

Please fax, ring or write your bookings to us. We extend a warm welcome to you.

Eliza's Manor House *B&B* *Christchurch Central* Lynn Smith 82 Bealey Avenue City Central Christchurch	**Tel:** (03) 366 8584 **Fax:** (03) 366 4946 **E:** elizas@ihug.co.nz **W:** www.bnb.co.nz/hosts/ elizasmanorhouse.html	**Cost:** Double $90-$150 Single $80-$130 Visa/MC Amex Diners **Beds:** 4 King/Twin 4 Queen 1 Double 3 Twin 1 Single (10 bdrm) **Bath:** 2 Ensuite 6 Private 2 Guests share

Christchurch City

The Armagh Lodge situated in a quiet residential area of the central city, is a spacious 1910 villa with the original ornate plaster ceilings, beautiful lead light windows and surrounded by a large garden. We are a 5-10min walk to the main shopping and restaurant area and many attractions, such as the tram, convention centre, town hall, Centennial Pool and Arts centre. We have several cats and discourage smoking indoors. Our guests are guaranteed a quiet and comfortable stay in a relaxed atmosphere.

Armagh Lodge
Guesthouse
Christchurch Central
Ruth Mclachlan
257 Armagh Street
PO Box 13785 Christchurch

Tel: (03) 366 0744
Fax: (03) 374 6359
Mob: 025 626 2347
Tollfree: 0800 007 257
E: armaghlodge@xtra.co.nz
W: www.bnb.co.nz/hosts/ armaghlodge.html

Cost: Double $65-$75
Single $45-$50
Child 1/2 price Visa/MC
Beds: 6 Double 11 Single
(10 bdrm)
Bath: 3 Ensuite 3 Guests share

Christchurch City

Home-Lea is a charming character home built circa 1920, and is superbly situated, just a 10 min walk from the city centre and an excellent selection of restaurants. Our guest rooms are spacious, have good beds and pleasant decor. The guest lounge has a warm open fire in the winter and tea, coffee, biscuits and fruit available at all times. Pauline and Gerald are happy to share their extensive knowledge of local attractions. Their special interests are travel, yachting and music. Email/fax facilities available for guests.

Home-Lea
B&B
Christchurch Central
Pauline & Gerald Oliver
195 Bealey Ave
Christchurch

Tel: (03) 379 9977
Fax: (03) 379 4099
Tollfree: 0800 355 321
E: homelea@xtra.co.nz
W: www.bnb.co.nz/hosts/ homelea.html

Cost: Double $85-$110
Single $50-$75
Child $15 Dinner B/A
Visa/MC Amex Diners
Beds: 1 King 2 Queen
5 Single (5 bdrm)
Bath: 2 Ensuite 2 Guests share

Christchurch City

ORARI was built in 1893. Of Kauri construction with beautifully proportioned rooms, Orari is situated within easy walking distance of the Arts Centre, the Botanic Gardens, Museum, Hagley Park, Town Hall, Casino, Convention Centre, and Cathedral Square. Featuring 10 bedrooms with private bathrooms, off street parking and wheel chair access, it provides comfortable, friendly accommodation for travellers, business people and small group conferences. Enjoy the convenience of the inner city in an elegant heritage home. Children are welcome as guests but Orari is unsuitable for pets.

Orari B&B
B&B
Christchurch Central
Jenny Brown
42 Gloucester St Christchurch 1

Tel: (03) 365 6569
Fax: (03) 365 2525
E: jenny@orari.net.nz
W: www.orari.net.nz

Cost: Double $135-$210
Single $120-$135
Visa/MC Amex
Beds: 10 Queen 5 Single
(10 bdrm)
Bath: 8 Ensuite 2 Private

Christchurch City

In the heart of Christchurch (Cathedral Square), Apartment 37 is unique offering warm friendly hospitality and elegant accommodation in a grand historic building with central city convenience. In addition enjoy many extras including Sky TV, tea/coffee making facilities, complimentary wine/sherry, and access to in-building facilities (lap pool, gymnasium, spa, sauna). Walk to Christchurch's vibrant attractions - Arts Centre, museum, botanic gardens, Hagley park, shops, cafes and entertainment or use transport right on door step. Perfect for holidays or business. Please phone for directions.

Apartment 37	**Tel:** (03) 377 7473	**Cost:** Double $125-$145
B&B	**Fax:** (03) 377 7863	Visa/MC
Christchurch Central	**Mob:** 025 622 0849	**Beds:** 1 Queen 1 Twin (2 bdrm)
Lynne & David	**E:** apartment37@xtra.co.nz	**Bath:** 2 Ensuite
Apartment 37, PO Box 177	**W:** www.bnb.co.nz/hosts/	
Old Government Buildings	apartment.html	
Cathedral Square, Christchurch		

Christchurch City

The Devon is a personal guest house located in the heart of beautiful Christchurch city, which offers elegance and comfort in the style of an olde worlde English manor. Just 5 minute's walk to Christchurch Cathedral, Town Hall, and Convention Centre, casino, museum, hospital and botanical gardens in Hagley Park. TV lounge, tea & coffee making facilities. Off street parking.

Devon B&B Hotel	**Tel:** (03) 366 0398	**Cost:** Double $95-$120
B&B Guest House	**Fax:** (03) 366 0398	Single $70-$95 Child $15
500m S of Central City	**E:** bandbdevonhotel@xtra.co.nz	$20 Extra Adults
Sandra & Benjamin Humphrey	**W:** www.devonbandbhotel.co.nz	Visa/MC Amex Diners
69 Armagh Street		**Beds:** 9 Queen 13 Single
Christchurch		(10 bdrm)
		Bath: 4 Ensuite 6 Guests share

Southshore - Christchurch

Twenty minutes from the city, Southshore lies between the ocean and the Avon Estuary. Sheltered by the dunes wilderness, our comfortable home is a quiet retreat set in an interesting seaside garden from where a private track over the dunes provides easy access to miles of safe, sandy beach. Nearby, the Estuary walkway offers expansive views and varied bird life. We are non-smokers, semi-retired with interests in gardening, vintage cars, embroidery and our cat. Please phone for reservations. Airport pickup available.

Southshore Homestay	**Tel:** (03) 388 4067	**Cost:** Double $75-$95
B&B Homestay	**Fax:** (03) 365 3775	Single $60-$75
10km E of Christchurch	**E:** posmerch@posmerch.co.nz	Dinner $25pp Visa/MC
Jan & Graham Pluck	**W:** www.bnb.co.nz/hosts/	**Beds:** 1 Queen 2 Single
71A Rockinghorse Road	southshorehomestay.html	(2 bdrm)
South Shore Christchurch 7		**Bath:** 1 Ensuite 1 Family share

CANTERBURY

Richmond - Christchurch

•Beautiful river setting   •Family suite   •1928 Art Deco style home.
"You really can live by the river! What a jolly life...." 'Wind in the Willows'.
Your perfect end to a wonderful journey - relax & unwind, read or chat, make yourself at home.

Enjoy a choice of 1 large suite or 2 large rooms. We value our home's 1920/30's architecture & style,
and mix it with plenty of contemporary art & books. Excellent large, firm beds.
Breakfast is fresh & generous - organic bread, cereals, fresh fruit, eggs, good coffee & teas.
And it is 'jolly' here.... Christchurch is bulging with
good things - food & wine, bookshops, clothes,
antiques and a lively arts scene.

We are happy to add our personal experience to
enhance your stay. Shuttle or taxi service to gate from
air/rail/coach. Sam is our elderly black Labrador.
Also available: mountain bike, off street parking &
laundry.

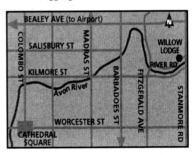

*Central city: walk/20 min.
*Airport/rail: car/20 min.
*Central city: car/5 min.

Willow Lodge	**Tel:** (03) 389 9395	**Cost:** Double $100-$140
B&B Homestay	**Fax:** (03) 381 5395	Single $70-$80
1.5km E of Cathedral Square	**E:** willow@inet.net.nz	Child $25
Grania McKenzie	**W:** www.bnb.co.nz/hosts/	Visa/MC Amex Diners
71 River Road	willowlodgerichmond.html	**Beds:** 1 King/Twin 2 Queen
Avonside		1 Single (3 bdrm)
Christchurch 1		**Bath:** 1 Ensuite 2 Private

Avonside - Christchurch

Enjoy the quiet peaceful surroundings of our beautiful
hidden garden and two-storey home, close to public
transport, eating facilities and restaurants. You are assured
of a warm friendly welcome and excellent accommodation
at affordable prices. Wander through nearby parks or along
the banks of the River Avon. Day trips can be arranged.
City, beaches and golf course are only minutes away. We
are ideally sited to explore Christchurch and its environs.
Discounts for longer stays. Off-street parking and
complimentary pick-up. Phone for directions.

Avon Park Lodge
B&B Homestay
4km E of Christchurch
Murray & Richeena Bullard
144A Kerrs Road
Avonside Christchurch

Tel: (03) 389 1904
Mob: 025 641 9692
E: avonparklodge@zfree.co.nz
W: www.bnb.co.nz/hosts/
avonparklodge.html

Cost: Double $85 Single $55
Child by arrangement
Dinner by arrangement
Visa/MC
Beds: 1 Queen 1 Twin (2 bdrm)
Bath: 1 Guests share

Woolston - Christchurch

Welcome. Kiwi hospitality. Smoke free sunny home in
quiet cul-de-sac. Garden with seating. Guests carport.
Comfortable beds, electric blankets, hair drier. Generous
breakfast in dining room with cathedral ceilings. 10 mins by
car to city and beaches. Bus handy. Courtesy transport from
Railway Station. Airport shuttle service. From Cathedral
Square take Gloucester Street to roundabout at Linwood
Avenue. turn right. Pass Eastgate Mall to traffic lights end
of avenue of trees. Right into Hargood Street. First left into
Clydesdale, first left Lomond Place.

Treeview
B&B Homestay
5km E of Christchurch
Kathy & Laurence Carr
6 Lomond Place
Woolston Christchurch 6

Tel: (03) 384 2352
W: www.bnb.co.nz/hosts/
treeview.html

Cost: Double $65
Single $45
Child $20 Dinner $20
Beds: 1 Double 2 Single (2 bdrm)
Bath: 1 Guests share

St Martins - Christchurch

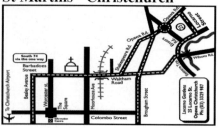

Locarno Gardens
Homestay Two Luxury
Self-catering Apartments
Christchurch Central
Aileen & David Davies
25 Locarno Street
Christchurch 8002

Tel: (03) 332 9987
Fax: (03) 332 9687
Mob: 025 399 747
E: locarno@xtra.co.nz
W: www.cottagestays.co.nz/
begonia/cottage.htm

Cost: Double $85-$95
Extra Person $20
Continental Breakfast
Optional Extra
Beds: 1 Super King 1 Queen
1 Twin (2 bdrm)
Bath: 2 Ensuite

St Martins - Christchurch

ESPECIALLY FOR YOU, QUALITY ACCOMODATION WITH A PERSONAL TOUCH. Away from the "hustle & bustle" close to the city centre, in an easy to find tree-lined street. That's us! Our ensuite room is generous in size, has a fridge, jug, microwave etc.
Our popular boutique studio room is artistic, with lots of wood and art.
If you wish you can cater for yourself. The No-Breakfast rate is $60. We have enjoyed New Zealand for almost 15 years.
Our children are 9 and 12. Gerda works in Mental Health. Having guests is a little like family who have come to stay.

KLEYNBOS Homestay B&B	**Tel:** (03) 332 2896	**Cost:** Double &70-$85
4km S of Christchurch City Centre	**E:** bandb@voyager.co.nz	Single $45-$65
Gerda De Kleyne &	**W:** www.bnb.co.nz/hosts/	Visa/MC
Hans Van Den Bos	kleynbosbb.html	**Beds:** 1 Queen 1 Double
59 Ngaio Street		1 Single (3 bdrm)
Christchurch		**Bath:** 1 Ensuite 1 Guests share

St Martins - Christchurch

This holiday home is all yours and ready to move in. Very private. It is a spacious, stand-alone 1920 character house in top condition. You have two living areas, two toilets, three double bedrooms, a fully equipped new kitchen, a sunny garden, a new bathroom with shower and bath. The Grand Cottage is easy to find in a quiet street. Supermarket, bakery, busses, bank etc.on hand. Ideally positioned to enjoy the attractions of the city and the tranquillity of the Port Hills.

The Grand Cottage	**Tel:** (03) 332 2896	**Cost:** Double $85 plus $10 for
Holidayhome	**E:** bandb@voyager.co.nz	each extra person
4km S of Christchurch Central	**W:** www.bnb.co.nz/hosts/	Breakfast extra $15 pp or
Gerda & Hans (DeKleyne &	thegrandcottage.html	No Breakfast included
VanDenBos)		Min 2 nights Visa/MC
59 Ngaio Street		**Beds:** 2 Queen 2 Single
Christchurch		(3 bdrm)
		Bath: 1 Private

```
  59            | Gamblins rd.   | Brougham st-sh 73    inner city
                |                |                      centre
    Ngaio st.   |←
  Wilsons rd | Waltham rd       | Waltham rd-sh 74   Barbadoes st-sh74
  s←---
                                | Brougham st-sh74
```

Mt Pleasant - Christchurch

Enjoy our warm hospitality in the comfort of our modern home, spacious ad sunny with wonderful views of the city and Southern Alps. Close by sumner beach, Ferrymead historical Park, Mt Cavendish Gondola and a variety of restaurants. We are in our 40's with a 10 year old daughter, our travels have taken us throughout New Zealand and overseas. Our interests include 4 wheel driving the outdoors, tapestry and gardening. our travels have taken us throughout New Zealand and overseas. We provide complimentary tea and coffee and are a non smoking household. Please phone for directions.

Plains View	**Tel:** (03) 384 5558	**Cost:** Double $70-$85
Homestay	**Fax:** (03) 384 5558	Single $45
8km E of Christchurch	**Mob:** 025 211 3606	**Beds:** 1 Queen 1 Double
Robyn & Peter Fleury	**E:** Fleury@inet.net.nz	1 Single (3 bdrm)
2 Plains View	**W:** www.bnb.co.nz/hosts/	**Bath:** 1 Guests share
Mt Pleasant Christchurch 8	fleury.html	

Mt Pleasant - Christchurch

Away from the city smog. Quiet secluded comfort in homely cottage down private lane. Charming tranquil garden. Sunny bedrooms opening onto covered terrace (for breakfast al fresco!). Tea and coffee always available. Many cafes, pubs, good restaurants 5 minutes drive. Estuary where bird life abounds 2 minutes walk. Nearby scenic attractions include Sumner Beach, hills, walks, gondola, Lyttelton Harbour. City centre is 15 minutes. We enjoy company, have travelled extensively, enjoy creative pursuits, gardening, books. Two resident cats. Laundry facilities. Smoking outdoors. Please phone for directions.

The Cotterage	**Tel:** (03) 384 2898	**Cost:** Double $100
B&B Homestay	**Fax:** (03) 384 2898	Single $60
7km E of Christchurch Central	**W:** www.bnb.co.nz/hosts/	Child neg Dinner $20
Jennifer Cotter	thecotterage.html	Visa/MC
24B Soleares Avenue		**Beds:** 1 Queen 2 Single (2 bdrm)
Mt Pleasant Christchurch 8008		**Bath:** 1 Ensuite 1 Family share

Mt Pleasant - Christchurch

Welcome to Santa Maria, our centrally heated home with panoramic views of the Pacific Ocean through to the Southern Alps. Our comfortable guestroom has ensuite bathroom, tea/coffee making facilities and access to a sunny courtyard. Enjoy our tennis court, pool or visit the nearby beach village of Sumner with its excellent selection of cafes, restaurants, bars and movie theatres. Windsurf, paraglide, ride the Gondola or explore one of our many walkways. The choice is yours. Two adorable cats reside with us.

Santa Maria	**Tel:** (03) 384 1174	**Cost:** Double $100
B&B	**Fax:** (03) 384 6474	Single $70
8km SE of Christchurch Centre	**Mob:** 021 673 549	**Beds:** 1 Queen (1 bdrm)
Anne & Ian Harris	**E:** the-harris-family@xtra.co.nz	**Bath:** 1 Ensuite
57 Santa Maria Avenue	**W:** www.bnb.co.nz/hosts/	
Mt Pleasant Christchurch	santamaria.html	

Redcliffs - Christchurch

Relax and enjoy our comfortable home by the sea, situated approximately 15 minutes from the city, our home is "absolute water front ", on the Avon-Heathcote Estuary with magnificent views of the sea, birds and boating. We are non smoking and our guest facilities include a sunny double and single bedroom with its own ensuite and TV, plus a twin bedroom with family share bathroom. Local restaurants offer a choice of cuisine, continental breakfast is included in the Tariff, laundry facilities and off street parking.

Redcliffs on Sea
B&B Homestay
8km E of Christchurch
Cynthia & Lyndsey Ebert
125 Main Road
Redcliffs Christchurch 8

Tel: (03) 384 9792
Fax: (03) 384 9703
E: redcliffs@nzhomestay.co.nz
W: www.nzhomestay.co.nz/
ebert.htm

Cost: Double $100 Single $60
          Visa/MC
Beds: 1 Double 1 Single
          1 Twin (2 bdrm)
Bath: 1 Ensuite
          1 Family share

Sumner - Christchurch

Stroll along sumner's sandy beach, search rock pools or walk the many hillside flower strewn tracks. By night enjoy the numerous village cafes and restaurants or visit Christchurch city 15 minutes away. Relax in happy luxury at our comfortable double storey home or use us as a base for daily sightseeing trips to vineyards, hot springs, whale watching or mountains. Guests say "unparalleled hospitality!". Children are welcome. Free use of internet, surfboards and childrens beach toys. Pet free and non-smoking for those with allergies.

Marriner Lodge
B&B Guesthouse
8km E of Christchurch Central
Marilyn & Chris Marshall
20 Marriner Street
Sumner Christchurch

Tel: (03) 326 7883
Fax: (03) 326 7883
E: Christchurchbandb@clear.net.nz
W: www.bnb.co.nz/hosts/
marrinerlodge.html

Cost: Double $95-$115
          Single $70
          Child $10,
          5 - 12yrs Visa/MC
Beds: 2 Queen 1 Twin (3 bdrm)
Bath: 2 Ensuite 1 Private

Sumner - Christchurch

Enjoy the warmest hospitality in our spacious turn of the century Villa overlooking Sumner bay. Our home retains the graciousness of a bygone era while offering all modern comforts. In winter enjoy open fires, cosy farmhouse kitchen and on sunny days the verandah and turret. Spectacular sea views form Sumner to the Kaikouras. Our interest are food, wine, music, gardening, tramping, travel. The children have flown, but we still have three hens. 5 mins walk to beach; off street parking; laundry. Also self-contained beach front apartment.

Villa Alexandra
Self-contained Homestay
10km E of Christchurch
Wendy & Bob Perry
1 Kinsey Terrace
Christchurch 8

Tel: (03) 326 6291
Fax: (03) 326 6096
W: www.bnb.co.nz/hosts/
villaalexandra.html

Cost: Double $75-$95
          Single $60
          Child $10, free under 12yrs
          Dinner $25
Beds: 1 Queen 1 Double
          1 Twin (3 bdrm)
Bath: 1 Ensuite 2 Private

Sumner Beach - Christchurch

The Cave Rock Guest House is Christchurch's only seafront accommodation directly opposite Sumner's famous "Cave Rock". Your hosts Gayle and Norm Eade have been in the hospitality industry for 15 years and enjoy meeting people from overseas and within NZ. Our large double rooms have seaviews and are self contained. Both have colour TV, heating and ensuite bathrooms, and can sleep up to 4. Kitchen facilities available. Sumner Village is an ideal location, 15 minutes from Christchurch city, we have cafe/bars, shops, cinema, all walking distance. We have a very friendly Dalmatian dog.

Cave Rock Guest House	**Tel:** (03) 326 6844	**Cost:** Double $90
B&B Guesthouse	**Fax:** (03) 326 5600	Single $75
8km E of Christchurch	**Mob:** 025 360 212	Child $15 Visa/MC
Gayle & Norm Eade	**E:** eade@chch.planet.org.nz	**Beds:** 2 Queen (2 bdrm)
16 Esplanade	**W:** www.bnb.co.nz/hosts/	**Bath:** 2 Ensuite
Sumner Christchurch	caverockguesthouse.html	

Sumner - Christchurch

Chris, Anna and Dominic welcome you to Ocean View B&B. Twenty minutes from Christchurch city and is set in the popular seaside suburb of Sumner. Sumner's relaxing village atmosphere has much to offer the traveller. Take advantage of the views up the coast and out to sea from the guest rooms that have direct access to expansive verandas and decking positioned to capture the sun. Set on three acres of land providing a rural flavour. DIRECTIONS : Please telephone, e-mail or visit our brochure.

Ocean View	**Tel:** 0064 3 326 4888	**Cost:** Double $95-$130
B&B	**Fax:** 0064 3 326 4888	Single $55-$90
8km E of Christchurch	**E:** oceanview@clear.net.nz	Child neg
Christian and Anna van Uden	**W:** www.bnb.co.nz/hosts/	Visa/MC
65 Ocean View Terrace	user5.html	**Beds:** 1 Queen 1 Twin (2 bdrm)
Sumner Christchurch		**Bath:** 2 Private

Cashmere - Christchurch

Two storeyed home in quiet back section on Cashmere Hills. Lower storey is an independent suite comprising two hand basins, shower, lavatory, kingsize bed with electric blanket, two single bunks, television, telephone, heaters, and table and chairs. Tea/coffee making facilities. Non smokers only. I am a registered general nurse; obstetrics nurse; a university student studying for a degree in linguistics; and an English language teacher. The piano loves attention. Spanish and English are my favourite languages. 'Explorer' of foreign countries.

Homestay	**Tel:** 03 337 1423	**Cost:** Single $50
5km S of Christchurch	**W:** www.bnb.co.nz/hosts/	Child 1/2 price
Janet Milne	milne.html	Dinner $25 Shared $40
12A Hackthorne Road		**Beds:** 1 Queen 1 Twin 1 Single
Cashmere		(2 bdrm)
Christchurch		**Bath:** 1 Ensuite 1 Family share

Cashmere - Christchurch

Cashmere Heights - where a warm friendly welcome awaits you in a home where you can relax in comfort and quiet elegance.

Our home is on two levels and is in an exclusive suburb of Christchurch. Nestled high on the Port Hills amongst other high quality homes and 220 metres above sea level, Cashmere Heights captures the "Million dollar views" with 180 degrees unobstructed panorama from the Pacific Ocean, across the city and the Canterbury Plains to the playground of the South Island, the Southern Alps.

Our guest accommodation is located on a separate level of our home thereby ensuring total privacy and relaxation. All bedrooms are large and individually decorated in bold bright colours to enhance our desire to create and maintain a relaxing holiday and homely environment. All bedrooms are located to ensure all take advantage of the views.

We have a separate guest lounge which is large and offers tea/coffee facilities, home theatre entertainment system, reading area, computer station, phone and fax. Adjoining this lounge is a sun deck with outdoor furniture, barbecue and a spa pool.

A leisurely breakfast may be selected from the wide choices available and may be taken in the cafe style eatery, or weather permitting, al fresco on the sun deck or on the garden patio.

We are only 400 metres from the Historic "Sign of the Takahe Restaurant" and there are several other good restaurants close by. Also close by are numerous scenic walking trails.

We are aged in our early forties and have travelled extensively. We enjoy meeting people and welcoming guests into our home.

Our home is a non smoking home, which we share with our cat.

You may also wish to take advantage of our Tour service, Rover Tours NZ, which specialise in luxury customised tours. These are personally guided tours for a maximum of four persons anywhere in the South Island.

Cashmere Heights
Homestay
5km S of Christchurch
Karen & Barry Newman
6 Allom Lane
Cashmere Heights
Christchurch 2

Tel: (03) 332 1778
Fax: (03) 332 9399
Mob: 025 241 0911
E: rover@iconz.co.nz
W: www.bnb.co.nz/hosts/
cashmereheights.html

Cost: Double $150-$165
Single $110 B/A
Visa/MC Amex Diners
Beds: 3 King 6 Single (3 bdrm)
Bath: 1 Private

Cashmere - Christchurch

Our home is 5 minutes drive form the city center with million dollar views of Rural Canterbury and the Southern Alps. Easy flat access and parking, quiet and peaceful, it incorporates the charm of yesteryear with the conveniences of a modern home, complemented by David's prizewinning garden and Kathleen's exhibition patchwork quilts. Interests include Rotary, Zonta, Stamp collecting, Hiking, Gardening, Patchwork Quilting and Embroidery. Tim our friendly cat offers a special welcome. Flexible full home cooked breakfast. Directions: Please telephone or visit our web-page.

Burford Manor	**Tel:** (03) 337 1905	**Cost:** Double $120
B&B Homestay	**Fax:** (03) 337 1916	Single $90
5km S of Christchurch	**E:** burfords@xtra.co.nz	Visa/MC
Kathleen & David Burford	**W:** www.bnb.co.nz/hosts/	**Beds:** 2 Queen 2 Single
3 Lucknow Place	burfordmanor.html	(3 bdrm)
Cashmere 2 Christchurch		**Bath:** 1 Ensuite 2 Private

Huntsbury Hill - Christchurch

Our spacious elegantly restored 1920's Port Hills home has city and mountain views and is a tranquil base for City/ Banks Peninsula exploration, also for day trips to Kaikoura, Akaroa, Mt Hutt and West Coast. Offstreet parking. Bus at gate. Enjoy large bedrooms and cheerfully served breakfasts. Relax in a romantic garden with swimming pool or experience Paul's woodcraft workshop. Laundry, fax, BBQ, tea, coffee facilities. Apartment has separate entrance. We have a wide range of interests and enjoy listening to travellers' tales. Airport 20 mins. City 5 mins.

Huntsbury House	**Tel:** (03) 332 1020	**Cost:** Double $80-$120
Homestay S/C Apartment B&B	**Fax:** (03) 337 0666	Single $60-$90
2km SE of Christchurch Central	**E:** huntbnb@voyager.co.nz	Visa/MC
Paul Bennett & Anthea Clibborn	**W:** www.voyager.co.nz/~huntbnb	**Beds:** 1 King 1 Double
16 Huntsbury Avenue		3 Single (3 bdrm)
Huntsbury Hill Christchurch 2		**Bath:** 2 Ensuite 1 Family share

Halswell - Christchurch

Tranquil, cosy and convenient. Only 20 minutes from the city and near the Akaroa highway, our 1/2 acre garden on the Port Hills overlooks the rural setting of the Canterbury Plains to the Southern Alps. Choose the self-contained "Garden Lodge", yours for exclusive use, with 2 bedrooms (one with queen-sized bed, and one twin), toilet, shower, TV and cooking facilities, or, in our home, a room with twin beds. Our hobbies include gardening, fishing, fibre-arts, debating and Cass, our Golden Retriever.

Overton	**Tel:** (03) 322 8326	**Cost:** Double $80-$95
B&B Self-contained	**Fax:** (03) 322 8350	Single $45-$80
6km SE of Christchurch Central	**Mob:** 025 623 0831	Child $10 - $15
Judi & Joe Brizzell	**E:** brizzell.accom@xtra.co.nz	Dinner from $20 Visa/MC
241 Kennedys Bush Road	**W:** www.canterburypages.co.nz/	**Beds:** 1 Queen 4 Single (3 bdrm)
Halswell	overton	**Bath:** 1 Private
Christchurch 3		1 Family share

Lincoln - Christchurch

Our tranquil 10 acre farmlet nestles among mature trees with spectacular mountain views and easy city/airport access. Relax in our warm indoor spa/swimming pool conservatory before your busy day sightseeing. Spacious rooms with TV, coffee facilities, electric blankets, heating, hairdryers. Hearty breakfasts served with home grown produce. 3km golf course, university. Restaurants. Fay is a keen spinner - you're welcome to try your hand! Our retirement interests include golf, Rotary, skiing, genealogy. Lovable moggy named 'Muffin'. Map directions: www.webnz.com/bbnz/menteith.htm

Menteith Country Homestay	**Tel:** (03) 325 2395	**Cost:** Double $95-$105
Homestay Country	**Fax:** (03) 325 2469	Single $70
20km S of Christchurch Central	**Mob:** 021 131 5523	Visa/MC
Fay & Stephen Graham	**E:** menteith@clear.net.nz	**Beds:** 1 King/Twin 1 Queen
Springs Road (Rapid No 961)	**W:** www.bnb.co.nz/hosts/	(2 bdrm)
RD 6 Christchurch 8021	menteithcountryhomestay.html	**Bath:** 2 Ensuite

Tai Tapu - Christchurch

Country Retreat in two acre rambling garden. Character farmhouse. King/Twin and double bedrooms. Self contained unit with queen and single bed, ensuite bathroom. Numerous extras. Gourmet organic meals featuring our own meat, eggs, fruit, nuts and vegetables. Local fish and wine. Irish/Kiwi hospitality. Masses of animals and birds. Many rare breeds, black pigs, white peacocks donkeys, Dexter's and Dorset horns. Golden retrievers, fox terrier and cats. Full farmstay includes all meals, farm tour, animal feeding, horseriding. Croquet, boules, bicycles on site. Golf and vineyards locally.

Ballymoney Farmstay & Garden	**Tel:** (03) 329 6706	**Cost:** Double $135 Single $90
Farmstay & Self-contained	**Fax:** (03) 329 6709	Child neg Dinner $35 Full
20km SE of Christchurch	**Mob:** 025 604 8353	Farmstay $130 - $240
Merrilies & Peter Rebbeck	**E:** rebbeckpandm@hotmail.com	Visa/MC
Wardstay Road	**W:** www.bnb.co.nz/hosts/	**Beds:** 1 King/Twin 1 Queen
RD 2 Christchurch	ballymoney.html	1 Double 1 Single (3 bdrm)
		Bath: 2 Ensuite 1 Guests share

Tai Tapu - Christchurch

Erik and Paula offer warm relaxed Kiwi hospitality. Welcome to our comfortable country home, nestled in 2 1/2 acres of trees, garden/orchard. Superbly located for City and Country activities, 15 mins to Christchurch. Paula's specialty, home cooking with organic fruit and vegetables from our garden. Meal times flexible. Fully appointed rooms provide ultimate comfort. Relax in the spa and informal landscaped garden with gazebo's and large pond. Local wineries, restaurants, walking tracks, golf, all within 5 minutes. Discounts available for longer stays.

Pear Drop Inn	**Tel:** (03) 329 6778	**Cost:** Double $90
B&B Homestay	**Fax:** (03) 329 6661	Single $50
15km S of Christchurch	**Mob:** 021 1266 873	Child 1/2 price Dinner $25
Erik & Paula Gray	**E:** pear-drop-inn@zfree.co.nz	Visa/MC
Akaroa Highway 75	**W:** www.bnb.co.nz/hosts/	**Beds:** 1 King 1 Queen 4 Single
Tai Tapu, RD 2	peardropinn.html	(2 bdrm)
		Bath: 1 Ensuite 1 Guests share

Lyttelton

Historic Lyttelton, arrival point of the first European settlers. A bustling port town full of action and interest: restaurants, bars, historic buildings and walkways. Only 20 minutes to central Christchurch, but what a contrast! Welcome to Randolph House, built in 1870, lovingly restored and comfortably furnished. Enjoy the harbour views from our decks, a glass of wine at sunset, walk a short distance to dine in the lively atmosphere of the town. There's bed and then there's the breakfast. Superb!

B&B Self-contained Homestay
0.5km E of Lyttelton
Judy & Jonathan Elworthy
Randolph House
49 Sumner Road
Lyttelton

Tel: (03) 328 8877
Fax: (03) 328 8779
Mob: (025) 356 309
E: randolphhouse@xtra.co.nz
W: www.bnb.co.nz/hosts/
randolph.html

Cost: Double $100-$120
Single $80-$100 Child neg
Visa/MC Amex
Beds: 2 Double 2 Single
(3 bdrm)
Bath: 1 Ensuite 1 Guests share

Lyttelton

Dalcory House built 1859, has been a Boarding School, private residents, rental property, and hostel for naval rating's in WW2. Shonagh your hostess is a Cook, Nurse, Educator, Health manager and mother. Have a comfortable nights sleep in pleasant surroundings with a clear view of Lyttelton Port and Harbour, 5 minutes walk from the centre of Lyttelton. Shonagh and her young son will ensure your stay is comfortable and memorable.

Shonagh O'Hagan's Guest House
B&B
9km E of Christchurch
Shonagh O'Hagan
Dalcroy House
16 Godley Quay
Lyttelton

Tel: (03) 328 8577
Mob: (025) 346 351
E: shonagh.ohagan@xtra.co.nz
W: www.bnb.co.nz/hosts/
shonaghohagans.html

Cost: Double $100 Single $75
Child $20 Dinner $25
Visa/MC
Beds: 1 King/Twin 2 Queen
1 Double (3 bdrm)
Bath: 1 Guests share
2 Family share

Lyttelton

Look out over historic Lyttelton, the port for Christchurch. We live elsewhere but will greet you and leave you to the quiet enjoyment of our cosy self contained cottage. Hill trails and guided town walks available locally. Cafes, bars and restaurants are a short stroll away or use the full kitchen. Self serve continental breakfast. Phone & fax. Washer/dryer. No objection to well behaved pets. Small lawn with seat under a weeping willow. Note: This property is at the top of a flight of 55 steps, mobility essential.

Ebony Cottage
B&B Self-contained
5km SE of Christchurch
Michael & Susan Denny
57a Jacksons Road
Lyttelton

Tel: (03) 329 9009
Fax: (03) 329 9249
Mob: 025 6802445
E: cant.garden.nz@clear.net.nz
W: www.bnb.co.nz/hosts/
ebonycottage.html

Cost: Double $85
Single $75
Visa/MC
Beds: 1 Double (1 bdrm)
Bath: 1 Ensuite

Lyttelton

Lyttelton, the original settlement of Canterbury, has retained that special Romantic charm of ships and the sea. Explore its history in the Maritime Museum, visit the Time Ball, walk in the footsteps of the pioneers up the Bridle Path, or take advantage of the commanding view from our gracious Edwardian villa and watch the ballet of ships and boats as they go about their business.

Each elegantly furnished guest room offers spacious accommodation and privacy, whilst both of the modern ensuite bathrooms are luxuriously appointed; the Venice Suite with double spa bath.

You are welcome to relax in the former Ball-Room, whose huge bay window looks over the beautiful terraced garden to the hillsides of Lyttelton township, where the houses are reminiscent of a Mediterranean fishing village.

Fine teas, coffee and other refreshments are freely available in the Chart-Room with its spectacular harbour views. As evening approaches, complimentary drinks are served on the adjoining verandah.

Venture down the quaint laneways to the cafes and restaurants, then call us to save you the walk home.

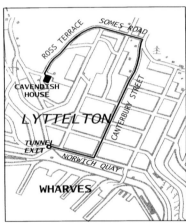

Cavendish House	Tel: (03) 328 9505	Cost: Double $130-$150
B&B Boutique B&B	Fax: (03) 328 9502	Single $110
0.5km NW of Lyttelton	Mob: 025 616 0266	Visa/MC Amex
Graham & Jenny Sorell	E: gsorell@xtra.co.nz	Beds: 1 King/Twin 1 Queen
10 Ross Terrace	W: www.bnb.co.nz/hosts/	(2 bdrm)
Lyttelton	cavendishhouse.html	Bath: 2 Ensuite

Governors Bay

Governor's Bay is one of the many scenic bays surrounding Lyttelton Harbour. Our hillside home has beautiful views over the bay. The area is noted for its gardens and walking tracks, and is ideally situated for exploring Banks Peninsula. Our guest wing has a large sunny bedroom with ensuite. French doors open to a private balcony. The room has a TV and tea/coffee making facilities. A wide range of cuisine is offered by local restaurants. We have a cat called Suzy. Directions: Please phone.

Orchard House
B&B Homestay
13km SE of Christchurch
Judy & Neil Wilkinson
Main Road, Governors Bay
RD 1, Lyttelton
Christchurch

Tel: (03) 329 9622
E: n.j.wilkinson@xtra.co.nz
W: www.bnb.co.nz/hosts/
orchardhouse.html

Cost: Double $100
Single $75
Beds: 1 Double (1 bdrm)
Bath: 1 Ensuite

Governors Bay - Banks Peninsula

Nestled in Governor's Bay, The Anchorage looks East, out to the headlands and Lyttelton Harbour. The upper deck is private and warm, offering 180 degree views of the bay. Upstairs guests enjoy a large private room with modern facilities, including a jacuzzi bath. Table-tennis is also available on the front patio. Kim and Mark, with their son (4) Raphael, warmly welcome you to their home. We are both practising artists with a passion for culture and entertaining. Governor's Bay is a delightful retreat 15 to 20 minutes drive over the hill from Christchurch. Many native birds, such as bellbirds, fantails and wood pigeons share in our garden.

The Anchorage
B&B Homestay
13km S of Christchurch
Kim & Mark Soltero
Please phone for directions

Tel: (03) 329 9051
E: anchoragenz@hotmail.com
W: www.bnb.co.nz/hosts/
theanchorage.html

Cost: Double $90
Single $60
Beds: 1 Queen (1 bdrm)
Bath: 1 Private

Teddington - Lyttelton Harbour

Lyttelton Harbour and the Port Hills create a dynamic panorama you can enjoy from our custom-built log chalet. Our smoke-free home has three guestrooms with a Queen bed and single bed each. We are both self-employed (woodworker and shadow puppeteer) and enjoy sharing a sail on Max's yacht. Our pet cat and sheep welcome guests enthusiastically. Whether relaxing on the veranda at Max's hand-crafted table or sipping wine in the spa bath, we are sure you will make good memories.

Bergli Hill Farmstay
Farmstay Self-contained
20km S of Christchurch
Rowena & Max Dorfliger
RD 1
Lyttelton

Tel: (03) 329 9118
Fax: (03) 329 9118
Mob: 025 829 410
E: bergli@ihug.co.nz
W: www.bnb.co.nz/hosts/
berglihillfarmstay.html

Cost: Double $90
Single $65
Dinner $25 B/A S/C $50
Visa/MC
Beds: 3 Queen 3 Single (3 bdrm)
Bath: 2 Ensuite 1 Family share

Church Bay - Diamond Harbour

Explore Banks Peninsula from Church Bay. Our cosy, ensuite unit overlooks Quail Island and our coastal garden. The room has a tea/coffee tray, home-made biscuits, books, TV. We are a non-smoking household with an unobtrusive cat. Philip and I are travelled, retired teachers who enjoy welcoming travellers to our wonderful area. Languages: German, Dutch (some Italian, Spanish).

Kai-o-ruru Bed & Breakfast
B&B Self-contained
35km S of Christchurch
Robin & Philip Manger
32 James Drive
Church Bay, RD 1
Lyttelton

Tel: (03) 329 4788
Fax: (03) 329 4788
E: manger@xtra.co.nz
W: www.bnb.co.nz/hosts/
kaiorurubedbreakfast.html

Cost: Double $85
Single $50
Dinner $25
Beds: 2 Single (1 bdrm)
Bath: 1 Ensuite

Akaroa - Paua Bay

Set in a private bay, our 900 acre sheep, deer and cattle farm is surrounded by coast-line, native bush and streams. You are spoilt for choice - Walk to the beach, enjoy seals and extensive bird life, join in seasonal farming activities or horse-riding. Swim in the pool, laze in the hammock and don't miss the secluded moonlit bath under the stars overlooking the pacific..... In the evening share a meal of fresh farm produce with relaxed conversation gathered around the large kitchen table.

Paua Bay Farmstay
Farmstay
12km E of Akaroa
Murray & Sue Johns
Postal - c/o 113 Beach Road
Akaroa Banks Peninsula

Tel: (03) 304 8511
Fax: (03) 304 8511
Mob: 021 133 8194
E: pauabay@inet.net.nz
W: www.bnb.co.nz/hosts/
pauabayfarmstay.html

Cost: Double $80
Single $50
Child neg Dinner $25
Beds: 1 Queen 1 Twin
(2 bdrm)
Bath: 1 Guests share

Akaroa

Our home is situated 1.5km up the Takamatua valley and only 5km from Akaroa. We farm sheep, cattle and deer, and usually have a menagerie of dogs, cats and orphaned pets around. Hanne is Danish and speaks that language fluently. We have both worked in Australia for 10 years. We offer spacious accommodation in a sheltered position and invite you to enjoy some good old fashioned country hospitality. A trip to the "Akaroa Seal Colony Safari" should be considered a must.

Farmstay
5km N of Akaroa
Hanne & Paul LeLievre
Box 4
Akaroa
Banks Peninsula

Tel: (03) 304 7255
Fax: (03) 304 7255
Mob: 025 942 070
E: Double.L@Xtra.co.nz
W: www.bnb.co.nz/hosts/
lelievre.html

Cost: Double $80
Single $45
Dinner $20 Visa/MC
Beds: 1 Double 1 Single
(1 bdrm)
Bath: 1 Ensuite

Akaroa - Barrys Bay

Experience the tranquillity of farm life while conveniently situated on the main road between Christchurch and Akaroa, at the French Farm/Wainui intersection allowing you to explore this intriguing volcanic peninsula with ease.

Our home is set amid rolling hills 400m along a meandering driveway, overlooking the Akaroa Harbour. Rosslyn is a large historic homestead built in the 1860's. It has been our family home and life style for four generations.

The homestead and farm buildings are rich in history including the original building that milled timber for the Christchurch Cathedral.

We take pride in offering quality home-grown and prepared produce from vegetables and fruit to preserves and baking. It is a pleasure for us to share our evening meal, served in the farm style kitchen at the family table. Breakfast ranges from, fresh fruit to full cooked with smoke cured bacon and home-made bread toasted on the embers.

Two large ground floor rooms have been refurbished to accommodate you in comfort. Each room has ensuite bathroom, firm queen bed, central heating, screened windows and antiques of the period. A spa room, laundry, e-mail and ph/fax are also available. French doors leading to expansive verandahs and informal gardens make the most of serene harbour views.

Our 160 cow-working dairy farm also runs deer and much loved pets, most of whom live outside. The streams are lined with bush attracting an abundance of native birds.

We look forward to welcoming you with a fresh pot of tea, coffee or cool drink served with home baking, hearing of your adventures, and help plan new ones for the remainder of your holiday.

Rosslyn Estate
B&B Farmstay Homestay
12km Akaroa
Ross, Lynette, Kirsty (9)
& Matt (7) Curry
Christchurch-Akaroa
Main Road (SH75)
Rapid #5797
Barrys Bay, Akaroa Harbour

Tel: (03) 304 5804
Fax: (03) 304 5804
E: Rosslyn@xtra.co.nz
W: www.bnb.co.nz/hosts/
rosslynestate.html

Cost: Double $110-$120
Single $90
Child neg
Dinner $25pp
Laundry no charge
Visa/MC
Beds: 2 Queen (2 bdrm)
Bath: 2 Ensuite

Okains Bay - Banks Peninsula

Do you want to experience the grace and charm of yesteryear, while enjoying the fine food and wine of NZ today? Do you want to revel in the peace of country life, but still be close to sights and activities? Then escape to 'Kawatea', an historic Edwardian homestead set in spacious gardens, and surrounded by land that has been in our family since the 1850s.

Built in 1900 from native timbers 'Kawatea' has been carefully renovated to add light and space without losing its old world charm. Elegantly decorated, the house features original stained glass windows, handcrafted furniture.

Linger over breakfasts of your choice in sunny conservatory. Join us for summer barbecues on the expansive verandahs, savouring seafood from the Bay, and creative country fare from our garden and farm. Gather around the dining table by the fire on cooler nights, sharing thoughts and experiences with our family and fellow travellers.

Participate in farm activities such as moving stock, feeding our pet sheep, lambing, calving or shearing. Wander our hillside farm, climbing to enjoy a breath taking panoramic view of Banks Peninsula. Relax or swim at Okains Bay, observe the birdlife on the estuary, or walk along the scenic coastline to secluded beaches and a seal colony with excellent photgraphic opportunities. Learn about Maori Culture and the life of early New Zealand settlers at the acclaimed Okains Bay Museum. Explore the township of Akaroa, with its strong French influence. Visit art galleries and craft shops, play golf or go horse riding, sample local wines and watch traditional cheeses being made. Take a harbour cruise, or swim with the rare Hector's dolphin.

We have been providing farmstays since 1988, and we pride ourselves on thoughtful personal service. Romantic weekends and special occasion dinners are also catered for. We hope you come as a visitor but leave as a friend.

Directions: Take Highway 75 from Christchurch through Duvauchelle. Turn left at the signpost marked Okains Bay- we are 11km on the right.

Kawatea
Farmstay
20km N of Akaroa
Judy & Kerry Thacker
Okains Bay
Banks Peninsula

Tel: (03) 304 8621
Fax: (03) 304 8621
E: marniek@encos.com
W: www.bnb.co.nz/hosts/
kawatea.html

Cost: Double $90-$120
Single $65-$75 Child B/A
Dinner $25 Visa/MC
Beds: 3 Queen 2 Single
(3 bdrm)
Bath: 1 Ensuite
1 Guests share

"La Belle Villa"

Akaroa

A warm welcome awaits you. Relax in the comfort of a bygone era, and appreciate the antiques in our picturesque historic villa. Built in the 1870's for a prominent business man it became one of the 1st doctor's surgeries in Akaroa and is now established on approx. 1/2 acre of beautiful, mature grounds, surrounded by rolling hills and lush scenery.

Enjoy the indoor/outdoor living, large private swimming pool and gently trickling stream. We offer warm, spacious bedrooms, large guest lounge, fabulous fires in winter, breakfast 'Al Fresco' in the summer if you choose with the birds and trees. We offer to make your stay with us special.

Separate Guest Lounge

It will be a pleasure to book you on to any cruises, fishing trips, swim with the dolphins, horse treks etc that you may require. Being centrally situated, restaurants, cafes, and wine bars and the beach are all walking distance. So too, you will find, are the majority of galleries, shops and excursions available in New Zealand's most charming, quaint and quintessential French township.

Outdoor Swimming Pool

La Belle Villa
B&B
80km SE of Christchurch
Deborah & Gordon Akaroa
113 Rue Jolie
Akaroa

Tel: (03) 304 7084
Fax: (03) 304 7084
Mob: 025 227 2084
W: www.bnb.co.nz/hosts/labellevilla.html

Cost: Double $90-$110
Single $70
Wimter rates apply
Beds: 1 King 2 Queen
1 Twin (4 bdrm)
Bath: 1 Ensuite 2 Private
1 Guests share

Akaroa Harbour

"Bossu" farm of 100 acres is on 2 kms of the harbour foreshore offering panoramic views of Akaroa and the surrounding countryside. Our farm tours are a specialty with sheep, cattle, forestry and a small vineyard. We also have a Jack Russell dog. We offer fishing, sightings of dolphin, penguin and nesting sea birds. A well used grass tennis court is a feature of our extensive garden. We enjoy golf, bridge, tennis and travel. Directions: first property on seaward side after Wainui.

Bossu
Farmstay
20km E of Akaroa
Rana & Garry Simes
Wainui
Akaroa, RD 2
Banks Peninsula

Tel: (03) 304 8421
Fax: (03) 304 8421
E: bossu@xtra.co.nz
W: www.bnb.co.nz/hosts/
bossu.html

Cost: Double $120
Single $75
Dinner $25
Beds: 1 Queen 3 Single
(3 bdrm)
Bath: 1 Private 1 Guests share

Akaroa

Enjoy the unique experience of staying in a fully restored, listed historic cottage, in a tranquil garden setting. Wake to the dawn chorus, the sound of the nearby stream and a generous breakfast hamper. The privacy and peace provide an ideal atmosphere for those seeking a romantic setting for a special break. The character and charm of the original cottage have been largely retained, while providing all essential amenities for guest comfort. The cottage is exclusively yours during your stay. Smoke-free. No children or pets.

Mill Cottage
B&B Boutique
1km NE of Akaroa
Joan & John Galt
Rue Grehan
Akaroa 8161

Tel: (03) 304 8007
Fax: (03) 304 8007
E: millcottage@xtra.co.nz
W: www.bnb.co.nz/hosts/
millcottage.html

Cost: Double $130
Single $100
Visa/MC
Beds: 1 Double
2 Single (3 bdrm)
Bath: 1 Private

Akaroa

Centrally located quiet, restful, historic home with category one listing. Also self-contained cottage at bottom of garden. Croquet lawn - petanque - full sized billiard table. 1 hectare garden and native bush, bordered by rocky stream. Email facilities. Laundry. Guest lounge with TV and tea/coffee making facilities. Continental/full breakfast, fresh fruit and home baking, crisp cotton damask linen. Fresh flowers. 1 family cat. Hair dryers, heated towel rails, toiletries. 5th generation local knowledge and history. Help with local interests and activities assured. Closed June/July.

Blythcliffe
B&B Self-contained Cottage
Akaroa Central
Rosealie & Jan Shuttleworth
37 Rue Balguerie
Akaroa 8161

Tel: (03) 304 7003
Fax: (03) 304 7003
Tollfree: 0800 393 877
E: blythcliffe@xtra.co.nz
W: www.blythcliffe.co.nz

Cost: Double $145
Single $125
S/C Cottage $150 Visa/MC
Beds: 3 Queen 1 Single
(4 bdrm)
Bath: 1 Ensuite 2 Private

Akaroa

'Loch-Hill' with magnificent sea-views overlooking Akaroa, and cluster of new fully self-contained luxurious cottages, nestled in surrounding bush, park and garden setting, offers privacy and tranquillity. Some large cottages have air-conditioning. Try our romantic honeymoon cottages with cozy log-fires and double spa-baths. Enjoy wonderful views form your balcony. Experience the hospitality of 'Loch-Hill' "Caid Mile Failte" (One hundred thousand welcomes). Explore or relax in these idyllic, secluded surroundings. Perfect for your holiday retreat, smaller business conference, or wedding group. Special rates available.

Loch Hill Country Cottages
Self-contained
1km N of Akaroa
Donna & David Kingan
PO Box 21
Main Highway Akaroa

Tel: (03) 304 7195
Fax: (03) 304 7672
Tollfree: 0800 456 244
E: lochhill@xtra.co.nz
W: www.lochill.co.nz

Cost: Double $90-$140
      Child $12 under 12 yrs
      Breakfast $10pp Visa/MC
Beds: 2 King/Twin 2 King
      8 Queen 4 Single (11 bdrm)
Bath: 5 Ensuite 3 Private

Akaroa Harbour

Superbly sited in a commanding position above the north end of Akaroa harbour, this newly-restored 1920's farmhouse offers peace, comfort and views to die for. On the main highway it's close to all the Peninsula's attractions. Go walking, cycling or boating, see the dolphins, or enjoy the fine restaurants. Then relax in the peaceful atmosphere of our smoke free home (the discreet tabby-cat won't disturb you). Expect a generous breakfast of fine fresh foods. Please phone for directions. The Akaroa/ Christchurch bus stops at our gate.

Cabbage Tree Corner
Country B&B
7km N of Akaroa
Prue Billings
RD 1
Akaroa

Tel: (03) 304 5155
Mob: 021 655 862
E: prueb@xtra.co.nz
W: www.breakfast.co.nz

Cost: Double $90-$100
      Single $70
      Visa/MC
Beds: 1 Double 2 Single
      (2 bdrm)
Bath: 2 Ensuite

Akaroa - Barrys Bay

Jennifer and Kevin offer self contained boutique lodgings on five acres of famrland in Barrys Bay 10 minutes from Akaroa. The 'Honey House' has two bedrooms, with separate bathroom and toilet. The (circa 1883) barn has one bedroom with separate bathroom and toilet.
Both lodgings have luxury bedding, tea and coffee making facilities, with fridge, TV, CD.
Enjoy the views over the old Maori Pa site on Onawe Peninisula, to the Akaroa heads. We offer a full menu breakfast served in your rooms, garden, or our cottage kitchen.

The Honey House
B&B Self-contained
10min Akaroa
Jennifer & Kevin Wilson
Barrys Bay, RD 2 Akaroa

Tel: (03) 304 7186
Fax: (03) 304 7186
E: honey.house@xtra.co.nz
W: www.bnb.co.nz/hosts/ thehoneyhouse.html

Cost: Double $120
      Single $70
      Visa/MC
Beds: 2 Queen 1 Double
      (3 bdrm)
Bath: 2 Private

Akaroa

Built in 1910 for a local merchant, Maison de la Mer is a two-storey villa sited directly opposite the beach and one minute from the Information Centre. Guests can easily walk to the village shops, restaurants, and cafes.

Two of the rooms have gorgeous harbour views, one with a double spa bath and dressing room and another with a private sitting room. All the rooms are elegantly furnished and have television and tea and coffee facilities.

A spacious lounge with an open fire and panoramic sea views is also available for guest use.

A full breakfast is served in the dining room or on the lawn during summer if desired. It is our aim to provide a warm welcome and excellent hospitality, and we can assure you of a very enjoyable stay.

We are a non smoking household, with a family pet.

Email facility is available to guests.

Maison de la Mer
B&B
80km SE of Christchurch
Alan & Laurice Bradford
1 Rue Benoit
Akaroa
Banks Peninsula

Tel: (03) 304 8907
Fax: (03) 304 8907
Mob: 025 373 940
E: maisondelamer@xtra.co.nz
W: www.maisondelamer.co.nz

Cost: Double $110-$165
Single $85
Visa/MC
Beds: 3 Queen 1 Single
(3 bdrm)
Bath: 3 Ensuite

CANTERBURY

Akaroa

The Maples is a charming historic two storey home
built in 1877, it is situated in a quiet peaceful garden
setting 3 mins walk from the cafes and water front.
We offer Queen size ensuited rooms upstairs and a
Garden room with Queen size bed and double sofa bed
that is ideal for anyone wanting a private retreat.
Relax in the guests' lounge which has television, a log
fire and complimentary tea and coffee. Breakfast
includes freshly baked Brioche, croissants, muffins,
also an English cooked.

The Maples
B&B
80km SE of Christchurch
Peter & Lesley Keppel
158 Rue Jolie
Akaroa

Tel: (03) 304 8767
Fax: (03) 304 8767
E: maplesakaroa@xtra.co.nz
W: www.bnb.co.nz/hosts/
themaples.html

Cost: Double $100
Single $75
Visa/MC
Beds: 3 Queen (3 bdrm)
Bath: 3 Ensuite

Akaroa

Our historic French designed home overlooks the beach
and harbour. Our central location means you are five
minutes walking distance from restaurants, galleries and
shops. Relax in the comfort of elegant furnishings,
peaceful garden with native birds and magnificent harbour
views. Enjoy a complimentary glass of wine in the evening
and a gourmet continental breakfast. Tea/coffee available
in the guest lounge We have a background in people
related businessess, enjoy travel and meeting people. We
look forward to making your stay in Akaroa memorable.

Lavaud House
B&B Homestay
80km SE of Christchurch
Theresa & Paul
83 Rue Lavaud
Akaroa

Tel: (03) 304 7121
Fax: (03) 304 7121
E: lavaudhouse@xtra.co.nz
W: www.nzhomestay.co.nz/
lavaudhouse.html

Cost: Double $110-$155
Single $90-$125
Visa/MC Amex
Beds: 1 King 2 Queen 1 Twin
(4 bdrm)
Bath: 3 Ensuite 1 Private

Akaroa

Majestic view - Romantic accommodation. Onuku Heights is
a charming 1860's Homestead, overlooking the harbour,
nestled in orchard and gardens, with an abundance of bird life,
surrounded by native bush reserves, streams and waterfalls on
300 ha sheep farm. Well maintained walking tracks, going up
to 700m altitude with breathtaking panoramic views. Our
property is part of Banks Peninsula Track. Enjoy comfortable
king size rooms with antiques and exquisite ensuite bathrooms.
Relax in our guest lounge with an open fire. Delicious
breakfasts. Candlelight dinner. Fine wines.

Onuku Heights - Historic
Farmstay
B&B Farmstay
5km S of Akaroa
Angelika Balsam & Eckhard
Keppler
Onuku Heights Akaroa

Tel: (03) 304 7112
Fax: (03) 304 7116
E:
onuku.heights@paradise.net.nz
W: www.onuku-heights.co.nz

Cost: Double $120
Single $110
Dinner $30 B/A Visa/MC
Beds: 2 King (2 bdrm)
Bath: 2 Ensuite

Akaroa

Wilderness House is a beautiful historic home set in a large traditional garden containing protected trees, old roses and private vineyard. Charming bedrooms, with their own character, feature fine linen, fresh flowers, tea/coffee and home baking. Elegant lounge opens to verandah and garden. Delicious continental and cooked breakfasts. We take particular care to make you feel comfortable, relaxed and welcome in our home. Join us for a glass of wine in the evening. Short stroll to harbour, restaurants and shops. Resident cats, Beethoven and Harry.

Wilderness House	**Tel:** (03) 304 7517	**Cost:** Double $150
Boutique B&B	**Fax:** (03) 304 7518	Single $100
80km SE of Christchurch	**Mob:** 021 669 381	Visa/MC
Jim & Liz Coubrough	**E:** info@wildernesshouse.co.nz	**Beds:** 1 King/Twin 3 Queen
42 Rue Grehan	**W:** www.wildernesshouse.co.nz	(4 bdrm)
Akaroa		**Bath:** 3 Ensuite 1 Private

Castle Hill - Christchurch, Canterbury

A carefree atmosphere prevails at "The Burn" nestled in the heart of the Southern Alps and arguably New Zealand's highest B&B. We have designed and built our alpine lodge to maximise mountain vistas. A great place to return after a days activity or just relax on the huge deck. There are a host of outdoor sports on hand e.g. hiking, mountain biking, tennis, rock climbing, caving, children's playground, alpine golf, ski touring, ski/snowboarding (7 areas), High Country fly fishing, salmon fishing (5 lakes and rivers). Professional guiding for fishing and alpine sports available in house. POA.

The Burn Alpine B&B	**Tel:** (03) 318 7559	**Cost:** Double $120
B&B Homestay	**Fax:** (03) 318 7558	Single $90
33km W of Springfield	**E:** theburn@xtra.co.nz	Child 1/2 price Dinner $25
Bob Edge & Phil Stephenson	**W:** www.theburn.co.nz	Visa/MC
11 Torlesse Place		**Beds:** 3 Double 2 Single (4 bdrm)
Castle Hill Village Christchurch		**Bath:** 2 Guests share

Glenroy - Darfield

Our historical home is located in the Canterbury Foothills. 20 minutes North of Mt Hutt, 45 minutes to Christchurch Airport. Join in farm activities or enjoy golf, fishing or skiing. We farm the rare and distinctive Belted Galloway cattle, some dairy goats, sheep, pigs and poultry. Horse wagon rides with Hank and Xena are optional and extra. Most foods are home grown, home cooked to ensure they are always fresh. Lots of tame animals to feed. Children and babies welcome. Email facilities available. Robyn is a qualified Ambulance Officer.

Kerrilea	**Tel:** (03) 318 6569	**Cost:** Double $90
B&B Farmstay	**Fax:** (03) 318 6569	Single $60
19km W of Darfield	**Mob:** 021 153 727	Child $40 Dinner $25
Robyn Prouse & Kerry	**E:** info@kerrilea.com	**Beds:** 2 King 1 Queen
Beveridge Beckwith Rd	**W:** www.kerrilea.com	2 Twin 4 Single (6 bdrm)
RD2 Coalgate Canterbury		**Bath:** 1 Ensuite 1 Family share

Darfield

Brian and Michelle warmly invite you to relax or have fun in their friendly, luxury family deer farm. Built in 1999, 25 minutes from Christchurch International Airport (on SH 73). • Shops/Restaurants • Ski-fields • Golf Courses • Beautiful Walkways • TransAlpine Scenic Train connection • Jetboat Rides • Wineries close by.

Meychelle Manor offers something special for guests from holidaymakers, honeymooners, business couples to children. We have a wide variety of farmyard and exotic animals. Lots of fun activities to do • Farm Tour • Childrens Playarea • Putt on Golf Green • Petanque • Help Brian feed deer and farmyard animals • Walk to ostriches • Scatter wheat for chickens • Feed ducks and fish in lake • Swim in indoor heated pool.

Guest lounge has a very comfortable leather lounge suite (very relaxing!), large screen TV, DVD home surround-sound theatre with large selection of movies and telescope. Also brochure and travel books to assist your travel plans. Three private, beautiful, warm rooms with comfortable super King/ Twin beds, clock radios, blow dryers with 2 ensuites and private bathroom, private access, lake and mountain views from balconies with cafe style seating.

Complimentary bottle of wine • Tea or Coffee • Iced Lemon Water and Chocolates at night • Modern Laundry facilities • Email • Internet access • Faxing • Transport to and from our local restaurants so you can enjoy a drink and not worry about driving. Enjoy a delicious breakfast (at a time convenient with you) of • Brian's home-made bread 'yum' • Jams • Cereals • Yoghurt • Venison Sausages • Tomatoes • Eggs • Hash Browns • Fruit Juice • Variety of Teas • Ground Coffee. End of the day enjoy the local cuisine or by arrangement experience Brian's roasted venison and Michelle's home-made pie.

We have 2 lovely, young girls, Chevonn and Chloe who adore meeting people but whom are also respectful of others. We ask guests not to smoke. Pets are not inside.
From our Visitors Book - "You made us feel part of your family", "We'll be back".
Please phone for reservation/directions. Happy travelling. We look forward to meeting you.

Meychelle Manor
Farmstay
35km W of Christchurch
Brian & Michelle Walker
State Highway 73
Kirwee/ Darfield

Tel: (03) 318 1144
Fax: (03) 318 1965
E: meychelle.m@net.nz
W: www.farmstaynewzealand.com

Cost: Double $170
Single $95
Child neg Dinner $50
Visa/MC
Beds: 3 King/Twin (3 bdrm)
Bath: 2 Ensuite 1 Private

Mt Hutt - Methven

Welcome to Tyrone Deer Farm, centrally situated in the Mount Hutt, Methven Rakaia Gorge area in the middle of the South Island, 5km from the Inland Tourist Route (Highway 72) making "Tyrone" an ideal stopover if heading south to Queenstown, north to Picton/Nelson or Highway 73 to the West Coast, one hour from Christchurch International Airport.

Positioned on the farm, our home has views of the mountains (Mt Hutt) which also builds the backdrop of grazing deer a few metres away.

As our family have left home, we have plenty of room for guests with electric blankets and duvets on beds, heater and hair dryer in the bedrooms, a lounge with open fire, TV , tea & coffee making facilities, a guest fridge.

Come and meet Guz our pet deer, her daughter $$ and 10.30 our cat. Laze in the garden, swim in our pool.

Dinner, by arrangement, join us for a home cooked evening meal served with New Zealand wine.

For the visitor the surrounding area provides adventures and sporting activities i.e. skiing Mt Hutt, Heliskiing (remote ranges), Jet boating Rakaia River, Ballooning, Tramping, Horse riding. Guides are available for hunting (Tahr, Chamois, Red Deer etc), also Trout and Salmon fishing (seasonal) Golf, numerous walks - scenic, bush garden and alpine.

Directions: 8km from Methven on the alternative Rakaia Gorge Route, 10 km from Rakaia Gorge Bridges please refer to map.

Tyrone Deer Farm
Farmstay
8km N of Methven
Pam & Roger Callaghan
Mt Hutt Station Road
RD 12, Rakaia
Methven/Rakaia Gorge
Alternative Route

Tel: (03) 302 8096
Fax: (03) 302 8099
Tollfree: 0800 42 84 38
E: tyronedeerfarm@xtra.co.nz
W: www.bnb.co.nz/hosts/
tyronedeerfarm.html

Cost: Double $100-$110
Single $75
Dinner $30pp
Beds: 1 Queen 1 Double 1 Twin
(3 bdrm)
Bath: 2 Ensuite 1 Private

Mt Hutt - Methven

A warm welcome awaits you at Green Gables which is minutes from Methven-Mt Hutt, a beautiful picturesque village, which has an impressive range of both summer and winter activities.

This is an area of freshness, adventure and enjoyment situated 1 hour from Christchurch the garden city of New Zealand and its International Airport. Queenstown 5 hours. Relax in our peaceful farmhouse.

The tastefully appointed guest wing is complete with ensuite facilities, super-king beds, wool underlays, electric blankets, heaters, hair dryers and clock radios. French doors opening from all bedrooms provide private access to all the guests bedrooms.

Green Gables presents magnificent views of Mt Hutt and the surrounding mountains.

Hand feed pet deer "Lucy" and her lovely fawn in a tranquil setting with white doves, Royal Danish White Deer. Meet "Max" the golden Labrador and "Harry" the silver-grey cat.

Dine in the evening with delicious New Zealand country cuisine and wine. Relax with an open fire and TV in our comfortable sitting room.

We delight in sharing our knowledge of this fascinating area, its history and its wide range of all seasons activities. * Salmon Fishing - Rakaia River * Fishing Guides * Skiing - Mt Hutt Transport from gate * Hot Air Ballooning * Scenic Bush Walks * Horse Riding * Breakfast served to suit your schedule * Trout Fishing - Lakes & Rivers * Hunting - Guides Available * Closest Farm Stay - Ski Area * Golf - Terrace Downs and Methven 18 hole courses - Club Hire * Open Gardens to Visit * Jet Boating * Restaurants nearby * NZAFHH * Host Link NZ.

Directions: Green Gables is on SH77, 4kms north west of Methven - Mt Hutt Village, or from Scenic Route 72 turn into SH77 - travel 5kms towards Methven-Mt Hutt Village. Green Gables is on right.

Green Gables Deer Farm
Farmstay
4km NW of Methven Village
Colleen & Roger Mehrtens
Waimarama Rd
Methven, RD 12
Rakaia

Tel: (03) 302 8308
Fax: (03) 302 8309
Tollfree: 0800 466 093
E: greengables@xtra.co.nz
W: www.nzfarmstay.com

Cost: Double $110-$130
Single $80-$100
Child $35 - $55
Dinner $40 Visa/MC
Beds: 2 Superking
1 Twin/Superking (3 bdrm)
Bath: 2 Ensuite 1 Private

Mt Hutt - Methven

ENJOY Being the only guests, our beautiful 4500 sq ft home- set amidst aged trees, 1.5 acres of rose garden and lawns, wonderful homegrown cuisine, pre dinner drinks- mouth watering NZ wine, "hands on" of our 400 acre Romney Sheep stud farm, fresh air-peace-tranqility-mountain views.

 Local activities include wonderful bush walks, ballooning, Methven's magnificent 18 hole golf course, skiing on Mt Hutt.

We will arrange transport if required. YOU MAY NEVER WANT TO LEAVE.

Directions: From Methven town centre, turn at the Medical Centre down Methven Chertsey Road, 6km on left.

Pagey's Farmstay
Farmstay
6km E of Methven
Shirley & Gene Pagey
Methven - Chertsey Road
Methven

Tel: (03) 302 1713
Fax: (03) 302 1714
E: pageys@ashburton.co.nz
W: www.bnb.co.nz/hosts/
pageysfarmstay.html

Cost: Double $80
        Single $50
        Child 1/2 price under
        12yrs Dinner $25pp
Beds: 1 Queen 1 Double
        4 Single (3 bdrm)
Bath: 1 Guests share

Lake Coleridge - Canterbury Highlands

Adventure and Hospitality in the South Island High Country. Ryton Station is a wonderful place for a personal experience of home hospitality on a working high country sheep station. Scenery is magnificent, the air and water crystal clear. 1 1/2 hours from Christchurch, accessible all year round. Fishing, walks, tramping, station activities, jet boating, 4x4 trips, skiing, peace and quiet. Variety of accommodation for families, groups, individuals. Provide own transport, no pets. Chalets price includes dinner. Lodge: self catering or meals in homestead, price on application

Ryton Station	**Tel:** (03) 318 5818	**Cost:** Double $200 Single $120
B&B Self/C Farmstay Lodge	**Fax:** (03) 318 5819	Child B/A
120km W of Christchuch	**Tollfree:** 0800 92 868	**Beds:** 6 King/Twin 6 Queen
Karen & Mike Meares	**E:** ryton@xtra.co.nz	1 Double (13 bdrm)
Harper Road	**W:** www.ryton.co.nz	**Bath:** 7 Ensuite 1 Private
Lake Coleridge		1 Guests share

Staveley - Mt Hutt

Welcome to our cattle and sheep farm nestled in the Foothills of Mid Canterbury. Relax in our warm comfortable homestead, surrounded by our large tranquil garden extending from the Staveley Village on 'Inland Scenic Route 72'. 75 minutes south west of Christchurch Airport, 10 minutes from Mt Hutt Ski Area, and en route to Mt Cook and Queenstown. Enjoy a walk around our farm, hand feed out pet sheep and meet "Bill" our large black cat. We delight passing on our knowledge of the Geology, History and Attractions in our area.

Awaiti Farmstay	**Tel:** (03) 303 0853	**Cost:** Double $120 Single $60
B&B Farmstay	**Fax:** (03) 303 0851	Child $35 Dinner $25
20km SW of Methven	**E:** graeme.a.c@xtra.co.nz	Visa/MC
Jan & Graeme Crozier	**W:** www.bnb.co.nz/hosts/	**Beds:** 1 King/Twin 1 King
Staveley RD 1 Ashburton	awaitifarmstay.html	1 Queen (3 bdrm)
		Bath: 2 Ensuite 1 Family share

Rakaia

A warm welcome is assured at St Ita's. Built in 1912 this spacious former convent is full of charm, set in an acre of grounds, and located on the western fringe of Rakaia. Nearby: Salmon fishing, horse trekking, golf, tennis, visiting local pubs and winery. Within 30 minutes: Skiing, bushwalks, jetboating, bird watching, Tranzalpine Express. Evening 3 course meals include local produce and NZ wines, Full breakfasts Share the open fire with our cat and golden retriever.

St Ita's Guesthouse	**Tel:** (03) 302 7546	**Cost:** Double $90
B&B Homestay Guesthouse	**Fax:** (03) 302 7546	Single $60
Ken & Miriam Cutforth	**Mob:** 025 233 4670	Dinner $25pp Visa/MC
Barrhill/Methven Road	**E:** st.itas_rakaia@xtra.co.nz	**Beds:** 2 Double 4 Single
Rakaia Village	**W:** www.bnb.co.nz/hosts/	(3 bdrm)
Canterbury	stitasguesthouse.html	**Bath:** 3 Ensuite

Ashburton

Our homestead which captures the sun in all rooms is cosy and inviting. It is situated in a sheltered garden where you can enjoy peace, tranquillity and fresh country air or indulge in a game of tennis. All guest rooms have comfortable beds, electric blankets, reading lamps and tea/coffee making facilities. Laundry and ironing facilities available. Dinner is by arrangement and features traditional New Zealand cuisine. Including home grown meat and vegetables. Breakfast is served with delicious home made jams and preserves.

We have a 220 acre irrigated sheep and cattle farm. You may like to join in farm activities or be taken for a farm tour; sheep shearing demostration available (in season).

As we have both travelled extensively in New Zealand, Australia, United Kingdom, Europe, North America and Zimbabwe. We would like to offer hospitality to fellow travellers. Our hobbies include meeting people, travel, reading, photography, gardening, sewing, cake decorating, rugby, cricket, Jim belongs to the Masonic Lodge and Karen is involved in Community Affairs.

For the weary traveller a spa pool is available. For young children we have a cot and high chair. There is a power point for camper vans.

CARRADALE FARM "WHERE PEOPLE COME AS STRANGERS AND LEAVE AS FRIENDS"

Carradale Farm
B&B Farmstay
8km W of Ashburton
Karen & Jim McIntyre
Ferriman's Rd
RD 8, Ashburton

Tel: (03) 308 6577
Fax: (03) 308 6548
Mob: 025 338 044
E: carradale@ashburton.co.nz.
W: www.ashburton.co.nz/
carradale

Cost: Double $90-$100
Single $60 Child 1/2 price
Caravan powerpoint $25
Dinner $25 Visa/MC
Beds: 1 Double 2 Twin (3 bdrm)
Bath: 1 Ensuite 2 Private

Ashburton

Our comfortable home is situated in a quiet street with the added pleasure of looking onto a rural scene. We are 10-15 mins walk from town or 3-5 mins to riding for the disabled grounds or river walkway. Guest rooms have comfortable beds with electric blankets. We welcome the opportunity to meet and greet visitors and wish to make your stay a happy one. Your hosts are semi-retired hobbies general/varied from meeting people to walking etc. Request visitors no smoking inside home. Laundry facilities available.

Homestay	**Tel:** (03) 308 3534	**Cost:** Double $70
Pat & Dave Weir	**E:** d&pweir@xtra.co.nz	Single $40
1 Sudbury Street	**W:** www.bnb.co.nz/hosts/	Dinner $20 Visa/MC
Ashburton Central	weir.html	**Beds:** 1 Double 2 Single
		(2 bdrm)
		Bath: 1 Family share

Ashburton

Weatherly House is a villa built in 1910 with a "Come In"atmosphere and set in private gardens, with off-street parking and is only a 15 minute walk to town and most amenities, 5 minutes from Ashfords Craft Village. Ashburton is a service town for a large agricultural area, there are five golf courses within half an hour of town and various exciting experiences to enjoy in this district. For your comfort hot drinks etc are always available, a cosy fire in the lounge and electric blankets on all beds.

Weatherly House	**Tel:** (03) 308 9949	**Cost:** Double $70 Single $40
B&B Homestay	**Fax:** (03) 308 9949	Child neg Dinner $20
Helen Thomson	**W:** www.bnb.co.nz/hosts/	Visa/MC
359 West Street	weatherlyhouse.html	**Beds:** 1 Queen 1 Double
(State Highway 1)		2 Single (2 bdrm)
Ashburton		**Bath:** 1 Guests share

Take it easy.

Don't try to travel too far in one day

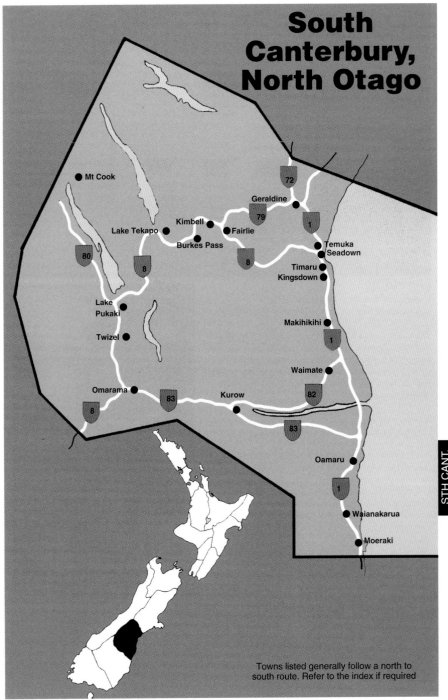

South Canterbury, North Otago

Mt Cook

72

Geraldine

79

Kimbell
Lake Tekapo
Fairlie
Burkes Pass

80

8

8

Temuka
Seadown

Timaru
Kingsdown

Lake
Pukaki

Makihikihi

1

Twizel

Waimate

Omarama

83

Kurow

82

8

83

Oamaru

1

Waianakarua

Moeraki

Towns listed generally follow a north to
south route. Refer to the index if required

Geraldine

Experience New Zealand history on thirty seven tranquil acres near the base of the Four Peaks Range.

The Crossing is a beautifully restored and furnished English style manor house built in 1908. Our spacious lounges have open fires and comfortable seating. A shaded verandah overlooks the lovely gardens, where you can relax and read or enjoy a leisurely game of croquet or petanque.

Enjoy dinner and your choice of beverages in our fully licensed restaurant. Dinners by prior arrangement.

The Crossing is your perfect base for exploring the central South Island. Local attractions include fishing for salmon and trout, white water rafting, nature treks in Peel Forest, and ski fields are nearby. Golfers, spend a week and play fourteen uncrowded courses each within one hours drive. All have low green fees and welcome visitors.

We are located on the main route between Christchurch and Queenstown or Mount Cook. Directions: Signposted on SH 72/79 approx 3 km north of Geraldine, turn into Woodbury Road, then 1 km on right hand side. Children over 12 welcome.

The Crossing
Guest Lodge
3km N of Geraldine
Richard & Barbara Sahlie
124 Woodbury Rd
RD 21
Geraldine

Tel: (03) 693 9689
Fax: (03) 693 9789
E: srelax@xtra.co.nz
W: www.bnb.co.nz/hosts/
thecrossing.html

Cost: Double $160-$190
Single $140-$170
Extra Person $30
Visa/MC/BC
Beds: 1 Queen 2 Queen + single
(3 bdrm)
Bath: 3 Ensuite

Geraldine

"Camberdown" is on Highway 79 between Geraldine and Fairlie, two hours from Christchurch. Our farm is situated in lush green country with mountain views. Bird life abounds in areas of native bush. Relax on our sunny verandah with our cat and spaniel. Susan enjoys patchwork and needlework. Where possible we offer guests homegrown produce. Home made bread, jam, preserves are part of our delicious meals Non - smoking household.

Camberdown
Farmstay
22km SW of Geraldine
Susan & Colin Sinclair
2013 Geraldine/Fairlie Highway
Beautiful Valley, RD 21
Geraldine

Tel: (03) 697 4849
Fax: (03) 697 4849
W: www.bnb.co.nz/hosts/
camberdown.html

Cost: Double $110
Single $80
Dinner $25pp Visa/MC
Beds: 1 Queen 2 Single
(2 bdrm)
Bath: 2 Guests share

Geraldine

We have a charming two storey, character home set in a cottage garden where our cat "Fergus Roe" loves to hide. You will be warmly welcomed on arrival and a refreshing cup of tea or coffee is available in the guest lounge at all times. We are a short stroll to the cafes and restaurants in the charming village of Geraldine which is the ideal first stop from Christchurch (137km) as you travel towards the Southern Lakes and mountains.

Forest View
B&B Homestay
0.5km S of Geraldine
Liz & Ron Jolliffe
128 Talbot Street
Geraldine
South Canterbury

Tel: (03) 693 9928
Fax: (03) 693 9928
Mob: 025 623 6384
Tollfree: 0800 572 740
E: forest.view@xtra.co.nz
W: www.bnb.co.nz/hosts/
forestview.html

Cost: Double $70-$90
Single $55
Dinner $20 by arrangement
Visa/MC Amex
Beds: 1 King 2 Double (3 bdrm)
Bath: 1 Ensuite 1 Private
1 Guests share

Temuka

Ashfield is set on 4 acres of woodlands, 10 minutes walk from shops and restaurants. Built in in 1883 Ashfield features marble fireplaces and gilt mirrors, and a full size snooker table. Two of our upstairs bedrooms open up to a balcony with lovely views of the mountains. We enjoy spending the evening with guests by the open fire. In close proximity are skifields. salmon and trout fishing. So join us for a wonderful stay in a lovely setting. Two cats and two outside dogs. Guests welcome to use laundry.

Ashfield B&B
B&B Homestay
20km N of Timaru
Ann & Martin Bosman
71 Cass Street
Temuka

Tel: (03) 615 6157
Fax: (03) 615 9062
W: www.bnb.co.nz/
hosts/ashfieldbb.html

Cost: Double $88-$100
Single $50-$65
Child neg
Visa/MC Amex Diners
Beds: 1 King 2 Queen 1 Double
(4 bdrm)
Bath: 1 Ensuite 1 Guests share

Timaru - Kingsdown

'Mountain View' is a farmlet on Talbot Road, 200 metres from State Highway 1. Blue and white Bed and Breakfast signs on highway. Semi-retired farmers have hosted for 17 years - pet deer and sheep. Home is situated in tranquil garden overlooking farmland with wonderful views of mountains - quiet - off road parking. Electric blankets - private bathrooms - laundry facilities. Home made bread, jams and cookies. Nearby fishing, golf courses, swimming and walk to sea coast. Day trips comfortably taken to Mt Cook, Hydro Lakes and Ski Fields.

Mountain View Homestay
B&B Rural Homestay
3km S of Timaru
Mary & Graeme Bell
23 Talbot Road
Kingsdown, RD 1, Timaru

Tel: (03) 688 1070
Fax: (03) 688 1069
E: mvhomestay@xtra.co.nz
W: www.bnb.co.nz/hosts/
mountainview.html

Cost: Double $80 Single $55
Child 1/2 price under 12yrs
Dinner $25 by arrangement
Visa/MC
Beds: 1 Double 4 Single (3bdrm)
Bath: 2 Private 1 Family share

Timaru Central

Welcome to our spacious character brick home built in the 1920's and situated in a beautiful garden with a grass tennis court. A secluded property with off street parking and views of the surrounding sea and mountains. Centrally situated, only 5 minutes from the beach and town with an excellent choice of cafes and restaurants. On arrival tea is served on our sunny verandah. Hosts have lived and worked extensively overseas, namely South Africa, U.K and the Middle East, and enjoy music, theatre, tennis and golf. Dinner by arrangement.

Homestay
Margaret & Nevis Jones
16 Selwyn Street
Timaru

Tel: (03) 688 1400
Fax: (03) 688 1400
W: www.bnb.co.nz/hosts/
jonestimaru.html

Cost: Double $80
Single $50 Child 1/2 price
Dinner $25 Visa/MC
Beds: 2 Double 2 Single
(3 bdrm)
Bath: 2 Ensuite 1 Guests share

Timaru - Seadown

Our Homestay is approximately 10 minutes north of Timaru, situated 4.8 kms on Seadown Road off State Highway 1 at Washdyke - second house on left past Pharlap Statue. We have hosted on our farm for 11 years - now retired and have a country farmlet with some farm animals, with views of farmland and mountains. Day trips to Mt Cook, Hydro Lakes and ski fields, fishing, golf course few minutes away. Electric blankets on all beds - laundry facilities available. Interests are farming, gardening, spinning and overseas travel.

Country Homestay
Homestay Country Homestay
4.8km N of Timaru
Margaret and Ross Paterson
491 Seadown Road
Seadown, RD 3
Timaru

Tel: (03) 688 2468
Fax: (03) 688 2468
W: www.bnb.co.nz/hosts/
countryhomestay.html

Cost: Double $75 Single $50
Child 1/2 price Dinner $20
Visa/MC Amex Diners
Beds: 1 Double 2 Single
(3 bdrm)
Bath: 1 Guests share

Timaru

Ethridge Gardens is a beautiful character home built in 1911 set in romantic English style gardens. We offer the very best in hospitality. Guests are encouraged to relax in our spacious sitting room which leads on to the terrace and garden with heated swimming pool. TV in main bedroom. Tea, coffee, chocolates and fresh flowers and robes in the bedrooms. Afternoon tea and complimentary wine, aperitifs on arrival. Excellent restaurants nearby. Children, pets welcome. Wynne is mayor of Timaru, Nan is a renowned NZ gardener.

Ethridge Gardens
B&B
Timaru Central
Nan & Wynne Raymond
10 Sealy Street
Timaru

Tel: (03) 684 4910
Fax: (03) 684 4910
Mob: 025 365 365
W: www.bnb.co.nz/hosts/
ethridgegardens.html

Cost: Double $120
Single $90
Child $40 Visa/MC
Beds: 1 Queen 1 Twin 1 Single
(3 bdrm)
Bath: 1 Private

Timaru

We are retired and offer superior homestay in a classic two storeyed home with a delightful garden situated in a quiet street in central Timaru - 5 minutes walk to the town centre, restaurants and Caroline Bay. The main guest bedroom has 1king/twin and the smaller bedroom has 2 single beds. Laundry facilities are available and a courtesy car can meet guests. We have many interests and look forward to meeting and offering our hospitality to those who prefer homestays.

Bidwill House
Homestay
Timaru Central
Dorothy & Ron White
15 Bidwill Street
Timaru

Tel: (03) 688 5856
Fax: (03) 688 5870
Mob: 025 238 8122
E: bookin@xtra.co.nz
W: www.bnb.co.nz/hosts/
bidwillhouse.html

Cost: Double $90 Single $70
Child 1/2 price
Dinner $15 - $25 b/a
Visa/MC
Beds: 1 King/Twin 2 Single
(2 bdrm)
Bath: 1 Private

Timaru

Welcome to Ballyagan. Our home is among trees and gardens with native birds, small farm walk, pet sheep, cat and dog. Bedrooms have electric blankets and bedside lamps. Restaurants 5 mins to Pleasant Point vintage trains and golf course. We serve Devonshire afternoon tea, herbal-tea and fresh percolated coffee. Samlpe our local wine. Mount Cook ski fields and fishing within reasonable distance. Tea making, laundry facilities available. We enjoy meeting and hosting guests. Directions: SH8 7km from Washdyke. 5km from Pleasant Point. B&B Homestay sign at gate.

Ballyagan
B&B Homestay
5km N of Pleasant Point
Gail & Bill Clarke
State Highway 8 Levels
RD 4, Timaru

Tel: (03) 614 8221
Fax: (03) 614 8221
Mob: 025 653 7663
W: www.bnb.co.nz/
hosts/ballyagan.html

Cost: Double $75 Single $50
Child 1/2 price
Dinner $20 by arrangement
Visa/MC
Beds: 1 Double 4 Single (3 bdrm)
Bath: 1 Guests share 1 Family share

Timaru

Okare is a substantial Edwardian brick residence built in 1909 and offers discerning travellers and small families visiting the region comfortable accommodation with warm welcoming hospitality. Okare offers substantial sunny living spaces for our guests, upstairs there is a super King/twin and two twin rooms with share bathroom and a Double with twin spa-bath ensuite, downstairs a queen room with private facilities. We are situated only five minutes walk from a selection of restaurants, Boudicca's our own, offers a charge back facility. We have a baby and two huskies for your entertainment.

Okare Boutique Accommodation	**Tel:** (03) 688 0316	**Cost:** Double $95-$125 Single $80
Homestay	**Fax:** (03) 688 0368	Child $40 Visa/MC
Malcolm Smith	**Mob:** 025 229 7301	**Beds:** 1 King 1 Queen 1 Double
11 Wai-iti Road	**E:** okare@xtra.co.nz	4 Single (5 bdrm)
Timaru	**W:** www.bnb.co.nz/hosts/	**Bath:** 1 Ensuite 1 Private
	okare.html	1 Guests share

Timaru

Welcome to our warm and comfortable modern home which is a storey and a half, with good views across the City and Mountains. Our home is smoke and pet free and not suitable for children. Tea or coffee is available on arrival. Dinner by arrangement, guest lounge also available, double bedroom opens onto sundeck and secluded garden. Off street parking, laundry facilities available. We have many interests and look forward to offering our hospitality to overseas and local travellers. Please phone for reservations and directions.

Grand View	**Tel:** (03) 686 2044	**Cost:** Double $93
Homestay	**Mob:** 025 355 125	Single $55
Timaru Central	**E:** ronhull@xtra.co.nz	Dinner $25 Visa/MC
Jill & Ron Hull	**W:** www.bnb.co.nz/hosts/	**Beds:** 1 Queen 1 Twin (2 bdrm)
186A Morgans Road	grandview.html	**Bath:** 1 Guests share
Timaru		

Timaru

Our spacious home on 9 acres enjoys the best of both worlds - country living only 3 1/2 kms from the centre of Timaru. Set in 1 1/2 acres of established gardens (in Friars NZ Gardens to visit) with a magnificent view of Mt Cook we offer a relaxed atmosphere, heated swimming pool (summer), private spa pool, Sky TV in bedroom, dinner by arrangement. We run coloured sheep, the wool of which Margaret spins and knits. We enjoy golfing, boating and meeting people. Our family are all away. Children welcome. Phone for directions.

Ranui	**Tel:** (03) 686 1288	**Cost:** Double $85 Single $60
Farmstay Homestay	**Fax:** (03) 686 1285	Child 1/2 price
3.5km NW of Timaru	**Mob:** 025 321 458	Dinner $25 Visa/MC
Margaret & Kevin Cosgrove	**E:** ranui@timaru.com	**Beds:** 2 Queen 1 Double
5 Kellands Hill	**W:** www.bnb.co.nz/hosts/	(3 bdrm)
Timaru	ranui.html	**Bath:** 2 Guests share

Timaru

The "Craigmore Farmhouse" accommodation is within the Manager's Residence. Sheep, deer and cattle are farmed on this limestone hill country. A limestone quarry is operating locally. A commercial Peony area is on the river flat. Export blooms are colourful in November, early December. Maori Rock Art, Cabbage trees, public walkways and a 9 hole golf course are close by. A neighbouring antique business is open September to May. Late September, spring is celebrated amongst daffodils at a Market Day in the Craigmore Homestead Garden.

Craigmore Farmhouse
Farmstay
26km SW of Timaru
Raewyn & Kerry Swann
Craigmore Hill Road
2RD, Timaru

Tel: (03) 612 9822
Fax: (03) 612 9822
Mob: 025 337 718
W: www.bnb.co.nz/hosts/
craigmorefarmhouse.html

Cost: Double $110 - $120
Single $70 Dinner $25
Beds: 1 King 1 Queen 1 Single
(3 bdrm)
Bath: 1 Ensuite 1 Private
1 Guests share

Makikihi - Waimate

Welcome to Alford Farm situated halfway between Dunedin and Christchurch. June and Ken offer Kiwi hospitality, comfortable beds, electric blankets, delicious meals and a relaxed atmosphere in a smoke free home. Enjoy a complimentary farm tour and see our farm dog performing. We raise cattle and deer. Visitors are welcome to view or participate in farm activities. We enjoy Square Dancing, hosting and gardening. Please feel free to call. 4kms south of Makikihi turn inland into Lower Hook Road. Alford Farm is 2nd on right (2kms).

Alford Farm
Farmstay
37km S of Timaru
June & Ken McAuley
Lower Hook Road
RD 8
Waimate

Tel: (03) 689 5778
Fax: (03) 689 5779
Mob: 025 267 6008
E: alfordfarmstays@paradise.net.nz
W: www.bnb.co.nz/hosts/
alfordfarm.html

Cost: Double $75
Single $50
Dinner $20 Visa/MC
Beds: 1 Double 2 Single
(2 bdrm)
Bath: 1 Family share

Fairlie

Our farm consists of 400 acres producing fat lambs, cattle and deer, with numerous other animals and bird life. The house is situated in a large English style garden with many mature trees in a tranquil setting. In the area are two skifields, golf courses, walkways and scenic drives. Informative farm tours available. Our interests include golf, gardening and music. Directions: Travel 1 km from town centre, along Tekapo highway, then turn left into Nixon's Road when two more kilometers will bring you to the "Fontmell" entrance.

Fontmell
Farmstay Homestay
3km W of Fairlie
Anne & Norman McConnell
Nixons Road 169
RD 17, Fairlie

Tel: (03) 685 8379
Fax: (03) 685 8379
W: www.bnb.co.nz/hosts/
fontmell.html

Cost: Double $80-$100
Single $55 Child $25
Dinner $20
Beds: 2 Double 4 Single
(3 bdrm)
Bath: 1 Guests share

STH CANT, NTH OTAGO

Fairlie

Welcome to the MacKenzie Country. Our new home is situated 2 hours south of Christchurch and 3 1/2 hours north of Queenstown on the main highway. We are on a 50 acre hobby farm block with spectacular views of the mountains. Our 2 guest apartments have their own lounges with tea making facilities, but we hope you will join us for refreshments and a chat. We are interested in hunting and tramping. Our fare includes mainly home made and local produce. Relax with us and our resident puss Snoopy.

Braelea Countrystay
B&B Homestay
3km E of Fairlie
Sandra, Les & Gerry Riddle
State Highway 79
Fairlie
South Canterbury

Tel: (03) 685 8366
Fax: (03) 685 8943
Mob: 025 203 5151
Tollfree: 0800 222 723
E: braeleabandb@hotmail.com
W: www.bnb.co.nz/hosts/
braeleacountrystay.html

Cost: Double $90-$140
Single $60 Child neg
Dinner $20pp Visa/MC
Beds: 1 King/Twin 1 King
1 Queen 2 Single
(3 bdrm)
Bath: 2 Private

Kimbell - Fairlie

Welcome to my one acre paradise; a haven of peace and tranquility offering quality country comfort and hospitality. I am a well travelled writer with a passion for mountains, literature and good conversation. I enjoy cooking and gardening and use home grown produce wherever possible. Take time out for fishing, skiing, walking, golf or water sports. Relax in the garden, complete with stream and cat, or come with us to some of our favourite places. Complimentary refreshments on arrival. Laundry facilities and internet access available.

Rivendell Lodge
Country Homestay
8km W of Fairlie
Joan Gill
Stanton Road
Kimbell, RD 17, Fairlie

Tel: (03) 685 8833
Fax: (03) 685 8825
Mob: 025 819 189
E: Rivendell.lodge@xtra.co.nz
W: www.fairlie.co.nz/rivendell

Cost: Double $95 Single $55
Child neg Dinner $30
Visa/MC
Beds: 2 Queen 3 Single
(3 bdrm)
Bath: 2 Private 1 Family share

Kimbell - Fairlie

Our homestead is an elegant early 1900's villa tastefully restored with the comfort of modern amenities. Heated rooms open onto verandahs overlooking the garden where there are numerous quiet spots to sit and relax and view the surrounding mountains. We have the usual menagerie of farm animals including pet lambs, hens, pigs, house cows, mares and foals, sheep dog and cocker spaniel as well as the household moggy. Locally there is skiing, golf, fishing and tramping. Our home is smoke free with children most welcome.

Poplar Downs
Farmstay Homestay
7km W of Fairlie
Shirl & Robin Sinclair
Mt Cook Road
Kimbell, RD 17
Fairlie

Tel: (03) 685 8170
Fax: (03) 685 8210
E: bigred@es.co.nz
W: www.bnb.co.nz/hosts/
poplardowns.html

Cost: Double $90
Single $60
Child neg Dinner $25
Visa/MC
Beds: 1 King/Twin 1 Double
(2 bdrm)
Bath: 1 Ensuite 1 Private

Kimbell - Fairlie

Imagine - your own fully self contained chalet set in
secluded privacy on 10 acres. Escape and unwind in an
atomosphere of peace and tranquillity. Breakfast in the sun
or dine at dusk on the large private deck surrounded by
panoramic views of mountians and countryside. Enjoy the
proximity to skiing, tramping, fishing, and golf. Ideal for
couples, families or groups alike. We have an assortment of
animals and plenty of room for children to play. All
ingredients for a full country breakfast included in tariff.

The School House
B&B Self-contained
8k W of Fairlie
Carolyn Todd
Kimbell-Park, Stanton Road
Kimbell 17 RD, Fairlie

Tel: (03) 685 8152
Fax: (03) 685 8154
Mob: 025 837 596
E: kimbell-park@xtra.co.nz
W: kimbell-park.co.nz

Cost: Double $95
Single $50
Child negotiable Visa/MC
Beds: 4 Single 1 Queen
(2 bdrm)
Bath: 1 Private

Burkes Pass

Come and share with us our unique glacier stone homestead
with exceptional character set in 17 acres. We are nestled in
a picturesque valley, with views of Mount Dobson and
close to Lake Tekapo. We are on the main tourist route
approximately halfway between Christchurch and
Queenstown. There is a small restaurant at Burkes Pass
settlement. Our interests include photography, crafts and
travel. We have one cat, a friendly collie and pet sheep. As
well as the Lodge, self-contained railway carriage
accommodation is available.

Dobson Lodge
B&B Country Homestay
23km E of Lake Tekapo
Margaret & Keith Walter
Dobson Lodge
RD 17, Burkes Pass

Tel: (03) 685 8316
Fax: (03) 685 8316
E: dobson_lodge@xtra.co.nz
W: www.mtcook.org.nz/
dobsonlodge/

Cost: Double $95, $120, $160
Single $70-$100 Child neg
Dinner $25pp Visa/MC
Beds: 2 Queen 1 Double
1 Single (3 bdrm)
Bath: 2 Ensuite 1 Family share

Lake Tekapo

Holbrook is a high country sheep station of 14,000 hectares
(35,000 acres) on State Highway 8 between Burkes Pass
and Lake Tekapo. Our cottage is near our homestead, is
fully self contained, warm, spacious and comfortable. We
provide electric blankets, feather duvets, log fire, telephone,
TV, automatic washing machine, cot and highchair and
everything necessary to make your stay with us an
enjoyable experience. There is a small lake available for
trout fishing near our cottage. Breakfast optional and extra.
Dinner by arrangement.

Holbrook Cottage
Self-contained
12km E of Lake Tekapo
Lesley & Alister France
PO Box 4
Fairlie

Tel: (03) 685 8535
Fax: (03) 685 8534
Mob: 025 387 974
E: lesley@holbrook.co.nz
W: www.kiwi-nz.com

Cost: Double $90
Breakfast $10 -$14
$15 per extra person
Beds: 1 Queen 6 Single
(3 bdrm)
Bath: 1 Guests share

STH CANT,
NTH OTAGO

Lake Tekapo

Experience tranquillity and a touch of mountain magic. A warm and friendly welcome. Comfortable home, mountain and lake views. Rimu panelling, heart timber furniture, attractive decor, blending with the McKenzie Country. Bedrooms in private wing overlooking garden, two opening onto balcony. Mt Cook one hour away. Walkways nearby. Views of skifield. Our cat "Missy" welcomes you. Five minutes to shops and restaurants. From SH8 turn into Lakeview Heights and follow green B&B sign into Barbara Hay Street. Then right and see our Freda Due Faur sign.

Freda Du Faur House
B&B
40km E of Fairlie
Dawn & Barry Clark
1 Esther Hope Street
Lake Tekapo

Tel: (03) 680 6513
W: www.bnb.co.nz/hosts/
fredadufaurhouse.html

Cost: Double $99 Single $65
Child under 5 half price
Visa/MC
Beds: 1 Queen 1 Double
2 Single (3 bdrm)
Bath: 1 Guests share

Lake Tekapo

Built by Grant, our three storied home with expansive balconies offers panoramic views of the Southern Alps, Mt John, Lake Tekapo and surrounding mountains. All rooms are spacious and comfortable, with guest lounge and separate guest entrance. A NZ native garden adds an attractive feature. Restaurants in township. Our two daughters are 11 & 13 years, we live on the ground floor with two cats thus separate from our guest accommodation. Grant is a professional flyfishing guide (NZPFGA) and offers guided tours.

Creel House
B&B
43km W of Fairlie
Grant & Rosemary Brown
36 Murray Place
Lake Tekapo

Tel: (03) 680 6516
Fax: (03) 680 6659
E: creelhouse.l.tek@xtra.co.nz
W: www.bnb.co.nz/hosts/
creelhouse.html

Cost: Double $130-$140
Single $70
Off-season $100 double/twin
Visa/MC
Beds: 2 Queen 1 Twin (3 bdrm)
Bath: 1 Ensuite 2 Private

Lake Pukaki - Mt Cook

A quiet place to stop, halfway between Christchurch and Queenstown or Christchurch and Dunedin via Waitaki Valley. 40 minutes to Mt Cook. The 18,000 acre property has been in the family 80 years. Merino sheep graze to 6,000 feet, Hereford cattle. Views of the Southern sky the homestead is set in tranquil gardens afternoon tea/drinks served on the veranda, have a cat and dog. Twizel has a bank, doctor, restaurants, shops. Dinner by arrangement. Please phone for bookings and directions. Cot available.

Rhoborough Downs
Homestay
12km N of Twizel
Roberta Preston
Lake Pukaki
PB, Fairlie

Tel: (03) 435 0509
Fax: (03) 435 0509
Tollfree: 0800 420 007
E: ra.preston@xtra.co.nz
W: www.bnb.co.nz/hosts/
rhoboroughdowns.html

Cost: Double $90
Single $50
Child $30 Dinner $25
Beds: 1 Double 3 Single
(3 bdrm)
Bath: 1 Guests share

Lake Pukaki

"A place of unsurpassed beauty" located on the shores of Lake Pukaki with magnificent views of Mount Cook and the Southern Alps. Our local stone home blends in with the natural peaceful surrounds. Your host, an ex RAF pilot, has rich pioneering and surprisingly wide experiences. This high country farm, in the family since 1914, runs mainly cattle with crops grown for self-sufficiency. This is your great opportunity to experience true farm life with friendly hosts and a good natured corgi and cat.

Tasman Downs Station	**Tel:** (03) 680 6841	**Cost:** Double $100 Single $60
Farmstay	**Fax:** (03) 680 6851	Dinner $30pp
27km Lake Tekapo	**W:** www.bnb.co.nz/hosts/	**Beds:** 1 Double 2 Single
Linda, Bruce & Ian Hayman	tasmandownsstation.html	(2 bdrm)
Lake Tekapo		**Bath:** 1 Private
		1 Family share

Twizel

Haere Mai ki Aoraki (Welcome to Aoraki Lodge). If you prefer a casual informal atmosphere with friendly genuine "kiwi" hosts then Aoraki Lodge is the place for you. Relax in our warm, sunny home and enjoy our private garden. Kerry is of Maori descent and would love to share with you her knowledge of Maori culture and history. Steve is a wellknown flyfishing guide and can offer helpful advice and information on all the attractions in the area. We look forward to meeting you.

Aoraki Lodge	**Tel:** (03) 435 0300	**Cost:** Double $110-$130
Homestay	**Fax:** (03) 435 0305	Single $80 Dinner $40pp
Kerry & Steve Carey	**Mob:** 021 142 8229	Visa/MC
32 Mackenzie Drive	**E:** aorakilodge@xtra.co.nz	**Beds:** 1 Queen 2 Double
Twizel/Mt Cook 8773	**W:** www.bnb.co.nz/hosts/	4 Single (4 bdrm)
	aorakilodge.html	**Bath:** 4 Ensuite 1 Family share

Twizel

Welcome to our lovely, large Homestay Lodge, only 45 minutes from Mt Cook. Luxuriously appointed guest rooms feature ensuites with spa baths. Guests are invited to join us for a complimentary pre-dinner drink before sharing a delicious 3 course dinner complemented by New Zealand wine (by prior arrangement) or dining at one of several nearby restaurants. Our black Labrador, Megan and donkey, Monty, will extend a warm welcome. "The Loft" - a large self-contained loft above our garage sleeps up to 7. Directions: Please phone

Heartland Lodge	**Tel:** (03) 435 0008	**Cost:** Double $140 Single $90
Homestay + Self-contained	**Fax:** (03) 435 0387	Child neg Dinner $45 B/A
Loft	**Mob:** 025 927 778	'Loft' from $70
2km W of Twizel	**Tollfree:** 0800 164 666	Visa/MC Amex Diners
Dave & Jenny Pullen	**E:** european@xtra.co.nz	**Beds:** 2 King Double/Twin
19 North West Arch	**W:** www.bnb.co.nz/hosts/	(2 bdrm)
Twizel, South Canterbury	heartlandlodge.html	**Bath:** 2 Ensuite

STH CANT, NTH OTAGO

Omarama

Omarama Station is a merino sheep and cattle property adjacent to the Omarama township. The 100 year old homestead is nestled in a small valley in a tranquil parklike setting of willows, poplars and a fast flowing stream (good fly fishing), pleasant walking environs, and interesting historical perspective to the high country as this was the original station in the area. Swimming pool and a pleasant garden. An opportunity to experience day to day farming activities. Dinner by arrangement.

Omarama Station	**Tel:** (03) 438 9821	**Cost:** Double $100 Single $60
Farmstay	**Fax:** (03) 438 9822	Child $20 - $50
1km S of Omarama	**E:** wardell@paradise.net.nz	Dinner $30
Beth & Dick Wardell	**W:** www.bnb.co.nz/hosts/	**Beds:** 2 Queen 2 Single
Omarama	omaramastation.html	(3 bdrm)
North Otago		**Bath:** 1 Ensuite 1 Private

Kurow

The perfect place for those wanting to get away from traffic noises, enjoy home cooked meals, have a comfortable bed, relax and be treated as one of the family. Our 4000 acre high country farm has merino sheep and beef cattle. Either on farm or nearby is horse riding, four wheel drive farm tour, walking/tramping, fishing (guide available), golf. ALSO AVAILABLE - SELF CONTAINED COTTAGE, $15pp. Full kitchen, linen supplied. DIRECTIONS: Situated at end of Gards Road which 10km east of Kurow on right or 13 km west of Duntroon on left.

Glenmac	**Tel:** (03) 436 0200	**Cost:** Double $70-$90 Single $35-$45
Self-contained Farmstay	**Fax:** (03) 436 0202	Child 1/2 price Dinner $20
Campervans or tents	**Mob:** 025 222 1119	S/C $15pp Visa/MC
60km W of Oamaru	**E:** glenmac@xtra.co.nz	**Beds:** 1 Queen 2 Double 1 Twin
Kaye & Keith Dennison	**W:** www.farmstaynewzealand.co.nz	(4 bdrm)
RD 7K, Oamaru		**Bath:** 1 Ensuite 1 Guests share
		1 Family share

Kurow

Western House, built in 1871, as an accomodation house is surrounded by extensive garden and orchard with mountain views. Enjoy wood fires, fresh flowers, hearty breakfasts and wholesome dinners. A warm welcome awaits guests for an enjoyable stay with us and our cat simba. Attractions: Trout and salmon fishing (guide available), golf (clubs on-site), tennis, squash, walks, mountain biking, 4WD, swimming pool, beehive tours, and historic water wheel built 1899.

Western House	**Tel:** (03) 436 0876	**Cost:** Double $100-$120
B&B Self-contained Homestyle	**Fax:** (03) 436 0872	Single $90 Dinner $35
2.7km E of Kurow	**E:** mbparish@xtra.co.nz	Visa/MC
Bridgette & Michael Parish	**W:** www.westernhouse.co.nz	**Beds:** 1 Queen 1 Double
Highway 83		1 Twin 1 Single (4 bdrm)
Kurow		**Bath:** 1 Ensuite 1 Private
North Oago		1 Guests share

Oamaru

Our modern home is situated high above the North end of Oamaru with superb views to the east and the mountains in the west. We have four children, all happily married, and an ever increasing number of grand children. We have been home hosting for the last ten years and although recently retired from farming, still enjoy the buzz of meeting new friends. Our interests include gardening and tramping.

Wallfield	**Tel:** (03) 437 0368	**Cost:** Double $70
Homestay	**Mob:** 025 284 7303	Single $40
Pat & Bill Bews	**E:** b&pbews@xtra.co.nz	**Beds:** 1 Double 2 Single
126 Reservoir Road	**W:** www.bnb.co.nz/hosts/	(2 bdrm)
Oamaru	wallfield.html	**Bath:** 1 Guests share

Oamaru

Want to be pampered? "Tara" is the place for you. Enjoy the comfort and luxuries of our character Oamaru stone home. "Tara" boasts all day sun and the privacy to soak up the country atmosphere. Nestled amongst eleven acres of roses, mature trees and rural farmland "Tara" is the perfect place to unwind. Our livestock include Alpacas, coloured sheep, donkeys and an aviary. We also have a Burmese cat and a Lassie Collie. My husband Baxter and I will ensure your visit is an enjoyable experience.

Tara	**Tel:** (03) 434 8187	**Cost:** Double $85
Homestay	**Fax:** (03) 434 8187	Single $50
8km SW of Oamaru	**E:** smith.tara@xtra.co.nz	Dinner $25 B/A
Marianne & Baxter Smith	**W:** www.tarahomestay.com	**Beds:** 2 Single (1 bdrm)
Springhill Road		**Bath:** 1 Private
3 ORD, Oamaru		

Oamaru

We have a charming, character home surrounded by gardens, in a quiet street near the main highway. Our guest bedrooms are well appointed. Tea or coffee is available. Dinner by arrangement is preceded by drinks beside the fire. We have travelled, and enjoy meeting people, especially visitors to New Zealand. Oamaru has many fine, stone, Victorian buildings. Enjoy one of Oamaru's many lovely walks, the attractive public gardens, or visit our art gallery, museum or penguin colony. A warm welcome awaits you. Family cat.

Homestay	**Tel:** (03) 434 9628	**Cost:** Double $120 Single $75
Oamaru Central	**W:** www.bnb.co.nz/hosts/	Dinner $35
Jenny & Gerald Lynch-Blosse	lynchblosse.html	**Beds:** 1 Double 2 Single
11 Stour Street		(2 bdrm)
South Hill, Oamaru		**Bath:** 1 Private 1 Family share

STH CANT, NTH OTAGO

Oamaru - Waianakarua

Spacious, Oamaru-stone, Homestead in the country with
beautiful views. Two open fires in winter (one in book-lined
Snug). Really comfortable beds, music, books, peace, for
your enjoyment. Roses and wisteria bloom beside large
verandahs overlooking acres of sloping, green lawns. A
sparkling river and huge forest, on our boundary. Song-
birds enchant and our two Retrievers, McDuff and Adam
delight in greeting. Mishka the ginger pussycat follows on
behind. Our surrounding fields shelter hens, steers and fruit
trees. Larger parties catered with Glen Dendron (sleeps six).

Glen Foulis	**Tel:** (03) 439 5559	**Cost:** Double $90 Single $55
Homestay	**Fax:** (03) 439 5220	Child $30 Campervans $25
25km S of Oamaru	**Mob:** 021 940 777	Dinner $12 - $25 Visa/MC
Margaret & John Munro	**E:** hjm@wxc.net.nz	**Beds:** 1 King/Twin
39 Middle Ridge Road	**W:** www.bnb.co.nz/hosts/	2 Single (2 bdrm)
Waianakarua	glenfoulis.html	**Bath:** 1 Guests share
ORD 9, Oamaru		1 Family share

Oamaru

A unique private pole house nestled into the side of a
hill with panoramic views of the town and ocean.
Catering for business executives and independent free
travellers. I specialise in charter deep sea fishing on
my own boat "Dolphin'. Local interests are: Penguin
viewing, Whitestone Buildings. Bookings essential.
After a three hour drive from Christchurch International Airport my guests have found "Innwoodleigh" to
be relaxing and quiet. All have marvelled at the view.
Fully serviced exclusive private level with satellite TV.

Innwoodleigh	**Tel:** (03) 437 0829	**Cost:** Double $110
B&B Homestay	**Fax:** (03) 437 0829	Single $55
2km N of Oamaru	**Mob:** 025 299 4731	**Beds:** 1 Double 2 Single
Howard Bradley	**W:** www.bnb.co.nz/hosts/	(2 bdrm)
39 Forth Street	innwoodleigh.html	**Bath:** 1 Private
Oamaru		

Waianakarua - Oamaru

As caring hosts we aim to provide unique experiences for
guests. Quality, modern facilities, panoramic views, large
developing garden, bush and riverside walks, farm and district
tours. Private golf course available. Following lifetime
involvement in large scale farming and forestry , we now
enjoy developing our garden, nursery and small sheep farm,
Interests include overseas travel, reading, Lions and floral art.
Close to famous Moeraki boulders, penguin and seal colonies,
beaches, forests and Oamaru's historic buildings. Do join us
for dinner. We don't mind short notice.

Glen Dendron	**Tel:** (03) 439 5288	**Cost:** Double $90 Single $55
B&B Farmstay	**Fax:** (03) 439 5288	Child $30 Dinner $25
30km S of Oamaru	**Mob:** 021 615 287	Visa/MC
Anne & John Mackay	**E:** anne.john.mackay@xtra.co.nz	**Beds:** 1 Queen 4 Single
284 Breakneck Road	**W:** www.bnb.co.nz/hosts/	(3 bdrm)
ORD 9, Oamaru	glendendron.html	**Bath:** 2 Guests share

Oamaru

Unique private family home, built early 1900's, solid Oamaru limestone walls. Close to town, restaurants, and the Blue Penguin Colony. Three rooms, ensuite, private and shared facilities. Nature, fishing and garden tours can be arranged. Electric blankets and feather duvets. Own TV or share our spacious living areas. Wrap around smoking verandah. Breakfast in our spacious conservatory (Wintergarden). Off street parking. We pride ourselves on our home baking and preserves. Sherry (our cat), Wenda and John welcome you to our home.

Clyde House
B&B Homestay
15min walk Oamaru Central
Wenda & John Eason
32 Clyde St
Oamaru

Tel: (03) 437 2774
Fax: (03) 437 2774
Mob: 025 603 1363
E: eason.clydehouse@xtra.co.nz
W: www.clydehouse.co.nz

Cost: Double $80-$95
　　　　Dinner $25 Child $25
　　　　Studio Unit $150 Visa/MC
Beds: 1 King 1 Queen 1 Double
　　　　1 Single (3 bdrm)
Bath: 1 Guests share 1 Ensuite
　　　　1 Private 1 Family share

Oamaru

We look forward to sharing our retirement haven with visitors from overseas and New Zealand. Our modern home and separate guest flat are set in a peaceful and private large garden. Feed the gold fish and pamper Oscar our cat. Our guest flat is sunny, warm and comfortable. We have travelled overseas and enjoy helping visitors discover our district's best kept secrets! Like yellow and blue eyed penguins, gardens, Moeraki Boulders, beaches, pool, fishing and golf - the list goes on.

Springbank
Self-contained Homestay
3km S of Oamaru
Joan & Stan Taylor
60 Weston Road
Oamaru

Tel: (03) 434 6602
Fax: (03) 434 6602
Mob: 025 669 2902
W: www.bnb.co.nz/hosts/
springbank.html

Cost: Double $75
　　　　Single $40
Beds: 1 Double 1 Twin
　　　　(1 bdrm)
Bath: 1 Private

Moeraki - Oamaru

Indulge yourself and enjoy warm hospitality at our country retreat by the sea. We invite you to join us for a traditional New Zealand dinner then relax by the fire in our charming 1920's homestead. Breakfast with the bellbirds then stroll along the beautiful beach to Moeraki Boulders and quaint fishing village. Sheep farm tours a speciality. Stay with us while you explore the penguins, seals, historic Oamaru, golf courses and antique shops nearby. We are enroute to Christchurch, Dunedin, Queenstown and Mt. Cook.

Moeraki Boulder Downs
Farmstay - B&B
B&B Farmstay
38km S of Oamaru
Jan & Ken Wheeler
State Highway 1, Moeraki
RD 2, Palmerston

Tel: (03) 439 4855
Fax: (03) 439 4355
Mob: 025 614 6396
E: farmstay@moerakiboulders.co.nz
W: www.moerakiboulders.co.nz

Cost: Double $80-$90
　　　　Single $50
　　　　Child $35 Dinner $25
　　　　Visa/MC
Beds: 1 Queen 3 Single
　　　　(2 bdrm)
Bath: 1 Guests share

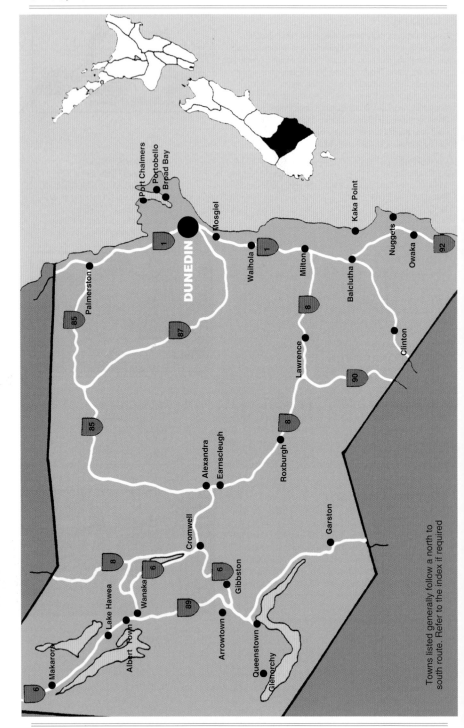

Towns listed generally follow a north to south route. Refer to the index if required

Makarora

Nestled in native bush, our unique home and cottage are secluded and quiet. Originally from the United States, we have lived in Makarora for over 25 years and like sharing our mountain retreat and enjoying good food and conversation. Many activities are available locally, including jetboat trips, scenic flights, bird watching, guided fishing, and bush walks. We can provide mountain bikes, fishing rods and sea kayaks for use on Lake Wanaka. Laundry facilities are available. 10% discount for stays of 3 days or longer.

Larrivee Homestay	**Tel:** (03) 443 9177	**Cost:** Homestay: Double $110
Homestay	**E:** andipaul@xtra.co.nz	Single $80
Self-contained Cottage	**W:** www.bnb.co.nz/hosts/	Cottage: Double $100
65km N of Wanaka	larrivee.html	$20 each extra
Andrea and Paul		Dinner $35 BYO
Makarora via Wanaka		**Beds:** 4 Double 2 Single (4 bdrm)
		Bath: 1 Private 1 Guests share

Lake Hawea

I am a retired school teacher - now a craft dyer of silk, a spinner and cross-country skier. My three-storied A-frame is in a sheltered compound with many specimen trees. One guest room has an ensuite, the other opens to a balcony; both have mountain views. Access via a circular staircase. Washing machine available. Lake Hawea two minutes walk away. I have a cat and small dog. Directions: From Wanaka-Haast Rd turn off to Lake Hawea - past hotel to store - see A-frame through Archway.

Sylvan Chalet	**Tel:** (03) 443-1343	**Cost:** Double $70
Homestay	**Mob:** 025 224 9192	Single $35
15km N of Wanaka	**E:** lyallc@xtra.co.nz	Child $20
Lyall Campbell	**W:** www.inow.co.nz/	**Beds:** 1 Double 2 Single
4 Bodkin St	sylvanchalet	(2 bdrm)
Lake Hawea, RD 2 Wanaka		**Bath:** 1 Ensuite 1 Family share

Lake Hawea

We are a retired English couple, well travelled and actively involved in outdoor pursuits. Our main interests are flyfishing, tramping and skiing, but we happily share our local knowledge of all the opportunities this wonderful area offers. Situated at the eastern foot of Haast Pass, close to Mt Aspiring National Park and local skifields, our comfortable modern home features sundeck overlooking secluded garden with mountain views. Lakeshore 5 minutes stroll. All inclusive stays/excursions negotiated to individual requirements. Dinner by arrangement. 7 Day restaurant nearby.

HILLKIRK HOUSE

HillKirk House	**Tel:** (03)443 1655	**Cost:** Double $85 Single $50
B&B Homestay	**Fax:** (03) 443 1655	Child 1/2 price under 12
13km N of Wanaka	**W:** www.bnb.co.nz/hosts/	Dinner $25
Doreen & Mike Allen	hillkirkhouse.html	**Beds:** 1 King 4 Single
117 Noema Terrace		(2 bdrm)
Lake Hawea Central Otago		**Bath:** 1 Ensuite 1 Family share

Wanaka

Relax with us in our warm comfortable home ideally
situated Centre Wanaka. Magnificent lake and mountain
views, just 3 minutes walk to shops and restaurants. We
both enjoy golf, skiing, boating, outdoor activities. Peter is
keen fly fisherman. Good comfortable beds, electric
blankets, hairdryers, heaters, smoke free home. Tea, coffee,
muffins, homemade biscuits any time. We offer a cooked
breakfast. We both enjoy helping people, hosted guests for
16 years. "Kim" our Labrador is everyone's friend.
Directions: 4 blocks back Lake Front, opposite school.
Reservations: Freephone 0800 443799

Lake Wanaka Homestay	**Tel:** (03) 443 7995	**Cost:** Double $90 Single $55
Homestay	**Fax:** (03) 443 7945	Child neg
Wanaka Central	**Tollfree:** 0800 443 799	**Beds:** 1 Double 2 Single (2 bdrm)
Peter & Gailie Cooke	**E:** wanakahomestay@xtra.co.nz	**Bath:** 1 Guests share
85 Warren Street Wanaka	**W:** www.wanakahomestay.co.nz	1 Family share

Wanaka

Located only 2 minutes drive from the centre of Wanaka, the
careful blending of the old and the new create at Oak Ridge a
holiday experience unique in terms of comfort, design,
location and ambience. Central to the development is a
purpose-built hunting, fishing and skiing lodge. The existing
lodge was extensively remodelled (July 2000) and new
wings added to provide a range of accommodation designed
to cater for the most judicious traveller. Fully licensed
restaurant & bar offering sumptuous a la carte dining.

Oak Ridge Lake Wanaka	**Tel:** (03) 443 7707	**Cost:** Double $160-$240 Single
Boutique Accommodation	**Fax:** (03) 443 7750	$144-$216 Child neg
2km Wanaka Central	**Tollfree:** 0800 869 262	Fully licensed restaurant/bar
Rowland & Nora Hastings and	**E:** info@oakridge.co.nz	Visa/MC Amex
John & Beth Haryett	**W:** www.oakridge.co.nz	**Beds:** 12 King/Twin (12 bdrm)
cnr Cardrona Valley &		**Bath:** 12 Ensuite
Studholme Roads		
PO Box 220 Wanaka		

Wanaka

The challenge - portray Wanaka and our homestay in 85 words!
Wanaka is: magical; tranquil; dramatic; refreshing; exhilarating;
captivatingly beautiful. **Wanaka has:** activities both challenging
and restful, fascinating history, distinctive micro-climate, ecological
diversity, mountain light ever changing. **Our homestay offers:**
informative welcoming hosts, warmth and comfort, lake and
mountain views, adjacent park with lake access, mountain bikes to
ride. **We are:** ex-teachers with musical, sporting, photographic and
Rotary interests; well travelled both nationally and internationally,
qualified to help with NZ itineraries.

Aspiring Images	**Tel:** (03) 443 8358	**Cost:** Double $100-$110
Homestay	**Fax:** (03) 443 8327	Single $60-$75 Child $25
Wanaka	**Mob:** 025 378 503	Dinner $35 B/A Visa/MC
Betty & George Russell	**E:** grussell@xtra.co.nz	**Beds:** 1 King/Twin 1 Double
26 Norman Terrace	**W:** www.bnb.co.nz/hosts/	(2 bdrm)
Wanaka	aspiringimages.html	**Bath:** 1 Ensuite 1 Private
		1 Guests share

Wanaka

We enjoyed home hosting for many years on our farm near Wanaka and took pleasure helping our guests discover the charms of the area. We welcome you to our new home set on an acre in a quiet cul-de-sac with wonderful views of Lake Wanaka and mountains bordering a reserve on the shores of the lake. As the house was purpose built for home hosting guests enjoy their own luxuriously furnished private wing with a sitting room and beautifully landcaped courtyard. Recommendation, "lovely interesting hosts, superb stay".

Atherton House
Roy & Kate Summers
3 Atherton Place
Wanaka
Otago

Tel: (03) 443 8343
Fax: (03) 443 8343
Mob: 025 228 1982
E: roy.kate@xtra.co.nz
W: www.bnb.co.nz/hosts/
athertonhouse.html

Cost: Double $120
Single $110
Dinner $45 Visa/MC
Beds: 1 Queen 1 Twin
(2 bdrm)
Bath: 2 Ensuite

Wanaka

Without exception, our guests acclaim our panoramic view the best in Wanaka. This glorious grandstand action scene from lounge and bedrooms equals any spectacular mountain vista in New Zealand. Our home overlooks the lake and is an easy five minute walk to shops, restaurants and all facilities. We assure you of a quiet, comfortable relaxed and enjoyable stay in friendly surroundings. Plenty of secure on-site parking. No pets. Up little street opposite Post Office, turn left along Lismore Street to 102 opposite pine tree.

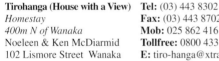

Tirohanga (House with a View)
Homestay
400m N of Wanaka
Noeleen & Ken McDiarmid
102 Lismore Street Wanaka

Tel: (03) 443 8302
Fax: (03) 443 8702
Mob: 025 862 416
Tollfree: 0800 433 554
E: tiro-hanga@xtra.co.nz
W: www.bnb.co.nz/hosts/
tirohanga.html

Cost: Double $100-$110
Single $75
Beds: 2 King/Twin
(2 bdrm)
Bath: 2 Ensuite

Lake Wanaka

Our new home "Beacon Point" B & B is surrounded by 1 acre of lawn and garden for your enjoyment. It leads to a walking track to the village around the edge of the lake with snow capped mountains in winter. Private spacious studio with ensuite, Queen and single beds (2 rooms), kitchen, T.V, and sundeck. Studio equiped with every need for a perfect stay. We are very flexable and enjoy planning your days with you. Our intrests include farming, forestry, fly fishing, real estate, boating, gardening and our grandchildren. Turn right at lake - Lakeside Road - then to Beacon Point Road 302.

Beacon Point
B&B Self-contained Homestay
Wanaka
Diana & Dan Pinckney
302 Beacon Point Road
PO Box 6 Lake Wanaka

Tel: (03) 443 1253
Fax: (03) 443 1254
Mob: 025 246 0222
E: dan.pinckney@harcourts.co.nz
W: www.bnb.co.nz/hosts/
beaconpoint.html

Cost: Double $90-$120
Child $30 Dinner $30
Beds: 1 Queen 1 Twin
(2 bdrm)
Bath: 2 Private

Wanaka

We take pride in offering a friendly, comfortable home. Share breakfast and our awesome lake and mountain views with us. Also explore our extensive garden which provides a tranquil environment for relaxing. Recent guests' comments: '..surely one of the best B&Bs in NZ', '..nicest hosts we have encountered. I'll always remember the long breakfast talks', '..No Contest. The best 2 nights stay I've had in NZ. Long live the best pancake house'. We offer a drink and muffins on your arrival. Smokefree home.

Harpers
B&B Homestay
1km N of Wanaka
Jo & Ian Harper
95 McDougall Street
Wanaka

Tel: (03) 443 8894
Fax: (03) 443 8834
E: harpers@xtra.co.nz
W: www.bnb.co.nz/hosts/
harpers.html

Cost: Double $100
Single $60 Visa/MC
Beds: 1 King/Twin
2 Single (2 bdrm)
Bath: 1 Ensuite
1 Guests share

Wanaka

Our home is set in a developing two acres about five minutes drive from Wanaka. All beds have electric blankets, tea and coffee is freely available. We have extensive views of surrounding mountains. Children are welcome. Child care by arrangement. Our nearby tree collection has an accent on autumn colour. Local walks a speciality. Organic fruit both in season and preserved. We have twin twelve year old girls, a small dog, and two cats. No smoking inside please. Please phone for directions.

Stonehaven
Homestay Rural
4km S/ of Wanaka
Deirdre & Dennis
Halliday Lane
RD 2 Wanaka

Tel: (03) 443 9516
Fax: (03) 443 9513
E: moghul@xtra.co.nz
W: www.stonehaven.co.nz

Cost: Double $95
Single $60
Child $20 neg Visa/MC
Beds: 1 Queen 1 Double
2 Single (2 bdrm)
Bath: 1 Ensuite 1 Private

Wanaka

Temasek House offers its guests the luxury of their own separate upper floor area equipped with TV, log fire, coffee and tea making facilities, extensive reading collection, large sun-deck, small kitchenette and most importantly for travellers - a washing machine and dryer (small additional charge). We survive downstairs with our two young children. They try to organise everything - although if it gets overwhelming, we can lock them away with the cat! We try to keep fit - you are welcome to join us for a run, make use of our bikes , or even accompany us to the local gym.

Temasek House
B&B Self-contained Homestay
Wanaka Central
Poh Choo & David Turner
7 Huchan Lane
Wanaka 9192

Tel: (03) 443 1288
Fax: (03) 443 1288
Mob: 025 277 9594
E: temasek.house@xtra.co.nz
W: www.wanakahomestay.co.nz/
temasek.html

Cost: Double $105 Single $55
Child $20 Twin $90
Visa/MC
Beds: 2 King/Twin 1 Queen
1 Double (3 bdrm)
Bath: 1 Ensuite 1 Guests share

Wanaka

Fifty years ago, a spectacular garden was created at Dublin Bay on the tranquil shores of Lake Wanaka. Its beauty still blooms today against a backdrop of the majestic Southern Alps. Accommodation is private, comfortable and elegantly decorated.

The Stone Cottage offers two self-contained loft apartments with breathtaking views over lake Wanaka to snow clad alps beyond. Featuring your own bathroom, bedroom, kitchen, living room and balcony. Television, fax and email available. Private entrance.

Enjoy breakfast at leisure, made from fresh ingredients from your well stocked fully equipped kitchen, Pre dinner drinks, delicious 3 course dinner and NZ wines or a gourmet picnic hamper is available by arrangement.

Walk along the beach just 4 minutes from The Stone Cottage or wander in the enchanting garden. Guests can experience trout fishing, nature walks, golf, boating, horse riding, wine tasting and ski fields nearby.

Only 10 minutes from Wanaka, this is the perfect retreat for those who value privacy and the unique beauty of this area.

Relax in the magic atmosphere at The Stone Cottage and awake to the dawn bird chorus of native bellbirds and fantails.

The Stone Cottage
B&B Self-contained
10km N of Wanaka
Belinda Wilson
Wanaka
RD 2
Central Otago

Tel: (03) 443 1878
Fax: (03) 443 1276
E: stonecottage@xtra.co.nz
W: www.bnb.co.nz/hosts/
thestonecottage.html

Cost: Double $200-$220
Single $175
Child 1/2 price
Dinner $60 Visa/MC
Beds: 1 King 2 Double
2 Single (2 bdrm)
Bath: 2 Private

Wanaka

Welcome to our modern home in Wanaka where we will greet you with tea or coffee in our smoke-free house and settle you in your spacious ground-floor accommodation. After farming near Wanaka, we built this house over looking the mountains and lake, and so have a good knowledge of the area. Through our membership of Lake Wanaka Tourism we are kept informed of all tourist activities in the area. Our interests are golf, gardening, travel and meeting people. We have no resident children or pets.

Hunt's Homestay
Homestay
2min N of Wanaka
Bill & Ruth Hunt
56 Manuka Crescent
Wanaka 9192
Central Otago

Tel: (03) 443 1053
Fax: (03) 443 1355
Mob: 025 265 0114
E: hunts.homestay@xtra.co.nz
W: www.inow.co.nzhuntshomestay

Cost: Double $100
Single $60
Child & Dinner B/A
Visa/MC
Beds: 1 Queen 2 Single
(2 bdrm)
Bath: 1 Guests share

Wanaka

Purpose built for bed & breakfast accommodation, rooms are large with own dressing rooms and ensuite bathrooms. Beds are luxuriously fitted with quality linen, feather duvets and electric blankets. Decor accented with native timber, fresh flowers, Italian art, Belgium rugs, Scottish leather and English linens. Wide open views of lake and mountains , a walk to lake edge for fishing, swimming or secluded relaxation. Central heating plus two fireplaces keep us cosy. Breakfast is varied and generous. We have two Pharaoh Hound dogs you may choose to meet. We certainly look forward to meeting you.....

Anubis Lodge
Homestay Lodge
Wanaka Central
Michele and Bob Mercer
264 Beacon Point Road
Wanaka

Tel: (03) 443 7807
Fax: (03) 443 7803
Mob: 025 221 7387
E: m.b.mercer@xra.co.nz
W: www.wanakahomestay.co.nz

Cost: Double $145
Single $100
Visa/MC
Beds: 2 King 1 Queen
2 Single (3 bdrm)
Bath: 3 Ensuite

Wanaka

We welcome visitors to Wanaka, enjoy sharing our natural surroundings with others. We have a large peaceful home where our guests can experience not only the austerity of the lake and mountains around them, but also experience the ambience of Wanaka itself. guest room with super king bed has adjoining TV lounge with TV, tea coffee facilities, private bathroom. Good laundry facilities. We wish your stay in Wanaka will be a very happy one. Directions: please ring for directions. We enjoy your company.

Lake Wanaka Home Hosting
B&B Homestay
2km N of Wanaka Central
Joyce & Lex Turnbull
19 Bill's Way
Wanaka

Tel: (03) 443 9060
Fax: (03) 443 1626
Mob: 025 228 9160
E: lex.joy@xtra.co.nz
W: www.lakewanaka
homehosting.co.nz

Cost: Double $100-$125
Single $65
Child $25 Dinner $30
Beds: 1 King/Twin 1 Double
1 Twin (3 bdrm)
Bath: 2 Private

Wanaka

Northridge is situated on a ridge with stunning views of the Lake and Mountains and within walking distance to restaurants, shops and the lakefront. Our quality 4brm 2 storey stone & natural timber home lends itself to indoor/ outdoor living, where you can have refreshments served whilst taking in the breathtaking views. All rooms are large and beds are complete with wool underlays, feather duvets and quality linen. Our home is centrally heated and has a fireplace to ensure warmth & comfort for those cosy winter evenings. Come & share our piece of paradise with us.

Northridge	**Tel:** (03) 443 8835	**Cost:** Double $120-$140
B&B	**Fax:** (03) 443 1835	Single $85 Visa/MC
Richie & Sue Heathfield /	**Mob:** 025 950 436	**Beds:** 2 Queen 2 Single
Atkinson	**E:** s.atkinson@xtra.co.nz	(3 bdrm)
11 Botting Place	**W:** www.wanakahomestay.co.nz	**Bath:** 1 Ensuite 1 Private
PO Box 376 Wanaka	/northridge.html	1 Guests share

Wanaka

'Crofthead' - named after the family farm - is situated right on the edge of picturesque Lake Wanaka. Stroll along the lake front to shops and restaurants which are within easy walking distance. Our modern timber and stacked stone home is set in a peaceful English cottage garden complete with mature trees and masses of roses. We offer uninterrupted mountain and lake views, secluded courtyard areas for relaxed outdoor living, cosy log fire, spa bath and washing and drying facilities.

Crofthead B&B	**Tel:** (03) 443 8883	**Cost:** Double $100-$110
Boutique B&B Accommodation	**Fax:** (03) 443 6683	Single $60-$70
Wanaka Central	**W:** www.bnb.co.nz/hosts/	**Beds:** 1 Queen
Joan & Rodger Cross	croftheadbb.html	2 Single (2 bdrm)
20 Mt Aspiring Road		**Bath:** 1 Ensuite 1 Private
Wanaka		

Wanaka

The township's newest boutique lodge, constructed from local timbers and stone, this 'in-town retreat' is set in a peaceful oasis surrounded by natural springs, landscaped gardens- yet only a 3 minute stroll from the centre of Wanaka. Savour our special breakfast buffet and afternoon tea in the sunny dining room or from your private deck/ courtyard- all with stunning views. Or unwind with apertifs in the sumptuous lounge withs its blazing log fire. Wanaka Springs- a unique experience of informal sophistication for the discerning traveller. New Zealand Tourism Awards Finalist 2001/2002 for Hosted Accommodation.

		Cost: Double $190-$250
		Adjacent Luxury Home
Wanaka Springs Lodge	**Tel:** (03) 443 8421	Rental $350
Boutique Lodge	**Fax:** (03) 443 8429	Visa/MC Amex Diners
Wanaka Central	**Mob:** 025 903 175	**Beds:** 5 Queen 3 Twin (8 bdrm)
Linzi & Brian Ebbage - Thomas	**E:** relax@wanakasprings.com	**Bath:** 8 Ensuite
21 Warren Street	**W:** www.wanakasprings.com	
Wanaka 9192 Central Otago		

Wanaka

Nestled in the heart of Wanaka, Te Wanaka Lodge is a two minute walk to the lake, restaurants, shops and golf course. Tastefully decorated with fishing and skiing memorabilia, Te Wanaka Lodge has a distinctive Alpine ambience.

On a hot summer's day laze under our walnut tree with a cool drink from the House Bar, or in winter relax by the warmth of our log fire after enjoying a soak in our secluded garden hot tub.

- All bedrooms with ensuite and private balcony
- Full cooked breakfast included
- House Bar specialising in local beers and wines
- Sky TV, video, CD and book library
- Off street parking
- Ski drying room and laundry service
- Full business facilities

Te Wanaka Lodge
B&B Luxury Lodge
Wanaka Central
Graeme & Andy Oxley
23 Brownston Street
Wanaka

Tel: (03) 443 9224
Fax: (03) 443 9246
Mob: 021 345 996
Tollfree: 0800 WANAKA
      0800 92 62 52
E: tewanakalodge@xtra.co.nz
W: www.tewanaka.co.nz

Cost: Double $140-$175
     Single $130-$155
     S/C Cottage $175 - $190
     Visa/MC Amex
Beds: 8 Queen 4 Twin (12 bdrm)
Bath: 12 Ensuite

Wanaka

Parklands Lodge, nestled on 10 acres of rural land 6km from Wanaka, has spectacular mountain views, a refuge from the hustle and bustle of urban life. We have a guest dining room, 2 lounge rooms, cosy fires, laundry facilities, spa, swimming pool, BBQ area and a 5 hole pitch and putt golf course and a self-contained apartment. We have a golden labrador dog. Guests are served a continental and cooked breakfast. Wanaka is a destination on its own with great activities and only 45 min by car from Queenstown.

Parklands Lodge
B&B Luxury Lodge S/C Apt.
6km from Wanaka
60km E of Queenstown
Margaret and Lawrence Mikkelsen
Ballantyne Road
RD2 Wanaka

Tel: +(64-3) 443 7305
Fax: +(64-3) 443 7345
Mob: 025 955 160
E: parklandslodge@xtra.co.nz
W: www.parklandswanaka.co.nz

Cost: Double $210 Single $185
Child $20.00 Dinner $35.00
S/C. $225 Visa/MC Amex
Beds: 3 King/Twin 2 Queen
2 Twin (6 bdrm)
Bath: 4 Ensuite
1 Guests share

Wanaka

Smiths Settlement Bed and Breakfast   OPENING JANUARY 2002   A secluded private location nestled beside the Cardrona River in a rural setting. Two double bedrooms, one with an ensuite. Just 5 minutes to the base of the Cardrona Resort Skifield ,The historic Cardrona Hotel and the Wairau Nordic Skifield. Only 10 minutes to Wanaka and 45 minutes to Queenstown.   Come and enjoy a relaxing stay with us .   We have two Golden Retriever dogs and three cats that will just love all your attention.

Smiths Settlement B&B
B&B
16 KM S of Wanaka
Chris & Mat Andrews
Cardrona Valley Road
R.D. 2 Wanaka

Tel: 03 4436680
Fax: 03 4436690
Mob: 025 836261
E: MAT-CHRIS.A@xtra.co.nz
W: www.bnb.co.nz/hosts/
smithssettlementbb.html

Cost: Double $100
Single $80
Beds: 1 Double (2 bdrm)
Bath: 1 Ensuite 1 Family share

Wanaka

"Riversong" ... named after the soft lament of nearby Clutha River, is situated at historic Albert Town, five minutes from Wanaka. Riversong is the heart of Central Otago's natural and scenic beauty, trout fishing, three skifields, Mt Aspiring National Park, and much more. My background is healthcare and Ian's law. We invite you to share the comfort of our home and garden and Ian's knowledge of the region's fishing. We are committed to providing a friendly and relaxed atmosphere. We have two outside lab dogs. Directions: Albert Town is 6km north of Wanaka on State Highway 6 to Haast. Turn downriver at bridge over Clutha Riverand travel to end of Wicklow Terrace. Property signposted.

Riversong
B&B Homestay
6km N of Wanaka
Ann Horrax
5 Wicklow Terrace
Albert Town, RD 2 Wanaka

Tel: (03) 443 8567
E: info@happyhomestay.co.nz
W: www.happyhomestay.co.nz

Cost: Double $100
Single $75
Dinner B/A Visa/MC
Beds: 1 King/Twin 1 Single
(2 bdrm)
Bath: 1 Guests share

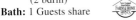

Wanaka

We welcome guests to our lovely home on six developing acres with river boundary. Just 100 metres from SH 84 and 2.5km from Lake Wanaka and township. We offer you our friendly, peaceful environment with mountain and rural views. In winter, warm and cosy by the fires, or in summer cool outdoor living. We have 2 cats and an extremely friendly small dog. Our boat is available for charter fishing or lake cruising. Our son is an experienced trout fishing guide. Dinner available by arrangement.

Riverside
B&B Homestay
2.5km E of Wanaka
Lesley & Norman West
27 Riverbank Road
RD 2
Wanaka

Tel: (03) 443 1522
Fax: (03) 443 1522
Mob: 025 601 4640
E: n.l.west@paradise.net.nz
W: www.bnb.co.nz/hosts/
riverside.html

Cost: Double $95
    Single $60
Beds: 1 Queen 2 Twin
    (2 bdrm)
Bath: 1 Guests share

Wanaka

Welcome to our new home in Wanaka that offers the most spectacular views. Breathtaking and uninterrupted lake, town and mountains. Relax in our guest lounge or on your own private balcony and soak up the wonderful sights. After experiencing some of Wanaka's many attractions enjoy a pre-dinner drink before venturing on a 2 minutes stroll to one of our many delightful restaurants. Or stay home to a delicious 3 course meal which is available by prior arrangements. Each room has electric blankets and TV.

Ponderosa B&B
B&B
Wanaka central
Janice & Mark Cochrane
10 Lismore Street
Wanaka

Tel: (03) 443 4644
Fax: (03) 443 4645
Mob: 025 928 820
W: www.bnb.co.nz/hosts/
ponderosabb.html

Cost: Double $250-$280
    Single $150-$200
    Child 1/2 price
    Dinner $60 B/A Visa/MC
Beds: 1 Queen 1 Twin (2 bdrm)
Bath: 1 Ensuite 1 Guests share

Cromwell

Apricots and Hospitality are our specialty. We offer good food and company and welcome you to join us anytime. Enjoy the privacy of our spacious guest room with ensuite, TV, fridge and teamaking facilities. Private entrance and verandahs overlooks gardens and Lake Dunstan. Queenstown, Wanaka High adventure experiences 45 minutes drive, or relaxing visits to vineyards, orchards in around Cromwell. Lakeside walks with Jessica May, Golden Labrador or fireside chats with feline George. Excellent golfing nearby your choice - Members Lions International. Laundry - Smoke free - unsuitable for children.

Cottage Gardens
Orchardstay
1km N of Cromwell
Jill & Colin McColl
3 Alpha Street
Cromwell Central Otago

Tel: (03) 445 0628
Fax: (03) 445 0628
E: eco@xtra.co.nz
W: www.bnb.co.nz/hosts/
cottagegardens.html

Cost: Double $75
    Single $40-$55
    Dinner $20 Visa/MC
Beds: 1 Twin 4 Single (3 bdrm)
Bath: 1 Ensuite
    2 Family share

Cromwell - Northburn

You are invited to stay at my peaceful and modern lakeside home located in Central Otago, a rapidly expanding wine growing region. Panoramic views from your sunny room include Lake Dunstan and surrounding mountains. Both rooms have total privacy with their own entrances. One has its own deck, tea making facilities, fridge, microwave and TV. Another room has twin beds, TV and sitting room. I enjoy making pottery in my studio and supply local galleries. I have two friendly pets, a dog Guinness and cat, Tom.

Quartz Reef Creek B&B	**Tel:** (03) 445 0404	**Cost:** Double $100 Single $60
B&B Self-contained	**Fax:** (03) 445 0404	Twin Room $90
4km N of Cromwell	**W:** www.bnb.co.nz/hosts/	Visa/MC
June Boulton	boulton.html	**Beds:** 1 Queen 1 Twin 1 Single
Quartz Reef Creek		(2 bdrm)
RD 3, Northburn, State Highway		**Bath:** 1 Ensuite 1 Private
8 Cromwell		

Cromwell

Welcome to Hiburn Farmstay, ideally situated between main tourist attractions yet off the beaten track at Cromwell, The Centre of beautiful Central Otago. Farming 400 hectares with Merino sheep and deer. Guests are welcome to join in and farm activities always included. Amazing working sheepdogs, great home cooking, children welcome. No pets. Peaceful and quiet, an ideal place to explore this region. Interests include sport, curling, gardening, handcrafts, sheepdog competitions. We treat our guests as friends and invite you to share our paradise.

Hiburn	**Tel:** (03) 445 1291	**Cost:** Double $90 Single $60
Farmstay	**Fax:** (03) 445 1291	Child $30 Dinner $20
10km NW of Cromwell	**Tollfree:** 0800 205 104	**Beds:** 1 Double 2 Single
Claire & Jack Davis	**E:** hiburn@xtra.co.nz	(2 bdrm)
RD 2	**W:** www.bnb.co.nz/hosts/	**Bath:** 1 Guests share
Cromwell Central Otago	hiburn.html	

Cromwell

Friendly hospitality awaits you at our home privately situated beside Lake Dunstan. We are ex-Southland farmers and have a cat "Ollie". Our interests include "Lions", fishing, boating, gardening and crafts. Bedrooms have attached balconies, fridge, tea and coffee facilities. Guests share our living areas, spa pool and laundry. Local attractions: orchards, vineyards, gold diggings, fishing, boating, walks, 4 ski fields nearby. Enjoy dinner with us or just relax in the peaceful surroundings. No smoking indoors please. Directions: 5km north of Cromwell Bridge on SH8.

Lake Dunstan Lodge	**Tel:** (03) 445 1107	**Cost:** Double $100-$110
Homestay Lodge	**Fax:** (03) 445 3062	Single $60 Child neg
6km N of Cromwell	**Mob:** 025 311 415	Dinner $25pp B/A
Judy & Bill Thornbury	**W:** www.bnb.co.nz/hosts/	Visa/MC Amex
Northburn	lakedunstanlodge.html	**Beds:** 1 Queen 3 Single (3 bdrm)
RD 3 Cromwell		**Bath:** 1 Ensuite 1 Guests share

Cromwell - Lowburn

Let our home be your home for your visit to Central Otago - beautiful in all seasons! Our spacious home is on 4 acres, almost surrounded by a working orchard and with mountain views and glimpse of Lake Dunstan. Each comfortable non-smoking guestroom has ensuite, TV, telephone and tea/coffee-making facilities. Breakfast is served when it suits you. We have two Siamese cats, a Labrador dog and our interests include meeting people, travel, fishing and exploring Central Otago. Please ring ahead to make a reservation.

Walnut Grove
B&B Homestay
1.5km N of Cromwell
Adrian & Olivia Somerville
State Highway 6
Lowburn, RD 2, Cromwell
Rapid No 67

Tel: (03) 445 1112
Fax: (03) 445 1115
Mob: 025 774 695
E: walnut.grove@xtra.co.nz
W: www.walnutgrove.co.nz

Cost: Double $120
　　　Single $105
　　　Visa/MC
Beds: (2 bdrm)
Bath: 2 Ensuite

Cromwell - Bannockburn

Living among the golden hills of Bannockburn, we welcome you to our new home and relaxing garden environment. Enjoy the privacy of our guest living that include 2 rooms and big bathroom, TV, hairdryer, tea/coffee, laundry facilities available. Breakfast is served to suit you. We are surrounded by local wineries, vineyards and historic Bannockburn gold mine sites. Maurice is a Scenic Artist with work shown in galleries and exhibitions. Janette likes meeting people and offers the Dutch language. Please phone ahead to make a reservation.

Aurum
B&B Self-contained Homestay
6km Cromwell
Janette & Maurice Middleditch
RD 2, Bannockburn
Lawrence Street - Short Street

Tel: (03) 445 2024
Fax: (03) 445 2027
W: www.bnb.co.nz/hosts/
aurum.html

Cost: Double $95
　　　Single $70
　　　Visa/MC
Beds: 1 Queen 1 Double
　　　(2 bdrm)
Bath: 1 Guests share

Arrowtown

We are a retired business couple who have travelled extensively. We welcome our guests to a peaceful, spacious, sunny self-contained upstairs suite complete with kitchen, and a balcony with panoramic views of surrounding mountains and the famous Millbrook golf resort. Meet our friendly Cocker Spaniel. Extra continental breakfast with freshly baked bread, jams etc is provided in your suite; or join us for a cooked starter. Complimentary laundry, road bikes, gold mining gear, BBQ etc. Our courtesy car is an Archbishop's 1924 Austin drophead coupe.

Bains Homestay
Self-contained Homestay
18km NE of Queenstown
Ann & Barry Bain
R32 Butel Road
Arrowtown Otago

Tel: (03) 442 1270
Fax: (03) 442 1271
Mob: 025 274 3360
E: bainshomestay@ihug.co.nz
W: www.dotco.co.nz/
bainshomestay

Cost: Double $90-$105
　　　Child neg Visa/MC
Beds: 1 Queen 4 Single
　　　(2 bdrm)
Bath: 1 Ensuite 1 Private

Arrowtown

Rowan Cottage is situated in a quiet tree lined street with views to the mountains and hills. We are 10 minutes walk to the town and 20 minutes drive to Queenstown. We have a lovely cottage garden to relax and have coffee and homemade goodies. We are well travelled and can advise you on things to see and do in our beautiful part of the country. Guests comments: Wonderful Hospitality - Very Comfortable - Excellent Breakfasts.

Rowan Cottage	**Tel:** (03) 442 0443	**Cost:** Double $80
Homestay	**Mob:** 025 622 8105	Single $50
19km E of Queenstown	**W:** www.bnb.co.nz/hosts/	Dinner $25pp
Elizabeth & Michael Bushell	rowancottage.html	**Beds:** 1 Double 2 Single
9 Thomson Street		(2 bdrm)
Arrowtown		**Bath:** 1 Guests share

Arrowtown

Our spacious home overlooking Millbrook Country Club and the Wakatipu Basin, offers spectacular views from every window. Although only 5 minutes walk from the town centre, our outlook is totally rural. We have a warm and comfortable home with plenty of space inside and out. During the Summer join us for a glass of wine beside our heated swimming pool, which is there for your use. Free use of laundry. Freephone: 0800 184 990

Arrowtown Homestay	**Tel:** (03) 442 1747	**Cost:** Double $100
Homestay	**Fax:** (03) 442 1787	Single $50
Arrowtown	**Tollfree:** 0800 184 990	**Beds:** 1 King 2 Single (2 bdrm)
Anne & Arthur Gormack	**E:** agormack@xtra.co.nz	**Bath:** 2 Private
18 Stafford Street	**W:** www.bnb.co.nz/hosts/	
Arrowtown	arrowtownhomestay.html	

Arrowtown

Daphne and Bill, retired business couple, have restored and renovated their quaint cute and cosy 100 year old cottage, nestled in an attractive garden, surrounded by spectacular hills, mountains. Bill retired from Ford Dealer Industry; Have both travelled widely; Can inform on all local attractions and offer our warm hospitality, completely private ensuite facilities. 3 minutes from historic Arrowtown, 15 minutes to Queenstown. Try Daph's home preserves. Comments: "Highlight of our trip". "Thanks for Memory". 6 year old cat named Maggie. Directions: Polly-Anna sign at front gate.

Polly-Anna Cottage	**Tel:** (03) 442 1347	**Cost:** Double $85-$90
B&B Self-contained	**Fax:** (03) 442 1307	Single $55-$60 Child $20
20km N of Queenstown	**Mob:** 025 220 3974	Dinner $25 Visa/MC
Daphne & Bill MacLaren	**W:** www.bnb.co.nz/hosts/	**Beds:** 1 Double 2 Single (2 bdrm)
43 Bedford Street Arrowtown	pollyannacottage.html	**Bath:** 1 Ensuite 1 Private

Arrowtown

A friendly welcome awaits you with tea or coffee on the patio of our home overlooking Arrowtown which is a popular holiday destination because of its charm and tranquillity. We are only 20 minutes drive from Queenstown where all the venturesome attractions are found. We have travelled widely and are keen trampers, and enjoy gardening, golf, computing and helping other people to enjoy the beauty of our area. Laundry is complimentary. Off street parking. We have a cat. Please phone, Fax or E mail for bookings.

Homestay	**Tel:** (03) 442 1092	**Cost:** Double $85
20km N of Queenstown	**Fax:** (03) 442 1092	Single $55 Dinner $25
Wicky & Norman Smith	**E:** norman@queenstown.co.nz	**Beds:** 1 Queen 2 Single
13 Stafford Street	**W:** www.bnb.co.nz/hosts/	(2 bdrm)
Arrowtown	smitharrowtown.html	**Bath:** 1 Guests share

Arrowtown

Located in the historic part of Arrowtown. Arrowtown Lodge and Hiking Company is only 200 metres from the centre of Arrowtown where guests can enjoy a good selection of restaurants, cafes and pubs. Arrowtown Lodge was completed in 1999 and is built in the old style using schist and mud brick. The four cottage style suites have king or queen size beds, TV, tea and coffee making facilities, hair driers, heated floors, guest phones, private guest entrance and off street car parking. Children welcome. Ancient Labrador resident. Guided walks available.

Arrowtown Lodge & Hiking Co	**Tel:** (03) 442 1101	**Cost:** Double $120-$150
B&B B&B Lodge	**Fax:** (03) 442 1108	Single $70-$100
Arrowtown Central	**Tollfree:** 0800 258 802	Visa/MC Amex
John & Margaret Wilson	**E:** hiking@queenstown.co.nz	**Beds:** 2 King/Twin 2 Queen
7 Anglesea Street	**W:** www.arrowtownlodge.co.nz	(4 bdrm)
Arrowtown		**Bath:** 4 Ensuite

Arrowtown

You will be made very welcome at my home which is centrally located on the main road, entering Arrowtown from Queenstown. I am three blocks from the Arrowtown village centre. My accommodation for guests has a private entrance, double bedroom, small sitting room with TV and tea/coffee making facilities. Also a private bathroom with laundry facilities. Delicious continental or full breakfast is served in the dining room upstairs. Elderly cat in residence. Off street parking. Only 20 minutes drive to Queenstown.

Self-contained	**Tel:** (03) 442 1126	**Cost:** Double $90
Arrowtown Central	**Mob:** 025 344 738	Single $70
Pam Miller	**W:** www.bnb.co.nz/hosts/	Dinner n/a
23 Berkshire Street	miller.html	**Beds:** 1 Queen (1 bdrm)
Arrowtown		**Bath:** 1 Private

Arrowtown

Listed as an Historic Feature, the Old Nick is so called because it was the constable's cottage & office for the region - the property adjoins the old jail. Cosy and warm, it is built of half meter-thick stone walls and high ceilings & is 2 minutes' walk from the shops & restaurants of Historic Arrowtown, - close enough to walk, far enough to be tranquil. Join us for generous cooked breakfast in our grand farmhouse kitchen and relax by the open fireplace in spacious lounge. Complimentary laundry, BBQ. Share our hospitality with our 4 year old son Daniel.

Arrowtown Old Nick	**Tel:** (03) 442 0066	**Cost:** Double $120-$150
B&B Self-contained	**Fax:** (03) 442 0066	Single $90-$120
Central Arrowtown	**Mob:** 025 239 6091	Visa/MC
Marie & Steve Waterhouse	**E:** host@oldnick.co.nz	**Beds:** 4 King/Twin
70 Buckingham Street	**W:** www.oldnick.co.nz	(4 bdrm)
Arrowtown		**Bath:** 3 Ensuite 1 Private

Arrowtown - Gibbston Valley

Nestling among the grape vines in the Gibbston Valley is our stone cottage - offering a comfortable relaxed holiday in the country yet 1 kilometre from the main Queenstown-Cromwell highway. The cottage has been restored from an historic stable sitting in a garden of trees from the era. The area offers beautiful Central Otago scenery and gives easy access to local wineries and ski-fields. Only 10 minutes to Arrowtown with its golf courses, historic buildings and many restaurants. Our Labrador JR/Fox terrier and Siamese cat are eager to see you.

Coal Pit Vineyard	**Tel:** (03) 442 5339	**Cost:** Double $95
Self-contained Homestay	**Fax:** (03) 442 5339	Single $70
15km E of Arrowtown	**W:** www.bnb.co.nz/hosts/	Child $15 Dinner $25pp
Claire & Alan Perry	coalpitvineyard.html	**Beds:** 1 Queen 2 Single
Gibbston Coal Pit Road,		(2 bdrm)
RD 1 Queenstown		**Bath:** 1 Private

Arrowtown - Queenstown

Golden Hills is a superior, distinctive home surrounded by a three acre award winning garden. It has four large bedrooms each with its own bathroom and all the extras one would expect in this charming, spacious, sunfilled house. Email, phone, fax, refreshments, laundry and library included. The farm has thirty acres and is easy to find on main Highway 6. Travelling from North: continue past Arrowtown turn off 300 metres. Travelling from South: turn right at Frankton onto Highway 6, drive 11km, well signposted. Welcome!

Golden Hills Homestead	**Tel:** (03) 442 1427	**Cost:** Double $110-$130
B&B Farmstay	**Fax:** (03) 4421 427	Single $80 Child 1/2 price
4km S of Arrowtown	**Mob:** 025 238 8388	**Beds:** 4 Queen 2 Single
Patricia Sew Hoy	**E:** goldhill@queenstown.co.nz	(4 bdrm)
Golden Hills RD 1, Highway 6	**W:** www.bnb.co.nz/hosts/	**Bath:** 3 Ensuite 1 Private
Queenstown	goldenhills.html	

Arrowtown - Queenstown

Willowbrook is a 1914 farmhouse at the foot of Coronet Peak in the beautiful Wakatipu Basin. The setting is rural, historical and distinctly peaceful, and with the attractions of Queenstown only 15 minutes away, Willowbrook can truly claim to offer the best of both worlds.

The old homestead has been beautifully renovated and while the character of the original house has been retained, it now boasts such modern comforts as central heating, Sky TV and a luxurious spa pool. Guest rooms all contain a bed (or beds) more comfortable than you would find in most hotels and are ensuite or have a private bathroom.

The front deck is an ideal spot to sit back and watch hanggliders drifting down from Coronet Peak while in the colder months, enjoying one of the open fires in the lounge following an apres-ski spa can be addictive.

We have a tennis court in the garden and are within easy reach of 4 skifields and 3 golf courses. An Anglo/Japanese couple with a wealth of 'cross cultural experiences', we are only too happy to help with local bookings and itineraries in general.

Directions: We are on Malaghan Road (the 'back road' between Queenstown and Arrowtown). From Queenstown, take Gorge Road out through Arthurs Point, make no turns and after about 15 minutes, look for our sign on your right. From the north, turn right at Lake Hayes, go 5km and turn left into Malaghan Road. Millbrook Resort is on your left and we are 3 1/2 km further along the road, also on the left.

Coming Soon: "The Shearers Quarters" - a cosy self-contained cottage.

Willowbrook
Guesthouse
4km W of Arrowtown
Tamaki & Roy Llewellyn
Malaghan Road
RD 1
Queenstown

Tel: (03) 442 1773
Fax: (03) 442 1773
Mob: 025 516 739
E: info@willowbrook.net.nz
W: www.willowbrook.net.nz

Cost: Double $120-$140
Single $105-$125
Child POA
Visa/MC Amex Diners JCB
Beds: 1 King 1 Queen 2 Single
(3 bdrm)
Bath: 2 Ensuite 1 Private

Arrowtown - Queenstown

You are warmly invited to stay with us in our modern, classic style country home set in a sunny, sheltered two acre garden. Relax in a private, tranquil setting or enjoy a game of tennis on our court. The house is single storeyed with good access and easy parking. There is a spacious, elegant guest room (ensuite) with its own entrance, and a choice of twin or double bedroom. Located halfway between Arrowtown and Queenstown. Nearby attractions include cafes, restaurants, wineries, skifields and golf courses. Come and enjoy this unique area.

Birchwood	**Tel:** (03) 442 3499	**Cost:** Double $110-$140
B&B Homestay	**Fax:** (03) 442 3498	Single $100
11km N of Queenstown	**Tollfree:** 0800 36 45 50	Child 1/2 price Visa/MC
Richard and Lynne Farrar	**E:** bnb@birchwood.net.nz	**Beds:** 1 King 1 Double
78 Lower Shotover Road	**W:** www.birchwood.net.nz	2 Single (3 bdrm)
RD 1 Queenstown		**Bath:** 1 Ensuite 1 Private

Queenstown

The Retreat is one of the longest established in New Zealand, and Ileen is an internationally acclaimed specialist in Natural Healing. Recharge your energies in the renowned magical garden tucked away in 4 acres of total seclusion. Balcony bedrooms fully appointed with all the extras providing the ultimate in comfort. Lounge, sun decks, organically grown foods and deep tissue massage is available. Directions: Approaching Queenstown downhill, turn right at 2nd round-a-bout into Gorge Road + 1km to shops on left - 2 signposts up Bowen Street to the Retreat.

Bush Creek Health Retreat	**Tel:** (03) 442 7260	**Cost:** Double $120
Homestay Health Retreat	**Fax:** (03) 442 7250	Single $60
1km N of Queenstown	**W:** www.bnb.co.nz/hosts/	Child 1/2 price
Ileen Mutch	bushcreek.html	**Beds:** 1 Queen 4 Single
21 Bowen Street		(3 bdrm)
Queenstown		**Bath:** 2 Guests share

Queenstown

Our home in a sunny situation overlooking Lake Wakatipu has guest rooms with handbasins, electric blankets, bedside lamps and heaters. Bathroom with separate toilet. Also laundry facilities. We are retired farmers having hosted tourists for a number of years. Dinner, including wine, is available by arrangement. Full cooked breakfast available if required. Shopping centre, restaurant, airport, coach stop, golf, tennis, jet boating and Milford Sound coach all within 1km. Pick up from airport, coach stop or Queenstown if required. Smoking only outdoors please. Please phone for directions.

Colston House	**Tel:** (03) 442 3162	**Cost:** Double $100
Homestay	**W:** www.bnb.co.nz/hosts/	Single $60 Child $30
7km E of Queenstown	colstonhouse.html	Dinner $25pp
Lois & Ivan Lindsay		**Beds:** 1 King 2 Single
2 Boyes Crescent		(2 bdrm)
Frankton Queenstown		**Bath:** 1 Guests share

Queenstown

Description: Sited dramatically above the Shotover River. Trelawn Place a superior country lodge is only 4kms from Queenstown.

Five comfortably appointed ensuite rooms furnished with country chintz and antiques. Guest sitting room with open fire, shady vine covered verandas.

Guest Laundry Facilities.

Your well travelled hosts Nery and Michael, Molly the cat, and the corgis welcome you.

Our Honeymoon Cottage has two bedrooms.

Directions: Take HW 6a into Queenstown, right at the second roundabout into Gorge Road, travel 4km toward Arthurs Point.

Trelawn Place
B&B Self-contained
4km N of Queenstown
Nery Howard & Michael Clark
PO Box 117
412 Gorge Road
Queenstown

Tel: (03) 442 9160
Fax: (03) 442 9160
E: trelawn@ihug.co.nz
W: www.trelawnb-b.co.nz

Cost: Double $180-$250
S/C $250 Visa/MC
Beds: 1 King/Twin 2 King
2 Queen (5 bdrm)
Bath: 4 Ensuite 1 Private

Queenstown

A 130 year old stone stable, converted for guest accommodation, and listed by the New Zealand Historic Places Trust, shares a private courtyard with our home.

The "Garden Room" and "Lake Room" are in the house, all providing convenience and comfort with fantastic lake and mountain views.

Our home is in a quiet cul-de-sac and set in a garden abundant with rhododendrons and native birds. It is less than 100 metres from the beach where a small boat and canoe are available for guests' use. The famous Kelvin Heights Golf Course is close and tennis courts, bowling greens and ice skating rink are in the adjacent park.

All tourist facilities, shops and restaurants are within easy walking distance, less than 5 minutes stroll on well lit footpaths.

All rooms are well heated with views of garden, lake or mountains. Tea and coffee making facilities are available at all times. Guests share our spacious living areas and make free use of our library and laundry.

A courtesy car is available to and from the bus depots. We can advise about and are booking agents for all sightseeing tours. Do allow an extra day or two for all the activities in the Queenstown region. When it is convenient for us, and by prior arrangement, guests will enjoy 3 course dinners served with New Zealand wines. The choice includes lamb, venison, fresh fish and chicken.

Breakfast is often served in the courtyard. No smoking indoors.

Your hosts, with a farming background, have bred Welsh ponies and now enjoy weaving, cooking, gardening, sailing and the outdoors.

We have an interest in a successful vineyard and enjoy drinking and talking about wine. We enjoy meeting people and have travelled extensively overseas.

Directions: Follow State Highway 6a (Frankton Road) to where it veers right at the Millenium Hotel. Continue straight ahead. Brisbane Street ("no exit") is 2nd on left. Phone if necessary.

The Stable
Homestay
Queenstown Central
Isobel & Gordon McIntyre
17 Brisbane Street
Queenstown

Tel: (03) 442 9251
Fax: (03) 442 8293
E: gimac@queenstown.co.nz
W: www.thestablebb.com

Cost: Double $120-$160
Single $60-$100
Dinner $50 Visa/MC
Beds: 1 King/Twin 1 Double
1 Single (3 bdrm)
Bath: 1 Ensuite 1 Private
1 Guests share

Queenstown

Our apartment is fully self-contained and occupies the middle floor of our home. A full breakfast is supplied if requested for $95 (double) or for the apartment only the tariff is $80. We have other beds available for groups of more than two people. There is a panoramic view of Lake Wakatipu and the surrounding mountains from the visitor's balcony and all rooms. Directions: Turn up Suburb Street off Frankton Road, then first right into Panorama Tce.

Braemar House	**Tel:** (03) 442 7385	**Cost:** Double $95
B&B Self-contained	**Fax:** (03) 442 4385	Single $60
1.5km E of Queenstown Central	**Mob:** 025 651 1035	Child 1/2 price
Ann & Duncan Wilson		**Beds:** 1 Double 1 Single
56 Panorama Terrace		(1 bdrm)
Queenstown		**Bath:** 1 Private

Queenstown

Welcome to our new home in Queenstown, purpose built to accommodate guests in a beautiful setting. At Birchall House, you enjoy a magnificent 200 degree view of Lake Wakatipu and surrounding mountains, and are within walking distance of town centre. Our guest accommodation is spacious, private with separate entrance, centrally heated, smoke-free, electric blankets on all beds. A continental or cooked breakfast is available. Off-street parking, courtesy transport to/from the airport or bus terminal. From Frankton Road, turn up Suburb Street, then first right into Panorama Terrace. Access via Sunset Lane.

Birchall House	**Tel:** (03) 442 9985	**Cost:** Double $110-$125
Self-contained Homestay	**Fax:** (03) 442 9980	Single $90
Queenstown Central	**E:** birchall.house@xtra.co.nz	**Beds:** 1 Double 2 Single
Joan & John Blomfield	**W:** www.bnb.co.nz/hosts/	(2 bdrm)
118 Panorama Terrace	birchallhouse.html	**Bath:** 1 Private
Larchwood Heights Queenstown		

Queenstown

We offer relaxed kiwi hospitality in rural environment with mountain views and lovely gardens. Accommodation: GARDEN COTTAGE with queen bed, ensuite, patio; GUEST WING, queen or twin, private bathroom. Laundry facilities. We are able to help with sightseeing arrangements. Our interests are golf, gardening, family, fishing and walking our dog Meg while BJ our cat prefers to lie in the sun. Directions from North 2km before Frankton Grant Rd & Mailbox on SH6. From South right at Frankton on SH6 2km to Grant Rd.

Collins Homestay	**Tel:** (03) 442 3801	**Cost:** Double $90 Single $70
B&B Self-contained Homestay	**E:** rcollins@queenstown.co.nz	Garden Cottage $100
8km NE of Queenstown	**W:** www.bnb.co.nz/hosts/	Visa/MC
Pat & Ron Collins	collins.html	**Beds:** 2 Queen 2 Single
Grant Road		(3 bdrm)
RD 1 Queenstown		**Bath:** 1 Ensuite 1 Private

Queenstown

Bed & Breakfast
NUMBER 12

.... a quiet convenient location

Queenstown

We would like you to come and share our conveniently situated house in a no exit street. You only have a 5 minute stroll to the town centre. Our home has mountain and lake views. Our home is warm and sunny, windows double glazed and we have central heating for the winter months. Our bedrooms have TVs,coffee/tea making facilities. Email & laundry is available.

We have a solar heated swimming pool (Dec/March) the sun deck and BBQ are for your use. Our sun room is available for your comfort.

Guests have the choice of either a full or continental breakfast in our dining room with its panoramic views. Once settled in you will seldom need to use your car again. There are several easy walking routes into the town centre, restaurants, shops and tourist centres. We are very close to the lake and our botanical gardens. Whilst you are with us we will be happy to advise on tourist activities and site seeing and make any arrangements you would wish. Barbara has a nursing/ social work background and Murray is a retired chartered accountant. We have an interest in classical/ choral music.

Directions: Highway 6a into Queenstown - the Millennium Hotel will be on your right, do NOT turn right at the sign Town Centre but continue straight ahead Brisbane St is second on the left and we are on the left.

Number Twelve
B&B Self-contained Homestay
Queenstown Central
Barbara & Murray Hercus
12 Brisbane Street
Queenstown

Tel: (03) 442 9511
Fax: (03) 442 9755
E: hercusbb@queenstown.co.nz
W: www.number12bb.co.nz

Cost: Double $120 Single $80
Dinner by prior
arrangement $45
Visa/MC
Beds: 2 King 2 Twin (2 bdrm)
Bath: 1 Ensuite 1 Private

Queenstown

A unique New Zealand home for you to share. We are a"B&B with no B". However bring your own food and use the excellent kitchen and great bbq area. Tea, coffee and milk is complimentary. Linen, towels, duvets and electric blankets are on all beds. Share bathroom facilities. Famously Fantastic views - 180 degrees panorama - sunrise to sunset - lake, mountains, valleys. The ambience is casual and informal. Enjoy the company of other travellers. The house is situated adjacent to a bush reserve with native birdlife and song abundant. A peaceful haven just 10 minutes pleasant walk to village centre.

Scallywags Guesthouse	**Tel:** (03) 442 7083	**Cost:** Double $55
Guesthouse	**Fax:** (03) 442 5885	Single $45
0.8km from Queenstown	**W:** www.bnb.co.nz/hosts/	**Beds:** 3 Queen 3 Twin
Evan Jenkins	scallywagsguesthouse.html	(6 bdrm)
27 Lomond Cres. Queenstown		**Bath:** 2 Guests share

Queenstown

Brecman Lodge is homestyle NZ hospitality at its best. Brecman Lodge is situated on the corner of Brecon and Man Streets, opposite the top of the Brecon Street steps, just above Queenstown's town centre. Brecman Lodge is friendly, warm and comfortable with single, twin and family accommodation. Upstairs is a bathroom and two bedrooms; one room has a double bed and the other has two single beds. Downstairs consists of guest lounge, bedroom with two single beds and a guest share bathroom.

Brecman Lodge	**Tel:** (03) 442 8908	**Cost:** Double $90
B&B	**Fax:** (03) 442 8904	Single $70
Queenstown Central	**W:** www.bnb.co.nz/hosts/	Visa/MC
Pat & Kevin MacDonell	brecmanlodge.html	**Beds:** 1 Double 5 Single
15 Man Street Queenstown		(3 bdrm)
		Bath: 1 Guests share
		1 Family share

Queenstown

Adelaide Street Guest House is perfectly situated just 35 metres from the shores of the beautiful Lake Wakatipu in the heart of Queenstown, just a short scenic walk to the centre of town. The sundecks, spacious lounge and most or our rooms enjoy breathtaking views of the lake and golf course enveloped by stunning mountain ranges. All rooms are heated and have electric blankets and duvets. Tea and coffee available anytime. Colourful sunsets in summer. Skiing in Winter. Book with us for tours and sightseeing.

Adelaide Street Guest House	**Tel:** (03) 442 6207	**Cost:** Double $70-$90
B&B	**Fax:** (03) 442 6202	Single $47-$59 King with
1/2km N of Queenstown	**E:** adelaide ehouse@xtra.co.nz	ensuite $110 Visa/MC
Dave, Mandy & family Wright	**W:** www.bnb.co.nz/hosts/	**Beds:** 2 King 2 Double 2 Twin
PO Box 998	ahomeawayfromhome.html	4 Single (6 bdrm)
27 Adelaide Street		**Bath:** 1 Ensuite 2 Guests share
Queenstown		1 Family share

Queenstown Central

"The best small B&B hotel in which we have stayed" comment our returning guests. Our elevated position has wonderful views over the town centre, lake and mountains. A delux breakfast menu served in our lakeview dining room is included, plus our very popular, complimentary cocktail hour each evening, hosted in either the fireside sitting room or rose filled courtyard. Guest laundry, bag storage, TV, hairdryer are supplied. Experience our unique style of hospitality, local knowledge and cheerful staff. Owner Louise Kiely, an ex restauranter & world traveller.

Queenstown House
Boutique Hotel
200m N of Queenstown
69 Hallenstein Street
Queenstown

Tel: (03) 442 9043
Fax: (03) 442 8755
Mob: 025 324 146
E: queenstown.house@xtra.co.nz
W: www.queenstownhouse.co.nz

Cost: Double $185-$295
Single $185
Visa/MC Amex
Beds: 10 King/Twin
4 Queen
Bath: 14 Ensuite

Queenstown

Welcome to our home in a quiet location, walking distance to town. Enjoy this panoramic view while you breakfast. One couple - personal attention. Spacious comfortable room with separate entrance and garden patio. Queen bed, own bathroom, TV, fridge and tea/coffee biscuits. Interests - music, gardening, sport, travel. We will enjoy your company but respect your privacy. Off street parking. Airport and bus transfers. Directions Turn right up Suburb Street off Frankton Road which is the main road into Queenstown then first right into Panorama Terrace.

Monaghans
B&B Homestay
800m Queenstown
Elsie & Pat Monaghan
4 Panorama Terrace
Queenstown

Tel: (03) 442 8690
Fax: (03) 442 8620
E: patmonaghan@xtra.co.nz
W: www.bnb.co.nz/hosts/
monaghans.html

Cost: Double $90
Single $70
Beds: 1 Queen (1 bdrm)
Bath: 1 Ensuite

Queenstown

A warm welcome to Anna's Cottage. Myrna a keen gardener and golfer, Ken with a love of fishing. Enjoy the peaceful garden setting and mountain views. Full kitchen facilities and living room combined. Washing machine. Tastefully decorated throughout, the bedroom is furnished with Sheridan linen. Only a few minutes from the centre of Queenstown. Private drive and parking at cottage. Attached to the end of our home The Rose Suite, self-contained, 1 Queen bed with ensuite, small kitchen, washing machine, furnished with Sheridan linen.

OTAGO, NTH CATLINS

Anna's Cottage & Rose Suite
Self-contained
Queenstown Central
Myrna & Ken Sangster
67 Thompson Street
Queenstown

Tel: (03) 442 8994
Fax: (03) 441 8994
Mob: 025 626 2165
W: www.bnb.co.nz/hosts/
annascottage.html

Cost: Double $95-$110
Single $80
breakfast $10 extra Visa/MC
Beds: 2 Queen (2 bdrm)
Bath: 2 Private

Queenstown

I offer friendly hospitality in a warm and comfortable home. It is a 3 minutes walk to central Queenstown - you don't have to climb any hills, but there is still a lovely view. Off-street parking and laundry facilities are available. Each room has its own TV and tea/coffee making facility. I serve a full breakfast menu, available from 6 - 9 am. I am happy to help your organise your local activities and make local reservations for you.

Turner Lodge
B&B
Queenstown Central
Hazel Seeto
Corner Gorge Road & Turner Street
Queenstown

Tel: (03) 442 9432
Fax: (03) 442 9409
Tollfree: 0800 488 763
E: turnerlodge@xtra.co.nz
W: www.bnb.co.nz/hosts/turnerlodge.html

Cost: Double $110
    Single $70
    Visa/MC
Beds: 1 Queen 2 Double
    2 Single (3 bdrm)
Bath: 3 Ensuite

Queenstown

Discover a luxury Bed & Breakfast just 150 metres form the historic centre of Queenstown. The Dairy Guesthouse has 11 private rooms with en-suite, two lounge rooms, one with wood fire, separate TV lounge, ski storage, 6-seater hydrotherapy spa, and parking. Its focus is an original 1920's general store - from which the guesthouse takes its name. Begin each day with a sumptuous breakfast served in the Old Dairy from where you can view the beautiful surrounding mountains. NZ Tourism Awards Finalist 2001. No pets. No children under 12.

The Dairy Guest House
Boutique Accommodation
100m Queenstown
Sarah & Brian Holding
10 Isle Street
Queenstown

Tel: (03) 442 5164
Fax: (03) 442 5164
Mob: 025 204 2585
Tollfree: 0800 33 33 93
E: TheDairy@xtra.co.nz
W: www.bnb.co.nz/hosts/thedairyguesthouse.html

Cost: Double $260-$295
    Visa/MC Amex
Beds: 7 King/Twin 4 Queen
    (11 bdrm)
Bath: 11 Ensuite

Queenstown

Our 2 girls, 1 cat and 2 bantams welcome other children to share their playground. This tranquil home with off street parking has outstanding views over Lake Wakatipu and Queenstown. The fully self contained 2 bedroom cottage garden unit with full kitchen and laundry facilities has proved immensely popular with guests - especially those with children. Includes breakfast. A superking or twin room with private bathroom is in the house. Enjoy a generous continental breakfast including fresh baked bread and real coffee at your leisure. Complimentary tea, coffee and also laundry facilities. Guests say "Excellent value for money!"

B&B & Self-contained
1.5km NE of Queenstown
Ruth Campbell
10 Wakatipu Heights
Queenstown

Tel: (03) 442 9190
Fax: (03) 442 4404
Mob: 021 116 8801
E: roosterretreat@xtra.co.nz
W: www.bnb.co.nz/hosts/campbell.html

Cost: Double $100 Single $50
    S.C Unit $200 Visa/MC
Beds: 1 King/Twin 1 Queen
    1 Double 1 Single (3 bdrm)
Bath: 1 Private 1 Guests share

Queenstown

Haus Helga overlooks Lake Wakatipu and the Remarkables Mountains and provides the "best view in all of New Zealand". Our luxurious home has extra large tastefully furnished guest rooms, each with a private deck or terrace. The self-contained suite includes a large kitchen/living/dining room. Our Voglauer guest room includes handpainted Austrian furniture and an ensuite with corner spa bath. We are now in our sixth year in operation and feel truly fortunate to have made so many great new friends, our wonderful guests.

Haus Helga
B&B
3km E of Queenstown
Helga & Ed Coolman
107 Wynyard Crescent
Fernhill, Queenstown

Tel: (03) 442 6077
Fax: (03) 442 4957
E: haushelga@xtra.co.nz
W: www.bnb.co.nz/hosts/
haushelga.html

Cost: Double $195-$295
Extra Adult $50 Child $30
Visa/MC
Beds: 1 King/Twin 3 Queen
2 Single (4 bdrm)
Bath: 4 Ensuite 4 Private

Queenstown

A warm welcome awaits you at Larch Hill. Our comfort-able and relaxing home-stay is just 3 min. drive from the centre of town. Public transport stops at the drive way. All rooms have Lake and Mountain views. In Winter, there is a roaring log-fire awaiting your return from a days skiing or sightseeing. Maria provides three course dinners by prior arrangement. We have pleasure in organising any Queenstown experiences. We speak also Italian, German and Dutch. Directions: From HW6a turn into Goldfield Heights at Sherwood Manor. Second left is Panners Way.

Larch Hill Home-stay B&B
B&B Homestay
Queenstown Central
Maria & Chris Lamens
16 Panners Way
Goldfields, Queenstown

Tel: (03) 442 4811
Fax: (03) 441 8882
E: chris@larchhill.com
W: www.larchhill.com

Cost: Double $105-$140
Single $85 Dinner $40
Apartment $150 Visa/MC
Beds: 2 King 1 Queen 1 Twin
(4 bdrm)
Bath: 2 Ensuite 2 Private

Queenstown

The Stone House, built in 1874 of local stone and lovingly restored, provides charming accommodation for a maximum of eight guests. Steve and Jo Weir offer guests their advice on the best of Queenstown's sightseeing, shopping and dining options. This old style inn is equipped with modern amenities, and all rooms feature direct-dial telephones, radio alarms, bathrobes and hair dryers. Lake views, fire-side evening drinks, Baz the cat, and a jacuzzi are provided for our guests, with the added bonus of central Queenstown on the doorstep.

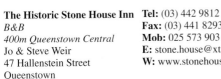

The Historic Stone House Inn
B&B
400m Queenstown Central
Jo & Steve Weir
47 Hallenstein Street
Queenstown

Tel: (03) 442 9812
Fax: (03) 441 8293
Mob: 025 573 903
E: stone.house@xtra.co.nz
W: www.stonehouse.co.nz

Cost: Double $220-$250
Visa/MC
Beds: 3 King 1 Queen
(4 bdrm)
Bath: 3 Ensuite 1 Private

Queenstown

Neil & Karen warmly welcome you to the elegant Coronet View Homestay, located in the Heart of Queenstown, New Zealand's adventure, holiday and shopping playground.

Enjoy an award winning local wine in the courtyard where there is a flower garden, jacuzzi, and swimming pool and where you will probably find our friendly Persian cats.

Wake-up in to the panoramic views of the lake and mountains in your spacious ensuite rooms, with exquisite home-made quilts.

You will be served freshly baked croissants, danish pastries, bagels, scones, blueberry muffins and other delights from our own bakery.

Coronet View Homestay B&B
B&B Homestay
1/2km NW of central
Karen & Neil Dempsey
28-30 Huff Street
Queenstown

Tel: (03) 442 6766
Fax: (03) 442 6766
Mob: 025 320 895
E: dempsey@coronetview.com
W: www.bnb.co.nz/hosts/
coronetview.html

Cost: Double $165-$240
Single $150-$240
Dinner $15 - $45
Hamper Lunches $10 - $50
Child POA Visa/MC
Beds: 9 King/Twin 1 Queen
1 Twin (11 bdrm)
Bath: 11 Ensuite

Queenstown

Browns Boutique Hotel was opened in August 2000.
Located only two blocks walk from downtown
Queenstown with views over Queenstown Bay to the
Remarkables. Every guest room is well appointed,
spacious and boasts a super king size bed along with
French doors opening onto balconies over the
courtyard. All rooms have their own generous sized
ensuite including showers and baths (excluding two
paraplegic rooms). The bathrooms are fully tiled and
feature Italian and German fittings.

Browns Boutique Hotel	**Tel:** (03) 441 2050	**Cost:** Double $190-$220
B&B	**Fax:** (03) 441 2060	Single $150-$180
Central Queenstown	**Mob:** 025 222 0681	Visa/MC Amex Diners
Nigel & Bridget Brown	**E:** stay@brownshotel.co.nz	**Beds:** 10 King/Twin (10 bdrm)
26 Isle Street	**W:** www.brownshotel.co.nz	**Bath:** 10 Ensuite
Queenstown		

Queenstown

Nestled on Queenstown Hill in a quiet cull-de-sac is
our sunny warm modern home, offering magnificent
unobstructed 180 degree views over town and lake.
Our guest room opens out to the garden and the same
view. It is only a 10 minutes downhill walk to town.
We are a non smoking, widely travelled retired couple
who enjoy meeting people, love art and music. We
have a piano waiting to be played. Because of our
former occupations we adore good food and wine.
Welcome to Salmond Place.

Homestay	**Tel:** (03) 441 1447	**Cost:** Double $140
Irene & George Mertz	**Fax:** (03) 441 1383	Single $120
11 Salmond Place (off Kent	**Mob:** 025 659 2609	Visa/MC
Street)	**W:** www.bnb.co.nz/hosts/	**Beds:** 1 Double (1 bdrm)
Queenstown	mertz.html	**Bath:** 1 Private

Queenstown - Glenorchy

Lake Haven offers quality accommodation and warm
hospitality at our secluded Lakefront property with
stunning lake and bush clad mountain views.
Glenorchy is the base for several world famous
walking tracks eg, Routeburn, renowned for its Trout
fishing and a large range of activities. Ronda and John
are longtime locals and are happy to assist you in
exploring and enjoying our unique and beautiful area.
Children welcome. Laundry facilities. Fishing guide
available. Glenorchy - Gateway to paradise.

Lake Haven	**Tel:** (03) 442 9091	**Cost:** Double $120 Single $70
B&B Homestay	**Fax:** (03) 442 9801	Child B/A Dinner B/A
40mins Queenstown	**E:** lakehaven@xtra.co.nz	Visa/MC
Ronda & John	**W:** www.bnb.co.nz/hosts/	**Beds:** 2 King/Twin 1 Twin
Benmore Place	lakehaven.html	(3 bdrm)
Glenorchy		**Bath:** 3 Ensuite

Garston

We are organic gardeners and our other interests include lawn bowls, sailing, gliding and alternative energy. Garston is New Zealand's most inland village with the Mataura River (famous for its fly fishing) flowing through the valley, surrounded by the Hector Range and the Eyre Mountains. A fishing guide is available with advance notice. For day trips, Garston is central to Queenstown, Te Anau, Milford Sound or Invercargill. We look forward to meeting you.

B&B Self-contained Homestay
50km S of Queenstown
Bev & Matt Menlove
17 Blackmore Road
Private Bag
Garston 9660

Tel: (03) 248 8516
E: glidesth@voyager.co.nz
W: www.bnb.co.nz/hosts/
menlove.html

Cost: Double $70
Single $40
Dinner $20
Beds: 1 Double 1 Single
(1 bdrm)
Bath: 1 Ensuite

Alexandra - Earnscleugh

Our self-contained guest accommodation offers you privacy and comfort. Combined with a warm welcome into our home, you can share with us, the peaceful and relaxing setting our our cherry orchard. While at Iversen , you can experience the grandeur and contrasts of the Central Otago landscape, walk the thyme covered hills, visit local wineries or just relax. Directions: From Alexandra or Clyde, travel on Earnscleugh Road, turn into Blackman Road and look for our sign on the left. Advanced bookings preferred.

Iversen
Self-contained Orchardstay
6km W of Alexandra
Robyn & Roger Marshall
47 Blackman Road
RD 1 Alexandra

Tel: (03) 449 2520
Fax: (03) 449 2519
Mob: 025 384 348
W: www.bnb.co.nz/hosts/
iversen.html

Cost: Double $90
Single $60
Dinner $25 B/A
Child B/A Visa/MC
Beds: 2 Queen (2 bdrm)
Bath: 1 Guests share

Alexandra

Welcome to our new home set in a small productive vineyard with commanding views of the surrounding hills. We are a professional couple with grown family and share our home with a Burmese cat and a springer spaniel, all non smokers. Complimentary wine and cheese served early evening and laundry and tea and coffee making facilities available. You can enjoy the privacy, views, spa and our wine cellar. If you are looking for privacy, tranquillity and executive accommodation you have found us.

Hawkdun Rise Vineyard Stay
B&B Vineyard Homestay
6km N of Alexandra
Judy & Roy Faris
Hawkdun Rise
Letts Gully Road, Alexandra

Tel: (03) 448 7782
Fax: (03) 448 7752
Mob: 025 337 072
E: rfaris@clear.net.nz
W: www.vineyardstay.co.nz

Cost: Double $120
Single $90
Visa/MC
Beds: 2 Queen 1 Double
(3 bdrm)
Bath: 2 Ensuite 1 Guests share

Alexandra

Nestled in a peaceful sheltered valley our country homestead offers superior accommodation only minutes from Alexandra. A new Cape Cod design house, spacious rooms an air of elegance, luxurious suite for guests, ensuite, formal dining room and spacious lounge. Rest, enjoy the crystal clear air and absorb the tranquil atmosphere. Stroll amongst the trees, orchard and gardens of the established house site. Excellent local restaurants for dinner or enjoy a meal in our own dining room. We enjoy the company of our little dog Ollie.

Ardshiel
Farmstay Homestay
3km NE of Alexandra
Ian & Joan Stewart
Letts Gully
Alexandra

Tel: (03) 448 9136
Fax: (03) 448 9136
Mob: 025 732 973
E: ij.stewart@xtra.co.nz
W: www.bnb.co.nz/hosts/
ardshiel.html

Cost: Double $110
    Single $85
Beds: 1 King 1 Double
    2 Single (2 bdrm)
Bath: 1 Ensuite 1 Guests share

Alexandra - Central Otago

Your accredited Kiwi hosts, Mary and Keith, welcome you to our secluded home where spectacular views offer some idea of the grandeur and contrasts to be found here, in the heart of Central Otago. We are an hour's drive from Queenstown and Wanaka, close to rivers, lakes and dams, sporting facilities, goldmining ruins, wineries, orchards, galleries, restaurants and shops. Relax in privacy, or join us on verandah, sitting room or garden, while the laundry does itself, and our cat (and if you have children) sleep peacefully.

Duart
Homestay
3.5km N of Alexandra
Mary & Keith McLean
Bruce's Hill
Highway 85, RD 3
Alexandra

Tel: (03) 448 9190
Fax: (03) 448 9190
E: duart.homestay@xtra.co.nz
W: www.bnb.co.nz/hosts/
duart.html

Cost: Double $80 Single $45
    Child $30 Dinner $20 B/A
Beds: 1 Double 1 Twin 1 Single
    (3 bdrm)
Bath: 1 Private 1 Family share

Roxburgh - Millers Flat

An easy 2-hour drive from Dunedin, Wanaka, Queenstown and Invercargill, Millers Flat is an attractive village in farming and fruitgrowing country, well-equipped with recreational facilities, easy access to fishing, walking tracks, gardens to visit, and the well-known community-owned store, "Faigan's". We live on 10 acres in a 110 year old house of rammed-earth construction. Our guest accommodation is a 2-storey building of more recent vintage, formerly Wallace's architectural studio, an interesting composition of space and light, comfortably-heated, with tea/coffee making facilities. Please phone ahead for directions.

The Studio
B&B Self-contained
16km S of Roxburgh
Sheena & Wallace Boag
Millers Flat, RD 2, Roxburgh

Tel: (03) 446 6872
Fax: (03) 446 6872
W: www.bnb.co.nz/hosts/
thestudio.html

Cost: Double $75 Single $45
    Child $20 Visa/MC
Beds: 2 Single (1 bdrm) and
    double bed settee (upstairs)
Bath: 1 Ensuite

Roxburgh - Ettrick

Clearburn Station is a 7000 acre property with a Homestead. Block and Hill Country Run stocked with Merino sheep and cattle and operated as a family partnership with son John and his wife Linda and children. Guest accommodation is a detached self contained unit with electric blankets, heaters, fridge, TV and tea making facilities. Guests are very welcome to join in the farm activities during their stay. Restaurant, golf course and fishing are within 5 mins drive. Directions: Please phone. 1 3/4 hour drive from Dunedin.

Clearburn Station	**Tel:** (03) 446 6712	**Cost:** Double $85
B&B Self-contained Farmstay	**Fax:** (03) 446 6774	Single $50
10km S of Roxburgh	**E:** JL.Lambeth@xtra.co.nz	Child B/A Dinner $20 B/A
Margaret & Ian Lambeth	**W:** www.bnb.co.nz/hosts/	**Beds:** 2 Single (1 bdrm)
Dalmuir Road	clearburnstation.html	**Bath:** 1 Ensuite
RD 2, Roxburgh		

Roxburgh

Nestled in the Teviot Valley centre of NZ's cherry and apricot growing region, the Seed Farm comprises a two storeyed cottage and separate stables set amidst two acres of cottage garden. The buildings all carry Historic Places Trust 2 classification reflecting their historic significance to the district. The stables have been converted and offer four self-contained bedrooms with TV, tea making facilities etc. The cottage contains a restaurant offering an eclectic menu in an olde world ambience.

The Seed Farm	**Tel:** (03) 446 6824	**Cost:** Double $100
Country Inn	**Fax:** (03) 446 6024	Single $80
9km S of Roxburgh	**W:** www.bnb.co.nz/hosts/	Dinner B/A Visa/MC
Raewyn & John Lane	theseedfarm.html	**Beds:** 3 Queen 2 Single
4760 Roxburgh-Ettrick Road		(4 bdrm)
RD 2, Roxburgh		**Bath:** 4 Ensuite

Lawrence

My home is situated on the main road near the picnic ground with its avenue of poplars. My garden is special to me, the home is 100 years old, has character, charm and a lived in feeling. It's home to Ambrose Pumpkin my cats and Holly a miniature Foxie. Guestrooms are restful with fresh flowers, fruit and breakfast included hot bread, croissants, home-made jams. Free-range eggs. There is a lovely peaceful atmosphere in our early gold mining town.

The Ark	**Tel:** (03) 485 9328	**Cost:** Double $90
B&B	**Fax:** (03) 485 9222	Single $45
45 min N of Balclutha	**E:** lawrence.infocentre@xtra.co.nz	Child 1/2 price
Frieda Betman	**W:** www.thearknz.homestead.com	**Beds:** 2 Double 1 Twin 1 Single
8 Harrington Place (Main Road)		(4 bdrm)
		Bath: 1 Family share

Palmerston

Set in 50 acres with rambling gardens and park-like grounds, Centrewood offers complete peace and privacy. Our guest-suite (2 bedrooms, bathroom, spacious living room) is available only for single party bookings and affords elegant accommodation including billiards, piano and kitchenette. Adjacent is a cliff-top walk allowing easy viewing of seals and penguins and nearby sandy beaches. On site attractions include rose-gardens, tennis, native bird-watching. As Ernest Lord Rutherford's great-granddaughter Jane has a collection of Rutherford memorabilia. Dinner by arrangement. Nearby attractions: Moeraki Boulders, Dunedin 40 minutes.

Centrewood
Homestay Boutique Lodge
8km S of Palmerston
Drs Jane & David Loten
RD 1, Palmerston

Tel: (03) 465 1977
Fax: (03) 465 1977
E: david.loten@xtra.co.nz
W: www.bnb.co.nz/hosts/
centrewood.html

Cost: Double $150 Single $120
Dinner $40 Visa/MC
Beds: 2 Queen 1 Single
(2 bdrm)
Bath: 1 Private

Broad Bay - Otago Peninsula

"CHY~AN~DOWR" ("House by the Water") a quality B&B located on scenic Otago Peninsula with panoramic harbour views. The upstairs guest area is spacious and private with comfortable bedrooms, guest lounge and a sunroom with expansive harbour views. "SLEEPY HOLLOW", our peaceful, private SELF-CONTAINED COTTAGE has the same home comforts and is situated in a quiet rural location, a five minute drive from our house. We emigrated from Holland in 1981 and we enjoy welcoming people into our home. Smoke-free accommodation. We also have a cat.

Chy-an-Dowr
B&B Self-contained
16km E of Dunedin
Susan & Herman van Velthoven
687 Portobello Road
Broad Bay, Dunedin

Tel: (03) 478 0306
Fax: (03) 478 0306
Mob: 025 270 5533
E: hermanvv@xtra.co.nz
W: www.visit-dunedin.co.nz/
chyandowr.html

Cost: Double $100-$135
Visa/MC
Beds: 1 King/Twin 2 Queen
1 Double 1 Single
(5 bdrm)
Bath: 2 Private/Guests share

Dunedin - Otago Peninsula

Captains Cottage is on the waterfront set in bush with spectacular views enroute to Albatross, Penguin and Seal Colonies. Christine and Robert are wildlife film makers, Robert having filmed for BBC, National Geographic and Discovery has many a tale to tell. Our local and wildlife knowledge can help plan your stay. Come in our boat fishing or view the unique bird and marine life. If you enjoy great food, hospitality, BBQ's or relaxing by our fire come and share our interesting home with us.

Captains Cottage
Homestay
8km N of Dunedin
Christine & Robert Brown
422 Portobello Road
RD 2
Dunedin

Tel: (03) 476 1431
Fax: (03) 476 1431
Mob: 021 352 734
E: wildfilm@actrix.co.nz
W: www.bnb.co.nz/hosts/
captainscottage.html

Cost: Double $135
Single $100
Dinner $25
Beds: 1 Double 2 Single
(2 bdrm)
Bath: 1 Ensuite 1 Private
1 Guests share

Broad Bay - Otago Peninsula

Private cottage. Built 1905 as fisherman's retreat. Right on
Otago Harbour. Picket-fence, mature bush-gardens.
Vignettes of harbour from verandah. Full of old-world
nostalgia -original matai floors , interesting collectibles a
Bakelite phone (but no TV!) With luxurious towels, fresh
linen, a comfortable bed - it's a real travellers' oasis.
Generous hamper breakfasts are a speciality. "The owners
have thought of just about everything" Gourmet Travellers
Magazine. "If you spend only one night at The Cottage,
you'll be sorry.... a few days is best" (Grace Magazine).

The Cottage
Self-contained
18km E of Dunedin
Lesley Hirst & Janet Downs
7 Frances Street
Broad Bay, Dunedin

Tel: (03) 478 0073
Fax: (03) 478 0272
Mob: 025 381 291
E: thecottage@xtra.co.nz
W: www.visit-dunedin.co.nz/
thecottage.html

Cost: Double $95 without
breakfast,
$125 with special
breakfast
Beds: 1 Double (1 bdrm)
Bath: 1 Ensuite

Portobello Village - Otago Peninsula

Adjacent to our home is an historic villa set in a 1/2
acre of beautiful gardens with sea views & rural
outlook. Luxury accommodation with ENSUITES,
spacious guest lounge & dining area, return verandahs, off street parking. Situated overlooking Lathum
Bay, opposite the 1908 Cafe & Restaurant. Albatross,
penguins, seals, bird watching, Larnach Castle, scenic
walks & drives name only a few of the attractions we
are most central to on the pituresque Otago Peninsula. Our son Jackson is 3yrs old.

Peninsula Bed & Breakfast
B&B
25min Dunedin
Rachel & Mike Kerr
4 Allans Beach Road
Portobello, Otago Peninsula

Tel: (03) 478 0909
Fax: (03) 478 0909
E:
otago_peninsula@hotmail.com
W: www.bnb.co.nz/hosts/
peninsulahomestaybb.html

Cost: Double $85-$125
Single $75-$115
Child $5 - $20 Visa/MC
Beds: 3 Queen 1 Twin
(4 bdrm)
Bath: 2 Ensuite 1 Guests share

Port Chalmers - Dunedin

Betty & Bob welcome you to our spacious renovated
stonehouse in a peaceful rural setting only 30 mins from
Dunedin. The view looking out across the Otago harbour is
spectacular. You can feed and mingle with the animals.
Emu's Aplaca's peacocks etc. A good surfing beach and
walking tracks. Then relax in our heated spa pool. We have
3 friendly cats. Three course farm-style meals available
Morning and afternoon teas complimentary with home
baking. Children and campervans welcome. We look
forward to meeting you.

Atanui
Farmstay Homestay
20km NE of Dunedin
Bob & Betty Melville
Heywards Point Road
RD 1, Port Chalmers
Dunedin

Tel: (03) 482 1107
Fax: (03) 482 1107
E: atanui@actrix.gen.nz
W: www.bnb.co.nz/hosts/
atanui.html

Cost: Double $100-$120
Single $80-$100
Child 1/2 price
Dinner $25 Visa/MC
Beds: 1 Queen 1 Twin
(2 bdrm)
Bath: 1 Ensuite 1 Guests share

Broad Bay - Otago Peninsula

Modern self contained cottage accommodation includes bedroom, kitchen-dining room, bathroom-shower. Laundry available. Off-street parking. All living areas have glass ranchslider doors opening onto an elevated deck offering unobstructive changing harbour views from sunrise to sunset. Accommodation set in fern garden, Rhododendrons, NZ native bush, etc. Albatross, penguins, seals, scenic walks, Larnach castle all nearby. Hosts Christine, Bill and Mika the cat welcome you. Our sign of 'B&B 741' is just past Broad Bay.

Fern Grove Garden	**Tel:** (03) 478 0321	**Cost:** Double $95-$125
Self-contained	**Mob:** 025 298 3110	Visa/MC
15km E of Dunedin	**E:** strang@southnet.co.nz	**Beds:** 1 Queen 1 Single
Bill & Christine Strang	**W:** www.bnb.co.nz/hosts/	(1 bdrm)
741 Portobello Road	ferngrovegarden.html	**Bath:** 1 Private
Dunedin		

Portobello - Otago Peninsula

Cosy, fully self contained cottage on owner's section. Stunning views of Otago Harbour and Quarantine Island. Ideally located for touring the Otago Peninsula. Close to the albatross colony, yellow eyed penguins and Larnach Castle. Restaurant, hotel, takeaway, cafe and shop are 3 minutes walk away. Ground floor comprises kitchen/lounge/diner, shower/toilet and access to large sun decks. The bedroom is located on the first floor and benefits from a small turret. TV, music, books provided. No pets. Hosts have children aged 4 & 9.

Silverlea Cottage	**Tel:** (03) 478 0140	**Cost:** Double $120
Self-contained	**E:** shhemu@xtra.co.nz &	Single $110
20km E of Dunedin	www.silverleacottages.com	Visa/MC
Shaun & Helen Murphy	**W:** www.bnb.co.nz/hosts/	**Beds:** 1 Double 2 Single
7 Blackwell Street	silverlea.html	(1 bdrm)
Portobello, Otago Peninsula		**Bath:** 1 Private

Dunedin

Our quiet turn-of-the-century villa sits in broad, flower-bordered lawns backed by native bush with beautiful, tuneful birds. All rooms have electric heating, comfortable beds with electric blanket, and antiques, while the Queen room has an adjoining balcony. Close to by is Moana Pool, the glorious Edwardian house, "Olveston", and Otago Golf Course. Our special breakfast will set you up for the day. We have a courtesy car, a Burmese and a Siamese cat. It is NOT SUITABLE FOR CHILDREN OR SMOKERS.

Magnolia House	**Tel:** (03) 467 5999	**Cost:** Double $85
B&B	**Fax:** (03) 467 5999	Single $60
2km W of Dunedin	**E:** mrsuth@paradise.net.nz	**Beds:** 1 Queen 1 Double
Joan & George Sutherland	**W:** www.bnb.co.nz/hosts/	2 Single (3 bdrm)
18 Grendon Street	magnoliahouse.html	**Bath:** 2 Guests share
Maori Hill		
Dunedin 9001		

Dunedin

Let us introduce you to the cultural heritage of one of New Zealand's oldest cities, and to the unique wildlife and coastal grandeur of Otago Peninsula. Your comfort will be asssured in a luxury guest bedroom in the residence of our motel complex. As Sue and I operate the adjoining motel please specify homestay accommodation when booking. Laundry facilities and off-street parking available. We are situated 8 minutes drive from the centre of the city at the base of the Otago Peninisula. Please ring for directions.

Arcadian Homestay	**Tel:** (03) 455 0992	**Cost:** Double $90
B&B Homestay	**Fax:** (03) 455 0237	Single $80
3.5km Dunedin Centre	**Tollfree:** 0508 272 2342	Visa/MC Amex Diners
Sue & Dick Williman	**E:** williman@voyager.co.nz	**Beds:** 2 Queen (2 bdrm)
85 Musselburgh Rise	**W:** www.voyager.co.nz/~williman	**Bath:** 2 Ensuite
Dunedin		

Dunedin

We are situated in a quiet suburb overlooking Otago Harbour and surrounding hills. Within easy reach of all local attractions. Lovely garden or harbour views from all rooms. Children very welcome. Directions: Drive into city on one-way system watch for Highway 88 sign follow Anzac Avenue onto Ravensbourne Rd. Continue approx 5 kms to St Leonards turn left at Playcentre opposite Boatshed into Pukeko St then left into Kaka Rd, straight ahead to Kiwi St turn left into No. 6.

Harbourside B&B	**Tel:** (03) 471 0690	**Cost:** Double $75-$85
B&B Homestay	**Fax:** (03) 471 0063	Single $45
7km NE of Dunedin	**W:** www.bnb.co.nz/hosts/	Child $15 Dinner $25
Shirley & Don Parsons	harboursidebb.html	Visa/MC Diners
6 Kiwi Street		**Beds:** 1 Queen 1 Double
St Leonards		3 Single (2 bdrm)
Dunedin		**Bath:** 1 Ensuite 1 Family share

Dunedin

Deacons Court is a charming superior spacious Victorian Villa 1km walking distance from the city centre and on a bus route. We offer you friendly but unobtrusive hospitality in a quiet secure haven. Guests can relax in our delightful sheltered back garden and conservatory. All our bedrooms are large, have ensuite or private bathrooms, heaters & electric blankets. Complimentary 24hr tea or coffee, ample free parking and laundry service available. We cater for non-smokers and have an unobtrusive cat. Family groups welcome.

Deacons Court	**Tel:** (03) 477 9053	**Cost:** Double $110
B&B	**Fax:** (03) 477 9058	Single $70
Dunedin Central	**Tollfree:** 0800 268 252	King $120 Visa/MC
Keith Heggie & Gail Marmont	**E:** Deacons@es.co.nz	**Beds:** 1 King 1 Queen
342 High Street	**W:** www.deaconscourt.	1 Double 3 Single
Dunedin	bizland.com	(3 bdrm)
		Bath: 2 Ensuite 1 Private

Dunedin

Relax at Castlewood and experience the character and charm of a bygone era. Castlewood offers superior homestay accommodation in a gracious restored 1912 Tudor style town house located a mere 10 minutes walk away from Dunedin's leading attractions and city centre. Delight in Castlewood's sunny fragrant walled garden. Your hosts Peter & Donna appreciate the needs of discerning travellers and offer sumptuous continental breakfast, plus guests sauna. Peter is a skilled artist, and author of "Great Escapes". For further information, references and maps, view http://www.castlewood.co.nz

Castlewood	**Tel:** (03) 477 0526	**Cost:** Double $100 Single $70
B&B Homestay	**Fax:** (03) 477 0526	Ensuite $145 Visa/MC
800m w of Dunedin Central	**E:** relax@castlewood.co.nz	**Beds:** 2 Queen 1 Twin 1 Single
Donna & Peter Mitchell	**W:** www.castlewood.co.nz	(3 bdrm)
240 York Place, Dunedin		**Bath:** 1 Ensuite 1 Private
		1 Guests share

Dunedin

We welcome you to our restored Victorian residence on the edge of the green belt. We offer you warmth, elegance and informality. In all bedrooms we provide heating, cotton and feather bedding, TV, telephone and freshly ground coffee. Our blue suite incorporates an ensuite, a sun room and the opportunity for intimate dining overlooking the city and harbour. With notice, a sumptuous three course meal prepared from Otago produce will be served in the guest dining room. We thank you for not smoking.

Glenfield House	**Tel:** (03) 453 5923	**Cost:** Double $135-$175
Bed & Breakfast Inn	**Fax:** (03) 453 5984	Single $110-$135
2km SW of Dunedin Central	**W:** www.bnb.co.nz/hosts/	Visa/MC Amex Diners
Cal Johnstone & Wendy Gunn	glenfieldhouse.html	**Beds:** 2 Queen 2 Double
3 Peel St, Mornington		(4 bdrm)
Dunedin		**Bath:** 2 Ensuite 1 Guests share

Dunedin

We are a retired couple who issue a warm welcome to you our guests. Directions: Follow Port Chalmers Highway 88 eg Anzac Ave and Ravensbourne Road to Adderley Tce turning uphill behind the Hotel. Entering the first bend be alert for signpost on right for Taupo Street and Lane. Turn downhill and right into our drive. Your bedroom with private toilet is on this level. Bathroom and living areas upstairs. We and Beethoven the Budgie look forward to meeting you. Come in and relax..

Harbour Lookout	**Tel:** (03) 471 0582	**Cost:** Double $65
Homestay	**Mob:** 025 263 7244	Single $40
3km NE of Dunedin	**E:** jasmin@clear.net.nz	**Beds:** 2 Single (1 bdrm)
Ron & Maire Graham	**W:** www.bnb.co.nz/hosts/	**Bath:** 1 Family share
3 Taupo Street	harbourlookout.html	
Ravensbourne		
Dunedin		

Dunedin

Welcome to Dunedin & Albatross Inn! Our beautiful late Victorian House is ideally located on the main street close to the University, gardens, museum, shops and restaurants.

Our attractive rooms have ensuite bathrooms, telephone, TV, radio, tea/coffee, warm duvets and electric blankets on modern beds. Extra firm beds upon request. Very quiet rooms at rear of house. Several rooms have kitchenette and fridge. Enjoy your breakfast in front of the open fire in our lounge. We serve freshly baked bread and muffins, fresh fruit salad, yoghurt, juices, cereals, teas, freshly brewed coffee.

Nigel & I are both Dunedin born and have an extensive knowledge of the city. We are happy to recommend and book tours for you. All wildlife tours pick up and drop off here. We can recommend many great places to eat, most just a short walk down George Street.

Nearby laundry, non-smoking, cot and highchair.

Our visitor book says! "The convenience of your location is wonderful, you can walk everywhere! Combined with a gorgeous house, such friendly hosts" *Joe & Cathy Wallace, Georgia, USA*. "This is everything a B&B ought to be... our only regret is leaving... Thank you Kerry & Nigel for organising 3 wonderful days and making our stay so special!" *Dianna & William McDowey, England.*

Homepage: www.albatross.inn.co.nz. Winter special $69 Double - special conditions apply. Complimentary e-mail and internet and mountain bikes..

Albatross Inn
B&B Private Hotel
Dunedin Central
Kerry, Nigel and daughters Zoe & Joanna
770 George Street
Dunedin

Tel: (03) 477 2727
Fax: (03) 477 2108
Tollfree: 0800 441 441
E: albatross.inn@xtra.co.nz
W: www.albatross.inn.co.nz

Cost: Double $75-$125
        Single $65-$85
        Child $15
        Visa/MC Amex Diners
Beds: 1 King 4 Queen 3 Double
        5 Single (8 bdrm)
Bath: 8 Ensuite

Dunedin

Beyond our cottage style entrance is a delightful and sizeable character family home built in 1903. There is a welcoming, warm atmosphere with relaxing decor. The family dog is a small dachshund. The beds have quality mattresses, duvets and electric blankets. Large guest lounge with tea and coffee making facilities. There is a north facing garden, off street parking and a bus stop at the door. It is a short distance to local shops, restaurants, Moana Pool and the centre of town. Refer:kincaple homestay on website welcometodunedin.co.nz

Kincaple	**Tel:** (03) 477 4384	**Cost:** Double $85-$120
B&B Homestay	**Fax:** (03) 477 4380	Single $60
2km W of Dunedin	**Mob:** 025 2488 968	Visa/MC
Delys Cox	**Tollfree:** 0800 269 384 pin 4774	**Beds:** 1 King 1 Twin (2 bdrm)
215 Highgate,	**E:** kincaple@xtra.co.nz	**Bath:** 1 Ensuite
Roslyn, Dunedin	**W:** welcometodunedin.co.nz/	1 Family share
	kincaplehomestay/	

Dunedin

Nisbet Cottage offers superior accommodation in quiet surroundings with panoramic views of Dunedin. Enjoy our comfortable rooms, the large sun deck, and the guest lounge with open fireplace. Meet Basil, our cat. Restaurant and bus stop nearby. As experienced Eco-tour operators we can help plan your stay. For a taste of real nature join our Sunrise Penguin Walk. Directions: From Highcliff Road (the high road to Larnach Castle), turn left into Every Street, 1st right into Albion Street and 1st left into Elliffe Place.

Nisbet Cottage	**Tel:** (03) 454 5169	**Cost:** Double $110-$135
B&B Eco Tours	**Fax:** (03) 454 5369	Single $100-$110
7km E of Dunedin Central	**E:** stay@nznatureguides.com	Visa/MC Amex
Hildegard & Ralf Lubcke	**W:** www.bnb.co.nz/hosts/	**Beds:** 1 Super King 1 Queen
6A Elliffe Place	nisbetcottage.html	2 Single (3 bdrm)
Shiel Hill, Dunedin		**Bath:** 3 Ensuite

Dunedin

Eileen and Wallie would like to welcome visitors to Dunedin to their smoke-free home, situated in a quiet street just off Stuart Street and opposite Roberts Park. We have travelled extensively ourselves and understand how visitors feel when they arrive in a new town. Our home is in short walking distance to Dunedin's stately home "Olveston", the Moana swimming Complex and just over one kilometre to the town centre. The guest bedrooms, situated on the top floor for privacy and quietness, are warm and sunny .

Cill Chainnigh	**Tel:** (03) 477 4963	**Cost:** Double $90
B&B	**Fax:** (03) 477 4965	Single $55
1km S of Dunedin	**Mob:** 025 228 7840	**Beds:** 1 Double 2 Single
Eileen & Wallie Waudby	**E:** wallie.waudby@xtra.co.nz	(2 bdrm)
33 Littlebourne Road	**W:** www.bnb.co.nz/hosts/	**Bath:** 1 Guests share
Roslyn, Dunedin	cillchainnigh.html	

Dunedin

Enjoy the relaxed atmosphere of our Spanish style home and marvel at the panoramic views over St Clair and St Kilda beaches, the Otago Peninsula, Harbour Basin and the hill suburbs of Dunedin City. Dunedin has many architecturally significant buildings, an internationally recognised art gallery and museum. Other local attractions include the Otago Peninsula Wildlife, Albatross Colony and Larnachs Castle. The Carisbrook International Rugby/ Cricket Ground is within easy walking distance. The house is situated down a private drive with off street parking. A friendly welcome awaits.

Homestay
3km Dunedin City Centre
Jenny & Bill Smith
117 Easther Cres
Kew, Dunedin

Tel: (03) 455 5731
Mob: 025 267 6853
W: www.bnb.co.nz/hosts/
smithdunedin.html

Cost: Double $85
    Single $60
    Twin $80
Beds: 1 King 2 Single (2 bdrm)
Bath: 1 Guests share

Dunedin

In its peaceful setting just two minutes off the Northern Motorway you'll find Dalmore Lodge. Our Larchwood home offers views of harbour, Pacific Ocean, city lights, Botanical Gardens, and hills. A three minute drive/20 minute walk takes you into the main business/shopping area. Public transport available end of driveway. We will meet you to/from airport, train, bus by prior arrangement (extra minimal cost) . Off street parking. Please no smoking indoors. Loraine, Mike and our cat Teagan look forward to your visit.

Dalmore Lodge
B&B Homestay
3.2km N of Dunedin Central
Loraine & Mike Allpress
9 Falkirk Street
Dalmore, Dunedin

Tel: (03) 473 6513
Fax: (03) 473 6512
Mob: 025 287 1517
E: dalmore.lodge@actrix.gen.nz
W: www.bnb.co.nz/hosts/
dalmorelodge.html

Cost: Double $85-$90 Single $60
    Child $15 Visa/MC
Beds 1 Queen 1 Double
    1 King/Twin 1 Single
    (4 bdrm)
Bath: 1 Private 1 Guests share

Dunedin

Our home is a modern interpretation of a traditional Scottish house, and set in 1 acre of gardens and lawns, with indoor/ outdoor living. Awake to the sound of abundant bird life in a quiet and secure neighbourhood. We serve delicious healthy breakfasts. Two luxury bedrooms complete with one queen and one single bed. All rooms have tea-making facilities, TV, heaters, electric blankets. Separate facilities with modern guest bathroom. Relax far from the madding crowd. All non smoking, no pets and not suitable for young children.

Alloway
B&B Homestay
4.5km SE of Dunedin Central
Lorraine & Stewart Harvey
65 Every Street
Andersons Bay, Dunedin

Tel: (03) 454 5384
Fax: (03) 454 5364
Tollfree: 0800 387 245
E: alloway@xtra.co.nz
W: www.bnb.co.nz/hosts/
harvey.html

Cost: Double $95-$120
    Single $85-$110
    Visa/MC
Beds: 2 Queen 2 Single
    (2 bdrm)
Bath: 1 Guests share

Dunedin

Hulmes Court and Hulmes Too are two beautiful homes situated right in the heart of Dunedin, only a few minutes walk from the Visitor Centre, restaurants, shops and theatres. Tennyson Street is a quiet side Street and the property has private gardens, trees, decks and sitting areas, a tranquil retreat from the hustle and bustle so near by.

The Victorian Hulmes Court is one of the oldest and most historic homes in Dunedin. It was built in the 1860's by the first provincial surgeon Edward Hulme who helped found the Otago Medical School. Hulmes Too is a large Edwardian home built next to Hulmes Court on the grounds of the original estate. For the first time in over a century the properties are back together again.

Hulmes Court & Too have a variety of rooms which cater for all tastes from the economical cute single Rose room at $60 per night to our large and grand en suite rooms in Hulmes Too at $150 per night.

Your host Norman owns an advertising business, is interested in history, philosophy, geography and has stood for parliament twice. At the same time Norman at 35 and his staff are youthful and full of energy. We have journeyed widely and know what travellers need: peace, relaxation, comfortable beds, warmth, continental breakfasts, friendly service and good information. In addition, we provide complimentary laundry, internet & email, BBQ, mountain bikes and off-street parking. We have a cute black cat called Solstice and we enjoy children staying with us.

Hulmes Court	**Tel:** (03) 477 5319	**Cost:** Double $95-$150
B&B	**Fax:** (03) 477 5310	Single $60-$95
Dunedin Central	**Mob:** 025 351 075	Child please inquire
Norman Wood	**Tollfree:** 0800 448 563	Visa/MC Amex Diners
52 Tennyson street	**E:** normwood@earthlight.co.nz	**Beds:** 1 King 10 Queen 4 Twin
Dunedin	**W:** www.hulmes.co.nz	1 Single (12 bdrm)
		Bath: 6 Ensuite 3 Guests share

Dunedin

Our spacious Edwardian villa, at the gateway to Otago Peninsula, is six minutes from central Dunedin. We offer a private lounge/dining area with Sky Television, upstairs bedrooms and sitting area with tea/coffee facilities. Our knowledge of local attractions and restaurants is at our guests' disposal. A complimentary daily paper and evening port/wine is offered. We cater for older children, and offer a cheeseboard and tasting of Central Otago wine by arrangement. Laundry facilities and off-street parking is available. Our family has pet dogs.

Ardgowan
B&B
3.5km E of Dunedin
Ken & Margaret Turner
218 Musselburgh Rise
Musselburgh, Dunedin

Tel: (03) 456 0411
E: kturner@southnet.co.nz
W: www.bnb.co.nz/hosts/
ardgowan.html

Cost: Double $100-$160
Single $70-$100
Visa/MC
Beds: 1 King/Twin 2 King
1 Queen (3 bdrm)
Bath: 2 Ensuite 1 Private

Dunedin - Harington Point

Enjoy very comfortable self-contained or B&B units overlooking Otago Harbour. Local wildlife includes Albatross, Penguins, Seals, Shags and Sealions. The area has many historic features. Two minute walk to the beach for a leisurely stroll - spectacular sunsets. Golf course, restaurant and cafes close by. Bourke has 7 year experience with Penguin Conservation and Sharon works at the Albatross Centre. We have two daughters, a dog called Missy and three pet sheep. Let our local knowledge enhance your stay on the Peninsula.

Harington Point Accommodation
B&B Motel S/C Cottage
30km N of Dunedin
Bourke & Sharon Thomas
932 Harington Point Road
RD 2, Dunedin

Tel: (03) 478 0287
Fax: (03) 478 0089
Mob: 025 398 080
E: southlight@clear.net.nz
W: www.bnb.co.nz/hosts/
haringtonpoint.html

Cost: Double $85-$95
Dinner $25 B/A
S/C Cottage $110
Visa/MC
Beds: 4 Queen 4 Twin (8 bdrm)
Bath: 6 Ensuite 2 Guests share

Dunedin

Arden Street House B&B (Opening Dec 2001)
Comfortable 1930s bungalow 2 minutes to Botanical gardens, 10 minutes university 20min walk to centre town.Sunny Garden, views over countryside. double or twin rooms from $45, single from $35 Whanau suite (own facilites + 4 bedrooms) $160. Your host Joyce Lepperd her family and cat enjoy travellers stories in their comfortable and quirky home. Great continental breakfast included .

Arden Street House
B&B
3km s of TOWN
Joyce Lepperd
36 Arden Street Dunedin
Dunedin

Tel: (03) 473 8860
Fax: (03) 473 8861
E: joyce-1@clear.net,nz
W: www.bnb.co.nz/hosts/
dunedinlodge.html

Cost: Double $45 to $55
Single $35 to $45
Full breakfast extra cost
Beds: 4 Double 2 Single
Bath: 1 Guests share
1 Family share

Dunedin

Experience a taste of early Dunedin. This heritage home in the centre of the city was built on the High Street Cable Car route in 1908 to provide first class accommodation to its residents. Today it is still an impressive home with spectacular views of the city and harbour. The three upstairs guest rooms are carefully restored to preserve their character for visitors, who delight in the many features in the home. A courtesy van can meet you at the bus or train if required.

Highbrae Guesthouse	**Tel:** (03) 479 2070	**Cost:** Double $85-$110
B&B Homestay	**Fax:** (03) 479 2100	Single $65 Child $10
Dunedin	**Mob:** 025 328 470	Visa/MC Amex
Stephen & Fienie Clark	**W:** www.bnb.co.nz/hosts/	**Beds:** 1 King 1 Queen 1 Twin
376 High Street	highbraeguesthouse.html	(3 bdrm)
City Rise, Dunedin		**Bath:** 1 Guests share

Mosgiel

Welcome to our English-style cottage home. Built in 1913 and used as the Vicarage for 46 years, before passing to private owners who made sympathetic restorations. The outstanding feature is the exquisitely balanced garden, laid out in 'rooms'. Two upstairs guest rooms and bathroom enjoy a commanding view of the garden. Warm Oregan panelling and leadlight windows enhance the atmosphere. Situated in Mosgiel, close to the Airport, just 15 minutes from Dunedin. We are a retired Christian couple who enjoy gardening, architecture, tramping and history.

The Old Vicarage	**Tel:** (03) 489 8236	**Cost:** Double $65-$85
Homestay	**Fax:** (03) 489 8236	Single $45
14km S of Dunedin	**E:** l.l.woodfield@clear.net.nz	Visa/MC
Lois & Lance Woodfield	**W:** www.bnb.co.nz/hosts/	**Beds:** 1 Queen 2 Single
14 Mure Street	theoldvicarage.html	(2 bdrm)
Mosgiel, Otago		**Bath:** 1 Guests share

Waihola

We have a very comfortable home situated in a quiet street, only 15 minutes drive to Dunedin Airport. Our double room has Queen sized bed with ensuite, teamaking facilities, TV, fridge and heater. Lake Waihola is popular for boating, fishing and swimming. We have one friendly cat. We enjoy meeting people and ensure a very pleasant stay. Please phone.

B&B Self-contained Homestay	**Tel:** (03) 417 8218	**Cost:** Double $65
40km S of Dunedin	**Fax:** (03) 417 8287	Single $40
Lillian & Trevor Robinson	**Mob:** 025 545 935	Dinner $20 B/A Visa/MC
Sandown Street, Rapid No 13	**W:** www.bnb.co.nz/hosts/	**Beds:** 1 Queen 2 Single
Waihola	robinson.html	(2 bdrm)
South Otago		**Bath:** 1 Ensuite 1 Family share

Waihola

"Ivy Cottage" is on the northern end of the "Southern Scenic Route". Guests enjoy uninterrupted views of Lake Waihola, farmlands, forests. An excellent base for day trips. North, Dunedin's Albatross, Heritage, South, "The Catlins" scenic beauty; West, Central Otago's orchards, vineyards; East, Taieri Mouth & Pacific coastline. Waihola features Wetlands, Limestone fossils, aquatic recreation. "The Shed" our detached accommodation has ensuites, tea facilities, TV, heating and laundry. Dining options include our cuisine with wines or Waihola restaurants. "Bud" is our friendly golden retriever. Wheel chair friendly.

Ivy Cottage - Lake Waihola	**Tel:** (03) 417 8946	**Cost:** Double $70 Single $50
B&B Homestay Lakeside Cottage	**Fax:** (03) 417 8966	Child $20 under 14yrs
40km S of Dunedin	**W:** www.bnb.co.nz/hosts/	Dinner $25 2 nights $125
Bryan & Robin Leckie	ivycottagelakewaihola.html	Visa/MC
Rapid No7, State Highway 1		**Beds:** 1 Double 1 Twin (2 bdrm)
Waihola, Otago		**Bath:** 2 Ensuite

Balclutha

Join our family at "Balcairn" a 500 acre sheep, beef and deer working farm and enjoy the quiet, peaceful surroundings of life in the country. Guests are welcome to join in whatever farm activity is happening on the day or enjoy a farm tour. Our location is an ideal stopover for guests travelling through the beautiful Catlins Scenic Reserve with its wonderful wildlife. We have a family cat "Jonty". Campervan point available. Guests can be met from public transport. No smoking in our home please.

Balcairn	**Tel:** (03) 418 1385	**Cost:** Double $80
Self-contained Farmstay	**Fax:** (03) 418 4385	Single $45
22km NW of Balclutha	**E:** balcairn@xtra.co.nz	Dinner $25 by arrangement
Helen & Ken Spittle	**W:** www.bnb.co.nz/hosts/	Child $20
Blackburn Road	balcairn.html	**Beds:** 2 Double 2 Single
Hillend, RD 2		(2 bdrm)
Balclutha		**Bath:** 1 Guests share

Balclutha

We welcome guests to our comfortable country home with large garden, swimming pool, and beautiful views of green pasture and river flats. We farm 530 acres running 800 deer, 150 cattle and 1000 sheep. We offer our guests an extra option of a Jet boat ride or Fishing Trips with Alan, an experienced fisherman on the Clutha River, in our commercial boat Blue Mountain Jet. We are centrally located for people travelling to the Catlins, Queenstown or Te Anau. Directions: Please telephone.

Argyll Farmstay	**Tel:** (03) 415 9268	**Cost:** Double $80 Single $45
Farmstay	**Fax:** (03) 415 9268	Child neg Dinner $25
26km W of Balclutha	**Mob:** 025 318 241	Visa/MC
Trish & Alan May	**E:** argyllfm@ihug.co.nz	**Beds:** 1 Queen 1 Twin 2 Single
Clutha River Road, Clydevale	**W:** www.bnb.co.nz/hosts/	(2 bdrm)
RD 4, Balclutha	argyllfarmstay.html	**Bath:** 1 Guests share

Balclutha

Welcome to Breadalbane, 1300 acres of rolling farm land, with sheep, deer and farm forestry, located within two minutes of the Southern Scenic Route and Telford Polytechnic. Relax in peaceful surroundings in our large country garden, or stroll along the farm lane enjoying the panoramic views. Our home is well heated, all beds have electric blankets, each room has tea/coffee making facilities, with TV in the double room. Complimentary laundry available. We have a friendly corgi dog and cat. Farm Tour by arrangement. Phone for directions.

Breadalbane	**Tel:** (03) 418 2568	**Cost:** Double $80 Single $45
B&B Farmstay	**Fax:** (03) 418 2591	Child $20 Dinner $25
5km S of Balclutha	**Mob:** 025 651 4215	S/C House at Kaka Point $60
Carolynne & Ken Stephens	**W:** www.bnb.co.nz/hosts/	$10 each extra person
293 Freezing Works Road	breadalbane.html	**Beds:** 1 Double 2 Twin (3 bdrm)
RD 3 Balclutha		**Bath:** 1 Guests share

Balclutha

Experience the peace and charm of yesteryear in historic Benhar. We offer quality and comfort in our character home and extensive gardens. Our guestrooms are spacious and comfortably furnished, complete with individual robes and hairdryers. A leisurely continental breakfast with homemade breads and muffins can be enjoyed in our lounge or garden. Situated at the gateway to the Catlins, 40 mins. from Dunedin airport, your comfort is our objective. Your hosts, Noel and Kate, along with Thomas, our household cat, welcomes you to our home, Lesmahagow.

Lesmahagow	**Tel:** (03) 418 2507	**Cost:** Double $85-$100
B&B Homestay	**Mob:** 025 578 465	Single $65-$85 Child $20
4km N of Balclutha	**Tollfree:** 0800 301 224	Dinner $25 Lunches B/A
Noel & Kate O'Malley	**E:** lesmahagow@xtra.co.nz	**Beds:** 1 Queen 3 Double
Main Road	**W:** www.lesmahagow.co.nz	2 Single (4 bdrm)
Benhar		**Bath:** 2 Guests share
RD 2, Balclutha		1 Family share

Clinton

We welcome you to our warm spacious home, set on 45 acres of farmland surrounded by Podocarp bush. Unwind from your travel in peace and tranquillity. Follow walkways through 5 acres of native flora with some Podocarp trees being over 500 years old. Listen to the Bell birds, Fantails and wood pigeons. If you wish Roy will be happy to introduce you to our farm animals or take you for a game of bowls. We also have a pet cat who won't annoy you, and a frisky foxy. Please phone or book in advance.

Wairuna Bush	**Tel:** (03) 415 7222	**Cost:** Double $80
Farmstay Country B&B	**E:** kath.carruthers@xtra.co.nz	Single $40
33km S of Balclutha	**W:** www.bnb.co.nz/hosts/	Dinner $25 B/A
Kathleen & Roy Carruthers	wairunabush.html	**Beds:** 1 Queen 1 Double
Clinton		1 Twin (3 bdrm)
RD		**Bath:** 1 Guests share
South Otago		

Clinton

Introducing Strathearn's cosy self-contained cottage, "Grandma's House". Strathearn is an established 3000ac family operated sheep and beef farm. Join with us, our two kids, pets - kunekunes, alpaca, hens, ducks, cat & dog - and unwind whilst experiencing farm activities and hill vistas, or fishing the renowned Waipahi and Mataura Rivers. Breakfast at your leisure from our full breakfast hamper (sugar-free if required). Children welcome, cot available. "Grandma's House" overlooks SH1 between Clinton and Waipahi, making Strathearn halfway to everywhere Southern - Catlins, Fiordland, Invercargill, Dunedin and Central Otago.

Strathearn Cottage Farmstay
B&B Self-contained Farmstay
8.2km W of Clinton
Ngaire & Warwick Taylor
Strathearn Road, Wairuna RD
Clinton

Tel: (03) 415 7444
Mob: 025 392 938
E: wf_na_taylor@xtra.co.nz
W: www.bnb.co.nz/hosts/
strathearn.html

Cost: Double $85 Single $55
Child $10 (6 - 10yrs)
Under 5 free Visa/MC Amex
Beds: 1 Double 1 Twin
(1 bdrm)
Bath: 1 Private

Nuggets - The Catlins

Why go elsewhere when the Nuggets has it all. Base yourself here. New Zealand's largest selection of wildlife. Seals, sealions, penguins and birdlife. Two private luxury self-contained units, centrally heated, beautiful views and absolutely on the water's edge. Your host is a Wildlife Ranger and professional photographer. We cater for enthusiasts who care for the protection of our wildlife. Sleep to the roar of waves and walk our deserted beach. Dinner served in your unit. Breakfast in our home. Only accommodation on Nugget Road.

Nugget Lodge
Self-contained
24km S of Balclutha
Kath & Noel Widdowson
Nugget Road
RD 1, Balclutha
South Otago

Tel: (03) 412 8783
Fax: (03) 412 8784
E: lighthouse@nuggetlodge.co.nz
W: www.nuggetlodge.co.nz

Cost: Double $95 Dinner $35pp
Breakfast $15pp
Visa/MC/Bankcard
accepted
Beds: 1 Queen 1 Double
1 Single (2 bdrm)
Bath: 2 Ensuite

Kaka Point - The Catlins

A fully self contained sunny Bed & Breakfast unit in a tranquil bush garden setting, with sea view, bell birds and tuis. Bedroom with twin beds, plus double divan in lounge. Wheelchair facilities. Five minutes from a beautiful sandy beach for swimming or long walks. next door to scenic reserve and bush walks. You can have breakfast in the garden with the birds, or a visit from Baxter the cat if you wish. Non smoking. Laundry facilities available. Cooking facilities.

Rata Cottage
B&B Self-contained
21km S of Balclutha
Jean Schreuder
31 Rata Street
Kaka Point
South Otago

Tel: (03) 412 8779
Mob: 025 607 5790
W: www.bnb.co.nz/hosts/
ratacottage.html

Cost: Double $60
Single $55
Child $7
Beds: 1 Twin (1 bdrm)
Bath: 1 Ensuite

Owaka - The Catlins

Welcome ..... Situated within walking distance to the beautiful Purakaunui Falls, Alan enjoys taking people around our 1900 acre sheep, cattle and deer farm. Our home offers warm, comfortable accommodation. One guest bedroom has an ensuite, and day-room opening to a large garden. A private bathroom services other guest rooms. We enjoy dining with our guests. The Catlins area features the yellow-eyed penguin. Directions: Take Highway 92 to Owaka from Balclutha or Invercargill. From Owaka follow the signs to Purakaunui Falls.

Greenwood
Farmstay or Self-contained
at Papatowai Beach
15km S of Owaka
Alan & Helen-May Burgess
739 Purakaunui Falls Road
Owaka, South Otago

Tel: (03) 415 8259
Fax: (03) 415 8259
Mob: 025 384 538
E: greenwoodfarm@xtra.co.nz
W: www.bnb.co.nz/hosts/
greenwood.html

Cost: Double $75-$85 Single $55
Child 1/2 price Dinner $28
S/C cottage (sleeps 8) $65p/n
(2 people) $10 extra person
Beds: 1 Queen 3 Single (3 bdrm)
Bath: 1 Ensuite 1 Private
1 Family share

Owaka - The Catlins

Our 2000-acre farm is situated in an area renowned for its bush and coastal scenery, within walking distance of the beautiful Purakaunui Falls. Our farm runs sheep, cattle, deer and horses. As well as seeing normal farm activities, horse riding, bush walks and fishing trips are available in the district. We live in a comfortable farmhouse with a cat, as our family have all left home, and enjoy eating local delicacies. Children very welcome. Directions: Follow signs to Purakaunui Falls - we are the closest house to them.

Tarara Downs
Farmstay
16 S of Owaka
Ida & John Burgess
857 Puaho Road
RD 2, Owaka

Tel: (03) 415 8293
Fax: (03) 415 8293
Mob: 025 215 1428
E: tarara@ihug.co.nz
W: www.bnb.co.nz/hosts/
tararadowns.html

Cost: Double $55-$70 Single $45
Child 1/2 price Dinner $20
Beds: 1 Double 2 Single
(2 bdrm)
Bath: 1 Ensuite
1 Family share

If you would like dinner
most hosts require 24 hours notice.

Owaka - The Catlins

There are NO strangers here, only friends we haven't met.
Situated 100 metres from beach, with Hooker sealions.
Close to all Catlins scenery, waterfalls, walks, spoonbill
colony. Golf course, 3kms, chip and putt on property.
Private penguin viewing with Catlins Natural Wonders.
Delicious breakfast, all homemade goodies. Organically
grown vegetables from garden served with fabulous meals,
special diets catered for. Directions: Follow signs "towards"
Pounawea, at golf club go "across" bridge turn right to
Newhaven, at Suratbay Road (3km metal) first house on left.

Kepplestone-By-The-Sea	**Tel:** (03) 415 8134	**Cost:** Double $65-$95
B&B Self-contained Homestay	**Fax:** (03) 415 8137	Single $60
6km E of Owaka	**Mob:** 025 6767 253	Dinner B/A
Gay & Arch Maley	**Tollfree:** 0800 105 134	**Beds:** 1 King/Twin 1 Queen
9 Surat Bay Road	**E:** kepplestone@xtra.co.nz	2 Single (3 bdrm)
Newhaven, Owaka 9251	**W:** www.bnb.co.nz/hosts/	**Bath:** 2 Ensuite
	kepplestonebythesea.html	1 Family share

Owaka

Our 450 acre sheep and cattle grazing unit is situated 15
minutes from Nugget Point and 10 minutes from Cannibal
Bay. Relax in our cosy private cottage set in a 2 acre
developing garden. Alternatively enjoy the comfortable
relaxed atmosphere of our non-smoking home shared by
our 2 Burmese cats, miniature poodle and occasionally ,
foreign exchange students. Our interests include training
sheepdogs, handcrafts, gardening, reading, horses,
grandchildren and meeting people. Breakfast with us or in
private. Evening meals by arrangement. Bookings
essential. Please phone after 4 pm.

Hillview	**Tel:** (03) 415 8457	**Cost:** Double $75 Single $40
B&B Self-contained Farmstay	**Fax:** (03) 415 8650	Child $20 Dinner from $20
6km N of Owaka	**Mob:** 025 201 9115	Visa/MC
Kate & Bruce McLachlan	**E:** hillviewcatlins@xtra.co.nz	**Beds:** 2 Queen 4 Single
Hunt Road	**W:** www.bnb.co.nz/hosts/	(4 bdrm)
Katea, RD 2, Owaka	hillview.html	**Bath:** 2 Guests share

Owaka - The Catlins

We farm a 1500 acre property carrying sheep, cattle and deer. We have a friendly fox terrier called 'Boon'. Fishing trips may be arranged. Golf equipment available, 9 hole golf course 10 minute drive. We are near Kaka Point renowned for beach, lighthouse and viewing of the yellow-eyed penguins and seals. Directions: Take Highway 92 from Balclutha towards Owaka, first turn right past Sawmill. Matuanui Road - No Exit. From Owaka turn left before Sawmill up gravel road Matuanui Road - No Exit.

Farmstay
11km N of Owaka
Kathryn & Bruce Wilson
Glenomaru
RD 1
Balclutha

Tel: (03) 415 8282
Fax: (03) 415 8282
W: www.bnb.co.nz/hosts/ wilson.html

Cost: Double $60
Single $35
Child 1/2 price Dinner $20
Beds: 1 Double 4 Single
(3 bdrm)
Bath: 2 Family share

Owaka - The Catlins

Welcome to our warm and comfortable home, which is situated on a 25 acre farmlet, surrounded by colourful, peaceful gardens with splendid unspoilt views. Located in the heart of the Catlins, renowned for its wildlife and spectacular scenery, we are within walking distance of Owaka township with its restaurants, museum and other amenities. Our guests are encouraged to dine with us for the evening meal when we enjoy quality local food and wine. We are involved in community activities and enjoy meeting people.

J T's Bed & Breakfast
B&B Countrystay
200m N of Owaka
John & Thelma Turnbull
Main Road
Owaka

Tel: (03) 415 8127
Fax: (03) 415 8129
Mob: 025 649 7693
E: jtowaka@ihug.co.nz
W: www.bnb.co.nz/hosts/ jts.html

Cost: Double $75
Single $50
Child half price Dinner $25
Beds: 1 Queen 1 Twin
(2 bdrm)
Bath: 1 Guests share

Don't try to travel too far in one day.
Take time to enjoy the company
of your hosts and other locals.

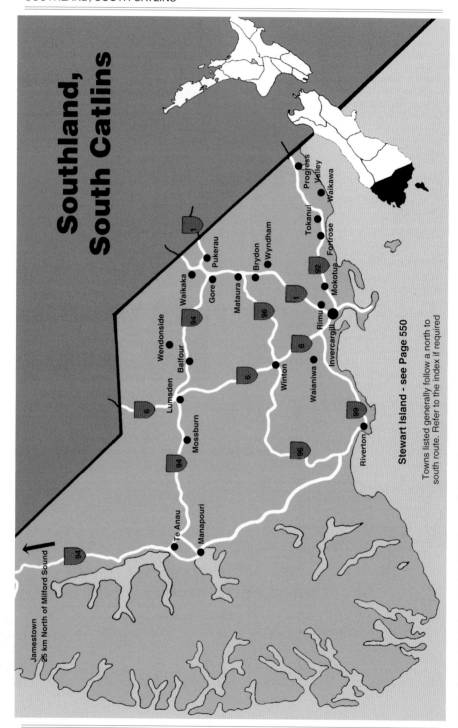

Southland,
South Catlins

Stewart Island - see Page 550

Towns listed generally follow a north to
south route. Refer to the index if required

Jamestown
25 km North of Milford Sound

Milford Sound - Jamestown

Established in this unique wilderness area by Charlie in 1995 this is arguably the most remote wilderness B&B and homestay in NZ. Accesible from Milford Sound by aeroplane (20 minute flight and 2 hour walk) or direct by helicopter (15 minute flight). "Charlies Place" is nestled in the beautiful and historic ghost town of Jamestown Bay at Lake McKerrow surrounded by the beautiful podocarp rainforest and fantastic mountainous scenery of Fiordland National Park. Charlies Brochures and transport details obtainable Air Fiordland offices in Te Anau.

Charlies Place
B&B Homestay Wilderness
Homestay
25km N of Milford Sound
Charlie Paterson

Tel: (03) 249 7505
A/H: (07) 332 2093
Fax: (03) 249 7080
Mob: 025 893 570
E: airfiord@airfiordland.com
W: www.webfactor.co.nz/
charlies-place

Cost: Double $110
Single $55
Dinner $35 Homestay $105
Season Nov to April
Beds: 1 Double 1 Twin
(2 bdrm)
Bath: 1 Ensuite 1 Family share

Te Anau

A warm welcome to our deer farm, just 5 minutes drive from Te Anau township and one kilometre off the Milford Highway. David, besides farming, works in the Deer industry, while I teach at the local Primary School. Our children are away from home now, but our cat and dog enjoy meeting our visitors. Your accommodation, which has mountain and lake views, is a self contained bed-sitting room with ensuite, TV, tea/

Farmstay
Teresa & Dave Hughes
123 Sinclair Road
RD 1
Te Anau

Tel: (03) 249 7581
Fax: (03) 249 7589
Mob: 025 344 016
E: daveandteresa@paradise.net.nz
W: www.bnb.co.nz/hosts/
hughes.html

Cost: Double $80
Single $55
Beds: 2 Single (1 bdrm)
Bath: 1 Ensuite

Te Anau

You are surrounded by "Million Dollar" views while enjoying the comfort of our large modern family home. Electric blankets, heaters in rooms. Traditional farm style meals. Excellent base for day trips to Milford or Doubtful Sound. A two night stay is recommended. Farm tour prior to dinner of our 348ha farm which has 3700 sheep and approx 100 cattle. Excellent fishing rivers within a few minutes drive as are great walking tracks, golf course etc. We have a cat. Smoke free home. Directions: Please phone.

Farmstay
20km E of Te Anau
Dorothy & Donald Cromb
Tapua
RD 2
Te Anau

Tel: (03) 249 5805
Fax: (03) 249 5805
Mob: 025 201 9109
E: Tapua.Cromb@xtra.co.nz
W: www.bnb.co.nz/hosts/
cromb.html

Cost: Double $110
Single $70
Dinner $25pp Visa/MC
Beds: 1 King/Twin 1 Twin
(2 bdrm)
Bath: 1 Guests share

Te Anau

Rob, Nancy and Chardonnay our Burmese cat welcome you to our quiet and tranquil home facing a park, five minutes walk to the lake and town centre. We are a couple retired from farming and enjoy meeting people. Our modern home includes a courtyard barbecue and gardens. Te Anau is a special place to visit with the magnificent scenery of the Fiordland National Park including spectacular Milford and Doubtful Sounds. All tours are picked up and delivered to the door. Off street parking and storage available.

Rob & Nancy's Place
Self-contained Homestay
R & N Marshall
13 Fergus Square
Te Anau

Tel: (03) 249 8241
Fax: (03) 249 7397
Mob: 025 226 1820
E: rob.nancy@xtra.co.nz
W: www.bnb.co.nz/hosts/
robnancysplace.html

Cost: Double $90-$110
   Single $65 Visa/MC
Beds: 2 King 2 Single (3 bdrm)
Bath: 1 Ensuite
   1 Guests share

Te Anau

Our 750 acre farm is 5ks (3 miles) north of Te Anau on the Milford Sound Highway. Our smoke free home and accommodation is on a terrace with fantastic panoramic views of lake and mountains. Guest rooms are separate form the house in a garden setting, with all the facilities to make your stay warm and comfortable. We enjoy guests joining us for breakfast and evenings of friendship and conversation. We have friendly tame sheep. To find us, turn right into Sinclair Road, then immediately right into Driveway.

Perenuka Farm
Self-contained Farmstay
5km N of Te Anau
Margaret & Les Simpson
RD 1
Te Anau

Tel: (03) 249 7841
Fax: (03) 249 7841
E: perenuka@xtra.co.nz
W: http://webnz.com/bbnz/
perenuka.htm

Cost: Double $95-$105
   Visa/MC
Beds: 2 Queen (2 bdrm)
Bath: 2 Ensuite

Te Anau

Our country homestay, 3 km from Te Anau, has detached, self contained cottage, privacy assured, peaceful rural setting and spectacular views of surrounding mountains. We are ideally situated for your Fiordland experience. Having for many years both worked on the Milford track and driven visitors to Milford Sound we are able to offer the very best advice for you Te Anau- Fiordland visit. Our pets- donkey, pony, sheep, pig, goats, terriers (2) are waiting to greet you!! Welome to Te Anau-Fiordland. Please contact us for reservations.

The Farmyard
Homestay Country Homestay
3km S of Te Anau
Helen & Ray Willett
Charles Nairn Road -24
Te Anau 9681

Tel: (03) 249 7833
Fax: (03) 249 7830
Mob: 025 289 0939
E: helenraywillett@actrix.co.nz
W: www.bnb.co.nz/hosts/
thefarmyard.html

Cost: Double $90-$100
Beds: 1 Double 1 Single
   (1 bdrm)
Bath: 1 Ensuite

Te Anau - Manapouri

Exclusively yours, in a tranquil setting, is a delightful sunlit self-contained cottage with courtyard garden, beautiful mountain backdrop overlooking the (famous trout fishing) Mararoa River. Murray and I with our two teenage children live on a sheep/cattle farm close to both Te Anau and Manapouri, Murray enjoys sharing his extensive knowledge of fishing and the region. I love gardening and helping with your travel plans if you wish. Bookings can be made for local tourist excursions. Looking forward to meeting you; travel safely. - Marie.

Christies Cottage	**Tel:** (03) 249 6695	**Cost:** Double $90
B&B Self-contained Farmstay	**Fax:** (03) 249 6695	Extra adult $15 Child neg
8km N of Manapouri	**E:** mchristie@xtra.co.nz	Visa/MC
Marie & Murray Christie	**W:** www.christiescottage.co.nz	**Beds:** 1 Double 2 Single
Hillside/Manapouri Road		(2 bdrm)
Te Anau		**Bath:** 1 Private

Te Anau

"House of Wood" with natural timber throughout interior is a uniquely designed two storey wooden house with outside balconies and beautiful views. We know the Otago/ Southland area extremely well and can help you make the most of your time here. Now our three daughters have left home we have more time for woodturning, walking and spinning. Along with Kaidy our Westhighland Terrier, we welcome you to our smokefree home which is in a quiet residential area. Please phone for directions.

House of Wood	**Tel:** (03) 249 8404	**Cost:** Double $95-$110
Homestay	**Fax:** (03) 249 7676	Single $80
Te Anau Central	**Mob:** 025 220 4356	**Beds:** 1 Queen 1 Double
Elaine & Trevor Lett	**E:** houseofwood@extra.co.nz	2 Single (3 bdrm)
44 Moana Crescent	**W:** www.bnb.co.nz/hosts/	**Bath:** 1 Ensuite 1 Guests share
Te Anau	houseofwood.html	

Te Anau

Situated opposite Department of Conservation headquarters, 10 min. walk to shops and restaurants. Comfortable pleasant rooms feature Queen or Twin. Family room - 1 King plus Twin. All ensuite, TV and tea making. Courtesy car to restaurants or meeting coaches. Off street parking and luggage storage for track walks or overnight kayaking. Agents for excursions to Milford and Doubtful Sounds. We have two Burmese cats. Directions: as you approach town, turn left where sign posted off Highway 94. First house on right. Off season rates. Guests laundry.

The Cats Whiskers	**Tel:** (03) 249 8112	**Cost:** Double $125-$135
B&B	**Fax:** (03) 249 8112	Single $95 Child 1/2 price
1km S of Te Anau	**E:** i.t.maher@paradise.net.nz	Visa/MC
Irene & Terry Maher	**W:** www.webnz.co.nz/bbnz/	**Beds:** 1 King 2 Queen
2 Lakefront Drive	catwh.htm	4 Single (3 bdrm)
Te Anau		**Bath:** 3 Ensuite

Te Anau

John, Carolyn and Casey (14) all enjoy meeting people, (our 2 elder sons have left home to pursue their chosen careers). We share our home with 2 friendly cats (Joe and Milo) and Misty our mischevious German Wirehair dog who will play fetch till you drop! Casey, our daughter now has a Golden Retreiver pup (Meg) which she is training - she is soft and adorable and very cheeky. Other pets include pet lambs which you are welcome to bottle feed and our pet deer Shirley who is always looking for something extra to eat!

Carolyn is a keen gardener and a superb cook with local venison or fresh Fiordland fish - a favourite. Nobody has ever left our place hungry!

John operates a contracting business in our local farming community. His interests include winter squash and he is also an active member of our local Lion's Club. His first love though is hunting and fishing in Fiordland so is well qualified to offer guided fishing on our local rivers for brown and rainbow trout, wether it be fly fishing or spin fishing for the novice who just wants a day out - we can accommodate you and supply all necessary gear!

Our country property overlooks the scenic Mararoa river which is itself famous for its trout fishing and just a 5 min walk away. We live at "The Key", a small rural community on the main Queenstown, Te Anau highway (15 mins to Te Anau). Surrounded by sheep, beef and deer farms and majestic mountains it makes an ideal base to explore Fiordland. For your convenience we also offer a booking service for any of the local tourist trips and are more than happy to provide information or advice to plan your stay.

We offer a courtesy car for anybody travelling by bus. We also offer free of charge evening bike rides, bush walks and fishing - for anyone wanting a real "Country" experience. Your accommodation is a warm, sunny and modern self-contained cottage with plenty of room and character and fully equiped for a comfortable stay. Your cottage has a beautiful country view and privacy if you prefer, or you are welcome to join us at your leisure for some good old country hospitality - we'd love to see you!

Country Cottage
Self-contained Farmstay
26km E of Te Anau
Carolyn & John Klein
The Key
RD 2
Te Anau

Tel: (03) 249 5807
Fax: (03) 249 5807
E: kleinbnb@ihug.co.nz
W: www.fishfiordland.com

Cost: Double $80
　　　Single $55
　　　Child neg Dinner $25
　　　Visa/MC
Beds: 1 Queen 3 Single
　　　(2 bdrm)
Bath: 1 Private

Te Anau

Shakespeare House is a well established Bed & Breakfast where we keep a home atmosphere with personal service. We are situated in a quiet residential area yet are within walking distance of shops, lake and restaurants. Our rooms are ground floor and with the choice of King, Double or Twin beds. Each room has private facilities, TV, tea/coffee making. Tariff includes continental or delicious cooked breakfast. Guest laundry available. Winter rates May to September. Along with Brothersoul our pussy we welcome you to Te Anau.

Shakespeare House	**Tel:** (03) 249 7349	**Cost:** Double $80-$112
B&B S/C Guesthouse	**Fax:** (03) 249 7629	Single $60-$80
1km N of Te Anau Centre	**Tollfree:** 0800 249 349	Child $5 - $15 Visa/MC
Margaret & Jeff Henderson	**E:** marg.shakespeare.house	**Beds:** 4 King 3 Double
10 Dusky Street	@xtra.co.nz	4 Single (8 bdrm)
PO Box 32, Te Anau	**W:** www.bnb.co.nz/hosts/	**Bath:** 8 Ensuite
	shakespearehouse.html	

Te Anau

Jeff, an aircraft engineer, and Jan, who works from home as a freelance journalist and marketing consultant, welcome you to their small farmlet on the edge of Fiordland, just five minutes drive from Te Anau. Relax outdoors in the garden and enjoy the peace and comfort of our rural location between visiting Milford or Doubtful Sounds, or walking one of the many nearby tracks. Our family includes a Cairn Terrier, and two cats. We can advise tours and sightseeing and make bookings where needed.

Kepler Cottage	**Tel:** (03) 249 7185	**Cost:** Double $120
B&B Farmstay Rural Homestay	**Fax:** (03) 249 7186	Single $90
5km S of Te Anau	**Mob:** 025 314 076	Visa/MC
Jan & Jeff Ludemann	**E:** kepler@teanau.co.nz	**Beds:** 1 Queen 3 Single
William Stephen Road	**W:** www.fiordland.org.nz/html/	(3 bdrm)
Te Anau	kepler.html	**Bath:** 1 Ensuite 1 Private

Te Anau

This accommodation is a very comfortable, large self-contained farmhouse. All rooms are well equipped - Log burner, TV, good kitchen, auto washing machine, phone. It has a private country setting and is an excellent base for families or groups to explore Fiordland from. We are a keen farming family with cattle, sheep dogs and pets. Our farm is situated at the base of the Takitimu Mountains 15 mins from Manapouri, 25 mins from Te Anau. Good scenery,

Grassy Creek	**Tel:** (03) 249 8553	**Cost:** Double $90
Self-contained Farmstay	**Fax:** (03) 249 8333	Single $20
45km E of Te Anau	**E:** ray.mcconnell@xtra.co.nz	**Beds:** 2 Double 6 Single
Carol & Ray McConnell	**W:** www.bnb.co.nz/hosts/	(4 bdrm)
RD 1	grassycreek.html	**Bath:** 2 Private
Te Anau		

Te Anau

Lynwood Park is a developing 6 acre garden set amidst my families 450 acre sheep, cattle and deer farm Our home was built to ensure guests have privacy and comfort. Each guest has a private entrance, TV, fridge, tea/coffee making facilities. We offer the use of our Barbecue, laundry facilities and childrens play area which Daniella looks forward to sharing with you. I am able to advise or arrange most activities to make your holiday a memorable experience. Come as guests - leave as friends.

Lynwood Park	**Tel:** (03) 249 7990	**Cost:** Double $90
B&B	**Fax:** (03) 249 7990	Single $70
8km S of Te Anau	**Mob:** 021 129 5626	Child $30 Visa/MC
Trina & Daniella Baker	**E:** lynwood.park@xtra.co.nz	**Beds:** 2 Queen 3 Single
RD 2, Te Anau	**W:** www.bnb.co.nz/hosts/	(3 bdrm)
	lynwoodpark.html	**Bath:** 2 Ensuite

Te Anau

Virginia an Gerhard and our two children welcome you to our new Bed & Breakfast (20 years experience in hospitality, we speak German). Privacy with comfort, quiet spacious, ensuited bedrooms, quality beds, individual heating and television. Gourmet breakfast buffet of home-made breads, jams, fresh fruits, home-bottled fruits, yoghurt, brewed coffee, special teas, mouthwatering pancakes with maple syrup and more. Centrally located, bookings arranged for all tours, pick-up at gate. Guest lounge with Internet access, laundry, off-street parking and luggage storage.

Cosy Kiwi	**Tel:** (03) 249 7475	**Cost:** Double $85-$99
B&B	**Fax:** 0064 3 249 8471	Single $60-$70
Te Anau Central	**Tollfree:** 0800 249 700	Child neg Visa/MC
Virginia and Gerhard Hirner	**E:** cosykiwi@xtra.co.nz	**Beds:** 3 King/Twin 4 Queen
186 Milford Road	**W:** www.bnb.co.nz/hosts/	9 Single (7 bdrm)
Te Anau 9681	cosykiwi.html	**Bath:** 7 Ensuite

Te Anau

Genuine Kiwi hospitality in a magic setting 5 minutes from Te Anau. Hand feed tame fallow deer, meet two friendly cats. Sit on the veranda of our fully self contained cabin and enjoy watching deer with a lake and mountain view. The two room cabin has cooking facilities, fridge, microwave, TV, 1 Queen, 1 double plus bathroom. Our modern two storey smoke-free home is set in an extensive garden. Two downstairs guest bedrooms. Lex is a keen fly fisherman and average golfer, while I love to garden. Directions: Please phone.

Rose 'n' Reel	**Tel:** (03) 249 7582	**Cost:** Double $90
Self-contained Farmstay	**Fax:** (03) 249 7582	Single $60
2km E of Te Anau	**Mob:** 025 545 723	Visa/MC
Lyn & Lex Lawrence	**E:** rosenreel@xtra.co.nz	**Beds:** 1 Queen 1 Double
Benloch Lane	**W:** www.fiordland.org.nz/htm/	1 Single (3 bdrm)
RD 2, Te Anau	rosenreel.html	**Bath:** 1 Private 1 Guests share

Te Anau

Fiordland Lodge comprises two specially designed log cabins which have been built in the traditional method with sun dried logs that have been hand peeled. The interior is completed with recycled New Zealand native timbers.

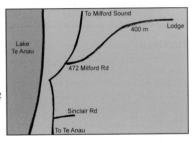

The lodge is situated on our 40 acre farm, with stunning views overlooking Lake Te Anau and the mountains of Fiordland National Park beyond. The cabins are fully self-contained, including a kitchen. There is a queen sized bed downstairs, and two/three single beds upstairs. The grounds are landscaped with barbecue area. Transport can be arranged from Te Anau.

Ron is a licenced professional guide. He specialises in Wilderness fly fishing, supplying all fishing equipment as required, plus tuition for the less experienced. Ron also provides nature guiding services for birdwatching, natural history and geology. Guided hunting is also available for all species of wild game.

Ron's expertise is unique. He was a National Park Ranger for 25 years, 17 of those in Fiordland. Together we enjoy the outdoors. We have three teenage children, a cat and a dog.

Directions: Follow the Te Anau-Milford Highway 5km north of Te Anau, a short distance past Sinclair Road. Turn up the drive at No. 472, and continue as far as you can go keeping right (400m) to the top of the hill.
NOTE that off-season rate apply May 1st - September 30th.

Fiordland Lodge
Self-contained
5km N of Te Anau
Robynne & Ron Peacock
472 Te Anau - Milford Highway
RD 1
Te Anau

Tel: (03) 249 7832
Fax: (03) 249 7832
E: fiordlandguidesltd@xtra.co.nz
W: www.fiordlandguides.co.nz

Cost: Double $140
Single $120
Child $20 extra adult $30
Visa/MC
Beds: 2 Queen 5 Single
(4 bdrm)
Bath: 2 Private

Te Anau

A unique holiday experience awaits you at Davaar Country Lodge, nestled in the foothills of the Takitimu Mountains near Milford Sound in Fiordland. 'Davaar' is a 2800 acre (1100 hectare) sheep and cattle station, located in an idyllic rural setting on state highway 94, just 20 minutes east of Te Anau, at The Key.

The Lodge is exclusively yours and is fully self-contained with comprehensive kitchen and laundry facilities. A wood-burning log fire and electric blankets on all the beds make Davaar Country Lodge a cozy, warm retreat. We provide a continental style breakfast including fresh farm eggs, which is available in the lodge for you to breakfast at your leisure.

The lodge is perfect for tourists, families, mountain-bikers, trampers and hunters, it is also great for anyone just looking for a real Kiwi experience. Located on the Mararoa River, with the Oreti River and Mavora lakes nearby, it is a fisherman's paradise. A fishing or hunting guide can be arranged on request. 'Davaar' offers a wonderful combination of country hospitality with the freedom to suit your own special vacation needs.

Here you can get off the beaten track and explore some of New Zealand's most spectacular back country. Your hosts James and Fiona Macdonald look forward to welcoming you. We are really easy to find, situated on the main route between Queenstown and Milford Sound. Please phone for further directions.

Davaar Country Lodge
Self-contained Farmstay
26km E of Te Anau
James & Fiona Macdonald
RD 2
Te Anau

Tel: (03) 249 5838
Fax: (03) 249 5839
E: davaar@xtra.co.nz
W: www.bnb.co.nz/hosts/
davaarcountrylodge.html

Cost: Double $85
Single $60
Child $15
Beds: 1 Queen 3 Single
(2 bdrm)
Bath: 1 Private

Te Anau

Hosts Jane and Ross, Mac the Jack Russell, Molly the sheep & the 2 Moggy's. Two new, superior cottages, spacious & very appealing. Cooking facilities, ensuites, TV's, decks, laundry. Magnificent lake & mountain views from cottages. Rural, private and tranquil garden settings. Join us for breakfast and in the evenings for company. Walk down our farm to the river & lake (15 mins). Name & B&B sign at gate-1.5kms from Te Anau. We guarantee you warm hospitality, quality accommodation, and generous breakfasts.

The Croft	**Tel:** (03) 249 7393	**Cost:** Double $95-$110
B&B Self-contained Rural	**Fax:** (03) 249 7393	Visa/MC
Lifestyle	**E:** rossjane.mcewan@xtra.co.nz	**Beds:** 2 Queen 1 Single
1.5km N of Te Anau	**W:** www.thecroft.co.nz	(2 bdrm)
Jane & Ross McEwan		**Bath:** 2 Ensuite
Te Anau Milford Sound Road		
RD 1, Te Anau		

Te Anau

The Matai Lodge is ideally located in a quiet residential area just 2 mins walk to the lake and 5 mins to the town centre. It offers clean friendly homestyle accommodation in a smoke free environment. Full and substantial cooked and continental breakfasts, are served in the dining lounge area with tea and coffee. Cookies always available along with fresh fruit. All rooms are on the ground floor, have hot + cold vanity units, electric blankets and heaters. Te Anau is the hub of Fiordland a World Heritage national Park.

Matai Lodge	**Tel:** (03) 249 7360	**Cost:** Double $76
Guesthouse	**Fax:** (03) 249 7360	Single $55
Te Anau Central	**Tollfree:** 0800 249 736	Visa/MC
Linda & Rod James	**E:** matailodge@hotmail.com	**Beds:** 1 Queen 2 Double
42 Mokonui Street	**W:** www.bnb.co.nz/hosts/	9 Single (7 bdrm)
Te Anau	matailodgeteanau.html	**Bath:** 2 Guests share

Te Anau - Manapouri

Our 900 acre sheep, cattle and deer farm offers a farm tour after 6 pm, and views of Lake Manapouri, fiordland mountains, and the Te Anau Basin. Day trips to Doubtful and Milford Sounds, visits to Te Anau, Glow-worm Caves, or hikes on the many walking tracks, in fiordland are all within easy reach. Having travelled in the UK, Europe, Canada, Hong Kong and Singapore, we enjoy meeting guests from all over the world. We and Harriet the cat look forward to welcoming you to our home.

Crown Lea	**Tel:** (03) 249 8598	**Cost:** Double $130-$150
Farmstay	**Fax:** (03) 249 8598	Single $100
20 minutes -Manapouri, 30	**Mob:** 025 227 8366	Dinner $25
minutes-T	**E:** crownlea@xtra.co.nz	**Beds:** 1 King/Twin 1 Queen
Florence & John Pine	**W:** www.bnb.co.nz/hosts/	1 Twin (3 bdrm)
Gillespie Road	crownlea.html	**Bath:** 1 Ensuite 2 Private
RD 1, Te Anau		

Manapouri

We Don, Joy, Rosie our Sky Terrier and kittie extend a
warm welcome to all who choose to stay in our quiet and
tranquil home situated by the Waiau River Manapouri.
Each guest room has wonderful views, through the trees of
the river,mountains and lake. French doors open to cottage
gardens. Warm comfortable beds, tea and coffee
facilities.We request no smoking inside The Cottage.
Excellent breakfasts. Full breakfast available Your laundry
washed and dried ($6).Scan a photo to send home via email
no charge.

The Cottage
B&B Homestay
20km S of Te Anau
Don & Joy MacDuff
Waiau St
Manapouri

Tel: (03) 249 6838
Fax: (03) 249 6839
Mob: 021 130 3136
Tollfree: 0800 677 866
E: don.joymacduff@xtra.co.nz
W: www.bnb.co.nz/hosts/
thecottagemanapouri.html

Cost: Double $75-$90
Single $55-$65
Visa/MC
Beds: 2 Queen 1 Single
(2 bdrm)
Bath: 2 Ensuite

Mossburn

Our modern home on 301 hectares, 3000 sheep 200 beef
cattle is situated half-way between Invercargill and Te Anau,
which can be reached in 1 hour. We enjoy meeting people,
will provide quality accommodation, farm fresh food in a
welcoming friendly atmosphere. You can join in farm
activities, farm tour or just relax. The Aparima River is
adjacent to the property. Murray's a keen fly fisherman.
Guiding available. Pet Bichon Frise. Evening meal on
request. Directions please phone/fax. 24 hours notice to
avoid disappointment

Farmstay
25km S of Mossburn
Joyce & Murray Turner
RD 1
Otautau
Southland

Tel: (03) 225 7602
Fax: (03) 225 7602
E: murray.joyce@xtra.co.nz
W: www.bnb.co.nz/hosts/
turner.html

Cost: Double $70
Single $40
Child $20 Dinner $30
Beds: 1 Double 4 Single
(3 bdrm)
Bath: 1 Guests share

Lumsden

We have a 480 hectare farm which runs sheep, cattle
and deer. Surrounding our comfortable warm home,
we have a large garden with a selection of specimen
trees, rhododendrons, roses, peonys and perennials.
The golf course is 3km away - golf clubs are available-
a good fishing river nearby. We have hiked in our
mountains a lot and can give advise on where and what
to see. If you wish a four wheel drive trip is available.

Josephville Gardens
Self-contained Farmstay
9km S of Lumsden
Annette & Bob Menlove
Rapid sign 824
State Highway 6, RD 4
Lumsden

Tel: (03) 248 7114
Fax: (03) 248 7114
Mob: 025 204 9753
E: bobannette@menlove.net
W: www.bnb.co.nz/hosts/
josephvillegardens.html

Cost: Double $80
Single $70
Dinner $25
Beds: 2 Double 4 Single
(4 bdrm)
Bath: 2 Private 1 Family share

Winton

Enjoy your own comfortable fully equipped three bedroom house plus separate bunkhouse for energetic children. Set in historical garden on a sheep and flower farm, in the heart of Southland. Flowers bloom October to May. Tennis court on property, trout river 2 minutes away, excellent golf course 10 minutes @ $15 per round! Fishing guides available. Central to all southern parks, coasts & adventures. Good central location for daytrips everywhere in region.

Nethershiel Farm Cottage
Self-contained Farmstay
10mins N of Winton
Mrs Henderson & staff
710 Riverside No 3 Rd
Winton 9662

Tel: (03) 236 0791
Fax: (03) 236 0101
Mob: 025 340 598
E: nethershiel.farm@xtra.co.nz
W: www.nethershielfarm.co.nz

Cost: Double $75
Single $50
Child $20 under 12yrs
Visa/MC
Beds: 2 Queen 2 Single
(3 bdrm)
Bath: 1 Private

Balfour

Welcome to our 650 acre sheep and deer farm. Relax in our garden, enjoy a farm tour with mountain views or a game of tennis. Trout fish the Mataura, Oreti or Waikaia rivers. Fishing guide can be arranged on request. Enjoy a relaxing dinner with fine food, wine and conversation. Breakfast is served with fresh baked bread, home-made yoghurt, muesli, jams and preserves. Interests include handcrafts, tennis, photography and fishing. We have 3 school-age children and 2 cats. Smoke free home.

Hillcrest
Farmstay
3km N of Balfour
Liz & Ritchie Clark
206 Old Balfour Road
RD 1, Balfour

Tel: (03) 201 6165
Fax: (03) 201 6165
E: clarkrl@esi.co.nz
W: www.bnb.co.nz/hosts/
hillcrestbalfour.html

Cost: Double $100
Single $70
Dinner $20pp
Beds: 2 King/Twin (2 bdrm)
Bath: 1 Private 1 Family share

Most of our B&Bs are non smoking.

Wendonside

Experience "Ardlamont", a 4th generation 1200 acre sheep and beef farm offering panoramic views of Northern Southland. Gourmet meals a specialty, served with fine New Zealand wines. Tour the farm, then return to the renovated comforts of our 90 year old homestead. Having travelled widely we enjoy welcoming visitors into our home. Our 3 teenage children attend university/boarding school in Dunedin. Two of New Zealand's best trout rivers only five minutes away. 15 minutes off SH94 (Queenstown - Gore - Dunedin route) Well worth the detour.

Ardlamont Farm	**Tel:** (03) 202 7774	**Cost:** Double $80
Farmstay	**Fax:** (03) 202 7774	Single $50
15km N of Riversdale	**E:** ardlamont@xtra.co.nz	Child $20 Dinner $30
Dale & Lindsay Wright	**W:** www.bnb.co.nz/hosts/	**Beds:** 1 Double 2 Single
110 Wendonside Church Rd Nth	ardlamontfarm.html	(2 bdrm)
Wendonside, RD 7, Gore		**Bath:** 1 Private

Waikaka

Venture off highway 1 for the refreshment of a quiet rural visit. Turn off highway 90 at the windmill. Drive 10 kilometres on the Waikaka Road to the T corner. Turn left, then right on to Nicholson Road. Veer right on to Robertson Road. Our 800 acre sheep and beef farm on a ridge above the Waikaka River offers superb views, a farm tour, sports facilities in nearby Waikaka and warm hospitality. Our name is on the mailbox at the top of the hill.

Blackhills Farmstay	**Tel:** (03) 207 2865	**Cost:** Double $80 Single $40
B&B Farmstay	**Fax:** (03) 207 2865	Child $20 Dinner $25 B/A
30km N of Gore	**Mob:** 025 209 1563	**Beds:** 1 King/Twin 1 Queen
Dorothy & Tom Affleck	**W:** www.bnb.co.nz/hosts/	(2 bdrm)
192 Robertson Road	blackhillsfarmstay.html	**Bath:** 1 Guests share
RD 3, Gore		1 Family share
Southland		

Pukerau - Gore

Relax with us in our warm comfortable home set in a mature garden with a rural outlook. We are just minutes away from several rivers including the Mataura which is well known for Brown Trout fishing. Fishing guide available on request. Growing a variety of orchids is our main interest, we run a few pet sheep. We enjoy meeting people and have travelled extensively ourselves. Complimentary tea & coffee available. Smokefree accommodation.

Connor Orchids	**Tel:** (03) 205 3896	**Cost:** Double $70
Homestay Country Homestay	**Fax:** (03) 205 3896	Single $45
12km E of Gore	**Mob:** 025 669 1362	Dinner B/A Visa/MC
Dawn & David Connor	**Tollfree:** 0800 372 484	**Beds:** 1 Queen 2 Single
1158 State Highway 1	**E:** ddconnor@esi.co.nz	(2 bdrm)
Pukerau	**W:** www.bnb.co.nz/hosts/	**Bath:** 1 Private
Southland	connororchids.html	1 Guests share

Gore

Sandy and Tricia are semi-retired farmers living on 43 acres where we have sheep, farm dog and hens. We are 10 minutes from Gore on the road to Dolamore Park where there are several bush walking tracks. Golf course and fishing rivers a short drive away. We enjoy meeting people, sport, reading and gardening. Laundry facilities, cot and highchair available. A Bichon Frise dog and a cat share our home. No smoking indoors please. Please phone for directions.

Irwin's Farmstay
Farmstay Homestay
6km W of Gore
Sandy & Trish Irwin
Croydon Bush
RD 7, Gore

Tel: (03) 208 6260
W: www.bnb.co.nz/hosts/
irwinsfarmstay.html

Cost: Double $70
Single $45
Child neg
Dinner $25pp B/A
Beds: 1 Queen 4 Single
(3 bdrm)
Bath: 1 Guests share

Mataura - Gore

John & Helen farm sheep and deer, on our 50 acre farmlet. We live 5 minutes, from one of the best brown trout fishing rivers in the world. Drive 1 hour south to the sea side and 1 1/2 hours northwest to lakes and ski fields. We both play golf, and enjoy gardening. Fishing guide, horse riding and garden tours can be arranged with prior notice. Over the past years, we have enjoyed sharing our spacious home and garden with lots of overseas guests. Enjoy the South.

Kowhai Place
Farmstay
12km S of Gore
JR & HM Williams
291 Glendhu Road
RD Gore

Tel: (03) 203 8774
Fax: (03) 203 8774
E: kowhaiplace@hotmail.com
W: www.bnb.co.nz/hosts/
kowhaiplace.html

Cost: Double $80 Single $45
Child 1/2 price
Dinner $20 B/A
Beds: 2 Queen 4 Single
(4 bdrm)
Bath: 1 Private 1 Guests share
1 Family share

The best thing about a homestay is
that you share the family's living area.

Wyndham

Beverly and Doug assure you of a warm welcome to the Modern Farm house set in 265 hectare sheep farm. We are situated on the hills above Wyndham only 3.65 km, set in quiet and peaceful surroundings.

Farm tour included in tarif. Feeding the animals and sheep shearing when in season. Doug will demonstrate his sheep dogs working.

Beverly a registered nurse enjoys cooking, floral art, knitting, gardening and travel. We enjoy meeting people and both are of a friendly deposition, with a sense of humour.

"Each bedroom has a View and is tastefully furnished to meet your needs." "Genuine home cooking""Special Diets on request." "Packed Lunches if required" you are most welcome to join us for the evening meal, which is $30pp. We love sharing Christmas Day with guests, enquiries welcome.

FISHERMANS RETREAT; The Mataura, Wyndham and Mimihau Rivers are renowned for its abundance of Brown trout. Each of these Rivers are only a short 5Km away. Doug, a keen experienced fisherman is only too happy to share his knowledge of these rivers with you. Enjoy the Mad Mataura evening Rise a site to experience.

Gateway to Catlins, Only two hours from Queenstown, Te Anau and Dunedin.

Laundry, Fax and email facilities available.

Directions: Come to Wyndham, follow signs to Mokoreta.

Smiths Farmstay	**Tel:** (03) 206 4840	**Cost:** Double $90-$120
Farmstay	**Fax:** (03) 206 4847	Single $65
3.65km E of Wyndham	**Mob:** 025 286 6920	Dinner $30 Child Neg
Beverly and Doug Smith	**E:** beverly@smithsfarmstay.co.nz	Visa/MC
365 Wyndham - Mokoreta Road,	**W:** www.smithsfarmstay.co.nz	**Beds:** 2 King/Twin 1 Queen
RD 2		1 Twin (4 bdrm)
Wyndham		**Bath:** 1 Ensuite 1 Private
Southland		1 Guests share

Progress Valley - South Catlins

Ours is a great location close to fossil-forest at Curio Bay. We farm 1000 acres running, 3000 sheep, 500 deer, 150 cattle with 3 sheepdogs. Dinner is local fish, beef, venison or lamb raised on our farm and organic vegetables, followed by homemade desserts, and breakfast according to your needs. Directions: 32 km south Papatowai turn left into Progress Valley drive 2km. 4km north Waikawa turn right, then left onto Manse Road, then right to 174 Progress Valley Road. Ask about our s/c cottage at Waikawa.

Catlins Farmstay B&B
B&B Self-contained Farmstay
6km N of Waikawa
June & Murray Stratford
174 Progress Valley Road
South Catlins
Southland

Tel: (03) 246 8843
Fax: (03) 246 8844
E: catlinsfarmstay@xtra.co.nz
W: www.nzhomestay.co.nz/ stratford.htm

Cost: Double $95-$110 Single $55
Child $25 Dinner $30
S/C $70 per night Visa/MC
Beds: 1 Queen 1 Double 2 Single
(3 bdrm)
Bath: 1 Ensuite 1 Guests share
1 Family share

Fortrose - The Catlins

Greenbush Bed and Breakfast is ideally located off the Southern Scenic Route from Fortrose. Within 30 minutes drive from Greenbush you can enjoy Curio Bay, Waipapa Point and Slope Point the southern most point in the South Island. Greenbush is nestled in two acres of garden. you will wake to the song of birds and magnificent views of green rolling countryside. Enjoy our private beach access, lake and farm tour.

Greenbush
B&B Farmstay
50km SE of Invercargill
Ann & Donald McKenzie
298 Fortrose - Otara Road
Fortrose, RD 5, Invercargill

Tel: (03) 246 9506
Fax: (03) 246 9505
Mob: 025 239 5196
E: info@greenbush.co.nz
W: www.greenbush.co.nz

Cost: Double $120
Single $65
Child neg Dinner $30 B/A
Beds: 1 Double 1 Twin
(2 bdrm)
Bath: 1 Ensuite 1 Private

Waikawa Harbour - South Catlins

Bayfarm is a tranquil retreat situated in native forest overlooking Waikawa Harbour South Catlins. We farm sheep and cattle on 1200 acres. Dinner-fresh home grown produce. Non smokers preferred. Our interests include tramping, sailing, golf and meeting people. Fantail cottage is a modern self catering cottage for two adults, it has an extensive kitchen, queen bed, TV and ensuite. It is 150 metres from the homestead and completely private.

Bay Farm
B&B Self-contained Farmstay
80km SE of Invercargill
Alison & Bruce Yorke
595 Yorke Road
RD 1, Tokanui
Southland

Tel: (03) 246 8833
Fax: (03) 246 8833
Mob: 025 260 9203
E: BAYFARM@xtra.co.nz
W: www.bayfarm.co.nz

Cost: Double $90
Single $55
Self Catering $90
Dinner $25 Visa/MC
Beds: 1 Queen 1 Double
2 Single (3 bdrm)
Bath: 2 Private 1 Family share

SOUTHLAND, STH CATLINS

Mokotua

Fernlea Bed and Breakfast was the SOUTHLAND
SUPREME TOURISM AWARD WINNER 2000-2001.
Anne's cottage is nestled in its own private cottage garden - it
is completely self contained and can sleep four people. It is a
dairy farm of 300 acres and home to 180 Holstein cows.
Located 20 minutes from Invercargill on the Southern Scenic
route it's an ideal location for visitors to relax and enjoy a
taste of NZ farm life on their journey to discover the Catlins.
Directions: From Invercargill on SH92 turn left at Mokotua
Garage 20km from Invercargill.

Fernlea
Self-contained Farmstay Cottage
20km NE of Invercargill
Anne & Brian Perkins
Mokotua, RD 1
Invercargill on Southern Scenic
Route

Tel: (03) 239 5432
Fax: (03) 239-5432
Mob: 025 313 432
E: fernlea@southnet.co.nz
W: www.fernlea.co.nz

Cost: Double $100
    Child $10
    Dinner $30 B/A
Beds: 1 Double (1 bdrm)
Bath: 1 Private

Invercargill

If you are travelling in the Scenic South enjoy the peace and
tranquillity of a comfortable country home set in a large 4
acre garden which was placed first in the 2000 SOUTH-
ERN PRIDE BEAUTIFICATION AWARD for large
garden. With fresh flowers, cotton sheets, personal service,
private bathrooms, Tudor Park is the place to stay. 'The
best beds in NZ' is a regular comment. We are close to
Invercargill, Stewart Island and just off SH6 to Te Anau and
Queenstown. Please book ahead if possible.

Tudor Park
Farmstay Country stay
15km N of Invercargill
Joyce & John Robins
21 Lawrence Road
RD 6, Invercargill

Tel: (03) 221 7150
Fax: (03) 221 7150
Mob: 025 310 031
E: tudorparksouth@hotmail.com
W: www.bnb.co.nz/hosts/
tudorpark.html

Cost: Double $150 Single $80
    Twin $100 Child neg
    Dinner From $30 Visa/MC
Beds: 1 King/Twin 1 Double
    1 Twin (3 bdrm)
Bath: 1 Ensuite 2 Private

Invercargill - Rimu

Welcome to our warm and comfortable home, surrounded
by colourful gardens, We are semi-retired, graze cattle and
sheep, have two cats, enjoy meeting people, play golf, love
to cook, home baking a specialty, all meals prepared from
farm fresh produce and vegetables from our large garden.
Gateway to Catlins, Stewart Island, Fiordland, Queenstown.
Directions: From Invercargill travel 7 km toward Dunedin
turn right at Clapham Road, turn left, then right, cross
railway line, travel straight ahead for 4km, AJ Thomson on
mail box, number 375.

Southern Home Hospitality
B&B Farmstay Homestay
12km E of Invercargill
Margaret & Alan Thomson
Rimu No 375
RD 1, Invercargill

Tel: (03) 230 4798
Fax: (03) 230 4798
E: margalanthomson@actrix.net
W: www.bnb.co.nz/hosts/
southernhomehospitality.html

Cost: Double $90 Single $60
    Child $12 Dinner $30
Beds: 1 Queen 2 Single
    (2 bdrm)
Bath: 1 Private/Guests share

Invercargill

Our Bed & Breakfast Hotel is in a quiet street and close to the centre of town. Bedrooms have ensuite facilities, telephone, tea and coffee, and central heating throughout. We provide a full cooked breakfast up to 9 am, served in the dining room. You can walk to the city centre, museum, parks, golf course, aquatic centre in ten to fifteen minutes. We can arrange trips to Stuart Island and make a call to your next B&B. Your hosts: Marian and Harry Keil. We have two cats.

Montecillo Travel Lodge	**Tel:** (03) 218 2503	**Cost:** Double $90
B&B Hotel	**Fax:** (03) 218 2506	Single $72
Invercargill Central	**Tollfree:** 0800 66 68 32	Child $12 Dinner $25
M & H Keil	**W:** www.bnb.co.nz/hosts/	Visa/MC Amex Diners
PO Box 141	montecillotravellodge.html	**Beds:** 2 Queen 3 Double
240 Spey Street		6 Single (6 bdrm)
Invercargill		**Bath:** 6 Ensuite 6 Guests share

Invercargill

THE OAK DOOR. The Stuarts: Bill (a kiwi) and Lisa (a Canadian) welcome you to their unique home built by them. Set in native bush and attractive gardens. Come! Relax! Enjoy the tranquility and hospitality after touring the Southern Scenic Route. BEGIN IN THE SOUTH - TRAVEL NORTH AND HOME!! AIRPORT (2KM) Connections: Stewart Island and all points north. INVERCARGILL CITY CENTRE (5KM) Well-serviced, restaurants-gardens-State of art sport facilities-Olympic pool-5 Golf courses-tours-clubs and pubs etc. NOTES: No smoking No pets. Children welcome.

The Oak Door	**Tel:** 64 3 213 0633	**Cost:** Double $80
B&B	**Fax:** 64 3 213 0633	Single $60
5km W of Invercargill	**E:** blstuart@xtra.co.nz	Child POA
Lisa & Bill Stuart	**W:** www.bnb.co.nz/hosts/	**Beds:** 1 Queen 1 Double
22 Taiepa Road	theoakdoor.html	2 Single (3 bdrm)
Otatara, RD 9, Invercargill		**Bath:** 2 Guests share

Invercargill - Waikiwi

We enjoy meeting people and wish to make your stay as pleasant and comfortable as possible. Our home is five min's drive from the centre of Invercargill. On the main highway to/(from) Queenstown or Te Anau. Bus stops to Centre City. Visits to Stewart Island arranged. Catlands Information available. Guests have comfortable lounge, open fire, tea, coffee and TV facilities, conservatory, electric blankets on beds, off street parking. House is a non-smoking zone.

Aarden House	**Tel:** (03) 215 8825	**Cost:** Double $70-$80
B&B	**Fax:** (03) 215 8826	Single $45-$55
Dorothy & Raymond Shaw	**W:** www.bnb.co.nz/hosts/	**Beds:** 1 Queen 3 Single
193 North Road	aardenhouse.html	(2 bdrm)
Invercargill		**Bath:** 1 Guests share

Invercargill

Enjoy Bed & Breakfast on a deer farm. Situated in a unique
rural setting only 1 kilometer from city boundary. See
farmed deer and sheep. Guests welcome to tour of the
farm. Ideal stopover on Southern Scenic/Catlins Route
and the New Stewart Island National Park Easy access to
the Hump Ridge and Fiordland walking tracks. Alex is a
vintage car & machinery enthusiast and can arrange good
viewing. Directions: Find Tweed Street - travel East. Cross
Rockdale Road. We are 1 kilometer on right. Look for
"The Grove" sign.

The Grove Deer Farm	**Tel:** (03) 216 6492	**Cost:** Double $90 Single $50
B&B Farmstay	**Fax:** (03) 216 6492	Child neg Visa/MC
1km E of Invercargill	**E:** the_grove@xtra.co.nz	**Beds:** 1 Queen 4 Single
Alex & Eileen Henderson	**W:** www.bnb.co.nz/hosts/	(3 bdrm)
154 Oteramika Road	thegrovedeerfarm.html	**Bath:** 1 Guests share
RD 1, Invercargill		1 Family share

Invercargill - Waianiwa

We are 1 km from the Southern Scenic Route, fifteen
minutes from Invercargill and well placed for sightseeing,
fishing and golf. Annfield, originally built in 1866, has
recently been renovated to retain character and include
modern facilities. We are semi-retired, grow flowers for
export, keep coloured sheep and also Dexter cattle. Our cat
and two dogs are allowed limited access inside. We enjoy
meeting people and love to share dinner or a light meal,
including our own produce. Complimentary laundry
facilities. Directions - please phone

Annfield Flowers	**Tel:** (03) 235 2690	**Cost:** Double $80
Country Homestay	**Fax:** (03) 235 2745	Dinner $25
18km W of Invercargill	**E:** annfield@ihug.co.nz	Light meal $15 Visa/MC
Margaret & Mike Cockeram	**W:** www.bnb.co.nz/hosts/	**Beds:** 1 King/Twin (1 bdrm)
126 Argyle-Otahuti Road	annfieldflowers.html	**Bath:** 1 Ensuite
Waianiwa, RD 4, Invercargill		

Invercargill

Southland hospitality at its best awaits you at our warm and
friendly home. Our farm is 700 acres carrying 3000 sheep
and 80 cattle. We are a farming and shearing family.
Shearing videos available to watch. Farm Tour available.
Our farm is 30 minutes from Bluff. Transport to Stewart
Island can be arranged. Our home and garden is relaxing
and very peaceful. Being travellers ourselves we enjoy
meeting visitors. Stay as long as you wish. A home cooked
meal is always available. A welcome assured.
Directions: From Invercargill SH 92 approx 15 mins. look
for Long Acres Farmstay Sign.

Long Acres Farmstay	**Tel:** (03) 216 4470	**Cost:** Double $80 Single $50
Self-contained Farmstay	**Fax:** (03) 216 4470	Child neg Dinner $25
10km E of Invercargill	**Mob:** 025 228 1308	S/C $90
Helen & Graeme Spain	**W:** www.bnb.co.nz/hosts/	**Beds:** 2 Double 3 Single (4 bdrm)
Waimatua	longacres.html	**Bath:** 1 Private
RD 11, Invercargill		1 Family share

Invercargill

Gala Lodge, ideally situated for visitors to Invercargill, overlooks beautiful Queens Park, City centre, Museum and Information centre. The home has well appointed, upstairs bedrooms (electric blankets provided). Downstairs, kitchen and two guest lounges. Spacious gardens, ample car parking. Hosts background - Farming, Police work, Education & Training, Gardening. Interests - Reading, Genealogy, handcrafts, travel. Many years hosting students of many nationalities including Japan and China. We provide a relaxing, friendly base, support in welfare and travel arrangements. Courtesy car available. Most buses stop here. You are very welcome.

Gala Lodge	**Tel:** (03) 218 8884	**Cost:** Double $80 Single $50
B&B Homestay	**Fax:** (03) 218 9148	Dinner $25
Invercargill Central	**E:** charlie.ireland@xtra.co.nz	**Beds:** 1 Queen 2 Twin 1 Single
Jeanette & Charlie Ireland	**W:** www.bnb.co.nz/hosts/	(3 bdrm)
177 Gala Street, Invercargill	galalodge.html	**Bath:** 1 Guests share 1 Family

Invercargill

Our home is warm and comfortable with underfloor heating and electric blankets. Neville owns a wholesale fruit and vegetable market so fresh produce is assured. Joan has been involved for years with catering and enjoys cooking, so we would love to share an evening meal with you. We are keen golfers and members of the Invercargill Golf Club rated in the top 10 courses in NZ. City and Airport pick-ups can be arranged. 5 minutes drive from the City Centre on North Road.

Stoneleigh Homestay	**Tel:** (03) 215 8921	**Cost:** Double $90 Single $60
Homestay	**Fax:** (03) 215 8491	Dinner $25
5km N of Invercargill Central	**W:** www.bnb.co.nz/hosts/	**Beds:** 1 Queen 3 Single
Joan & Neville Milne	stoneleighhomestay.html	(3 bdrm)
15 Stoneleigh Lane		**Bath:** 1 Guests share
Invercargill		

Invercargill

Relax and enjoy our warm and comfortable home in a sheltered garden setting. Our 10 acre farmlet is situated on the outskirts of Invercargill. We are retired farmers, our interests include: keen golfers, gardening, horses, travel and meeting people. We have underfloor heating, electric blankets, pleasant outdoor areas and meals of fresh home grown produce, private guest area with television, fridge, tea and coffee making facilities. We are 5 minutes drive from Invercargill along State Highway One. Sign at Kennington corner.

The Manor	**Tel:** (03) 230 4788	**Cost:** Double $90 Single $60
B&B Homestay	**Mob:** 025 667 0904	Child negotiable
6km NE of Invercargill	**W:** www.bnb.co.nz/hosts/	Dinner $25 B/A Visa/MC
Pat & Frank Forde	themanor.html	**Beds:** 1 Queen 1 Double
9 Drysdale Road		2 Single (3 bdrm)
Myross Bush, RD 2, Invercargill		**Bath:** 1 Guests share

Riverton

We welcome you to our 350 acres sheep farm which is situated on the Southern Scenic Route. Our sunny and well heated home is surrounded by flower and vegetable gardens with views of Stewart Island. Riverton is a fishing port and is one of the oldest settlements in New Zealand. You may share dinner with us or if you prefer just Bed & Breakfast. Laundry facilities are available. We enjoy sharing our home and farm with visitors and a friendly stay is assured. Directions: Please phone.

Self-contained & Farmstay	**Tel:** (03) 234 8460	**Cost:** Double $80 Single $45
5km E of Riverton	**Fax:** (03) 234 8460	Dinner $15 - $20 B/A
Elaine & Ian Stuart	**Mob:** 025 203 3825	Visa/MC
Otaitai Bush	**W:** www.bnb.co.nz/hosts/	**Beds:** 1 Queen 2 Single
RD 3	stuart.html	(2 bdrm)
Riverton		**Bath:** 1 Ensuite 1 Private

Riverton

Relax and enjoy our comfortable home by the sea, situated on the waterfront with our 3 double bedrooms opening onto a sunny veranda with peaceful water and garden views. We also have a private upstairs studio unit with spa bath and views from the mountains to the sea. Come and enjoy a relaxed homestyle stay. We are only 20 minutes from Invercargill on the Southern Scenic Route. Enjoy a meal at Riverton's great cafes. Laundry facilities available. We look forward to meeting you.

93 Towack	**Tel:** (03) 234 8732	**Cost:** Double $60-$120
B&B Self-contained	**Fax:** (03) 234 8732	Visa/MC
35km S of Invercargill	**E:** rbjmdore@actrix.co.nz	**Beds:** 3 Queen 1 Double
Jocelyn and Russell Dore	**W:** www.bnb.co.nz/hosts/	(4 bdrm)
93 Towack Street	dore.html	**Bath:** 1 Ensuite 1 Guests share
Riverton		1 Family share

Stewart Island

The Nest is situated on Lonnekers Point overlooking Halfmoon Bay and Lonnekers Beach.

Beautiful Island, we know so well
Where freedom, love and peace do dwell
Haven of refuge in time of strife
Heavenly place to enjoy sweet life

We look forward to your visit.

The Nest	**Tel:** (03) 219 1310	**Cost:** Double $160
Homestay	**Fax:** (03) 219 1310	Single $80
22km Invercargill	**E:** thenest@es.co.nz	Visa/MC
Lorraine Squires	**W:** www.bnb.co.nz/hosts/	**Beds:** 1 Queen 1 Double
PO Box 88	thenest.html	(2 bdrm)
Halfmoon Bay		**Bath:** 1 Ensuite 1 Private
Stewart Island		

Stewart Island

Overlooking a beautiful sheltered beach, you can stay in our comfortable B&B/Homestay (ensuite) or one of two self-catering houses. With bush surrounds and superlative sea views, our accommodation is modern, private, centrally heated with conservatories and well-equipped kitchens. Courtesy transfer on arrival. Explore the Island's superb scenery, history, mammals, pelagic and land birds on nature walks off the beaten track with DOC Concessionaires Bruce & BJ; or catch a fish from our new 36' luxury launch. We look forward to helping you discover Stewart Island.

**Thorfinn Charters
& Accommodation**
*B&B Self-contained Homestay
10 mins walk to Oban*
Barbara McKay & Bruce Story
PO Box 43, Halfmoon Bay
Stewart Island

Tel: (03) 219 1210
Fax: (03) 219 1210
Mob: 025 201 1336
E: thorfinn@southnet.co.nz
W: www.thorfinn.co.nz

Cost: Double $100 Single $70
Dinner B/A S/C $100 - 200
Extra adult $20 Visa/MC
Beds: 2 Double 1 Single
(2 bdrm)
Bath: 1 Ensuite
1 Family share

Stewart Island

Our modern home on a bush clad point has panoramic views of Halfmoon Bay and islands beyond. Rooms have ensuites, tea/coffee and TV. Relax and watch boats in the Bay, or native birds feed on our balcony. Courtesy transfers but only 5 minutes walk. We are a fifth generation Stewart Island family. Tourism Southland Hospitality winner. STEWART ISLAND HOLIDAY HOMES private, refurbished, self-contained, set in bush with abundance of native birds. Sea views, well equipped, centrally heated. Four star Qualmark grading, Courtesy transfers.

Goomes B&B
B&B & Self-contained
5min walk from Oban
Jeanette & Peter Goomes
PO Box 36, Halfmoon Bay
Stewart Island

Tel: (03) 219 1057
Fax: (03) 219 1057
W: www.bnb.co.nz/hosts/
goomesbb.html

Cost: Double $140 Single $120
S/C $100/night
Extra adult$25
Visa/MC Amex
Beds: 2 Queen 1 Single
(2 bdrm)
Bath: 2 Ensuite

The difference between a hotel and a B&B
is that you don't hug the
hotel staff when you leave.

Schedule of Standards

General
Local tourism and transport information available to guests
Property appearance neat and tidy, internally and externally
Absolute cleanliness of the home in all areas used by the guests
Absolute cleanliness of kitchen, refrigerator and food storage areas
Roadside identification of property
Smoke alarms
Hosts accept responsibility to comply with local body bylaws
Pets & children must be mentioned in *NZ B&B Book* listing
Host will be present to welcome and farewell guests

Bedrooms
Each bedroom solely dedicated to guests with:
Heating
Light controlled from the bed
Wardrobe space with variety of hangers
Drawers
Mirror
Power point
Waste paper basket
Drinking glasses
Night light or torch for guidance to bathroom if not adjacent to bedroom
Opaque blinds or curtains on all windows where appropriate
Good quality mattresses in sound condition on a sound base
Clean bedding appropriate to the climate, with extra available
Clean pillows with additional available

Bathroom & toilet facilities
At least one bathroom adequately ventilated and equipped with:
Bath or shower
Wash handbasin and mirror
Wastebasket in bathroom
Lock on bathroom and toilet doors
Electric razor point if bedrooms are without a suitable power point
Soap, towels, bathmat, facecloths, fresh for each new guest
Towels changed or dried daily for guests staying more than one night
Sufficient toilet and bathroom facilities to serve family and guests adequately
Towel rail per guest in the bathroom or bedroom

Meals
Beverages: water, milk, tea, coffee should be offered
If fruit juice is offered it must be 100% pure juice
Breakfast: A generous breakfast must be provided

Index